Lecture Notes in Computer Science 13160

Founding Editors

Gerhard Goos
Juris Hartmanis

The series Lecture Notes in Computer Science (LNCS), including its subseries Lecture Notes in Artificial Intelligence (LNAI) and Lecture Notes in Bioinformatics (LNBI), has established itself as a medium for the publication of new developments in computer science and information technology research, teaching, and education.

LNCS enjoys close cooperation with the computer science R & D community, the series counts many renowned academics among its volume editors and paper authors, and collaborates with prestigious societies. Its mission is to serve this international community by providing an invaluable service, mainly focused on the publication of conference and workshop proceedings and postproceedings. LNCS commenced publication in 1973.

Pedro Lopez-Garcia · John P. Gallagher ·
Roberto Giacobazzi
Editors

Analysis, Verification and Transformation for Declarative Programming and Intelligent Systems

Essays Dedicated to Manuel Hermenegildo
on the Occasion of His 60th Birthday

 Springer

Editors
Pedro Lopez-Garcia ⓘ
IMDEA Software Institute
Pozuelo de Alarcón, Madrid, Spain

John P. Gallagher ⓘ
Roskilde University
Roskilde, Denmark

Roberto Giacobazzi ⓘ
Università di Verona
Verona, Italy

ISSN 0302-9743   ISSN 1611-3349 (electronic)
Lecture Notes in Computer Science
ISBN 978-3-031-31475-9   ISBN 978-3-031-31476-6 (eBook)
https://doi.org/10.1007/978-3-031-31476-6

This Springer imprint is published by the registered company Springer Nature Switzerland AG
The registered company address is: Gewerbestrasse 11, 6330 Cham, Switzerland

Preface

This volume is published in honour of Manuel Hermenegildo, on the occasion of his 60th birthday. Throughout his career, Manuel has been at the forefront of the fields of logic programming, constraint programming, parallel programming, program analysis, program transformation, and programming environment design. Many of these areas are reflected in the papers in this Festschrift and in the presentations made at the AVERTIS symposium, held in Madrid on November 29, 2019, and at the MH60 workshop, held in Porto on October 8, 2019.

Manuel grew up in Madrid and received a degree in Electrical Engineering from the Universidad Politécnica de Madrid (UPM). He moved to the University of Texas at Austin (UT Austin) and obtained a masters in Electrical and Computer Engineering, followed by a Ph.D. from the same university. He established himself early as a researcher who was comfortable at all levels of the computing stack, from electronics and computer architecture to very high-level programming languages and their semantics. He undertook his Ph.D. at UT Austin while also at the Microelectronics and Computer Technology Corporation (MCC), a joint industry/academy research centre established in response to the Japanese 5th Generation project. Declarative programming and parallel computing were major topics at MCC, and Manuel combined them in his own work on AND-parallel execution of logic programs. After three more years at MCC, he spent three more years in Texas, both as a researcher at MCC and as (adjunct) assistant and later associate professor at UT Austin. Following this, he returned to Spain in 1990 to take up a faculty position at UPM, where he founded the CLIP (Computational Logic, Implementation, and Parallelism) research group and where he became full professor in 1994.

During the years following his Ph.D., he explored models for the parallel and concurrent execution of more expressive variants of logic programming languages including, for example, constraints. At the same time, and motivated by the need to detect opportunities for parallelism at compile time, instead of through expensive run-time tests, his interests widened to include the static analysis of (constraint) logic programs. He devised a generic algorithm for the abstract interpretation of logic programs, into which different abstract domains could be plugged. This seminal work was very influential in other researchers' efforts to perform static analysis of logic programs, and became the core of the advanced programming environment developed at the CLIP group, the Ciao logic programming system, which uses program analysis and transformation as the core techniques to optimise, debug, and verify programs. Always an engineer at heart, Manuel continuously and actively participated in the design and implementation of the Ciao logic programming system, including its analysis and transformation tools and its programming environment.

Manuel has always been a strong advocate of logic programming, arguing that its declarative semantics, coupled with flexible procedural semantics, offered the best framework for realising the vision of an advanced development environment. Expressiveness, efficiency, and usefulness in real-world tasks were (and are) the driving forces behind his research. He was an active member of the Association for Logic Programming (ALP) and was first elected to the ALP executive committee in 1993 and later as ALP President, from 2005 to 2009. To this day, he continues to be involved with the ALP as Secretary and Director.

He has also been a member of the editorial boards of different journals as well as program chair of many conferences and workshops on implementation, analysis, and verification of logic programming, such as ICLP, LOPSTR, FLOPS, PADL, and PPDP – always focussing on ensuring the quality of the scholarly works presented at these venues. Apart from logic programming events, he has been involved in leading conferences on programming languages, analysis, and verification more generally, including being program chair of SAS and VMCAI and general chair of POPL.

As a relatively young science, computing has sometimes struggled to obtain public research funding in competition with the established disciplines. Manuel has worked tirelessly to raise the profile of computer science in Spain, taking on the job of Director of the Spanish National Research Directorate for two years in 2000, while somehow maintaining his research activities. As an extension to his national activities, Manuel was deeply involved in representing Spain in European Union funding programs.

In 2003 Manuel returned partly to the USA to take on the Prince of Asturias Chair in Information Science and Technology at the University of New Mexico, where he extended his research activities and group, all of which gave rise to many collaborations and results, including three Ph.D. theses, in addition to laying new avenues for collaboration between Spain and the USA.

In the early 2000s, the Madrid regional government began to plan a network of research institutes of the highest international stature. Manuel's research achievements and his experience in research policy was vital in ensuring that Computer Science was adequately represented in these plans. In 2007, he was appointed as the Founding Scientific Director of the IMDEA Software Institute, a position he held for 10 years, during which the Institute was established and grew to be the world-class research institution it is now.

Manuel has been given many awards, including the National "Aritmel" Prize for Scientific Merit in Computer Science, 2005, and the National "Julio Rey Pastor" Prize for Research in Mathematics and Information and Communication, 2006. He has been appointed to many other positions of high responsibility, clearly showing the trust he has within the research community: Elected member of the Academia Europæa; President of the Scientific Advisory Board of Inria; President of the Association for Logic Programming; and Member of the Scientific Advisory Board of the Schloß Dagstuhl International Center. In 2022 he was elected a Fellow of the ACM for contributions to program analysis, verification, parallelism, logic programming, and the IMDEA Software Institute.

Throughout his scientific career, Manuel has had hundreds of research collaborators. All of them know his amazing capacity for detailed work, thoroughness, and expert contributions at all the stages of a piece of work, from its inception to the final product. Manuel has in abundance all the skills needed for successful collaboration: extensive knowledge, innovative ideas, interpersonal skills, a positive attitude, capacity for encouragement, a sense of humour, and the ability to turn a potential conflict into a constructive discussion. In short, working with him is a pleasure and a source of inspiration. Those who perhaps know this best are his 15 Ph.D. students: Kalyan Muthukumar, Yow-Yan Lin, María García de la Banda, Francisco Bueno, Germán Puebla, Pedro López-García, Manuel Carro, Daniel Cabeza, Jorge Navas, Amadeo Casas, Mario Méndez, José Francisco Morales, Pablo Chico de Guzmán, Nataliia Stulova, and Isabel García.

To Manuel Hermenegildo, the scholar, teacher, engineer, manager, administrator, leader, and friend, with deep admiration, gratitude, and affection. Happy birthday!

July 2022   Pedro Lopez-Garcia
                                                                                      John Gallagher
                                                                                 Roberto Giacobazzi

Organization

Editors

Pedro López-García   IMDEA Software Institute and Spanish Council
for Scientific Research, Spain

John P. Gallagher   Roskilde University, Denmark, and IMDEA
Software Institute, Spain

Roberto Giacobazzi   University of Verona, Italy

Contents

Strategies in Conditional Narrowing Modulo SMT Plus Axioms

Luis Aguirre⬤, Narciso Martí-Oliet$^{(\boxtimes)}$⬤, Miguel Palomino, and Isabel Pita⬤

Departamento de Sistemas Informáticos y Computación, Facultad de Informática,
Universidad Complutense de Madrid, Madrid, Spain
{luisagui,narciso,miguelpt,ipandreu}@ucm.es

Abstract. This work presents a narrowing calculus that uses strategies to solve reachability problems in order-sorted conditional rewrite theories whose underlying equational logic is composed of some theories solvable via a satisfiability modulo theories (SMT) solver plus some combination of associativity, commutativity, and identity. Both the strategies and the rewrite rules are allowed to be parameterized, i.e., they may have a set of common constants that are given a value as part of the solution of a problem. A proof tree based interpretation of the strategy language is used to prove the soundness and weak completeness of the calculus.

Keywords: Narrowing · Strategies · Reachability · Rewriting logic · SMT · Unification

1 Introduction

Rewriting logic is a computational logic that was developed thirty years ago [11]. The semantics of rewriting logic [2] has a precise mathematical meaning, allowing mathematical reasoning for proving properties, providing a flexible framework for the specification of concurrent systems.

A system is specified in rewriting logic as a rewrite theory $\mathcal{R} = (\Sigma, E, R)$, with (Σ, E) an underlying equational theory, which in this work will be *order-sorted equational logic*, where terms are given as an algebraic data type, and R is a set of *rules* that specify how the system can derive one term from another.

Strategies allow modular separation between the rules that specify a system and the way that these rules are applied. In this work we will use a subset of the Maude strategy language [5,10,20], and we will give an interpretation of its semantics.

A *reachability problem* has the form $\exists \bar{x}(t(\bar{x}) \rightarrow^* t'(\bar{x}))$, with t, t' terms with variables in $\bar{x}$, or a conjunction $\exists \bar{x} \bigwedge_i (t_i(\bar{x}) \rightarrow^* t'_i(\bar{x}))$. In the general case where

Partially supported by projects TRACES (TIN2015-67522-C3-3-R), ProCode (PID 2019-108528RB-C22), and by Comunidad de Madrid as part of the program S2018/TCS-4339 (BLOQUES-CM) co-funded by EIE Funds of the European Union.

© Springer Nature Switzerland AG 2023
P. Lopez-Garcia et al. (Eds.): Hermenegildo Festschrift 2022, LNCS 13160, pp. 1–20, 2023.
https://doi.org/10.1007/978-3-031-31476-6_1

$t(\bar{x})$ is not a ground term, a technique known as *narrowing* [7] that was first proposed as a method for solving equational problems (*unification*), has been extended to cover also reachability problems [15]. One of the weaknesses of narrowing is the state space explosion associated to any reachability problem where arithmetic equational theories are involved. *Satisfiability modulo theories* (SMT) solvers [17] may mitigate this state space explosion.

This paper extends our previous work [1], where we developed a sound and weakly complete, i.e., complete with respect to normalized answers, narrowing calculus when $\mathcal{R} = (\Sigma, E_0 \cup B, R)$, with E_0 a subset of the theories handled by SMT solvers and B a set of *axioms* for the other algebraic data types. Here we introduce: (i) the use of strategies to further reduce the state space, and (ii) the support for *parameters* in the specifications, i.e., a subset of the variables in them, either SMT or not, to be considered as *common constants* that need to be given a value in the reachability problem. We have defined a strategy language suitable for narrowing, given a proof tree based interpretation of the semantics of the strategy language, and developed a completely new narrowing calculus that includes the strategy language and the use of parameters. Under certain requirements, the calculus is proven to be sound and weakly complete.

The work is structured as follows: Sect. 2 presents basic definitions and properties for order-sorted equational deduction and unification. Section 3 presents rewriting modulo built-in subtheories and axioms (R/E). In Sect. 4 the concepts of built-in subtheory, abstraction, B-extension, and rewrite theory closed under B-extensions are introduced. Also, the relation $\rightarrow_{R,B}$ is presented. This relation is closely related to the narrowing calculus to be developed in Sect. 7. Then the equivalence of R/E-rewriting and R, B-rewriting, for rewrite theories closed under B-extensions, is proved. In Sect. 5 the strategy language and its semantics are presented; then, an interpretation of this semantics is proved. In Sect. 6 we define the concept of parameterized reachability problem and its solution. In Sect. 7 the narrowing calculus for reachability is introduced. Then the soundness and weak completeness of the calculus are proved, as well as its completeness for some rewrite theories. Section 8 shows an example of the use of the calculus. In Sect. 9, related work, conclusions, and future lines of investigation for this work are presented. The technical report TR-02/2021, with more definitions, explanations, examples, and all the related proofs, together with the prototype with the running example, can be found at http://maude.ucm.es/cnarrowing.

2 Preliminaries

Familiarity with term rewriting and rewriting logic [2] is assumed. Several definitions and results from [19] are included in this section. The technical report TR-02/2021 holds other definitions, required in the proofs.

2.1 Running Example

Example 1. Toast cooking will be used as a running example. A toast is well-cooked if both sides of the toast have been cooked for exactly cookTime (abbre-

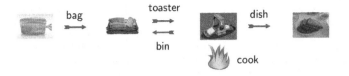

Fig. 1. Running example. Toast cooking

viated to ct) seconds. No overcooking is allowed. Fresh toasts are taken from a toast bag, and they are cooked using a frying pan that can toast up to two toasts simultaneously, well-cooking one side of each toast in the pan. There is a bin, where fresh toasts are put when taken from the bag. A toast in the pan can be returned to the bin, being flipped in this process. Finally, there is a dish where well-cooked toasts can be output. There is a limit of failTime (ft) seconds to reach the desired final state. In this example, ct and ft will be the parameters, i.e., they are the variables that represent the common constants of the specification that must be given a value either by the conditions of the problem or by its solution (Fig. 1).

A Toast (abbreviated to t) can be either a RealToast (rt), represented as an ordered pair of natural numbers, each one with sort Integer (i), storing the seconds that each side has already been toasted, or an EmptyToast (et) which has a constant zt, representing the absence of Toasts; a Pan (p) is an unordered pair of Toasts; a Kitchen (k) has a timer, represented by a natural number, and a Pan; a Bin (b) is a multiset of Toasts; the bag and the dish are represented by natural numbers, the number of RealToasts in each one; the System (s) has a bag, a Bin, a Kitchen, and a dish. When a RealToast is in the pan, the side being toasted is represented by the first integer of the ordered pair. We will use two auxiliary functions, cook and toast (in lowercase).

2.2 Order-Sorted Equational Logic

Definition 1 (Kind completion). *A poset of sorts $(S, \leq)$ whose connected components are the equivalence classes corresponding to the least equivalence relation $\equiv_\leq$ containing $\leq$ is kind complete iff for each $s \in S$ its connected component has a top sort, denoted $[s]$, called the kind of s.*

Definition 2 (Order-sorted signature). *An order-sorted (OS) signature is a tuple $\Sigma = (S, \leq, F)$ where: (1) $(S, \leq)$ is a kind complete poset of sorts; (2) $F = \{\Sigma_{s_1...s_n,s}\}_{(s_1...s_n,s) \in S^* \times S}$ is an $S^* \times S$-indexed family of sets of function symbols, where for each function symbol f in $\Sigma_{s_1...s_n,s}$ there is a function symbol f in $\Sigma_{[s_1]...[s_n],[s]}$; and (3) Σ is sensible, i.e., if f is a function symbol in $\Sigma_{s_1...s_n,s}$, f is also a function symbol in $\Sigma_{s'_1...s'_n,s'}$, and $[s_i] = [s'_i]$ for $i = 1, \ldots, n$ then $[s] = [s']$.*

When each connected component of $(S, \leq)$ has exactly one sort, the signature is many-sorted. When $f \in \Sigma_{\epsilon,s}$, ϵ being the empty word, we call f a constant with type s and write $f \in \Sigma_s$ instead of $f \in \Sigma_{\epsilon,s}$.

Example 2. In the cooking example, omitting the implied kind for each connected component of S, $\Sigma = (S, \leq, F)$ is:
$S = \{\texttt{Integer}, \texttt{RealToast}, \texttt{EmptyToast}, \texttt{Toast}, \texttt{Pan}, \texttt{Kitchen}, \texttt{Bin}, \texttt{System}\}$,
$\leq = \{(\texttt{RealToast}, \texttt{Toast}), (\texttt{EmptyToast}, \texttt{Toast}), (\texttt{Toast}, \texttt{Bin})\}$,
$F = \{\{[\_,\_]\}_{\texttt{i\,i,rt}}, \{\_\_\}_{\texttt{t\,t,p}}, \{\_;\_\}_{\texttt{b\,b,b}}, \{\_;\_\}_{\texttt{i\,p,k}}, \{\texttt{cook}\}_{\texttt{k\,i,[k]}}, \{\texttt{toast}\}_{\texttt{t\,i,[t]}},$
  $\{\_/\_/\_/\_\}_{\texttt{i\,r\,k\,i,s}}, \{\texttt{zt}\}_{\texttt{et}}\}$.
The notation used in F has the following meaning: $\{[\_,\_]\}_{\texttt{i\,i,rt}}$ means that
$[\_,\_]$ is a mix-fix function symbol such that if i_1 and i_2 are terms with sort
$\texttt{Integer}$ then $[i_1, i_2]$ is a term with sort $\texttt{RealToast}$.

A function symbol f in $\Sigma_{s_1 \ldots s_n, s}$ is displayed as $f : s_1 \ldots s_n \to s$, its *rank*
declaration. An S-sorted set $\mathcal{X} = \{\mathcal{X}_s\}_{s \in S}$ of variables satisfies $s \neq s' \Rightarrow \mathcal{X}_s \cap \mathcal{X}_{s'} = \emptyset$, and the variables in $\mathcal{X}$ are disjoint from all the constants in Σ. Each
variable in $\mathcal{X}$ has a subscript indicating its sort, i.e., x_s has sort s.

The sets $\mathcal{T}_{\Sigma, s}$ and $\mathcal{T}_{\Sigma}(\mathcal{X})_s$ denote, respectively, the set of Σ-terms with sort
s and the set of Σ-terms with sort s when the variables in $\mathcal{X}$ are considered
extra constants of Σ. The notations $\mathcal{T}_{\Sigma}$ and $\mathcal{T}_{\Sigma}(\mathcal{X})$ are used as a shortcut for
$\bigcup_{s \in S} \mathcal{T}_{\Sigma, s}$ and $\bigcup_{s \in S} \mathcal{T}_{\Sigma}(\mathcal{X})_s$ respectively. It is assumed that Σ has non-empty
sorts, i.e., $\mathcal{T}_{\Sigma, s} \neq \emptyset$ for all sorts s in S. We write $vars(t)$ to denote the set of
variables in a term t in $\mathcal{T}_{\Sigma}(\mathcal{X})$. This definition is extended in the usual way to
any other structure, unless explicitly stated. If $vars(A) = \emptyset$, where A is any
structure, then A is said to be *ground*. A term where each variable occurs only
once is said to be *linear*.

Positions in a term t: when a term t is expressed in functional notation as
$f(t_1, \ldots, t_n)$, it can be pictured as a tree with *root* f at position ϵ and *children*
t_i at position i, for $1 \leq i \leq n$. The inner positions of t are referred as lists of
nonzero natural numbers separated by dots. The set of positions of t is written
$pos(t)$. The set of non-variable positions of t is written $pos_{\Sigma}(t)$. $t|_p$ is the subtree
of t below position p. $t[u]_p$ is the replacement in t of $t|_p$ with u. $t[\ ]_p$ is a *term
with hole* that is equal to t except that in the position p there is a special symbol
$[\ ]$, the hole. For positions p and q, we write $p \leq q$ if there is a position r such
that $q = p.r$. Given any *ordered list* $\bar{u} = u_1, \ldots, u_n$, we call $\hat{u} = \{u_1, \ldots, u_n\}$.

Definition 3 (Preregularity). *Given an order-sorted signature Σ, for each
natural number n, for every function symbol f in Σ with arity n, and for every
tuple $(s_1, \ldots, s_n)$ in S^n, let $S_{f, s_1 \ldots, s_n}$ be the set containing all the sorts s' that
appear in rank declarations in Σ of the form $f : s'_1 \ldots s'_n \to s'$ such that $s_i \leq s'_i$,
for $1 \leq i \leq n$. If whenever $S_{f, s_1, \ldots, s_n}$ is not empty it is the case that $S_{f, s_1, \ldots, s_n}$
has a least sort, then Σ is said to be preregular.*

Preregularity guarantees that every Σ-term t has a *least sort*, denoted $ls(t)$,
i.e., for any rank declaration $f : s_1 \ldots s_n \to s$ that can be applied to t it is true
that $ls(t) \leq s$.

A *substitution* $\sigma : \mathcal{X} \to \mathcal{B}$, where $\mathcal{B} \subseteq \mathcal{T}_{\Sigma}(\mathcal{X})$ is a superset of the *range*
of σ, defined below, is a function that matches the identity function in all $\mathcal{X}$
except for a finite set called its *domain*, $dom(\sigma)$. We represent the application
of a substitution σ to a variable x in $\mathcal{X}$ as $x\sigma$. Substitutions are written as

$\sigma = \{x^1_{s_1} \mapsto t_1, \cdots, x^n_{s_n} \mapsto t_n\}$, where $dom(\sigma)$ is $\{x^1_{s_1}, \ldots, x^n_{s_n}\}$ and the range of σ is $ran(\sigma) = \bigcup^n_{i=1} vars(t_i)$. If $ran(\sigma) = \emptyset$ then σ is *ground*. We write $\sigma : \mathcal{D} \to \mathcal{B}$, where $\mathcal{D} \subset \mathcal{X}$ is finite, to imply that $dom(\sigma) = \mathcal{D}$. The *identity* substitution, where $dom(\sigma) = \emptyset$, is displayed as *none*. A substitution σ where $dom(\sigma) = \{x^1_{s_1}, \ldots, x^n_{s_n}\}$ $(n \geq 0)$, $x^i_{s_i}\sigma = y^i_{s_i} \in \mathcal{X}$, for $1 \leq i \leq n$, and $y^i_{s_i} \neq y^j_{s_j}$ for $1 \leq i < j \leq n$ is called a *renaming*. The restriction $\sigma_\mathcal{V}$ of σ to a set of variables $\mathcal{V}$ is defined as $x\sigma_\mathcal{V} = x\sigma$ if $x \in \mathcal{V}$ and $x\sigma_\mathcal{V} = x$ otherwise. The *deletion* $\sigma_{\backslash\mathcal{V}}$, where $\mathcal{V} \subseteq \mathcal{X}$ is defined as $x\sigma_{\backslash\mathcal{V}} = x\sigma$ if $x \in dom(\sigma)\backslash\mathcal{V}$ and $x\sigma_{\backslash\mathcal{V}} = x$ otherwise. Substitutions are homomorphically extended to terms in $\mathcal{T}_\Sigma(\mathcal{X})$ and also to any other syntactic structures. The *composition* of σ and σ' is denoted by $\sigma\sigma'$, with $x(\sigma\sigma') = (x\sigma)\sigma'$ (left associativity). Their *closed composition*, denoted by $\sigma\cdot\sigma'$, is defined as $\sigma\cdot\sigma' = (\sigma\sigma')_{\backslash ran(\sigma)}$. If $\sigma\sigma = \sigma$ then we say that σ is *idempotent*.

A *context* $\mathcal{C}$ is a λ-term of the form $\lambda x^1_{s_1} \cdots x^n_{s_n}.t$, with $t \in \mathcal{T}_\Sigma(\mathcal{X})$ and $\{x^1_{s_1}, \ldots, x^n_{s_n}\} \subseteq vars(t)$. A Σ-equation has the form $l = r$, where $l \in \mathcal{T}_\Sigma(\mathcal{X})_{s_l}$, $r \in \mathcal{T}_\Sigma(\mathcal{X})_{s_r}$, and $s_l \equiv_\leq s_r$. A conditional Σ-equation has the form $l = r$ if C with $l = r$ a Σ-equation and C a conjunction of Σ-equations. We call a Σ-equation $l = r$: *regular* iff $vars(l) = vars(r)$; *sort-preserving* iff for each substitution σ and sort s, $l\sigma$ in $\mathcal{T}_\Sigma(\mathcal{X})_s$ implies $r\sigma$ in $\mathcal{T}_\Sigma(\mathcal{X})_s$ and vice versa; *left (or right) linear* iff l (resp. r) is linear; *linear* iff it is both left and right linear.

A set of equations E is said to be regular, or sort-preserving, or (left or right) linear, if each equation in it is so.

2.3   Order-Sorted Equational Theories

Definition 4 (OS equational theory). *An* OS equational theory *is a pair* $\mathcal{E} = (\Sigma, E)$, *where* Σ *is an* OS signature *and* E *is a finite set of (possibly conditional)* Σ-equations of the forms $l = r$ or $l = r$ if $\bigwedge^n_{i=1} l_i = r_i$. *All the variables appearing in these* Σ-equations are interpreted as universally quantified.

Example 3. The OS equational theory for the toast example has $\Sigma = (S, \leq, F)$ and E is the set E_0 of equations for integer arithmetic (not displayed), together with the equations:
$(x_b; y_b); z_b = x_b; (y_b; z_b)$, $x_b; y_b = y_b; x_b$, $x_b; \mathsf{zt} = x_b$, $x_t y_t = y_t x_t$
stating that Bin is a multiset of Toasts and that the position of the Toasts in the Pan is irrelevant.

Definition 5 (Equational deduction). *Given an* OS equational theory $\mathcal{E} = (\Sigma, E)$ *and a* Σ-equation $l = r$, $E \vdash l = r$ *denotes that* $l = r$ *can be deduced from* $\mathcal{E}$ *using the rules in* [12].

An OS equational theory $\mathcal{E} = (\Sigma, E)$ has an *initial algebra* $(\mathcal{T}_{\Sigma/E}$ or $\mathcal{T}_\mathcal{E})$, whose elements are the equivalence classes $[t]_\mathcal{E}$ of ground terms in $\mathcal{T}_\Sigma$ identified by the equations in E.

We denote by $\mathcal{T}_{\Sigma/E}(\mathcal{X})$, or $\mathcal{T}_\mathcal{E}(\mathcal{X})$, the algebra whose elements are the equivalence classes of terms in $\mathcal{T}_\Sigma(\mathcal{X})$ identified by the equations in E.

The deduction rules for OS equational logic specify a sound and complete calculus, i.e., for all Σ-equations $l = r$, $E \vdash l = r$ iff $l = r$ is a logical consequence of E (written $E \vDash l = r$) [12]; then we write $l =_E r$.

A theory inclusion $(\Sigma, E) \subseteq (\Sigma', E')$ is called *protecting* iff the unique Σ-homomorphism $\mathcal{T}_{\Sigma/E} \longrightarrow \mathcal{T}_{\Sigma'/E'}|_{\Sigma}$ to the Σ-*reduct of the initial algebra* $\mathcal{T}_{\Sigma'/E'}$, i.e., the elements of $\mathcal{T}_{\Sigma'/E'}$ that consist only in function symbols from Σ, is a Σ-isomorphism, written $\mathcal{T}_{\Sigma/E} \simeq \mathcal{T}_{\Sigma'/E'}|_{\Sigma}$.

2.4   Unification

Given an OS equational theory (Σ, E), the E-*subsumption* preorder $\ll_E$ on $\mathcal{T}_{\Sigma}(\mathcal{X})$ is defined by $t \ll_E t'$ if there is a substitution σ such that $t =_E t'\sigma$. For substitutions σ, ρ and a set of variables $\mathcal{V}$ we write $\rho_{\mathcal{V}} \ll_E \sigma_{\mathcal{V}}$, and say that σ is more general than ρ with respect to $\mathcal{V}$, if there is a substitution η such that $dom(\sigma) \cap dom(\eta) = \emptyset$, $ran(\rho_{\mathcal{V}}) = ran((\sigma\eta)_{\mathcal{V}})$, and $\rho_{\mathcal{V}} =_E (\sigma\eta)_{\mathcal{V}}$. When $\mathcal{V}$ is not specified, it is assumed that $\mathcal{V} = dom(\rho)$ and $\rho =_E \sigma \cdot \eta$. Then σ is said to be more general than ρ. When E is not specified, it is assumed that $E = \emptyset$.

Given an OS equational theory (Σ, E), a *system of equations* F is a conjunction of Σ-equations $\bigwedge_{i=1}^{n} l_i = r_i$. An E-*unifier* for F is a substitution σ such that $l_i\sigma =_E r_i\sigma$, for $1 \leq i \leq n$.

Definition 6 (Complete set of unifiers [18]). *For F a system of equations and $vars(F) \subseteq \mathcal{W}$, a set of substitutions $CSU_E^{\mathcal{W}}(F)$ is said to be a complete set of E-unifiers of F away from $\mathcal{W}$ iff each substitution σ in $CSU_E^{\mathcal{W}}(F)$ is an E-unifier of F, for any E-unifier ρ of F there is a substitution σ in $CSU_E^{\mathcal{W}}(F)$ such that $\rho_{\mathcal{W}} \ll_E \sigma_{\mathcal{W}}$, and for each substitution σ in $CSU_E^{\mathcal{W}}(F)$, $dom(\sigma) \subseteq vars(F)$ and $ran(\sigma) \cap \mathcal{W} = \emptyset$.*

The notation CSU_E is used when $\mathcal{W}$ is the set of all the variables that have already appeared in the current calculation.

3   Conditional Rewriting Modulo Built-Ins and Axioms

Definition 7 (Signature with built-ins [19]). *An OS signature $\Sigma = (S, \leq, F)$ has* built-in subsignature *$\Sigma_0 = (S_0, \leq, F_0)$ iff (i) $\Sigma_0 \subseteq \Sigma$, (ii) Σ_0 is many-sorted, (iii) S_0 is a set of minimal elements in $(S, \leq)$, and (iv) if $f : w \to s \in F_1$, where $F_1 = F \backslash F_0$, then $s \notin S_0$ and f has no other typing in Σ_0.*

We let $\mathcal{X}_0 = \{\mathcal{X}_s\}_{s \in S_0}$, $\mathcal{X}_1 = \mathcal{X} \backslash \mathcal{X}_0$, $S_1 = S \backslash S_0$, $\Sigma_1 = (S, \leq, F_1)$, $\mathcal{H}_\Sigma(\mathcal{X}) = \mathcal{T}_\Sigma(\mathcal{X}) \backslash \mathcal{T}_{\Sigma_0}(\mathcal{X}_0)$, and $\mathcal{H}_\Sigma = \mathcal{T}_\Sigma \backslash \mathcal{T}_{\Sigma_0}$.

The restriction of $\mathcal{T}_{\Sigma/E}$ to $\mathcal{H}_\Sigma$ is denoted by $\mathcal{H}_{\Sigma/E}$ or $\mathcal{H}_\mathcal{E}$, and the restriction of $\mathcal{T}_{\Sigma/E}(\mathcal{X})$ to $\mathcal{H}_\Sigma(\mathcal{X})$ is denoted by $\mathcal{H}_{\Sigma/E}(\mathcal{X})$ or $\mathcal{H}_\mathcal{E}(\mathcal{X})$.

Definition 8 (Rule). *Given an OS signature $(\Sigma, S, \leq)$ with built-in subsignature (Σ_0, S_0), a* rule *is an expression with the form $c : l \to r$ if $\bigwedge_{i=1}^{n} l_i \to r_i \mid \phi$, where: (i) c is the alphanumeric label of the rule, (ii) l, the head of the rule, and r are terms in $\mathcal{H}_\Sigma(\mathcal{X})$, with $ls(l) \equiv_\leq ls(r)$, (iii) for each pair l_i, r_i, $1 \leq i \leq n$,*

l_i is a term in $\mathcal{H}_\Sigma(\mathcal{X})\backslash\mathcal{X}$ and r_i is a term in $\mathcal{H}_\Sigma(\mathcal{X})$, with $ls(l_i) \equiv_\leq ls(r_i)$, and (iv) $\phi \in QF(\mathcal{X}_0)$, the set of quantifier free formulas made up with terms in $\mathcal{T}_{\Sigma_0}(\mathcal{X}_0)$, the comparison function symbols $=$ and $\neq$, and the connectives $\vee$ and $\wedge$.

The symbol $\neg$ (that can be defined with respect to $=$, $\neq$, $\vee$, and $\wedge$) will also appear in this work. All the variables in $vars(c)$ are interpreted as universally quantified. Three particular cases of the general form are admitted: $c : l \rightarrow r$ if $\bigwedge_{i=1}^n l_i \rightarrow r_i$, $c : l \rightarrow r$ if ϕ, and the unconditional case $c : l \rightarrow r$.

Definition 9 (B-preregularity). *Given a set of Σ-equations B, a preregular OS signature Σ is called B-preregular iff for each Σ-equation $u = v$ in B and substitution σ, $ls(u\sigma) = ls(v\sigma)$.*

Definition 10 (Conditional rewrite theory with built-in subtheory).
A conditional rewrite theory $\mathcal{R} = (\Sigma, E, R)$ with built-in subtheory and axioms (Σ_0, E_0) consists of: (1) an OS equational theory (Σ, E) where: (i) $\Sigma = (S, \leq, F)$ is an OS signature with built-in subsignature $\Sigma_0 = (S_0, \leq, F_0)$, (ii) $E = E_0 \cup B$, where E_0 is the set of Σ_0-equations in E, the theory inclusion $(\Sigma_0, E_0) \subseteq (\Sigma, E)$ is protecting, B is a set of regular and linear equations, called axioms, each equation having only function symbols from F_1 and kinded variables, (iii) there is a procedure that can compute $CSU_B(F)$ for any system of equations F, (iv) Σ is B-preregular, and (2) a finite set of uniquely labeled rules R.

Condition number 2 will be relaxed, but not totally removed, later in this work. From now on, we will write "rewrite theory" as a shortcut for "conditional rewrite theory with built-in subtheory and axioms".

The transitive (resp. transitive and reflexive) closure of the relation $\rightarrow_R^1$, inductively defined below, is denoted $\rightarrow_R^+$ (resp. $\rightarrow_R^*$).

Definition 11 (R-rewriting). *Given a rewrite theory $\mathcal{R} = (\Sigma, E_0 \cup B, R)$, a term t in $\mathcal{H}_\Sigma$, a position p in $Pos(t)$, a rule $c : l \rightarrow r$ if $\bigwedge_{i=1}^n l_i \rightarrow r_i \mid \phi$ in R, and a substitution $\sigma : vars(c) \rightarrow \mathcal{T}_\Sigma$, the one-step transition $t \rightarrow_R^1 t[r\sigma]_p$ holds iff $t = t[l\sigma]_p$, $l_i\sigma \rightarrow_R^* r_i\sigma$, for $1 \leq i \leq n$, and $E_0 \vDash \phi\sigma$.*

We write $t \xrightarrow[c,p,\sigma]{\quad 1 \quad} R\, t[r\sigma]_p$ when we need to make explicit the rule, position, and substitution. Any of these items can be omitted when it is irrelevant. We write $t \xrightarrow[c\sigma]{\quad 1 \quad} R\, v$ to express that there exists a substitution δ such that $t \xrightarrow[c,\sigma\cdot\delta]{\quad 1 \quad} R\, v$.

Example 4. In the toast example, E_0 is the theory for integer arithmetic, B is the set of axioms in Example 3, and R is:
$[kitchen] : y_i; h_{rt}\, v_t \rightarrow \mathsf{cook}(y_i; h_{rt}\, v_t, z_i)$ if $z_i > 0$
$[cook] : \mathsf{cook}(y_i; h_{rt}\, v_t, z_i) \rightarrow y_i + z_i; h'_{rt}\, v'_t$ if
$\qquad \mathsf{toast}(h_{rt}, z_i) \rightarrow h'_{rt} \wedge \mathsf{toast}(v_t, z_i) \rightarrow v'_t$
$[toast1] : \mathsf{toast}(\mathsf{zt}, z_i) \rightarrow \mathsf{zt}$
$[toast2] : \mathsf{toast}([a_i, b_i], z_i) \rightarrow [a_i + z_i, b_i]$ if $a_i \geq 0 \wedge a_i + z_i = \mathsf{ct}_i$
$[bag] : n_i/x_b/g_k/ok_i \rightarrow (n_i - 1)/[0, 0]; x_b/g_k/ok_i$ if $n_i > 0$

$[pan] : n_i/h_{rt}; x_b/y_i; zt\ v_t/ok_i \rightarrow n_i/x_b/y_i; h_{rt}\ v_t\ /ok_i$
$[bin] : n_i/x_b/y_i; [a_i, b_i]\ v_t/ok_i \rightarrow n_i/[b_i, a_i]; x_b/y_i; zt\ v_t\ /ok_i$
$[dish] : n_i/x_b/y_i; [ct_i, ct_i]\ v_t/ok_i \rightarrow n_i/x_b/y_i; zt\ v_t/ok_i + 1$

The transitive closure of the relation $\rightarrow^1_{R/E}$, inductively defined below, is denoted $\rightarrow^+_{R/E}$. The relation $\rightarrow_{R/E}$ is defined as $\rightarrow_{R/E} = \rightarrow^+_{R/E} \cup =_E$.

Definition 12 (R/E-rewriting). *Given a rewrite theory* $\mathcal{R} = (\Sigma, E_0 \cup B, R)$, *terms* t, u, *and* v *in* $\mathcal{H}_\Sigma$, *and a rule* $c : l \rightarrow r$ *if* $\bigwedge^n_{i=1} l_i \rightarrow r_i \mid \phi$ *in* R, *if there exist a position* p *in* $Pos(u)$, *and a substitution* $\sigma : vars(c) \rightarrow \mathcal{T}_\Sigma$ *such that* $t =_E u = u[l\sigma]_p$, $u[r\sigma]_p =_E v$, $l_i\sigma \rightarrow_{R/E} r_i\sigma$, *for* $1 \le i \le n$, *and* $E_0 \models \phi\sigma$ *then we say that the* one-step modulo transition $t \rightarrow^1_{R/E} v$ *holds.*

We write $t \xrightarrow[c,u,p,\sigma]{1}_{R/E} v$ when we need to make explicit the rule, matching term, position, and substitution. Any of these items can be omitted.

Rewriting modulo is *more expressive* than rewriting (see example 3.9 in [1]).

4   Abstractions, B-extensions, and R, B-Rewriting

Two simpler relations, $\rightarrow^1_{R,B}$ and $\rightarrow_{R,B}$ [13] are defined in this section which, under several requirements, are equivalent to $\rightarrow^1_{R/E}$ and $\rightarrow_{R/E}$, allowing us to solve reachability problems using a narrowing calculus based on $\rightarrow_{R,B}$.

4.1   Abstractions

Definition 13 (Abstraction of built-in [19]). *If* Σ *is a signature with built-in subsignature* Σ_0, *then an* abstraction of built-in *is a context* $\mathcal{C} = \lambda x^1_{s_1} \cdots x^n_{s_n}.t^\circ$, *with* $n \ge 0$, *such that* $t^\circ \in \mathcal{T}_{\Sigma_1}(\mathcal{X})$ *and* $\{x^1_{s_1}, \ldots, x^n_{s_n}\} = vars(t^\circ) \cap \mathcal{X}_0$. *For pairs of terms we write* $abstract_{\Sigma_1}((u,v)) = \langle \lambda(\bar{x}, \bar{y}).(u^\circ, v^\circ); (\theta^\circ_u, \theta^\circ_v); (\phi^\circ_u, \phi^\circ_v) \rangle$.

Lemma 1 shows that there exists an abstraction that provides a canonical decomposition of any term in $\mathcal{T}_\Sigma(\mathcal{X})$.

Lemma 1 (Existence of a canonical abstraction [19]). *Let* Σ *be a signature with built-in subsignature* Σ_0. *For each term* t *in* $\mathcal{T}_\Sigma(\mathcal{X})$ *there exist an abstraction of built-in* $\lambda x^1_{s_1} \cdots x^n_{s_n}.t^\circ$ *and a substitution* $\theta^\circ : \mathcal{X}_0 \rightarrow \mathcal{T}_{\Sigma_0}(\mathcal{X}_0)$ *such that (i)* $t = t^\circ\theta^\circ$ *and (ii)* $dom(\theta^\circ) = \{x^1_{s_1}, \ldots, x^n_{s_n}\}$ *are pairwise distinct and disjoint from* $vars(t)$; *moreover, (iii)* t° *can always be selected to be* S_0-*linear and with* $\{x^1_{s_1}, \ldots, x^n_{s_n}\}$ *disjoint from an arbitrarily chosen finite subset* $\mathcal{Y}$ *of* $\mathcal{X}_0$.

Definition 14 (Abstract function [19]). *Given a term* t *in* $\mathcal{T}_\Sigma(\mathcal{X})$ *and a finite subset* $\mathcal{Y}$ *of* $\mathcal{X}_0$, *define* $abstract_{\Sigma_1}(t, \mathcal{Y})$ *as* $\langle \lambda x^1_{s_1} \cdots x^n_{s_n}.t^\circ; \theta^\circ; \phi^\circ \rangle$ *where the context* $\lambda x^1_{s_1} \cdots x^n_{s_n}.t^\circ$ *and the substitution* θ° *satisfy the properties (i)-(iii) in Lemma 1 and* $\phi^\circ = \bigwedge^n_{i=1}(x^i_{s_i} = x^i_{s_i}\theta^\circ)$. *If* $t \in \mathcal{T}_{\Sigma_1}(\mathcal{X} \backslash \mathcal{X}_0)$ *then* $abstract_{\Sigma_1}(t, \mathcal{Y}) = \langle \lambda.t; none; true \rangle$. *We write* $abstract_{\Sigma_1}(t)$ *when* $\mathcal{Y}$ *is the set of all the variables that have already appeared in the current calculation, so each* $x^i_{s_i}$ *is a fresh variable. For pairs of terms we use the compact notation* $abstract_{\Sigma_1}((u,v)) = \langle \lambda(\bar{x}, \bar{y}).(u^\circ, v^\circ); (\theta^\circ_u, \theta^\circ_v); (\phi^\circ_u, \phi^\circ_v) \rangle$.

Definition 15 (Set of topmost Σ_0-positions [1]). *Let $\mathcal{R} = (\Sigma, E_0 \cup B, R)$ be a rewrite theory with built-in subtheory (Σ_0, E_0), and t a term in $\mathcal{H}_\Sigma(\mathcal{X})$. The set of topmost Σ_0 positions of t, $top_{\Sigma_0}(t)$, is $top_{\Sigma_0}(t) = \{p \mid p \in Pos(t) \wedge t|_p \in \mathcal{T}_{\Sigma_0}(\mathcal{X}_0) \wedge \exists i \in \mathbb{N}, q \in Pos(t) \; s.t. \; p = q.i \wedge t|_q \in \mathcal{H}_\Sigma(\mathcal{X})\}$.*

4.2   B-Extensions

The concept of *B-extension*, together with its properties, has been studied in [13]. Now, we allow for repeated labels in rules; later we will restrict this repetition. We will use subscripts or apostrophes, e.g. c_1 or c', when we need to refer to a specific rule with label c.

Definition 16 (Rewrite theory closed under B-extensions). *Let $\mathcal{R} = (\Sigma, E_0 \cup B, R)$ be a rewrite theory, where R may have repeated labels, and let $c : l \rightarrow r$ if C be a rule in R. Assume, without loss of generality, that $vars(B) \cap vars(c) = \emptyset$. If this is not the case, only the variables of B will be renamed; the variables of c will never be renamed. We define the set of B-extensions of c as the set:*
$$Ext_B(c) = \{c : u[l]_p \rightarrow u[r]_p \; if \; C \mid u = v \in B \cup B^{-1} \wedge p \in Pos_\Sigma(u) - \{\epsilon\} \wedge$$
$$CSU_B(l, u_p) \neq \emptyset\} \; where, \; by \; definition, \; B^{-1} = \{v = u \mid u = v \in B\}.$$
All the rules in $Ext_B(c)$ have label c. Given two rules $c : l \rightarrow r$ if C and $c_1 : l' \rightarrow r'$ if C, c subsumes c_1 iff there is a substitution σ such that: (i) $dom(\sigma) \cap vars(C) = \emptyset$, (ii) $l' =_B l\sigma$, and (iii) $r' =_B r\sigma$.

We say that $\mathcal{R}$ is closed under B-extensions *iff for any rule with label c in R, each rule in $Ext_B(c)$ is subsumed by one rule with label c in R.*

Meseguer [13] shows an algorithm that given a rewrite theory $\mathcal{R} = (\Sigma, E_0 \cup B, R)$ constructs a superset R that is finite and closed under B-extensions, called a *finite closure under B-extensions of* $\mathcal{R}$.

Definition 17 (Finite closure under B-extensions of a rule). *Given an equational theory $(\Sigma, E_0 \cup B)$, with built-in subtheory (Σ_0, E_0), and a rule with label c, we denote by c_B the set of rules in any finite closure under B-extensions of the rewrite theory $\mathcal{R} = (\Sigma, E_0 \cup B, \{c\})$.*

Definition 18 Associated rewrite theory closed under B-extensions). *Given a rewrite theory $\mathcal{R}_1 = (\Sigma, E_0 \cup B, R)$ with no repeated rule labels, its associated rewrite theory closed under B-extensions is any rewrite theory $\mathcal{R}_2 = (\Sigma, E_0 \cup B, \bigcup_{c \in R} c_B)$.*

Rewriting modulo does not change if we use a rewrite theory or any of its associated rewrite theories closed under B-extensions.

Lemma 2 (Equivalence of R/E-rewriting and R_B/E-rewriting). *If $\mathcal{R}_B = (\Sigma, E_0 \cup B, R_B)$ is an associated rewrite theory of $\mathcal{R} = (\Sigma, E_0 \cup B, R)$ closed under B-extensions, then $\rightarrow^1_{R/E} = \rightarrow^1_{R_B/E}$ and $\rightarrow_{R/E} = \rightarrow_{R_B/E}$.*

Our definition of the relation $\to^1_{R,B}$ will require the use of a single representative for all the instances of each E_0-equivalence class that may appear in the top_{Σ_0} positions of the subterm that we are rewriting.

Definition 19 (Representative of a Σ_0-term over a set of Σ_0 terms). *Let t be a term in $\mathcal{T}_{\Sigma_0}$ and let $\hat{u} = \{u_1, \ldots, u_n\} \subseteq \mathcal{T}_{\Sigma_0}$ such that $t \in \hat{u}$. We define the Σ_0-representative of t over $\hat{u}$ as $rep^\circ_{\hat{u}}(t) = u_{min(\{i | u_i =_{E_0} t\})}$.*

Definition 20 (Representative of a term over a set of Σ_0 terms). *Let t be a term in $\mathcal{T}_\Sigma$, where $top_{\Sigma_0}(t) = \hat{p}$, and let $\hat{u} \subseteq \mathcal{T}_{\Sigma_0}$ such that $t|_{\hat{p}} \subseteq \hat{u}$. We define the representative of t over $\hat{u}$, as $rep_{\hat{u}}(t) = t[rep^\circ_{\hat{u}}(t|_{\bar{p}})]_{\bar{p}}$.*

Definition 21 (Representative of a term). *Let t be a term in $\mathcal{T}_\Sigma$, where $top_{\Sigma_0}(t) = \hat{p}$. We define the representative of t as $rep(t) = rep_{t|_{\hat{p}}}(t)$.*

The transitive closure of the relation $\to^1_{R,B}$, inductively defined below, is denoted $\to^+_{R,B}$. The relation $\to_{R,B}$ is defined as $\to_{R,B} = \to^+_{R,B} \cup =_E$.

Definition 22 (R, B-rewriting). *Given a rewrite theory $\mathcal{R} = (\Sigma, E_0 \cup B, R)$, terms t, v in $\mathcal{H}_\Sigma$, and a rule $c : l \to r$ if $\bigwedge_{i=1}^n l_i \to r_i \mid \phi$ in R, if $abstract_{\Sigma_1}(l) = \langle \lambda \bar{x}.l^\circ; \theta^\circ; \phi^\circ \rangle$ and there exist a position p in $pos_{\Sigma_1}(t)$ and a substitution $\sigma : \bar{x} \cup vars(c) \to \mathcal{T}_\Sigma$ such that $rep(t|_p) =_B l^\circ \sigma$, $v =_E t[r\sigma]_p$, $l_i\sigma \to_{R,B} r_i\sigma$, for $1 \leq i \leq n$, and $E_0 \vDash (\phi \wedge \phi^\circ)\sigma$, then we say there is a one-step transition $t \to^1_{R,B} v$.*

We write $t \xrightarrow[c,p,\sigma \ R,B]{1} v$ when we need to make explicit the rule, position, and substitution. Any of these items can be omitted when it is irrelevant.

Definition 23 (Normalized substitution). *Given a rewrite theory $\mathcal{R} = (\Sigma, E, R)$ with built-in subtheory (Σ_0, E_0), a substitution σ is R/E-normalized (resp. R, B-normalized) iff for each variable x in $dom(\sigma)$ there is no term t in $\mathcal{T}_\Sigma(\mathcal{X})$ such that $x\sigma \to^1_{R/E} t$ (resp. $x\sigma \to^1_{R,B} t$).*

Theorem 1 (Equivalence of R/E and R, B-rewriting). *If $\mathcal{R} = (\Sigma, E_0 \cup B, R)$ is an associated rewrite theory of $\mathcal{R}_0 = (\Sigma, E_0 \cup B, R_0)$ closed under B-extensions, then $\to^1_{R,B} = \to^1_{R/E}$ and $\to_{R,B} = \to_{R/E}$.*

5   Strategies

In this section we present the combinators of a strategy language suitable for narrowing, which is a subset of the Maude strategy language for rewriting [5, 10, 20], a set-theoretic semantics for the language, and an interpretation of this semantics.

A *call strategy* is a name given to a strategy to simplify the development of more complex strategies. A *call strategy definition* is a user-defined association of a strategy to one call strategy.

A rewrite theory $\mathcal{R} = (\Sigma, E, R)$ and a set of call strategy definitions for $\mathcal{R}$, written $Call_\mathcal{R}$, have an associated set of *derivation rules* $\mathcal{D}_{\mathcal{R}, Call_\mathcal{R}}$ that will be defined and used in the following.

5.1   Goals, Derivation Rules and Proof Trees

Definition 24 (Goals). *An* open goal *has the form* $t \rightarrow v/ST$, *where* t, *its* head, *and* v *are terms in* $\mathcal{H}_\Sigma$, *and* ST *is a strategy; a* closed goal *has the form* $\overline{G}$, *with* G *an open goal.*

Definition 25 (Derivation rule). *A derivation rule, has the form* $\overline{G}$ *or* $\frac{G_1 \cdots G_n}{G}$, *where* G, *its* head, *and each* G_i, $1 \leq i \leq n$, *are open goals.*

Definition 26 (Proof tree). *Given a rewrite theory* $\mathcal{R} = (\Sigma, E, R)$ *and a set of call strategy definitions* $Call_\mathcal{R}$, *a proof tree* T *is inductively defined as either: (i) an open or closed goal,* G *or* $\overline{G}$, *or (ii) a derivation tree* $\frac{T_1 \cdots T_n}{G}$, *constructed by application of the derivation rules in* $\mathcal{D}_{\mathcal{R},Call_\mathcal{R}}$, *where each* T_i, $1 \leq i \leq n$, *is a proof tree. The* head *of* T *is* G *in all cases, and we write* $head(T) = G$. T *is said to be* closed *if it has no open goals on it. We denote by* $V_\mathcal{R}$ *the set of all the variables appearing in* R *and* B, $V_{Call_\mathcal{R}}$ *the set of all the variables appearing in* $Call_\mathcal{R}$, *and* $V_{\mathcal{R},Call_\mathcal{R}} = V_\mathcal{R} \cup V_{Call_\mathcal{R}}$.

Definition 27 (Application of a derivation rule to an open goal). *Given any open goal* $t \rightarrow v/ST$ *in a proof tree and a derivation rule with head* $t' \rightarrow v'/ST$ *such that* $t =_E t'$ *and* $v =_E v'$, *the application of the rule to the open goal consists in putting the derivation rule in place of the open goal, but replacing* t' *with* t *and* v' *with* v *anywhere in the rule.*

5.2   Strategies and Their Semantics

The semantics that defines the result of the application of a strategy to the equivalence class of a term is given by a function (in mix-fix notation) $\_@\_ :$ $Strat_{\mathcal{R},Call_\mathcal{R}} \times \mathcal{H}_{\Sigma/E} \longrightarrow \mathcal{P}(\mathcal{H}_{\Sigma/E})$, with $\mathcal{R} = (\Sigma, E_0 \cup B, R)$ and $E = E_0 \cup B$, where $[v]_E$ is an element of $ST @ [t]_E$ if and only if a closed proof tree, c.p.t. from now on, with head $t \rightarrow v/ST$ can be constructed using the derivation rules in $\mathcal{D}_{\mathcal{R},Call_\mathcal{R}}$, also defined below. We will use this set of strategies for narrowing, which is a subset of the Maude strategy language for rewriting [5,10,20]:

1. `Idle and fail`. These are constant strategies that always belong to $Strat_{\mathcal{R},Call_\mathcal{R}}$. While the first one always succeeds, returning the same equivalence class, the second one always fails. For each $[t]_E \in \mathcal{H}_{\Sigma/E}$ there is a derivation rule $\overline{t \rightarrow t/\texttt{idle}} \in \mathcal{D}_{\mathcal{R},Call_\mathcal{R}}$. There are no derivation rules for `fail`.

2. **Rule application.** If $c : l \rightarrow r \text{ if } \bigwedge_{j=1}^m l_j \rightarrow r_j \mid \psi$ is a rule in R, $m \geq 0$, γ is a substitution such that $dom(\gamma) \subseteq vars(c)$, and $\overline{ST} = ST_1, \ldots, ST_m$ is an ordered list of strategies then $RA = c[\gamma]\{\overline{ST}\}$ is a rule application in $Strat_{\mathcal{R},Call_\mathcal{R}}$. For each substitution $\delta : vars(c\gamma) \rightarrow \mathcal{T}_\Sigma$ such that $E_0 \vDash \psi\gamma\delta$, each term u in $\mathcal{H}_\Sigma$, and each position p in $pos(u)$ such that $u|_p = l\gamma\delta$ there is a derivation rule $\frac{l_1\gamma\delta \rightarrow r_1\gamma\delta/ST_1\delta \cdots l_m\gamma\delta \rightarrow r_m\gamma\delta/ST_m\delta}{u \rightarrow u[r\gamma\delta]_p/RA}$ in $\mathcal{D}_{\mathcal{R},Call_\mathcal{R}}$.

3. **Top.** It is possible to restrict the application of a rule in R only to the top of the term. This is useful for structural rules, that are applied to the whole state, or for the strategies applied on the conditional part of a rule.

If $c : l \rightarrow r$ if $\bigwedge_{j=1}^{m} l_j \rightarrow r_j \mid \psi$ is a rule in R, $m \geq 0$, γ is a substitution, such that $dom(\gamma) \subseteq vars(c)$, $\overline{ST} = ST_1, \ldots, ST_m$ is an ordered list of strategies, and we call $RA = c[\gamma]\{\overline{ST}\}$, then $\mathtt{top}(RA)$ is a strategy in $Strat_{\mathcal{R}, Call_{\mathcal{R}}}$. For each substitution $\delta : vars(c\gamma) \rightarrow \mathcal{T}_\Sigma$ such that $E_0 \vDash \psi\gamma\delta$, there is a derivation rule $\frac{l_1\gamma\delta \rightarrow r_1\gamma\delta / ST_1\delta \cdots l_m\gamma\delta \rightarrow r_m\gamma\delta / ST_m\delta}{l\gamma\delta \rightarrow r\gamma\delta / \mathtt{top}(RA)}$ in $\mathcal{D}_{\mathcal{R}, Call_{\mathcal{R}}}$.

4. **Call strategy.** Call strategy definitions allow the use of parameters and the implementation of recursive strategies. We list the semantics for their *invocations*, for any pair of terms t and v in $\mathcal{H}_\Sigma$ such that $ls(t) \equiv_\leq ls(v)$:

   – If $\mathtt{sd}$ $CS(\bar{x}) := ST \in Call_{\mathcal{R}}$, where $\bar{x} = x_{s_1}^1, \ldots, x_{s_n}^n$, $n \geq 0$, are the *parameters* of CS, $t_1, \ldots, t_n$ are terms in $\mathcal{T}_\Sigma(\mathcal{X} \backslash V_{\mathcal{R}, Call_{\mathcal{R}}})$, with sorts $s_1, \ldots, s_n$ respectively, and we call $\bar{t} = t_1, \ldots, t_n$, then the call strategy invocation $CS(\bar{t})$ is a strategy in $Strat_{\mathcal{R}, Call_{\mathcal{R}}}$. If $\rho = \{\bar{x} \mapsto \bar{t}\}$ then for every renaming γ such that $dom(\gamma) \cap \backslash\hat{x} = \emptyset$ there is a derivation rule $\frac{t \rightarrow v / ST(\gamma \cup \rho)}{t \rightarrow v / CS(t)}$ in $\mathcal{D}_{\mathcal{R}, Call_{\mathcal{R}}}$.

   – If $\mathtt{csd}$ $CS(\bar{x}) := ST$ if $C \in Call_{\mathcal{R}}$, where everything is as in the previous case, $C = \bigwedge_{j=1}^{m}(l_j = r_j) \wedge \phi$, $m \geq 0$, and $\delta : vars(C(\gamma \cup \rho)) \rightarrow \mathcal{T}_\Sigma$ is a substitution such that $\bar{l}(\gamma \cup \rho)\delta =_E \bar{r}(\gamma \cup \rho)\delta$ and $E_0 \vDash \phi(\gamma \cup \rho)\delta$, then there is a derivation rule $\frac{t \rightarrow v / ST(\gamma \cup \rho\delta)}{t \rightarrow v / CS(t)}$ in $\mathcal{D}_{\mathcal{R}, Call_{\mathcal{R}}}$.

5. **Tests.** A test strategy TS has the form $\mathtt{match}\ u$ s.t. $\bigwedge_{j=1}^{m}(l_j = r_j) \wedge \phi$. It checks a property on an equivalence class $[t]_E$ in $\mathcal{H}_{\Sigma/E}$. The test returns $\{[t]_E\}$ if the property holds, else $\emptyset$. For each equivalence class $[t]_E$ in $\mathcal{H}_{\Sigma/E}$ and ground substitution δ such that $t =_E u\delta$, $\bar{l}\delta =_E \bar{r}\delta$, and $E_0 \vDash \phi\delta$, there is a derivation rule $\frac{}{t \rightarrow t / TS}$ in $\mathcal{D}_{\mathcal{R}, Call_{\mathcal{R}}}$.

6. **If-then-else.** An if-then-else strategy IS has the form $\mathtt{match}\ u$ s.t. $\phi\ ?\ ST_1 : ST_2$. It uses the quantifier-free formula ϕ as test. For each pair of equivalence classes $[t]_E$ and $[v]_E$ in $\mathcal{H}_{\Sigma/E}$ and each substitution $\delta : vars(u) \cup vars(\phi) \rightarrow \mathcal{T}_\Sigma$ such that $t =_E u\delta$, if $E_0 \vDash \phi\delta$, then $\frac{t \rightarrow v / ST_1\delta}{t \rightarrow v / IS} \in \mathcal{D}_{\mathcal{R}, Call_{\mathcal{R}}}$, and if $E_0 \vDash \neg\phi\delta$ then $\frac{t \rightarrow v / ST_2\delta}{t \rightarrow v / IS} \in \mathcal{D}_{\mathcal{R}, Call_{\mathcal{R}}}$. The restriction to SMT conditions will ensure the completeness of the narrowing calculus since, in general, a reachability condition cannot be proved false.

7. **Regular expressions.** Another way of combining strategies is the use of regular expressions: ; (concatenation), | (union), and + (iteration). $ST*$ is defined as $\mathtt{idle} \mid ST+$. Let ST and ST' be strategies, and let t, v and u be terms in $\mathcal{H}_\Sigma$ such that $ls(t) \equiv_\leq ls(u) \equiv_\leq ls(v)$. Then, we have rules $\frac{t \rightarrow u / ST_1 \quad u \rightarrow v / ST_2}{t \rightarrow v / ST_1 \ ; ST_2}$, $\frac{t \rightarrow v / ST_1}{t \rightarrow v / ST_1 \mid ST_2}$, $\frac{t \rightarrow v / ST_2}{t \rightarrow v / ST_1 \mid ST_2}$, $\frac{t \rightarrow v / ST}{t \rightarrow v / ST+}$, and $\frac{t \rightarrow v / ST \ ; ST+}{t \rightarrow v / ST+}$ in $\mathcal{D}_{\mathcal{R}, Call_{\mathcal{R}}}$. The scope of this work is restricted to concatenated strategies that have no variables in common.

8. **Rewriting of subterms.** The $\mathtt{matchrew}$ combinator allows the selection of a subterm to apply a rule. $\mathtt{Matchrew}$ strategies have the form $MS = \mathtt{matchrew}\ u$ s.t. $\bigwedge_{j=1}^{m}(l_j = r_j) \wedge \phi$ by $x_{s_1}^1$ using $ST_1, \ldots, x_{s_n}^n$ using ST_n, where $\bar{x} = x_{s_1}^1, \ldots, x_{s_n}^n$ are the *match parameters* of MS. We will also use the short-form $MS = \mathtt{matchrew}\ u$ s.t. $\bar{l} = \bar{r} \wedge \phi$ by $\bar{x}$ using $\overline{ST}$. For each n-tuple $(t_1, \ldots, t_n)$ of terms in $\mathcal{H}_\Sigma^n$ such that $ls(\bar{t}) \leq \bar{s}$, and each substitution

δ such that $u\delta \in \mathcal{T}_{\Sigma}$, $\{l_j\delta, r_j\delta\}_{j=1}^{m} \subset \mathcal{T}_{\Sigma}$, $\bar{l}\delta =_E \bar{r}\delta$, $\phi\delta \in \mathcal{T}_{\Sigma}$, and $E_0 \vDash \phi\delta$,
there is a derivation rule $\dfrac{x_{s_1}^1\delta \to t_1/ST_1\delta \cdots x_{s_n}^n\delta \to t_n/ST_n\delta}{u\delta \to u\delta[t]_{\bar{p}}/MS}$ in $\mathcal{D}_{\mathcal{R}, Call_{\mathcal{R}}}$.

5.3 Interpretation of the Semantics

We enumerate some of the properties of the semantics for each c.p.t. T formed
using the rules in $\mathcal{D}_{\mathcal{R}, Call_{\mathcal{R}}}$, with head $t \to v/ST$:

1. This is the main property: $t \to_{R/E} v$.
2. If $ST = \texttt{idle}$ then $[t]_E = [v]_E$.
3. If $ST = c[\gamma]$ then $t \xrightarrow[c\gamma]{1}_{R/E} v$.
4. If $ST = CS$, where $\texttt{sd } CS := ST_1 \in Call_{\mathcal{R}}$, then $[v]_E \in ST_1@[t]_E$.
5. If $ST = c[\gamma]\{ST_1, \ldots, ST_m\}$, with $c : l \to r \text{ if } \bigwedge_{j=1}^{m} l_j \to r_j \mid \psi$ a rule
   in R, then there is a substitution δ such that $[r_i\gamma\delta]_E \in ST_i\delta @ [l_i\gamma\delta]_E$, for
   $1 \le i \le m$, and $t \xrightarrow[c,\gamma\delta]{1}_{R/E} v$.
6. If $ST = \texttt{matchrew } u \text{ s.t. } \bar{l} = \bar{r} \wedge \phi \text{ by } \bar{x} \text{ using } \overline{ST}$, where $u = u[x_{s_1}^1, \ldots, x_{s_n}^n]_{\bar{p}}$
   then there exist a substitution δ, where $\delta_{V_{u,\phi,\bar{l},\bar{r}}}$ is ground, and terms $t_1, \ldots, t_n$
   in $\mathcal{H}_{\Sigma}$ such that $t =_E u\delta$, $\bar{l}\delta =_E \bar{r}\delta$, $E_0 \vDash \phi\delta$, $[t_i]_E \in ST_i\delta @ [x_{s_i}^i\delta]_E$, for
   $1 \le i \le n$, and $v =_E u\delta[t]_{\bar{p}}$.

6 Reachability Problems

In this section we present the concept of reachability problem, together with its
solutions and the properties that a solution to one of these problems has. From
now on, we will consider as valid those rewrite theories $\mathcal{R} = (\Sigma, E_0 \cup B, R)$
whose axioms B are any combination of **associativity**, **commutativity**, and
identity (*ACU rewrite theories*).

Definition 28 (Reachability problem). *Given a rewrite theory $\mathcal{R} = (\Sigma, E_0 \cup B, R)$ and a set of call strategy definitions $Call_{\mathcal{R}}$, a reachability problem
is an expression P with the form $\bigwedge_{i=1}^{n} u_i \to v_i/ST_i \mid \phi \mid V, \nu$, where u_i and v_i
are terms in $\mathcal{H}_{\Sigma}(\mathcal{X})$, ST_i is a strategy in $Strat_{\mathcal{R}, Call_{\mathcal{R}}}$, $\phi \in QF(\mathcal{X}_0)$, $V \subset \mathcal{X}$ is
the finite set of parameters of the problem, i.e., variables that have to be given a
ground value, and ν is a substitution such that $dom(\nu) \subseteq V$ and $ran(\nu)$ consists
only of new variables. We define $vars(P) = vars(\bar{u}, \bar{v}, \phi)$. V must always verify:
(1) $vars(P) \subseteq V$, $vars(B) \cap V = \emptyset$, and $V_{\mathcal{R}} \cap V_{Call_{\mathcal{R}}} \subseteq V$, (2) concatenated
and iterated strategies may have in common only variables from V, and (3) V
cannot contain: (i) any variable in $dom(\gamma)$ for any strategy $c[\gamma]$ that may appear
in $Call_{\mathcal{R}}$ or ST_i, $1 \le i \le n$, (ii) any variable in $\hat{x}$ for any call strategy definition $\texttt{sd } C(\bar{x})$ or $\texttt{csd } C(\bar{x})$ that may appear in $Call_{\mathcal{R}}$, or (iii) any variable in
$matchParam(\overline{ST}) \cup matchParam(Call_{\mathcal{R}})$.*

Definition 29 (Instances). *Given a rewrite theory* $\mathcal{R} = (\Sigma, E_0 \cup B, R)$, *a set of call strategy declarations* $Call_{\mathcal{R}}$, *and a substitution* σ *such that* $vars(B) \cap (dom(\sigma) \cup ran(\sigma)) = \emptyset$, *the instance* $\mathcal{R}^\sigma$ *of* $\mathcal{R}$ *is the rewrite theory that results from the simultaneous replacement of every instance in* R *of any variable* $x \in dom(\sigma)$ *with* $x\sigma$, $Call_{\mathcal{R}}^\sigma$ *is the set of call strategy declarations that results from the simultaneous replacement of every instance in* $Call_{\mathcal{R}}$ *of any variable* $x \in dom(\sigma)$ *with* $x\sigma$, *and* $Strat_{\mathcal{R}, Call_{\mathcal{R}}}^\sigma$ *is their set of associated strategies. For every strategy* ST *in* $Strat_{\mathcal{R}, Call_{\mathcal{R}}}$ *we denote by* ST^σ *its corresponding strategy in* $Strat_{\mathcal{R}, Call_{\mathcal{R}}}^\sigma$. *We denote by* $\mathcal{D}_{\mathcal{R}, Call_{\mathcal{R}}}^\sigma$ *the associated set of derivation rules.*

Although the label, say c, of an instantiated rule remains the same, we will use superscripts, say c^σ, to distinguish the instances of a rule.

Definition 30 (Solution of a reachability problem). *Given a rewrite theory* $\mathcal{R} = (\Sigma, E_0 \cup B, R)$ *and a set of call strategy definitions* $Call_{\mathcal{R}}$, *a solution of the reachability problem* $P = \bigwedge_{i=1}^n t_i \rightarrow v_i / ST_i \mid \phi \mid V, \nu$ *is a substitution* $\sigma : V \rightarrow \mathcal{T}_\Sigma$ *such that* $\sigma = \nu \cdot \sigma'$ *for some substitution* σ', $E_0 \vDash \phi\sigma$, *and* $[v_i\sigma]_E \in ST_i^\sigma @[t_i\sigma]_E$ *(hence* $t_i\sigma \rightarrow_{\mathcal{R}^\sigma/E} v_i\sigma$), *for* $1 \leq i \leq n$.

7 Strategies in Reachability by Conditional Narrowing Modulo SMT and Axioms

In this section, the narrowing calculus for reachability with strategies is introduced, and its soundness and weak completeness are stated.

Definition 31 (Instance of a set of variables). *Given a set of variables* V *and a substitution* ν, *we call* $V^\nu = (V \backslash dom(\nu)) \cup ran(\nu_V)$.

Definition 32 (Reachability goal and instantiation). *Given a rewrite theory* $\mathcal{R} = (\Sigma, E_0 \cup B, R)$ *and a set of call strategy definitions* $Call_{\mathcal{R}}$, *a reachability goal* G *is an expression with the form (1)* $(\bigwedge_{i=1}^n u_i' \rightarrow v_i' / ST_i \mid \phi')^\nu \varrho_\nu \mid V, \nu$, *or (2)* $(u_1'|_p \rightarrow^1 x_k, u_1'[x_k]_p \rightarrow v_1' / ST_1 \wedge \bigwedge_{i=2}^n u_i' \rightarrow v_i' / ST_i \mid \phi')^\nu \varrho_\nu \mid V, \nu$, *where* ν *and* ϱ_ν *are substitutions,* $dom(\nu) \subseteq V$, $dom(\varrho_\nu) \cap (V \cup V^\nu) = \emptyset$, $V \subset \mathcal{X}$ *is finite, call* $(\bar{u}, \bar{v}, \phi) = (\bar{u}', \bar{v}', \phi')^\nu \varrho_\nu$, $n \geq 1$, u_i' *and* v_i' *are terms in* $\mathcal{H}_\Sigma(\mathcal{X})$, $ST_i \in Strat_{\mathcal{R}, Call_{\mathcal{R}}}$, *for* $1 \leq i \leq n$, *and* $\phi \in QF(\mathcal{X}_0)$; *also, in the second case,* $p \in pos(u_1)$, $k = [ls(u_1|_p)]$, *the kind of the least sort of* $u_1|_p$, $x_k \notin V_{\bar{u}', \bar{v}', \phi', \overline{ST}} \cup V \cup ran(\nu) \cup dom(\varrho_\nu) \cup ran(\varrho_\nu)$, *and* ST_1 *has the form* $RA; ST$, *with* RA *a rule application.*

In the first case, each one of the elements in the conjunctions is an open goal, for which we define $V_{u \rightarrow v/ST} = V_{u,v}$, *and* $V_G = V_{\bar{u}, \bar{v}, \phi} \cup V^\nu$; *in the second case, we say that* x_k *is the connecting variable of the goal and we define* $V_G = \{x_k\} \cup V_{\bar{u}, \bar{v}, \phi} \cup V^\nu$. *We will write 'goal' as a synonym of 'reachability goal'.*

Definition 33 (Instance of a goal). *If* G *is a goal of the form* $(\bigwedge_{i=1}^n S_i \mid \phi)^\nu \varrho_\nu \mid V, \nu$ *and* σ *is a substitution such that* $dom(\sigma) \cap V^\nu \neq \emptyset$, *then we define the instance* $G\sigma$ *of* G, *where* $\mu = (\nu\sigma)_V$ *and* $\varrho_\mu = (\varrho_\nu\sigma)_{V_G \backslash V}$, *as* $G\sigma = (\bigwedge_{i=1}^n S_i \mid \phi)^\mu \varrho_\mu \mid V, \mu$.

When $dom(\sigma) \cap V^\nu = \emptyset$, σ is directly applied to every term and formula in G thus avoiding circularity in this definition.

Definition 34 (Admissible goals). *Only two types of goals are admitted in our work: (a) those goals coming from a reachability problem $\bigwedge_{i=1}^{n} u_i \rightarrow v_i/ST_i \mid \phi \mid V, \nu$, which is transformed into the goal $\bigwedge_{i=1}^{n} u_i\nu \rightarrow v_i\nu/ST_i^\nu; \mathtt{idle} \mid \phi\nu \mid V, \nu$, with $\varrho_\nu = none$, and (b) those goals generated by repeatedly applying the inference rules for reachability (see excerpt in Fig. 2) to one goal of type (a).*

The notation $G \leadsto_{[r],\sigma} G'$, a *narrowing step*, will be used to indicate that rule $[r]$ has been applied with substitution σ to G, yielding G'.

Definition 35 (Solution of a goal). *Given a rewrite theory $\mathcal{R} = (\Sigma, E_0 \cup B, R)$, a set of call strategy definitions $Call_\mathcal{R}$ for $\mathcal{R}$, and a goal G, a substitution $\sigma : vars(G) \rightarrow T_\Sigma$, where $\nu' = (\nu\sigma)_V$ and $\varrho_{\nu'} = (\varrho_\nu\sigma)_{\backslash V}$, is a solution of G iff:*

1. *if $G = \bigwedge_{i=1}^{n} u_i \rightarrow v_i/ST_i^\nu \varrho_\nu \mid \phi \mid V, \nu$ then $E_0 \models \phi\sigma$ and $[v_i\sigma]_E \in ST_i^{\nu'} \varrho_{\nu'} @[u_i\sigma]_E$ (hence $u_i\sigma \rightarrow_{R^{\nu'}/E} v_i\sigma$), for $1 \leq i \leq n$, and*

2. *if $G = u_1|_p \rightarrow^1 x_k, u_1[x_k]_p \rightarrow v_1/ST_1^\nu \varrho_\nu \wedge \bigwedge_{i=2}^{n} u_i \rightarrow v_i/ST_i^\nu \varrho_\nu \mid \phi \mid V, \nu$, where $ST_1 = RA; ST$, then $E_0 \models \phi\sigma$, $[x_k\sigma]_E \in RA^{\nu'} \varrho_{\nu'} @[u_1\sigma|_p]_E$, $[v_1\sigma]_E \in ST^{\nu'} \varrho_{\nu'} @[u_1[x_k]_p\sigma]_E$, and $[v_i\sigma]_E \in ST_i^{\nu'} \varrho_{\nu'} @[u_i\sigma]_E$, for $2 \leq i \leq n$.*

We call $nil \mid \phi \mid V, \nu$, where ϕ is satisfiable and $\nu : \mathcal{X} \rightarrow T_\Sigma(\mathcal{X})$ such that $dom(\nu) \subseteq V$, an *empty goal*. Given $\mathcal{R}$ and $\mathcal{R}_B$, a reachability problem $P = \bigwedge_{i=1}^{n} u_i \rightarrow v_i/ST_i \mid \phi \mid V, \nu$ is solved by applying the inference rules for reachability (see excerpt in Fig. 2), starting with $G = \bigwedge_{i=1}^{n} u_i\nu \rightarrow v_i\nu/(ST_i^\nu; \mathtt{idle}) \mid \phi\nu \mid V, \nu$ in a top-down manner, until an empty goal is obtained.

Figure 2 is an excerpt of the calculus rules. We briefly explain rule $[w]$ (matchrew): we rename the matching parameters from $\bar{z}$ to the fresh variables $\bar{x}$ with γ. Once abstracted u and $t[\bar{x}]_{\bar{p}}$ to u° and t° and B-unified u° and t° with σ, we search for a unifier of $\bar{l}\gamma\sigma$ and $\bar{r}\gamma\sigma$, say α, using the $\mathtt{idle}$ strategy. Once found, the open goals $(\bar{x}\sigma \rightarrow \bar{y}/\overline{ST}\gamma\sigma)\alpha$, where $\bar{y}$ is fresh, will find a substitution β that makes $[y_i\beta]_E$ an element of $ST_i\gamma\sigma\alpha\beta@[x_i\sigma\alpha\beta]_E$, for $1 \leq i \leq n$, and go on trying to find solutions for the open goal $(t[\bar{y}]_{\bar{p}} \rightarrow v/ST)\sigma\alpha\beta$.

Definition 36 (Narrowing path and computed answer). *Given $\mathcal{R}_B = (\Sigma, E_0 \cup B, R_B)$, an associated rewrite theory of $\mathcal{R} = (\Sigma, E_0 \cup B, R)$ closed under B-extensions, , and a reachability goal G with set of parameters V and substitution ν_0, if there is a narrowing path $G \leadsto_{\sigma_1} G_1 \leadsto_{\sigma_2} \cdots \leadsto_{\sigma_{n-1}} G_{n-1} \leadsto_{\sigma_n} nil \mid \psi \mid V, \nu$ then we write $G \leadsto_\sigma^* nil \mid \psi \mid V, \nu$, where $\sigma = \sigma_1 \cdots \sigma_n$, and we call $\nu \mid \psi$ a computed answer for G.*

Theorem 2 (Soundness of the Calculus for Reachability Goals). *Given an associated rewrite theory $\mathcal{R} = (\Sigma, E_0 \cup B, R)$ closed under B-extensions and a reachability goal G, if $\nu \mid \psi$ is a computed answer for G then for each substitution $\rho : V^\nu \rightarrow T_\Sigma$ such that $\psi\rho$ is satisfiable, $\nu \cdot \rho$ is a solution for G.*

– [d1] idle

$$\frac{u \to v/\texttt{idle} \ (\wedge \ \Delta) \mid \phi \mid V, \nu}{(\Delta \sigma) \mid \psi \mid V, (\nu \sigma)_V}$$

where $abstract_{\Sigma_1}((u,v)) = \langle \lambda(\bar{x}, \bar{y}).(u^\circ, v^\circ); (\theta^\circ_u, \theta^\circ_v); (\phi^\circ_u, \phi^\circ_v) \rangle$, σ in
$CSU_B(u^\circ = v^\circ)$,
$vars(\psi) \subseteq vars((\phi \wedge \phi^\circ_u \wedge \phi^\circ_v)\sigma)$, $E_0 \vdash \psi \Leftrightarrow (\phi \wedge \phi^\circ_u \wedge \phi^\circ_v)\sigma$, and ψ is satisfiable

– [p2] plus

$$\frac{u \to v/ST_1+ \, ; ST \ (\wedge \ \Delta) \mid \phi \mid V, \nu}{u \to v/ST_1 \, ; ST_1+ \, ; ST \ (\wedge \ \Delta) \mid \phi \mid V, \nu}$$

– [i1] if then else

$$\frac{u \to v/\texttt{match } t \ \texttt{s.t. } \phi' \ ? \ ST_1 : ST_2 \, ; ST \ (\wedge \ \Delta) \mid \phi \mid V, \nu}{(u \to v \ /ST_1 \, ; ST \ (\wedge \ \Delta))\sigma \mid \psi \mid V, (\nu \sigma)_V}$$

where $abstract_{\Sigma_1}((u,t)) = \langle \lambda(\bar{x}, \bar{y}).(u^\circ, t^\circ); (\theta^\circ_u, \theta^\circ_t); (\phi^\circ_u, \phi^\circ_t) \rangle$, σ in
$CSU_B(u^\circ = t^\circ)$,
$vars(\psi) \subseteq vars((\phi \wedge \phi' \wedge \phi^\circ_u \wedge \phi^\circ_t)\sigma)$, $E_0 \vdash \psi \Leftrightarrow (\phi \wedge \phi' \wedge \phi^\circ_u \wedge \phi^\circ_t)\sigma$, and ψ is
satisfiable

– [t] transitivity

$$\frac{u \to v/RA \, ; ST \ (\wedge \ \Delta) \mid \phi \mid V, \nu}{u \to^1 x_k, x_k \to v/RA \, ; ST \ (\wedge \ \Delta) \mid \phi \mid V, \nu}$$

where RA is a rule application, $u \in \mathcal{H}_\Sigma(\mathcal{X}) \setminus \mathcal{X}$, $k = [ls(u)]$, and x_k fresh variable

– [r] rule application

$$\frac{u|_p \to^1 x_k, u[x_k]_p \to v/c[\gamma]\{ST_1, \ldots, ST_n\} \, ; ST \ (\wedge \ \Delta) \mid \phi \mid V, \nu}{(\bigwedge^n_{i=1}(l_i\gamma \to r_i\gamma/ST_i; \texttt{idle}) \wedge u[r\gamma]_p \to v \ /ST \ (\wedge \ \Delta))\sigma \mid \psi \mid V, (\nu \sigma)_V}$$

where $c : l \to r$ if $\bigwedge^n_{i=1}(l_i \to r_i) \mid \phi'$ fresh version, except for $dom(\gamma) \cup V^\nu$, of a
rule c in R^ν,
$abstract_{\Sigma_1}((u|_p, l\gamma)) = \langle \lambda(\bar{u}, \bar{y}).(u^\circ, l^\circ); (\sigma^\circ_u, \sigma^\circ); (\phi^\circ_u, \phi^\circ_l) \rangle$, σ in $CSU_B(u^\circ = l^\circ)$,
$\sigma = \sigma' \cup \{x_k \mapsto r\gamma\sigma'\}$, $vars(\psi) \subseteq vars((\phi \wedge \phi^\circ_u \wedge \phi^\circ_l \wedge (\phi'\gamma))\sigma)$,
$E_0 \vdash \psi \Leftrightarrow (\phi \wedge \phi^\circ_u \wedge \phi^\circ_l \wedge (\phi'\gamma))\sigma$, and ψ is satisfiable

– [w] matchrew

$$\frac{u \to v/\texttt{matchrew } t[\bar{z}]_{\bar{p}} \ \texttt{s.t. } \bigwedge^m_{j=1}(l_j = r_j) \wedge \phi' \ \texttt{by } \bar{z} \ \texttt{using } \overline{ST} \, ; ST \ (\wedge \ \Delta) \mid \phi \mid V, \nu}{(\bigwedge^m_{j=1}(l_j\gamma \to r_j\gamma/\texttt{idle}) \wedge \bigwedge^n_{i=1}(x_i \to y_i/ST_i\gamma; \texttt{idle}) \wedge t[\bar{y}]_{\bar{p}} \to v/ \ ST \ (\wedge \ \Delta))\sigma \mid \psi \mid V, (\nu \sigma)_V}$$

where $\bar{z} = z_1, \ldots, z_n$, $\bar{x}$ and $\bar{y}$ fresh versions of $\bar{z}$, $\gamma = \{z_i \mapsto x_i\}^n_{i=1}$,
$abstract_{\Sigma_1}((u, t[\bar{x}]_{\bar{p}})) = \langle \lambda(\bar{w}, \bar{w}').(u^\circ, t^\circ); (\theta^\circ_u, \theta^\circ_t); (\phi^\circ_u, \phi^\circ_t) \rangle$,
σ in $CSU_B(u^\circ = t^\circ)$, $vars(\psi) \subseteq vars((\phi \wedge \phi' \wedge \phi^\circ_u \wedge \phi^\circ_t)\sigma)$,
$E_0 \vdash \psi \Leftrightarrow (\phi \wedge \phi' \wedge \phi^\circ_u \wedge \phi^\circ_t)\sigma$, and ψ is satisfiable

– [c2] call strategy

$$\frac{u \to v/CS(\bar{t}) \, ; ST \ (\wedge \ \Delta) \mid \phi \mid V, \nu}{\bigwedge^m_{j=1}(l_j\gamma \to r_j\gamma/\texttt{idle}) \wedge u \to v/ST_2\gamma \, ; ST \ (\wedge \ \Delta) \mid \psi \mid V, \nu}$$

where csd $CS(\bar{x}) := ST_1$ if C in $Call^\nu_\mathcal{R}$, $\gamma = \{\bar{x} \mapsto \bar{t}\}$,
ST_2 if $\bigwedge^m_{j=1}(l_j = r_j) \wedge \phi$ fresh version of ST_1 if C, except for $dom(\gamma) \cup V^\nu$,
$vars(\psi) \subseteq vars(\phi'\gamma \wedge \phi)$, $E_0 \vdash \psi \Leftrightarrow \phi'\gamma \wedge \phi$, and ψ is satisfiable

Fig. 2. Inference rules for reachability modulo SMT plus B with strategies (excerpt)

Theorem 3 (Weak Completeness of the Calculus for Reachability Goals). *Given an associated rewrite theory* $\mathcal{R} = (\Sigma, E_0 \cup B, R)$ *closed under B-extensions and a reachability problem* $P = \bigwedge_{i=1}^{n} u_i \to v_i / ST_i \mid \phi \mid V, \mu$, *where* μ *is R/E-normalized, if* $\sigma : V \to \mathcal{T}_\Sigma$ *is a R/E-normalized solution for P then there exist a formula* $\psi \in QF(\mathcal{X}_0)$ *and two substitutions, say λ and ρ, such that* $\bigwedge_{i=1}^{n} u_i \mu \to v_i \mu / ST_i^\mu; \mathtt{idle} \mid \phi\mu \mid V, \mu \rightsquigarrow_\lambda^+ nil \mid \psi \mid V, \nu$, $\sigma =_E \nu \cdot \rho$, *and $\psi\rho$ is satisfiable, where* $\nu = (\mu\lambda)_V$.

The proof of both theorems can be found in the technical report TR-02/2021 at http://maude.ucm.es/cnarrowing.

8   Example

In this example, where $\mathtt{ct} = 20$ (cooktime) and $\mathtt{ft} = 61$ (failtime), from an initial system with an empty toaster, an empty dish, and at most one toast in the bin, we want to reach a final system where there are three toasts in the dish and all the remaining elements are empty. We choose $Call_\mathcal{R}$ to consist of the following call strategy definitions:

- sd test := match $N/B/Y; V\,W/OK$ s.t. $Y < \mathtt{ft}$
- sd cook1 := matchrew $N/B/K/OK$ s.t. $K = Y; RV$ by K using kitchCook
- sd kitchCook := top(kitchen[$none$]) ; top(cook[$none$]{toasts, toasts})
- sd toasts := top(toast1[$none$]) | top(toast2[$none$])
- sd noCook := top(bin[$none$]) | top(pan[$none$]) | top(dish[$none$])
- sd loop := (noCook | (cook1 ; test ; noCook))+
- sd solve := top(bag[$none$]) ; top(bag[$none$]); (top(bag[$none$])|idle); loop.

The (symbolic) reachability problem is: $P = N / T / 0 ; \mathtt{zt\,zt} / 0 \to 0 / \mathtt{zt} / Y ; \mathtt{zt\,zt} / 3 / \mathtt{solve} \mid N > 0 \wedge N < 3 \mid \{\mathtt{ct}, \mathtt{ft}, N, T, Y\}, \{\mathtt{ct} \mapsto 20, \mathtt{ft} \mapsto 61\}$.

In P we use the strategy solve. As there must be either two or three toasts in the bag, we impose the application of the rule bag twice, followed by the nondeterministic strategy top(bag[$none$])|idle, and we use the variable T with sort Toast to represent the bin, since both EmptyToast and RealToast are subsorts of Toast, subsort of Bin, so T covers both initial cases: the one without toasts in the bin and the one with one toast in the bin. The concatenation of the strategy test after each invocation of cook1, comparing the timer against ft, renders the search state space finite.

Among the answers returned by the prototype we have:

a - $\mathtt{ct} \mapsto 20, \mathtt{ft} \mapsto 61, N \mapsto 3, Y \mapsto 60, T \mapsto \mathtt{zt}$,
b - $\mathtt{ct} \mapsto 20, \mathtt{ft} \mapsto 61, N \mapsto 2, Y \mapsto 60, T \mapsto [0, 0]$,
c - $\mathtt{ct} \mapsto 20, \mathtt{ft} \mapsto 61, N \mapsto 2, Y \mapsto 40, T \mapsto [20, 20]$, and
d - $\mathtt{ct} \mapsto 20, \mathtt{ft} \mapsto 61, N \mapsto 2, Y \mapsto 40 + U + V, T \mapsto [C, D]$ *such that*
$\quad C + U = 20 \wedge D + V = 20 \wedge U + V \le 20 \wedge U > 0 \wedge V > 0$,

stating that we need 60 s when (a) 3 toasts are in the bag or (b) 2 toasts are in the bag and one fresh toast is in the bin. The required amount of time can be smaller: (c) 40 s if the toast in the bin is well-cooked or, if it is not, (d) 40 s plus the remaining toasting time for the toast in the bin, as long as this remaining time is not above 20 s.

9   Conclusions and Related Work

In our previous work [1], we extended the admissible conditions in [19] by: (i) allowing for reachability subgoals in the rewrite rules and (ii) removing all restrictions regarding the variables that appear in the rewrite rules. A narrowing calculus for conditional narrowing modulo $E_0 \cup B$ when E_0 is a subset of the theories handled by SMT solvers, B are the axioms not related to the algebraic data types handled by the SMT solvers, and the conditions in the rules in the rewrite theory are either rewrite conditions or quantifier-free SMT formulas, was presented, and the soundness and weak completeness of the calculus, as well as the completeness of the calculus for topmost rewrite theories was proved.

The current work extends the previous one by adding two novel features: (1) the use of strategies, to drive the search and reduce the state space, and (2) the support for parameters both in the rewrite theories and in the strategies, that allows for the resolution of some reachability problems that could not be specified in the previous calculi that we had developed. A calculus for conditional narrowing modulo $E_0 \cup B$ with strategies and parameters has been presented, and the soundness and weak completeness of the calculus have been proved. To the best of our knowledge, a similar calculus did not previously exist in the literature.

The strategy language that we have proved suitable for our narrowing calculus in this work is a subset of the Maude strategy language [5,10,20]. This strategy language and a connection with SMT solvers have been incorporated into the latest version of the Maude language [4], which is being used to develop the prototype for the calculus in this work.

Conditional narrowing without axioms for equational theories with an order-sorted type structure has been thoroughly studied for increasingly complex categories of term rewriting systems. A wide survey can be found in [16]. The literature is scarce when we allow for extra variables in conditions (e.g., [8]) or conditional narrowing modulo axioms (e.g., [3]).

Narrowing modulo order-sorted unconditional equational logics is covered by Meseguer and Thati [15], being currently used for cryptographic protocol analysis.

The idea of constraint solving by narrowing in combined algebraic domains was presented by Kirchner and Ringeissen [9], where the supported theories had unconstrained equalities and the unconditional rewrite rules had constraints from an algebraic built-in structure.

Escobar, Sasse, and Meseguer [6] have developed the concepts of variant and folding variant narrowing, a narrowing strategy for order-sorted unconditional rewrite theories that terminates on those theories having the *finite variant property*, but it has no counterpart for conditional rewrite theories and it does not allow the use of constraint solvers or strategies.

Foundations for order-sorted conditional rewriting have been published by Meseguer [13]. Cholewa, Escobar, and Meseguer [3] have defined a new hierarchical method, called layered constraint narrowing, to solve narrowing problems in order-sorted conditional equational theories, an approach similar to ours, and given new theoretical results on that matter, including the definition of constrained variants for order-sorted conditional rewrite theories, but with no specific support for SMT solvers.

Order-sorted conditional rewriting with constraint solvers has been addressed by Rocha et al. [19], where the only admitted conditions in the rules are quantifier-free SMT formulas, and the only non-ground terms admitted in the reachability problems are those whose variables have sorts belonging to the SMT sorts supported.

In [14], Meseguer studies reachability in Generalized Rewrite Theories, that include constructors and variants, using equational theories beyond our setup of $E_0 \cup B$ (that only asks for strict B-coherence), but with no rewrite conditions in the rules. Frozenness is used as a type of strategy.

Future work will focus in broadening the applicability of the calculus. One line of work will involve the development of a narrowing calculus for $E_0 \cup (E_1 \cup B)$ unification with strategies, where E_1 is a non-SMT equational theory; another line of work will study the extension of the strategies and reachability problems supported by the calculus.

References

1. Aguirre, L., Martí-Oliet, N., Palomino, M., Pita, I.: Conditional narrowing modulo SMT and axioms. In: Vanhoof, W., Pientka, B. (eds.) Proceedings of the 19th International Symposium on Principles and Practice of Declarative Programming, Namur, Belgium, 09–11 October 2017, pp. 17–28. ACM (2017). http://doi.acm.org/10.1145/3131851.3131856
2. Bruni, R., Meseguer, J.: Semantic foundations for generalized rewrite theories. Theor. Comput. Sci. **360**(1-3), 386–414 (2006). http://dx.doi.org/10.1016/j.tcs.2006.04.012
3. Cholewa, A., Escobar, S., Meseguer, J.: Constrained narrowing for conditional equational theories modulo axioms. Sci. Comput. Program. **112**, 24–57 (2015). https://doi.org/10.1016/j.scico.2015.06.001
4. Durán, F., et al.: Programming and symbolic computation in Maude. J. Log. Algebr. Meth. Program. **110**, 100497 (2020). https://doi.org/10.1016/j.jlamp.2019.100497
5. Eker, S., Martí-Oliet, N., Meseguer, J., Verdejo, A.: Deduction, strategies, and rewriting. In: Archer, M., de la Tour, T.B., Muñoz, C. (eds.) Proceedings of the 6th International Workshop on Strategies in Automated Deduction, STRATEGIES 2006, Seattle, WA, USA, 16 August 2006. Electronic Notes in Theoretical Computer Science, vol. 174, no. 11, pp. 3–25. Elsevier (2007). http://dx.doi.org/10.1016/j.entcs.2006.03.017
6. Escobar, S., Sasse, R., Meseguer, J.: Folding variant narrowing and optimal variant termination. J. Logic Algebraic Program. **81**(7-8), 898–928 (2012). http://dx.doi.org/10.1016/j.jlap.2012.01.002
7. Fay, M.: First-order unification in an equational theory. In: Proceedings of the 4th Workshop on Automated Deduction, Austin, pp. 161–167. Academic Press (1979)
8. Giovannetti, E., Moiso, C.: A completeness result for E-unification algorithms based on conditional narrowing. In: Boscarol, M., Carlucci Aiello, L., Levi, G. (eds.) Foundations of Logic and Functional Programming. LNCS, vol. 306, pp. 157–167. Springer, Heidelberg (1988). https://doi.org/10.1007/3-540-19129-1_7

9. Kirchner, H., Ringeissen, C.: Constraint solving by narrowing in combined algebraic domains. In: Hentenryck, P.V. (ed.) Logic Programming, Proceedings of the Eleventh International Conference on Logic Programming, Santa Marherita Ligure, Italy, 13–18 June 1994, pp. 617–631. MIT Press (1994)

10. Martí-Oliet, N., Meseguer, J., Verdejo, A.: Towards a strategy language for Maude. In: Martí-Oliet, N. (ed.) Proceedings of the Fifth International Workshop on Rewriting Logic and its Applications, WRLA 2004, Barcelona, Spain, 27 March–4 April 2004. Electronic Notes in Theoretical Computer Science, vol. 117, pp. 417–441. Elsevier (2004). https://doi.org/10.1016/j.entcs.2004.06.020

11. Meseguer, J.: Rewriting as a unified model of concurrency. In: Baeten, J.C.M., Klop, J.W. (eds.) CONCUR 1990. LNCS, vol. 458, pp. 384–400. Springer, Heidelberg (1990). https://doi.org/10.1007/BFb0039072

12. Meseguer, J.: Membership algebra as a logical framework for equational specification. In: Presicce, F.P. (ed.) WADT 1997. LNCS, vol. 1376, pp. 18–61. Springer, Heidelberg (1998). https://doi.org/10.1007/3-540-64299-4_26

13. Meseguer, J.: Strict coherence of conditional rewriting modulo axioms. Theor. Comput. Sci. **672**(C), 1–35 (2017). https://doi.org/10.1016/j.tcs.2016.12.026

14. Meseguer, J.: Generalized rewrite theories, coherence completion, and symbolic methods. J. Log. Algebraic Meth. Program. **110** (2020). https://doi.org/10.1016/j.jlamp.2019.100483

15. Meseguer, J., Thati, P.: Symbolic reachability analysis using narrowing and its application to verification of cryptographic protocols. Higher-Order and Symbolic Comput. **20**(1-2), 123–160 (2007). http://dx.doi.org/10.1007/s10990-007-9000-6

16. Middeldorp, A., Hamoen, E.: Completeness results for basic narrowing. Appl. Algebra Eng. Commun. Comput. **5**, 213–253 (1994). http://dx.doi.org/10.1007/BF01190830

17. de Moura, L., Bjørner, N.: Z3: an efficient SMT solver. In: Ramakrishnan, C.R., Rehof, J. (eds.) TACAS 2008. LNCS, vol. 4963, pp. 337–340. Springer, Heidelberg (2008). https://doi.org/10.1007/978-3-540-78800-3_24

18. Plotkin, G.: Building in equational theories. Mach. Intell. **7**, 73–90 (1972)

19. Rocha, C., Meseguer, J., Muñoz, C.A.: Rewriting modulo SMT and open system analysis. J. Log. Algebr. Meth. Program. **86**(1), 269–297 (2017). https://doi.org/10.1016/j.jlamp.2016.10.001

20. Rubio, R., Martí-Oliet, N., Pita, I., Verdejo, A.: Parameterized strategies specification in Maude. In: Fiadeiro, J.L., Tutu, I. (eds.) WADT 2018. LNCS, vol. 11563, pp. 27–44. Springer, Cham (2019). https://doi.org/10.1007/978-3-030-23220-7_2

Optimizing Maude Programs via Program Specialization

María Alpuente[1], Demis Ballis[2], Santiago Escobar[1], Jose Meseguer[3],
and Julia Sapiña[1(✉)]

[1] VRAIN, Universitat Politècnica de València, Valencia, Spain
{alpuente,sescobar,jsapina}@upv.es
[2] DMIF, Università degli Studi di Udine, Udine, Italy
demis.ballis@uniud.it
[3] University of Illinois at Urbana-Champaign, Urbana, IL, USA
meseguer@illinois.edu

Abstract. We develop an automated specialization framework for rewrite theories that model concurrent systems. A rewrite theory $\mathcal{R} = (\Sigma, E \uplus B, R)$ consists of two main components: an order-sorted equational theory $\mathcal{E} = (\Sigma, E \uplus B)$ that defines the system states as terms of an algebraic data type and a term rewriting system R that models the concurrent evolution of the system as state transitions. Our main idea is to partially evaluate the underlying equational theory $\mathcal{E}$ to the specific calls required by the rewrite rules of R in order to make the system computations more efficient. The specialization transformation relies on *folding variant narrowing*, which is the symbolic operational engine of Maude's equational theories. We provide three instances of our specialization scheme that support distinct classes of theories that are relevant for many applications. The effectiveness of our method is finally demonstrated in some specialization examples.

1 Introduction

Maude is a high-performance, concurrent functional language that efficiently implements Rewriting Logic (RWL), a logic of change that unifies a wide variety of models of concurrency [38]. Maude is endowed with advanced symbolic reasoning capabilities that support a high-level, elegant, and efficient approach to programming and analyzing complex, highly nondeterministic software systems [24]. Maude's symbolic capabilities are based on equational unification and *narrowing*, a mechanism that extends term rewriting by replacing pattern matching with unification [49], and they provide advanced logic programming features such as unification modulo user-definable equational theories and symbolic reachability analysis in rewrite theories. Intricate computing problems may be effectively and naturally solved in Maude thanks to the synergy of

This work has been partially supported by the EC H2020-EU grant agreement No. 952215 (TAILOR), grants RTI2018-094403-B-C32 and PID2021-122830OB-C42 funded by MCIN/AEI/10.13039/501100011033 and by "ERDF A way of making Europe", by Generalitat Valenciana under grant PROMETEO/2019/098, and by the Department Strategic Plan (PSD) of the University of Udine—Interdepartmental Project on Artificial Intelligence (2021-25).

© Springer Nature Switzerland AG 2023
P. Lopez-Garcia et al. (Eds.): Hermenegildo Festschrift 2022, LNCS 13160, pp. 21–50, 2023.
https://doi.org/10.1007/978-3-031-31476-6_2

these recently developed symbolic capabilities and classical Maude features, such as: (i) rich type structures with sorts (types), subsorts, and overloading; (ii) equational rewriting modulo various combinations of axioms such as associativity (A), commutativity (C), and identity (U); and (iii) classical reachability analysis in rewrite theories.

Partial evaluation (PE) is a program transformation technique that automatically specializes a program to a part of its input that is known statically (at *specialization time*) [23, 33]. Partial evaluation conciliates generality with efficiency by providing automatic program optimization. In the context of logic programming, partial evaluation is often called partial deduction and allows to not only instantiate input variables with constant values but also with terms that may contain variables, thus providing extra capabilities for program specialization [35, 36]. Early instances of this framework implemented partial evaluation algorithms for different narrowing strategies, including lazy narrowing [12], innermost narrowing [15], and needed narrowing [2, 16].

The *Narrowing-driven partial evaluation* (NPE) scheme for functional logic program specialization defined in [14, 15] and implemented [1] in is strictly more powerful than the PE of both logic programs and functional programs thanks to combining functional reduction with the power of logic variables and unification by means of narrowing. In the *Equational narrowing-driven partial evaluation* (EQNPE) scheme of [7], this enhanced specialization capability was extended to the partial evaluation of order-sorted equational theories. Given a signature Σ of program operators together with their type definition, an equational theory $\mathcal{E} = (\Sigma, E \uplus B)$ combines a set E of equations (that are implicitly oriented from left to right and operationally used as simplification rules) on Σ and a set B of commonly occurring axioms (which are implicitly expressed in Maude as operator attributes using the `assoc`, `comm`, and `id:` keywords) that are essentially used for B-matching[1]. To be executable in Maude, the equational theory $\mathcal{E}$ is required to be *convergent* (i.e., the equations E are confluent, terminating, sort-decreasing, and coherent modulo B). This ensures that every input expression t has one (and only one) *canonical* form $t\downarrow_{\vec{E},B}$ up to B-equality.

This paper addresses the specialization of *rewrite theories* $\mathcal{R} = (\Sigma, E \uplus B, R)$ whose system transitions are specified by rewrite rules R on top of an underlying equational theory $\mathcal{E} = (\Sigma, E \uplus B)$. Altogether, the rewrite theory $\mathcal{R}$ specifies a concurrent system that evolves by rewriting states using *equational rewriting*, i.e., rewriting with the rewrite rules in R *modulo* the equations and axioms in $\mathcal{E}$ [38]. In Maude, rewrite theories can also be *symbolically* executed by narrowing at *two levels*: (i) narrowing with the (typically non-confluent and non-terminating) rules of R modulo $\mathcal{E} = (\Sigma, E \uplus B)$; and (ii) narrowing with the (explicitly) oriented equations $\vec{E}$ modulo the axioms B. They both have practical applications: (i) narrowing with R modulo $\mathcal{E} = (\Sigma, E \uplus B)$ is useful for solving *reachability goals* [43] and *logical model checking* [29]; and (ii) narrowing with $\vec{E}$ modulo B is useful for $\mathcal{E}$-unification and variant computation [31]. Both levels of narrowing should meet some conditions: (i) narrowing with R modulo $\mathcal{E}$ is performed in a "topmost" way (i.e., the rules in R rewrite the global system state) and there must be a finitary equational unification algorithm for $\mathcal{E}$; and (ii) narrowing with $\vec{E}$ modulo B requires that B is a theory with a finitary unification algorithm and that

---

[1] For example, assuming a commutative binary operator $*$, the term $s(0) * 0$ matches within the term $X * s(Y)$ *modulo* the commutativity of symbol $*$ with matching substitution $\{X/0, Y/0\}$.

$\mathscr{E}$ is convergent. When $(\Sigma, E \uplus B)$ additionally has the property that a finite complete set of most general *variants*[2] exists for each term, known as the *finite variant property* (FVP), $\mathscr{E}$-unification is finitary and *topmost* narrowing with R modulo the equations and axioms can be effectively performed.

For variant computation and (variant-based) $\mathscr{E}$-unification, the *folding variant narrowing* (or FV-narrowing) strategy of [31] is used in Maude, whose termination is guaranteed for theories that satisfy the FVP (also known as *finite variant theories*). Another important class of rewrite theories are those that satisfy the so-called *constructor finite variant property* (CFVP), i.e., they have a finite number of most general *constructor* variants [40]. Many relevant theories have the FVP, including theories of interest for Boolean satisfiability and theories that give algebraic axiomatizations of cryptographic functions used in communication protocols, where FVP and CFVP are omnipresent. CFVP is implied by FVP together with *sufficient completeness* modulo axioms (SC); that is, all function calls (i.e., input terms) reduce to *values* (i.e., ground constructor terms [27,32]).

Given the rewrite theory $\mathscr{R} = (\Sigma, E \uplus B, R)$, the key idea of our method is to specialize the underlying equational theory $\mathscr{E} = (\Sigma, E \uplus B)$ to the precise use that the rules of R make of the operators that are defined in $\mathscr{E}$. This is done by partially evaluating $\mathscr{E}$ with respect to the *maximal* (or outermost) function calls that can be retrieved from the rules of R, in such a way that $\mathscr{E}$ gets rid of any possible over-generality and the functional computations given by $\mathscr{E}$ are thus greatly compacted. Nevertheless, while the transformation highly contracts the system states, we deliberately avoid making any states disappear since both reachability analysis and logical model checking generally require the whole search space of rewrite theories to be searched (i.e., all system states).

Our specialization algorithm follows the classic control strategy of logic specializers [36], with two separate components: 1) the local control (managed by an unfolding operator [13]) that avoids infinite evaluations and is responsible for the construction of the residual equations for each specialized call; and 2) the global control (managed by an abstraction operator) that avoids infinite iterations of the partial evaluation algorithm and decides which specialized functions appear in the transformed theory. A postprocessing compression transformation is finally performed that highly compacts the functional computations occurring in the specialized rewrite theory while keeping the system states as reduced as possible.

We provide three different implementations of the unfolding operator based on FV-narrowing that may include some distinct extra control depending on the FVP/CFVP behavior of the equational theory $\mathscr{E}$. More precisely, we distinguish the following three cases:

1. $\mathscr{E}$ does not fulfill the finite variant property: a subsumption check is performed at each FV-narrowing step that compares the current term with all previous narrowing redexes in the same derivation. The subsumption checking relies on the *order-sorted equational homeomorphic embedding* relation of [8] that ensures all infinite FV-narrowing computations are safely stopped;

---

[2] A *variant* [22] of a term t in the theory $\mathscr{E}$ is the canonical (i.e., irreducible) form of $t\sigma$ in $\mathscr{E}$ for a given substitution σ; in symbols, it is represented as the pair $(t\sigma\downarrow_{\vec{E},B}, \sigma)$.

2. $\mathcal{E}$ satisfies the finite variant property: FV-narrowing trees are always finite for any input term, and therefore they are completely deployed; and

3. $\mathcal{E}$ satisfies the finite variant property and is also sufficiently complete: we supplement unfolding with an extra "sort downgrading" transformation in the style of [41] that safely rules out variants that are not constructor terms. This means that all specialized calls get *totally evaluated* and the maximum compression is achieved, thereby dramatically reducing the search space for the construction of the specialized theories.

It is worth noting that our specialization system is based on the Maude's narrowing engine and, hence, it respects the limitations and applicability conditions of the current narrowing implementation. In particular, Maude's narrowing (and thus our specializer) does not support conditional equations, built-in operators and special equational attributes (e.g., owise). However, advances in narrowing and unification for Maude will enlarge the class of rewrite theories that our specialization technique handles.

It is a great pleasure for us to honor Manuel Hermenegildo in this Festschrift. Many of the themes and techniques we present—beginning with partial evaluation, and including as well the solving of constraints in user-definable algebraic domains—are themes to which Manuel and his collaborators have made outstanding contributions. More broadly, we share also with him the passion for logically-based programming language design, so as to integrate within a solid mathematical framework various programming paradigms. Science is, should be, a dialogue. We look forward to continue the pleasure of such a dialogue with Manuel—which some of us initiated with him decades ago—and to his new outstanding contributions in the years to come.

Plan of the Paper. In Sect. 2, we introduce a leading example that illustrates the optimization of rewrite theories that we can achieve by using our specialization technique, which we formalize in Sect. 3. In Sect. 4, we focus on finite variant theories that are sufficiently complete and we demonstrate that both properties, SC and FVP, are preserved by our transformation scheme. In Sect. 5, we instantiate the specialization scheme for the three classes of equational theories already mentioned: theories whose terms may have an infinite number of most general variants, or a finite number of most general variants, or a finite number of most general constructor variants. The proposed methodology is illustrated in Sect. 6 by describing several specializations of the bank account specification of Sect. 2 and by presenting some experiments with the partial evaluator Presto that implements our technique. In Sect. 7, we discuss some related work and we conclude. The complete code of a non-trivial specialization example together with its computed optimizations are given in Appendix.

2   A Leading Example

Let us motivate the power of our specialization scheme by optimizing a simple rewrite theory that is inspired by [41]. The considered example has been engineered to fulfill the conditions for the applicability of all the three instances of our specialization framework.

Example 1. Consider a rewrite theory that specifies a bank account system with managed accounts. The system automates a simple investment model for the beginner investor that, whenever the account balance exceeds a given investment threshold, the excess balance is automatically moved to investment funds. The system allows deposits and withdrawals to occur non-deterministically, where each withdrawal occurs in two steps: the withdrawal is initiated through a withdrawal request provided that the amount to be withdrawn is less than or equal to the current account balance. Later on, the actual withdrawal is completed. On the contrary, deposits are single-step operations that need to consume explicit deposit messages to be performed. This asymmetric behaviour is due to the fact that the amount in a deposit operation is unbounded, while a withdrawal request is always limited by the account balance. For simplicity, the external operation of the investment portfolio is not considered in the model.

A managed account is modelled as a term

```
< bal: n pend: x overdraft: b threshold: h funds: f >
```

where n is the current balance, x is the amount of money that is currently pending to be withdrawn, b is a Boolean flag that indicates whether or not the account is in the red, h is a fixed upper threshold for the account balance, and funds represents the amount to be invested by the account manager. Messages of the form d(m) and w(m) specify deposit and withdrawal operations, where m is the amount of money to be, respectively, deposited and withdrawn. A bank account state (or simply state) is a pair act # msgs, where act is an account and msgs a multiset of messages. Monetary values in a state are specified by natural numbers in Presburger's style[3]. State transitions are formalized by the three rewrite rules in Fig. 1 (namely, w-req, w, and dep) that respectively implement withdrawal requests, (actual) withdrawals, and deposits.

```
rl [w-req] : < bal: n + m + x pend: x overdraft: false threshold: n + m + x + h funds: f > # msgs
               => < bal: n + m + x pend: x + m overdraft: false threshold: n + h funds: f > #
                  w(m) , msgs .

rl [w] : < bal: n pend: x overdraft: false threshold: n + h funds: f > # w(m),msgs
            => [ m > n ,
               < bal: n pend: x overdraft: true threshold: n + h funds: f > # msgs,
               < bal: n - m pend: x - m overdraft: false threshold: n + h funds: f > # msgs ] .

rl [dep] : < bal: n pend:x overdraft: false threshold: n + m + h funds: f > # d(m),msgs .
             => << bal: n + m pend: x overdraft: false threshold: n + m + h funds: f >> # msgs .
```

Fig. 1. Rewrite rules that model a simple bank account system.

The intended semantics of the three rules is as follows. The rule w-req non-deterministically requests to draw money whenever the account balance covers the request. The requested amount m is added to the amount of pending withdraw requests and the withdraw message w(m) is generated. The rule w implements actual withdrawal of money from the account. When the balance is not enough, the account is blocked by

---

[3] In [40], natural numbers are encoded by using two constants 0 and 1 and an ACU operator + so that a natural number is either the constant 0 or a finite sequence 1 + 1 ... + 1.

setting overdraft to true and the withdrawal attempt fails (for simplicity, the excess of balance that is moved to investment funds is never moved back). If not in overdraft, money can be deposited in the account by processing the deposit message d(m) using rule dep.

The auxiliary functions that are used by the three rules implement the pre-agreed, automated investment policy for a given threshold. They update the account's state by means of an equational theory whose operators and equations are shown in Fig. 2. The equational theory extends Presburger's arithmetic with the operators over natural numbers _>_ and _-_, together with the if-then-construct [_,_, _] and an auxiliary version «...» of the operator <...> that ensures that the current balance n is below the current threshold h; otherwise, it sets the balance to n mod h and increments the funds by n div h, where div is the division for natural numbers and mod is the remainder of the division; both operations are encoded by successive subtractions. Roughly speaking, this operator allows money to be moved from the bal attribute to the funds attribute, whenever the balance exceeds the threshold h. Note that the amount of money in the investment funds is measured in h units (1, 2, ...), which indicate the client's wealth category (the higher the category, the greater the investment advantages). The attribute variant is used to identify the equations to be considered by the FV-narrowing strategy.

The considered equational theory has neither the FVP nor the CFVP since, for instance, the term « bal: n pend: x overdraft:false threshold: h funds: f » has an infinite number of (incomparable) most general (constructor) variants

```
--- Encoding of natural numbers with constants 0,1 and ACU operator +
ops 0 1 : -> Nat [ctor] .
op _+_ : Nat Nat -> Nat [ctor assoc comm id: 0] .

--- greater-than operator
op _>_ : Nat Nat -> Bool .
eq m + n + 1 > n = true [variant] .
eq n > n + m = false [variant] .

--- monus  function
op _-_ : Nat Nat -> Nat .
eq n - (n + m) = 0 [variant] .
eq (n + m) - n = m [variant] .

--- if-then-else construct
op [_,_,_] : Bool State State -> State .
eq [ true,s,s' ] = s [variant] .
eq [ false,s,s' ] = s' [variant] .

--- Account balance simplification
op << bal:_ pend:_ overdraft:_ threshold:_ funds:_ >> : Nat Nat Bool Nat Nat -> Account .
eq << bal: n + h pend: m overdraft: b threshold: h funds: f >>
       = << bal: n pend: m overdraft: false threshold: h funds: f + 1 >> [variant] .
eq << bal: n pend: m overdraft: false threshold: n + h funds: f >>
       = < bal: n pend: m overdraft: false threshold: n + h funds: f > [variant] .
```

Fig. 2. Companion equational theory for the bank account system.

```
( < bal: n' pend: x overdraft: false threshold: h funds: f + 1 >,{n/(n' + h)})
                  .
                  .
( < bal: n' pend: x overdraft: false threshold: h funds: f + 1 + ...+ 1 >,{n/(n' + h +...+ h)})


( < bal: n' pend: x overdraft: false threshold: h funds: f + 1 >,{n/(n' + h)})
                  .
                  .
( < bal: n' pend: x overdraft: false threshold: h funds: f + 1 + ...+ 1 >,{n/(n' + h +...+ h)})


eq f0($4,$5 + $4,$1 + $4,$6,$2,$3)
     = < bal: $5 pend: $1 overdraft: false threshold: $5 + $4 + $6 funds: $2 > # $3 [ variant ] .
eq f0($5 + $3,$5 + $3 + $4,$5,$6,$1,$2)
     = < bal: $4 pend: 0 overdraft: false threshold: $5 + $3 + $4 + $6 funds: $1 > # $2 [ variant ] .
eq f0(1 + $5 + $4,$5,$1,$6,$2,$3)
     = < bal: $5 pend: $1 overdraft: true threshold: $5 + $6 funds: $2 > # $3 [ variant ] .

rl [w-req-s] : < bal: n + x + m pend: x overdraft: false threshold: n + h funds: f > # msgs
             => < bal: n + x + m pend: x + m overdraft: false threshold: n + h funds: f > # msgs,w(m) .
rl [w-s]  : < bal: n pend: x overdraft: false threshold: n + h funds: f > # msgs,w(m)
             => f0(m,n,x,h,f,msgs) .
rl [dep-s] : < bal: n pend: x overdraft: false threshold: n + m + h funds: f > # msgs,d(m)
             => < bal: n + m pend: x overdraft: false threshold: n + m + h funds: f > # msgs .
```

Fig. 3. Specialized bank account system.

Nonetheless, this is not an obstacle to applying our specialization technique as it can naturally handle theories that may not fulfill the FVP, whereas the total evaluation method of [41] can only be applicable to theories that satisfy both, FVP and SC. Actually, in this specific case, the application of our technique generates the highly optimized rewrite theory that is shown in Fig. 3, which improves several aspects of the input bank account theory. First, the specialized equational theory is much more compact (3 equations vs 8 equations); indeed, all of the original defined functions are replaced by a much simpler, newly introduced function f0 that is used to update bank accounts. Furthermore, f0 exhibits an optimal performance since any call is normalized in just one reduction step, thereby providing fast bank account updates. Actually, the partially evaluated equational theory runs one order of magnitude faster than the original one, as shown in Sect. 6. This happens because the right-hand sides of the equations defining f0 are constructor terms; hence, they do not contain any additional function call that must be further simplified.

Second, the specialized equational theory satisfies the FVP, which enables $\mathcal{E}$-unification, complete variant generation, and also symbolic reachability in the specialized bank account system via narrowing with rules modulo $\mathcal{E}$ while they were not feasible in the original rewrite theory.

Third, the original rewrite rules have also been simplified: the new deposit rule dep-s gets rid of the operator «bal:_ pend:_ overdraft:_ threshold:_ funds:_ », while the rewrite rule w-s replaces the complex nested call structure in the right-hand side of the rule w with a much simpler and equivalent call to function f0.

A detailed account of the specialization process for this example is given in Sect. 6.

3   Specialization of Rewrite Theories

In this section, we briefly present the specialization procedure $\mathrm{NPER}_{\mathscr{A}}^{\mathscr{U}}$, which allows a rewrite theory $\mathscr{R} = (\Sigma, E \uplus B, R)$ to be optimized by specializing the underlying equational theory $\mathscr{E} = (\Sigma, E \uplus B)$ with respect to the calls in the rewrite rules R. The procedure $\mathrm{NPER}_{\mathscr{A}}^{\mathscr{U}}$ extends the equational, narrowing-driven partial evaluation algorithm $\mathrm{EQNPE}_{\mathscr{A}}^{\mathscr{U}}$ of [7], which applies to equational theories and is parametric on an unfolding operator $\mathscr{U}$ that is used to construct finite narrowing trees for any given expression, and on an abstraction operator $\mathscr{A}$ that guarantees global termination.

3.1   Narrowing and Folding Variant Narrowing in Maude

Equational, $(R, E \uplus B)$-narrowing computations are natively supported by Maude version 3.0 for unconditional rewrite theories. Before explaining how narrowing computations are handled within our framework, let us introduce some technical notions and notations that we need.

Let Σ be a *signature* that includes typed operators (also called function symbols) of the form $f \colon s_1 \ldots s_m \to s$ where s_i, and s are sorts in a poset $(S, <)$ that models subsort relations (e.g. $s < s'$ means that sort s is a subsort of s'). Σ is assumed to be *preregular*, so each term t has a least sort under $<$, denoted $ls(t)$. Binary operators in Σ may have an axiom declaration attached that specifies any combinations of algebraic laws such as associativity (assoc), commutativity (comm), and identity (id). By $ax(f)$, we denote the set of algebraic axioms for the operator f. By $\mathscr{T}_{\Sigma}(\mathscr{X})$, we denote the usual non-ground term algebra built over Σ and the set of (typed) variables $\mathscr{X}$. By $\mathscr{T}_{\Sigma}$, we denote the ground term algebra over Σ. By notation $x : s$, we denote a variable x with sort s. Any expression $\overline{t_n}$ denotes a finite sequence $t_1 \ldots t_n$, $n \geq 0$, of terms. A *position* w in a term t is represented by a sequence of natural numbers that addresses a subterm of t (Λ denotes the empty sequence, i.e., the root position). Given a term t, we let $Pos(t)$ denote the set of positions of t. We denote the usual prefix preorder over positions by $\leq$. By $t_{|w}$, we denote the *subterm* of t at position w. By $root(t)$, we denote the operator of t at position Λ.

A *substitution* σ is a sorted mapping from a finite subset of $\mathscr{X}$ to $\mathscr{T}_{\Sigma}(\mathscr{X})$. Substitutions are written as $\sigma = \{X_1 \mapsto t_1, \ldots, X_n \mapsto t_n\}$. The identity substitution is denoted by id. Substitutions are homomorphically extended to $\mathscr{T}_{\Sigma}(\mathscr{X})$. The application of a substitution σ to a term t is denoted by $t\sigma$. The restriction of σ to a set of variables $V \subset \mathscr{X}$ is denoted by $\sigma_{|V}$. Composition of two substitutions is denoted by $\sigma\sigma'$ so that $t(\sigma\sigma') = (t\sigma)\sigma'$.

A Σ-*equation* (or simply equation, where Σ is clear from the context) is an unoriented pair $t = t'$, where $t, t' \in \mathscr{T}_{\Sigma,s}(\mathscr{X})$ for some sort $s \in S$. An equational theory is a pair $(\Sigma, E \uplus B)$ that consists of a signature Σ, a set E of Σ-equations, and a set B of equational axioms (e.g., associativity, commutativity, and identity) declared for some binary operators in Σ. The equational theory $\mathscr{E}$ induces a congruence relation $=_{\mathscr{E}}$ on $\mathscr{T}_{\Sigma}(\mathscr{X})$.

A term t is more (or equally) general than t' modulo $\mathscr{E}$, denoted by $t \leq_{\mathscr{E}} t'$, if there is a substitution γ such that $t' =_{\mathscr{E}} t\gamma$. A substitution θ is more (or equally) general than σ modulo $\mathscr{E}$, denoted by $\theta \leq_{\mathscr{E}} \sigma$, if there is a substitution γ such that $\sigma =_{\mathscr{E}} \theta\gamma$, i.e., for all $x \in \mathcal{X}, x\sigma =_{\mathcal{E}} x\theta\gamma$. Also, $\theta \leq_{\mathcal{E}} \sigma$ $[V]$ iff there is a substitution γ such that, for all $x \in V, x\sigma =_{\mathcal{E}} x\theta\gamma$. An $\mathcal{E}$-unifier for a Σ-equation $t = t'$ is a substitution σ such that $t\sigma =_{\mathcal{E}} t'\sigma$.

Similarly to equational rewriting, where syntactic pattern-matching is replaced with matching modulo $\mathcal{E}$ (or $\mathcal{E}$-matching), in equational narrowing syntactic unification is replaced by *equational* unification (or $\mathcal{E}$-unification). More precisely, in a topmost[4] rewrite theory $\mathcal{R} = (\Sigma, E \uplus B, R)$, with $\mathcal{E} = (\Sigma, E \uplus B)$, equational narrowing is supported in Maude by means of a *three-layer* machinery [21]:

1. An $(R, E \uplus B)$-narrowing step from s to t with a rule $l \Rightarrow r$ in R can be performed iff there is a $\mathcal{E}$-unifier θ of the equation $s = l$ such that $t = r\theta$.
2. In turn, each $\mathcal{E}$-unification problem $s =_{\mathcal{E}}^{?} l$ of Point 1 is solved by using *folding variant* narrowing in the equational theory $\mathcal{E}$ that computes a finite, minimal and complete set of $\mathcal{E}$-unifiers for $s = l$ under suitable requirements [31]. Following [44], this is done by *equationally* narrowing the term $s =?= l$ (that encodes the unification problem $s =_{\mathcal{E}}^{?} l$) to an extra constant tt for denoting *success* in the rewrite theory $\mathcal{R}_0 = (\Sigma \cup \{=?=, tt\}, B, \vec{E} \cup \{\varepsilon\})$, where the extra[5] rewrite rule $\varepsilon = (X =?= X \Rightarrow tt)$ has been added to $\vec{E}$ in order to mimic unification of two terms (modulo B) as a narrowing step[6] that uses ε.
3. For each folding variant narrowing step using a rule in $\vec{E}$ modulo B in Point 2, B-unification algorithms are employed, allowing any combination of symbols that satisfy any combination of associativity, commutativity, and identity axioms [25].

Example 2. Consider the (partial) specification of integer numbers defined by the equations $E = \{X + 0 = X, X + s(Y) = s(X + Y), p(s(X)) = X, s(p(X)) = X\}$, where variables X, Y are of sort Int, operators p and s respectively stand for the predecessor and successor functions, and B contains the commutativity axiom $X + Y = Y + X$. Also consider that the program signature Σ contains a binary state constructor operator $\|\_,\_\|$: Int Int $\rightarrow$ State for a new sort State that models a simple network of processes that are either performing a common task (denoted by the first component of the state) or have finished the task (denoted by the second component). The system state $t = \|s(0), s(0) + p(0)\|$ can be rewritten to $\|0, s(0)\|$ (modulo the equations of E and the commutativity of $+$) using the following rule that specifies the system dynamics:

$$\|A, B\| \Rightarrow \|p(A), s(B)\|, \text{ where A and B are variables of sort Int} \tag{1}$$

Also, a (topmost) narrowing reachability goal from $\|V + V, 0 + V\|$ to $\|p(0), s(0)\|$ succeeds (in one step) with computed substitution $\{V \mapsto 0\}$, which is essentially calculated by first computing an $\mathcal{E}$-unifier σ of the input term $\|V + V, 0 + V\|$ and the left-hand side $\|A, B\|$ of rule (1), $\sigma = \{A/(V + V), B/V\}$. Second, an $\mathcal{E}$-unifier σ' is computed

---

[4] Besides the topmost assumption for $\mathcal{R}$, we also consider the classical executability restriction that the set R of rules is coherent with E modulo B (intuitively, this ensures that a rewrite step with R can always be postponed in favor of deterministically rewriting with E modulo B).

[5] In an order-sorted setting, multiple equations are actually used to cover any possible sort in $\mathcal{R}$.

[6] For example, by using ε, the term $s(0) * 0 =?= U * s(V)$ FV-narrows to tt (modulo commutativity of $*$), and the computed narrowing substitution does coincide with the unifier modulo commutativity of the two argument terms, i.e., $\{U \mapsto 0, V \mapsto 0\}$.

between the instantiated right-hand side $\|p(V+V), s(V)\|$ and the target state $\|p(0), s(0)\|$, $\sigma' = \{V \mapsto 0\}$. Third, the composition $\sigma\sigma' = \{A \mapsto 0+0, B \mapsto 0, V \mapsto 0\}$ is simplified into $\{A \mapsto 0, B \mapsto 0, V \mapsto 0\}$ and finally restricted to the variable V in the input term, yielding $\{V \mapsto 0\}$. Note that this narrowing derivation might signal a possible programming error in rule (1) since the number of processes in the first component of the state becomes negative.

The main idea of folding variant narrowing is to "fold" the search space of all FV-narrowing computations by using subsumption modulo B. That is, folding variant narrowing avoids computing any variant that is a substitution instance modulo B of a more general variant. Note that this notion is quite different from the classical folding operation of Burstall and Darlington's fold/unfold transformation scheme [20], where unfolding is essentially the replacement of a call by its body, with appropriate substitutions, and folding is the inverse transformation, i.e., the replacement of some piece of code by an equivalent function call. In [31], folding variant narrowing was proved to be complete and minimal for variant generation w.r.t. $(\vec{E}, B)$-normalized substitutions and it terminates for all inputs provided that the theory has the FVP.

FV-narrowing derivations correspond to sequences $t_0 \leadsto_{\sigma_0, \vec{e}_0, B} t_1 \leadsto_{\sigma_1, \vec{e}_1, B}$ $\cdots \leadsto_{\sigma_n, \vec{e}_{n-1}, B} t_n$, where $t \leadsto_{\sigma, \vec{e}, B} t'$ (or simply $t \leadsto_\sigma t'$ when no confusion can arise) denotes a transition (modulo the axioms B) from term t to t' via the *variant equation e* (i.e., an oriented equation $\vec{e}$ that is enabled to be used for FV-narrowing thanks to the attribute $\mathtt{variant}$) using the *equational unifier* σ. Assuming that the initial term t is normalized, each step $t \leadsto_{\sigma, \vec{e}, B} t'$ (or variant narrowing step) is followed by the simplification of the term into its normal form by using all equations in the theory, which may include not only the variant equations in the theory but also (non-variant) equations (e.g., built-in equations in Maude). The composition $\sigma_0\sigma_1\sigma_{n-1}$ of all the unifiers along a narrowing sequence leading to t_n (restricted to the variables of t_0) is the computed substitution of this sequence. The set of all FV-narrowing computations for a term t in $\mathscr{E}$ can be represented as a tree-like structure, denoted by $VN_\mathscr{E}^\circlearrowright(t)$, that we call the FV-narrowing tree of t in $\mathscr{E}$.

An equational theory has the *finite variant property* (FVP) (or it is called a *finite variant theory*) iff there is a finite and complete set of most general variants for each term. Intuitively, the $(\vec{E}, B)$-variants of t are the "irreducible patterns" $(t\sigma)\!\downarrow_{\vec{E}, B}$ to which t can be narrowed, with computed substitution σ, by applying the oriented equations $\vec{E}$ modulo B. For instance, there is an infinite number of variants for the term $(0 + Y\!:\!\mathtt{Int})$ in the equation theory of Example 2; e.g., $(Y\!:\!\mathtt{Int}, id)$, $(0, \{Y\!:\!\mathtt{Int} \mapsto 0\})$, $(s(0), \{Y\!:\!\mathtt{Int} \mapsto s(0)\})$, $(s(Z\!:\!\mathtt{Int}), \{Y\!:\!\mathtt{Int} \mapsto s(Z\!:\!\mathtt{Int})\})$, $(p(0), \{Y\!:\!\mathtt{Int} \mapsto p(0)\})$, $\ldots$

A preorder relation of generalization between variants provides a notion of *most general variant* and also a notion of completeness of a set of variants. Formally, a variant (t, σ) is *more general* than a variant (t', σ') w.r.t. an equational theory $\mathscr{E}$ (in symbols, $(t, \sigma) \leq_\mathscr{E} (t', \sigma')$) iff $t \leq_\mathscr{E} t'$ and $\sigma \leq_\mathscr{E} \sigma'$. For the term $0 + Y\!:\!\mathtt{Int}$, the most general variant is $(Y : \mathtt{Int}, id)$ since any other variant can be obtained by equational instantiation.

Example 3. Consider the definition of the (associative and commutative) Boolean conjunction operator $\wedge$ given by $E = \{X \wedge \text{true} = X, X \wedge \text{false} = \text{false}\}$, where variable X belongs to sort Bool and constants true and false stand for the corresponding Boolean values. There are five most general variants modulo associativity and commutativity for the term $X \wedge Y$, which are: $\{(X \wedge Y, \text{id}), (Y, \{X \mapsto \text{true}\}), (X, \{Y \mapsto \text{true}\}), (\text{false}, \{X \mapsto \text{false}\}), (\text{false}, \{Y \mapsto \text{false}\})\}$.

The theory of Example 3 satisfies the FVP, whereas the equational theory of Example 2 does not have the FVP since there is an infinite number of most general variants for the term $X : \text{Int} + Y : \text{Int}$. It is generally undecidable whether an equational theory has the FVP [19]; a semi-decision procedure is given in [39] (and implemented in [9]) that works well in practice and another technique based on the dependency pair framework is given in [31]. The procedure in [39] works by computing the variants of all flat terms $f(X_1, \ldots, X_n)$ for any n-ary operator f in the theory and pairwise-distinct variables $X_1, \ldots, X_n$ (of the corresponding sort); the theory does have the FVP iff there is a finite number of most general variants for every such term [39].

3.2   Partial Evaluation of Equational Theories

Given a convergent equational theory $\mathscr{E} = (\Sigma, E \uplus B)$ and a set Q of terms (henceforth called *specialized calls*), we define a transformation $\text{EQNPE}_{\mathscr{A}}^{\mathscr{U}}$ that derives a new equational theory $\mathscr{E}'$ which computes the same answers (and values) as $\mathscr{E}$ for any input term t that is a recursive instance (modulo B) of the specialized calls in Q. This means that all of the subterms of t (including itself) are a substitution instance of some term in Q. The transformation $\text{EQNPE}_{\mathscr{A}}^{\mathscr{U}}$ has two parameters, an *unfolding operator* $\mathscr{U}$ and an *abstraction operator* $\mathscr{A}$, whose precise meaning is clarified below.

The equational theory $\mathscr{E}$ to be specialized is *decomposed as a simple rewrite theory* $\vec{\mathscr{E}} = (\Sigma, B, \vec{E})$ (henceforth $\vec{\mathscr{E}}$ is called a *decomposition* of $\mathscr{E}$), whose only equations are the equational axioms in B and where the equations in E are explicitly oriented from left to right as the set $\vec{E}$ of rewrite rules. The axioms B satisfy the following extra assumptions [30]: 1) *regularity*, i.e., for each $t = t'$ in B, we have that the set of variables in t and t' is the same, 2) *linearity*, i.e., for each $t = t'$ in B, each variable occurs only once in t and in t'; 3) *sort-preservation*, i.e., for each $t = t'$ in B and substitution σ, $ls(t\sigma) = ls(t'\sigma)$, and furthermore, all variables in t and t' have a common top sort; and 4) B has a finitary and complete unification algorithm, which implies that B-matching is decidable.

The transformation consists of iterating two consecutive actions:

i) Symbolic execution (*Unfolding*). A finite, possibly partial folding variant narrowing tree for each input term t of Q^7 is generated. This is done by using the unfolding operator $\mathscr{U}(Q, \vec{\mathscr{E}})$ that determines when and how to stop the derivations in the FV-narrowing tree.

---

[7] For simplicity, we assume that Q is normalized w.r.t. the equational theory $\mathscr{E}$. If this were not the case, for each $t \in Q$ that is not in canonical form such that $t \downarrow_{\vec{E},B} = C(\overline{t_i})$, where $C()$ is the (possibly empty) constructor context of $t \downarrow_{\vec{E},B}$ and $\overline{t_i}$ are the maximal calls in $t \downarrow_{\vec{E},B}$, we would replace t in Q with the normalized terms $\overline{t_i}$ and add a suitable "bridge" equation $t = C(\overline{t_i})$ to the resulting specialization.

ii) Search for regularities (*Abstraction*). In order to guarantee that all calls that may occur at runtime are *covered* by the specialization, every (sub-)term in any leaf of the tree must be *equationally closed* w.r.t. Q. This notion extends the classical PD closedness by:

1) considering B-equivalence of terms;
2) considering a natural partition of the signature as $\Sigma = \mathscr{D} \uplus \Omega$, where Ω are the *constuctor* symbols, which are used to define the (irreducible) values of the theory, and $\mathscr{D} = \Sigma \setminus \Omega$ are the *defined* symbols, which are evaluated away by equational rewriting.
3) recursing over the term structure (in order to handle nested function calls). Roughly speaking, a term u is equationally closed modulo B w.r.t. Q iff either: (i) it does not contain defined function symbols of $\mathscr{D}$, or (ii) there exists a substitution θ and a (possibly renamed) $q \in Q$ such that $u =_B q\theta$ and the terms in θ are recursively Q-closed. For instance, given a defined binary symbol $\bullet$ that does not obey any structural axioms, the term $t = a \bullet (Z \bullet a)$ is equationally closed w.r.t. $Q = \{a \bullet X, Y \bullet a\}$ or $\{X \bullet Y\}$, but it is not with Q being $\{a \bullet X\}$; however, it would be closed if $\bullet$ were commutative.

Given the set $\mathscr{L}$ of leaves in the FV-narrowing trees for the partially evaluated calls in Q, in order to properly add to Q the non-closed (sub-)terms occurring in the terms of $\mathscr{L}$, an abstraction operator $\mathscr{A}(Q, \mathscr{L}, B)$ is applied that yields a new set of terms which may need further evaluation. The abstraction operator $\mathscr{A}(Q, \mathscr{L}, B)$ ensures that the resulting set of terms "covers" (modulo B) the calls previously specialized and that equational closedness modulo B is preserved throughout successive abstractions.

Steps i) and ii) are iterated as long as new terms are generated, and the abstraction operator $\mathscr{A}$ guarantees that only finitely many expressions are evaluated, thus ensuring global termination.

Note that the algorithm does not explicitly compute a partially evaluated equational theory. It does so implicitly, by computing a (generally augmented) set Q' of partially evaluated terms that unambiguously determine the desired partial evaluation of the equations in E as the set E' of *resultants* $t\sigma = t'$ associated with the derivations in the narrowing tree from a root $t \in Q'$ to a leaf t' with computed substitution σ, such that the closedness condition modulo B w.r.t. Q' is satisfied for all function calls that appear in the right-hand sides of the equations in E'. We assume the existence of a function $\text{GENTHEORY}(Q', (\Sigma, E \uplus B))$ that delivers the partially evaluated equational theory $\mathscr{E}' = (\Sigma', E' \uplus B')$ univocally determined by Q' and the original equational theory $\mathscr{E} = (\Sigma, E \uplus B)$, with $\Sigma' = \Sigma$ and $B' = B$.

3.3 The NPER$_{\mathscr{A}}^{\mathscr{U}}$ Scheme for the Specialization of Rewrite Theories

The specialization of the (topmost) rewrite theory $\mathscr{R} = (\Sigma, E \uplus B, R)$ is achieved by partially evaluating its underlying equational theory $\mathscr{E} = (\Sigma, E \uplus B)$ w.r.t. the rules R, which is done by using the partial evaluation procedure EQNPE$_{\mathscr{A}}^{\mathscr{U}}$ of Sect. 3.2. By providing suitable unfolding (and abstraction) operators, different instances of the specialization scheme can be defined.

Algorithm 1. Symbolic Specialization of Rewrite Theories $\text{NPER}_{\mathscr{A}}^{\mathscr{U}}(\mathscr{R})$

Require:

A rewrite theory $\mathscr{R} = (\Sigma, E \uplus B, R)$, an unfolding operator $\mathscr{U}$

1: **function** $\text{NPER}_{\mathscr{A}}^{\mathscr{U}}(\mathscr{R})$

2: $\quad R' \leftarrow \{(l \downarrow_{\vec{E},B}) \Rightarrow (r \downarrow_{\vec{E},B}) \mid l \Rightarrow r \in R\}$

3: $\quad Q \leftarrow mcalls(R')$

$\quad$ *Phase 1. Partial Evaluation*

4: $\quad Q' \leftarrow \text{EQNPE}_{\mathscr{A}}^{\mathscr{U}}((\Sigma, E \uplus B), Q)$

5: $\quad (\Sigma, E' \uplus B) \leftarrow \text{GENTHEORY}(Q', (\Sigma, E \uplus B))$

$\quad$ *Phase 2. Compression*

6: $\quad$ Let ρ be an independent renaming for Q in

7: $\qquad \Sigma'' \leftarrow (\Sigma \setminus \{f \mid f \text{ occurs in } E \setminus E'\}) \cup \{root(\rho(t)) \mid t \in Q\}$

8: $\qquad B'' = \{ax(f) \in B \mid f \in \Sigma \cap \Sigma''\}$

9: $\qquad E'' \leftarrow \bigcup_{t \in Q} \{\rho(t)\theta = RN_\rho(t') \mid t\theta = t' \in E'\}$

10: $\qquad R'' \leftarrow \{RN_\rho(l) \Rightarrow RN_\rho(r) \mid l \Rightarrow r \in R'\}$

$$
\text{where } RN_\rho(t) = \begin{cases} c(\overline{RN_\rho(t_n)}) & \text{if } t = c(\overline{t_n}) \text{ with } c : \overline{s_n} \to s \in \Sigma \text{ s.t. } c \in \Omega, \, ls(t) = s, \, n \geq 0 \\ \rho(u)\theta' & \text{if } \exists \theta, \exists u \in Q' \text{ s.t. } t =_B u\theta \text{ and } \theta' = \{x \mapsto RN_\rho(x\theta) \mid x \in Dom(\theta)\} \\ t & \text{otherwise} \end{cases}
$$

11: **return** $\mathscr{R}' = (\Sigma'', E'' \uplus B'', R'')$

The $\text{NPER}_{\mathscr{A}}^{\mathscr{U}}$ procedure is outlined in Algorithm 1. Roughly speaking, the procedure consists of two phases.

Phase 1) *Partial Evaluation.* It applies the $\text{EQNPE}_{\mathscr{A}}^{\mathscr{U}}$ algorithm to specialize the equational theory $\mathscr{E} = (\Sigma, E \uplus B)$ w.r.t. a set Q of specialized calls that consists of all of the *maximal functions calls* that appear in the $(\vec{E}, B)$-normalized version R' of the rewrite rules of R. We must normalize the rules in R before initializing Q because, for each t in Q, the FV-narrowing tree for t is not rooted by t but by $t \downarrow_{\vec{E},B}$; hence, we would lose the connection between the partially evaluated functions and the rules of R if the rules were not correspondingly normalized.

Given $\Sigma = (\mathscr{D} \uplus \Omega)$, a maximal function call in a term t is any outermost subterm of t that is rooted by a defined function symbol appearing in the equations of E. Given a rewrite rule $s \Rightarrow t$ of R, by $mcalls(s \Rightarrow t)$, we denote the set of all the maximal function calls that occur in s and t. By abuse, $mcalls(R)$ is the set of all maximal calls in the rewrite rules of R.

This phase produces the new set of specialized calls Q' from which the partial evaluation $\mathscr{E}' = (\Sigma', E' \uplus B')$ of $\mathscr{E}$ w.r.t. Q is univocally derived by executing $\text{GENTHEORY}(Q', (\Sigma, E \uplus B))$.

Phase 2) *Compression.* It consists of a refactoring transformation that computes a new, much more compact equational theory $\mathscr{E}'' = (\Sigma'', E'' \uplus B'')$ where the equations of E' are simplified by renaming similar expressions w.r.t. an independent renaming function ρ that is derived from the set of specialized calls Q' so that unused symbols, unneeded axioms, and unnecessary repetition of variables are removed.

More precisely, for each t of sort s in Q' such that its root symbol is f, we define $\rho(t) = f_t(\overline{x_n : s_n})$, where $\overline{x_n}$ are the distinct variables in t in the order of their first occurrence and $f_t : \overline{s_n} \to s$ is a new function symbol that does not occur in Σ or Q' and is different from the root symbol of any other renamed term $\rho(t')$, for $t' \in Q'$.

Given the renaming ρ, the compression algorithm computes a new equation set E'' by replacing each call in E' by a call to the corresponding renamed function according to ρ. Note that, while the independent renaming suffices to rename the left-hand sides of the equations in E' (since they are mere instances of the specialized calls), the right-hand sides must be renamed by recursively replacing each call in the given expression by a call to the corresponding renamed function (according to ρ). This is done by means of the function RN_ρ.

Furthermore, a new rewrite rule set R'' is also produced by consistently applying RN_ρ to the $(\vec{E}, B)$-normalized rewrite rules of R'. Specifically, each rewrite rule $l \Rightarrow r$ in R' is transformed into the rewrite rule $RN_\rho(l) \Rightarrow RN_\rho(r)$, in which every maximal function call t in the rewrite rule is recursively renamed according to the independent renaming ρ taking into account the term equivalences given by B.

Given the rewrite theory $\mathscr{R} = (\Sigma, E \uplus B, R)$ and its specialization $\mathscr{R}' = \mathrm{NPER}_{\mathscr{A}}^{\mathscr{U}}(\mathscr{R})$, all of the executability conditions that are satisfied by $\mathscr{R}$ are also satisfied by $\mathscr{R}' = (\Sigma', E' \uplus B', R')$, including the fact that $\vec{\mathscr{E}}' = (\Sigma', B', \vec{E}')$ is a decomposition and that R' is (ground) coherent w.r.t. E' modulo B'. Also, because of the correctness and completeness of $\mathrm{EQNPE}_{\mathscr{A}}^{\mathscr{U}}$, which states a strong correspondence between the variant computations of $\mathscr{E}$ and $\mathscr{E}'$ [7], the renaming function ρ that is used to generate $\mathscr{R}'$ is a bisimulation between the transition systems $(\mathscr{T}_{\Sigma/(E \uplus B)}, \to_{R/(E \uplus B)})$ and $(\mathscr{T}_{\Sigma'/(E' \uplus B')}, \to_{R'/(E' \uplus B')})$.

4 Total Evaluation and Constructor Variants

In [41], a theory transformation $\mathscr{R} \mapsto \mathscr{R}_{l,r}^{\Omega}$ is defined that relies on the division of Σ as $\mathscr{D} \uplus \Omega$ together with the notion of *most general constructor variant* that we describe in the following. Roughly speaking, $\mathscr{R}_{l,r}^{\Omega}$ is obtained from $\mathscr{R}$ by transforming each rewrite $l \Rightarrow r$ in $\mathscr{R}$ into a totally evaluated rule $l' \Rightarrow r'$, where l' and r' are constructor Ω-terms. More precisely, any call appearing in l (resp. r) to a function that is defined in $\mathscr{E}$ is replaced in l' (resp. r') by its constructor normal form w.r.t. $\mathscr{E}$.

4.1 Constructor Term Variants, Sufficient Completeness, and the CFVP

In order-sorted equational logic, the notion of constructor symbols and constructor terms are more intricate and essential than in standard term rewriting. Let us denote by $[t]_B$ the B-equivalence class of t, i.e., terms t' that are B-equivalent to t, in symbols $t' =_B t$ for all $t' \in [t]_B$. Given a decomposition $(\Sigma, B, \vec{E})$, quite often the signature Σ has a natural division as a disjoint union $\Sigma = \mathscr{D} \uplus \Omega$, where the elements of the *canonical algebra* $\mathscr{C}_{\vec{E},B} = \{[t\downarrow_{\vec{E},B}]_B \mid t \in \mathscr{T}_\Sigma\}$ (that is, the values computed by $\vec{E}, B$-simplification) are Ω-terms, whereas the function symbols $f \in \mathscr{D}$ are viewed as defined functions which are evaluated away by $\vec{E}, B$-simplification. The subsignature Ω (with same poset of sorts as Σ) is then called a *constructor subsignature* of Σ. We call a decomposition $(\Sigma, B, \vec{E})$

sufficiently complete with respect to the constructor subsignature Ω iff for each $t \in \mathscr{T}_\Sigma$ we have: (i) $t\downarrow_{\vec{E},B} \in \mathscr{T}_\Omega$; and (ii) if $u \in \mathscr{T}_\Omega$ and $u =_B v$, then $v \in \mathscr{T}_\Omega$. Condition (ii) ensures that if any element in a B-equivalent class is a Ω-term, all other elements in the class are also Ω-terms. We also say that $(\Sigma, B, \vec{E})$ is *sufficiently complete* w.r.t. Ω and input term $t \in \mathscr{T}_\Sigma$ if conditions (i) and (ii) hold for t. In the following, the ctor operator attribute of Maude is used to highlight the constructor symbols of an equational theory so that the constructor subsignature can be easily read off the Maude code.

A decomposition $\vec{\mathscr{E}} = (\Sigma, B, \vec{E})$ *protects* another decomposition $\vec{\mathscr{E}}_0 = (\Sigma_0, B_0, \vec{E}_0)$ iff $\mathscr{E}_0 \subseteq \mathscr{E}$, i.e., $\Sigma_0 \subseteq \Sigma$, $B_0 \subseteq B$, $E_0 \subseteq E$, and for all $t, t' \in \mathscr{T}_{\Sigma_0}(\mathscr{X})$ we have: (i) $t =_{B_0} t' \Longleftrightarrow t =_B t'$, (ii) $t = t\downarrow_{\vec{E}_0, B_0} \Longleftrightarrow t = t\downarrow_{\vec{E}, B}$, and (iii) $\mathscr{C}_{\vec{E}_0, B_0} = \mathscr{C}_{\vec{E}, B}|_{\Sigma_0}$, where $\mathscr{C}_{\vec{E}, B}|_{\Sigma_0}$ agrees with $\mathscr{C}_{\vec{E}, B}$ in the interpretation of all sorts and operations in Σ_0 and discards everything in $\Sigma \setminus \Sigma_0$. The decomposition $\vec{\mathscr{E}}_\Omega = (\Omega, B_\Omega, \vec{E}_\Omega)$ is a *constructor* decomposition of $\vec{\mathscr{E}} = (\Sigma, B, \vec{E})$ iff 1) $\vec{\mathscr{E}}$ protects $\vec{\mathscr{E}}_\Omega$; and 2) $\vec{\mathscr{E}}$ is sufficiently complete w.r.t. its constructor subsignature Ω.

Throughout the paper, we assume that the set B of axioms respects the constructors in any decomposition $\vec{\mathscr{E}} = (\Sigma, B, \vec{E})$. In other words, if an axiom in B can be applied to a constructor term, then the result is a constructor term.

Example 4. Consider the following Maude functional module that encodes an equational theory $\mathscr{E} = (\Sigma, E \uplus B)$ for natural numbers modulo 2, with an equation that collapses natural numbers into the canonical forms 0 and s(0).

```
fmod OS-NAT/2 is
  sorts Nat Zero One .
  subsort Zero One < Nat .
  op 0 : -> Zero [ctor] .
  op s : Zero -> One [ctor] .
  op s : Nat -> Nat .
  eq s(s(0)) = 0 [variant] .
endfm
```

Let us denote by $\vec{\mathscr{E}} = (\Sigma, B, \vec{E})$ the decomposition of the considered theory. The signature Σ can be naturally decomposed into $\mathscr{D} \uplus \Omega$, where

$$\mathscr{D} = \{s : \mathtt{Nat} \to \mathtt{Nat}\} \text{ and } \Omega = \{0 :\to \mathtt{Zero}, s : \mathtt{Zero} \to \mathtt{One}\}.$$

Then, the decomposition $(\Omega, \emptyset, \emptyset)$ is a constructor decomposition of $\vec{\mathscr{E}}$.

Given $\Sigma = \mathscr{D} \uplus \Omega$, it is possible to strengthen the notion of term variants to that of *constructor variants* [40].

Definition 1 (Constructor Variant [40]). *Let $\vec{\mathscr{E}} = (\Sigma, B, \vec{E})$ be a decomposition and let $(\Omega, B_\Omega, \vec{E}_\Omega)$ be a constructor decomposition of $\vec{\mathscr{E}}$. Given a term $t \in \mathscr{T}_\Sigma(\mathscr{X})$, we say that a variant (t', θ) of t is a constructor variant if $t' \in \mathscr{T}_\Omega(\mathscr{X})$ (i.e., the set of non-ground constructor terms).*

The following example illustrates the notion of constructor variant in Maude.

Example 5. Consider the functional module OS-NAT/2 of Example 4 and the term s(X), with X:Nat. There exist only two most general variants for s(X) in the equational theory $\mathscr{E}$ encoded by OS-NAT/2: namely, $(0, \{X \mapsto s(0)\})$ and $(s(X), id)$. The former is also a constructor variant since the constructor 0 belongs to the constructor subsignature Ω of $\mathscr{E}$. Conversely, the latter is not a constructor variant since s : Nat → Nat in s(X) is a defined symbol. Nonetheless, note that there exists the constructor variant $(s(Y), X \mapsto Y : \text{Zero})$, where the sort of variable X:Nat is downgraded to sort Zero, which is a constructor variant that is less general than $(s(X), id)$.

The notion of most general variant can be trivially extended to constructor variants. By $[\![t]\!]^{\Omega}_{\vec{E},B}$, we denote the set of most general constructor variants for the term t. Given an equational theory $\mathscr{E} = (\Sigma, E \uplus B)$, we say that $\mathscr{E} = (\Sigma, E \uplus B)$ has the *constructor finite variant property* (CFVP) (or it is called a *finite constructor variant theory*) iff for all $t \in \mathscr{T}_{\Sigma}(\mathscr{X})$, $[\![t]\!]^{\Omega}_{\vec{E},B}$ is a finite set. By abuse, we often say that a decomposition $(\Sigma, B, \vec{E})$ has the FVP (resp. CFVP) when $\mathscr{E} = (\Sigma, E \uplus B)$ is a finite variant theory (resp. a constructor finite variant theory).

An algorithm for computing the complete set of most general constructor variants $[\![t]\!]^{\Omega}_{\vec{E},B}$ is provided in [40] for a decomposition $(\Sigma, B, \vec{E})$ that satisfies the FVP, has a constructor decomposition $(\Omega, E_{\Omega}, B_{\Omega})$, and satisfies the extra *preregular-below* condition [40], which essentially ensures that Σ does not contain any overloaded symbol with a constructor typing that lies below a defined typing for the same symbol. Roughly speaking, the algorithm has two phases. First, the signature Σ of $(\Sigma, B, \vec{E})$ is refined into a new signature Σ^c that introduces a new sort $\sharp s$ for each sort s in the sort poset of Σ. Also, this sort refinement is extended to subsort relations, and constructor operators to precisely identify the constructor terms of the decomposition. Two functions, $(\_)^{\bullet}$ and its inverse $(\_)_{\bullet}$, are respectively used to map sorts of Σ to sorts of Σ^c and sorts of Σ^c to sorts of Σ. These functions are homomorphically extended to terms and substitutions in the usual way. Then, $[\![t]\!]^{\Omega}_{\vec{E},B}$ is distilled from the set of most general variants $[\![t]\!]_{\vec{E},B}$ by using unification modulo B in the following way:

$$[\![t]\!]^{\Omega}_{\vec{E},B} = \{(t'\tau^{\bullet}, (\sigma\tau^{\bullet})_{|Var(t)}) \mid (t', \sigma) \in [\![t]\!]_{\vec{E},B}, \tau \in CSU_B(t' = x:(ls(t'))_{\bullet})\}$$

where $CSU_B(t = t')$ denotes the complete set of unifiers of $t = t'$ modulo B.

Example 6. Consider the FVP functional module OS-NAT/2 of Example 4. Its associated decomposition has a constructor decomposition as shown in Example 4, and also meets the *preregular below* condition. Indeed, although the successor operator in OS-NAT/2 is overloaded, its constructor typing s : Zero → One is below the defined typing s : Zero → One, since Zero < Nat and One < Nat. Hence, the algorithm in [40] can be used to compute $[\![t]\!]^{\Omega}_{\vec{E},B}$.

The complete set of most general constructor variants for s(X:Nat)

$$[\![s(X)]\!]^{\Omega}_{\vec{E},B} = \{\{(0, X \mapsto s(0)), (s(X'), X \mapsto X' : \text{Zero})\}$$

is derived from $[\![s(X)]\!]_{\vec{E},B} = \{\{(0, X \mapsto s(0)), (s(X), id)\}$ as follows.

The constructor variant $(0, X \mapsto s(0))$ is a variant in $[\![s(X)]\!]_{\vec{E},B}$ and the (trivial) unification problem $0 = Y : \sharp \text{Zero}$ provides a unifier $\tau^\bullet$ that leaves $(0, X \mapsto s(0))$ unchanged.

The constructor variant $(s(X'), X \mapsto X' : \text{Zero})$ derives from the variant $v = (s(X), id) \in [\![s(X)]\!]_{\vec{E},B}$ by solving the unification problem $s(X) = Y : \sharp \text{Nat}$ which yields the computed unifier $\tau = \{X \mapsto X' : \sharp \text{Zero}, Y \mapsto s(X')\}$; hence, $\tau^\bullet = \{X \mapsto X' : \text{Zero}, Y \mapsto s(X')\}$, and finally by applying $\tau^\bullet$ to v, we get $(s(X'), \{X \mapsto X' : \text{Zero}\})$.

For any decomposition $(\Sigma, B, \vec{E})$, note that FVP implies CFVP when there exists a constructor decomposition of $(\Sigma, B, \vec{E})$.

The following result establishes that the FVP and/or SC nature of an input equational theory is preserved by the $\text{NPER}^{\mathcal{U}}_{\mathcal{A}}$ transformation.

Theorem 1 (FVP and SC preservation). *Let $\mathcal{R} = (\Sigma, E \uplus B, R)$ be a rewrite theory with $\mathcal{E} = (\Sigma, E \uplus B)$ such that $\vec{\mathcal{E}} = (\Sigma, B, \vec{E})$ is a decomposition. Let $\mathcal{R}' = \text{NPER}^{\mathcal{U}}_{\mathcal{A}}(\mathcal{R})$ be a specialization of $\mathcal{R}$ under the renaming ρ such that $\mathcal{R}' = (\Sigma', E' \uplus B', R')$. Let $Q = \{t \mid s \mapsto t \in \rho\}$ so that $\mathcal{E}' = (\Sigma', E' \uplus B')$ is Q-closed modulo B'. Then, it holds that*

1. *If $\vec{\mathcal{E}}$ satisfies the FVP, then $\vec{\mathcal{E}}'$ satisfies the FVP;*
2. *Given $\Sigma = \mathcal{D} \uplus \Omega$, if $\vec{\mathcal{E}}$ satisfies SC w.r.t. Ω, then $\vec{\mathcal{E}}'$ satisfies SC w.r.t. Ω for every input term that is Q-closed modulo B'.*

4.2   Total Evaluation of Rewrite Theories

The total evaluation transformation $\mathcal{R} \mapsto \mathcal{R}^{\Omega}_{l,r}$ is achieved by computing the set of most general constructor variants $[\![\langle l, r \rangle]\!]^{\Omega}_{\vec{E},B}$, for each $l \Rightarrow r$ in $\mathcal{R}$. More specifically, $\mathcal{R}$ is transformed into $\mathcal{R}^{\Omega}_{l,r}$ by replacing the set of rewrite rules of $\mathcal{R}$ with

$$R^{\Omega}_{l,r} = \{l' \to r' \mid l \to r \in R \wedge (\langle l', r' \rangle, \sigma) \in [\![\langle l, r \rangle]\!]^{\Omega}_{\vec{E},B}\}$$

Correctness of the transformation $\mathcal{R} \mapsto \mathcal{R}^{\Omega}_{l,r}$ (or more precisely, the isomorphism between the ground canonical algebras of $\mathcal{R}$ and $\mathcal{R}^{\Omega}_{l,r}$) is established in [41] and is ensured when the equational theory $\mathcal{E} = (\Sigma, E \uplus B)$ in $\mathcal{R}$ satisfies the FVP, has a constructor decomposition $(\Omega, B_{\Omega}, E_{\Omega})$, and satisfies the *preregular below* condition.

Example 7. Consider a rewrite theory $\mathcal{R}$ that includes a single rewrite rule

```
rl [ Y:Nat ] => [ s(Y:Nat) ] .
```

and the finite variant equational theory $\mathcal{E} = (\Sigma \cup \{[\_] : \text{Nat} \to \text{State}\}, E \uplus B)$ that extends the equational theory of Example 4 with the constructor operator $[\_] : \text{Nat} \to \text{State}$. Note that the decomposition $\vec{\mathcal{E}} = (\Sigma \cup \{[\_] : \text{Nat} \to \text{State}\}, B, \vec{E})$ of $\mathcal{E}$ has a constructor decomposition $(\Omega, \emptyset, \emptyset)$ where $\Sigma = \Omega \uplus \mathcal{D}$ with $\Omega = \{[\_] : \text{Nat} \to \text{State}, s : \text{Zero} \to \text{One}, 0 :\to \text{Zero}\}$ and $\mathcal{D} = \{s : \text{Nat} \to \text{Nat}\}$, and clearly satisfies the *preregular below* condition for the very same argument exposed in Example 6. Hence, the transformation $\mathcal{R} \mapsto \mathcal{R}^{\Omega}_{l,r}$ can be applied to $\mathcal{R}$ thereby specializing the original rule into the two following rewrite rules

```
rl [ s(0) ] => [ 0 ] .
rl [ X:Zero ] => [ s(X:Zero) ] .
```

which are obtained from the computation of $[\![\langle[\texttt{Y}:\texttt{Nat}],[\texttt{s}(\texttt{Y}:\texttt{Nat})]\rangle]\!]^{\Omega}_{\vec{E},B}$.

In Sect. 5, we show how the $\mathscr{R} \mapsto \mathscr{R}^{\Omega}_{l,r}$ transformation can be mimicked as an instance of our NPER$^{\mathscr{U}}_{\mathscr{A}}$ scheme and we formulate two additional instances of the generic algorithm that can deal with a rewrite theory that does not satisfy the FVP and/or SC. Furthermore, sometimes we can transform a theory that satisfies SC but not FVP into a specialized theory that satisfies both SC and FVP so that the above transformation can be applied.

5   Instantiating the Specialization Scheme for Rewrite Theories

Given a rewrite theory $\mathscr{R} = (\Sigma, E \uplus B, R)$, with $\mathscr{E} = (\Sigma, B, \vec{E})$ being a decomposition of $(\Sigma, E \uplus B)$, the equational theory $\mathscr{E}$ in $\mathscr{R}$ may or may not meet sufficient completeness (SC) or the finite variant property (FVP). In this section, we particularize the specialization scheme of Sect. 3 by considering the following three[8] possible scenarios:

1. $\mathscr{E}$ meets SC and the FVP (hence, it has the CFVP);
2. $\mathscr{E}$ does not meet SC but it meets the FVP;
3. $\mathscr{E}$ does not meet the FVP.

Recall the parameterized NPER$^{\mathscr{U}}_{\mathscr{A}}$ algorithm of Sect. 3.3 relies on two generic operators: an unfolding operator $\mathscr{U}$ that defines the unfolding rule used to determine when and how to terminate the construction of the narrowing trees; and an abstraction operator $\mathscr{A}$ that is used to guarantee that the set of terms obtained during partial evaluation (i.e., the set of deployed narrowing trees) is kept finite and progressively covers (modulo B) all of the specialized calls. The instantiation of the scheme requires particularizing these two parameters in order to specify a terminating, correct and complete partial evaluation for $\mathscr{E}$. In the following, we provide three different implementations for the tandem $\mathscr{U}/\mathscr{A}$, and we show how they work in practice on some use cases that cover all three scenarios.

5.1   Unfolding Operators

Let us first provide three possible implementations of the unfolding operator $\mathscr{U}$ that are respectively able to deal with: (a) equational theories that satisfy the SC and FVP (hence, satisfy the CFVP); (b) any equational theory that satisfies the FVP; and (c) equational theories that do not satisfy the FVP. Since $(\Sigma, B, \vec{E})$ is a decomposition of $(\Sigma, E \uplus B)$, all the considered implementations adopt the folding variant narrowing strategy to build the narrowing trees which are needed to specialize the input theory.

---

[8] The case when $\mathscr{E}$ satisfies SC but not the FVP is not considered because there is no technique to compute the finite set of most general constructor variants in this case, which is a matter for future research.

(a) Consider the case when $\mathscr{E} = (\Sigma, E \uplus B)$ satisfies all of the conditions required for the correctness of the transformation $\mathscr{R} \mapsto \mathscr{R}^{\Omega}_{l,r}$. In particular, $\mathscr{E}$ is SC and has the FVP. Let Σ^c be the sort-refinement of the signature Σ presented in Sect. 4.1, where $(\_)_{\bullet}$ (resp., $(\_)^{\bullet}$) is the function that maps the sorts of Σ into the sorts of Σ^c (resp., the sorts of Σ^c into the sorts of Σ). Then, we define the following unfolding operator that totally evaluates Q in the decomposition $\vec{\mathscr{E}}$

$$\mathscr{U}_{cfvp}(Q, \vec{\mathscr{E}}) = \bigcup_{t \in Q} \{(x : s)\sigma^{\bullet} \mid t \leadsto^{*}_{\sigma, \vec{E}, B} x : (s_{\bullet}) \wedge t\sigma \neq x\sigma \wedge s = ls(t)\}$$

(b) When the equational theory $\mathscr{E}$ does not satisfy SC but does satisfy the FVP, FV-narrowing trees are always finite objects that can be effectively constructed in finite time. Therefore, in this specific case, we define the following unfolding operator that constructs the complete FV-narrowing tree for any possible call.

$$\mathscr{U}_{fvp}(Q, \vec{\mathscr{E}}) = \bigcup_{t \in Q} \{t' \mid t \leadsto^{!}_{\sigma, \vec{E}, B} t' \in VN^{\circlearrowleft}_{\vec{\mathscr{E}}}(t)\}$$

where $t \leadsto^{!}_{\sigma, \vec{E}, B} t'$ denotes a FV-narrowing derivation from t to the term t' to which no FV-narrowing steps can be applied.

(c) Finally, when $\mathscr{E}$ does not meet the finite variant property, $\mathscr{U}_{fvp}(Q, \vec{\mathscr{E}})$ cannot be applied since the FVN strategy may lead to the creation of an infinite narrowing tree for some specialized calls in Q. In this case, the unfolding rule must implement a form of local control that stops the expansion of infinite derivations in the FV-narrowing tree. A solution to this problem has already been provided in [7] by means of an unfolding operator that computes a finite (possibly partial) FV-narrowing tree fragment for every specialized call t in Q. Narrowing derivations in the tree are stopped when no further FV-narrowing step can be performed or potential non-termination is detected by applying a subsumption check at each FV-narrowing step. The subsumption check is based on an *equational order-sorted* extension of the classical homeomorphic embedding relation [8] that is commonly used to ensure termination of symbolic methods and program optimization techniques.

Roughly speaking, a homeomorphic embedding relation is a structural preorder under which a term t is greater than (i.e., it embeds) another term t', written as $t \triangleright t'$, if t' can be obtained from t by deleting some parts, e.g., $s(s(X+Y) * (s(X)+Y))$ embeds $s(Y * (X+Y)))$. Embedding relations have become very popular to ensure termination of *symbolic* transformations because, provided the signature is finite, for every infinite sequence of terms $t_1, t_2, \ldots$, there exist $i < j$ such that $t_i \trianglelefteq t_j$. In other words, the embedding relation is a well-quasi order (wqo) [34]. Therefore, when iteratively computing a sequence $t_1, t_2, \ldots, t_n$, finiteness of the sequence can be guaranteed by using the embedding as a whistle: whenever a new expression t_{n+1} is to be added to the sequence, we first check whether t_{n+1} embeds any of the expressions already in the sequence. If that is the case, we say that $\trianglelefteq$ whistles, i.e., it has detected (potential) non-termination and the computation has to be stopped. Otherwise, t_{n+1} can be safely added to the sequence and the computation can proceed.

By $\mathscr{U}_{\overline{fvp}}(Q,\vec{\mathscr{E}})$, we denote this unfolding operator whose full formalization is given in [7].

5.2 Abstraction Operators

We consider two implementations of the abstraction operator: the first one deals with equational theories that are sufficiently complete and satisfy the finite variant property, while the second one covers the other two possible scenarios that we highlighted at the beginning of Sect. 5.

(a) When the equational theory $\mathscr{E}$ satisfies SC and has the FVP so that the unfolding operator $\mathscr{U}_{cfvp}(Q,\vec{\mathscr{E}})$ is applied, there is no need for an abstraction process. By construction of the $\mathscr{U}_{cfvp}(Q,\vec{\mathscr{E}})$ operator, the leaves of the tree are constructor terms; hence, they do not include any uncovered function call that needs to be abstracted by a further iteration of the partial evaluation process as constructor terms are trivially B-closed w.r.t. Q. Therefore, in this case, we can simply define $\mathscr{A}_{cfvp}(Q,\mathscr{L},B) = Q$, thus returning the very same set of specialized calls Q.

(b) As for the remaining cases, there is no guarantee that the leaves of the narrowing trees are B-closed w.r.t. the specialized calls in Q. Indeed, when the equational theory $\mathscr{E}$ does not satisfy either sufficient completeness or the finite variant property, the operators $\mathscr{U}_{fvp}(Q,\vec{\mathscr{E}})$ and $\mathscr{U}_{\overline{fvp}}(Q,\vec{\mathscr{E}})$ might deliver uncovered function calls to be abstracted. To overcome this problem, we simply resort to the abstraction procedure of [7], which relies on an *equational order sorted extension* of the pure, syntactical least general generalization algorithm [10] so that not too much precision is lost despite the abstraction.

Roughly speaking, the syntactic generalization problem for two or more expressions, in a pure syntactic and untyped setting, means finding their *least general generalization*, i.e., the least general expression t such that all of the given expressions are instances of t under appropriate substitutions. For instance, the expression *sibling(X,Y)* is a generalizer of both *sibling(john,sam)* and *sibling(tom,sam)*, but their least general generalizer is *sibling(X,sam)*.

In [10], the notion of least general generalization is extended to the order-sorted modulo axioms setting, where function symbols can obey any combination of associativity, commutativity, and identity axioms (including the empty set of such axioms). For instance, the least general generalizer of *sibling(sam,john)* and *sibling(tom,sam)* is still *sibling(X,sam)*, when *sibling* is a commutative symbol. In general, there is no unique lgg in the framework of [10], due to both the order-sortedness and to the equational axioms. Nonetheless, for the case of modular combinations of associativity and commutativity axioms, there is always a finite, minimal, and complete set of equational lggs (E-lggs) so that any other generalizer has at least one of them as a B-instance.

Therefore, in the case when the equational theory $\mathscr{E}$ does not satisfy either sufficient completeness or the finite variant property, we consider the abstraction operator

$\mathscr{A}_{Elgg}(Q, \mathscr{L}, B)$, which returns a set Q' of specialized calls that abstracts the set $Q \cup \mathscr{L}$ by using the generalization process formalized in [7] that ensures that Q' is B-closed w.r.t. $Q \cup \mathscr{L}$.

The use of folding variant narrowing in the definition of the three unfolding operators $\mathscr{U}_{\overline{fvp}}$, $\mathscr{U}_{fvp}$, and $\mathscr{U}_{cfvp}$, together with the abstraction operators $\mathscr{A}_{cfvp}$ and $\mathscr{A}_{Elgg}$, provides good overall behavior regarding both the elimination of intermediate data structures and the propagation of information.

6 Specializing the Bank Account System

In this section, we describe the precise specialization process that obtains the specialized bank account system of Example 1. For convenience, we denote by $\mathscr{R}_b$ the rewrite theory that specifies the bank account system. $\mathscr{R}_b$ includes the three rewrite rules of Fig. 1 and the equational theory $\mathscr{E}_b$ of Fig. 2. The theory $\mathscr{E}_b$ also contains algebraic axioms associated with two operators: 1) the associative and commutative, constructor operator $\_+\_$: Nat Nat -> Nat with identity 0 (used to model natural numbers); and 2) the associative and commutative, constructor operator $\_,\_$: MsgConf MsgConf -> MsgConf with identity mt (used to model multisets of deposit and withdrawal messages). The whole Maude specification of the bank account system is given in Appendix A.

As shown in Example 1, $\mathscr{E}_b$ is not a finite variant theory; therefore, the specialization of $\mathscr{R}_b$ can only be performed by using the unfolding operator $\mathscr{U}_{\overline{fvp}}$ despite the fact that it is sufficiently complete. Indeed, the other two operators (namely, $\mathscr{U}_{fvp}$ and $\mathscr{U}_{cfvp}$) are only applicable to equational theories that satisfy the finite variant property. In other words, the specialization of $\mathscr{R}_b$ is achieved by using the NPER$_{\mathscr{A}}^{\mathscr{U}}$ scheme instance with $\mathscr{U} = \mathscr{U}_{\overline{fvp}}$ and $\mathscr{A} = \mathscr{A}_{Elgg}$.

The specialization algorithm starts Phase 1 by normalizing the rewrite rules of $\mathscr{R}_b$ (Line 2 of Algorithm 1) w.r.t. $\mathscr{E}_b$. In this specific case, normalization only affects the dep rewrite rule, while w-req and w rules are left unchanged. The normalized version of dep is

```
rl [dep-n] : < bal: n pend: x overdraft: false threshold: n + m + h funds: f > # msgs,d(m)
         => < bal: n + m pend: x overdraft: false threshold: n + m + h funds: f > # msgs .
```

Rule normalization allows a first optimization to be achieved since the dep rule is simplified into dep-n by removing the operator ‹ bal:_ pend:_ overdraft:_ threshold:_funds:_ › from the right-hand side of the dep rule. At this point, all the maximal function calls are extracted from the normalized rules and stored in the set Q (Line 3 of Algorithm 1). Note that only the right-hand side of the w rule contains calls to the underlying equational theory $\mathscr{E}_b$. More precisely, the set Q of maximal function calls is $Q = \{rhs(\mathtt{w})\}$, where $rhs(\mathtt{w})$ is the right-hand side of w. The algorithm proceeds by partially evaluating $\mathscr{E}_b$ w.r.t. Q by an instance of the EQNPE$_{\mathscr{A}}^{\mathscr{U}}$ scheme with $\mathscr{U}_{\overline{fvp}}$ (in tandem with $\mathscr{A}_{Elgg}$) (Line 4 of Algorithm 1) and Phase 1 terminates by generating a rather complex and textually large specialized equational theory $\mathscr{E}_b'$ that contains 17 equations as shown in Appendix B. In Phase 2, the algorithm compresses the computed equational theory $\mathcal{E}_b'$ into a more compact theory $\mathcal{E}_b''$ that just contains four newly introduced functions (namely, f1, f2, f3, f4) that rename common nested calls and remove unused symbols. Furthermore, it propagates the computed renaming to the rewrite rules to let them access the new functions of $\mathcal{E}_b''$. The resulting specialization $\mathcal{R}_b'$ for $\mathcal{R}_b$ is shown in Appendix C.

It is worth noting that the equational theory $\mathcal{E}_b''$ in $\mathcal{R}_b'$ has the finite variant property. This can be automatically proven by using the FVP checker in [9] on $\mathcal{E}_b''$, or by simply observing that the functions f1, f2, f3, f4 are all defined by non-recursive equations and do not contain nested function calls in their left-hand sides, which suffices to ensure the FVP for $\mathcal{E}_b''$ [11]. Furthermore, the constructor decomposition of $\mathcal{E}_b''$ has a signature which is trivially preregular below the signature of $\mathcal{E}_b''$, since there are no overloaded operators with both a constructor typing and a defined typing. Additionally, by Theorem 1 $\mathcal{E}_b''$ is sufficiently complete.

Therefore, $\mathcal{R}_b'$ can be further specialized by applying the $\mathrm{NPER}_{\mathscr{A}}^{\mathscr{U}}$ scheme instantiated with $\mathscr{U} = \mathscr{U}_{cfvp}$ and $\mathscr{A} = \mathscr{A}_{cfvp}$. The final outcome is the optimized and extremely compact specialization $\mathcal{R}_b''$ shown in Example 1 (Fig. 3) that only includes three equations modeling the new invented function f0.

As a final remark, $\mathcal{R}_b''$ can be further optimized by a simple post-processing unfolding transformation that achieves the very same total evaluation of [41]. It suffices to encode each rewrite rule $l \Rightarrow r$ in $\mathcal{R}_b''$ with a term $l \mid r$ (where $\_ \mid \_$ is a fresh operator not appearing in the equational theory) and solve the reachability goal $l \mid r \rightsquigarrow_\sigma (x : ls(l)_\bullet \mid y : ls(r)_\bullet)$. The instantiated leaves $l' \mid r'$ are *constructor* terms $(x : s)\sigma^\bullet \mid (y : s)\sigma^\bullet$ that correspond to the totally evaluated rules $l' \Rightarrow r'$.

For instance, the w-s rewrite rule in $\mathcal{R}_b''$ can be totally evaluated by solving the reachability goal with initial state

```
< bal: n pend: x overdraft: false threshold: n + h funds: f > # msgs,w(m) | f0(m,n,x,h,msgs)
```

that yields the specialized and totally evaluated withdrawal rules:

```
rl [w-s-1] : < bal: n + m + x pend: m overdraft: false threshold: n + m + x + h funds: f >
              # msgs, w(m + x)
              => < bal: n pend: 0 overdraft: false threshold: n + m + x + h  funds: f > # msgs .

rl [w-s-2] : < bal: n + m pend: m + x overdraft: false threshold: n + m + h funds: f > # msgs, w(m)
              => < bal: n pend: x overdraft: false threshold: n + m + h funds: f > # msgs .

rl [w-s-3] : < bal: n pend: y overdraft: false threshold: n + h  funds: f > # msgs, w(1 + n + x)
              => < bal: n pend: y overdraft: true threshold: n + h  funds: f > # msgs .
```

The transformation leaves w-req-s and dep-s unchanged because these rules do not contain any function call to be unfolded.

Our specialization framework has been implemented in the Presto system [46], which provides all the functionality previously described in this paper. Table 1 contains some experiments that we have performed with an extension of the rewrite theory of Example 1 that is given by the Maude module Fully-Managed-Account, where deposits are fully automated by increasing balance accounts with a huge amount in a single step. Therefore there is no need to explicitly provide deposit messages in the input terms. By doing so, we avoid to feed Presto with huge input terms (with millions

Table 1. Benchmarks for the fully managed bank account system.

Size	Fully-Managed-Account		FMA-Specialized			FMA-Specialized-FVP			FMA-Specialized-CFVP			FMA-Specialized-TE		
	Rls/Eqs	T(ms)	Rls/Eqs	T(ms)	Speedup	Rls/Eqs	T(ms)	Speedup	Rls/Eqs	T(ms)	Speedup	Rls/Eqs	T(ms)	Speedup
100K	3/14	1,398	3/17	65	21.51	3/3	63	22.19	3/3	63	22.19	5/0	96	14.56
500K		7,175		337	21.29		308	23.30		308	23.30		483	14.86
1M		14,472		680	21.28		602	24.04		599	24.16		998	14.50
5M		72,096		3,469	20.78		3,068	23.50		3,053	23.61		5,049	14.28
10M		141,919		6,805	20.86		6,149	23.08		6,127	23.16		10,162	13.97

of deposits) whose parsing time might heavily affect the overall performance of the specialization process, thereby providing a more precise and fair experimental analysis.

Specifically, four distinct specializations of the rewrite theory under examination have been computed. Since the original specification Fully-Managed-Account does not satisfy the FVP, we first computed the specialized rewrite theory FMA-Specialized by using the tandem $\mathcal{U}_{\overline{fvp}}/\mathcal{A}_{Elgg}$. The obtained specialization does satisfy all of the conditions that are required to be further specialized by using either the tandem $\mathcal{U}_{fvp}/\mathcal{A}_{Elgg}$ or $\mathcal{U}_{cfvp}/\mathcal{A}_{cfvp}$ (in particular, it satisfies SC and has the FVP); hence, we have also independently computed the two corresponding (re-)specializations, FMA-Specialized-FVP and FMA-Specialized-CFVP. Also, we derived the total evaluation FMA-Specialized-TE from FMA-Specialized-CFVP.

For each experiment, we recorded the execution time $T_{\mathcal{R}'}$ of each specialization for five rewrite sequences with an increasing number of rewrite rule applications (from 100 thousands to 10 millions of applications). The considered sequences originate from the very same input term, hence input processing impacts on each experiment in the same way. Then, we compared $T_{\mathcal{R}'}$ with the execution time $T_{\mathcal{R}}$ in the original specification. These parameters allow us to precisely measure the degree of equational optimization achieved by Presto for a given rewrite theory. Indeed, the relative speedups for each specialization are computed as the ratio $T_{\mathcal{R}}/T_{\mathcal{R}'}$. We also measured the size of each specialization as the number of its rewrite rules and equations.

Our figures show an impressive performance improvement in all of the considered experiments, with an average speedup of 20.52. In the worst case, we get a totally evaluated rewrite theory FMA-Specialized-TE that runs 13.97 times faster than the original system, while the highest speedup (24.16) is achieved by the (doubly special-ized) theory FMA-Specialized-CFVP. Interestingly, the totally evaluated specification FMA-Specialized-TE is the most compact one (5 rules and 0 equations), nonetheless it provides the smallest, yet significant ($\sim$14%), optimization. This happens because all the equations have been removed from FMA-Specialized-TE so that all of the equa-tional computations are now *embedded* into system computations that are performed by applying rewrite rules, which is notoriously less efficient in Maude than the determinis-tic rewriting with equations. We also note that, since FMA-Specialized satisfies both SC and the FVP, for this particular benchmark the rewrite theories that are obtained by (re-)specializing FMA-Specialized using $\mathcal{U}_{fvp}$ and $\mathcal{U}_{cfvp}$ essentially achieve the same optimization.

Full details of these benchmarks together with further experiments are available at http://safe-tools.dsic.upv.es/presto.

7 Related Work and Conclusion

In the related literature, there are very few semantic-preserving transformations for rewrite theories. Since Maude is a reflective language, many tools are built in Maude that rely on theory transformations that preserve specific properties such as invariants or termination behavior. Full-Maude [21], Real-Time Maude [45], MTT [26], and Maude-NPA [28] are prominent examples. Equational abstraction [17,42] reduces an infinite state system to a finite quotient of the original system algebra by introducing some extra equations that preserve certain temporal logic properties. Explicit coherence [50] between rules, equations and axioms is necessary for executability purposes and also relies on rewrite theory transformations [41]. Also the semantic $\mathbb{K}$-framework [47] and the model transformations of [48] are based on sophisticated program transformations that both preserve the reduction semantics of the original theory. Nonetheless they do not aim to program optimization.

It is worth noting that our first transformation (for sufficiently complete, finite variant theories) must not be seen as a simple recast, in terms of partial evaluation, of the theory transformation of [41] since it has at least two extra advantages: 1) it seamlessly integrates the transformation of [41] within a unified, automated specialization framework for rewrite theory optimization; and 2) we have shown how we can automatically transform an equational theory that does not satisfy the FVP into a CFVP theory that can then be totally evaluated, while the original theory could not.

Our specialization technique can have a tremendous impact on the symbolic analysis of concurrent systems that are modeled as rewrite theories in Maude. The main reason why our technique is so effective in this area is that it not only achieves huge speedup for relevant classes of rewrite theories, but it can also cut down an infinite folding variant narrowing space to a finite one for the underlying equational theory $\mathcal{E}$. By doing this, any $\mathcal{E}$-unification problem can be finitely solved and symbolic, narrowing-based analysis with R modulo $\mathcal{E}$ can be effectively performed. Moreover, in many cases, the specialization process transforms a rewrite theory whose operators obey algebraic axioms, such as associativity, commutativity, and unity, into a much simpler rewrite theory with no structural axioms so that it can be run in an independent rewriting infrastructure that does not support rewriting or narrowing modulo axioms. This allows some costly analyses that may require significant (or even unaffordable) resources, both in time and space, to be effectively performed.

Finally, further applications could benefit from the optimization of variant generation that is achieved by Presto. For instance, an important number of applications (and tools) are currently based on narrowing-based variant generation: for example, the protocol analyzers Maude-NPA [28], Tamarin [37], AKiSs [18], Maude debuggers and program analysers [3–6], termination provers, model checkers, variant-based satisfiability checkers, coherence and confluence provers, and different applications of symbolic reachability analysis [24].

A   Full Specification of the Bank Account System

```
fmod NAT-PRES-MONUS is
  pr TRUTH-VALUE .
  sorts Nat NzNat Zero .
  subsort Zero NzNat < Nat .
  op 0 : -> Zero [ctor] .
  op 1 : -> NzNat [ctor] .
  op _+_ : NzNat Nat -> NzNat [ctor assoc comm id: 0] .
  op _+_ : Nat Nat -> Nat [ctor assoc comm id: 0] .
  vars n m : Nat .
  vars b b' : Bool .
  op _>_ : Nat Nat -> Bool .
  eq m + n + 1 > n = true [variant] .
  eq n > n + m = false [variant] .
  op _>=_ : Nat Nat -> Bool .
  eq m + n >= n =  true [variant] .
  eq n >= m + n + 1 = false [variant] .
  op _-_ : Nat Nat -> Nat .
  eq n - (n + m) = 0 [variant] .
  eq (n + m) - n = m [variant] .
endfm

mod MANAGED-ACCOUNT is
  pr NAT-PRES-MONUS .
  sorts Account Msg MsgConf State .
  subsort Msg < MsgConf .
  op < bal:_pend:_overdraft:_threshold:_funds:_ > : Nat Nat Bool Nat Nat -> Account [ctor] .
  op << bal:_pend:_overdraft:_threshold:_funds:_ >> : Nat Nat Bool Nat Nat -> Account .
  op mt : -> MsgConf [ctor] .
  op w : Nat -> Msg [ctor] .
  op d : Nat -> Msg [ctor] .
  op _,_ : MsgConf MsgConf -> MsgConf [ctor assoc comm id: mt] .
  op _#_ : Account MsgConf -> State [ctor] .
  op [_,_,_] : Bool State State -> State .
  vars n m x h : Nat .
  var b : Bool .
  vars s s' : State .
  var msgs : MsgConf .
  eq [true,s,s'] = s [variant] .
  eq [false,s,s'] = s' [variant] .
  eq << bal: (n + h) pend: m overdraft: b:Bool threshold: h funds: f >>
   = << bal: n pend: m overdraft: b:Bool threshold: h funds: f + 1 >> [variant] .
  eq << bal: n pend: m overdraft: b:Bool threshold: n + h funds: f >>
   = < bal: n pend: m overdraft: b:Bool threshold: n + h funds: f > [variant] .

  rl [w-req] : < bal: n + m + x pend: x overdraft: false threshold: n + h funds: f > # msgs
          => < bal: n + m + x pend: x + m overdraft: false threshold: n + h funds: f >
                 # w(m),msgs .

  rl [w] : < bal: n pend: x overdraft: false threshold: n + h funds: f > # w(m),msgs
      => [ m > n,
           < bal: n pend: x overdraft: true threshold: n + h funds: f > # msgs,
           < bal: (n - m) pend: (x - m) overdraft: false threshold: n + h funds: f > # msgs ]   .

  rl [dep] : < bal: n pend: x overdraft: false threshold: n + m + h funds: f >
                 # d(m),msgs
          => << bal: (n + m) pend: x overdraft: false threshold: n + m + h funds: f >> # msgs .
endm
```

B   Specialization of the Bank Account System $\mathscr{R}_b$

```
eq [$5 > $1,
    < bal: $1 pend: $5 + $6 overdraft:true limit: $1 + $2 funds: $3 > # $4,
    < bal: $1 - $5 pend: ($5 + $6) - $5 overdraft: false limit: $1 + $2 funds: $3 > # $4]
 = [$5 > $1,
    < bal: $1 pend: $5 + $6 overdraft: true limit: $1 + $2 funds: $3 > # $4,
    < bal: $1 - $5 pend: $6 overdraft: false limit: $1 + $2 funds: $3 > # $4] [ variant ] .

eq [$5 > $5,
    <bal: $5 pend: $1 + $5 overdraft:true limit: $5 + $2 funds: $3 > # $4,
    < bal: 0 pend: $1 overdraft: false limit: $5 + $2 funds: $3 > # $4]
 = < bal: 0 pend: $1 overdraft: false limit: $5 + $2 funds: $3 > # $4 [ variant ] .

eq [$5 > $1 + $5,
    < bal: $1 + $5 pend: $5 + $6 overdraft:true limit: $1 + $5 + $2 funds: $3 > # $4,
    < bal: ($1 + $5) - $5 pend: ($5 + $6) - $5 overdraft: false limit: $1 + $5 + $2
      funds: $3 > # $4]
 = < bal: $1 pend: $6 overdraft: false limit: $1 + $5 + $2 funds: $3 > # $4 [ variant ] .

eq [$5 > $5 + $6,
    < bal: $5 + $6 pend: $1 + $5 overdraft: true limit: $5 + $6 + $2 funds: $3 > # $4,
    < bal: ($5 + $6) - $5 pend: $1 overdraft: false limit: $5 + $6 + $2 funds: $3 > # $4]
 = < bal: $6 pend: $1 overdraft: false limit: $5 + $6 + $2 funds: $3 > # $4 [ variant ] .

eq [($4 + $5) > $4,
    < bal: $4 pend: $4 + $5 + $6 overdraft: true limit: $4 + $1 funds: $2 > # $3,
    < bal: $4 - $4 + $5 pend: ($4 + $5 + $6) - $4 + $5 overdraft: false limit: $4 + $1
      funds: $2 > # $3]
 = [($4 + $5) > $4,
    < bal: $4 pend: $4 + $5 + $6 overdraft: true limit: $4 + $1 funds: $2 > # $3,
    < bal: 0 pend: $6 overdraft: false limit: $4 + $1 funds: $2 > # $3] [ variant ] .

eq [($4 + $5) > $4 + $5,
    < bal: $4 + $5 pend: $4 overdraft: true limit: $4 + $5 + $1 funds: $2 > # $3,
    < bal: 0 pend: 0 overdraft: false limit: $4 + $5 + $1 funds: $2 > # $3]
 = < bal: 0 pend: 0 overdraft: false limit: $4 + $5 + $1 funds: $2 > # $3 [ variant ] .

eq [($4 + $5) > $4 + $5 + $6,
    < bal: $4 + $5 + $6 pend: $4 overdraft: true limit: $4 + $5 + $6 + $1 funds: $2 > # $3,
    < bal: ($4 + $5 + $6) - $4 + $5 pend: 0 overdraft: false limit: $4 + $5 + $6 + $1
      funds:$2 > # $3]
 = < bal: $6 pend: 0 overdraft: false limit: $4 + $5 + $6 + $1 funds: $2 > # $3 [ variant ] .

eq [($5 + $6) > $1,
    < bal: $1 pend: $5 overdraft: true limit: $1 + $2 funds: $3 > # $4,
       < bal: $1 - $5 + $6 pend: $5 - $5 + $6 overdraft: false limit: $1 + $2 funds: $3 > # $4]
 = [($5 + $6) > $1,
    < bal: $1 pend: $5 overdraft: true limit: $1 + $2 funds: $3 > # $4,
    < bal: $1 - $5 + $6 pend: 0 overdraft: false limit: $1 + $2 funds: $3 > # $4] [ variant ] .

eq [($5 + $6) > $1 + $5 + $6,
    < bal: $1 + $5 + $6 pend: $5 overdraft: true limit: $1 + $5 + $6 + $2 funds: $3 > # $4,
    < bal: ($1 + $5 + $6) - $5 + $6 pend: $5 - $5 + $6 overdraft: false limit: $1 + $5 + $6 + $2
      funds: $3 > # $4]
 = < bal: $1 pend: 0 overdraft: false limit: $1 + $5 + $6 + $2 funds: $3 > # $4 [ variant ] .

rl [dep] : < bal: n pend: x overdraft: false threshold: n + m + h funds: f > # msgs,d(m)
 => < bal: n + m pend: x overdraft: false threshold: n + m + h funds: f > # msgs.
rl [w] : < bal: n pend: x overdraft: false threshold: n + h funds: f > # msgs,withdraw(m)
 => [m > n,< bal: n pend: x overdraft: true threshold: n + h funds: f >
      # msgs, < bal: n - m pend: x - m overdraft: false threshold: n + h funds: f >
      # msgs] .
rl [w-req] : < bal: n + m + x pend: x overdraft: false threshold: n + m + x + h funds: f > # msgs
 => < bal: n + m + x pend: m + x overdraft: false threshold: n + m + x + h funds: f > # msgs,w(m) .
```

C Specialization of the Bank Account System $\mathcal{R}_b$ with Compression

```
eq f0($5, $5 + $6, $1, $2, $3, $4)
  = < bal: $6 pend: $1 overdraft: false threshold: $5 + $6 + $2 funds: $3 > # $4 [ variant ] .

eq f0(1 + $1 + $6, $1, $2, $3, $4, $5)
  = < bal: $1 pend: 1 + $1 + $2 + $6 overdraft: true threshold: $1 + $3 funds: $4 > # $5 [ variant ] .

eq f1($5, $1, $5 + $6, $2, $3, $4) = f0($5, $1, $6, $2, $3, $4) [ variant ] .

eq f1($5, $1 + $5, $5 + $6, $2, $3, $4)
  = < bal: $1 pend: $6 overdraft: false threshold: $1 + $5 + $2 funds: $3 > # $4 [ variant ] .

eq f1($4 + $5, $4, $4 + $5 + $6, $1, $2, $3) = f2($4, $5, $6, $1, $2, $3) [ variant ] .

eq f1($5 + $6, $1, $5, $2, $3, $4) = f3($5, $6, $1, $2, $3, $4) [ variant ] .

eq f1($5 + $6, $1 + $5 + $6, $5, $2, $3, $4)
  = < bal: $1 pend: 0 overdraft: false threshold: $1 + $5 + $6 + $2 funds: $3 > # $4 [ variant ] .

eq f1(1 + $1 + $6, $1, $2, $3, $4, $5)
  = < bal: $1 pend: $2 overdraft: true threshold: $1 + $3 funds: $4 > # $5 [ variant ] .

eq f1($4 + $5 + $6 + $7, $4 + $5, $4 + $6, $1, $2, $3)
  = f4($4, $5, $6, $7, $1, $2, $3) [ variant ] .

eq f2($1, 1 + $6, $2, $3, $4, $5)
  = < bal: $1 pend: 1 + $1 + $2 + $6 overdraft: true threshold: $1 + $3 funds: $4 > # $5 [ variant ] .

eq f2($5, 0, $1, $2, $3, $4)
  = < bal: 0 pend: $1 overdraft: false threshold: $5 + $2 funds: $3 > # $4 [ variant ] .

eq f3($4, $5, $4 + $5 + $6, $1, $2, $3)
  = < bal: $6 pend: 0 overdraft: false threshold: $4 + $5 + $6 + $1 funds: $2 > # $3 [ variant ] .

eq f3($4 + $6, 1 + $5 + $7, $4 + $5, $1, $2, $3)
  = < bal: $4 + $5 pend: $4 + $6 overdraft: true threshold: $4 + $5 + $1 funds: $2 > # $3 [ variant ] .

eq f3(1 + $4 + $6, $5 + $7, $4 + $5, $1, $2, $3)
  = < bal: $4 + $5 pend: 1 + $4 + $6 overdraft: true threshold: $4 + $5 + $1 funds: $2 > # $3 [ variant ] .

eq f4($4, $5, $6, 1 + $7, $1, $2, $3)
  = < bal: $4 + $5 pend: $4 + $6 overdraft: true threshold: $4 + $5 + $1 funds: $2 > # $3 [ variant ] .

eq f4($4, $5, 0, 0, $1, $2, $3)
  = < bal: 0 pend: 0 overdraft: false threshold: $4 + $5 + $1 funds: $2 > # $3 [ variant ] .

eq f4($4, $5, 1 + $6, $7, $1, $2, $3)
  = < bal: $4 + $5 pend: 1 + $4 + $6 overdraft: true threshold: $4 + $5 + $1 funds: $2 > # $3 [ variant ] .

rl [w]  : < bal: n pend: x overdraft: false threshold: n + h funds: f > # msgs,w(m)
  => f1(m, n, x, h, f, msgs) .
rl [dep] : < bal: n pend: x overdraft: false threshold: n + m + h funds: f > # msgs,d(m)
  => < bal: n + m pend: x overdraft: false threshold: n + m + h funds: f > # msgs.
rl [w-req] : < bal: n + m + x pend: x overdraft: false threshold: n + m + x + h funds: f > # msgs
  => < bal: n + m + x pend: m + x overdraft: false threshold: n + m + x + h funds: f > # msgs,w(m) .
```

References

1. Albert, E., Alpuente, M., Falaschi, M., Vidal, G.: Indy User's Manual. Technical report DSIC-II/12/98, Department of Computer Systems and Computation, Universitat Politècnica de València (1998)
2. Albert, E., Alpuente, M., Harms, M., Vidal, G.: A partial evaluation framework for curry programs. In: Ganzinger, H., McAllester, D., Voronkov, A. (eds.) LPAR 1999. LNCS (LNAI),

vol. 1705, pp. 376–395. Springer, Heidelberg (1999). https://doi.org/10.1007/3-540-48242-3_23

3. Alpuente, M., Ballis, D., Baggi, M., Falaschi, F.: A fold/unfold transformation framework for rewrite theories extended to CCT. In: Gallagher, J., Voigtländer, J. (eds.) ACM SIGPLAN Workshop on Partial Evaluation and Program Manipulation (PEPM 2010), pp. 43–52. ACM. https://doi.org/10.1145/1706356.1706367

4. Alpuente, M., Ballis, D., Frechina, F., Sapiña, J.: Assertion-based analysis via slicing with ABETS (system description). Theory Pract. Logic Program. **16**(5–6), 515–532 (2016)

5. Alpuente, M., Ballis, D., Frechina, F., Sapiña, J.: Debugging Maude programs via runtime assertion checking and trace slicing. J. Log. Algebr. Methods Program. **85**, 707–736 (2016)

6. Alpuente, M., Ballis, D., Romero, D.: A rewriting logic approach to the formal specification and verification of web applications. Sci. Comput. Program. **81**, 79–107 (2014)

7. Alpuente, M., Cuenca-Ortega, A., Escobar, S., Meseguer, J.: A partial evaluation framework for order-sorted equational programs modulo axioms. J. Log. Algebr. Methods Program. **110**, 1–36 (2020)

8. Alpuente, M., Cuenca-Ortega, A., Escobar, S., Meseguer, J.: Order-sorted homeomorphic embedding modulo combinations of associativity and/or commutativity axioms. Fund. Inform. **177**(3–4), 297–329 (2020)

9. Alpuente, M., Cuenca-Ortega, A., Escobar, S., Sapiña, J.: Inspecting Maude variants with GLINTS. Theory Pract. Logic Program. **17**(5–6), 689–707 (2017)

10. Alpuente, M., Escobar, S., Espert, J., Meseguer, J.: A modular order-sorted equational generalization algorithm. Inf. Comput. **235**, 98–136 (2014)

11. Alpuente, M., Escobar, S., Iborra, J.: Termination of narrowing revisited. Theoret. Comput. Sci. **410**(46), 4608–4625 (2009)

12. Alpuente, M., Falaschi, M., Julián, P., Vidal, G.: Specialization of lazy functional logic programs. In: Proceedings of the ACM SIGPLAN Symposium on Partial Evaluation and Semantics-Based Program Manipulation (PEPM 1997), pp. 151–162. Association for Computing Machinery (1997)

13. Alpuente, M., Falaschi, M., Moreno, G., Vidal, G.: Safe folding/unfolding with conditional narrowing. In: Hanus, M., Heering, J., Meinke, K. (eds.) ALP/HOA -1997. LNCS, vol. 1298, pp. 1–15. Springer, Heidelberg (1997). https://doi.org/10.1007/BFb0026999

14. Alpuente, M., Falaschi, M., Vidal, G.: A unifying view of functional and logic program specialization. ACM Comput. Surv. **30**(3es), 9es (1998)

15. Alpuente, M., Falaschi, M., Vidal, G.: Partial evaluation of functional logic programs. ACM Trans. Program. Lang. Syst. **20**(4), 768–844 (1998)

16. Alpuente, M., Lucas, S., Hanus, M., Vidal, G.: Specialization of functional logic programs based on needed narrowing. Theory Pract. Logic Program. **5**(3), 273–303 (2005)

17. Bae, K., Escobar, S., Meseguer, J.: Abstract logical model checking of infinite-state systems using narrowing. In: Proceedings of the 24th International Conference on Rewriting Techniques and Applications (RTA 2013). Leibniz International Proceedings in Informatics (LIPIcs), vol. 21, pp. 81–96. Schloss Dagstuhl - Leibniz-Zentrum für Informatik (2013)

18. Baelde, D., Delaune, S., Gazeau, I., Kremer, S.: Symbolic verification of privacy-type properties for security protocols with XOR. In: Proceedings of the 30th International Symposium on Computer Security Foundations (CSF 2017), pp. 234–248. IEEE Computer Society Press (2017)

19. Bouchard, C., Gero, K.A., Lynch, C., Narendran, P.: On forward closure and the finite variant property. In: Fontaine, P., Ringeissen, C., Schmidt, R.A. (eds.) FroCoS 2013. LNCS (LNAI), vol. 8152, pp. 327–342. Springer, Heidelberg (2013). https://doi.org/10.1007/978-3-642-40885-4_23

20. Burstall, R.M., Darlington, J.: A transformation system for developing recursive programs. J. ACM **24**(1), 44–67 (1977)

21. Clavel, M., et al.: Maude Manual (Version 3.0). Technical report, SRI International Computer Science Laboratory (2020). http://maude.cs.uiuc.edu
22. Comon-Lundh, H., Delaune, S.: The finite variant property: how to get rid of some algebraic properties. In: Giesl, J. (ed.) RTA 2005. LNCS, vol. 3467, pp. 294–307. Springer, Heidelberg (2005). https://doi.org/10.1007/978-3-540-32033-3_22
23. Danvy, O., Glück, R., Thiemann, P.: Partial Evaluation, International Seminar, Dagstuhl Castle, Germany. Springer, Heidelberg (1996). https://doi.org/10.1007/3-540-61580-6
24. Durán, F., et al.: Programming and symbolic computation in Maude. J. Log. Algebr. Methods Program. **110**, 100497 (2020)
25. Durán, F., Eker, S., Escobar, S., Martí-Oliet, N., Meseguer, J., Talcott, C.: Associative unification and symbolic reasoning modulo associativity in Maude. In: Rusu, V. (ed.) WRLA 2018. LNCS, vol. 11152, pp. 98–114. Springer, Cham (2018). https://doi.org/10.1007/978-3-319-99840-4_6
26. Durán, F., Lucas, S., Meseguer, J.: MTT: the Maude termination tool (system description). In: Armando, A., Baumgartner, P., Dowek, G. (eds.) IJCAR 2008. LNCS (LNAI), vol. 5195, pp. 313–319. Springer, Heidelberg (2008). https://doi.org/10.1007/978-3-540-71070-7_27
27. Durán, F., Meseguer, J., Rocha, C.: Ground confluence of order-sorted conditional specifications modulo axioms. J. Log. Algebr. Methods Program. **111**, 100513 (2020)
28. Escobar, S., Meadows, C., Meseguer, J.: Maude-NPA: cryptographic protocol analysis modulo equational properties. In: Aldini, A., Barthe, G., Gorrieri, R. (eds.) FOSAD 2007-2009. LNCS, vol. 5705, pp. 1–50. Springer, Heidelberg (2009). https://doi.org/10.1007/978-3-642-03829-7_1
29. Escobar, S., Meseguer, J.: Symbolic model checking of infinite-state systems using narrowing. In: Baader, F. (ed.) RTA 2007. LNCS, vol. 4533, pp. 153–168. Springer, Heidelberg (2007). https://doi.org/10.1007/978-3-540-73449-9_13
30. Escobar, S., Meseguer, J., Sasse, R.: Variant narrowing and equational unification. Electron. Notes Theor. Comput. Sci. **238**(3), 103–119 (2009)
31. Escobar, S., Sasse, R., Meseguer, J.: Folding variant narrowing and optimal variant termination. J. Logic Algebraic Program. **81**(7–8), 898–928 (2012)
32. Gnaedig, I., Kirchner, H.: Computing constructor forms with non terminating rewrite programs. In: Proceedings of the 8th ACM SIGPLAN Conference on Principles and Practice of Declarative Programming (PPDP 2006), pp. 121–132. Association for Computing Machinery (2006)
33. Jones, N.D., Gomard, C.K., Sestoft, P.: Partial Evaluation and Automatic Program Generation. Prentice-Hall, Hoboken (1993)
34. Leuschel, M.: Improving homeomorphic embedding for online termination. In: Flener, P. (ed.) LOPSTR 1998. LNCS, vol. 1559, pp. 199–218. Springer, Heidelberg (1999). https://doi.org/10.1007/3-540-48958-4_11
35. Lloyd, J.W., Shepherdson, J.C.: Partial evaluation in logic programming. J. Logic Program. **11**(3–4), 217–242 (1991)
36. Martens, B., Gallagher, J.: Ensuring global termination of partial deduction while allowing flexible polyvariance. In: Proceedings of the 12th International Conference on Logic Programming (ICLP 1995), pp. 597–611. The MIT Press (1995)
37. Meier, S., Schmidt, B., Cremers, C., Basin, D.: The TAMARIN prover for the symbolic analysis of security protocols. In: Sharygina, N., Veith, H. (eds.) CAV 2013. LNCS, vol. 8044, pp. 696–701. Springer, Heidelberg (2013). https://doi.org/10.1007/978-3-642-39799-8_48
38. Meseguer, J.: Conditional rewriting logic as a unified model of concurrency. Theoret. Comput. Sci. **96**(1), 73–155 (1992)

39. Meseguer, J.: Variant-based satisfiability in initial algebras. In: Artho, C., Ölveczky, P.C. (eds.) FTSCS 2015. CCIS, vol. 596, pp. 3–34. Springer, Cham (2016). https://doi.org/10. 1007/978-3-319-29510-7_1
40. Meseguer, J.: Variant-based satisfiability in initial algebras. Sci. Comput. Program. **154**, 3–41 (2018)
41. Meseguer, J.: Generalized rewrite theories, coherence completion, and symbolic methods. J. Log. Algebr. Methods Program. **110**, 100483 (2020)
42. Meseguer, J., Palomino, M., Martí-Oliet, N.: Equational abstractions. Theoret. Comput. Sci. **403**(2–3), 239–264 (2008)
43. Meseguer, J., Thati, P.: Symbolic reachability analysis using narrowing and its application to verification of cryptographic protocols. Higher-Order Symb. Comput. **20**(1–2), 123–160 (2007)
44. Middeldorp, A., Hamoen, E.: Counterexamples to completeness results for basic narrowing (extended abstract). In: Kirchner, H., Levi, G. (eds.) ALP 1992. LNCS, vol. 632, pp. 244–258. Springer, Heidelberg (1992). https://doi.org/10.1007/BFb0013830
45. Ölveczky, P.C., Meseguer, J.: The real-time Maude tool. In: Ramakrishnan, C.R., Rehof, J. (eds.) TACAS 2008. LNCS, vol. 4963, pp. 332–336. Springer, Heidelberg (2008). https://doi.org/10.1007/978-3-540-78800-3_23
46. The Presto Website (2020). http://safe-tools.dsic.upv.es/presto
47. Roşu, G.: $\mathbb{K}$: a semantic framework for programming languages and formal analysis tools. In: Dependable Software Systems Engineering. NATO Science for Peace and Security Series - D: Information and Communication Security, vol. 50, pp. 186–206. IOS Press (2017)
48. Rodríguez, A., Durán, F., Rutle, A., Kristensen, L.M.: Executing multilevel domain-specific models in Maude. J. Object Technol. **18**(2), 4:1–4:21 (2019)
49. Slagle, J.R.: Automated theorem-proving for theories with simplifiers, commutativity, and associativity. J. ACM **21**(4), 622–642 (1974)
50. Viry, P.: Equational rules for rewriting logic. Theoret. Comput. Sci. **285**(2), 487–517 (2002)

Automated Synthesis of Software Contracts with KINDSPEC

María Alpuente[iD] and Alicia Villanueva[(✉)][iD]

Valencian Research Institute for Artificial Intelligence, VRAIN,
Universitat Politècnica de València, Valencia, Spain
{alpuente,alvilga1}@upv.es

Abstract. In this paper, we describe KINDSPEC, an automated tool that synthesizes software contracts from programs that are written in a significant fragment of C that supports pointer-based structures, heap manipulation, and recursion. By relying on a semantic definition of the C language in the $\mathbb{K}$ semantic framework, KINDSPEC leverages the symbolic execution capabilities of $\mathbb{K}$ to axiomatically explain any program function. This is done by using observer routines in the same program to characterize the program states before and after the function execution. The generated contracts are expressed in the form of logical axioms that specify the precise input/output behavior of the C routines, including both general axioms for default behavior and exceptional axioms for the specification error behavior. We summarize the main services provided by KINDSPEC, which also include a novel refinement facility that improves the quality and accuracy of the synthesized contracts. Finally, we provide an experimental evaluation that assesses its effectiveness.

Keywords: Contract inference · Symbolic execution · Abstract subsumption · Exceptions

1 Introduction

Software contracts provide mathematical specification for the terms of the service that software components can provide. Contracts on software are essentially written by using program preconditions and postconditions, which are similar to Hoare formulas that formalize the mutual obligations and benefits of the software units or routines [34]. Contract checking can improve software reliability but requires contracts to always be guaranteed to be consistent with the program code, which places a heavy burden on programmers and hinders its applicability. Moreover, while exceptional (or error) behavior specification should be integral to the contract, error specification is highly prone to introduction of mistakes and oversight.

This research was partially supported by TAILOR, a project funded by EU Horizon 2020 research and innovation programme under GA No 952215, grant RTI2018-094403-B-C32 funded by MCIN/AEI/10.13039/501100011033 and by "ERDF A way of making Europe", and by Generalitat Valenciana PROMETEO/2019/098.

© Springer Nature Switzerland AG 2023
P. Lopez-Garcia et al. (Eds.): Hermenegildo Festschrift 2022, LNCS 13160, pp. 51–71, 2023.
https://doi.org/10.1007/978-3-031-31476-6_3

This paper presents KINDSPEC, an automated contract synthesis tool that is based on abstract *symbolic execution* for a significant fragment of C called KERNELC [18]. KERNELC supports recursive function and data structure definition, pointers, and dynamic memory allocation and deallocation (`malloc` and `free` routines), but it lacks pointer arithmetic and the possibility to import external code. The contracts that we synthesize essentially consist of logical assertions that characterize the behavior of a program function in terms of what can be observed in the states before and after the function execution. The inferred axioms include default (general) rules and exceptions to these rules that specify exceptional (or error) behavior; e.g., undesirable use cases or execution side effects.

The overall quality of programs and specifications can be fairly improved by systematically dealing with errors and exceptions. While several mainstream languages such as C++ and Java provide built-in support for exception handling, the C ANSI/ISO standard does not foresee any high-level way to define, throw, and catch exceptions [1]. The usual way for handling errors in C is to define special error return values through program constants, with the caller's duty being to check the returned value and to take appropriate action [21]. A known disadvantage of this practice is that it obscures the program control flow and is highly prone to oversight. Since exception failures can account for up to 2/3 of system crashes and 50% of security vulnerabilities [22], the capability to infer exceptional axioms from program code can be very helpful in this regard.

KINDSPEC implements an extension of the contract-discovering technique developed in [2,3], which is based on symbolic execution, a well-known program analysis technique that runs programs by using *symbolic* input values rather than actual (concrete) values [5,30]. By abstractly representing inputs as symbols, symbolic execution can simultaneously explore multiple paths that a program could take, resorting to constraint solvers to construct actual instances that would exercise the path. Roughly speaking, in the discovery methodology of [2], given a function f of a program P, and a root-to-leaf path from the pre-state s to the post-state s' in the symbolic execution tree for f in P, an implicative axiom $(p \Rightarrow q)$ is synthesized that *explains* the symbolic path from s to s'. Essentially, the antecedent p (resp. consequent q) of the axiom consists of a sequence of equations of the form $o(x_1, \ldots x_m) = v_s$ (resp. $o(x_1, \ldots x_m) = v_{s'}$) where each v_s (resp. $v_{s'}$) is the result of applying the m-ary *observer* function o of P to s (resp. s'). For example, for the case of a classical function `push(x,t)` that piles up an element `x` at the top of a given bounded stack `t`, the inferred logical axiom describes the expected behavior that, provided `t` was not full, the new top element is `x` and the stack size is increased by one: `size(t)=n` $\wedge$ `isfull(t)=0` $\wedge$ `top(t)=?e` $\Rightarrow$ `size(t)=n+1` $\wedge$ `isfull(t)=?b` $\wedge$ `top(t)=x`, where `?e` and `?b` stand for symbolic values.

The symbolic infrastructure of KINDSPEC is built on top of the rewriting-based, programming language definitional framework $\mathbb{K}$, which facilitates the development of executable semantics of programming languages and related formal analysis techniques and tools, such as type inferencers or program verifiers

[38]. In [2], the recent symbolic execution capabilities of $\mathbb{K}$ –that are available from $\mathbb{K}$ 3.4 on– were enriched with two new features not provided by $\mathbb{K}$: 1) lazy initialization, to effectively handle symbolic memory objects; and 2) abstract subsumption, to ensure termination without imposing fixed depth bounds. Due to abstraction, some of the inferred axioms cannot be guaranteed to be correct and are kept apart as candidate (or overly general) axioms.

KINDSPEC builds upon a previous, preliminary prototype presented in [2] and improves it in several ways: 1) we have fairly improved the maturity and robustness of the tool, giving support to more precise abstract domains that allow us to deal more accurately with complex dynamic allocated data structures such as linked lists and doubly-linked lists (including circular/cyclic lists); 2) we improved the accuracy of the inferred contracts by extending the original refinement process implemented in KINDSPEC that gets rid of less general axioms with new functionality for supporting axiom trusting and falsification; 3) we have extended the coverage of the analysis with the capability to infer axioms that express exceptional behavior; this not only improves the quality of the specification but may also suggest suitable program fixes that prevent execution failures to occur due to the faults. The KINDSPEC tool is publicly available at http://safe-tools.dsic.upv.es/kindspec2_2.

Manuel's pioneering work on concurrent logic programming with assertions has been a source of inspiration for our research on semantics of concurrent languages and symbolic execution since we met in the 1990s. The aim of this work is to honor Manuel with this paper that contributes to further advancing the intertwining between these areas.

2 Inferring Software Contracts with KINDSPEC

The wide interest in formal specifications as helpers for a variety of analysis, validation, and verification tools has resulted in numerous approaches for (semi-)automatically computing different kinds of specifications that can take the form of contracts, snippets, summaries, process models, graphs, automata, properties, rules, interfaces, or component abstractions. In this work, we focus on input-output relations; given a precondition for the state, we infer which modifications in the state are implied, and we express the relations as logical implications that reuse the program functions themselves. In order to achieve this, the inference technique of KINDSPEC relies on a classification scheme for program functions where a function may be a *modifier* or an *observer*, or it can play both roles. As defined in [31], observers are operations that can be used to inspect the state of an object, while modifiers change it. Since the C language does not enforce data encapsulation, we cannot presume purity of any function. Hence, we do not assume the traditional premise that observer functions do not modify the program state and we consider as observer any function whose return type is different from void.

Symbolic execution of a function call can be represented as a tree-like structure where each branch corresponds to a set of possible execution paths. At any time of the execution, KINDSPEC's symbolic execution engine maintains a state $s = (pc, stmt, \sigma, h, \phi)$, where pc (the program counter), $stmt$ (the next statement to evaluate), σ (the symbolic program store that associates program variables with symbolic expressions), and h (the symbolic heap used to store dynamically allocated objects) are akin to standard configurations used in operational semantics. As for the path constraint ϕ, it is a formula that expresses a set of assumptions that are generated whenever a branching condition on primitive fields is taken in the execution to reach $stmt$. Intuitively, when symbolic execution reaches a conditional control flow statement, the logical condition that enables each branch is conjuncted to the accumulated path constraint of each diverging path. When the executed path ends, the associated path constraint represents the condition that input values must satisfy in order for the execution to reach the current program point.

To provide for contract discovering, we enriched the symbolic states supported by the symbolic $\mathbb{K}$ framework with a new component ι (called the initial heap) that is aimed to keep track of the heap constraints that are generated during *lazy initialization*. Roughly speaking, when an instruction performs a first access to an uninitialized object reference field, the symbolic execution forks the current state with three different heap configurations, in which the field is respectively initialized with: (1) `null`, (2) a reference to a new object with all symbolic attributes, and (3) a previously introduced concrete object of the desired type.

In order to synthesize a contract for the function of interest f, a symbolic call to f is executed with a sequence $x_1, \ldots x_n$ of fresh variables (simply denoted by $\overline{x_n}$) as arguments and initial path constraint `true`, yielding as a result a set $\mathcal{F}$ of final states. Then, for each state F in $\mathcal{F}$, an instantiated initial state $I = (0, f(\overline{x_n}), \emptyset, \iota, \phi)$ which stands for the program state before executing f, is built by joining together the initial call $f(\overline{x_n})$ with the path constraint ϕ and the lazy initialization constraint ι that are both retrieved from the final state F. The symbolic execution path from I to F is then described by means of an axiom $(p \Rightarrow q)$, which is obtained by:

1. symbolically running every (*feasible*) m-ary program observer o on both states I and F, over any subsequence of m arguments taken from $\overline{x_n}$ and all its possible permutations. The *feasible* observers are those having a subset of f's arguments as parameters. Each observer execution contributes an equational explanation $o(\overline{x_m}) = v_I$ (resp. $o(\overline{x_m}) = v_F$) to the premise p (resp. the consequent q) of the synthesized axiom.
2. Adding to q a last equation $ret = v$, where v is the value returned by the function f at the final symbolic execution state F.

The expectation that observation functions exist or can easily be written is reasonable. Observer calls are independently executed on I (resp. F) so that they cannot contaminate each other. Those observer calls that are found out to modify the given state are disregarded since the observation could have corrupted the observed behavior. Also, we note that lazy initialization is never applied during the symbolic execution of observer functions since they would be exploring fresh states beyond the analyzed symbolic execution configurations. When it is not the case that all of the symbolic execution branches for $o(\overline{x_m})$ return the same value, the observation is inconclusive and a symbolic equation $o(\overline{x_m}) =?v$ is built, for fresh symbolic variable $?v$.

Specification of Exceptional Behavior. Error specification and handling has traditionally been a challenge to the theory of abstract data types [36], which is considered a major tool for writing hierarchical, modular, implementation-independent specifications [24]. The main reason for this is that initial algebra semantics considers errors just as ordinary data and then spends much effort to discriminate errors from correct data. Our error handling approach borrows some ideas from *order-sorted* semantics, which supports many different styles for dealing with errors [26]. Roughly speaking, at the semantic level we provide the semantic definition of the language with an explicit *error supersort (supertype)* S for each program type T, such that error handling is naturally achieved by overloading every program operator $f : T_1, T_2, \ldots T_n \to T$ in the corresponding error supertypes, i.e., $f : S_1, S_2, \ldots S_n \to S$. By this means, error return values belong to the supertype S and are valid results for the evaluation of operator f although they are not compatible with correct data return values of T. This is comparable in a sense to the handling of errors in the ACSL contract specification language [6], where special error return values are introduced in the C semantics.

In [25], Goguen suggests including all exceptional behaviors and error messages directly in the specifications by providing as much information as is helpful about what is wrong or exceptional. In order to identify exceptional state behavior and errors directly from the program code, we have enriched the symbolic execution of [2] so that exceptional behavior is integral to the inferred contract specification. First, we have identified the most common undesirable (or erroneous) behaviors that may occur while running a KERNELC[1] program and provided each of them with an error code, as shown in Table 1. Then, we created a new predefined KERNELC data type (universal supertype) consisting of the set of error codes, and we redefined the KERNELC semantic rules such that error return values of the form $(errorCode, pc)$ are allowed for all types, where the program counter pc aims to identify the precise statement of the program code that caused the error. Finally, we provided overloaded definitions of the program functions as explained in Sect. 1. By this means, every circumstance where an exception is triggered is witnessed by the corresponding error return value, which is not only useful for debugging purposes but can also be used to ascertain suitable program patches that avoid the errors. KINDSPEC internally represents each error e (e.g., null dereference, division by zero, etc.) as the repair problem $(e, pc, \mathcal{V})$, with $\mathcal{V}$ being the set of affected variables, whose solutions would represent a particular program fix. By the time being, such a fix just consists of suggesting the insertion of safety checks on the variables of $\mathcal{V}$ at the right program points to avoid e. The general problem of automated program repair

---

[1] Some standard C syntactic errors such as IRT are not statically detected by $\mathbb{K}$, thus they show up at (symbolic) execution time.

Table 1. Most common exceptions added to the KINDSPEC definition of KERNELC.

Error code	Exception	Description
NPE	*Null Pointer Error*	Null dereferencing
DBZ	*Division By Zero*	Division of any number by 0
VVA	*Void Value Access*	Access to a non-pointer value of type `void`
NMS	*Non-valid Malloc Size*	Calling `malloc` with a negative or zero object size
NOD	*Null Object Destruction*	Calling `free` over a `null` reference
UMA	*Undefined Memory Access*	Access to an undefined memory segment (e.g., immediately after a pointer declaration)
OOS	*Out Of Scope*	Access to a variable that is out of scope
IRT	*Incorrect Return Type*	Type of return value does not match the function profile
IAT	*Incompatible Assign Types*	Mismatch between type of variable and assigned value
NEF	*Non-Existing Function*	The called function is not defined or declared
UAC	*Unsuitable Call Arguments*	Function call does not match the function profile

for heap-manipulating programs is another major endeavour that has received increasing attention (see, e.g., [20,41]) and we left for future work.

In [8], exception handling and error recovery cases are specified by means of "declarations" that separate the correct values and the error values into two different subsets of their carrier sets. The semantic approach that we adopt is more akin to [36], which differentiates compile-time *sorts* from run-time *types*, where compile-time sorts are used to agglutinate both error and correct values (with the error values being interpreted as meta-level data) while run-time types are restricted to correct values. Similarly, our approach allows errors to be dealt with at *inference time* (at symbolic execution level) even if the generated logical axioms are unsorted.

The Inferred Contract. Given the set $IA = \{p_1 \Rightarrow q_1, \ldots, p_n \Rightarrow q_n\}$ of inferred axioms and the subset $EA \subseteq IA$ of exceptional axioms, let us denote as DA the set of default axioms, $DA = (IA - EA)$. The resulting contract is given by $<Pre, Post, Loc>$, where: 1) Pre is the function precondition given by $(\bigvee p \mid (p \Rightarrow q) \in DA)$ that represents the admissible program input data; 2) $Post$ is the function postcondition given by IA; and 3) Loc is a set of references to memory *locations* (function parameters and data-structure pointers and fields) whose value might be affected by the function execution. The Loc component of the contract is comparable to the `assignable` clause in standard contract specification languages such as ACSL or JML, while the Pre and $Post$ components are similar to the ACSL pre- and post-conditions in contracts with *named behaviors* [6].

Since we are using abstraction, some inferred axioms for function f cannot be guaranteed to be correct and are kept apart as *candidate* axioms. A refinement post-processing is implemented in KINDSPEC that 1) allows the user *trust* that a candidate axiom is, in fact, true, and then adds the axiom to the final contract; 2) provides support for semi-automated (testing-based) candidate axiom falsification, removing those candidate axioms for which an instance is refuted; and 3) filters out some redundant elements from the surviving axioms by detecting axiom subsumption. In order to deal with arithmetic, we adopt a constrained representation $p \wedge c \Rightarrow p' \wedge c'$ of axioms, where p and p' are conjunctions of equations of the form $o(\overline{x_m}) = y$, and c and c' are integer arithmetic constraints (e.g., $y = z + 1 \wedge z \geq 1$). This constrained representation is easily achieved by flattening each equation $o(\overline{x_m}) = t$, with t being a nonvariable term, to the constrained form $o(\overline{x_m}) = y \wedge y = t$. Then we check axioms for constraint subsumption [35]: a constraint c_1 is said to subsume[2] c_2 if c_2 implies c_1 (e.g., the constraint $y = z + 1 \wedge z \geq 1$ subsumes $y = 2$). The notion of constraint subsumption is naturally extended to constrained axioms in the obvious way: we say that a constrained axiom $p_1 \wedge c_1 \Rightarrow p_1' \wedge c_1'$ subsumes another constrained axiom $p_2 \wedge c_2 \Rightarrow p_2' \wedge c_2'$, if $p_1 \cup p_2'$ is a subset of $p_1' \cup p_2$ modulo renaming γ, and the constraint $(c_1 \wedge c_2')\gamma$ subsumes $(c_2 \wedge c_1')\gamma$ (by abuse we consider any conjunction p of equations $e_1 \wedge \ldots \wedge e_n$ as the equation set $\{e_1, \ldots, e_n\}$). Although checking for subsumption is not generally an easy task, we are able to make most common cases run fast by applying standard heuristics that can detect failures early [39]. Also, in some cases KINDSPEC further simplifies the final set of axioms by applying some simple, commonly occurring constraint generalization patterns to compute more general axioms under constraint subsumption.

3   KINDSPEC at a Glimpse

In this section, we outline the main features of the KINDSPEC tool. A starting guide that contains a complete description of all the settings and detailed sessions can be found at the tool homepage.

The granularity of the specification units (contracts) that can be generated by KINDSPEC is at the level of one function, as in many state-of-the-art contract specification approaches.

Given a program file and selected program function, the output of KINDSPEC is a structured Java object that represents the inferred contract. The contract can be either exported into a human-readable text file through the Save option of the File menu) or saved in serialized format (through the Export contract option) that can be then processed automatically by other techniques or tools.

Let us describe the graphical user interface (GUI) of the tool, as shown in Fig. 1. In the upper part of the right-hand side section of the input panel, a KERNELC program can be uploaded from the computer or selected from a drop-down list of built-in program examples. In the lower part of this section, all of

---

[2] From a model-theoretic viewpoint, this is to say that the solution set of c_1 contains the solution set of c_2.

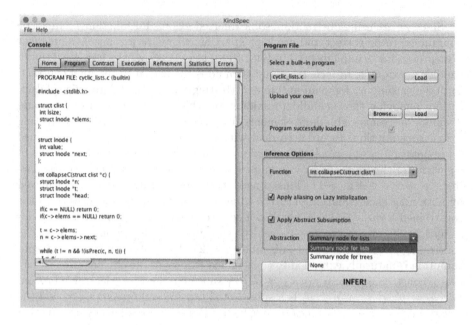

Fig. 1. Graphical interface of KINDSPEC.

the functions from the considered program are automatically loaded so that the
user can select the function for which the contract is to be inferred. Two extra
inference options are provided for enabling/disabling aliasing and/or abstract
subsumption (explained in the following subsections). Once everything is set, the
contract inference process is triggered by pressing the INFER! button. All of the
process details are available through several tabs at the Console that is shown on
the left-hand side section of the input panel: 1) the input Program; 2) the inferred
Contract; 3) Execution intermediate outcomes (e.g., the symbolic execution tree
for the considered function and the raw axiom set that is generated prior to
any subsequent refinement); 4) the candidate axioms that can be selected for
the Refinement process that admits *trusting* (i.e., explicitly marking as correct
some candidate axioms), gets rid of many redundant and spurious axioms, and
achieves in some cases falsification (i.e., disproving a candidate axiom); 5) some
Statistics of interest, including the elapsed symbolic execution time, inference
time, and number of inferred axioms; and 6) any eventual Errors that might
have arisen during KINDSPEC execution. Note that the Refinement tab does not
only show information, but also offers interactive entry points (through buttons)
to the axiom refinement features of KINDSPEC.

3.1 A Running Example

Figure 2 shows a fragment of a KERNELC program that implements an abstract
data type for representing single-linked cyclic lists. The program code is composed of five functions: 1) the function `collapseC(c)` implicitly assumes c is a

singly-linked cyclic list (i.e., either a circular list or a lasso) and deletes all of the elements in the cycle except the first one, which becomes a self-cycle; 2) the function isN(c) returns 1 if the pointer c references to NULL memory; 3) isE(c) returns 1 if c points to an empty list (i.e., c->elems is NULL); 4)lenC(c) counts up the number of elements in the circular segment of c; and 5) the auxiliary function isPrec(c, n, t) that is used to identify the beginning of a cycle and proceeds by checking whether the node referenced by the pointer n precedes the node pointed by t in c.

```
 1  #include <stdlib.h>                         37  int isN(struct clist *c) {
 2                                              38   return c == NULL; }
 3  struct lnode {                              39
 4   int value;                                 40  int isE(struct clist *c) {
 5   struct lnode *next;                        41   return c->elems == NULL; }
 6  };                                          42
 7  struct clist {                              43  int lenC(struct clist *c) {
 8   int lsize;                                 44   struct lnode *n;
 9   struct lnode *elems;                       45   struct lnode *t;
10  };                                          46   struct lnode *head;
11                                              47   int counter;
12  int collapseC(struct clist *c) {           48
13   struct lnode *n;                           49   if(c == NULL) return 0;
14   struct lnode *t;                           50   if(c->elems == NULL) return 0;
15   struct lnode *head;                        51
16                                              52   t = c->elems;
17   if(c == NULL) return 0;                    53   n = c->elems->next;
18   if(c->elems == NULL) return 0;             54   while (t!=n && !(isPrec(c,n,t))) {
19                                              55    t = n;
20   t = c->elems;                              56    n=n->next; }
21   n = c->elems->next;                        57
22   while (t!=n && !(isPrec(c,n,t))) {         58   head = n;
23    t = n;                                    59   n = head->next;
24    n=n->next; }                              60   counter = 1;
25                                              61   while(n != head) {
26   head = n;                                  62    counter++;
27   n = head->next;                            63    n = n->next; }
28   while(n != head) {                         64
29    t = n;                                    65   return counter;
30    n = n->next;                              66  }
31    free(t);                                  67
32    c->lsize--; }                             68  int isPrec(struct clist *c, struct lnode *n,
33                                                               struct lnode *t) {
34   head->next = head;                         69  [...] }
35   return 1; }
36
```

Fig. 2. KERNELC implementation of a cyclic list data type.

Since C does not ensure purity of functions, any program function can be chosen for contract generation. We have selected collapseC for the running example.

Setting the Inference Options. Let us describe the inference options that are available in the right-hand side section of the panel.

Aliasing on Lazy Initialization. As we previously discussed in Sect. 2, when a symbolic address is accessed for the first time, three lazy initialization cases are considered: 1) null; 2) a reference to a new object of its respective type, and 3) a reference to an already existing object in the heap, which allows cyclic data structures to be dealt with. This avoids requiring any a priori bound size for symbolic input structures. In the third case, lazy initialization generates a new path for each object of the same type that already exists in the heap. In order to avoid state blow-up, the Apply aliasing on Lazy Initialization option can be enabled on demand, with a due loss of precision on cyclic data structures, in exchange for efficiency, when disabled.

Abstract Subsumption. Symbolic execution of code containing loops or recursion may result in an infinite number of paths if the termination condition depends on symbolic data. A classical solution is to establish a bound to the depth of the symbolic execution tree by specifying the maximum number of unfoldings for each loop and recursive function. As a better approach, KINDSPEC implements the abstract subsumption technique of [4] that determines the length of the symbolic execution paths in a dynamic way by using abstraction.

Following the classical abstract interpretation approach, programs are (symbolically) executed in KERNELC by using *abstract* (approximated) data and operators rather than concrete ones. With regard to the data abstraction, when dealing with linked lists and trees we consider *summary nodes* for approximating a number of nodes in the list or tree [4]. For system states, the state abstraction function α is defined as a source-to-source transformation that approximates both primitive data and heaps. The abstract value of a primitive type object field e in an abstract (summary) node n^α is the set $\{v_1, \ldots v_k\}$ that contains the k distinct valuations v_i, $i = 1 \ldots k$, of e in the m individual nodes that are approximated by n^α, with $k \leq m$. A relation $\sqsubseteq^\alpha$ between abstract states is naturally induced such that, given two abstract states s and s', $s' \sqsubseteq^\alpha s$ whenever the set of concrete states represented by s' is included in the set of concrete states that are represented by s. Checking $\sqsubseteq^\alpha$ generally implies reasoning about logical subsumption (implication) for constraints involving primitive data, for which the Z3 SMT solver is used.

In the abstract symbolic execution of a program function, before entering a loop at the current (abstract) state s', $s' \sqsubseteq^\alpha s$ is checked for every comparable predecessor (abstract) state s of s' in the same branch. If the check succeeds, the execution of the loop stops.

With regard to the program functions, and particularly the observers, for each observer function a corresponding abstract version operates on summary nodes and preserves the original behavior. For instance, consider an observer neg(c,n) that returns 1 when n points to a node of the list c that contains a negative number in the value field, and returns 0 otherwise. The abstract version of this observer may access an abstract list that contains a summary node at the position pointed to by n. In such a case, it returns 1 only if all the concrete values in the abstract value field of the summary node are negative, 0 when all of them are positive, and a symbolic value ?v otherwise.

3.2   KINDSPEC **Output**

KINDSPEC provides two main outputs: 1) the contract $<Pre, Post, Loc>$ for the selected function; and 2) a list of (not necessarily correct) *Candidate* axioms.

Figure 3 shows the synthesized contract and candidate axioms for our running example (with enabled aliasing and abstract subsumption) as they are displayed.

```
PRECONDITION Pre:
(isN(c)=0 ^ lenC(c)=0 ^ isE(c)=1) || (isN(c)=0 ^ lenC(c)=1 ^ isE(c)=0) ||
(isN(c)=0 ^ lenC(c)=2 ^ isE(c)=0) || (isN(c)=0 ^ lenC(c)=3 ^ isE(c)=0)
-----------------------------------------------------------------
POSTCONDITION Post:
A1: (isN(c)=0 ^ lenC(c)=(NPE, 56) ^ isE(c)=0) =>
    (isN(c)=0 ^ lenC(c)=(NPE, 56) ^ isE(c)=0 ^ ret=(NPE, 24))
A2: (isN(c)=0 ^ lenC(c)=0 ^ isE(c)=1) => (isN(c)=0 ^ lenC(c)=0 ^ isE(c)=1 ^ ret=0)
A3: (isN(c)=1 ^ lenC(c)=0 ^ isE(c)=(NPE, 41)) =>
    (isN(c)=1 ^ lenC(c)=0 ^ isE(c)=(NPE, 41) ^ ret=0)
A4: (isN(c)=0 ^ lenC(c)=1 ^ isE(c)=0) => (isN(c)=0 ^ lenC(c)=1 ^ isE(c)=0 ^ ret=1)
A5: (isN(c)=0 ^ lenC(c)=2 ^ isE(c)=0) => (isN(c)=0 ^ lenC(c)=1 ^ isE(c)=0 ^ ret=1)
A6: (isN(c)=0 ^ lenC(c)=3 ^ isE(c)=0) => (isN(c)=0 ^ lenC(c)=1 ^ isE(c)=0 ^ ret=1)
-----------------------------------------------------------------
LOCATIONS Loc:
c->lsize
c->elems
c->elems->next
c->elems->next->next
c->elems->next->next->next
-----------------------------------------------------------------
CANDIDATE AXIOMS Post#:
C1: (isN(c)=0 ^ isE(c)=0 ^ lenC(c)=?10 + 2 ^ ?10 >= 2) =>
    (isN(c)=0 ^ isE(c)=0 ^ lenC(c)=?10 ^ ?10 >= 2 ^ ret=1) ^
C2: (isN(c)=0 ^ isE(c)=0 ^ lenC(c)=?10 + 2 ^ ?10 >= 2) =>
    (isN(c)=0 ^ isE(c)=0 ^ lenC(c)=1 ^ ret=1)
```

Fig. 3. Inferred contract for the `collapseC` function in Fig. 2.

First, the precondition is shown as the disjunction of all the initial scenarios for which the contract is defined (admissible inputs). Following the C convention, note that the value 0 is used to represent the boolean value `false`, whereas the value 1 stands for `true`. The postcondition consists of the generated axioms that describe all (successful and exceptional) inferred program behaviors. We note that one single axiom might correspond to a number of branches in the symbolic execution tree of the function. The third contract component is the set of overwritten program locations in the final symbolic states, which are identified and harvested as a by-product of the symbolic execution.

Every axiom $(p \Rightarrow q)$ that describes exceptional behavior can be easily identified since it contains (in either p or q) at least one equation $l = (errorCode, pc)$, where *errorCode* is an error identifier (see Table 1) and pc is the last executed instruction that triggered the exception. In Fig. 3, the exceptional axiom `A1` describes an execution scenario where, starting from a list `c` that is neither null nor empty, both the observer `lenC` and the target function `collapseC` itself return an exception. The associated program counters, 56 and 24, correspond to individual instructions `n = n->next` attempting to access the `next` field of a null pointer n. In fact, this may happen in the case when c is not cyclic, although cyclicity of c was taken for granted in the data type implementation. The exceptional axiom A3 characterizes the case when the input argument is a reference that points to a null position, which causes isE to trigger an exception. As for the axiom A2, it specifies that, whenever the input list is empty, nothing is deleted and the list is still empty after the execution. Axioms A4 to A6 specify the cases when the list contained a cycle (whose length is respectively equal to 1, 2, and 3) and it was actually collapsed.

With regard to the (overly-general) candidate axioms C1 and C2, they result from cutting down an infinite loop by means of abstract subsumption and can be later refined as follows: 1) First, for those candidate axioms that are suspicious to have spurious instances, a *falsification* subprocess can be triggered. This process is undertaken by i) building initial configurations that satisfy the axiom antecedent; ii) running the modifier function on those initial configurations; and iii) checking if the results comply with the axiom consequent. The initial configurations (input values) are currently generated interactively (with specific values provided by the user). If the falsification check succeeds, the axiom is considered to be *falsified* and is consequently left out. 2) However, some candidate axioms might be indeed correct (hence they cannot be falsified). To deal with this, users are allowed to mark *trusted* candidates as correct, so that they become a part of the contract. 3) Finally, redundant axioms are removed by means of a subsumption checking process that gets rid of duplicate axioms and less general instances. In our leading example, candidate C1 is spurious and can be trivially falsified for any input list, whereas C2 is correct and can be trusted. Moreover, a generalization of C2 can then be computed that subsumes A4-6. Generalizations are achieved by recognizing families of axioms such as C2 and A4-6, which are sets of axioms where all observer equations of the antecedent and consequent are equal modulo renaming except for one observer (arithmetic constraints can differ too), and then hypothesizing a more general axiom that can be used to replace all of the family axioms. This is done by simply trying some frequent patterns for constraint generalization; e.g., the constraint ?lo>= 1 generalizes a series of constraints ?lo=1; ... ; ?lo=i; ?lo>i, with i >=2, when these constraints appear in the antecedent of i different axioms. However, since generalization for arithmetic constraints is still an open problem, some of our constraint generalization patterns might not lead to correct generalizations and Z3 is queried to check if the involved constraints are actually equivalent. In the case when the verification fails, the user is prompted to either accept or reject the generated hypothesis. In the example, after simplifying (lenC(c)=?lo+2 ^ ?lo>=2) in the antecedent of C2 into (lenC(c)=?lo ^ ?lo>3), and flattening the equations lenC(c)=v of A4-6 as (lenC(c)=?lo ^ ?lo=v), for v=1 to v=3, we can recognize the pattern ?lo=1; ?lo=2; ?lo=3; ?lo>3 that is logically equivalent to ?lo>=1. Then, the following hypothesis H1 is generated that subsumes C2 and A4-A6:

```
(isN(c)=0^lenC(c)=?lo^isE(c)=0^?lo>= 1) =>
                    (isN(c)=0^lenC(c)=1^isE(c)=0^ret=1) .
```

At the end of the process, the final contract hence consists of axioms A1-3 and H1.

The errors reported by the exceptional axioms A1 and A3 may be later used for providing provisional program patches by using the program counter *pc* to determine the right program point to insert the patch. In our leading example, regarding the exception (NPE, 56) in axiom A1, a simple patch may consist in guarding the offending memory access with an appropriate check so that the guarded access is safe. This can be easily done replacing the sentence n = n->next; on line 56 by the guarded assignment if(n != NULL) {n = n->next;} else {break;}

4   System Architecture

The architecture of the KINDSPEC tool is depicted in Fig. 4. It essentially consists of a main module that orchestrates the inference by invoking a number of specialized components as follows:

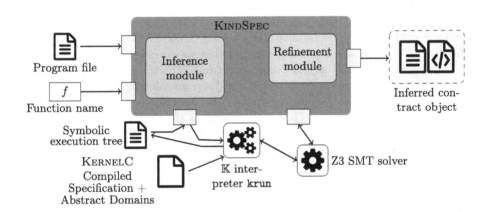

Fig. 4. Architecture of the KINDSPEC system.

1. The K interpreter (named **krun**) symbolically executes the compiled K specification of the KERNELC language and relies on the SMT Solver Z3 for pruning infeasible execution branches. Z3 is also used to simplify the path conditions and optimize the process. The K interpreter runs in Linux and MacOS X.
2. The inference module builds the axioms that explain the initial and final states of the symbolic execution paths and generates the inferred contract by piecing together the function pre-condition, post-condition, and affected program locations. Since the elapsed time for each execution of the K interpreter is rather high (15–20 s each, on average), in order to improve performance, our implementation exploits multithreading, with an independent thread for each symbolic execution path.

3. The refinement module applies the refinement post-processing, which consists in duplicate elimination, trusting, (test-based) falsification of overly general axioms, and axiom subsumption checking to get rid of less general axioms.

KINDSPEC is currently able to infer contracts for KERNELC programs with the summary node abstraction for linked data structures such as lists. Nevertheless, the implemented infrastructure has been designed to support further abstract domains and other languages for which a K semantics is given.

The implementation of KINDSPEC contains about 7500 lines of Java source code for the back-end and 2300 lines of K code for the extended, abstract KERNELC language specification. The abstract domain and operators have been integrated into the abstract KERNELC semantic definition written in K. Since summary nodes occur in the memory heap during symbolic execution, this means that abstractions are directly handled by K's symbolic engine.

5   Experiments

We evaluated KINDSPEC on a set of classical contract inference benchmark programs that size in the hundreds or tens of lines of code. Our test platform was an Intel Core2 Quad CPU Q9300(2.50 GHz) with 6 GB of RAM running K v3.4 on Maude v2.6. Table 2 summarizes the figures that we obtained for programs that contain (both cyclic and acyclic) data structures. The specific feature that we test within each example is described in the *Program* column. The *LOC* column shows the program size (in lines of code). The *Function* column indicates the name of the target function. The *#Obs* column is the number of observer program functions. The *#Paths* column shows the number of root-to-leaf symbolic paths in the deployed trees, while the *#Axms* column reflects how many *different* axioms are retrieved from the final states of the paths. The *#Cand ax* column indicates the number of overly general axioms, and the *Final contract* column indicates the final number of correct axioms that are distilled as a result of the whole process. It might happen that this number is smaller than *#Axms* due to the reduction given by generalized candidate axioms subsuming more specific axioms.

With respect to the time cost, specification inference is known to be expensive for accurate and strong properties. We distinguish between the amount of time taken for the symbolic execution of methods performed by K and the elapsed time of the processing applied by our inference algorithm. The time spent in K's symbolic execution ranges from 1 min. to 5 min. depending on the quantity and complexity of the method definitions and the number of cores in the user's CPU. On the other hand, the time taken for actual inference of contracts (once the symbolic execution trees have been deployed) ranges from approximately 150 ms to 300 ms. Our results are very encouraging since they show that KINDSPEC can infer compact and general contracts for programs that deal with common data structures without fixing the size of dynamic data structures or limiting the number of iterations to ensure termination. The tool infers contracts for

Table 2. Experimental results for KINDSPEC on programs manipulating lists.

Program	LOC	Function	#Obs	#Paths	#Axms	#Cand ax	Final contract
cyclic_lists.c (running example)	95	collapseC	3	22	8	2	4
insert.c (linked lists)	120	insert	5	17	10	3	5
insert_excp.c (version with errors)	90	insert	5	16	9	3	4
deallocate.c (reduction of heap size)	59	deallocate	2	5	5	1	2
reverse.c (heap mutation)	70	reverse	4	7	6	1	3
del_circular.c (circular lists)	69	delCircular	3	13	7	1	4
append.c (2 symbolic lists, 1 loop)	60	append	3	32	32	10	4

challenging programs that have recursive predicates, linked and doubly-linked lists, and circular/cyclic lists. Assuming the program contains an appropriate set of observers, KINDSPEC is able to infer accurate contracts for all of our benchmarks.

Let us provide a brief discussion of relative benefits w.r.t. existing tools for related tasks. Most of the tools that implement contract inference techniques that are described in the related literature are no longer publicly available for use or experimentation. In the following, we compare KINDSPEC with the three available tools Daikon [19] (which is based on testing), *Angelic Verifier* [16] (which implements a weakest precondition calculus), and the commercial tool for proving memory safety of C code Infer [10] (which infers separation logic assertions[3] aimed to ease the identification of program bugs).

Table 3 illustrates a comparison of key features of the considered tools. There is a column for each tool, and the nine rows stand for the accepted *input language(s)*; the artifacts that have to be provided as *tool input*; the *specification type* (either full contracts or just function preconditions) and its nature, i.e., whether it is described at *function-level* (meaning that it is expressed in

---

[3] In separation logic [37], heap predicates are constituted by "separated" sub-formulae which hold for disjoint parts of the heap. They represent either individual memory cells, which are encoded by using points-to heap predicates (i.e., $e_1 \mapsto e_2$ represents that the heap contains a cell at address e_1 with contents e_2), or sub-heaps (*heaplets*), which are encoded by predicates that collapse various heap locations.

Table 3. Comparison between KINDSPEC and other competing tools.

	KINDSPEC	Daikon	*AngelicVerifier*	Infer
Input language	C	C, .NET, Java, Perl, Eiffel	C, Java	C, .NET, Java
Tool input	Source code (C) + function name	Source code (Daikon)+ test cases	Intermediate code (Boogie) + input specification	Intermediate code (SIL)
Specification type	Function-level contracts	Heap-level contracts	Function-level preconditions	Heap-level contracts
Error cases	Yes	No	No	No
Technology	Abst. Symb. Exec. in $\mathbb{K}$	Instrumentation + Testing	Weakest prec. calculus	Abst. interp. + Bi-abduction
GUI	Yes (desktop)	No	No	Yes (online)
Last update	2020	2021	2018	2021
Operating system	Linux, MacOS X	Windows, Linux, MacOS X	Windows, Linux	Windows, Linux, MacOS X
Standalone	Yes	No	No	Yes

terms of the observer program functions) or at *heap-level* (that strictly capture the heap assignments); whether *error* (or exception) *cases* are captured in the specification; the underlying inference *technology*; the availability of a *GUI*; the date of the *last update* of the tool; *operating system* compatibility;[4] and finally, whether it is a *standalone* artifact. As shown in Table 3, KINDSPEC leverages symbolic execution infrastructure to generate meaningful specifications for heap-manipulating C code. Actually, only KINDSPEC delivers high (function-)level whole contracts, easier to read by the user, that moreover cope with exceptional behavior in an explicit way.

Daikon [19] (and the no longer available DySy [14]) aims to obtain (heap-level) properties by extensive testing. Daikon works by running an instrumented program over a given test suite, then storing all the values taken by the program variables at both the start and the end of these runs.[5] Microsoft's *Angelic Verifier* [16] applies a weakest precondition calculus to infer likely (function-level) preconditions from a given set of program traces that failed to be verified (and thus were considered as *uncertain*), aimed to retry the verification task. The contract discovery tool Infer applies to very large programs that can be written in several source languages (C, .NET languages, and Java) but focuses

---

[4] We tested the tools in Windows (versions 7 and 10), Linux (Ubuntu 18.04) and MacOS X (10.13 High Sierra).

[5] In contrast, DySy relied in concolic execution (a combination of symbolic execution with dynamic testing) to obtain more precise (heap-level) axiomatic properties for non-instrumented programs.

on pointer safety properties concerning the heap. Unlike KINDSPEC, it reasons over a semantic, analysis-oriented Smallfoot Intermediate Language (SIL) that represents source programs in a simpler instruction set describing the program's effect on symbolic heaps [41]. This is similar to *AngelicVerifier*, which relies on the intermediate language Boogie, designed for verification. While several compilers translate to Boogie programs that are written in high-level languages supporting heap manipulation (e.g., C), the inferred preconditions are expressed in terms of Boogie, thus lacking a direct correspondence to the source language.

While Infer synthesizes Hoare triples that imply memory safety and can identify potential flaws (which is indeed its main feature), no precondition is synthesized for failing attempts to establish safety; these findings are simply returned to the user in the form of a bug report. Also, the contracts generated by Infer are not accessible to users through the web interface of the tool. A last distinguished feature of our tool is the refinement functionality that provides interactive support, through a graphical user interface, for axiom falsification and trusting.

6   Conclusion and Related Work

Let us briefly discuss those strands of research that have influenced our work the most, independently of the current availability of a companion automated tool. Our axiomatic representation is inspired by Axiom Meister [40] (currently unavailable), which relied on a model checker for (bounded) symbolic execution of .NET programs and generates either Spec# specifications or parameterized unit tests. Similarly to [40], we aim to infer rich, *function-level* characterizations that are easily understandable; however, we generate simpler and more accurate formulas that avoid reasoning with the global heap because the different pieces of the heap that are reachable from the function argument addresses are also kept separate in $\mathbb{K}$. Moreover, our approach is generic, and thus potentially transferable with reasonable effort to other programming languages for which a semantic definition is formalized in $\mathbb{K}$.

Besides Daikon [19] and DySy [14], other approaches based on testing led to the development of AutoInfer [42] for inferring heap-level postconditions, the invariant discovery tool DIDUCE [28], the QUICKSPEC tool [13] that distils equational laws concerning Haskell functions, and the (never released) experimental prototype of Henkel and Diwan [29] that generalizes the results of running tests on Java class interfaces as an algebraic specification.

An alternative approach to software specification discovery is based on inductive machine learning (ML) such as the PSYCO project for Java Pathfinder [23] (that combines ML with symbolic execution to synthesize temporal interfaces for Java classes in the form of finite-state automata), and ADABU [15] (that mines state-machine models of object behavior from runs of Java programs).

Regarding the specific thread of research that concerns the inference of specifications for heap-manipulating programs with dynamic data structures, special mention deserve *angelic verification* [16] and the distinct separation logic-based approaches, from the early *footprint* analysis technique that discovers program preconditions [11] to the automatic deep-heap analysis tool Infer [9]. Typical properties that can be inferred by these tools regard safe memory access or the absence of memory leaks. No longer maintained are Infer's predecessor, Abductor [12], and the shape analysis tool SpInE that synthesizes heap summaries à la Hoare [27]. Also based on separation logic are [32,33], which rely on symbolic execution with abstraction to provide verified program repair and (heap-level) invariant generation, respectively.

This work improves existing approaches and tools in several ways besides those mentioned in Sect. 5. While testing-based approaches and learning-based approaches are limited to ascertain properties that *have not been previously falsified* by a (finite) number of examples or tests, KINDSPEC is able to guarantee correctness/completeness under some conditions in many practical scenarios [2]; moreover, the correctness of the delivered specifications can also be ensured by using the existing $\mathbb{K}$ formal analysis tools. In comparison to classical symbolic methods, we do not need to fix the size of arrays and dynamic structures or limit the number of iterations to ensure termination in the presence of loops; instead, we handle unbounded structures by means of lazy initialization and ensure termination of symbolic execution procedures by using abstraction. Finally, our experiments in Sect. 5 show that KINDSPEC infers rich contracts for challenging programs having recursive predicates and complex, dynamically allocated nested data structures such as singly/doubly linked lists, being them circular/cyclic or not, which are handled by few competing tools. In order to improve accuracy and applicability of our tool, in future work we plan to extend the supported abstract domains to cope with more sophisticated data structures [7,17] and provide support for automated verification.

References

1. ANSI/ISO IEC 9899:1999 Standard for C Language (C99), Technical Corrigendo 3 (2007)
2. Alpuente, M., Pardo, D., Villanueva, A.: Symbolic abstract contract synthesis in a rewriting framework. In: Hermenegildo, M.V., Lopez-Garcia, P. (eds.) LOPSTR 2016. LNCS, vol. 10184, pp. 187–202. Springer, Cham (2017). https://doi.org/10.1007/978-3-319-63139-4_11
3. Alpuente, M., Pardo, D., Villanueva, A.: Abstract contract synthesis and verification in the symbolic K framework. Fundam. Inform. **177**(3–4), 235–273 (2020)
4. Anand, S., Păsăreanu, C.S., Visser, W.: Symbolic execution with abstraction. STTT **11**(1), 53–67 (2009). https://doi.org/10.1007/s10009-008-0090-1
5. Baldoni, R., Coppa, E., D'Elia, D., Demetrescu, C., Finocch, I.: A survey of symbolic execution techniques. ACM Comput. Surv. **51**(3), 1–39 (2018)
6. Baudin, P., et al.: ACSL: ANSI/ISO C Specification Language, version 1.4 (2010). https://frama-c.com/download/acsl_1.4.pdf
7. Berdine, J., et al.: Shape analysis for composite data structures. In: Damm, W., Hermanns, H. (eds.) CAV 2007. LNCS, vol. 4590, pp. 178–192. Springer, Heidelberg (2007). https://doi.org/10.1007/978-3-540-73368-3_22

8. Bidoit, M.: Algebraic specification of exception handling and error recovery by means of declarations and equations. In: Paredaens, J. (ed.) ICALP 1984. LNCS, vol. 172, pp. 95–108. Springer, Heidelberg (1984). https://doi.org/10.1007/3-540-13345-3_8

9. Calcagno, C., Distefano, D.: Infer: an automatic program verifier for memory safety of C programs. In: Bobaru, M., Havelund, K., Holzmann, G.J., Joshi, R. (eds.) NFM 2011. LNCS, vol. 6617, pp. 459–465. Springer, Heidelberg (2011). https://doi.org/10.1007/978-3-642-20398-5_33

10. Calcagno, C., et al.: Moving fast with software verification. In: Havelund, K., Holzmann, G., Joshi, R. (eds.) NFM 2015. LNCS, vol. 9058, pp. 3–11. Springer, Cham (2015). https://doi.org/10.1007/978-3-319-17524-9_1

11. Calcagno, C., Distefano, D., O'Hearn, P.W., Yang, H.: Footprint analysis: a shape analysis that discovers preconditions. In: Nielson, H.R., Filé, G. (eds.) SAS 2007. LNCS, vol. 4634, pp. 402–418. Springer, Heidelberg (2007). https://doi.org/10.1007/978-3-540-74061-2_25

12. Calcagno, C., Distefano, D., O'Hearn, P.W., Yang, H.: Compositional shape analysis by means of bi-abduction. J. ACM **58**(6), 26:1–26:66 (2011). https://doi.org/10.1145/2049697.2049700

13. Claessen, K., Smallbone, N., Hughes, J.: QUICKSPEC: guessing formal specifications using testing. In: Fraser, G., Gargantini, A. (eds.) TAP 2010. LNCS, vol. 6143, pp. 6–21. Springer, Heidelberg (2010). https://doi.org/10.1007/978-3-642-13977-2_3

14. Csallner, C., Tillmann, N., Smaragdakis, Y.: DySy: dynamic symbolic execution for invariant inference. In: Proceedings of the ICSE 2008, pp. 281–290. ACM (2008). https://doi.org/10.1145/1368088.1368127

15. Dallmeier, V., Lindig, C., Wasylkowski, A., Zeller, A.: Mining object behavior with ADABU. In: Proceedings of the WODA 2006, pp. 17–24. ACM (2006). https://doi.org/10.1145/1138912.1138918

16. Das, A., Lahiri, S.K., Lal, A., Li, Y.: Angelic verification: precise verification modulo unknowns. In: Kroening, D., Păsăreanu, C.S. (eds.) CAV 2015. LNCS, vol. 9206, pp. 324–342. Springer, Cham (2015). https://doi.org/10.1007/978-3-319-21690-4_19

17. Distefano, D., O'Hearn, P.W., Yang, H.: A local shape analysis based on separation logic. In: Hermanns, H., Palsberg, J. (eds.) TACAS 2006. LNCS, vol. 3920, pp. 287–302. Springer, Heidelberg (2006). https://doi.org/10.1007/11691372_19

18. Ellison, C., Roşu, G.: An executable formal semantics of C with applications. In: Proceedings of the POPL 2012, pp. 533–544. ACM (2012). https://doi.org/10.1145/2103656.2103719

19. Ernst, M.D., et al.: The daikon system for dynamic detection of likely invariants. Sci. Comput. Prog. **69**(1–3), 35–45 (2007). https://doi.org/10.1016/j.scico.2007.01.015

20. Gazzola, L., Micucci, D., Mariani, L.: Automatic software repair: a survey. IEEE Trans. Soft. Eng. 45, 34–67 (2018). https://doi.org/10.1109/TSE.2017.2755013

21. Gehani, N.H.: Exceptional C or C with exceptions. Softw.: Pract. Exp. **22**(10), 827–848 (1992). https://doi.org/10.1002/spe.4380221003, https://onlinelibrary.wiley.com/doi/abs/10.1002/spe.4380221003

22. Gherghina, C., David, C.: A specification logic for exceptions and beyond. In: Bouajjani, A., Chin, W.-N. (eds.) ATVA 2010. LNCS, vol. 6252, pp. 173–187. Springer, Heidelberg (2010). https://doi.org/10.1007/978-3-642-15643-4_14

23. Giannakopoulou, D., Rakamarić, Z., Raman, V.: Symbolic learning of component interfaces. In: Miné, A., Schmidt, D. (eds.) SAS 2012. LNCS, vol. 7460, pp. 248–264. Springer, Heidelberg (2012). https://doi.org/10.1007/978-3-642-33125-1_18

24. Gogolla, M., Drosten, K., Lipeck, U.W., Ehrich, H.D.: Algebraic and operational semantics of specifications allowing exceptions and errors. Theor. Comput. Sci. **34**(3), 289–313 (1984). https://doi.org/10.1016/0304-3975(84)90056-2, http://www.sciencedirect.com/science/article/pii/0304397584900562
25. Goguen, J.: Abstract errors for abstract data types. In: Formal Description of Programming Concepts, pp. 491–522. North-Holland (1979)
26. Goguen, J.A., Meseguer, J.: Order-sorted algebra I: equational deduction for multiple inheritance, overloading, exceptions and partial operations. Theor. Comput. Sci. **105**(2), 217–273 (1992). https://doi.org/10.1016/0304-3975(92)90302-V, http://www.sciencedirect.com/science/article/pii/030439759290302V
27. Gulavani, B.S., Chakraborty, S., Ramalingam, G., Nori, A.V.: Bottom-up shape analysis using LISF. TOPLAS 2011 **33**(5), 17:1–17:41 (2011). https://doi.org/10.1145/2039346.2039349
28. Henkel, J., Diwan, A.: Discovering algebraic specifications from java classes. In: Cardelli, L. (ed.) ECOOP 2003. LNCS, vol. 2743, pp. 431–456. Springer, Heidelberg (2003). https://doi.org/10.1007/978-3-540-45070-2_19
29. Henkel, J., Reichenbach, C., Diwan, A.: Discovering documentation for java container classes. IEEE Trans. Softw. Eng. **33**(8), 526–543 (2007). https://doi.org/10.1109/TSE.2007.70705
30. King, J.C.: Symbolic execution and program testing. Commun. ACM **19**(7), 385–394 (1976). https://doi.org/10.1145/360248.360252
31. Liskov, B., Guttag, J.: Abstraction and Specification in Program Development. MIT Press, Cambridge (1986)
32. Logozzo, F., Ball, T.: Modular and verified automatic program repair. In: Proceedings of the OOPSLA 2012, pp. 133–146. ACM (2012). https://doi.org/10.1145/2384616.2384626
33. Magill, S., Nanevski, A., Clarke, E., Lee, P.: Inferring invariants in separation logic for imperative list-processing programs. In: Proceedings of the 3rd SPACE Workshop (2006)
34. Meyer, B.: Applying 'design by contract'. Computer **25**(10), 40–51 (1992). https://doi.org/10.1109/2.161279
35. Padmanabhuni, S., Ghose, A.K.: Inductive constraint logic programming: an overview. In: Antoniou, G., Ghose, A.K., Truszczyński, M. (eds.) PRICAI 1996. LNCS, vol. 1359, pp. 1–8. Springer, Heidelberg (1998). https://doi.org/10.1007/3-540-64413-X_25
36. Poigné, A.: Partial algebras, subsorting, and dependent types. In: Sannella, D., Tarlecki, A. (eds.) ADT 1987. LNCS, vol. 332, pp. 208–234. Springer, Heidelberg (1988). https://doi.org/10.1007/3-540-50325-0_11
37. Reynolds, J.C.: Separation logic: a logic for shared mutable data structures. In: Proceedings of the LICS 2002, pp. 55–74 (2002). https://doi.org/10.1109/LICS.2002.1029817
38. Roşu, G., Şerbănuţă, T.F.: An overview of the K semantic framework. J. Logic Algebraic Program. **79**(6), 397–434 (2010). https://doi.org/10.1016/j.jlap.2010.03.012, http://www.sciencedirect.com/science/article/pii/S1567832610000160
39. Schulz, S.: Simple and efficient clause subsumption with feature vector indexing. In: Bonacina, M.P., Stickel, M.E. (eds.) Automated Reasoning and Mathematics. LNCS (LNAI), vol. 7788, pp. 45–67. Springer, Heidelberg (2013). https://doi.org/10.1007/978-3-642-36675-8_3
40. Tillmann, N., Chen, F., Schulte, W.: Discovering likely method specifications. In: Liu, Z., He, J. (eds.) ICFEM 2006. LNCS, vol. 4260, pp. 717–736. Springer, Heidelberg (2006). https://doi.org/10.1007/11901433_39

41. van Tonder, R., Goues, C.: Static automated program repair for heap properties. In: Proceedings of the ICSE 2018, pp. 151–162. ACM (2018). https://doi.org/10.1145/3180155.3180250
42. Wei, Y., Furia, C.A., Kazmin, N., Meyer, B.: Inferring better contracts. In: Proceedings of the ICSE 2011, pp. 191–200. ACM (2011). https://doi.org/10.1145/1985793.1985820

Abstract Interpretation of Graphs

Patrick Cousot[iD]

Courant Institute of Mathematical Sciences, New York University
Visiting IMDEA Software, Madrid, Spain

pcousot@cims.nyu.edu

Dedicated to Manuel Hermenegildo
for his 60th birthday and many years of friendship

Abstract. Path problems in graphs can be solved by abstraction of a fixpoint definition of all paths in a finite graph. Applied to the Roy-Floyd-Warshall shortest path algorithm this yields a naïve n^4 algorithm where n is the number of graph vertices. By over-approximating the elementary paths and cycles and generalizing the classical exact fixpoint abstraction, we constructively derive the classical n^3 Roy-Floyd-Warshall algorithm.

1 Introduction

1.1 Objectives

[2,9,11,14,15] observed that various graph path algorithms can be designed and proved correct based on a common algebraic structure and then instantiated to various path problems up to homomorphisms. We show that this structure originates from the fixpoint characterization of the set of graph paths using the set of graph edges, the concatenation and union of sets of paths as basic operations. The common algebraic structure of graph path algorithms follows from the fact that these primitives and the fixpoint are preserved by abstraction with Galois connections. For example [19] designs Bellman–Ford–Moore algorithm [1, Sect. 2.3.4] by abstraction of a fixpoint definition of all graph paths (where a path is a vertex or a path concatenated with an arc).

The same approach for the Roy-Floyd-Warshall algorithm [1, Sect. 2.3.5], [12, p. 26–29], [13], and [18, p. 129] (where a path is an arc or the concatenation of a path with a path) yields a naïve algorithm in $O(n^4)$ where n is the number of vertices of the weighted finite graph (assumed to have no cycle of strictly negative weight). The derivation of the original Roy-Floyd-Warshall algorithm in $O(n^3)$ is tricky since it is based on the abstraction of an over-approximation of the elementary paths which is an under-approximation of all graph paths. It requires a generalization of the classical complete fixpoint abstraction to a different abstraction for each iterate and the limit.

© Springer Nature Switzerland AG 2023
P. Lopez-Garcia et al. (Eds.): Hermenegildo Festschrift 2022, LNCS 13160, pp. 72–96, 2023.
https://doi.org/10.1007/978-3-031-31476-6_4

1.2   Content

Fixpoint transfer theorems state the equality of the abstraction of a least fixpoint and the least fixpoint of an abstract function, under hypotheses such as the commutation of the abstraction function and the iterated function. Sect. **2** presents a new fixpoint transfer theorem that generalizes the well-known theorem on CPOs [6] to the case where, at each iterate, a different concrete function, abstract function, and abstraction function are used. Sect. **3** introduces directed graphs and their classic terminology (finite paths, subpaths, etc.), as well as the totally ordered group of weights. Sect. **4** expresses the (generally infinite) set of (finite) paths of a graph as least fixpoints, using four different possible formulations. Sect. **5** applies the (non extended) fixpoint transfer theorem to these fixpoints, thus exhibiting the common algebraic structure of path problems. Sect. **6** presents an application where the function associating to each pair of vertices the set of paths between them is presented in fixpoint form using a Galois isomorphism. Sect. **7** introduces path weights and a Galois connection between sets of paths and their smallest weight. Sect. **8** applies the (non extended) fixpoint transfer theorem to this Galois connection to find a (greatest) fixpoint characterization of the shortest path between every pair of vertices. However, the function iterated must consider, at each step, every vertex. As each step is performed for every pair of vertices and the number of steps equals the number of vertices, this leads to a $O(n^4)$ cost. Sect. **9** defines elementary (i.e., cycle-free) paths, and Sect. **10** provides four least fixpoint characterizations of them (similar to Sect. **4**). Sect. **11** is the crux of the article. It applies the new fixpoint transfer theorem from Sect. **2** to further simplify the functions iterated to only elementary path. It exploits the fact that each iteration step k uses a slightly different abstraction, that only considers paths using vertices up to vertex k. The commutation condition leads to especially lengthy proofs. The functions iterated in Sect. **11** remain costly as they take care to exactly enumerate elementary paths, pruning any other path. Sect. **12** considers iterating simpler, more efficient functions that do not perform the elementary path check after each concatenation and show that they compute an over-approximation of the set of elementary paths. Sect. **13** presents this fixpoint in a simple algorithmic form by computing iterations through a chaotic iteration scheme. Finally, Sect. **14** applies the path weight abstraction to convert the path enumeration algorithm from Sect. **13** into a shortest-patch algorithm, effectively retrieving exactly the cubic-time Roy-Floy-Warshall algorithm by calculational design. Sect. **15** concludes.

2   Fixpoint abstraction

We write $\mathsf{lfp}^{\sqsubseteq} f$ (respectively $\mathsf{lfp}_a^{\sqsubseteq} f$) for the $\sqsubseteq$-least fixpoint of f (resp. greater than or equal to a), if any. In fixpoint abstraction, it is sometimes necessary to abstract the iterates and their limit differently (similar to the generalization of Scott induction in [5]), as in the following

Theorem 1 (exact abstraction of iterates) *Let $\langle C, \sqsubseteq, \bot, \bigsqcup \rangle$ be a cpo, $\forall i \in \mathbb{N} . f_i \in C \to C$ be such that $\forall x, y \in C . x \sqsubseteq y \Rightarrow f_i(x) \sqsubseteq f_{i+1}(y)$ with iterates $\langle x^i, i \in \mathbb{N} \cup \{\omega\}\rangle$ defined by $x^0 = \bot$, $x^{i+1} = f_i(x^i)$, $x^\omega = \bigsqcup_{i \in \mathbb{N}} x^i$. Then these concrete iterates and $f \triangleq \dot{\bigsqcup}_{i \in \mathbb{N}} f_i$ are well-defined.*

Let $\langle \mathcal{A}, \preccurlyeq, 0, \curlyvee \rangle$ be a cpo, $\forall i \in \mathbb{N} . \overline{f}_i \in \mathcal{A} \to \mathcal{A}$ be such that $\forall \overline{x}, \overline{y} \in \mathcal{A}$. $\overline{x} \preccurlyeq \overline{y} \Rightarrow \overline{f}_i(\overline{x}) \preccurlyeq \overline{f}_{i+1}(\overline{y})$ with iterates $\langle \overline{x}^i, i \in \mathbb{N} \cup \{\omega\}\rangle$ defined by $\overline{x}^0 = 0$, $\overline{x}^{i+1} = \overline{f}_i(\overline{x}^i)$, $\overline{x}^\omega = \curlyvee_{i \in \mathbb{N}} \overline{x}^i$. Then these abstract iterates and $\overline{f} \triangleq \curlyvee_{i \in \mathbb{N}} \overline{f}_i$ are well-defined.

For all $i \in \mathbb{N} \cup \{\omega\}$, let $\alpha_i \in C \to \mathcal{A}$ be such that $\alpha_0(\bot) = 0$, $\alpha_{i+1} \circ f_i = \overline{f}_i \circ \alpha_i$, and $\alpha_\omega(\bigsqcup_{i \in \mathbb{N}} x_i) = \curlyvee_{i \in \mathbb{N}} \alpha_i(x_i)$ for all increasing chains $\langle x_i \in C, i \in \mathbb{N}\rangle$. It follows that $\alpha_\omega(x^\omega) = \overline{x}^\omega$.

If, moreover, $\forall i \in \mathbb{N} . f_i \in C \xrightarrow{uc} C$ is upper-continuous then $x^\omega = \mathsf{lfp}^\sqsubseteq f$. Similarly $\overline{x}^\omega = \mathsf{lfp}^\preccurlyeq \overline{f}$ when the $\overline{f}_i$ are upper-continuous. If both the f_i and $\overline{f}_i$ are upper-continuous then $\alpha_\omega(\mathsf{lfp}^\sqsubseteq f) = \alpha_\omega(x^\omega) = \overline{x}^\omega = \mathsf{lfp}^\preccurlyeq \overline{f}$.

A trivial generalization is to have a different (concrete and) abstract domain at each iteration and the limit (like *e.g.* in *cofibered domains* [20]).

Proof (of Th. 1) $x^0 \triangleq \bot \sqsubseteq x^1$ since $\bot$ is the infimum and if $x^i \sqsubseteq x^{i+1}$ then, by hypothesis, $x^{i+1} \triangleq f_i(x^i) \sqsubseteq f_{i+1}(x^{i+1}) = x^{i+2}$. Its follows that $\langle x^i, i \in \mathbb{N}\rangle$ is an $\sqsubseteq$-increasing chain so that its lub $x^\omega \triangleq \bigsqcup_{i \in \mathbb{N}} x^i$ is well-defined in the cpo $\langle C, \sqsubseteq \rangle$. The concrete iterates $\langle x^i, i \in \mathbb{N} \cup \{\omega\}\rangle$ are therefore well-defined.

For $x \in C$, reflexivity $x \sqsubseteq x$ implies $f_i(x) \sqsubseteq f_{i+1}(x)$ so $\langle f_i(x), i \in \mathbb{N}\rangle$ is an increasing chain which limit $f(x) \triangleq \bigsqcup_{i \in \mathbb{N}} f_i(x)$ is well-defined in the cpo $\langle C, \sqsubseteq \rangle$.

Similarly, the abstract iterates $\langle \overline{x}^i, i \in \mathbb{N} \cup \{\omega\}\rangle$ and $\overline{f}$ are well-defined.

Let us prove by recurrence on i that $\forall i \in \mathbb{N} . \alpha_i(x^i) = \overline{x}^i$.

- For the basis, $\alpha_0(x^0) = \alpha_0(\bot) = 0 = \overline{x}^0$.
- Assume, by induction hypothesis, that $\alpha_i(x^i) = \overline{x}^i$. For the induction step,

$$\alpha_{i+1}(x^{i+1})$$
$$= \alpha_{i+1}(f_i(x^i)) \qquad \text{⁅def. concrete iterates of the } f_i\text{⁆}$$
$$= \overline{f}_i(\alpha_i(x^i)) \qquad \text{⁅commutation } \alpha_{i+1} \circ f = \overline{f}_i \circ \alpha_i\text{⁆}$$
$$= \overline{f}_i(\overline{x}^i) \qquad \text{⁅ind. hyp.⁆}$$
$$= \overline{x}^{i+1} \qquad \text{⁅def. abstract iterates of the } \overline{f}_i\text{⁆}$$

It follows that $\alpha_\omega(x^\omega) = \alpha_\omega(\bigsqcup_{i \in \mathbb{N}} x^i) = \curlyvee_{i \in \mathbb{N}} \alpha_i(x^i) = \curlyvee_{i \in \mathbb{N}} \overline{x}^i = \overline{x}^\omega$.

If, moreover, $\forall i \in \mathbb{N} . f_i \in C \xrightarrow{uc} C$ is upper-continuous, then we have

$$f(x^\omega)$$
$$= \bigsqcup_{j \in \mathbb{N}} f_j(\bigsqcup_{i \in \mathbb{N}} x^i) \qquad \text{⁅def. } f \text{ and } x^\omega\text{⁆}$$
$$= \bigsqcup_{j \in \mathbb{N}} \bigsqcup_{i \in \mathbb{N}} f_j(x^i) \quad \text{⁅}\langle x^i, i \in \mathbb{N}\rangle \text{ is an } \sqsubseteq\text{-increasing chain and } f_i \text{ is upper-continuous⁆}$$
$$= \bigsqcup_{j \in \mathbb{N}} (\bigsqcup_{i<j} f_j(x^i) \sqcup \bigsqcup_{j=i} f_j(x^i) \sqcup \bigsqcup_{i>j} f_j(x^i)) \qquad \text{⁅case analysis⁆}$$

$$= \bigsqcup_{j \in \mathbb{N}} (f_j(x^j) \sqcup \bigsqcup_{i>j} f_j(x^i))$$

⟨since, by recurrence using $x_i \sqsubseteq x_{i+1} \Rightarrow f_i(x_i) \sqsubseteq f_{i+1}(x_{i+1})$, we have $i < j$
$\Rightarrow x_i \sqsubseteq x_j \Rightarrow f_i(x_i) \sqsubseteq f_j(x_j) \Rightarrow \bigsqcup_{i<j} f_j(x^i) \sqsubseteq f_j(x_j)$ and so, by def. lub $\bigsqcup$,
$\bigsqcup_{i<j} f_j(x^i) \sqcup \bigsqcup_{j=i} f_j(x^i) = f_j(x^j)$⟩

$$= (\bigsqcup_{j \in \mathbb{N}} f_j(x^j)) \sqcup (\bigsqcup_{j \in \mathbb{N}} \bigsqcup_{i>j} f_j(x^i)) \qquad \text{⟨def. lub } \bigsqcup\text{⟩}$$

$$= (\bigsqcup_{j \in \mathbb{N}} f_j(x^j)) \sqcup \bigsqcup_{j \in \mathbb{N}} \bigsqcup_{i \geqslant j} f_i(x^i)$$

⟨since, $j < i \Rightarrow x_j \sqsubseteq x_i \Rightarrow f_j(x_j) \sqsubseteq f_i(x_i)$ so $(\bigsqcup_{j \in \mathbb{N}} \bigsqcup_{i>j} f_j(x^i)) \sqsubseteq$
$(\bigsqcup_{j \in \mathbb{N}} \bigsqcup_{i>j} f_i(x^i)) = (\bigsqcup_{j \in \mathbb{N}} \bigsqcup_{i \geqslant j} f_i(x^i))$⟩

$$= (\bigsqcup_{j \in \mathbb{N}} f_j(x^j))$$

⟨$(\bigsqcup_{j \in \mathbb{N}} \bigsqcup_{i>j} f_j(x^i)) = (\bigsqcup_{j \in \mathbb{N}} f_j(x^j))$ by $\bigsqcup$ associative, commutative, and
idempotent⟩

$$= \bigsqcup_{i \in \mathbb{N}} x^{i+1} = x^0 \sqcup \bigsqcup_{j \in \mathbb{N}_*} x^j \qquad \text{⟨def. } x^{i+1} \text{ and } j = i + 1 \text{ is positive⟩}$$

$$= \bigsqcup_{i \in \mathbb{N}} x^i = x^\omega \qquad \text{⟨}x^0 = \bot \text{ is the infimum and def. } x^\omega\text{⟩}$$

Therefore x^ω is a fixpoint of f. Assume that $y \in C$ is a fixpoint of f. Let us prove by recurrence that $\forall i \in \mathbb{N} . x^i \sqsubseteq y$. For the basis $x^0 = \bot \sqsubseteq y$, by def. of the infimum $\bot$. Assume that $x^i \sqsubseteq y$ by induction hypothesis. Then

$$x^{i+1}$$

$$= f_i(x^i) \qquad \text{⟨def. abstract iterates⟩}$$

$$\sqsubseteq f_i(y) \qquad \text{⟨ind. hyp. } x^i \sqsubseteq y \text{ and } f_i \text{ upper-continuous hence increasing⟩}$$

$$\sqsubseteq \bigsqcup_{i \in \mathbb{N}} f_i(y) \qquad \text{⟨def. lub, if it exists⟩}$$

$$= f(y) \qquad \text{⟨}\langle f_i(y), i \in \mathbb{N}\rangle \text{ is increasing with well-defined limit } f(y) \triangleq \bigsqcup_{i \in \mathbb{N}} f_i(y)\text{⟩}$$

$$= y \qquad \text{⟨fixpoint hypothesis⟩}$$

It follows that $x^\omega \triangleq \bigsqcup_{i \in \mathbb{N}} x^i \sqsubseteq y$ proving that $x^\omega = \mathsf{lfp}^\sqsubseteq f$ is the $\sqsubseteq$-least fixpoint of f. □

Observe that the f_i can be chosen to be all identical equal to $f \in C \xrightarrow{uc} C$ in which case $x \sqsubseteq y \Rightarrow f_i(x) \sqsubseteq f_{i+1}(y)$ follows from f being upper-continuous hence monotonically increasing. Then $\alpha_\omega(\mathsf{lfp}^\sqsubseteq f) = \alpha_\omega(x^\omega) = \overline{x}^\omega$. Similarly, the choice $\overline{f}_i = \overline{f} \in \mathcal{A} \xrightarrow{uc} \mathcal{A}$ yields $\alpha_\omega(x^\omega) = \overline{x}^\omega = \mathsf{lfp}^\preccurlyeq \overline{f}$. If, moreover, all α_i are identical, we get the classical [6, theorem 7.1.0.4(3)]

> **Corollary 1 (exact fixpoint abstraction)** Let $\langle C, \sqsubseteq, \bot, \bigsqcup \rangle$ and $\langle \mathcal{A}, \preccurlyeq, 0, \curlyvee \rangle$ be cpos, $f \in C \xrightarrow{uc} C$, $\overline{f} \in \mathcal{A} \xrightarrow{uc} \mathcal{A}$, and $\alpha \in C \xrightarrow{uc} \mathcal{A}$ be upper-continuous, such that $\alpha(\bot) = 0$ and $\alpha \circ f = \overline{f} \circ \alpha$. Then $\alpha(\mathsf{lfp}^\sqsubseteq f) = \mathsf{lfp}^\preccurlyeq \overline{f} = \overline{x}^\omega$ where $\overline{x}^0 \triangleq 0$, $\overline{x}^{i+1} \triangleq \overline{f}_i(\overline{x}^i)$, and $\overline{x}^\omega \triangleq \curlyvee_{i \in \mathbb{N}} \overline{x}^i$.

By considering $\langle C, \sqsubseteq \rangle = \langle \mathcal{A}, \preccurlyeq \rangle$, $f = \overline{f}$, and the identity abstraction $\alpha(x) = x$, we get Tarski-Kleene-Scott's fixpoint theorem. Th. 1 and Cor. 1 easily extend to fixpoint over-approximation $\alpha(\mathsf{lfp}^{\sqsubseteq} f) \preccurlyeq \mathsf{lfp}^{\preccurlyeq} \overline{f}$.

3 Weighted graphs

3.1 Graphs

A (directed) *graph* or *digraph* $G = \langle V, E \rangle$ is a pair of a set V of *vertices* (or *nodes* or *points*) and a set $E \in \wp(V \times V)$ of *edges* (or *arcs*). A (directed) edge $\langle x, y \rangle \in V$ has *origin* x and *end* y collectively called *extremities* (so the graphs we consider are always directed). A graph is *finite* when the set of V of vertices (hence E) is finite.

A *path* π from y to z in a graph $G = \langle V, E \rangle$ is a <u>finite</u> sequence of vertices $\pi = x_1 \ldots x_n \in V^n$, $n > 1$, starting at *origin* $y = x_1$, finishing at *end* $z = x_n$, and linked by edges $\langle x_i, x_{i+1} \rangle \in E$, $i \in [1, n[$. Let $V^{>1} \triangleq \bigcup_{n>1} V^n$ be the sequences of vertices of length at least 2. Formally the set $\Pi(G) \in \wp(V^{>1})$ of all paths of a graph $G = \langle V, E \rangle$ is

$$\Pi(G) \triangleq \bigcup_{n>1} \Pi^n(G) \tag{1}$$
$$\Pi^n(G) \triangleq \{x_1 \ldots x_n \in V^n \mid \forall i \in [1, n[\, . \, \langle x_i, x_{i+1} \rangle \in E\} \qquad (n > 1)$$

The length $|\pi|$ of the path $\pi = x_1 \ldots x_n \in V^n$ is the number of edges that is $n - 1 > 0$. We do not consider the case $n = 1$ of paths of length 0 with only one vertex since paths must have at least one edge. A *subpath* is a strict contiguous part of another path (without holes and which, being strict, is not equal to that path).

The *vertices of a path* $\pi = x_1 \ldots x_n \in \Pi^n(G)$ of a graph G is the set $\mathbf{V}(\pi) = \{x_1 \ldots x_n\}$ of vertices appearing in that path π.

A *cycle* is a path $x_1 \ldots x_n \in \Pi^n(G)$ with $x_n = x_1$, $n > 1$. Self-loops *i.e.* $\langle x, x \rangle \in E$ yield a cycle $x \, x$ of length 1.

3.2 Totally ordered groups

A *totally (or linearly) ordered group* $\langle \mathbb{G}, \leqslant, 0, + \rangle$ is a group $\langle \mathbb{G}, 0, + \rangle$ with a total order $\leqslant$ on $\mathbb{G}$ satisfying the translation-invariance condition $\forall a, b, c \in \mathbb{G}$. $(a \leqslant b) \Rightarrow (a + c \leqslant b + c)$. An element $x \in \mathbb{G}$ of a totally ordered group $\langle \mathbb{G}, \leqslant, 0, + \rangle$ is said to be strictly negative if and only if $x \leqslant 0 \wedge x \neq 0$.

If $S \subseteq \mathbb{G}$ then we define $\min S$ to be the greatest lower bound of S in $\mathbb{G}$ or $-\infty$:

$$\min S = m \quad \Leftrightarrow m \in \mathbb{G} \wedge (\forall x \in S . m \leqslant x \wedge (\forall y \in S . y \leqslant x \Rightarrow y \leqslant m)$$
$$ = -\infty \Leftrightarrow \forall x \in S . \exists y \in S . y < x \qquad \text{(where } -\infty \notin \mathbb{G})$$
$$ = \infty \quad \Leftrightarrow S = \emptyset \qquad\qquad\qquad \text{(where } \infty \notin \mathbb{G})$$

So if $\mathbb{G}$ has no infimum $\min \mathbb{G} = \max \varnothing = -\infty \notin \mathbb{G}$. Similarly, $\max S$ is the least upper bound of S in $\mathbb{G}$, if any; $-\infty$ otherwise, with $\max \mathbb{G} = \min \varnothing = \infty \notin \mathbb{G}$ when $\mathbb{G}$ has no supremum. Extending $+$ by $x + \infty = \infty + x = \infty + \infty = \infty$ and $x + -\infty = -\infty + x = -\infty + -\infty = -\infty$ for all $x \in \mathbb{G}$, we have $\min\{x + y \mid x \in S_1 \wedge y \in S_2\} = \min S_1 + \min S_2$.

3.3 Weighted graphs

We now equip graphs with weights *e.g.* to measure the distance between vertices. A *weighted graph* on a totally ordered group $\langle \mathbb{G}, \leqslant, 0, + \rangle$ is a triple $\langle V, E, \omega \rangle$ of a set V of vertices and a set $E \in \wp(V \times V)$ of edges of a graph $\langle V, E \rangle$, and a weight $\omega \in E \to \mathbb{G}$ mapping edges $\langle x, y \rangle \in E$ to values $\omega(\langle x, y \rangle) \in \mathbb{G}$ taken in the totally ordered group $\mathbb{G}$.

4 Fixpoint characterization of the paths of a graph

The concatenation of sets of finite paths is

$$P \circledcirc Q \triangleq \{x_1 \ldots x_n y_2 \ldots y_m \mid x_1 \ldots x_n \in P \wedge y_1 y_2 \ldots y_m \in Q \wedge x_n = y_1\}. \quad (2)$$

We have the following well-defined fixpoint characterization of the paths of a graph [7, Sect. 4].

> **Theorem 2 (Fixpoint characterization of the paths of a graph)** *The paths of a graph $G = \langle V, E \rangle$ are*
>
> $$\Pi(G) = \mathsf{lfp}^{\subseteq} \overrightarrow{\mathscr{L}}_\Pi, \qquad \overrightarrow{\mathscr{L}}_\Pi(X) \triangleq E \cup X \circledcirc E \qquad \text{(Th.2.a)}$$
> $$= \mathsf{lfp}^{\subseteq} \overleftarrow{\mathscr{R}}_\Pi, \qquad \overleftarrow{\mathscr{R}}_\Pi(X) \triangleq E \cup E \circledcirc X \qquad \text{(Th.2.b)}$$
> $$= \mathsf{lfp}^{\subseteq} \overleftrightarrow{\mathscr{B}}_\Pi, \qquad \overleftrightarrow{\mathscr{B}}_\Pi(X) \triangleq E \cup X \circledcirc X \qquad \text{(Th.2.c)}$$
> $$= \mathsf{lfp}^{\subseteq}_E \widehat{\mathscr{P}}_\Pi, \qquad \widehat{\mathscr{P}}_\Pi(X) \triangleq X \cup X \circledcirc X \qquad \text{(Th.2.d)} \qquad \square$$

$\overrightarrow{\mathscr{L}}_\Pi$ stands for a forward definition of paths using a left-recursive transformer; $\overleftarrow{\mathscr{R}}_\Pi$ stands for a backward definition of paths using a right-recursive transformer; $\overleftrightarrow{\mathscr{B}}_\Pi$ stands for a bidirectional definition of paths using a right- and left-recursive transformer; $\widehat{\mathscr{P}}_\Pi$ stands for a recursive transformer using paths only which iterations are initialized by edges.

Proof (of Th. 2) We observe that $\bigcup_{i \in \Delta}(X_i \circledcirc E) = \bigcup_{i \in \Delta}\{\pi xy \mid \pi x \in X_i \wedge \langle x, y \rangle \in E\}$ $= \{\pi xy \mid \pi x \in \bigcup_{i \in \Delta} X_i \wedge \langle x, y \rangle \in E\} = (\bigcup_{i \in \Delta} X_i) \circledcirc E$ so that the transformer $\overrightarrow{\mathscr{L}}_\Pi$ preserves non-empty joins so is upper-continuous. Same for $\overleftarrow{\mathscr{R}}_\Pi$.

Let $\langle X_i, i \in \mathbb{N} \rangle$ be a $\subseteq$-increasing chain of elements of $\wp(V^{>1})$. $\circledcirc$ is componentwise increasing so $\bigcup_{i \in \mathbb{N}}(X_i \circledcirc X_i) \subseteq (\bigcup_{i \in \mathbb{N}} X_i \circledcirc \bigcup_{i \in \mathbb{N}} X_i)$. Conversely if $\pi \in (\bigcup_{i \in \mathbb{N}} X_i \circledcirc \bigcup_{i \in \mathbb{N}} X_i)$ then $\pi = \pi_i x \pi_j$ where $\pi_i x \in X_i$ and $x \pi_j \in X_j$. Assume $i \leqslant j$. Because $X_i \subseteq X_j$, $\pi_i x \in X_j$ so $\pi = \pi_i x \pi_j \in X_j \circledcirc X_j \subseteq \bigcup_{k \in \mathbb{N}} X_k \circledcirc X_k$ proving that $\bigcup_{i\in\mathbb{N}}(X_i \otimes X_i) \supseteq (\bigcup_{i\in\mathbb{N}} X_i \otimes \bigcup_{i\in\mathbb{N}} X_i)$. We conclude, by antisymmetry, that $\overrightarrow{\mathcal{B}}_\Pi$ and $\overrightarrow{\mathcal{P}}_\Pi$ are upper-continuous.

It follows, by Tarski-Kleene-Scott's fixpoint theorem, that the least fixpoints do exist.

We consider case (Th.2.c). By upper continuity, we can apply Cor. 1. Let us calculate the iterates $\langle \overrightarrow{\mathcal{B}}_\Pi{}^k, k \in \mathbb{N} \rangle$ of the fixpoint of transformer $\overrightarrow{\mathcal{B}}_\Pi$.

$\overrightarrow{\mathcal{B}}_\Pi{}^0 = \varnothing$, by def. of the iterates.

$\overrightarrow{\mathcal{B}}_\Pi{}^1(\varnothing) = \overrightarrow{\mathcal{B}}_\Pi(\overrightarrow{\mathcal{B}}_\Pi{}^0) = E = \Pi^2(G)$ contains the paths of length 1 which are made of a single arc. If the graph has no paths longer than mere arcs, all paths are covered after 1 iteration.

Assume, by recurrence hypothesis on k, that $\overrightarrow{\mathcal{B}}_\Pi{}^k = \bigcup_{n=2}^{2^{k-1}} \Pi^n(G)$ contains exactly all paths of G of length less than or equal to 2^{k-1}. We have

$$\overrightarrow{\mathcal{B}}_\Pi{}^{k+1} \triangleq \overrightarrow{\mathcal{B}}_\Pi(\overrightarrow{\mathcal{B}}_\Pi{}^k) \qquad \qquad \qquad \{\text{def. iterates}\}$$

$$= E \cup \overrightarrow{\mathcal{B}}_\Pi{}^k \otimes \overrightarrow{\mathcal{B}}_\Pi{}^k \qquad \qquad \{\text{def. } \overrightarrow{\mathcal{B}}_\Pi\}$$

$$= E \cup \{x_1 \ldots x_n y_2 \ldots y_m \mid x_1 \ldots x_n \in \overrightarrow{\mathcal{B}}_\Pi{}^k \wedge x_n y_2 \ldots y_m \in \overrightarrow{\mathcal{B}}_\Pi{}^k\} \quad \{\text{def. } \otimes\}$$

$$= E \cup \{x_1 \ldots x_n y_2 \ldots y_m \mid x_1 \ldots x_n \in \bigcup_{n=2}^{2^{k-1}} \Pi^n(G) \wedge x_n y_2 \ldots y_m \in \bigcup_{n=2}^{2^{k-1}} \Pi^n(G)\}$$

$$\qquad \qquad \qquad \qquad \qquad \qquad \qquad \{\text{ind. hyp.}\}$$

$$= E \cup \bigcup_{n=3}^{2^k} \Pi^n(G)$$

$\{(\subseteq)$ the concatenation of two paths of length at least 1 and at most 2^{k-1} is at least of length 2 and at most of length $2 \times 2^{k-1} = 2^k$.

$(\supseteq)$ Conversely, any path of length at most 2^k has either length 1 in E or can be decomposed into two paths $\pi = x_1 \ldots x_n$ and $\pi' = x_n y_2 \ldots y_m$ of length at most 2^{k-1}. By induction hypothesis, $\pi, \pi' \in \bigcup_{n=2}^{2^{k-1}} \Pi^n(G)$ $\}$

By recurrence on k, for all $k \in \mathbb{N}_*$, $\overrightarrow{\mathcal{B}}_\Pi{}^k = \bigcup_{n=2}^{2^{k-1}} \Pi^n(G)$ contains exactly all paths from x to y of length less than or equal to 2^{k-1}.

Finally, we must prove that the limit $\mathsf{lfp}^\subseteq \overrightarrow{\mathcal{B}}_\Pi = \bigcup_{k\in\mathbb{N}} \overrightarrow{\mathcal{B}}_\Pi{}^k$ is $\Pi(G)$ that is contains exactly all paths of G.

Any path in $\Pi(G)$ has a length $n > 0$ such that $n \leqslant 2^{k-1}$ for some $k > 0$ so belongs to $\overrightarrow{\mathcal{B}}_\Pi{}^n(\varnothing)$ hence to the limit, proving $\Pi(G) \subseteq \mathsf{lfp}^\subseteq \overrightarrow{\mathcal{B}}_\Pi$.

Conversely any path in $\mathsf{lfp}^\subseteq \overrightarrow{\mathcal{B}}_\Pi = \bigcup_{k\in\mathbb{N}} \overrightarrow{\mathcal{B}}_\Pi{}^k$ belongs to some iterate $\overrightarrow{\mathcal{B}}_\Pi{}^k$ which contains exactly all paths of length less than or equal to 2^k so belongs to $\Pi^{2^k}(G)$ hence to $\Pi(G)$, proving $\mathsf{lfp}^\subseteq \overrightarrow{\mathcal{B}}_\Pi \subseteq \Pi(G)$. By antisymmetry $\Pi(G) = \mathsf{lfp}^\subseteq \overrightarrow{\mathcal{B}}_\Pi$.

The equivalent form $\overrightarrow{\mathcal{P}}_\Pi$ follows from $\mathsf{lfp}^\subseteq f = \mathsf{lfp}^\subseteq \lambda x \cdot x \sqcup f(x)$ and $\mathsf{lfp}^\subseteq \lambda x \cdot a \sqcup f(x) = \mathsf{lfp}_a^\subseteq f$ when $a \sqsubseteq f(a)$. The proofs for (Th.2.a,b) are similar with the kth-iterate of the form $\bigcup_{n=2}^k \Pi^n(G)$. $\qquad \qquad \square$

5 Abstraction of the paths of a graph

A *path problem* in a graph $G = \langle V, E \rangle$ consists in specifying/computing an abstraction $\alpha(\Pi(G))$ of its paths $\Pi(G)$ defined by a Galois connection

$$\langle \wp(V^{>1}), \subseteq, \cup \rangle \xleftarrow[\alpha]{\gamma} \langle A, \sqsubseteq, \sqcup \rangle.$$

A path problem can be solved by a fixpoint definition/computation.

Theorem 3 (Fixpoint characterization of a path problem) *Let* $G = \langle V, E \rangle$ *be a graph with paths* $\Pi(G)$ *and* $\langle \wp(V^{>1}), \subseteq, \cup \rangle \xleftarrow[\alpha]{\gamma} \langle A, \sqsubseteq, \sqcup \rangle.$

$$\alpha(\Pi(G)) = \mathsf{lfp}^{\sqsubseteq} \overrightarrow{\mathcal{L}}^{\sharp}_{\Pi}, \qquad \overrightarrow{\mathcal{L}}^{\sharp}_{\Pi}(X) \triangleq \alpha(E) \sqcup X \overline{\circledcirc} \alpha(E) \qquad \text{(Th.3.a)}$$

$$= \mathsf{lfp}^{\sqsubseteq} \overrightarrow{\mathcal{R}}^{\sharp}_{\Pi}, \qquad \overrightarrow{\mathcal{R}}^{\sharp}_{\Pi}(X) \triangleq \alpha(E) \sqcup \alpha(E) \overline{\circledcirc} X \qquad \text{(Th.3.b)}$$

$$= \mathsf{lfp}^{\sqsubseteq} \overrightarrow{\mathcal{B}}^{\sharp}_{\Pi}, \qquad \overrightarrow{\mathcal{B}}^{\sharp}_{\Pi}(X) \triangleq \alpha(E) \sqcup X \overline{\circledcirc} X \qquad \text{(Th.3.c)}$$

$$= \mathsf{lfp}^{\sqsubseteq}_{\alpha(E)} \widehat{\mathcal{P}}^{\sharp}_{\Pi}, \qquad \widehat{\mathcal{P}}^{\sharp}_{\Pi}(X) \triangleq X \sqcup X \overline{\circledcirc} X \qquad \text{(Th.3.d)}$$

where $\alpha(X) \overline{\circledcirc} \alpha(Y) = \alpha(X \circledcirc Y).$ □

Proof (of Th. 3) All cases are similar. Let us check the commutation for (Th.3.c).

$\alpha(\overrightarrow{\mathcal{B}}_{\Pi}(X))$

$= \alpha(E \cup X \circledcirc X)$ $\langle$def. (Th.2.c) of $\overrightarrow{\mathcal{B}}_{\Pi}(X)\rangle$

$= \alpha(E) \sqcup \alpha(X \circledcirc X)$

            $\langle$the abstraction of Galois connections preserves existing joins$\rangle$

$= \alpha(E) \sqcup \alpha(X) \overline{\circledcirc} \alpha(X)$ $\langle$by hyp.$\rangle$

$= \overrightarrow{\mathcal{B}}^{\sharp}_{\Pi}(\alpha(X))$ $\langle$def. (Th.3.c) of $\overrightarrow{\mathcal{B}}^{\sharp}_{\Pi}\rangle$

We conclude by Th. 2 and exact least fixpoint abstraction Cor. 1. The equivalent form $\widehat{\mathcal{P}}^{\sharp}_{\Pi}$ follows from $\mathsf{lfp}^{\sqsubseteq} f = \mathsf{lfp}^{\sqsubseteq} \lambda x \cdot x \sqcup f(x)$ and $\mathsf{lfp}^{\sqsubseteq} \lambda x \cdot a \sqcup f(x) = \mathsf{lfp}^{\sqsubseteq}_{a} f$ when $a \sqsubseteq f(a)$.   □

An essential remark is that the fixpoint definitions of the set of paths in $\wp(V^{>1})$ of a graph $G = \langle V, E \rangle$ in Th. 2 based on the primitives E, $\cup$, and $\circledcirc$ are preserved in Th. 3 by the abstraction $\langle \wp(V^{>1}), \subseteq, \cup \rangle \xleftarrow[\alpha]{\gamma} \langle A, \sqsubseteq, \sqcup \rangle$ for the primitives $\alpha(E)$, $\sqcup$, and $\overline{\circledcirc}$ on A, which explains the origin of the observation by [2,14,15,9,11] that path problems all have the same algebraic structure.

6 Calculational design of the paths between any two vertices

As a direct application of Th. 3, let us consider the abstraction of all paths $\Pi(G)$ into the paths between any two vertices. This is $\mathsf{p} \triangleq \alpha^{\infty}(\Pi(G))$ with the projection abstraction

$$\alpha^{\circ\circ}(X) \triangleq \lambda(y,z) \cdot \{x_1 \dots x_n \in X \mid y = x_1 \wedge x_n = z\}$$
$$\gamma^{\circ\circ}(\mathsf{p}) \triangleq \bigcup_{\langle x,y \rangle \in V \times V} \mathsf{p}(x,y)$$

such that

$$\langle \wp(V^{>1}), \subseteq, \cup \rangle \xleftarrow[\alpha^{\circ\circ}]{\gamma^{\circ\circ}} \langle V \times V \to \wp(V^{>1}), \dot{\subseteq}, \dot{\cup} \rangle \tag{3}$$

where $\mathsf{p} \dot{\subseteq} \mathsf{p}' \Leftrightarrow \forall x, y \in V . \mathsf{p}(x,y) \subseteq \mathsf{p}'(x,y)$ and $(\dot{\bigcup}_{i \in \Delta} \mathsf{p}_i)(x,y) \triangleq \bigcup_{i \in \Delta}(\mathsf{p}_i(x,y))$ are defined pointwise.

By (1) and the abstraction in Galois connections preserves existing joins, we have

$$\mathsf{p}(y,z) \triangleq \bigcup_{n \in \mathbb{N}_*} \mathsf{p}^n(y,z) \tag{4}$$
$$\mathsf{p}^n(y,z) \triangleq \{x_1 \dots x_n \in \Pi^n(G) \mid y = x_1 \wedge x_n = z\}$$
$$= \{x_1 \dots x_n \in V^n \mid y = x_1 \wedge x_n = z \wedge \forall i \in [1,n[\, . \, \langle x_i, x_{i+1} \rangle \in E\}.$$

$\mathsf{p}(x,x)$ is empty if and only if there is no cycle from x to x (which requires, in particular, that the graph has no self-loops *i.e.* $\forall x \in V . \langle x, x \rangle \notin E$). We define the concatenation of finite paths

$$x_1 \dots x_n \odot y_1 y_2 \dots y_m \triangleq x_1 \dots x_n y_2 \dots y_m \qquad \text{if } x_n = y_1 \tag{5}$$
$$\triangleq \text{undefined} \qquad\qquad \text{otherwise}$$

As a direct application of the path problem Th. 3, we have the following fixpoint characterization of the paths of a graph between any two vertices [7, Sect. 5], which, by Kleene-Scott fixpoint theorem, yields an iterative algorithm (converging in finitely many iterations for graphs without infinite paths).

Theorem 4 (Fixpoint characterization of the paths of a graph between any two vertices) *Let $G = \langle V, E \rangle$ be a graph. The paths between any two vertices of G are $\mathsf{p} = \alpha^{\circ\circ}(\Pi(G))$ such that*

$$\mathsf{p} = \mathsf{lfp}^{\dot{\subseteq}} \vec{\mathscr{L}}_{\Pi}^{\circ\circ}, \qquad \vec{\mathscr{L}}_{\Pi}^{\circ\circ}(\mathsf{p}) \triangleq \dot{E} \dot{\cup} \mathsf{p} \overset{\dot{\odot}}{\odot} \dot{E} \qquad\qquad \text{(Th.4.a)}$$

$$= \mathsf{lfp}^{\dot{\subseteq}} \overleftarrow{\mathscr{R}}_{\Pi}^{\circ\circ}, \qquad \overleftarrow{\mathscr{R}}_{\Pi}^{\circ\circ}(\mathsf{p}) \triangleq \dot{E} \dot{\cup} \dot{E} \overset{\dot{\odot}}{\odot} \mathsf{p} \qquad\qquad \text{(Th.4.b)}$$

$$= \mathsf{lfp}^{\dot{\subseteq}} \overleftrightarrow{\mathscr{B}}_{\Pi}^{\circ\circ}, \qquad \overleftrightarrow{\mathscr{B}}_{\Pi}^{\circ\circ}(\mathsf{p}) \triangleq \dot{E} \dot{\cup} \mathsf{p} \overset{\dot{\odot}}{\odot} \mathsf{p} \qquad\qquad \text{(Th.4.c)}$$

$$= \mathsf{lfp}_{\dot{E}}^{\dot{\subseteq}} \overleftrightarrow{\mathscr{P}}_{\Pi}^{\circ\circ}, \qquad \overleftrightarrow{\mathscr{P}}_{\Pi}^{\circ\circ}(\mathsf{p}) \triangleq \mathsf{p} \dot{\cup} \mathsf{p} \overset{\dot{\odot}}{\odot} \mathsf{p} \qquad\qquad \text{(Th.4.d)}$$

where $\dot{E} \triangleq \lambda x, y \cdot (E \cap \{\langle x, y \rangle\})$ and $\mathsf{p}_1 \overset{\dot{\odot}}{\odot} \mathsf{p}_2 \triangleq \lambda x, y \cdot \bigcup_{z \in V} \mathsf{p}_1(x,z) \odot \mathsf{p}_2(z,y)$.

$\square$

Proof (of Th. 4) We apply Th. 3 with $\alpha^{\circ\circ}(E) = \lambda x, y \cdot (E \cap \{\langle x, y \rangle\}) = \dot{E}$ and

$$\alpha^{\circ\circ}(X \odot Y)$$
$$= \lambda(x,y) \cdot \{z_1 \dots z_n \in X \odot Y \mid x = z_1 \wedge z_n = y\} \qquad \text{⦃def. (3) of } \alpha^{\circ\circ}\text{⦄}$$

$$= \lambda(x,y) \cdot \{z_1 \ldots z_n \in \{x_1 \ldots x_k y_2 \ldots y_m \mid x_1 \ldots x_k \in X \wedge x_k y_2 \ldots y_m \in Y\} \mid x = z_1 \wedge z_n = y\}$$

$$\wr\text{def. (2) of } \circledcirc\wr$$

$$= \lambda(x,y) \cdot \bigcup_{z \in V} \{xx_2 \ldots x_{k-1} z y_2 \ldots, y_{m-1} y \mid xx_2 \ldots x_{k-1} z \in X \wedge z y_2 \ldots y_{m-1} y \in Y\}$$

$$\wr\text{def. } \in \text{ and } \cup \text{ with } x = x_1, \ y_m = y, \text{ and } z = x_k\wr$$

$$= \lambda(x,y) \cdot \bigcup_{z \in V} \{xx_2 \ldots x_{k-1} z \odot z y_2 \ldots y_{m-1} y \mid xx_2 \ldots x_{k-1} z \in X \wedge z y_2 \ldots y_{m-1} y \in Y\}$$

$$\wr\text{def. (5) of } \odot\wr$$

$$= \lambda(x,y) \cdot \bigcup_{z \in V} \{p \odot p' \mid p \in \alpha^{\infty}(X)(y,z) \wedge p' \in \alpha^{\infty}(Y)(z,y)\}$$

$$\wr\text{def. } \alpha^{\infty}(X) \text{ with } p = xx_2 \ldots x_{k-1} z \text{ and } p' = z y_2 \ldots y_{m-1} y\wr$$

$$= \alpha^{\infty}(X) \,\ddot{\circledcirc}\, \alpha^{\infty}(Y)$$

by defining $X \,\ddot{\circledcirc}\, Y \triangleq \lambda(x,y) \cdot \bigcup_{z \in V}\{p \odot p' \mid p \in X(y,z) \wedge p' \in Y(z,y)\} = \lambda(x,y) \cdot \bigcup_{z \in V} X(y,z) \circledcirc Y(z,y)$ by (2) and (5).   □

7   Shortest distances between any two vertices of a weighted graph

We now consider weighted graphs $\langle V, E, \omega \rangle$ on a totally ordered group $\langle G, \leqslant, 0, + \rangle$ and extend weights from edges to paths. The weight of a path is

$$\omega(x_1 \ldots x_n) \triangleq \sum_{i=1}^{n-1} \omega(\langle x_i, x_{i+1}\rangle) \tag{6}$$

which is 0 when $n \leqslant 1$ and $\sum_{i=1}^{n-1} \omega(\langle x_i, x_{i+1}\rangle)$ when $n > 1$, in particular $\omega(\langle x_1, x_2\rangle)$ when $n = 2$. The (minimal) weight of a set of paths is

$$\omega(P) \triangleq \min\{\omega(\pi) \mid \pi \in P\}. \tag{7}$$

We have $\omega(\bigcup_{i \in \Delta} P_i) = \min_{i \in \Delta} \omega(P_i)$ so a Galois connection

$$\langle \wp(\bigcup_{n \in \mathbb{N}_*} V^n), \subseteq \rangle \xrightleftharpoons[\omega]{\gamma_\omega} \langle G \cup \{-\infty, \infty\}, \geqslant \rangle$$

between path sets and the complete lattice $\langle G \cup \{-\infty, \infty\}, \geqslant, \infty, -\infty, \min, \max \rangle$ and $\gamma_\omega(d) \triangleq \{\pi \in \bigcup_{n \in \mathbb{N}_*} V^n \mid \omega(\pi) \geqslant d\}$.

Extending pointwise to $V \times V \to \wp(\bigcup_{n \in \mathbb{N}_*} V^n)$ with $\dot\omega(p)\langle x, y \rangle \triangleq \omega(p(x,y))$, $d \,\dot\leqslant\, d' \triangleq \forall x, y . d\langle x, y \rangle \leqslant d'\langle x, y \rangle$, and $\dot\geqslant$ is the inverse of $\dot\leqslant$, we have

$$\langle V \times V \to \wp(\bigcup_{n \in \mathbb{N}_*} V^n), \dot\subseteq \rangle \xrightleftharpoons[\dot\omega]{\dot\gamma_\omega} \langle V \times V \to G \cup \{-\infty, \infty\}, \dot\geqslant \rangle. \tag{8}$$

The distance $d(x, y)$ between an origin $x \in V$ and an extremity $y \in V$ of a weighted finite graph $G = \langle V, E, \omega \rangle$ on a totally ordered group $\langle \mathbb{G}, \leqslant, 0, + \rangle$ is the length $\omega(\mathsf{p}(x, y))$ of the shortest path between these vertices

$$d \triangleq \dot{\omega}(\mathsf{p})$$

where p has a fixpoint characterization given by Th. 4.

8   Calculational design of the shortest distances between any two vertices

The shortest distance between vertices of a weighted graph is a path problem solved by Th. 3, the composition of the abstractions and (8) and (3), and the path abstraction Th. 3. Th. 5 is based on (Th.3.d), (Th.3.a—c) provide three other solutions.

> **Theorem 5** *(Fixpoint characterization of the shortest distances of a graph)* Let $G = \langle V, E, \omega \rangle$ be a graph weighted on the totally ordered group $\langle \mathbb{G}, \leqslant, 0, + \rangle$. Then the distances between any two vertices are
>
> $$d = \dot{\omega}(\mathsf{p}) = \mathrm{gfp}^{\leqslant}_{E^\omega} \, \widehat{\mathscr{P}}^{\delta}_{G} \qquad where \qquad \text{(Th.5)}$$
> $$E^\omega \triangleq \lambda\,(x, y) \cdot [\![\,\langle x,\ y \rangle \in E \,?\, \omega(x, y) \,\vdots\, \infty\,]\!]$$
> $$\widehat{\mathscr{P}}^{\delta}_{G}(X) \triangleq \lambda\,(x, y) \cdot \min\{X(x, y), \min_{z \in V}\{X(x, z) + X(z, y)\}\} \qquad \square$$

Proof (of Th. 5) We apply Th. 3 with abstraction $\dot{\omega} \circ \alpha^{\circ\circ}$ so that we have to abstract the transformers in Th. 4 using an exact fixpoint abstraction of Cor. 1. The initialization and commutation condition yield the transformers by calculational design.

$-\quad \dot{\omega} \circ \alpha^{\circ\circ}(E)(x, y)$

$= \omega(E \cap \{\langle x, y \rangle\})$ ⦃as proved for Th. 4 and def. $\dot{\omega}$⦄

$= [\![\,\langle x, y \rangle \in E \,?\, \omega(x, y) \,\vdots\, \min \varnothing\,]\!]$ ⦃def. $\cap$, conditional, and ω⦄

$= [\![\,\langle x, y \rangle \in E \,?\, \omega(x, y) \,\vdots\, \infty\,]\!]$ ⦃def. $\min$⦄

$-\quad \dot{\omega} \circ \alpha^{\circ\circ}(X \otimes Y)(x, y)$

$= \dot{\omega}(\alpha^{\circ\circ}(X) \overset{\circ\circ}{\otimes} \alpha^{\circ\circ}(Y))(x, y)$ ⦃as proved for Th. 4⦄

$= \omega(\alpha^{\circ\circ}(X) \overset{\circ\circ}{\otimes} \alpha^{\circ\circ}(Y))(x, y))$ ⦃pointwise def. (8) of $\dot{\omega}$⦄

$= \omega(\bigcup_{z \in V} \alpha^{\circ\circ}(X)(x, z) \otimes \alpha^{\circ\circ}(Y)(z, y)))$ ⦃def. $\overset{\circ\circ}{\otimes}$ in Th. 4⦄

$= \min_{z \in V} \omega(\alpha^{\circ\circ}(X)(x, z) \otimes \alpha^{\circ\circ}(Y)(z, y)))$ ⦃Galois connection (7)⦄

$= \min_{z \in V} \omega(\{x_1 \dots x_n y_2 \dots y_m \mid x_1 \dots x_n \in \alpha^{\circ\circ}(X)(x, z) \wedge x_n y_2 \dots y_m \in \alpha^{\circ\circ}(Y)(z, y)\})$

                                                           ⦃def. (2) of $\otimes$⦄

$= \min_{z \in V}\{\omega(x_1 \dots x_n y_2 \dots y_m) \mid x_1 \dots x_n \in \alpha^{\circ\circ}(X)(x, z) \wedge x_n y_2 \dots y_m \in \alpha^{\circ\circ}(Y)(z, y)\})$

$$\langle \text{def. (7) of } \boldsymbol{\omega} \rangle$$

$$= \min_{z \in V} \{ \boldsymbol{\omega}(x_1 \ldots x_n) + \boldsymbol{\omega}(x_n y_2 \ldots y_m) \mid x_1 \ldots x_n \in \alpha^{\infty}(X)(x, z) \wedge x_n y_2 \ldots y_m \in \alpha^{\infty}(Y)(z, y) \})$$

$$\langle \text{def. (6) of } \boldsymbol{\omega} \rangle$$

$$= \min_{z \in V} \{ \boldsymbol{\omega}(x_1 \ldots x_n) + \boldsymbol{\omega}(y_1 y_2 \ldots y_m) \mid x_1 \ldots x_n \in \alpha^{\infty}(X)(x, z) \wedge y_1 y_2 \ldots y_m \in \alpha^{\infty}(Y)(z, y) \})$$

$$\langle \text{def. } \alpha^{\infty} \text{ so that } x_1 = x, \ x_n = y_1 = z, \text{ and } y_m = y \rangle$$

$$= \min_{z \in V} \min \{ \boldsymbol{\omega}(x_1 \ldots x_n) \mid x_1 \ldots x_n \in \alpha^{\infty}(X)(x, z) \} + \min \{ \boldsymbol{\omega}(y_1 y_2 \ldots y_m) \mid y_1 y_2 \ldots y_m \in \alpha^{\infty}(Y)(z, y) \}$$

$$\langle \text{min of a sum} \rangle$$

$$= \min_{z \in V} \min \{ \boldsymbol{\omega}(\pi_1) \mid \pi_1 \in \alpha^{\infty}(X)(x, z) \} + \min \{ \boldsymbol{\omega}(\pi_2) \mid \pi_2 \in \alpha^{\infty}(Y)(z, y) \}$$

$$\langle \text{letting } \pi_1 = x_1 \ldots x_n \text{ and } \pi_2 = y_1 y_2 \ldots y_m \rangle$$

$$= \min_{z \in V} \boldsymbol{\omega}(\alpha^{\infty}(X)(x, z)) + \boldsymbol{\omega}(\alpha^{\infty}(Y)(z, y))$$

$$\langle \text{def. (7) of } \dot{\boldsymbol{\omega}} \rangle$$

$$= \min_{z \in V} \dot{\boldsymbol{\omega}} \circ \alpha^{\infty}(X)(x, z) + \dot{\boldsymbol{\omega}} \circ \alpha^{\infty}(Y)(z, y)$$

$$\langle \text{pointwise def. (8) of } \dot{\boldsymbol{\omega}} \rangle$$

By Th. 3 and (Th.4.d), we get the transformer $\widehat{\mathscr{P}}_G^{\delta}$.   □

Of course the greatest fixpoint in Th. 5 is not computable for infinite graphs. For finite graphs, there is a problem with cycles with strictly negative weights. As shown by the graph $\langle \{x\}, \{\langle x, x \rangle, \boldsymbol{\omega} \rangle$ with $\boldsymbol{\omega}(\langle x, x \rangle) = -1$, the minimal distance between the extremities x and x of the paths $\{x^n \mid n > 1\}$ is $-\infty$. It is obtained as the limit of an infinite iteration for the greatest fixpoint in Th. 5. Following Roy-Floyd-Warshall, we will assume that the graph has no cycle with negative weight in which case the iterative computation of the greatest fixpoint in Th. 5 does converge in finite time to the shortest distance between any two vertices.

For a finite graph of n vertices, the computation of $\mathrm{gfp}_{\dot{\underline{\sqsubseteq}}\dot{\omega}}^{\dot{\leqslant}} \widehat{\mathscr{P}}_G^{\delta}$ in (Th.5) has to consider all pairs of vertices in n^2, for each such pair $\langle x, y \rangle$ the n vertices $z \in V$, and n iterations may be necessary to converge along an elementary path (with no cycles) going through all vertices, so considering elementary paths only, the computation would be in $O(n^4)$.

However, the iteration in Roy-Floyd-Warshall algorithm is much more efficient in $O(n^3)$, since it does not consider all elementary paths in the graph but only simple paths that over-approximate elementary paths, which simplifies the iterated function (from linear to constant time for each pair of vertices). Let us design the Roy-Floyd-Warshall algorithm by calculus.

9   Elementary paths and cycles

A cycle is *elementary* if and only if it contains no internal subcycle (*i.e.* subpath which is a cycle). A path is *elementary* if and only if it contains no subpath which is an internal cycle (so an elementary cycle is an elementary path). The only vertices that can occur twice in an elementary path are its extremities in which case it is an elementary cycle.

Lemma 1 (elementary path) *A path* $x_1 \ldots x_n \in \Pi^n(G)$ *is elementary if and only if*

$$\text{elem?}(x_1 \ldots x_n) \triangleq (\forall i, j \in [1, n] . (i \neq j) \Rightarrow (x_i \neq x_j)) \vee \qquad \text{(Lem.1)}$$
$$(x_1 = x_n \wedge \forall i, j \in [1, n[. (i \neq j) \Rightarrow (x_i \neq x_j)) \quad \text{(case of a cycle)}$$

is true.

Proof (of Lem. 1)

— The necessary condition (*i.e.* $x_1 \ldots x_n \in \Pi^n(G)$ is elementary implies that elem?$(x_1 \ldots x_n)$) is proved contrapositively.

$$\neg(\text{elem?}(x_1 \ldots x_n))$$
$$= \neg((\forall i, j \in [1, n] . (i \neq j) \Rightarrow (x_i \neq x_j)) \vee (x_1 = x_n \wedge \text{elem?}(x_1 \ldots x_n))) \quad \wr\text{def. elem?}\wr$$
$$= (\exists i, j \in [1, n] . i \neq j \wedge x_i = x_j) \wedge ((x_1 = x_n) \Rightarrow (\exists i, j \in [1, n[. i \neq j \wedge x_i \neq x_j))$$

$$\wr\text{De Morgan laws}\wr$$

By $\exists i, j \in [1, n] . i \neq j \wedge x_i = x_j$ the path $x_1 \ldots x_n$ must have a cycle, but this is not forbidden if $x_1 = x_n$. In that case, the second condition $(x_1 = x_n) \Rightarrow (\exists i, j \in [1, n[. i \neq j \wedge x_i \neq x_j)$ implies that there is a subcycle within $x_1 \ldots x_{n-1}$, so the cycle $x_1 \ldots x_{n-1} x_1$ is not elementary.

— Conversely, the sufficient condition (elem?$(x_1 \ldots x_n) \Rightarrow x_1 \ldots x_n \in \Pi^n(G)$ is elementary) is proved by *reductio ad absurdum*. Assume elem?$(x_1 \ldots x_n)$ and $x_1 \ldots x_n \in \Pi^n(G)$ is not elementary so has an internal subcycle.

– If $x_1 = x_n$, the internal subcycle is $x_1 \ldots x_{n-1} = \pi_1 a \pi_2 a \pi_3$ so $\exists i, j \in [1, n[. i \neq j \wedge x_i \neq x_j$ in contradiction with elem?$(x_1 \ldots x_n)$.
– Otherwise $x_1 \neq x_n$ and the internal subcycle has the form $x_1 \ldots x_n = \pi_1 a \pi_2 a \pi_3$ where, possibly $\pi_1 a = x_1$ or $a \pi_3 = x_n$, but not both, so $\exists i, j \in [1, n] . i \neq j \wedge x_i \neq x_j$ in contradiction with elem?$(x_1 \ldots x_n)$.

$\square$

10 Calculational design of the elementary paths between any two vertices

Restricting paths to elementary ones is the abstraction

$$\alpha^\partial(P) \triangleq \{\pi \in P \mid \text{elem?}(\pi)\}$$
$$\gamma^\partial(\overline{P}) \triangleq \overline{P} \cup \{\pi \in \wp(V^{>1}) \mid \neg\text{elem?}(\pi)\}$$

Notice that, by (Lem.1), cycles (such as x, x for a self-loop $\langle x, x \rangle \in E$) are not excluded, provided it is through the path extremities. This exclusion abstraction is a Galois connection.

$$\langle \wp(V^{>1}), \subseteq \rangle \xrightleftharpoons[\alpha^\partial]{\gamma^\partial} \langle \wp(V^{>1}), \subseteq \rangle$$

which extends pointwise between any two vertices

$$\langle V \times V \to \wp(V^{>1}), \subseteq \rangle \xrightleftharpoons[\dot\alpha^{\partial}]{\dot\gamma^{\partial}} \langle V \times V \to \wp(V^{>1}), \subseteq \rangle$$

The following Lem. 2 provides a necessary and sufficient condition for the concatenation of two elementary paths to be elementary.

> **Lemma 2 (concatenation of elementary paths)** *If $x\pi_1 z$ and $z\pi_2 y$ are elementary paths then their concatenation $x\pi_1 z \odot z\pi_2 y = x\pi_1 z\pi_2 y$ is elementary if and only if*
> $$\text{elem-conc?}(x\pi_1 z, z\pi_2 y) \triangleq (x \neq z \wedge y \neq z \wedge \mathbf{V}(x\pi_1 z) \cap \mathbf{V}(\pi_2 y) = \varnothing) \quad \text{(Lem.2)}$$
> $$\vee\, (x = y \neq z \wedge \mathbf{V}(\pi_1 z) \cap \mathbf{V}(\pi_2) = \varnothing)$$
> *is true.*

Proof (of Lem. 2) Assuming $x\pi_1 z$ and $z\pi_2 y$ to be elementary, we must prove that $\text{elem-conc?}(x\pi_1 z, z\pi_2 y)$ is true $\Leftrightarrow$ $x\pi_1 z \odot z\pi_2 y = x\pi_1 z\pi_2 y$ is elementary.

— We prove the necessary condition ($\pi_1 \odot \pi_2$ is elementary $\Rightarrow \text{elem-conc?}(\pi_1, \pi_2)$) by contraposition ($\neg\text{elem-conc?}(\pi_1, \pi_2) \Rightarrow \pi_1 \odot \pi_2$ has an internal cycle). We have

$$\neg((x \neq z \wedge y \neq z \wedge \mathbf{V}(x\pi_1 z) \cap \mathbf{V}(\pi_2 y) = \varnothing) \vee (x = y \wedge x \neq z \wedge y \neq z \wedge \mathbf{V}(\pi_1 z) \cap \mathbf{V}(\pi_2) = \varnothing))$$
$$= (x = z \vee y = z \vee (\mathbf{V}(x\pi_1 z) \cap \mathbf{V}(\pi_2 y) \neq \varnothing)) \wedge (x \neq y \vee x = z \vee y = z \vee \mathbf{V}(\pi_1 z) \cap \mathbf{V}(\pi_2) \neq \varnothing)) \qquad \langle \text{de Morgan laws} \rangle$$

- If $x = z$ then $x\pi_1 x\pi_2 y$ has a cycle and is not elementary;
- else, if $y = z$ then $x\pi_1 y\pi_2 y$ has a cycle and is not elementary;
- else $x \neq z \wedge y \neq z$, and then
  - either $x \neq z \wedge y \neq z \wedge x = y$ so $\mathbf{V}(\pi_1 z) \cap \mathbf{V}(\pi_2) \neq \varnothing$. There are two cases
    - either $\mathbf{V}(\pi_1) \cap \mathbf{V}(\pi_2) \neq \varnothing$ so $\pi_1 = \pi_1' a \pi_1''$ and $\pi_2 = \pi_2' a \pi_2''$ and therefore $\pi_1 \odot \pi_2 = x\pi_1 z\pi_2 y = x\pi_1' a\pi_1'' z\pi_2' a\pi_2'' x$ has an internal cycle $a\pi_1'' z\pi_2' a$,
    - or $z \in \mathbf{V}(\pi_2)$ so $\pi_2 = \pi_2' z\pi_2''$ and therefore $\pi_1 \odot \pi_2 = x\pi_1 z\pi_2 y = x\pi_1 z\pi_2' z\pi_2'' x$ has an internal cycle $z\pi_2' z$;
  - otherwise $x \neq z \wedge y \neq z \wedge x \neq y$ and we have $\mathbf{V}(x\pi_1 z) \cap \mathbf{V}(\pi_2 y) \neq \varnothing$. By cases.
    - If x appears in $\pi_2 y$ that is in π_2 since $x \neq y$ we have $\pi_2 = \pi_2' x\pi_2''$ and then $x\pi_1 z \odot z\pi_2 y = x\pi_1 z\pi_2 y = x\pi_1 z\pi_2' x\pi_2'' y$ has an internal cycle $x\pi_1 z\pi_2' x$;
    - Else, if $\mathbf{V}(\pi_1) \cap \mathbf{V}(\pi_2 y) \neq \varnothing$ then
      - Either $\mathbf{V}(\pi_1) \cap \mathbf{V}(\pi_2) \neq \varnothing$ so $\pi_1 = \pi_1' a\pi_1''$ and $\pi_2 = \pi_2' a\pi_2''$ and therefore $x\pi_1 z \odot z\pi_2 y = x\pi_1 z\pi_2 y = x\pi_1' a\pi_1'' z\pi_2' a\pi_2'' x$ has an internal cycle $a\pi_1'' z\pi_2' a$,
      - Or $y \in \mathbf{V}(\pi_1)$ so $\pi_1 = \pi_1' y\pi_1''$ and then $x\pi_1 z \odot z\pi_2 y = x\pi_1 z\pi_2 y = x\pi_1' y\pi_1'' z\pi_2 y$ has an internal cycle $y\pi_1'' z\pi_2 y$;
    - Otherwise, $z \in \mathbf{V}(\pi_2 y) \neq \varnothing$ and then
      - Either $z \in \mathbf{V}(\pi_2)$ so $\pi_2 = \pi_2' z\pi_2''$ and $x\pi_1 z \odot z\pi_2 y = x\pi_1 z\pi_2 y = x\pi_1 z\pi_2' z\pi_2'' y$ has an internal cycle $z\pi_2' z$,
      - Or $z = y$ and $x\pi_1 z \odot z\pi_2 y = x\pi_1 z\pi_2 y = x\pi_1 z\pi_2 z$ has an internal cycle $z\pi_2 z$.

— We prove that the condition is sufficient (elem-conc?$(\pi_1, \pi_2) \Rightarrow \pi_1 \odot \pi_2$ is elementary) by *reductio ad absurdum*. Assume $x\pi_1 z$, and $z\pi_2 y$ are elementary, elem-conc?$(x\pi_1 z, z\pi_2 y)$ holds, but that $x\pi_1 z \odot z\pi_2 y = x\pi_1 z\pi_2 y$ is not elementary.

- if the internal cycle is in $x\pi_1 z$ then, by hypothesis, $x = z$ so elem-conc?$(x\pi_1 z, z\pi_2 y)$ does not hold, a contradiction;
- else, if the internal cycle is in $z\pi_2 y$ then, by hypothesis, $z = y$ so elem-conc?$(x\pi_1 z, z\pi_2 y)$ does not hold, a contradiction;
- otherwise, the internal cycle is neither in $x\pi_1 z$ nor in $z\pi_2 y$ so $\mathbf{V}(x\pi_1 z) \cap \mathbf{V}(\pi_2 y) \neq \varnothing$. Since elem-conc?$(\pi_1, \pi_2)$ holds, it follows that $x = y \neq z \wedge \mathbf{V}(\pi_1 z) \cap \mathbf{V}(\pi_2) = \varnothing$ in contradiction with the existence of an internal cycle $a\pi'' \pi'_2 a$ requiring $\pi_1 z = \pi' a\pi''$ and $\pi_2 = \pi'_2 a\pi''_2$ so $a \in \mathbf{V}(\pi' a\pi'') \cap \mathbf{V}(\pi'_2 a\pi''_2) = \mathbf{V}(\pi_1 z) \cap \mathbf{V}(\pi_2) \neq \varnothing$.

□

We have the following fixpoint characterization of the elementary paths of a graph (converging in finitely many iterations for graphs without infinite paths).

Theorem 6 (Fixpoint characterization of the elementary paths of a graph) *Let $G = \langle V, E \rangle$ be a graph. The elementary paths between any two vertices of G are $\mathsf{p}^{\ni} \triangleq \alpha^{\infty} \circ \alpha^{\ni}(\Pi(G))$ such that*

$$\mathsf{p}^{\ni} = \mathsf{lfp}^{\subseteq} \overrightarrow{\mathcal{L}}^{\ni}_{\Pi}, \qquad \overrightarrow{\mathcal{L}}^{\ni}_{\Pi}(\mathsf{p}) \triangleq \dot{E} \,\dot{\cup}\, \mathsf{p} \,\dot{\odot}^{\ni}\, \dot{E} \qquad \text{(Th.6.a)}$$

$$= \mathsf{lfp}^{\subseteq} \overrightarrow{\mathcal{R}}^{\ni}_{\Pi}, \qquad \overrightarrow{\mathcal{R}}^{\ni}_{\Pi}(\mathsf{p}) \triangleq \dot{E} \,\dot{\cup}\, \dot{E} \,\dot{\odot}^{\ni}\, \mathsf{p} \qquad \text{(Th.6.b)}$$

$$= \mathsf{lfp}^{\subseteq} \overleftrightarrow{\mathcal{B}}^{\ni}_{\Pi}, \qquad \overleftrightarrow{\mathcal{B}}^{\ni}_{\Pi}(\mathsf{p}) \triangleq \dot{E} \,\dot{\cup}\, \mathsf{p} \,\dot{\odot}^{\ni}\, \mathsf{p} \qquad \text{(Th.6.c)}$$

$$= \mathsf{lfp}^{\subseteq}_{\dot{E}} \widehat{\mathcal{P}}^{\ni}_{\Pi}, \qquad \widehat{\mathcal{P}}^{\ni}_{\Pi}(\mathsf{p}) \triangleq \mathsf{p} \,\dot{\cup}\, \mathsf{p} \,\dot{\odot}^{\ni}\, \mathsf{p} \qquad \text{(Th.6.d)}$$

where $\dot{E} \triangleq \lambda x, y \cdot (E \cap \{\langle x, y \rangle\})$ in Th. 4 and $\mathsf{p}_1 \,\dot{\odot}^{\ni}\, \mathsf{p}_2 \triangleq \lambda x, y \cdot \bigcup_{z \in V} \{\pi_1 \odot \pi_2 \mid$
$\pi_1 \in \mathsf{p}_1(x, z) \wedge \pi_2 \in \mathsf{p}_2(z, y) \wedge$ elem-conc?$(\pi_1, \pi_2)\}$. □

The definition of $\mathsf{p}^{\ni}$ in Th. 6 is left-recursive in case (a), right recursive in case (b), bidirectional in case (c), and on paths only in case (d).

Proof (of Th. 6) We apply Th. 3 with abstraction $\dot{\alpha}^{\ni} \circ \alpha^{\infty}$ so that we have to abstract the transformers in Th. 4 using an exact fixpoint abstraction of Cor. 1. The commutation condition yields the transformers by calculational design.

$$\dot{\alpha}^{\ni}(\mathsf{p}_1 \,\overset{\circ\circ}{\odot}\, \mathsf{p}_2)$$

$$= \dot{\alpha}^{\ni}(\lambda x, y \cdot \bigcup_{z \in V} \mathsf{p}_1(x, z) \,\odot\, \mathsf{p}_2(z, y)) \qquad \text{?def. } \overset{\circ\circ}{\odot} \text{ in Th. 4?}$$

$$= \lambda x, y \cdot \alpha^{\ni}(\bigcup_{z \in V} \mathsf{p}_1(x, z) \,\odot\, \mathsf{p}_2(z, y)) \qquad \text{?pointwise def. } \dot{\alpha}^{\ni}?$$

$$= \lambda x, y \cdot \bigcup_{z \in V} \alpha^{\ni}(\mathsf{p}_1(x, z) \,\odot\, \mathsf{p}_2(z, y))$$

$\qquad\qquad$?join preservation of the abstraction in a Galois connection?

$$= \lambda x, y \cdot \bigcup_{z \in V} \alpha^{\partial}(\{\pi_1 \odot \pi_2 \mid \pi_1 \in p_1(x, z) \wedge \pi_2 \in p_2(z, y)\})$$

$$\langle \text{def. (2) of } \textcircled{\circ} \text{ and (5) of } \odot \rangle$$

$$= \lambda x, y \cdot \bigcup_{z \in V} \alpha^{\partial}(\{\pi_1 \odot \pi_2 \mid \pi_1 \in \alpha^{\partial}(p_1(x, z)) \wedge \pi_2 \in \alpha^{\partial}(p_2(z, y))\})$$

$$\langle \text{since if } \pi_1 \text{ or } \pi_2 \text{ are not elementary so is their concatenation } \pi_1 \odot \pi_2 \rangle$$

$$= \lambda x, y \cdot \bigcup_{z \in V} \{\pi_1 \odot \pi_2 \mid \pi_1 \in \alpha^{\partial}(p_1(x, z)) \wedge \pi_2 \in \alpha^{\partial}(p_2(z, y)) \wedge \text{elem-conc?}(\pi_1, \pi_2)\}$$

$$\langle \text{since, by Lem. 2, } \pi_1 \text{ and } \pi_2 \text{ being elementary, their concatenation } \pi_1 \odot \pi_2$$
$$\text{is elementary if and only if elem-conc?}(\pi_1, \pi_2) \text{ is true} \rangle$$

$$= \lambda x, y \cdot \bigcup_{z \in V} \{\pi_1 \odot \pi_2 \mid \pi_1 \in \dot{\alpha}^{\partial}(p_1)(x, z) \wedge \pi_2 \in \dot{\alpha}^{\partial}(p_2)(z, y) \wedge \text{elem-conc?}(\pi_1, \pi_2)\}$$

$$\langle \text{pointwise def. } \dot{\alpha}^{\partial} \rangle$$

$$= \dot{\alpha}^{\partial}(p_1) \, \dot{\textcircled{\circ}}^{\partial} \, \dot{\alpha}^{\partial}(p_2)$$

$$\langle \text{def. } \dot{\textcircled{\circ}}^{\partial} \text{ in Th. 6} \rangle \quad \square$$

11 Calculational design of the elementary paths between vertices of finite graphs

In finite graphs $G = \langle V, E \rangle$ with $|V| = n > 0$ vertices, elementary paths in G are of length at most $n+1$ (for a cycle that would go through all vertices of the graph). This ensures that the fixpoint iterates in Th. 6 starting from $\dot{\varnothing}$ do converge in at most $n+2$ iterates.

Moreover, if $V = \{z_1 \dots z_n\}$ is finite, then the elementary paths of the $k + 2^{\text{nd}}$ iterate can be restricted to $\{z_1, \dots, z_k\}$. This yields an iterative algorithm by application of the exact iterates multi-abstraction Th. 1 with[1]

$$\alpha_0^{\partial}(p) \triangleq p \tag{9}$$
$$\alpha_k^{\partial}(p) \triangleq \lambda x, y \cdot \{\pi \in p(x, y) \mid \mathbf{V}(\pi) \subseteq \{z_1, \dots, z_k\} \cup \{x, y\}\}, \qquad k \in [1, n]$$
$$\alpha_k^{\partial}(p) \triangleq p, \qquad\qquad\qquad\qquad\qquad\qquad\qquad\qquad\qquad k > n$$

By the exclusion abstraction and pointwise extension, these are Galois connections

$$\langle V \times V \to \wp(V^{>1}), \dot{\subseteq} \rangle \xrightarrow[\alpha_k^{\partial}]{\gamma_k^{\partial}} \langle V \times V \to \bigcup_{j=2}^{n+1} V^j, \dot{\subseteq} \rangle. \tag{10}$$

with $\gamma_k^{\partial}(p) \triangleq p$ for $k = 0$ or $k > n$ and $\gamma_k^{\partial}(p) \triangleq p \,\dot{\cup}\, \lambda x, y \cdot \{x\pi y \mid \mathbf{V}(x\pi y) \nsubseteq \{z_1, \dots, z_k\} \cup \{x, y\}\}$ when $k \in [1, n]$.

Applying Th. 1, we get the following iterative characterization of the elementary paths of a finite graph. Notice that $\dot{\textcircled{\circ}}_z$ in (Th.7.a) and (Th.7.b) does not require to test that the concatenation of two elementary paths is elementary while $\dot{\textcircled{\circ}}_z^{\partial}$ in (Th.7.c) and (Th.7.d) definitely does (since the concatenated elementary paths may have vertices in common). Notice also that the iteration $\langle \vec{\mathscr{L}}_{\pi}^{\partial \, k}, k \in [0, n+2] \rangle$ in (Th.7.a) is not the same as the iterates $\langle \vec{\mathscr{L}}_{\pi}^{\partial \, k}(\varnothing), k \in \mathbb{N} \rangle$

---

[1] This is for case (Th.7.d). For cases (a–c), we also have $\alpha_1^{\partial}(p) \triangleq p$ while the second definition is for $k \in [2, n+2]$.

of $\overrightarrow{\mathscr{L}}^{\partial}_{\Pi}$ from $\dot{\varnothing}$, since using $\dot{\odot}_z$ or $\dot{\odot}_z^{\partial}$ instead of $\dot{\odot}^{\partial}$ is the key to efficiency. This is also the case for (Th.7.b—d).

Theorem 7 *(Iterative characterization of the elementary paths of a finite graph)*   Let $G = \langle V, E \rangle$ be a finite graph with $V = \{z_1, \ldots, z_n\}$, $n > 0$. Then

$$\mathsf{p}^{\partial} = \mathsf{lfp}^{\subseteq} \overrightarrow{\mathscr{L}}^{\partial}_{\Pi} = \overrightarrow{\mathscr{L}}^{\partial}_{\pi}{}^{n+2} \quad where \tag{Th.7.a}$$

$$\overrightarrow{\mathscr{L}}^{\partial}_{\Pi}(\mathsf{p}) \triangleq \dot{E} \;\dot{\cup}\; \mathsf{p} \; \dot{\odot}^{\partial} \; \dot{E} \; in \; (Th.6.a) \quad and \quad \overrightarrow{\mathscr{L}}^{\partial}_{\pi}{}^0 \triangleq \dot{\varnothing}, \quad \overrightarrow{\mathscr{L}}^{\partial}_{\pi}{}^1 \triangleq \dot{E},$$

$$\overrightarrow{\mathscr{L}}^{\partial}_{\pi}{}^{k+2} \triangleq \dot{E} \;\dot{\cup}\; \overrightarrow{\mathscr{L}}^{\partial}_{\pi}{}^{k+1} \; \dot{\odot}_{z_{k+1}} \; \dot{E}, \quad k \in [0,n], \quad \overrightarrow{\mathscr{L}}^{\partial}_{\pi}{}^{k+1} = \overrightarrow{\mathscr{L}}^{\partial}_{\pi}{}^k, \quad k \geqslant n+2$$

$$= \mathsf{lfp}^{\subseteq} \overrightarrow{\mathscr{R}}^{\partial}_{\Pi} = \overrightarrow{\mathscr{R}}^{\partial}_{\pi}{}^{n+2} \quad where \tag{Th.7.b}$$

$$\overrightarrow{\mathscr{R}}^{\partial}_{\Pi}(\mathsf{p}) \triangleq \dot{E} \;\dot{\cup}\; \dot{E} \; \dot{\odot}^{\partial} \; \mathsf{p} \; in \; (Th.6.b) \quad and \quad \overrightarrow{\mathscr{R}}^{\partial}_{\pi}{}^0 \triangleq \dot{\varnothing}, \quad \overrightarrow{\mathscr{R}}^{\partial}_{\pi}{}^0 \triangleq \dot{E},$$

$$\overrightarrow{\mathscr{R}}^{\partial}_{\pi}{}^{k+2} \triangleq \dot{E} \;\dot{\cup}\; \dot{E} \; \dot{\odot}_{z_{k+1}} \; \overrightarrow{\mathscr{R}}^{\partial}_{\pi}{}^{k+1}, \quad k \in [0,n], \quad \overrightarrow{\mathscr{R}}^{\partial}_{\pi}{}^{k+1} = \overrightarrow{\mathscr{R}}^{\partial}_{\pi}{}^k, \quad k \geqslant n+2$$

$$= \mathsf{lfp}^{\subseteq} \overrightarrow{\mathscr{B}}^{\partial}_{\Pi} = \overrightarrow{\mathscr{B}}^{\partial}_{\pi}{}^{n+2} \quad where \tag{Th.7.c}$$

$$\overrightarrow{\mathscr{B}}^{\partial}_{\Pi}(\mathsf{p}) \triangleq \dot{E} \;\dot{\cup}\; \mathsf{p} \; \dot{\odot}^{\partial} \; \mathsf{p} \; in \; (Th.6.c) \quad and \quad \overrightarrow{\mathscr{B}}^{\partial}_{\pi}{}^0 \triangleq \dot{\varnothing}, \quad \overrightarrow{\mathscr{B}}^{\partial}_{\pi}{}^1 \triangleq \dot{E},$$

$$\overrightarrow{\mathscr{B}}^{\partial}_{\pi}{}^{k+2} \triangleq \dot{E} \;\dot{\cup}\; \overrightarrow{\mathscr{B}}^{\partial}_{\pi}{}^{k+1} \; \dot{\odot}^{\partial}_{z_{k+1}} \; \overrightarrow{\mathscr{B}}^{\partial}_{\pi}{}^{k+1}, \; k \in [0,n], \quad \overrightarrow{\mathscr{B}}^{\partial}_{\pi}{}^{k+1} = \overrightarrow{\mathscr{B}}^{\partial}_{\pi}{}^k, \; k \geqslant n+2$$

$$= \mathsf{lfp}^{\subseteq}_{\dot{E}} \widehat{\mathscr{P}}^{\partial}_{\Pi} = \widehat{\mathscr{P}}^{\partial}_{\pi}{}^{n+1} \quad where \tag{Th.7.d}$$

$$\widehat{\mathscr{P}}^{\partial}_{\Pi}(\mathsf{p}) \triangleq \mathsf{p} \;\dot{\cup}\; \mathsf{p} \; \dot{\odot}^{\partial} \; \mathsf{p} \; in \; (Th.6.d), \quad \widehat{\mathscr{P}}^{\partial}_{\pi}{}^0 \triangleq \dot{E},$$

$$\widehat{\mathscr{P}}^{\partial}_{\pi}{}^{k+1} \triangleq \widehat{\mathscr{P}}^{\partial}_{\pi}{}^k \;\dot{\cup}\; \widehat{\mathscr{P}}^{\partial}_{\pi}{}^k \; \dot{\odot}^{\partial}_{z_{k+1}} \; \widehat{\mathscr{P}}^{\partial}_{\pi}{}^k, \; k \in [0,n], \quad \widehat{\mathscr{P}}^{\partial}_{\pi}{}^{k+1} = \widehat{\mathscr{P}}^{\partial}_{\pi}{}^k, \; k \geqslant n+2$$

$$\mathsf{p}_1 \;\dot{\odot}_z\; \mathsf{p}_2 \triangleq \lambda\, x, y \cdot \{\pi_1 \odot \pi_2 \mid \pi_1 \in \mathsf{p}_1(x,z) \wedge \pi_2 \in \mathsf{p}_2(z,y) \wedge z \notin \{x,y\}\}, \; and$$

$$\mathsf{p}_1 \;\dot{\odot}^{\partial}_z\; \mathsf{p}_2 \triangleq \lambda\, x, y \cdot \{\pi_1 \odot \pi_2 \mid \pi_1 \in \mathsf{p}_1(x,z) \wedge \pi_2 \in \mathsf{p}_2(z,y) \wedge \mathsf{elem\text{-}conc?}(\pi_1, \pi_2)\}. \qquad \square$$

Proof (of Th. 7) — The proofs in cases (Th.7.c) and (Th.7.d) are similar. Let us consider (Th.7.d). Assume $V = \{z_1 \ldots z_n\}$ and let $\widehat{\mathscr{P}}^{\partial}_{\Pi}{}^{k+1} = \widehat{\mathscr{P}}^{\partial}_{\Pi}(\widehat{\mathscr{P}}^{\partial}_{\Pi}{}^k)$ be the iterates of $\widehat{\mathscr{P}}^{\partial}_{\Pi}$ from $\widehat{\mathscr{P}}^{\partial}_{\Pi}{}^0 = \dot{E}$ in (Th.6.d). To apply Th. 1, we consider the concrete cpo $\langle C, \subseteq \rangle$ and the abstract cpo $\langle \mathcal{A}, \subseteq \rangle$ to be $\langle C, \subseteq, \dot{E}, \dot{\cup} \rangle$ with $C \triangleq x \in V \times y \in V \rightarrow \{x\pi y \mid x\pi y \in E \cup \bigcup_{k=3}^{n+1} V^k \wedge x\pi y \text{ is elementary}\}$, and the functions $\widehat{\mathscr{P}}^{\partial}_{\pi k}(X) \triangleq X \;\dot{\cup}\; X \; \dot{\odot}^{\partial}_{z_{k+1}} \; X$, $k \in [1,n]$, and $\widehat{\mathscr{P}}^{\partial}_{\pi k}(X) \triangleq X$, $k = 0$ or $k > n$ which iterates from the infimum $\dot{E}$ are precisely $\langle \widehat{\mathscr{P}}^{\partial}_{\Pi}{}^k, i \in \mathbb{Z} \cup \{\omega\} \rangle$ where $\widehat{\mathscr{P}}^{\partial}_{\pi}{}^{\omega} = \dot{\bigcup}_{i \in \mathbb{Z}} \widehat{\mathscr{P}}^{\partial}_{\pi}{}^i = \widehat{\mathscr{P}}^{\partial}_{\pi}{}^{n+1} = \widehat{\mathscr{P}}^{\partial}_{\Pi}{}^k$, $k > n$.

- For the infimum $\widehat{\mathscr{P}}^{\partial}_{\pi 0} = \dot{E}$ the paths $x\pi y \in \dot{E}(x,y)$ of G which are elementary and have all intermediate states of π in $\varnothing = \{z_1, \ldots, z_0\}$ since π is empty.

- For the commutation, the case $k > n$ is trivial. Otherwise let $X \in \mathcal{A}$ so $x\pi y \in X(x,y)$ is elementary and has all states of π in $\{z_1, \ldots, z_k\}$

$$\alpha^{\partial}_{k+1}(\widehat{\mathscr{P}}^{\partial}_{\Pi}(X))$$
$$= \alpha^{\partial}_{k+1}(X \;\dot{\cup}\; X \; \dot{\odot}^{\partial} \; X) \qquad \qquad \qquad \{\text{def. (Th.6.d) of } \widehat{\mathscr{P}}^{\partial}_{\Pi} \}$$

$= \alpha_{k+1}^{\partial}(X) \,\dot{\cup}\, \alpha_{k+1}^{\partial}(X \,\dot{\odot}^{\partial}\, X)$ $\langle \alpha_{k+1}^{\partial}$ preserves joins in (10)$\rangle$

$= \alpha_{k}^{\partial}(X) \,\dot{\cup}\, \alpha_{k+1}^{\partial}(X \,\dot{\odot}^{\partial}\, X)$
     $\langle$def. (9) of α_{k+1}^{∂} and hypothesis that all paths in X have all intermediate states in $\{z_1, \ldots, z_k\}\rangle$

$= \alpha_{k}^{\partial}(X) \,\dot{\cup}\, \lambda\, x, y \cdot \{\pi \in X \,\dot{\odot}^{\partial}\, X(x, y) \mid \mathbf{V}(\pi) \subseteq \{z_1, \ldots, z_{k+1}\} \cup \{x, y\}\}$ $\langle$def. α_{k+1}^{∂} in (9)$\rangle$

$= \alpha_{k}^{\partial}(X) \dot{\cup} \lambda\, x, y \cdot \{\pi \in \bigcup_{z \in V}\{\pi_1 \odot \pi_2 \mid \pi_1 \in X(x, z) \wedge \pi_2 \in X(z, y) \wedge \text{elem-conc?}(\pi_1, \pi_2)\} \mid$
$\mathbf{V}(\pi) \subseteq \{z_1, \ldots, z_{k+1}\} \cup \{x, y\}\}$ $\langle$def. $\dot{\odot}^{\partial}$ in Th. 6$\rangle$

$= \alpha_{k}^{\partial}(X) \,\dot{\cup}\, \lambda\, x, y \cdot \bigcup_{z \in V}\{\pi_1 \odot \pi_2 \mid \pi_1 \in X(x, z) \wedge \pi_2 \in X(z, y) \wedge \text{elem-conc?}(\pi_1, \pi_2) \wedge$
$\mathbf{V}(\pi_1 \odot \pi_2) \subseteq \{z_1, \ldots, z_{k+1}\} \cup \{x, y\}\}$ $\langle$def. $\in\rangle$

$= \alpha_{k}^{\partial}(X) \,\dot{\cup}\, \lambda\, x, y \cdot \bigcup_{z \in V}\{x\pi_1 z\pi_2 y \mid x\pi_1 z \in X(x, z) \wedge z\pi_2 y \in X(z, y) \wedge$
$\text{elem-conc?}(x\pi_1 z, z\pi_2 y) \wedge \mathbf{V}(\pi_1) \cup \mathbf{V}(\pi_2) \cup \{z\} \subseteq \{z_1, \ldots, z_{k+1}\} \cup \{x, y\}\}$ $\langle$def. $\odot$, $\mathbf{V}$, and ind. hyp.$\rangle$

$= \alpha_{k}^{\partial}(X) \,\dot{\cup}\, \lambda\, x, y \cdot \{x\pi_1 z_{k+1}\pi_2 y \mid x\pi_1 z_{k+1} \in \alpha_{k}^{\partial}(X)(x, z_{k+1}) \wedge z_{k+1}\pi_2 y \in$
$\alpha_{k}^{\partial}(X)(z_{k+1}, y) \wedge \text{elem-conc?}(x\pi_1 z_{k+1}, z_{k+1}\pi_2 y)\}$

> $\langle(\supseteq)$ follows from taking $z = z_{k+1}$;   (11)
> $(\subseteq)$ For $z \in \{z_1, \ldots, z_k\}$, the paths in $\alpha_{k}^{\partial}(X)$ are elementary through $\{z_1, \ldots, z_k\}$, so if there exist paths $x\pi_1 z \in X(x, z)$ and $z\pi_2 y \in X(z, y)$ then either $x\pi_1 z\pi_2 x$ is also elementary through $\{z_1, \ldots, z_k\}$ and already therefore belongs to $\alpha_{k}^{\partial}(X)$ or it is not elementary and then does not pass the test elem-conc?$(x\pi_1 z_{k+1}, z_{k+1}\pi_2 y)$;
> Otherwise, if $z \in \{z_{k+2}, \ldots, z_n\}$, then the path $x\pi_1 z_{k+1}\pi_2 y$ is eliminated by $\mathbf{V}(\pi_1) \cup \mathbf{V}(\pi_2) \cup \{z\} \subseteq \{z_1, \ldots, z_{k+1}\} \cup \{x, y\}$;
> Finally, the only possibility is $z = z_{k+1}$, in which case all paths have the form $x\pi_1 z_{k+1}\pi_2 y$, are elementary, and with $\mathbf{V}(\pi) \subseteq \{z_1, \ldots, z_{k+1}\}$, as required by the def. of $\mathcal{A}$. It also holds for $\alpha_{k}^{\partial}(X)$ which is equal to $\alpha_{k+1}^{\partial}(X)$.
> $\rangle$

$= \alpha_{k}^{\partial}(X) \,\dot{\cup}\, \lambda\, x, y \cdot \{x\pi_1 z_{k+1} \odot z_{k+1}\pi_2 y \mid x\pi_1 z_{k+1} \in \alpha_{k}^{\partial}(X)(x, z_{k+1}) \wedge z_{k+1}\pi_2 y \in$
$\alpha_{k}^{\partial}(X)(z_{k+1}, y) \wedge \text{elem-conc?}(x\pi_1 z_{k+1}, z_{k+1}\pi_2 y)\}$ $\langle$def. $\odot\rangle$

$= \alpha_{k}^{\partial}(X) \,\dot{\cup}\, \lambda\, x, y \cdot \{\pi_1 \odot \pi_2 \mid \pi_1 \in \alpha_{k}^{\partial}(X)(x, z_{k+1}) \wedge \pi_2 \in \alpha_{k}^{\partial}(X)(z_{k+1}, y) \wedge$
$\text{elem-conc?}(\pi_1, \pi_2)\}$
     $\langle$by ind. hyp. all paths in $X(x, y)$ have the form $x\pi y\rangle$

$= \alpha_{k}^{\partial}(X) \,\dot{\cup}\, \alpha_{k}^{\partial}(X) \,\dot{\odot}_{z_{k+1}}^{\partial}\, \alpha_{k}^{\partial}(X)$ $\langle$def. $\dot{\odot}_{z_{k+1}}^{\partial}$ in (Th.7.d)$\rangle$

$= \widehat{\mathcal{F}}_{\pi k}^{\partial}(\alpha_{k}^{\partial}(X))$ $\langle$(Th.7.d)$\rangle$

We conclude by Th. 1.

— In cases (Th.7.a) and (Th.7.b), $\dot{\odot}_{z_{k+1}}^{\partial}$ can be replaced by $\dot{\odot}_{z_{k+1}}$ since in these cases the paths are elementary by construction. To see this, observe that for (Th.7.a), the iterates $\langle \mathscr{L}_{\pi}^{\partial\, k}(\emptyset),\, k \in \mathbb{N} \cup \{\omega\}\rangle$ are those of the functions

$\vec{\mathscr{L}}^{\partial}_{\pi 0}(X) \triangleq \dot{\varnothing}$, $\vec{\mathscr{L}}^{\partial}_{\pi 1}(X) \triangleq \dot{E}$, and $\vec{\mathscr{L}}^{\partial}_{\pi k}(X) \triangleq \dot{E} \dot{\cup} X \dot{\odot}^{\partial}_{z_{k-1}} \dot{E}$, $k \in [2, n+2]$, and $\vec{\mathscr{L}}^{\partial}_{\pi k}(X) \triangleq X$, $k > n$, so that we can consider the iterates from 1 to apply Th. 1.

- By (Th.6.a), the initialization is $\vec{\mathscr{L}}^{\partial}_{\Pi}(\dot{\varnothing}) \triangleq \dot{E} \dot{\cup} \dot{\varnothing} \dot{\odot}^{\partial} \dot{E} = \dot{E}$ such that all paths $x \pi y$ in $\dot{E}(x, y)$ are elementary with π empty so $\mathbf{V}(\pi) \subseteq \varnothing = \{z_1, \dots, z_0\}$.

- For the commutation, let $X \in \mathcal{A}$ such that all $x \pi y \in X(x, y)$ are elementary and have all states of π in $\{z_1, \dots, z_k\}$. Then

$\alpha^{\partial}_{k+2}(\vec{\mathscr{L}}^{\partial}_{\Pi}(X))$ \hfill $\wr$def. iterates$\wr$

$= \alpha^{\partial}_{k+2}(\dot{E} \dot{\cup} X \dot{\odot}^{\partial} \dot{E})$ \hfill $\wr$def. (Th.6.a) of $\vec{\mathscr{L}}^{\partial}_{\Pi}\wr$

$= \alpha^{\partial}_{k+2}(\dot{E}) \dot{\cup} \alpha^{\partial}_{k+2}(X \dot{\odot}^{\partial} \dot{E})$ \hfill $\wr\alpha^{\partial}_{k+2}$ preserves joins in $(10)\wr$

$= \dot{E} \dot{\cup} \lambda x, y \cdot \{\pi \in X \dot{\odot}^{\partial} \dot{E} \mid \mathbf{V}(\pi) \subseteq \{z_1, \dots, z_{k+2}\} \cup \{x, y\}\}$ \hfill $\wr$def. α^{∂}_{k+2} in $(9)\wr$

$= \dot{E} \dot{\cup} \lambda x, y \cdot \{\pi \in \bigcup_{z \in V} \{\pi_1 \odot \pi_2 \mid \pi_1 \in X(x, z) \wedge \pi_2 \in \dot{E}(z, y) \wedge \text{elem-conc?}(\pi_1, \pi_2)\} \mid$
$\mathbf{V}(\pi) \subseteq \{z_1, \dots, z_{k+2}\} \cup \{x, y\}\}$ \hfill $\wr$def. $\dot{\odot}^{\partial}$ in Th. $6\wr$

$= \dot{E} \dot{\cup} \lambda x, y \cdot \bigcup_{z \in V} \{\pi_1 \odot \pi_2 \mid \pi_1 \in X(x, z) \wedge \pi_2 \in \dot{E}(z, y) \wedge \text{elem-conc?}(\pi_1, \pi_2) \wedge \mathbf{V}(\pi_1 \odot$
$\pi_2) \subseteq \{z_1, \dots, z_{k+2}\} \cup \{x, y\}\}$ \hfill $\wr$def. $\in\wr$

$= \dot{E} \dot{\cup} \lambda x, y \cdot \bigcup_{z \in V} \{x \pi_1 z y \mid x \pi_1 z \in X(x, z) \wedge z y \in \dot{E}(z, y) \wedge \text{elem-conc?}(x \pi_1 z, z y) \wedge$
$\mathbf{V}(\pi_1) \cup \{z\} \subseteq \{z_1, \dots, z_{k+2}\} \cup \{x, y\}\}$ \hfill $\wr$def. $\odot$, $\mathbf{V}$, $\dot{E}$ in Th. 4, and ind. hyp.$\wr$

$= \dot{E} \dot{\cup} \lambda x, y \cdot \{x \pi_1 z_{k+2} \odot z_{k+2} \pi_2 y \mid x \pi_1 z_{k+2} \in \alpha^{\partial}_{k+1}(X)(x, z_{k+2}) \wedge z_{k+2} \pi_2 y \in \dot{E}(z_{k+2}, y) \wedge$
$\text{elem-conc?}(x \pi_1 z_{k+2}, z_{k+2} \pi_2 y)\}$ \hfill $\wr$by an argument similar to $(11)\wr$

$= \dot{E} \dot{\cup} \lambda x, y \cdot \{x \pi_1 z_{k+2} \odot z_{k+2} y \mid x \pi_1 z_{k+2} \in \alpha^{\partial}_{k+1}(X)(x, z_{k+2}) \wedge \langle z_{k+2}, y \rangle \in E \wedge$
$\text{elem-conc?}(x \pi_1 z_{k+2}, z_{k+2} y)\}$ \hfill $\wr$def. (9) of α^{∂}_{k+1} and $\dot{E}$ in Th. $4\wr$

$= \dot{E} \dot{\cup} \lambda x, y \cdot \{x \pi_1 z_{k+2} \odot z_{k+2} y \mid x \pi_1 z_{k+2} \in \alpha^{\partial}_{k+1}(X)(x, z_{k+2}) \wedge \langle z_{k+2}, y \rangle \in E\}$
$\wr$since $z_{k+2} \notin \mathbf{V}(\pi_1)$ by induction hypothesis path so that the path
$x \pi_1 z_{k+2} y$ is elementary$\wr$

$= \dot{E} \dot{\cup} \alpha^{\partial}_{k+1}(X) \dot{\odot}^{\partial}_{z_{k+2}} \dot{E}$ \hfill $\wr$def. $\dot{\odot}^{\partial}_{z_{k+2}}$ in Th. $7\wr$

$= \vec{\mathscr{L}}^{\partial}_{\pi k+2}(\alpha^{\partial}_{k+1}(X))$ \hfill $\wr$(Th.7.a)$\wr$ $\quad\square$

12 Calculational design of an over-approximation of the elementary paths between vertices of finite graphs

Since shortest paths are necessarily elementary, one could expect that Roy-Floyd-Warshall algorithm simply abstracts the elementary paths by their length. This is not the case, because the iterations in (Th.7.c) and (Th.7.d) for elementary paths are too expensive. They require to check elem-conc? in $\dot{\odot}^{\partial}$ to make sure that the concatenation of elementary paths does yield an elementary path. But we can over-approximate by replacing $\dot{\odot}^{\partial}$ by $\dot{\odot}$ since

Lemma 3 *The length of the shortest paths in a graph is the same as the length of the shortest paths in any subset of the graph paths provided this subset contains all elementary paths.*

Proof (of Lem. 3) If $\pi_1 x \pi_2 x \pi_3$ is a non-elementary path with an internal cycle $x \pi_2 x$ of the weighted graph $\langle V, E, \omega \rangle$ then $\pi_1 x \pi_3$ is also a path in the graph with a shorter weight, that is, by (6), $\omega(\pi_1 x \pi_3) < \omega(\pi_1 x \pi_2 x \pi_3)$. Since elementary paths have no internal cycles, it follows by definition of min and (7) that, for any subset P of the graph paths, we have $\omega(P) = \omega(P')$ whenever $\alpha^\partial(P) = \{\pi \in P \mid \text{elem}?(\pi)\} \subseteq P' \subseteq P$. $\qquad\square$

Corollary 2 *(Iterative characterization of an over-approximation of the elementary paths of a finite graph)* Let $G = \langle V, E \rangle$ be a finite graph with $V = \{z_1, \ldots, z_n\}$, $n > 0$. Then

$$\mathsf{p}^\partial = \mathsf{lfp}^{\dot\subseteq} \overrightarrow{\mathscr{B}}^\partial_\Pi \dot\subseteq \overrightarrow{\mathscr{B}}^{n+2}_\pi \qquad\qquad\qquad \text{(Cor.2.c)}$$

$$\text{where} \quad \overrightarrow{\mathscr{B}}^0_\pi \triangleq \dot\varnothing, \quad \overrightarrow{\mathscr{B}}^1_\pi \triangleq \dot{E}, \quad \overrightarrow{\mathscr{B}}^{k+2}_\pi \triangleq \dot{E} \,\dot\cup\, \overrightarrow{\mathscr{B}}^{k+1}_\pi \,\dot{\textstyle\bigodot}_{z_{k+1}}\, \overrightarrow{\mathscr{B}}^{k+1}_\pi$$

$$= \mathsf{lfp}^{\dot\subseteq}_{\dot{E}} \widehat{\mathscr{P}}^\partial_\Pi \dot\subseteq \widehat{\mathscr{P}}^{n+1}_\pi \qquad\qquad\qquad \text{(Cor.2.d)}$$

$$\text{where} \quad \widehat{\mathscr{P}}^0_\pi \triangleq \dot{E}, \quad \widehat{\mathscr{P}}^{k+1}_\pi \triangleq \widehat{\mathscr{P}}^k_\pi \,\dot\cup\, \widehat{\mathscr{P}}^k_\pi \,\dot{\textstyle\bigodot}_{z_k}\, \widehat{\mathscr{P}}^k_\pi \qquad\qquad \square$$

Proof (of Cor. 2) Obviously $\dot{\textstyle\bigodot}^\partial_z \dot\subseteq \dot{\textstyle\bigodot}_z$ so the iterates $\langle \overrightarrow{\mathscr{B}}^k_\pi, k \in [0, n+2] \rangle$ of (Cor.2.c) over-approximate those $\langle \overrightarrow{\mathscr{B}}^{\partial k}_\pi, k \in [0, n+2] \rangle$ of (Th.7.c). Same for (Th.7.d). $\qquad\square$

13   The Roy-Floyd-Warshall algorithm over-approximating the elementary paths of a finite graph

The Roy-Floyd-Warshall algorithm does <u>not</u> compute elementary paths in (Th.7.d) but the over-approximation of the set of elementary paths in (Cor.2.d), thus avoiding the potentially costly test in Th. 7 that the concatenation of elementary paths in $\dot{\textstyle\bigodot}^\partial_z$ is elementary.

> **Algorithm 12** *(Roy-Floyd-Warshall algorithm over-approximating the elementary paths of a finite graph)* Let $G = \langle V, E \rangle$ be a graph with $|V| = n > 0$ vertices. The Roy-Floyd-Warshall algorithm
>
> for $x, y \in V$ do
> $\mathsf{p}(x, y) := E \cap \{\langle x, y \rangle\}$
> done;
> for $z \in V$ do
>   for $x, y \in V \setminus \{z\}$ do
> $\mathsf{p}(x, y) := \mathsf{p}(x, y) \cup \mathsf{p}(x, z) \odot \mathsf{p}(z, y)$
>   done
> done
>
> computes an over-approximation of all elementary paths p of G.

Proof (of Algorithm 12) The first for iteration computes $\widehat{\mathscr{P}}^0_\pi \triangleq \dot{E}$ in (Cor.2.d). Then, the second for iteration should compute $\widehat{\mathscr{P}}^{k+1}_\pi \triangleq \widehat{\mathscr{P}}^k_\pi \dot{\cup} \widehat{\mathscr{P}}^k_\pi \dot{\odot}_{z_k} \widehat{\mathscr{P}}^k_\pi$ in (Cor.2.d) since $\mathsf{p}_1 \dot{\odot}_z \mathsf{p}_2 = \dot{\varnothing}$ in (Th.7.d) when $z \in \{x, y\}$, in which case, $\widehat{\mathscr{P}}^{k+1}_\pi = \widehat{\mathscr{P}}^k_\pi$, which is similar to the Jacobi iterative method. However, similar to the Gauss-Seidel iteration method, we reuse the last computed $\mathsf{p}(x, z)$ and $\mathsf{p}(z, y)$, not necessarily those of the previous iterate. For the convergence of the first n iterates of the second for iteration of the algorithm, the justification is similar to the convergence for chaotic iterations [4]. □

14   Calculational design of the Roy-Floyd-Warshall shortest path algorithm

The shortest path algorithm of Bernard Roy [16,17], Bob Floyd [10], and Steve Warshall [21] for finite graphs is based on the assumption that the graph has no cycles with strictly negative weights *i.e.* $\forall x \in V . \forall \pi \in \mathsf{p}(x, x) . \omega(\pi) \geqslant 0$. In that case the shortest paths are all elementary since adding a cycle of weight 0 leaves the distance unchanged while a cycle of positive weight would strictly increase the distance on the path. Otherwise, if the graph has cycles with strictly negative weights, the convergence between two vertices containing a cycle with strictly negative weights is infinite to the limit $-\infty$.

The essential consequence is that we don't have to consider all paths as in Th. 4 but instead we can consider any subset provided that it contains all elementary paths. Therefore we can base the design of the shortest path algorithm on Cor. 2. Observe that, although p may contain paths that are not elementary, d is precisely the minimal path lengths and not some strict over-approximation since

- p contains all elementary paths (so non-elementary paths are longer than the elementary path between their extremities), and

– no arc has a strictly negative weight (so path lengths are always positive and therefore the elementary paths are the shortest ones).

We derive the Roy-Floyd-Warshall algorithm by a calculation design applying Th. 1 for finite iterates to (Cor.2.d) with the abstraction $\dot{\omega}$ (or a variant when considering (Cor.2.c)).

– for the infimum $\dot{E}$ in (Cor.2.d), we have

$\dot{\omega}(\dot{E})\langle x, y\rangle$

$= \omega(\dot{E}(x, y))$ $\langle$pointwise def. $\dot{\omega}\rangle$

$= \omega(\llbracket \langle x, y\rangle \in E ? \{\langle x, y\rangle\} : \varnothing \rrbracket)$ $\langle$def. $\dot{E}$ in Th. 4$\rangle$

$= \llbracket \langle x, y\rangle \in E ? \omega(\{\langle x, y\rangle\}) : \omega(\varnothing) \rrbracket$ $\langle$def. conditional$\rangle$

$= \llbracket \langle x, y\rangle \in E ? \min\{\omega(\pi) \mid \pi \in \{\langle x, y\rangle\}\} : \infty \rrbracket$ $\langle$(7)$\rangle$

$= \llbracket \langle x, y\rangle \in E ? \omega(x, y) : \infty \rrbracket$ $\langle$(6)$\rangle$

– for the commutation with $\widehat{\mathscr{P}}_{\pi k+1}(X) \triangleq X \dot{\cup} X \dot{\odot}_{z_k} X$, we have

$\dot{\omega}(\widehat{\mathscr{P}}_{\pi k+1}(X))\langle x, y\rangle$

$= \dot{\omega}(X \dot{\cup} X \dot{\odot}_{z_k} X)\langle x, y\rangle$ $\langle$(Cor.2.d)$\rangle$

$= \min(\dot{\omega}(X)\langle x, y\rangle, \dot{\omega}(X \dot{\odot}_{z_k} X)\langle x, y\rangle)$

     $\langle$the abstraction $\dot{\omega}$ of Galois connection (8) preserves existing joins$\rangle$

Let us evaluate

$\dot{\omega}(X \dot{\odot}_{z_k} X)\langle x, y\rangle$

$= \omega((X \dot{\odot}_{z_k} X)(x, y))$ $\langle$pointwise def. $\dot{\omega}\rangle$

$= \omega(\{\pi_1 \odot \pi_2 \mid \pi_1 \in X(x, z_k) \land \pi_2 \in X(z_k, y) \land z_k \notin \{x, y\}\})$ $\langle$def. $\dot{\odot}_{z_k}$ in Th. 7$\rangle$

$= \min\{\omega(\pi_1 \odot \pi_2) \mid \pi_1 \in X(x, z_k) \land \pi_2 \in X(z_k, y) \land z_k \notin \{x, y\}\}$ $\langle$(7)$\rangle$

$= \min\{\omega(\pi_1) + \omega(\pi_2) \mid \pi_1 \in X(x, z_k) \land \pi_2 \in X(z_k, y) \land z_k \notin \{x, y\}\}$ $\langle$def. (6) of $\omega\rangle$

$= \llbracket z_k \in \{x, y\} ? \infty : \min\{\omega(\pi_1) \mid \pi_1 \in X(x, z_k)\} + \min\{\omega(\pi_2) \mid \pi_1 \in X(x, z_k) \land \pi_2 \in X(z_k, y)\} \rrbracket$ $\langle$def. min$\rangle$

$= \llbracket z_k \in \{x, y\} ? \infty : \min(\dot{\omega}(X)(x, z_k)) + \min(\dot{\omega}(X)(z_k, y)) \rrbracket$ $\langle$(7) and pointwise def. $\dot{\omega}\rangle$

so that $\dot{\omega}(\widehat{\mathscr{P}}_{\pi k+1}(X)) = \widehat{\mathscr{P}}_{\delta k}(\dot{\omega}(X))$ with $\widehat{\mathscr{P}}_{\delta k}(X)(x, y) \triangleq \llbracket z_k \in \{x, y\} ? X(x, y) : \min(X(x, y), X(x, z_k) + X(z_k, y)) \rrbracket$.

We have proved

Theorem 8 *(Iterative characterization of the shortest path length of a graph)* *Let* $G = \langle V, E, \omega \rangle$ *be a finite graph with* $V = \{z_1, \ldots, z_n\}$, $n > 0$ *weighted on the totally ordered group* $\langle \mathbb{G}, \leqslant, 0, + \rangle$ *with no strictly negative weight. Then the distances between any two vertices are*

$$\mathsf{d} = \dot{\omega}(\mathsf{p}) = \widehat{\mathscr{P}}^{n+1}_\delta \qquad where \tag{Th.8}$$

$$\mathscr{P}^0_\delta(x, y) \triangleq (\!(\langle x, y \rangle \in E ? \omega(x, y) \mathbin{\text{\tiny\$}} \infty)\!),$$

$$\widehat{\mathscr{P}}^{k+1}_\delta(x, y) \triangleq (\!(z_k \in \{x, y\} ? \widehat{\mathscr{P}}^k_\delta(x, y)$$
$$\mathbin{\text{\tiny\$}} \min(\widehat{\mathscr{P}}^k_\delta(x, y), \widehat{\mathscr{P}}^k_\delta(x, z_k) + \widehat{\mathscr{P}}^k_\delta(z_k, y)))\!) \qquad \square$$

and directly get the Roy-Floyd-Warshall distances algorithm.

Algorithm 13 (Roy-Floyd-Warshall shortest distances of a graph) $G = \langle V, E, \omega \rangle$ *be a finite graph with* $|V| = n > 0$ *vertices weighted on the totally ordered group* $\langle \mathbb{G}, \leqslant, 0, + \rangle$. *Let* $\mathsf{d} \in V \times V \to \mathbb{G} \cup \{-\infty, \infty\}$ *be computed by the Roy-Floyd-Warshall algorithm*

```
for x, y ∈ V do
    d(x, y) := if ⟨x, y⟩ ∈ E then ω(x, y) else ∞
done;
for z ∈ V do
    for x, y ∈ V do
        d(x, y) := min(d(x, y), d(x, z) + d(z, y))
    done
done.
```

The graph has no cycle with strictly negative weight if and only if $\forall x \in V$. $\mathsf{d}(x, x) \geqslant 0$, *in which case* $\mathsf{d}(x, y)$ *is the length of the shortest path from* x *to* y.

Proof (of Algorithm 13) Instead of calculating the next iterate $\widehat{\mathscr{P}}^{k+1}_\delta$ as a function of the previous one $\widehat{\mathscr{P}}^k_\delta$ (à la Jacobi), we reuse the latest assigned values (à la Gauss-Seidel), as authorized by chaotic iterations [4]. $\qquad \square$

15   Conclusion

We have presented a use of abstract interpretation which, instead of focusing on program semantics, focuses on algorithmics. It has been observed that graph algorithms have the same algebraic structure [3,9,11,14]. Abstract interpretation explains why.

Graph path algorithms are based on the same algebraic structure (e.g. [9, Ch. 2], [3, Table 3.1]) because they are abstractions of path finding algorithms which primitive structure $\langle \wp(V^{>1}), E, \cup, \circledcirc \rangle$ is preserved by the abstraction.

Some algorithms (*e.g.* based on (Th.6.a–b)) exactly abstract elementary paths and cycles and can therefore be designed systematically by exact fixpoint abstraction [6, theorem 7.1.0.4(3)] of the path finding fixpoint definitions. Other algorithms (such as the Roy-Floyd-Warshall or Dantzig [8] shortest path algorithms) consider fixpoint definitions of sets of paths over approximating the set of all elementary paths and cycles. We have seen for the Roy-Floyd-Warshall algorithm that the derivation of the algorithm is more complex and requires a different abstraction at each iterations (Th. 1 generalizing [6, theorem 7.1.0.4(3)]) based on a particular choice of different edges or vertices at each iteration plus chaotic iterations [4]. So from the observation of similarities, their algebraic formulation, we move to an explanation of its origin and its exploitation for the machine-checkable calculational design of algorithms.

Acknowledgement. I thank Antoine Miné and Jan Midtgaard for debugging a first version of this paper. I thank the anonymous referee to whom I borrowed the content section **1.2**.

This work was supported in part by NSF Grant CCF-1617717. Any opinions, findings, and conclusions or recommendations expressed in this material are those of the author and do not necessarily reflect the views of the National Science Foundation.

References

1. Bang-Jensen, J., Gutin, G.: Digraphs: Theory, Algorithms and Applications. Springer (2000)
2. Berge, C.: Théorie des graphes et ses applications. Dunod (1958)
3. Carré, B.: Graphs and Networks. Clarendon Press, Oxford (1979)
4. Cousot, P.: Asynchronous iterative methods for solving a fixed point system of monotone equations in a complete lattice. R.R. 88, Laboratoire IMAG, Université scientifique et médicale de Grenoble, Grenoble, France (Sep 1977), 15 p.
5. Cousot, P.: On fixpoint/iteration/variant induction principles for proving total correctness of programs with denotational semantics. In: LOPSTR 2019. Lecture Notes in Computer Science, vol. 12042, pp. 3–18. Springer (2019)
6. Cousot, P., Cousot, R.: Systematic design of program analysis frameworks. In: POPL. pp. 269–282. ACM Press (1979)
7. Cousot, P., Cousot, R.: Basic concepts of abstract interpretation. In: Jacquard, R. (ed.) Building the Information Society, pp. 359–366. Springer (2004)
8. Dantzig, G.B.: On the shortest route through a network. Manage. Sci. 6(2), pp. 187–190 (Jan 1960)
9. Derniame, J.C., Pair, C.: Problèmes de cheminement dans les graphes. Dunod (1971)
10. Floyd, R.W.: Algorithm 97: Shortest path. Commun. ACM 5(6), 345 (1962)
11. Gondran, M.: Algèbre linéaire et cheminement dans un graphe. Revue française d'automatique, informatique, recherche opérationnelle (R.A.I.R.O.) Recherche opérationnelle, tome 9 (V1), pp. 77–99 (1975)
12. Hansen, P., de Werra, D.: Connectivity, transitivity and chromaticity: The pioneering work of Bernard Roy in graph theory. In: Aiding Decisions with Multiple Criteria: Essays in Honor of Bernard Roy. pp. 23–44. Springer (2002)

13. Naur, P.: Proof versus formalization. BIT Numerical Mathematics 34(1), pp. 148–164 (1994)
14. Pair, C.: Sur des algorithmes pour les problèmes de cheminement dans les graphes finis, pp. 271–300. Dunod Paris, Gordon and Breach, New York (Jul 1966)
15. Pair, C.: Mille et un algorithmes pour les problèmes de cheminement dans les graphes. Revue Française d'Informatique et de Recherche opérationnelle (R.I.R.O.) B-3, pp. 125–143 (1970)
16. Roy, B.: Transitivité et connexité. C. R. Acad. Sci. Paris **249**, pp. 216–218 (1959)
17. Roy, B.: Cheminement et connexité dans les graphes, application aux problèmes d'ordonnancement. Metra, Paris, 2 edn. (1965)
18. Schrijver, A.: Combinatorial Optimization, Polyhedra and Efficiency, Algorithms and Combinatorics, vol. 24. Springer (2003)
19. Sergey, I., Midtgaard, J., Clarke, D.: Calculating graph algorithms for dominance and shortest path. In: MPC. Lecture Notes in Computer Science, vol. 7342, pp. 132–156. Springer (2012)
20. Venet, A.J.: Automatic analysis of pointer aliasing for untyped programs. Sci. Comput. Program. **35**(2), pp. 223–248 (1999)
21. Warshall, S.: A theorem on Boolean matrices. J. ACM **9**(1), pp. 11–12 (1962)

Applications of Muli: Solving Practical Problems with Constraint-Logic Object-Oriented Programming

Jan C. Dageförde(iD) and Herbert Kuchen$^{(\boxtimes)}$(iD)

ERCIS, Leonardo-Campus 3, 48149 Münster, Germany
{dagefoerde,kuchen}@uni-muenster.de

Abstract. The Münster Logic-Imperative Language (Muli) is a constraint-logic object-oriented programming language, suited for the development of applications that interleave constraint-logic search with deterministic, imperative execution. For instance, Muli can generate graph structures of neural networks using non-deterministic search, interleaved with immediate evaluation of each generated network regarding its fitness. Furthermore, it can be used for finding solutions to planning problems. In this paper, we explain and demonstrate how these application problems are solved using Muli.

Keywords: constraint-logic object-oriented programming · artificial neural networks · planning problems · applications

1 Motivation

Constraint-logic object-oriented programming augments object-oriented programming with concepts and features from constraint-logic programming [5]. As a result, logic variables, constraints, and non-deterministic application execution become available in an object-oriented context, facilitating the search for solutions to constraint-logic problems from an object-oriented application in an integrated way.

The **Mu**enster **L**ogic-**I**mperative language (Muli) is such a constraint-logic object-oriented language. Earlier publications on Muli focused on developing the language and its runtime environment, using artificial examples and constraint-logic puzzles for the purpose of demonstration and evaluation. With the current work, we demonstrate that Muli can be used for solving practical problems as well. We present and discuss the following application scenarios:

- The generation of graph structures for simple feed-forward neural networks designed to solve the pole balancing problem (see Sect. 3).
- Solving vehicle routing problems with dynamic constraint systems (see Sect. 4).

To start off, Sect. 2 introduces concepts of constraint-logic object-oriented programming with Muli. Concluding the paper, Sect. 5 presents related work, followed by final remarks in Sect. 6.

© Springer Nature Switzerland AG 2023
P. Lopez-Garcia et al. (Eds.): Hermenegildo Festschrift 2022, LNCS 13160, pp. 97–112, 2023.
https://doi.org/10.1007/978-3-031-31476-6_5

2   Constraint-Logic Object-Oriented Programming

As a rather novel paradigm, constraint-logic object-oriented programming languages feature the benefits of object-oriented programming while offering logic variables, constraints, and search, as known from constraint-logic programming. In this paper we use Muli, a constraint-logic object-oriented programming language based on Java [5].

Muli uses the **free** keyword to declare variables as *logic variables*. For example,

int operation **free**;

declares a logic variable with an integer type. Instead of assigning a constant value to operation, the logic (or free) variable will be treated symbolically, unless it is sufficiently constrained such that it can be safely substituted by a constant. Logic variables can be used interchangeably with other variables of the same type, so that they can be used in the formulation of arithmetic expressions or conditions [4]. Furthermore, they can be passed to methods as parameters.

Logic variables are used as part of *constraints*. For simplicity, Muli does not provide a dedicated language feature for imposing constraints. Instead, a constraint is derived from relational expressions, whenever their evaluation results in branching execution flows. As an abstract example, consider the following condition that involves the logic variable operation:

if (operation == 0) { s_1 } **else** { s_2 }.

Since operation is not sufficiently constrained, the condition can be evaluated to **true** as well as to **false** (but not both at the same time). Consequently, evaluating the condition causes the runtime environment to make a non-deterministic *choice*. From that point on, the runtime environment evaluates the available alternatives non-deterministically. When an alternative is selected, the runtime environment imposes the corresponding constraint. In the example above, when the runtime environment selects s_1 for further evaluation it imposes operation == 0, ensuring that later evaluations cannot violate the assumption that is made regarding the value of operation.

Search problems are specified in Muli by non-deterministic methods. In the sequel, we will call such methods *search regions*. Consider a problem that looks for integers e that can be expressed in two different ways as the sum of two positive integer cubes, including the smallest such number, which is the Hardy-Ramanujan number 1729. In fact, with our default search strategy the solution 1729 will be found first. The corresponding constraint is:

$$e = a^3 + b^3 = c^3 + d^3$$
$$\wedge\, a \neq c \wedge a \neq d$$
$$\wedge\, a, b, c, d, e \in \mathcal{N} - \{0\}$$

A Muli search region that calculates e using this constraint is implemented by the method **solve**() as depicted in Listing 1, assuming that there is a method $\text{cube}(n) = n^3$ and another method $\text{positiveDomain}(x_1, \ldots, x_n)$ that imposes the constraint $x_i \in \mathcal{N} - \{0\} \,\forall 1 \leq i \leq n$.

```
class Taxicab {
  int solve() {
    int a free, b free, c free, d free, e free;
    positiveDomain(a, b, c, d, e);
    if (a != c && a != d &&
        cube(a) + cube(b) == e &&
        cube(c) + cube(d) == e) {
      return e; }
    else throw Muli.fail(); } }
```

Listing 1. Muli search region that calculates numbers which can be expressed in two different ways as sums of cubes, including the Hardy-Ramanujan number.

The runtime environment realizes *search* transparently: It takes non-deterministic decisions at choices. Once a solution has been found, the runtime environment backtracks until the most recent choice is found that offers an alternative decision. Afterwards, it takes that alternative decision and continues execution accordingly. In the backend, the runtime environment leverages a *constraint solver* for finding appropriate values for logic variables that satisfy all imposed constraints. Furthermore, when a branch of a choice is selected, the solver checks whether the current constraint system has become inconsistent in order to cut off infeasible execution branches early. Found solutions are collected by the runtime environment and made available to the invoking application. Conceptually, following a sequence of decisions at choices, in combination with backtracking to take different decisions, produces a search tree that represents execution paths. In such a search tree, inner nodes are the choices whereas the leaves represent ends of alternative execution paths [7]. Execution paths in Muli end with a *solution*, e.g., a return value, or with a *failure*, e.g., if an execution path's constraint system is inconsistent. Moreover, applications sometimes require an *explicit failure* denoting the end of an execution path without a solution. An explicit failure is expressed by **throw** Muli.**fail**(), which is specifically interpreted by the runtime environment to end search and backtrack to the next alternative.

In Muli, execution of the main program is deterministic. In contrast, all non-deterministic search is *encapsulated*, thus giving application developers control over search. Muli.**muli**() accepts a search region, i.e. either a lambda expression or a reference to a method, and returns a stream of Solution objects. The search region that is passed to Muli.**muli**() is the method that will be executed non-deterministically. For instance, search for the Hardy-Ramanujan number from the example in Listing 1 is started with

```
Stream<Solution> solutions = Muli.muli(Taxicab::solve);,
```

thus offering a stream of solutions that can be consumed from the solutions variable. Muli uses the Java Stream API in order to evaluate solutions non-strictly, thus allowing applications to assess a returned solution individually before continuing search to obtain additional solutions [6]. This is made possible with the help of an adaptation of the trail structure of the Warren Abstract Machine (WAM) [27]. In contrast to the WAM trail, the Muli trail records changes to all elements of the execution state in order to be able to revert them. Furthermore, Muli features an inverse trail (or forward trail) that is leveraged when search at a specific point is resumed, i.e., when the consumer of the stream queries another element.

3   Generation of Graph Structures for Neural Networks

A current research trend in artificial neural networks (ANN) is that not only the weights of the inputs of each neuron are corrected via back-propagation, but also the structure of the network is adapted [18]. Thus, the goal is to find the smallest ANN producing an acceptable output quality. An application implemented in Muli can generate structures of directed acyclic graphs that define an ANN. In this section, we implement the application NNGenerator that demonstrates how the non-deterministic evaluation of Muli search regions can be used to systematically generate a set of feed-forward ANNs. Each generated ANN is then trained against a specific problem; in our case balancing a single pole on a moving cart as illustrated in Fig. 1 [2]. Every time that a network is generated, NNGenerator assesses the network's fitness in order to decide whether its output quality is acceptable, and continues the search for better ANN graph structures otherwise.

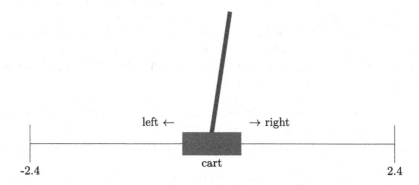

Fig. 1. The pole balancing problem as simulated by the CartPole-v1 implementation from OpenAI.

For the generated ANNs we use Python, because PyTorch [19] is a powerful Python-based library for the implementation of ANNs and because the OpenAI Gym collection of reinforcement learning tasks [17] provides a simulation environment for the pole balancing problem, namely *CartPole-v1*, implemented in Python. Moreover, this provides us with the opportunity to demonstrate that Muli applications can integrate applications written in other programming languages as well.

The *CartPole-v1* simulation provides a so-called environment that our application will interact with. As long as the pole is in balance, the environment accepts one of two actions, *left* and *right* (as illustrated in Fig. 1), that move the pole-balancing *cart* into a specific direction. As a result of an action, the environment updates its state and returns four observations:

- The position of the cart $\in [-2.4,\ 2.4]$,
- the velocity of the cart $\in [-\infty,\ \infty]$,
- the angle of the pole, and $\in [-41.8\,°,\ 41.8\,°]$, and
- the velocity of the tip of the pole $\in [-\infty,\ \infty]$.

These observations can be used to make a decision about a subsequent action. We generate feed-forward neural networks with reinforcement learning. Of these networks, two parameters are fixed: The input layer contains four nodes, one per observation, whereas the output layer contains two nodes, namely the probability of selecting the *left* action and that of selecting the *right* action, accordingly. The next step is decided by comparing the output nodes and choosing the action with the highest probability. The step is then passed to the environment. The structure of the hidden layer(s) is not fixed and will be generated by NNGenerator. The general structure of the intended ANNs is illustrated in Fig. 2a, and a concrete instance is exemplarily given in Fig. 2b.

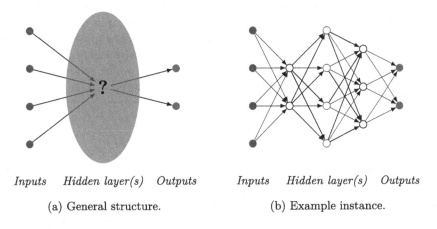

Inputs   Hidden layer(s)   Outputs   Inputs   Hidden layer(s)   Outputs

(a) General structure.   (b) Example instance.

Fig. 2. Feed-forward neural networks for solving the pole balancing problem.

We first describe the Muli application NNGenerator that generates graph structures for the hidden layers of ANNs, followed by a subsection with details on the neural network implementation using PyTorch. Afterwards, we experiment with NNGenerator and present the results.

3.1   Generating Neural Network Graph Structures from a Muli Application

The goal of the NNGenerator Muli application is to search for directed acyclic graphs that will constitute the hidden layers of the final neural networks, with the aim of producing the simplest graph structure. The simplest network has no hidden layer; i.e., all input nodes are directly connected to all output nodes. Starting from the simplest network, two operations that modify the graph are possible:

1. AddLayer Add a hidden layer (with one node as a starting point), or
2. AddNode   add a node to one of the existing hidden layers.

We can implement NNGenerator as a Muli search region that enumerates graphs by non-deterministically choosing one of these operations and, for the AddNode operation, by non-deterministically selecting one of the existing layers. As an implementation detail we add a third operation, Return, that returns the current graph structure as a solution. The other two operations recursively invoke the generation method in order to select the next operation. Listing 2 shows the recursive implementation of the generation method and exhibits the use of the free variable **int** operation **free** in conditions, thus implementing the non-deterministic choice for one of the three operations, as well as **int** toLayer **free** for selecting a layer in the AddNode case.

As the search region of Listing 2 does not have a termination criterion, an infinite number of solutions is found (i.e., infinitely many graphs with all numbers and sizes of layers). Returning all of them in a fixed array is impossible. However, Muli offers an encapsulated search operator that delivers solutions lazily and returns immediately after a solution has been found, while maintaining state such that search can be resumed for additional solutions on demand [6]. For our application, the operator is invoked as

```
Stream<Solution<Network>> solutions =
    Muli.muli(NNGenerator::generateNetwork);
```

As a result, individual solutions can be obtained from the solutions stream.

Another caveat of the application is the selected search strategy. Even though the Muli runtime environment takes non-deterministic decisions at choices, the decisions are not random. Instead, it will systematically traverse the choices of the search region. With a depth-first search strategy, this means that the generated graphs are probably bad solutions: First, a graph with no hidden layers; second, a graph with one hidden layer with a single node; third, a graph with two hidden layers and one node each, and so on. Under a depth-first search assumption and with the presented search region, there would never be layers with more than one node except for the input and output layers. Rewriting the search region does not help either, as that would only generate graphs with a single layer and an ever-increasing number of nodes on that layer. As a remedy, Muli offers the well-known iterative deepening depth-first search (IDDFS) strategy [7] ensuring that every number of layers and every size of each layer can

```
Network generateNetwork() {
  return generateNetwork( new Network(4, 2) ); }

Network generateNetwork(Network network) {
  int operation free;
  switch (operation) {
    case 0: // Return current network.
      return network;
    case 1: // Add layer.
      network.addLayer();
      return generateNetwork(network);
    default: // Add node. But where?
      if (network.numberOfLayers > 0) {
        int toLayer free;
        for (int layer = 0; layer < network.numberOfLayers;
                            layer++) {
          if (layer == toLayer) {
            network.addNode(layer);
            return generateNetwork(network);
          } else {
            // Add at a different layer!
          } }
        throw Muli.fail();
      } else {
        throw Muli.fail(); } } }
```

Listing 2. Muli search region that systematically generates graph structures by non-deterministic selection of operations.

eventually be considered. In order to use IDDFS we have to slightly modify the encapsulated search operator call:

```
Stream<Solution<Network>> solutions =
      Muli.muli(NNGenerator::generateNetwork,
              SearchStrategy.IterativeDeepening);
```

Listing 3 shows how the solution stream is used. The forEach consumer demands and obtains individual solutions from the stream. n.toPyCode() creates Python code that implements an ANN according to the generated graph (for details on what the code looks like see Sect. 3.2), and the helper method writeAndRun() writes the generated code into a .py script. Afterwards, the script is run via Runtime.getRuntime().exec(). We assume that the generated Python application prints the network's fitness after training and use to standard output, so that output is captured and stored in the fitness variable. In Listing 3 we consider a solution "good enough" (thus ending search) if its cumulative fitness value is greater than 400.

```
solutions.forEach(solution -> {
  Network n = solution.value;
    // Execute python script.
    String fitness = NNGenerator.writeAndRun(n.toPyCode());
    // Quit if a working neural network is found.
    if (Float.parseFloat(fitness) > 400) {
      System.out.println(n.toString());
      System.exit(0); } });
```

Listing 3. Processing the solution stream in Muli.

3.2 Using Generated Neural Networks to Solve the Pole Balancing Problem

In our feed-forward ANNs we assume that all layers are linear ones. In addition to that, between every layer we use dropout [24] to randomly cancel the effect of some nodes with a probability of 0.6, in combination with a rectified linear unit activation function ensuring that values are positive [10]. Finally, the output layer values are rescaled using the softmax activation function, ensuring that each output is in the range [0, 1] and that the sum of the two outputs is 1. Initially, the edge weights assume the default values provided by PyTorch for nn.Linear layers. Afterwards, the network is trained in order to learn weights such that the network can balance the pole for as long as possible. To that end, we use the Adam optimizer [11] with a learning rate of 0.01 and train the network using a monte-carlo policy gradient method for 500 episodes, each for a maximum of 500 steps. We process an entire episode and learn new weights based on the rewards obtained in throughout that episode, before continuing with the next episode.

The toPyCode() method of NNGenerator will generate Python code that implements ANNs according to the above specification of the network and to the structure that was generated. In the end, we do not want to generate full implementations of ANNs for every found graph. After all, major parts of the resulting programs are static and could therefore be implemented once and then be used as a library by all generated networks. We implement a Python class ENN that implements the ANN itself using PyTorch, and we provide two methods train() and use() that each accept an instance of ENN in order to work with it. The Muli application NNGenerator can generate small Python programs that import ENN, train(), and use(). The generated programs then instantiate the ENN class according to the parameters found by Muli and use the provided methods. Listing 4 provides an example of the code that is generated from the NNGenerator application, demonstrating that implementation details of the ANN are abstracted away into the library. Subsequently, we provide more details about the class and the methods.

In its constructor, the ENN class accepts three parameters: The number of input nodes, an ordered list containing the numbers of nodes on the inner layers,

```
net = ENN(ins = 4, hidden = [100, 50], out = 2)
train(net)
fitness = use(net)
print(fitness)
```

Listing 4. Structure of the Python program as generated by the NNGenerator Muli application. Note that the constructor parameters of ENN are shown exemplarily; they need to be substituted according to a specific configuration.

and the number of output nodes. For instance, the network illustrated in Fig. 2b is instantiated by invoking ENN(ins = 4, hidden = [2, 4, 3], outs = 2). Since the number of inner layers and the number of nodes on each layer is expressed as an array, ENN is able to construct an ANN with arbitrary hidden layers, allowing NNGenerator to specify the hidden layer. Listing 5 demonstrates how the constructor parameters, and the list of hidden layers in particular, are used to represent the network. In Listing 5, the forward() method specifies the sequential model, inserting the additional layers as described above.

```
class ENNPolicy(nn.Module):
  def __init__(self, ins, hidden, outs):
    # < some initialization omitted >
    lastnodes = ins
    for nodes in hidden:
      newlayer = nn.Linear(lastnodes, nodes, bias=False)
      self.layers.append(newlayer)
      lastnodes = nodes
    # Final layer:
    newlayer = nn.Linear(lastnodes, outs, bias=False)
    self.layers.append(newlayer)
    self.layerout = newlayer
  def forward(self, x):
    args = []
    for layer in self.layers[:-1]:
      args.append(layer)
      args.append(nn.Dropout(p=0.6))
      args.append(nn.ReLU())
    args.append(self.layers[-1])
    args.append(nn.Softmax(dim=-1))
    model = torch.nn.Sequential(*args)
    return model(x)
```

Listing 5. Python class ENN that creates hidden layers dynamically from the constructor parameters.

The `train()` method accepts the ENN instance and creates an Open AI Gym environment using the CartPole implementation. It then starts a training loop with 500 episodes. At the beginning of every episode, the environment is reset to an initial state. An episode ends either when the pole is out of balance, or when the maximum of 500 steps is reached. As soon as an episode ends, the network weights are learned according to the description above, thus preparing the network for the next episode.

The trained network is passed to the `use()` method that creates a new OpenAI Gym environment and performs a single simulation of the pole balancing problem, up to a maximum of 500 steps. In order to allow NNGenerator to judge the quality of a final, i.e., generated and trained, network, we define a fitness function based on the position of the cart that is applied after every step and summed over all steps that the pole is in balance:

$$f(position) = -0.1736 * position^2 + 1$$

$f(position)$ is 1 when the cart is at the centre and decreases to 0 when the cart is nearing one of the edges at -2.4 or 2.4. As a consequence, solutions that keep the pole near the centre, with just minor movement, are favoured. A perfect solution would keep the pole balanced for all 500 steps and $\sum_{i=1}^{500} f(position_i)$ is approximately 500. We augment the `use()` method to record the fitness values throughout all steps and to return the cumulative fitness value. The last two lines of Listing 4 demonstrate how the sum is printed to the standard output, so that it can be read and judged by NNGenerator.

3.3   Experiments

Table 1. Graph structures generated before the smallest neural network that solves the problem is found. For each network, the time spent on its generation (in milliseconds) and training (in seconds) are indicated as well as its fitness.

Nodes on first layer	Generation time [ms]	Training time [s]	Fitness	Solved
1	115.712	6.898	14.987	no
2	14.832	8.402	9.992	no
3	2.446	8.117	76.888	no
4	2.350	10.662	14.987	no
5	2.426	15.710	125.005	no
6	1.930	18.086	75.889	no
7	1.991	18.825	125.491	no
8	2.488	38.483	52.977	no
9	2.351	17.703	371.425	no
10	2.240	50.963	499.623	**yes**

We conducted two experiments with NNGenerator in order to evaluate Muli's ability to generate directed acyclic graphs. In the first experiment we were interested in the smallest ANN that is able to solve the pole balancing problem, i.e., whose cumulative fitness is greater than 400. The IDDFS search strategy ensures that the smallest ANN is found first. Incidentally, the structures that were generated until finding an adequate ANN all only have a single hidden layer. The smallest network capable of solving the problem has just ten nodes on a single hidden layer (Table 1). The generation of the first network takes longer than that of the other, larger ones. This can be attributed to the just-in-time compilation of the JVM that increases the speed of generating subsequent solutions. Moreover, it was also the first network to be generated at all, so that the generation time includes some initialization effort for the virtual machine and the search region. In contrast, subsequent graphs are created by local backtracking and/or by applying minor modification operations, so generating those is quicker.

Table 2. Times spent on generating (in milliseconds) and training (in seconds) the first 15 generated large neural networks that were able to solve the problem.

Hidden layers	Generation time [ms]	Training time [s]	Fitness
[400]	155.547	80.583	499.952
[350, 50]	0.044	35.114	499.390
[300]	0.060	94.019	499.653
[300, 100]	2.224	47.930	499.899
[250]	0.040	77.497	499.704
[250, 150]	1.474	126.405	499.569
[250, 50]	0.031	52.727	499.508
[200, 150]	0.042	98.520	499.298
[200, 100]	0.027	112.001	498.324
[200, 50, 100]	0.036	115.636	483.321
[150]	0.025	76.728	499.223
[150, 200]	0.025	73.006	498.517
[150, 150, 50]	0.028	80.517	498.564
[150, 50]	0.028	87.862	499.916
[100, 100, 50, 100]	0.036	101.163	499.540

In the second experiment we are interested in the ability to generate larger hidden layers. To that end, we multiply the number of nodes added in the AddNode step by 50. Moreover, we switch the order in which IDDFS takes decisions, thus favouring larger networks over smaller ones first. The first generated ANN is already able to solve the pole balancing problem. Therefore, execution could already be stopped after that according to the termination criterion in Listing 3. However, we are curious about additional solutions, so we remove that criterion. Table 2 exemplarily shows the first 15 generated networks that were able to solve the problem, i.e., whose cumulative fitness is greater than 400 each. In fact, all these networks exhibit a value of over 483, and most of them are able to reach a cumulative fitness greater than 499. Not shown in Table 2 are networks that are unable to solve the pole balancing problem. As an additional finding, both experiments indicate that the generation of graph structures with NNGenerator is faster than training the ANNs afterwards. This is expected since the structural modifications between two graph structures are minor, whereas each generated ANN has to be trained from scratch.

4   Solving a Dynamic Scheduling Problem with Constraint-Logic Object-Oriented Programming

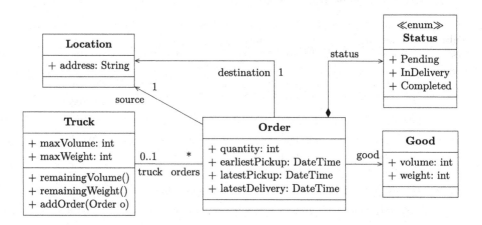

Fig. 3. Class structure that models our logistics planning problem.

Another application which can benefit from interleaved deterministic object-oriented computation and non-deterministic search can be found in logistics. Imagine a logistics company which runs a large number of trucks carrying goods from various sources to destinations. New orders arrive on the fly while trucks are running. Each order has a quantity of a certain good (that has a specific size and weight), a source location, a destination, an earliest and latest pick-up time, a latest delivery time, and so on. Moreover, the trucks have a maximum capacity w.r.t. volume and weight of goods that are transported at the same time. Consequently, the current set of orders imposes a set of constraints. The current schedule is based on a solution that satisfies these constraints and, optionally, on an optimal solution that maximizes the revenues of the accepted orders.

   The described problem is transferred into a class structure as illustrated in Fig. 3. Dispatching new orders to trucks results in additional constraints regarding size and weight, ensuring that trucks are not over capacity after scheduling. For an array of trucks, the constraints can be formulated with Muli using

```
boolean dispatch(Truck[] trucks, Order[] newOrders) {
  for (Order o : newOrders) {
    int selection free;
    domain(truck, 0, trucks.length-1);
    int orderWeight = o.quantity * o.good.weight;
    int orderVolume = o.quantity * o.good.volume;
    for (int truck = 0; truck < trucks.length; truck++) {
      if (truck == selection) {
        if (orderWeight <= trucks[truck].remainingWeight() &&
            orderVolume <= trucks[truck].remainingVolume()) {
          trucks[truck].addOrder(o);
        } else {
          throw Muli.fail(); } } } }
    // All orders dispatched; good to go.
    return true;
}
```

Listing 6. Muli code snippet to dispatch orders to trucks with non-deterministic search, modelling weight and volume constraints.

the code presented in Listing 6. Capacity violations result in an explicit failure, whereas a successful dispatch of all goods will result in the return value **true** and Truck-Order relationships are set via addOrder() accordingly. Constraints w.r.t. location and pickup/delivery timing are formulated analogously. The method domain(a, min, max) imposes constraints over a such that $min \leq a \leq max$.

The solution can be found by non-deterministic search and constraint solving, e.g., using the Muli.**muli**() encapsulated search operator. However, the encapsulated search does not only deliver a solution. It also delivers a representation of the search space for potential later use. After the solution has been found, deterministic computations are required for instance for keeping track of the current positions of the trucks and for communicating the determined schedule with truck drivers.

As soon as new orders arrive, a new solution of the now extended scheduling problem has to be found. As a consequence, this is a dynamic problem in which the entire set of constraints is not known prior to the start of an application. Instead, the set of constraints develops over time. Now, the additional constraints caused by the new order can be added to the saved representation of the search space and a new encapsulated search can be started producing a new solution (and a new representation of the search space). The possibility to continue search based on the previous solution facilitates faster search, as opposed to solving the constraint problem from scratch.

5   Related Work

There are several approaches that extend object-oriented (OO) programming or imperative programming with concepts from constraint-logic programming, see e.g. [8,14,21,25]. The integration of the two paradigms that these approaches achieve is not as smooth as the integration provided by Muli. Typically, these approaches show a clear syntactic and semantic separation of the imperative and object-oriented part. Moreover, none of these approaches provides encapsulated search.

An alternative to using Muli is to just call a constraint solver from an OO language, such as JaCoP or Choco from Java [12,20]. However, this also does not lead to a seamless integration of both paradigms. In particular, alternating deterministic OO computations and non-deterministic search are more cumbersome.

There are also approaches adding object-orientation to (constraint) logic languages [15,16,22,23,26]. However here, the object orientation is just syntactic sugar and constraint-logic features are used to simulate the object orientation. This typically causes some performance penalty compared to pure OO languages. Also, these languages keep the declarative flavour and do not provide assignments. Thus, they will hardly be considered by object-oriented programmers, whereas Muli is very close to Java and hence easier to use for developers who are used to object-oriented languages.

The general idea of Muli's encapsulated search was taken from the functional-logic programming language Curry [1,3,9,13]. However, in contrast to Curry, our encapsulated search can deal with side-effects, which causes the implementation to be quite different.

6   Conclusion and Outlook

With the present work we use the Muli programming language for the development of applications that solve practical search problems. As the first example, the NNGenerator application leverages non-deterministic execution for the systematic generation of directed acyclic graphs that are used to describe the structure of PyTorch-based ANNs. The networks generated by NNGenerator solve the pole balancing problem; this problem can be substituted for different ones as the ANNs are problem-agnostic. Moreover, NNGenerator runs and evaluates each generated network, judging whether one of them is good enough or whether to proceed search in order to find additional networks. As the second example, we discuss how to apply Muli to a scheduling problem from logistics, demonstrating how to model constraints in an constraint-logic object-oriented way.

The presented applications demonstrate the practical applicability of Muli. Compiler and runtime environment are publicly available as open source software on GitHub,[1] inviting others to use Muli in research or for their practical

---

[1] https://github.com/wwu-pi/muli.

applications. Future work will use Muli for further planning problems, refining the language and the runtime environment in the process.

References

1. Antoy, S., Jost, A.: A new functional-logic compiler for curry: sprite. In: LOPSTR 2016 (2016). https://doi.org/10.1007/978-3-319-63139-4_6
2. Barto, A.G., Sutton, R.S., Anderson, C.W.: Neuronlike adaptive elements that can solve difficult learning control problems. IEEE Trans. Syst. Man Cybern. **13**(5), 834–846 (1983). https://doi.org/10.1109/TSMC.1983.6313077
3. Kuchen, H. (ed.): LNCS, vol. 6816. Springer, Heidelberg (2011). https://doi.org/10.1007/978-3-642-22531-4
4. Dageförde, J.C., Kuchen, H.: An operational semantics for constraint-logic imperative programming. In: Seipel, D., Hanus, M., Abreu, S. (eds.) WFLP/WLP/INAP -2017. LNCS (LNAI), vol. 10997, pp. 64–80. Springer, Cham (2018). https://doi.org/10.1007/978-3-030-00801-7_5
5. Dageförde, J.C., Kuchen, H.: A compiler and virtual machine for constraint-logic object-oriented programming with Muli. J. Comput. Lang. **53**, 63–78 (2019). https://doi.org/10.1016/j.cola.2019.05.001
6. Dageförde, J.C., Kuchen, H.: Retrieval of individual solutions from encapsulated search with a potentially infinite search space. In: Proceedings of the 34th ACM/SIGAPP Symposium on Applied Computing, pp. 1552–1561. Limassol, Cyprus (2019). https://doi.org/10.1145/3297280.3298912
7. Dageförde, J.C., Teegen, F.: Structured traversal of search trees in constraint-logic object-oriented programming. In: Hofstedt, P., Abreu, S., John, U., Kuchen, H., Seipel, D. (eds.) INAP/WLP/WFLP -2019. LNCS (LNAI), vol. 12057, pp. 199–214. Springer, Cham (2020). https://doi.org/10.1007/978-3-030-46714-2_13
8. Doyle, J., Meudec, C.: IBIS: an interactive bytecode inspection system, using symbolic execution and constraint logic programming. In: 2nd PPPJ, pp. 55–58 (2003). https://doi.org/10.1145/957289.957307
9. Hanus, M., Kuchen, H., Moreno-Navarro, J.J.: Curry: a truly functional logic language. In: Workshop on Visions for the Future of Logic Programming (ILPS 1995), pp. 95–107 (1995)
10. Hara, K., Saito, D., Shouno, H.: Analysis of function of rectified linear unit used in deep learning. In: 2015 International Joint Conference on Neural Networks, pp. 1–8 (2015). https://doi.org/10.1109/IJCNN.2015.7280578
11. Kingma, D.P., Ba, J.L.: Adam: a method for stochastic optimization. In: 3rd International Conference on Learning Representations, ICLR 2015 - Conference Track Proceedings, pp. 1–15 (2015). https://arxiv.org/abs/1412.6980
12. Kuchcinski, K.: Constraints-driven scheduling and resource assignment. ACM Trans. Des. Autom. Electron. Syst. **8**(3), 355–383 (2003). https://doi.org/10.1145/785411.785416
13. Lux, W., Kuchen, H.: An efficient abstract machine for curry. In: Beiersdörfer, K., Engels, G., Schäfer, W. (eds.) Informatik 1999. Informatik aktuell, pp. 390–399. Springer, Heidelberg (1999). https://doi.org/10.1007/978-3-662-01069-3_58
14. Majchrzak, T.A., Kuchen, H.: Logic Java: combining object-oriented and logic programming. In: WFLP, pp. 122–137 (2011). https://doi.org/10.1007/978-3-642-22531-4_8

15. McCabe, F.G.: Logic and Objects. Prentice-Hall International Series in Computer Science, Prentice Hall (1992)
16. Moss, C.: Prolog++ - the power of object-oriented and logic programming. International Series in Logic Programming, Addison-Wesley (1994)
17. OpenAI: CartPole-v1 (2020). https://gym.openai.com/envs/CartPole-v1/
18. Palnitkar, R.M., Cannady, J.: A review of adaptive neural networks. In: IEEE SoutheastCon 2004. Proceedings, pp. 38–47 (2004). https://doi.org/10.1109/SECON.2004.1287896
19. Paszke, A., et al.: PyTorch: an imperative style, high-performance deep learning library. In: Wallach, H., Larochelle, H., Beygelzimer, A., Alché-Buc, F., Fox, E., Garnett, R. (eds.) Advances in Neural Information Processing Systems, vol. 32, pp. 8024–8035. Curran Associates, Inc. (2019)
20. Prud'homme, C., Fages, J.G., Lorca, X.: Choco documentation. TASC - LS2N CNRS UMR 6241, COSLING S.A.S. (2017). https://www.choco-solver.org
21. Renshaw, D.: Seer: symbolic execution engine for rust (2018). https://github.com/dwrensha/seer
22. Scott, R.: A Guide to Artificial Intelligence with Visual Prolog. Outskirts Press, Parker, Colorado (2010)
23. Shapiro, E., Takeuchi, A.: Object oriented programming in concurrent prolog. New Gener. Comput. **1**(1), 25–48 (1983). https://doi.org/10.1007/BF03037020
24. Srivastava, N., Hinton, G.E., Krizhevsky, A., Sutskever, I., Salakhutdinov, R.: Dropout: a simple way to prevent neural networks from overfitting. J. Mach. Learn. Res. **15**, 1929–1958 (2014)
25. Beckert, B., Hähnle, R. (eds.): LNCS, vol. 4966. Springer, Heidelberg (2008). https://doi.org/10.1007/978-3-540-79124-9
26. Van Roy, P., Brand, P., Duchier, D., Haridi, S., Schulte, C., Henz, M.: Logic programming in the context of multiparadigm programming: the Oz experience. Theory Pract. Log. Program. **3**(6), 717–763 (2003). https://doi.org/10.1017/S1471068403001741
27. Warren, D.H.D.: An abstract prolog instruction set. Tech. rep., SRI International, Menlo Park (1983)

Grammar Induction for Under-Resourced Languages: The Case of Ch'ol

Veronica Dahl[1], Gemma Bel-Enguix[2(✉)], Velina Tirado[2], and Emilio Miralles[1]

[1] Simon Fraser University, Burnaby, Canada
{veronica_dahl,emilio_miralles}@sfu.ca
[2] Universidad Nacional Autónoma de México, Mexico City, Mexico
gbele@iingen.unam.mx, velina.tiradoz@enallt.unam.mx

Abstract. We apply to the under-resourced language Ch'ol the Womb Grammar Model of grammar induction (WGM), thus called because given appropriate input it can generate grammars for different languages, much as human wombs can generate different races. The WGM is inferential, works for more than just specific tasks and needs neither a pre-specified model family, nor parallel corpora, nor any of the typical models of machine learning. It generates an understudied language's grammar using representative and correct input sentences in that language, together with its lexicon relevant to that input, all of which is parsed with respect to the correct grammar of a well-studied language, or alternatively, of a "universal" grammar. The errors that inevitably result serve to guide the production of the desired grammar. We present the main framework describing the model and the results of our experiments, inferring Ch'ol grammar from English grammar and suggest some future lines of research in the area.

Keywords: Grammatical inference · Under-resourced languages · Ch'ol · Prolog · Property Grammars (PG) · Constraint Handling Rule Grammars (CHRG)

1 Introduction and Related Work

Language diversity is being eroded at alarming speed: over 7,000 languages are spoken in the world, of which according to Ethnologue[1], 2895 are endangered. This means that 40% of the world's languages can disappear in a near future. Many of them are under-studied, because the number of linguists who can study them is notably insufficient and most of their efforts pour moreover into mainstream languages. Consequently, it is of utmost importance to develop efficient

---

[1] https://www.ethnologue.com/.

This paper has been supported by projects PAPIIT-UNAM TA400121, CONACYT CB A1-S-27780 and by V. Dahl's research grant from the Natural Sciences and Engineering Research Council of Canada NSERC grant 31611021.

© Springer Nature Switzerland AG 2023
P. Lopez-Garcia et al. (Eds.): Hermenegildo Festschrift 2022, LNCS 13160, pp. 113–132, 2023.
https://doi.org/10.1007/978-3-031-31476-6_6

and affordable methods to automatically generate the unknown grammars of under-resourced languages.

In the present state-of-the-art, most grammar induction models involve probabilities (so that learning a grammar amounts to selecting a model from a pre-specified model family) or statistical models of machine learning. With respect to precision, reliability and explanatory power, such models are inferior to inference-based models: they are prone to catastrophic failure, the only question being when, rather than if, they will fail; it is not technically feasible to produce from them, if required, an explanation that is understandable by a human; and they rely crucially upon extensive search on voluminous data sets, which typically vary dynamically, so results may be unstable. At such a cost, they can achieve impressive results when what matters is only to simulate linguistic understanding in the Turing test sense, but even in such cases, their reliance on Big Data requires computational and storage power which is not readily available in countries where languages are under-resourced, and hence their grammars are most needed.

Even in the developed world we would greatly benefit from methods that require more minimalistic machinery, since the tendency to under-fund universities and research institutions is becoming widespread everywhere, placing expensive methods out of their reach.

This status-quo was the motivation for developing Womb Grammars[2] [11], a purely inferential method for automatically learning the grammar of a (typically) under-resourced language from the known grammar of another language whose correct grammar we do have access to.

A first proof-of-concept with a real language in existence was provided in [1, 2], where a language was chosen – Yorùbá – whose grammar is in fact reasonably studied, so as to be able to verify the correctness of our results by comparing them with what Yorùbá scholars have established is the correct grammar of Yorùbá.

Other applications of Womb grammars to related but different problems have been studied: to language acquisition [5,12], to second Language Tutoring [4], and to interactions with ontologies [14].

In this article we report our results in a new application of the Womb Grammar method, this time to Ch'ol [3]. Although some grammars have been published about this Mayan language spoken in Chiapas [17,19], Ch'ol has not yet been fully studied. Therefore, we have followed a corpus-based strategy to test the results of our experiments. We have carried out a manual search of nominal phrases in a corpus of Ch'ol to finally take into account only those structures

---

[2] The name Womb Grammars came to Dahl's mind after chancing upon a quote by Churchill that praised Canadians as "virile people" (sic). The thought that such fallacies of composition could be repeated unblushingly, and that there were no female equivalents of expressions such as "seminal contribution", suggested to her that it was time to create praising associations with female-specific terms too. "Womb Grammars" hints at the analogy between human wombs, which can generate different races given appropriate input, and the system she was naming, which can generate different languages' grammars given appropriate linguistic input.

that have been found in such collection of texts. Additionally, we have tested their correctness with some native speakers.

With this work we hope to stimulate further work in resourcing, in the very cost-effective manner we show here, many more of the under-resourced languages that exist – in particular those in danger of quick disappearance.

The paper is structured as follows. In Sect. 2, we explain the linguistic and computational theories this work is based on. Section 3 explains the main features and working process of Womb Grammars. Section 4 is dedicated to Ch'ol and provides some rules that define the structure of NP in this language. The parameters and results of our experiments are shown in Sect. 5. The paper ends in Sect. 6 with conclusions and future work.

2   Linguistic and Computational Framework

In this section we present our linguistic and our computational framework before describing what Womb Grammars do, what they require and how they work.

2.1   Linguistic Framework: Property Grammars (PG)

Property grammars, or PG [6,7], conceive of parsing as a process of testing whether properties that should hold for a given constituent or between a pair of constituents are satisfied or not – e.g., a noun phrase containing just an adjective would fail the noun phrase property that says that a noun must contain a nominal head – namely a noun, a proper noun, or a pronoun; a determiner preceding a noun satisfies the property of normal ordering of such constituents in English, whereas one following it, as in "politicians the" would fail it. We can also think of properties as constraints – and extend this thinking into implementation tools for PG, as we have done for instance in [10], and as we do for the present application of PG into Womb Grammars. Parse trees can still be obtained as side effect of parsing, but in PG they are not essential, so some implementations don't even bother calculating them. Instead, PGs characterize the parse of a given input phrase in terms of *which properties that input satisfies*, and *which properties it fails to satisfy*. It follows that incorrect phrases can also be informatively parsed.

More specifically: in Womb Grammar parsing, both our input and our output grammars are described in terms of properties either of a single node (unary properties) or between pairs of sister nodes (binary properties) under a common mother node [6,7]. The allowable properties are just a handful, which we exemplify for English noun phrases as follows [15]:

1. *Constituency*. Identifies all the possible categories that can be immediate part of a syntactic linguistic structure (in graph theory terms, all possible children of a node). For an NP, since its possible immediate daughters are: determiner, noun, pronoun, proper name..., constituency will be satisfied for each of these, so we will list the unary properties constituency(det), constituency(pronoun), etc.

2. *Precedence.* Establishes an order between two constituents A and B that have the same parent, C. For C = NP, a determiner must precede a noun, an adjective must precede a noun... We note these as precedence(det,noun), etc.
3. *Obligatority.* A phrase's obligatory constituents are those that need to exist as immediate child for the phrase to be well-formed. In English, the obligatory constituents of a noun phrase are either a noun, a proper name or a pronoun. We note the alternative with ';', e.g. obligatory([n;pn;pron]).
4. *Requirement.* Used to express that if a constituent A is a child of C, then a constituent B must also be a child of C. For example, in a noun phrase, a noun requires a determiner, which is noted requirement(noun,det).
5. *Exclusion.* Used to express that if a constituent A is a child of C, then B cannot also be a child of C. In the structure of NP, nouns, pronouns and proper names exclude each other, so we note for instance exclusion(n,pn).
6. *Unicity.* Used to express that there can be only one constituent belonging to a given class A as a child of C. For instance, an NP cannot have more than one noun or pronoun or proper name – noted e.g. unicity(n).

The output, i.e., the result of parsing a phrase, is no longer a parse tree, but a list of satisfied properties together with a list of unsatisfied properties for a sample input phrase. This means in particular that where more traditional parsing schemes, such as Prolog grammars with their rewriting rules, used to silently fail faced to imperfect input, PGs succeed, and yield (in the list of satisfied properties) those results that were reachable, while pointing out (through the list of unsatisfied properties) the imperfections. PG grammars are therefore much more robust that traditional rewriting grammars.

2.2   Computational Framework: CHRG

CHRG, or Constraint Handling Rule Grammars [8], are the grammatical incarnation of CHR [16]. They provide syntactic sugar in the same way that DCG provide it to Prolog (i.e., by invisibly adding and handling boundaries between symbols to express symbol contiguity), plus extra functionalities, such as assumptive and abductive reasoning capabilities as developed by Dahl, Tarau and Christiansen [9,13] – however these will not occupy us here. Constituents can be skipped over with "...".

As in CHR, CHRG has three types of rules:

1. *Propagation rules,* such as `a,b::>c`, unify adjacent occurrences in the constraint store of grammar symbols a and b, and add c to the store, affected by the same unification.
2. *Simplification rules,* such as `a,b<:>c`, are similar to propagation but a and b will be deleted from the store.
3. *Simpagation rules* are similar to simplification rules except that symbols which are prefixed with ! are not deleted. E.g `a,!b<:>c` means a will be deleted but b and c stay.

3   The Womb Grammar Methodology

Womb Grammars are a method for inferring the grammar of a language knowing the grammar of another language. It transforms a given Property Grammar Description of a source language S (in this case, English) into the (PG Description of) a grammar for the target language T (in our case, Ch'ol).

This is done through grammar analysis plus transformation, starting from an imperfect initial grammar. We need to provide the system with:

1. A representative sample of correct input phrases for the subset of targeted language to be covered,
2. the pre-terminal lexical rules corresponding to the words used in that sample, and
3. the correct syntactic constraints of another language, stated in Property Grammar terms. They will serve as an imperfect model of the desired grammar.

For this initial, imperfect model, we can use either an existing language's correct grammar, or that of a "universal" grammar formed by listing all possible properties – even if contradicting – between pairs of daughters of a phrase in the target language. The former case defines the *hybrid model* of Womb Grammars; the latter, the *universal model*.

3.1   Analysis and Transformation

By analysing the failed properties resulting from parsing input in T, the WG model infers how to transform them so that they won't fail. The result is a grammar that accepts all representative phrases of the target language.

To do that, the source grammar must be correct and complete (for the subset of language covered) and the target 'corpus' must be correct and representative.

More specifically, the method consists of:

1. Replacing the lexical rules of the correct grammar by those of the *target language*, so that the syntactic rules for S (*source language*) call the lexicon of language T (the target).
2. Running the correct input phrases of language T by this curious grammar which is a hybrid of the syntax of S plus the lexicon of T.
3. Examining the errors that will be inevitably produced, and modifying the syntactic rules of the grammar so that no more errors are produced.

In other words, the WG method perfects the imperfect model we started from by correcting its syntactic properties informed by the errors produced, until the grammar contains only correct rules.

3.2   Implementing a PG Parser Through CHRG

We are now able to show some fragments of a PG parser for English noun phrases, to illustrate our above concepts.

Lexicon fragment:
```
[a]::>word(det,a).
[book]::>word(noun,book).
[blue]::>word(adjective,blue).
```

Grammar fragment:
```
g(np(precedence(adj,noun))).
```

Input Phrase:
```
[a,blue,book]
```

English Parser Fragment: (detects correct word ordering)
```
word(C1,_):(N1,_),...,word(C2,_):(_,N4),
g(np(precedence(C1,C2))), all(A,B) ::>
succeeds(np(precedence(C1,C2)),N1,N4,A,B).
```

3.3   Implementing a Hybrid-Model WG Parser Through CHRG

Since Ch'ol words will likely not evoke as much in readers' minds as those of a more familiar language, without loss of generality we exemplify implementation concepts here for a hypothetical case in which the source language is English and the target language is Spanish, just to illustrate our methodology in easier-to-understand terms.

For the sake of clarity, here we leave out a third argument that records features, such as number and gender.

Spanish lexicon fragment:
```
[libro] ::> word(noun,libro).
[azul] ::> word(adjective,azul).
```

English grammar fragment:
```
g(np(precedence(adj,noun))).
```

Spanish input phrase:
```
[libro,azul]
```

English parser fragment (rule detecting word mis-ordering):
```
word(C2,_):(N1,_),...,word(C1,_):(_, N4),
g(np(precedence(C1,C2))), all(A, B) ::>
fail(np(precedence(C1,C2)),N1,N4,A,B).
```

3.4   Heuristics for Analysing and Transforming Failed Properties

Since we have designed the input corpus to represent all possible structures of the phrases we cover (in our case, noun phrases), our analysis of the output will be indicative of precisely how we need to modify the starting grammar's properties in order to arrive at our desired grammar.

This analysis needs to involve all input phrases, and counts the number of times in which, for phrases relevant to a given property, that property fails. To exemplify, if the target language were Spanish, (where we would say: el libro azul – the book blue), the property that an adjective must precede the noun can be inferred from the failure *in all input phrases that contain the relevant constituents* of the property np(precedence(adj,noun)). However, a representative sample of Spanish noun phrases must include examples in which the order is actually reversed, because it is the case that when the adjective is short, it can precede the noun (e.g. un buen libro – a good book).

Features (such as number of syllables, tonality for languages that exhibit it, gender, number, ...) that can affect our properties are stored in the lexicon, and the system consults them when exceptions to a rule show up in the corpus. If some regularity can be found, it will be signalled in the output grammar. Of course this relies on the features that can affect properties having been identified when the lexicon is input. For this, we rely on our informants in the case of under-studied languages such as Ch'ol. Should informants be unable to identify some of such features, they won't be included in the lexicon and the system will therefore be unable to correctly apply this heuristic to them.

However, even linguists unfamiliar with the language will, upon examining the output themselves, be able to notice under which regularities properties that succeed in general fail in a few examples, since all failed and succeeded properties will have been laid out, ready for manual examination too. (N.B. This does not mean that our system *relies* on humans manually implementing heuristics: we only point out the availability of manual examination as a last resort safeguard in case informants have been unable to identify crucially needed features in their language – a situation no automated system can be expected to automatically correct).

In short, our heuristic's implementation automatically transforms a property into its converse if it fails for all examples in the corpus, deletes it altogether if it is satisfied in some cases and not others, but no regularity that could explain it can be found among those examples for which it fails, and in the case in which a regularity can be found, describes the property in conditional terms: "P holds if it is the case that..." (e.g. np(precedence(noun,adj)) holds unless the noun has no more syllables than the adjective).

Exceptions to a property can alternatively be expressed in terms of the Property Grammar primitive "relax", which serves to relax a property under certain conditions. For Ch'ol we have chosen to simply add a condition in the property's description itself, which makes the description more self contained: all the relevant elements are visible in the same description.

4   Ch'ol

Ch'ol is part of the western branch of the Mayan family, which is divided into
a) Cholan-tseltal languages and b) Tseltalan languages. Ch'ol belongs to the
former. It is spoken mainly in the state of Chiapas, in Mexico, where it has
251,800 speakers.

There are two identified dialects of Ch'ol, that have morphological and phono-
logical differences. But, according to Vazquez (2011), the main differences are
lexical.

In what follows, we introduce a short explanation of the main traits of the
language that can be of some interest for this work. We will be formulating the
property rules that will be used to check the correctness of the results.

4.1   Writing System

There is an agreement on an alphabet among writers: a, b, ch, ch', e, i, j, k, k',
l, m, ñ, o, p, p', r, s, t, ts, ts', ty, ty', u, w, x, y, ä, -. This alphabet simplifies
some of the graphemes used before, like 'k' instead of 'qu'. It also includes 'ty'
and its plosive form 'ty'. For simplicity, and to avoid codification problems, all
the graphemes have been simplified in our program. This does not affect the
performance of the system, at least at this initial level.

4.2   Morphology and Parts of Speech

Parts of Speech in Ch'ol do not exactly correspond to the ones in the indo-
european languages. To build a general grammar of Ch'ol, the following parts
of the speech: nouns (n), verbs (v), adjectives (adj), adverbs (adv), prepositions
(prep), pronouns (pron), numerals (num), classifiers (class), determinants (det),
person markers (poss) and quantifiers (quant) are commonly considered.

For the work in property grammars, some classes need clarification or small
adaptations.

As for nouns, there is a clear distinction for proper nouns (pn), that show a
very specific behavior, which differs from the rest of nouns. Therefore, n and pn
will be treated differently in this work.

Two of the categories do not have a clear correspondence in indo-european
languages: classifiers (class) and person markers (poss).

Classifiers (class) are always affixed either to the nouns or to the interroga-
tive form *jay* and they indicate some properties of the word they are attached
to. Their graphical treatment is not clear; orthographically, classifiers are not
independent. Some researchers do consider them as affixes, more than parts of
speech [19]. Therefore, classifiers are not considered to be part of the property
grammar of Ch'ol NP in this paper.

Mayan languages use two different sets of person markers commonly known as
Set A and Set B [19], which are mainly attached to verbs to show grammatical
relations. Set A is also used with noun roots to indicate the possessor [16].
Most linguistic studies have considered Set A as prefixes; although some others

describe them as proclitics, since they can attach to the modifiers. There even are texts where they are written as independent words. Considering this, we separate them in order to have a correspondence between Set A and the possessives in indo-european languages that we are using in this paper. Therefore, Set A are identified as poss, while Set B are considered as affixes.

The constituency order of Ch'ol is VOS (namely, verb, object, subject), although this is not a rigid order. This means there are several factors, as topicality, animacy, etc., that can have an influence in the order of the three main constituents. NPs with function of subject are not necessarily explicit because the verbs provide enough information to understand the sentence [18].

4.3 NP Structure

The present paper is focused on the analysis of the basic structure of the NP. This means that we deal only with simple NP structures that not include PP, NP and S as complements. Conjoined constituents (e.g. n → n conj n) are not considered either. Only the categories that are listed in the constituency properties will be taken into account.

In what follows, we present a property grammar for Ch'ol following the parameters introduced in Sect. 2.1. Ch'ol does not have a totally explicitly defined grammar. Therefore, the following properties have been inferred from a corpus.

The constituency properties for Ch'ol noun phrases are the following:

```
g(constituency(n)),
g(constituency(pn)),
g(constituency(pron)),
g(constituency(det)),
g(constituency(quant)),
g(constituency(adj)),
g(constituency(num)),
g(constituency(poss)).
```

There is only an obligation property:

```
g(obligatory([n;pn;pron])).
```

The following unicity properties have been formulated:

```
g(unicity(n)),
g(unicity(pn)),
g(unicity(pron)),
g(unicity(poss)).
```

We have inferred several exclusion properties:

```
g(exclusion(n,pn)),
g(exclusion(n,pron)),
g(exclusion(pron,pn)),
g(exclusion(pron,det)),
g(exclusion(pron,quant)),
g(exclusion(pron,adj)),
g(exclusion(pron,num)),
g(exclusion(pron,poss)),
g(exclusion(pn,quant)),
g(exclusion(pn,adj)),
g(exclusion(pn,num)),
g(exclusion(pn,poss)),
g(exclusion(num,quant)).
```

The properties of precedence establish the order of the constituents:

```
g(precedence(quant,n)),
g(precedence(num,n)),
g(precedence(adj,n)),
g(precedence(det,n)),
g(precedence(poss,n)),
g(precedence(det,pn)),
g(precedence(adj,poss)),
g(precedence(adj,quant)),
g(precedence(det,adj)),
g(precedence(det,poss)),
g(precedence(det,num)),
g(precedence(num,adj)),
g(precedence(quant,det)),
g(precedence(quant,poss)).
```

Finally, we formulated some properties of requirement:

```
g(requirement(adj,n)),
g(requirement(det,[n;pn])),
g(requirement(poss,n)),
g(requirement(num,n)),
g(requirement(quant,n)).
```

5 Experiments and Results

We have performed two different experiments. In the first one, which uses the hybrid system, Ch'ol – the target language – must be inferred from English – the source language. The second one uses the universal system, where the grammar of the target language (Ch'ol) is inferred from a universal grammar. The latter method had not been tried yet to infer the grammar of a real language.

5.1 Hybrid Womb Grammar

For this experiment we design a program with the following elements: a) a correct grammar of the source language (English) NPs, b) a set of correct NP examples from the target language (Ch'ol), with a PoS label.

Tables 1 and 2 show the results of the program. The correct property grammar of English that is provided to the system is shown in the first column. Table 1 contains the satisfied results that the system obtains for the grammar of Ch'ol, according to the correct Ch'ol phrase examples provided to the program, that can be found in Appendix Table 5. For example, "kolem kabäl xajlel" – adj, quant, n – translated as "many big stones". Table 2 contains the unsatisfied properties. The second column of both give the examples (or counter-examples) that illustrate the decision of the system.

There are six English properties that are violated by some of the phrase samples, whereas the others are satisfied in all the Ch'ol cases tested. The unsatisfied properties are all consistent with our expectations based on common English usage and the properties identified for Ch'ol. They are each violated by at least one of the counter examples from the second column of Table 2.

This implies for the precedence properties that the converse may be true. For example from `precedence(poss,adj)` being unsatisfied we know that an adjective can come before a possessive in a simple noun phrase. To infer that `precedence(adj,poss)` is a valid property in Ch'ol, we would need to ensure that it is never violated in a corpus sufficiently large to remove doubt.

The violation of the exclusion properties simply implies that those categories can coexist in a Ch'ol simple noun phrase.

Some expected properties for Ch'ol are missing from the resulting grammar. For example, based on the English grammar in which we have `exclusion(det, pn)`, we are unable to infer either `precedence(det, pn)` or `precedence(pn, det)`; the English grammar does not have either precedence property, so they never enter the system.

Therefore, the method has been able to analyze a set of examples according to the rules of a grammar (S) and generate the new grammar for them (T).

5.2 Universal Womb Grammar

The Universal Womb Grammar does not use the known grammar of a language S to infer the grammar of a language T. Instead, the program includes every possible property over the terminal vocabulary of T belonging to each of the six categories explained in Sect. 2.1: constituency, precedence, obligatority, requirement, exclusion and unicity. For our work, we only consider the properties involving the constituents we have defined.

Table 1. Results obtained with the Hybrid English method. First column: English grammar given to the system. Second column: examples for satisfied properties.

English grammar property satisfied by Ch'ol	Examples
g(obligatory(n;pn;pron))	
g(constituency(det))	
g(constituency(quant))	
g(constituency(adj))	
g(constituency(num))	
g(constituency(n))	
g(constituency(pn))	
g(constituency(pron))	
g(constituency(poss))	
g(precedence(det,n))	jiñi$_{det}$ me$_n$
g(precedence(adj,n))	jupem$_{adj}$ lakña$_n$
g(precedence(num,n))	jotikil$_{num}$ soko$_n$
g(precedence(quant,n))	kabäl$_{quant}$ xinich$_n$
g(precedence(poss,n))	i$_{poss}$ yijñam$_n$
g(precedence(num,adj))	juñtikil$_{num}$ jumpe$_{adj}$ lakña$_n$
g(precedence(det,adj))	jiñi$_{det}$ jumpe$_{adj}$ lakña$_n$
g(precedence(det,num))	jiñi$_{det}$ uxtikil$_{nem}$ reyob$_n$
g(requirement(num,[n]))	jotikil$_{num}$ soko$_n$
g(requirement(poss,[n]))	k$_{poss}$ weel$_n$
g(requirement(adj,[n]))	iik$_{adj}$ chuch$_n$
g(requirement(det,[n;pn]))	jiñi$_{det}$ tsi$_n$
g(requirement(quant,[n]))	kabäl$_{quant}$ kixtañujob$_n$
g(exclusion(pron,pn))	
g(exclusion(num,quant))	
g(exclusion(pn,quant))	
g(exclusion(pn,poss))	
g(exclusion(pron,n))	
g(exclusion(pron,adj))	
g(exclusion(pron,num))	
g(exclusion(pron,poss))	
g(exclusion(pron,det))	
g(exclusion(pron,quant))	
g(exclusion(n,pn))	
g(exclusion(pn,adj))	
g(exclusion(pn,num))	
g(unicity(n))	ja$_n$
g(unicity(pron))	joñoñ$_{pron}$
g(unicity(pn))	Juan$_{pn}$
g(unicity(poss))	

Table 2. Results obtained with the Hybrid English method. First column: English grammar given to the system. Second column: English grammar property Unsatisfied by Ch'ol.

English grammar property Unsatisfied by Ch'ol	Counterexamples
g(precedence(poss,adj))	$tyam_{adj}$ aw_{poss} ok_n
g(precedence(det,quant))	$kabäl_{quant}$ $jiñi_{det}$ ja_n
g(precedence(quant,adj))	$kolem_{adj}$ $kabäl_{quant}$ $xajlel_n$
g(precedence(poss,quant))	$kabäl_{quant}$ $tyak_{quant}$ k_{poss} $wakax_n$
g(exclusion(det,pn))	jiñi Tila
g(exclusion(det,poss))	$jiñi_{det}$ i_{poss} yum_m

The list of correct examples of the language T with which we test the Universal Womb Grammar model is the same that has been given to the program in the hybrid model (See Appendix Table 5).

Since the universal grammar contains all combinations of properties, the result can contain the complete set of properties for the target language, unlike the Hybrid English parser with the more restricted input grammar. We see this in column 1 of Table 3, where the recall, the number of rules of Ch'ol the program was able to capture, was 100%. Every one of the properties described in Sect. 4.3 was in the output.

There are additional unexpected properties inferred. In many cases exclusion between categories invalidates precedence rules; if a phrase cannot have both pronoun and proper name, there cannot be any precedence property between them. Pruning these cases, there are three additional unexpected properties for unicity of adj, num, and det, shown in column two. In each of the phrase samples where any of these appear, they appear alone. Therefore, they are inferred from the Universal grammar because they were never violated in the Ch'ol phrase samples. These can be accepted as valid Ch'ol properties until a counterexample is found to be added to the testing corpus.

This over-generation of properties and the resulting uncertainty highlights a key aspect of the Womb Grammars approach: a substantial, representative set of test phrases must be used to bolster confidence in the output grammar. For some less used languages this can be challenging, and a very limited set of examples may be given to the program. This leads to many combinations of constituents not being represented, and to the chance of missing counterexamples that would otherwise refine the result.

These results show that Universal Womb Grammars need some more development to prune the rules retrieved as valid but that cannot be inferred from the rules.

5.3 Comparative Results Hybrid vs. Universal

Although every property satisfied by the Hybrid Grammar corresponds to a property of the grammar that has been designed in Sect. 4.3, this formalism is

Table 3. Results obtained with the Universal method. First column: Properties inferred and expected based on independent study. Second column: Additional properties inferred, but not anticipated.

Ch'ol grammar property	Additional Inferred property
g(obligatory(n;pn;pron))	g(unicity(adj))
g(constituency(quant))	g(unicity(num))
g(constituency(adj))	g(unicity(det))
g(constituency(num))	
g(constituency(poss))	
g(constituency(det))	
g(constituency(pn))	
g(constituency(pron))	
g(constituency(n))	
g(precedence(quant, n))	
g(precedence(num, n))	
g(precedence(adj, n))	
g(precedence(det, n))	
g(precedence(poss, n))	
g(precedence(det, pn))	
g(precedence(adj, poss))	
g(precedence(adj, quant))	
g(precedence(det, adj))	
g(precedence(det, poss))	
g(precedence(det, num))	
g(precedence(num, adj))	
g(precedence(quant, det))	
g(precedence(quant, poss))	
g(requirement(num,[n]))	
g(requirement(poss,[n]))	
g(requirement(adj,[n]))	
g(requirement(det,[n;pn]))	
g(requirement(quant,[n]))	
g(exclusion(pron,pn))	
g(exclusion(num,quant))	
g(exclusion(pn,quant))	
g(exclusion(pn,poss))	
g(exclusion(pron,n))	
g(exclusion(pron,adj))	
g(exclusion(pron,num))	
g(exclusion(pron,poss))	
g(exclusion(pron,det))	
g(exclusion(pron,quant))	
g(exclusion(n,pn))	
g(exclusion(pn,adj))	
g(exclusion(pn,num))	
g(unicity(n))	
g(unicity(pron))	
g(unicity(pn))	
g(unicity(poss))	

not able to capture every property. However, the Universal Womb Grammar is able to infer a number of properties that have not been formulated by the hybrid version. Table 4 shows the comparative outcome:

Table 4. Set of rules of Ch'ol inferred by the program that do not belong to English

UWG	HWG	Defined in Ch'ol Grammar
g(precedence(adj,quant))	unsatisfied the reverse	Yes
g(precedence(adj,poss))	unsatisfied the reverse	Yes
g(precedence(det,pn))	not covered	Yes
g(precedence(det,poss))	not covered	Yes
g(precedence(quant,det))	unsatisfied the reverse	Yes
g(precedence(quant,poss))	unsatisfied the reverse	Yes
g(unicity(adj))	not covered	No
g(unicity(num))	not covered	No
g(unicity(det))	not covered	No

As the table shows, while HWG are not able to decide if an unsatisfied property of the source language can be reversed, in those examples, it seems that UWG are able to infer them. This seems to indicate that a possible future improvement for HWG is to add a component of analysis of the unsatisfied properties.

6 Conclusions and Future Work

We have contributed to the automatic induction of grammars that can be incorporated into modern technological and educational tools in order to help under-resourced languages acquire the resources needed, and thus help endangered languages survive. The process of inducing a target language's grammar proceeds mostly in automatic fashion, where the only human intervention required (other than running the program) is to enter an informant's representative sample of lexical categories in the target language, together with their features, as well as the (known) grammar which will be used as an imperfect starting model.

First, we have manually generated a grammar for a restricted but important subset of Ch'ol noun phrases. The fact that no full description of Ch'ol grammar exists may be a disadvantage because, at some point, it was not clear what the definition of the categories and structures had to be. However, this has made our work also more useful and relevant.

To complete our work, we have fine tuned our source grammar around the specific needs of Ch'ol. In a first stage, we took the same approach as was taken for Yorùbá, i.e., we used the Hybrid version of Womb Grammars, using English as the source language. This yielded reasonable results, but since the constituents of English and Ch'ol don't coincide exactly, we had to make appropriate adjustments, such as defining for Ch'ol the category of possessives that appears in the grammar of English. This may indicate that, in order to make the hybrid version of this system work in every not well-known language, we may need to make our source grammar very granular.

We then turned, in a second stage, to experimenting with the Universal Womb Grammar system, where all properties between all possible pairs of constituents of the target language are included as our starting point source "grammar" (note that this "universal grammar", while being highly useful, is not correct in theory, since it must include, by definition, properties that contradict each other).

In our experiments, we have seen that Universal Womb Grammars still need some adjustments to be able to restrict the results to the features that are represented in the examples. However, we think that this formalism is more adequate because of three reasons: a) constituents that are in the source but not in the target language can be safely ignored, which means we do not have to deal with extraneous constituents; b) constituents that are in the target language but not in the source are (most appropriately) taken into account right away when the target language's lexicon is entered, and c) the process of deriving properties that include all constituents of the target language is highly mechanizable when we proceed, as we do, phrase by phrase. We are at present studying the process of developing a front end to mechanize the development of a universal grammar from the given lexicon of a target language, in the hope that it can serve as a start point for all future applications of universal WG. Ultimately we would like to have a useful general toolkit that can be applied to fairly arbitrary target languages with as little necessary adaptations as possible.

As mentioned, we have studied only one of the two main dialects of Ch'ol, but since the differences between them are mostly lexical, our work stands to be almost directly applicable to the other dialect too. While we have not yet tested this hypothesis, if it proves as reasonable as is to be expected, our approach multiplies its promise, as it is likely the case that in many other different dialects of a same language, most differences may relate mainly to the lexicon.

Although Universal Womb Grammars have been already defined earlier [11], and their application embrionically studied for language acquisition, this paper presents the first real-language rendition of the working of this formalism for inducing unknown grammars. Ch'ol has been the first language whose simple NP structure has been inferred by using a Universal WG.

To check the performance of the system, we have been assisted by a linguist native speaker of Ch'ol. In Sect. 4, we have explained the main features of the NP in Ch'ol, formulating some property features that will help us to validate the results.

This being only our first approach to grammatical inference from Womb Grammar to a Mexican indigenous Language, there is of course room for improvement. First, we plan to extend our present coverage of Ch'ol nominal phrases by adding PP and NP as complements. In a second step, prepositional phrases, verb phrases and the whole sentence structure should be tackled. Ch'ol will give us many clues on how to collect elements for a universal grammar that can help to define the mechanisms to automatically infer the structure of Mayan languages and, in further steps, languages belonging to other families.

Regarding the choice of a source language, other considerations than whether we have an existing grammar for the source language are relevant, e.g.:

- Common sense would suggest that using source and target languages from the same linguistic family would tend to work best. Yet one of the results of our research that was surprising to us is how well English worked as a source language for a target language as dissimilar from English as Ch'ol. Obviously, conclusions from punctual experiments cannot be elevated to general conclusions about our method. It would be useful to compare what types of languages would perform best as providers of a source grammar for a given target language. This could be done empirically by running many tests, or through conceptual linguistic analyses, such as theoretically analysing the compatibility of the (known) linguistic constraints (perhaps within a theory other than Property Grammars) in a given source language, with respect to those (typically, unknown a priori) inferred by our method and corroborated as correct by native speakers or linguists – an approach that could at least throw light on the choice of other under-resourced languages in the same family as the already targeted one. As a side effect, it might also throw an empirically useful comparative light between Property Grammars and any other linguistic theory used for the said conceptual analysis.
- Meanwhile, when considering what target language to choose, we can reasonably speculate that languages with similar main characteristics might lend themselves better to the task. For instance, if we target a non-agglutinative language, using an agglutinative one as source might require the extra step of separating the different morphemes contained in a single lexical item so that we can more easily recognize them as parallel to the separate constituents that the target language represents them with. On the other hand, doing this extra step may not be prohibitive if we use one of the many agglutinative languages in which morphemes tend to remain unchanged after their unions.
- In general, the fact that for Womb Grammars, lexical items are the most important input required to infer the grammar of a source language would suggest that languages with the same, or similar set of constituents would be among the most promising to be used as source languages. It might also be helpful to choose a language from the same linguistic family, e.g. if the target language is a romance language, taking a romance language as source might be a good option. However, the method as we have so far tested it showed to be resilient in this respect: English worked well as source language not only for Ch'ol but for Yorùbá as well – i.e. for two target languages with quite different linguistic genealogies.

We hope this work will motivate more applications of Womb Grammars to the induction of other under-resourced languages, in the final aim of significantly increasing the survival chances for endangered languages, with obvious positive socio-economic potential impact.

Appendix I: Examples of Ch'ol Given to the Program, with the PoS Tagging and the English Translation

Table 5. Examples provided to the system

Ch'ol phrase	PoS	Translation
joñoñ	pron	I
lu	pron	everything
ja	n	water
xchumtälob	n	inhabitans
jiñi me	det, n	the deer
ili wits	det, n	this hill
jiñi Juan	det, pn	that Juan
jiñi Tila	det, pn	that Tila
yambä kin	adj, n	another day
iik chuch	adj, n	black squirrel
junkojt xwax	det, n	a vixen
jumpe xchumtäl,	det, n	an inhabitant
i bak,	poss, n	its bone
k weel,	poss, n	my meat
kabäl xiñich	quant, n	many ants
kabäl kixtañujob	quant, n	many people
sumukjax k waj	adj, poss, n	my delicious tortillas
tyam aw ok	adj, poss, n	your large feet
kolem kabäl xajlel	adj, quant, n	many big stones
jiñi jupem lakña	det adj n	that fat woman
jiñi k mut	det, poss, n	my chicken
jiñi i yum	det, poss, n	its owner
juntikil jupem lakña	num, adj, n	a fat woman
uxtikil i yalobilob	num, poss, n	his three children
i yuxpejlel, klesiaji	poss, num, n	his third temple
kabäl jiñi ja	quant, det, n	a lot of water
jiñi uxtikil reyob	det, num, n,	these three kings
jiñi uxpejl estado	det, num, n,	these three states
juan	pn	juan
kabäl tyak k wakax	quant, quant, poss, n	many some my cows

References

1. Adebara, I.: Using womb grammars for inducing the grammar of a subset of Yorùbá noun phrases. Ph.D. thesis, Department of Computing Science, Simon Fraser University, Burnaby, Canada (2015)
2. Adebara, I., Dahl, V.: Grammar induction as automated transformation between constraint solving models of language. In: Proceedings of the Workshop on Knowledge-based Techniques for Problem Solving and Reasoning Co-located with 25th International Joint Conference on Artificial Intelligence (IJCAI 2016), New York City, USA, 10 July 2016 (2016). https://ceur-ws.org/Vol-1648/paper6.pdf
3. Alejos, J., Martínez, N.: Ch'oles, 3rd edn., pp. 19–33. Comisión nacional para el desarrollo de los pueblos indígenas, México (2007). iSBN 0 471 40300
4. Becerra Bonache, L., Dahl, V., Miralles, J.E.: On second language tutoring through womb grammars. In: Rojas, I., Joya, G., Gabestany, J. (eds.) IWANN 2013. LNCS, vol. 7902, pp. 189–197. Springer, Heidelberg (2013). https://doi.org/10.1007/978-3-642-38679-4_18
5. Becerra-Bonache, L., Dahl, V., Miralles, J.E.: The role of universal constraints in language acquisition. In: Duchier, D., Parmentier, Y. (eds.) CSLP 2012. LNCS, vol. 8114, pp. 1–13. Springer, Heidelberg (2013). https://doi.org/10.1007/978-3-642-41578-4_1
6. Blache, P.: Property grammars and the problem of constraint satisfaction. In: ESSLLI-2000 Workshop on Linguistic Theory and Grammar Implementation (2000)
7. Blache, P.: Property grammars: a fully constraint-based theory. In: Christiansen, H., Skadhauge, P.R., Villadsen, J. (eds.) CSLP 2004. LNCS (LNAI), vol. 3438, pp. 1–16. Springer, Heidelberg (2005). https://doi.org/10.1007/11424574_1
8. Christiansen, H.: CHR grammars (2004)
9. Christiansen, H., Dahl, V.: V.: Assumptions and abduction in prolog. In: Workshop on Multiparadigm Constraint Programming Languages (MultiCPL 2004), Saint-Malo, France (2004). Workshop notes (2004)
10. Dahl, V., Blache, P.: Extracting selected phrases through constraint satisfaction. In: Proceedings of the Constraint Satisfaction and Language Processing SLP 2005 (2005)
11. Dahl, V., Miralles, E.: Womb grammars: Constraint solving for grammar induction. In: Sneyers, J., Frühwirth, T. (eds.) Proceedings of the 9th Workshop on Constraint Handling Rules. Technical report CW 624, pp. 32–40. Department of Computer Science, K.U. Leuven (2012)
12. Dahl, V., Miralles, E., Becerra, L.: On language acquisition through womb grammars. In: CSLP, pp. 99–105 (2012)
13. Dahl, V., Tarau, P., Li, R.: Assumption grammars for processing natural language. In: ICLP (1997)
14. Dahl, V., Tessaris, S., De Sousa Bispo, M.: Parsing as semantically guided constraint solving: the role of ontologies. Ann. Math. Artif. Intell. **82**(1), 161–185 (2018). https://doi.org/10.1007/s10472-018-9573-2
15. Duchier, D., Dao, T., Parmentier, Y.: Model-theory and implementation of property grammars with features. J. Log. Comput. **24**(2), 491–509 (2014). https://doi.org/10.1093/logcom/exs080
16. Frühwirth, T.: Theory and practice of constraint handling rules. J. Log. Program. **37**(1), 95–138 (1998). https://doi.org/10.1016/S0743-1066(98)10005-5

17. Warkentin, V., Scott, R.: Gramática ch'ol. Instituto Lingüístico de verano, México (1980)
18. Nichols, J.: Head-marking and dependent-marking grammar. Language **62**(1), 56–119 (1986). https://www.jstor.org/stable/415601
19. Vázquez Álvarez, J.: A grammar of Chol, a Mayan language. Ph.D. thesis, University of Texas (2011)

Answer Set Programming Made Easy

Jorge Fandinno[1,2] , Seemran Mishra[2] , Javier Romero[2] , and Torsten Schaub[2(✉)]

[1] University of Nebraska at Omaha, Omaha, USA
[2] University of Potsdam, Potsdam, Germany
smishra@uni-potsdam.de , torsten@cs.uni-potsdam.de

Abstract. We take up an idea from the folklore of Answer Set Programming (ASP), namely that choices, integrity constraints along with a restricted rule format is sufficient for ASP. We elaborate upon the foundations of this idea in the context of the logic of Here-and-There and show how it can be derived from the logical principle of extension by definition. We then provide an austere form of logic programs that may serve as a normalform for logic programs similar to conjunctive normalform in classical logic. Finally, we take the key ideas and propose a modeling methodology for ASP beginners and illustrate how it can be used.

1 Introduction

Many people like Answer Set Programming (ASP [20]) because its declarative approach frees them from expressing any procedural information. In ASP, neither the order of rules nor the order of conditions in rule antecedents or consequents matter and thus leave the meaning of the overall program unaffected. Although this freedom is usually highly appreciated by ASP experts, sometimes laypersons seem to get lost without any structural guidance when modeling in ASP.

We address this issue in this (preliminary) paper and develop a methodology for ASP modeling that targets laypersons, such as biologists, economists, engineers, and alike. As a starting point, we explore an idea put forward by Ilkka Niemelä in [25], although already present in [10,16] as well as the neighboring area of Abductive Logic Programming [7,9]. To illustrate it, consider the logic program encoding a Hamiltonian circuit problem in Listing 1.1. Following good practice in ASP, the problem is separated into the specification of the problem instance in lines 1–3 and the problem class in lines 5–10. This strict separation, together with the use of facts for problem instances, allows us to produce uniform[1] and elaboration tolerant[2] specifications. Building upon the facts of the problem instance, the actual encoding follows the guess-define-check methodology of ASP. A solution candidate is guessed in Line 5, analyzed by auxiliary definitions in Line 6 and 7, and finally checked through integrity constraints in lines 8–10.

A closer look reveals even more structure in this example. From a global perspective, we observe that the program is partitioned into facts, choices, rules, and integrity

---

[1] A problem encoding is *uniform*, if it can be used to solve all its problem instances.
[2] A formalism is *elaboration tolerant* if it is convenient to modify a set of facts expressed in the formalism to take into account new phenomena or changed circumstances [24].

© Springer Nature Switzerland AG 2023
P. Lopez-Garcia et al. (Eds.): Hermenegildo Festschrift 2022, LNCS 13160, pp. 133–150, 2023.
https://doi.org/10.1007/978-3-031-31476-6_7

```
1   node(1..4).              start(1).
2   edge(1,2). edge(2,3). edge(2,4). edge(3,1).
3   edge(3,4). edge(4,1). edge(4,3).
4
5   { hc(V,U) } :- edge(V,U).
6   reached(V) :- hc(S,V), start(S).
7   reached(V) :- reached(U), hc(U,V).
8   :- node(V), not reached(V).
9   :- hc(V,U), hc(V,W), U!=W.
10  :- hc(U,V), hc(W,V), U!=W.
```

Listing 1.1. A logic program for a Hamiltonian circuit problem

constraints, and in this order. From a local perspective, we note moreover that the predicates in all rule antecedents are defined beforehand. This structure is not arbitrary and simply follows the common practice that concept formation is done linearly by building concepts on top of each other. Moreover, it conveys an intuition on how a solution is formed. Importantly, such an arrangement of rules is purely methodological and has no impact on the meaning (nor the performance[3]) of the overall program. From a logical perspective, it is interesting to observe that the encoding refrains from using negation explicitly, except for the integrity constraints. Rather this is hidden in Line 5, where the choice on hc(V,U) amounts to the disjunction hc(V,U) $\lor \neg$hc(V,U), an instance of the law of the excluded middle. Alternatively, hc(V,U) can also be regarded as an abducible that may or may not be added to a program, as common in Abductive Logic Programming.

Presumably motivated by similar observations, Ilkka Niemelä already argued in [25] in favor of an ASP base language based on choices, integrity constraints, and stratified negation.[4] We also have been using such an approach when initiating students to ASP as well as teaching laypersons. Our experience has so far been quite positive and we believe that a simple and more structured approach helps to get acquainted with posing constraints in a declarative setting.

We elaborate upon this idea in complementary ways. First of all, we lift it to a logical level to investigate its foundations and identify its scope. Second, we want to draw on this to determine a syntactically restricted subclass of logic programs that still warrants the full expressiveness of traditional ASP. Such a subclass can be regarded as a normalform for logic programs in ASP. This is also interesting from a research perspective since it allows scientists to initially develop their theories in a restricted setting without regarding all corner-cases emerging in a full-featured setting. And last but not least, inspired by this, we want to put forward a simple and more structured modeling methodology for ASP that aims at beginners and laypersons.

---

[3] Shuffling rules in logic programs has an effect on performance since it affects tie-breaking during search; this is however unrelated to the ordering at hand.

[4] This concept eliminates the (problematic) case of recursion through negation.

2   Background

The logical foundations of ASP rest upon the logic of Here-and-There (HT [17]) along with its non-monotonic extension, Equilibrium Logic [26].

We start by defining the monotonic logic of *Here-and-There* (HT). Let $\mathcal{A}$ be a set of atoms. A *formula* φ over $\mathcal{A}$ is an expression built with the grammar:

$$\varphi ::= a \mid \bot \mid \varphi \wedge \varphi \mid \varphi \vee \varphi \mid \varphi \to \varphi$$

for any atom $a \in \mathcal{A}$. We also use the abbreviations: $\neg\varphi \overset{\text{def}}{=} (\varphi \to \bot)$, $\top \overset{\text{def}}{=} \neg\bot$, and $\varphi \leftrightarrow \psi \overset{\text{def}}{=} (\varphi \to \psi) \wedge (\psi \to \varphi)$. Given formulas φ, α and β, we write $\varphi[\alpha/\beta]$ to denote the uniform substitution of all occurrences of formula α in φ by β. This generalizes to the replacement of multiple formulas in the obvious way. As usual, a *theory* over $\mathcal{A}$ is a set of formulas over $\mathcal{A}$. We sometimes understand finite theories as the conjunction of their formulas.

An *interpretation* over $\mathcal{A}$ is a pair $\langle H, T \rangle$ of atoms (standing for "here" and "there", respectively) satisfying $H \subseteq T \subseteq \mathcal{A}$. An interpretation is *total* whenever $H = T$. An interpretation $\langle H, T \rangle$ *satisfies* a formula φ, written $\langle H, T \rangle \models \varphi$, if the following conditions hold:

$$\begin{aligned}
&\langle H, T \rangle \models p && \text{if } p \in H \\
&\langle H, T \rangle \models \varphi \wedge \psi && \text{if } \langle H, T \rangle \models \varphi \text{ and } \langle H, T \rangle \models \psi \\
&\langle H, T \rangle \models \varphi \vee \psi && \text{if } \langle H, T \rangle \models \varphi \text{ or } \langle H, T \rangle \models \psi \\
&\langle H, T \rangle \models \varphi \to \psi && \text{if } \langle H', T \rangle \not\models \varphi \text{ or } \langle H', T \rangle \models \psi \text{ for both } H' \in \{H, T\}
\end{aligned}$$

A formula φ is *valid*, written $\models \varphi$, if it is satisfied by all interpretations. An interpretation $\langle H, T \rangle$ is a *model* of a theory Γ, written $\langle H, T \rangle \models \Gamma$, if $\langle H, T \rangle \models \varphi$ for all $\varphi \in \Gamma$.

Classical entailment is obtained via the restriction to total models. Hence, we define the classical satisfaction of a formula φ by an interpretation T, written $T \models \varphi$, as $\langle T, T \rangle \models \varphi$.

A total interpretation $\langle T, T \rangle$ is an *equilibrium model* of a theory Γ if $\langle T, T \rangle$ is a model of Γ and there is no other model $\langle H, T \rangle$ of Γ with $H \subset T$. In that case, we also say that T is a *stable model* of Γ. We denote the set of all stable models of Γ by $SM[\Gamma]$ and use $SM_V[\Gamma] \overset{\text{def}}{=} \{ T \cap V \mid T \in SM[\Gamma] \}$ for their projection onto some vocabulary $V \subseteq \mathcal{A}$.

Since ASP is a non-monotonic formalism, it may happen that two different formulas share the same equilibrium models but behave differently in different contexts. The concept of *strong equivalence* captures the idea that two such formulas have the same models regardless of any context. More precisely, given two theories Γ and Π and a set $V \subseteq \mathcal{A}$ of atoms, we say that Γ and Π are V-*strongly equivalent* [2], written $\Gamma \cong_V \Pi$, if $SM_V[\Gamma \cup \Delta] = SM_V[\Pi \cup \Delta]$ for any theory Δ over $\mathcal{A}'$ such that $\mathcal{A}' \subseteq V$. For formulas φ and ψ, we write $\varphi \cong_V \psi$ if $\{\varphi\} \cong_V \{\psi\}$.

A *rule* is a (reversed) implication of the form

$$l_1 \vee \cdots \vee l_m \leftarrow l_{m+1} \wedge \cdots \wedge l_n \tag{1}$$

where each l_i is a literal, that is, either an atom or a negated atom, for $1 \leq i \leq n$. If $n = 1$, we refer to the rule as a *fact* and write it as l_1 by dropping the trailing implication symbol. A rule is said to be *normal* whenever $m = 1$ and l_1 is an atom. A negation-free normal rule is called *definite*. An *integrity constraint* is a rule with $m = 0$ and equivalent to $\bot \leftarrow l_{m+1} \wedge \cdots \wedge l_n$. Finally, the law of the excluded middle $a \vee \neg a$ is often represented as $\{a\}$ and called a *choice*. Accordingly, a rule with a choice on the left-hand side is called a *choice rule*. A *logic program* is a set of rules. It is called *normal*, if it consists only of normal rules and integrity constraints, and *definite* if all its rules are definite.

3   Logical Foundations

We begin by investigating the logical underpinnings of the simple format of logic programs discussed in the introductory section. Although the discussion of the exemplary logic program has revealed several characteristic properties, not all of them can be captured in a logical setting, such as order related features. What remains is the division of the encoding into facts, rules, choices, and integrity constraints. In logical terms, the first two amount to negation-free formulas, choices are instances of the law of the excluded middle, and finally integrity constraints correspond to double-negated formulas in HT. While the first two types of formulas are arguably simpler because of their restricted syntax, the latter's simplicity has a semantic nature and is due to the fact that in HT double negated formulas can be treated as in classical logic.

In what follows, we show that any formula can be divided into a conjunction of corresponding subformulas. This conjunction is strongly equivalent (modulo the original vocabulary) to the original formula and the translation can thus also be applied to substitute subformulas. Interestingly, the resulting conjunction amounts to a conservative extension of the original formula and the underlying translation can be traced back to the logical principle of extension by definition, as we show below.

To this end, we associate with each formula φ over $\mathcal{A}$ a new propositional atom x_φ. We then consider defining axioms of the form $(x_\varphi \leftrightarrow \varphi)$. We can now show that replacing any subformula φ by x_φ while adding a corresponding defining axiom amounts to a conservative extension of ψ.[5]

Proposition 1. *Let ψ and φ be formulas over $\mathcal{A}$ and $x_\varphi \notin \mathcal{A}$.*
    Then, $\psi \cong_\mathcal{A} (\psi[\varphi/x_\varphi] \wedge (\varphi \leftrightarrow x_\varphi))$.

Moreover, we get a one-to-one correspondence between the stable models of both formulas.

Proposition 2. *Let ψ and φ be formulas over $\mathcal{A}$ and $x_\varphi \notin \mathcal{A}$.*

1. *If $T \subseteq \mathcal{A}$ is a stable model of ψ, then $T \cup \{x_\varphi \mid T \models \varphi\}$ is a stable model of $(\psi[\varphi/x_\varphi] \wedge (\varphi \leftrightarrow x_\varphi))$.*
2. *If $T \subseteq (\mathcal{A} \cup \{x_\varphi\})$ is a stable model of $(\psi[\varphi/x_\varphi] \wedge (\varphi \leftrightarrow x_\varphi))$, then $T \cap \mathcal{A}$ is a stable model of ψ.*

---

[5] An extended version of the paper including all proofs can be found here: https://arxiv.org/abs/2111.06366.

Clearly, the above results generalize from replacing and defining a single subformula φ to several such subformulas.

With this, we can now turn our attention to negated subformulas: Given a formula ψ, let $N(\psi)$ stand for the set of all maximal negated subformulas occurring in ψ. This leads us to the following variant of Proposition 1.

Corollary 1. *Let ψ be a formula over $\mathcal{A}$ and $x_\varphi \notin \mathcal{A}$.*
Then, $\psi \cong_\mathcal{A} \psi[\varphi/x_\varphi \mid \varphi \in N(\psi)] \wedge \bigwedge_{\varphi \in N(\psi)}(\varphi \leftrightarrow x_\varphi)$.

Given that we exclusively substitute negated subformulas, we can actually treat the defining axiom as in classical logic. This is because in HT, we have $\langle H, T \rangle \models \neg\varphi$ iff (classically) $T \models \neg\varphi$. The classical treatment of the defining axiom is then accomplished by replacing $(\varphi \leftrightarrow x_\varphi)$ by $\neg\neg(\varphi \leftrightarrow x_\varphi)$ and $(\neg x_\varphi \vee x_\varphi)$. This results in the following decomposition recipe for formulas.

Definition 1. *Let ψ be a formula over $\mathcal{A}$ and $x_\varphi \notin \mathcal{A}$.*
Then, we define

$$\psi^\star = \psi[\varphi/x_\varphi \mid \varphi \in N(\psi)] \wedge \bigwedge_{\varphi \in N(\psi)}(\neg x_\varphi \vee x_\varphi) \wedge \bigwedge_{\varphi \in N(\psi)} \neg\neg(\varphi \leftrightarrow x_\varphi).$$

Example 1. Let ψ be $\neg a \rightarrow b \vee \neg\neg(c \wedge \neg d)$. Then,

$$N(\psi) = \{\neg a, \neg\neg(c \wedge \neg d)\}$$
$$\psi^\star = (x_{\neg a} \rightarrow b \vee x_{\neg\neg(c \wedge \neg d)}) \wedge$$
$$(x_{\neg a} \vee \neg x_{\neg a}) \wedge (x_{\neg\neg(c \wedge \neg d)} \vee \neg x_{\neg\neg(c \wedge \neg d)})$$
$$\neg\neg(\neg a \leftrightarrow x_{\neg a}) \wedge \neg\neg(\neg\neg(c \wedge \neg d) \leftrightarrow x_{\neg\neg(c \wedge \neg d)})$$

With the translation from Definition 1, we obtain an analogous conservative extension result as above.

Theorem 1. *Let ψ be a formula over $\mathcal{A}$.*
Then, we have $\psi \cong_\mathcal{A} \psi^\star$.

In analogy to Proposition 2, we get a one-to-one correspondence between the stable models of both formulas.

Theorem 2. *Let ψ be a formula over $\mathcal{A}$.*

1. *If $T \subseteq \mathcal{A}$ is a stable model of ψ, then $T \cup \{x_\varphi \mid \varphi \in N(\psi) \text{ and } T \models \varphi\}$ is a stable model of $\psi^\star$.*
2. *If $T \subseteq (\mathcal{A} \cup \{x_\varphi \mid \varphi \in N(\psi)\})$ is a stable model of $\psi^\star$, then $T \cap \mathcal{A}$ is a stable model of ψ.*

For instance, $\{b\}$ is a stable model of the formula $\psi = \neg a \rightarrow b \vee \neg\neg(c \wedge \neg d)$ from Example 1. From Theorem 1, $\{x_{\neg a}, b\}$ is a stable model of $\psi^\star$. Conversely, from the stable model $\{x_{\neg a}, b\}$ of $\psi^\star$, we get the stable model $\{b\}$ of ψ by dropping the new atoms.

4   Austere Answer Set Programming

In this section, we restrict the application of our formula translation to logic programs. Although we focus on normal programs, a similar development with other classes of logic programs, like disjunctive ones, can be done accordingly.

For simplicity, we write $\bar{a}$ instead of $x_{\neg a}$ for $a \in \mathcal{A}$ and let $\{\bar{a}\}$ stand for $\bar{a} \vee \neg\bar{a}$. Note that, for a rule r as in (1), the set $N(r)$ consists of negative literals only. The next two definitions specialize our translation of formulas to logic programs.

Definition 2. *Let r be a rule over $\mathcal{A}$ as in* (1) *with $m \geq 1$.*
Then, we define

$$r^\star = r[\neg a/\bar{a} \mid \neg a \in N(r)] \cup \bigcup_{\neg a \in N(r)} \{\{\bar{a}\} \leftarrow\} \cup \bigcup_{\neg a \in N(r)} \left\{ \begin{array}{l} \leftarrow a \wedge \bar{a} \\ \leftarrow \neg a \wedge \neg\bar{a} \end{array} \right\}$$

Definition 3. *Let P be a logic program over $\mathcal{A}$. Then, $P^\star = \bigcup_{r \in P} r^\star$.*

This translation substitutes negated literals in rule bodies with fresh atoms and adds a choice rule along with a pair of integrity constraints providing an equivalence between the eliminated negated body literals and the substituted atoms.

By applying the above results in the setting of logic programs, we get that a logic program and its translation have the same stable models when restricted to the original vocabulary.

Corollary 2. *Let P be a logic program over $\mathcal{A}$.*
Then, we have $P \cong_\mathcal{A} P^\star$

In other words, every stable model of a logic program can be extended to a stable model of its translation and vice versa.

Corollary 3. *Let P be a logic program over $\mathcal{A}$.*

1. *If $T \subseteq \mathcal{A}$ is a stable model of P, then $T \cup \{\bar{a} \mid \neg a \in N(P)$ and $a \notin T\}$ is a stable model of $P^\star$.*
2. *$T \subseteq (\mathcal{A} \cup \{\bar{a} \mid \neg a \in N(P)\}$ is a stable model of $P^\star$, then $T \cap \mathcal{A}$ is a stable model of P.*

For illustration, consider the following example.

Example 2. Consider the normal logic program P:

$$a \leftarrow$$
$$b \leftarrow \neg c$$
$$c \leftarrow \neg b$$
$$d \leftarrow a \wedge \neg c$$

Then, $P^\star$ is:

$$
\begin{array}{lll}
a \leftarrow & \{\bar{b}\} \leftarrow & \{\bar{c}\} \leftarrow \\
b \leftarrow \bar{c} & \leftarrow b \wedge \bar{b} & \leftarrow c \wedge \bar{c} \\
c \leftarrow \bar{b} & \leftarrow \neg b \wedge \neg\bar{b} & \leftarrow \neg c \wedge \neg\bar{c} \\
d \leftarrow a \wedge \bar{c} & &
\end{array}
$$

The stable models of P are $\{a, b, d\}$ and $\{a, c\}$ and the ones of $P^\star$ are $\{a, b, d, \bar{c}\}$ and $\{a, c, \bar{b}\}$, respectively.

The example underlines that our translation maps normal rules to definite ones along with choices and pairs of integrity constraints. In other words, it can be seen as a means for expressing normal logic programs in the form of programs with facts, definite rules, choice rules and integrity constraints over an extended vocabulary. We call this class of programs *austere logic programs*, and further elaborate upon them in the following.

4.1   Austere Logic Programs

We define austere logic programs according to the decomposition put forward in the introduction.

Definition 4 (Austere logic program). *An* austere logic program *is a quadruple* (F, C, D, I) *consisting of a set F of facts, a set C of choices,[6] a set D of definite rules, and a set I of integrity constraints.*

A set of atoms is a stable model of an austere logic program, if it is a stable model of the union of all four components.

In view of the above results, austere logic programs can be regarded as a normalform for normal logic programs.

Corollary 4. *Every normal logic program can be expressed as an austere logic program and vice versa.*

The converse follows from the fact that choice rules are expressible by a pair of normal rules [27].

In fact, the (instantiation of) Listing 1.1 constitutes an austere logic program. To see this observe that

- lines 1–3 provide facts, F, capturing the problem instance, here giving the specification of a graph;
- Line 5 provides choices, C, whose instantiation is derived from facts in the previous lines. Grounding expands this rule to several plain choice rules with empty bodies;
- lines 5–6 list definite rules, D, defining (auxiliary) predicates used in the integrity constraints;
- finally, integrity constraints, I, are given in lines 7–9, stating conditions that solutions must satisfy.

This example nicely illustrates a distinguishing feature of austere logic programs, namely, the *compartmentalization* of the program parts underlying ASP's guess-define-check encoding methodology (along with its strict separation of instance and encoding): The problem instance is described by means of

- the facts in F

and the problem encoding confines

- non-deterministic choices to C,
- the deterministic extension of the taken decisions to D, and

---

[6] That is, choice rules without body literals.

– the test of the obtained extension to I.

This separation also confines the sources of multiple or non-existing stable models to well-defined locations, namely, C and I, respectively (rather than spreading them over several circular rules; see below). As well, the rather restricted syntax of each compartment gives rise to a very simple operational semantics of austere logic programs, as we see in the next section.

4.2   Operational Semantics

In our experience, a major factor behind the popularity of the approach sketched in the introductory section lies in the possibility to intuitively form stable models along the order of the rules in a program. In fact, the simple nature of austere logic programs provides a straightforward scheme for computing stable models by means of the well-known immediate consequence operator, whose iteration mimics this proceeding. Moreover, the simplicity of the computation provides the first evidence of the value of austere logic programs as a normalform.

The operational semantics of austere logic programs follows ASP's *guess-define-check* methodology. In fact, the only non-determinism in austere logic programs is comprised of choice rules. Hence, once choices are made, we may adapt well-known deterministic bottom-up computation techniques for computing stable models. However, the results of this construction provide merely candidate solutions that still need to satisfy all integrity constraints. If this succeeds, they constitute stable models of the austere program.

Let us make this precise for an austere logic program (F, C, D, I) in what follows. To make choices and inject them into the bottom-up computation, we translate the entire set of choices, C, into a set of facts:

$$F_C = \{a \leftarrow \mid \{a\} \leftarrow \, \in C\}$$

A subset of F_C, the original facts F, along with the definite program D are then passed to a corresponding consequence operator that determines a unique stable model candidate. More precisely, the T_P operator of a definite program P is defined for an interpretation X as follows [23]:

$$T_P(X) = \{l_1 \mid (l_1 \leftarrow l_{m+1} \wedge \cdots \wedge l_n) \in P, \ X \models l_{m+1} \wedge \cdots \wedge l_n\}$$

With this, the candidate solutions of an austere program can be defined.

Definition 5. *Let (F, C, D, I) be an austere logic program over $\mathcal{A}$.*
We define a set $X \subseteq \mathcal{A}$ of atoms as a candidate stable model of (F, C, D, I), if X is the least fixpoint of $T_{F \cup C' \cup D}$ for some $C' \subseteq F_C$.

The existence of the least fixpoint is warranted by the monotonicity of $T_{F \cup C' \cup D}$ [23]. Similar to traditional ASP, several candidate models are obtained via the different choices of C'.

While the choice of C' constitutes the *guess* part and the definite rules in D the *define* part of the approach, the *check* part is accomplished by the integrity constraints in I.

Proposition 3. *Let* (F, C, D, I) *be an austere logic program over* $\mathcal{A}$ *and* $X \subseteq \mathcal{A}$.
Then, X *is a stable model of* (F, C, D, I) *iff* X *is a candidate stable model of* (F, C, D, I) *such that* $X \models I$.

We illustrate the computation of stable models of austere logic programs in the following example.

Example 3. Consider the austere logic program P

$$a \leftarrow$$
$$\{b\} \leftarrow$$
$$c \leftarrow b$$
$$\leftarrow a \wedge \neg c$$

We get the candidate stable models $\{a, b, c\}$ and $\{a\}$ from the first three rules depending on whether we choose b to be true or not, that is, whether we add the fact $b \leftarrow$ or not. Then, on testing them against the integrity constraint expressed by the fourth rule, we see that $\{a, b, c\}$ is indeed a stable model, since it satisfies the integrity constraint, while set $\{a\}$ is not a stable model since checking the integrity constraint fails.

A major intention of austere logic programs is to confine the actual guess and check of an encoding to dedicated components, namely, the choices in C and constraints in I. The definite rules in D help us to analyze and/or extend the solution candidate induced by the facts F and the actual choices in C'. The emerging candidate is then evaluated by the integrity constraints in I. This stresses once more the idea that the extension of a guessed solution candidate should be deterministic; it elaborates the guess but refrains from introducing any ambiguities. This is guaranteed by the definite rules used in austere programs.

Observation 1 *For any austere logic program* (F, C, D, I) *and* $C' \subseteq F_C$, *the logic program* $F \cup C' \cup D$ *has a unique stable model.*

This principle is also in accord with [25], where stratified logic programs are used instead of definite ones (see below).

5 Easy Answer Set Programming

Austere logic programs provide a greatly simplified format that reflects ASP's *guess-define-check* methodology [20] for writing encodings. Their simple structure allows for translating the methodology into an intuitive process that consists of making non-deterministic choices, followed by a deterministic bottom-up computation, and a final consistency check.

In what follows, we want to turn the underlying principles into a modeling methodology for ASP that aims at laypersons. To this end, we leave the propositional setting and aim at full-featured input languages of ASP systems like *clingo* [14] and *dlv* [19]. Accordingly, we shift our attention to predicate symbols rather than propositions and let the terms 'logic program', 'rule', etc. refer to these languages without providing a technical account (cf. [5, 12]). Moreover, we allow for normal rules instead of definite ones as well as aggregate literals in bodies in order to accommodate the richness of existing ASP modeling languages.

The admission of normal rules comes at the expense of losing control over the origin of multiple or non-existing stable models as well as over a deterministic development of guessed solutions. In fact, the idea of *Easy Answer Set Programming* (ezASP) is to pursue the principles underlying austere logic programs without enforcing them through a severely restricted syntax. However, rather than having the user fully absorb the loss in control, we shift our focus to a well-founded development of ASP encodings, according to which predicates are defined on top of previously defined predicates (or facts). This parallels the structure and the resulting operational semantics of austere logic programs.

To this end, we start by capturing dependencies among predicates [3].

Definition 6. *Let P be a logic program.*

- *A predicate symbol p depends upon a predicate symbol q, if there is a rule in P with p on its left-hand side and q on its right-hand side.*
  If p depends on q and q depends on r, then p depends on r, too.
- *The* definition *of a predicate symbol p is the subset of P consisting of all rules with p on their left-hand side.*

We denote the definition of a predicate symbol p in P by $def(p)$ and view integrity constraints as rules defining $\bot$.

Our next definition makes precise what we mean by a well-founded development of a logic program.[7]

Definition 7. *Let P be a logic program.*
We define a partition $(P_1, \ldots, P_n)$ *of P as a* stratification *of P, if*

1. $def(p) \subseteq P_i$ *for all predicate symbols p and some* $i \in \{1, \ldots, n\}$ *and*
2. *if p depends on q, $def(p) \subseteq P_i$, and $def(q) \subseteq P_j$ for some $i, j \in \{1, \ldots, n\}$, then*
   (a) $i > j$ *unless q depends on p, and*
   (b) $i = j$ *otherwise*

Any normal logic program has such a stratification. One way to see this is that mutually recursive programs can be trivially stratified via a single partition. For instance, this applies to both programs $\{a \leftarrow b, b \leftarrow a\}$ and $\{a \leftarrow \neg b, b \leftarrow \neg a\}$ in which a and b mutually depend upon each other. Accordingly, similar recursive structures in larger programs are confined to single partitions, as required by (*2b*) above.

With it, we are ready to give shape to the concept of an *easy logic program*.

Definition 8 (Easy logic program). *An easy logic program is a logic program having stratification* $(F, C, D_1, \ldots, D_n, I)$ *such that F is a set of facts, C is a set of choice rules, D_i is a set of normal rules for $i = 1, \ldots, n$, and I is a set of integrity constraints.*

As in traditional ASP, we often divide a logic program into facts representing a problem instance and the actual encoding of the problem class. For easy programs, this amounts to separating F from $(C, D_1, \ldots, D_n, I)$.

---

[7] The term *stratification* differs from the one used in the literature [3].

Clearly, an austere logic program is also an easy one.

Thus, the program in Listing 1.1 is also an easy logic program having the stratification

$$(\{1, 2, 3\}, \{5\}, \{6, 7\}, \{8, 9, 10\})$$

where each number stands for the rules in the respective line.

Predicates node/1, edge/2, and start/1 are only used to form facts or occur in rule bodies. Hence, they do not depend on any other predicates and can be put together in a single component, F. This makes sense since they usually constitute the problem instance. Putting them first reflects that the predicates in the actual encoding usually refer to them. The choices in C provide a solution candidate that is checked by means of the rules in the following components. In our case, the guessed extension of predicate hc/2 in Line 5 is simply a subset of all edges provided by predicate edge/2. Tests for being a path or even a cycle are postponed to the *define-check* part: The rules in $\{6, 7\}$, that is, D_1, define the auxiliary predicate reached/1, and aim at analyzing and/or extending our guessed solution candidate by telling us which nodes are reachable via the instances of hc/2 from the start node. The actual checks are then conducted by the integrity constraints, I, in the final partition $\{8, 9, 10\}$. At this point, the solution candidate along with all auxiliary atoms are derived and ready to be checked. Line 8 tests whether each node is reached in the solution at hand, while lines 9 and 10 make sure that a valid cycle never enters or leaves any node twice.

Finally, it is instructive to verify that strata $\{5\}$ and $\{6, 7\}$ cannot be reversed or merged. We observe that

– hc/2 depends on edge/2 only,

while

– reached/1 depends on hc/2, edge/2, start/1, and itself,

and no other dependencies. The rules defining hc/2 and reached/1 must belong to the same partition, respectively, as required by (*2a*) above. Thus, $\{5\} \subseteq P_i$ and $\{6, 7\} \subseteq P_j$ for some i, j. Because reached/1 depends on hc/2 and not vice versa, we get $i < j$. This dependency rules out an inverse arrangement, and the fact that it is not symmetric excludes a joint membership of both definitions in the same partition, as stipulated by (*2b*) above.

5.1 Modeling Methodology

The backbone of easy ASP's modeling methodology is the structure imposed on its programs in Definition 8. This allows us to encode problems by building concepts on top of each other. Also, its structure allows for staying in full tune with ASP's *guess-define-check* methodology [20] by offering well-defined spots for all three parts.

Easy logic programs tolerate normal rules in order to encompass full-featured ASP modeling languages. Consequently, the interplay of the guess, define, and check parts of an easy logic program defies any control. To tame this opening, we propose to carry over Observation 1 to easy logic programs: For any easy logic program

$(F, C, D_1, \ldots, D_n, I)$ and $C' \subseteq F_C$, the logic program $F \cup C' \cup D_1 \cup \cdots \cup D_n$ should have a unique stable model. Even better if this can be obtained in a deterministic way.

This leads us to the following advice on easy ASP modeling:

1. Compartmentalize a logic program into facts, F, choice rules, C, normal rules, $D_1 \cup \cdots \cup D_n$, and integrity constraints I,
   such that the overall logic program has stratification $(F, C, D_1, \ldots, D_n, I)$.
2. Aim at defining one predicate per stratum D_i and avoid cycles within each D_i for $i = 1, \ldots, n$.
3. Ensure that $F \cup C' \cup D_1 \cup \cdots \cup D_n$ has a unique stable model for any $C' \subseteq F_C$.

While the first two conditions have a syntactic nature and can thus be checked automatically, the last one refers to semantics and, to the best of our knowledge, has only sufficient but no known necessary syntactic counterparts. One is to restrict $D_1 \cup \cdots \cup D_n$ to definite rules as in austere programs, the other is to use stratified negation, as proposed in [25] and detailed in the next section.

Our favorite is to stipulate that $F \cup C' \cup D_1 \cup \cdots \cup D_n$ has a total well-founded model [28] for any $C' \subseteq F_C$ but unfortunately, we are unaware of any syntactic class of logic programs warranting this condition beyond the ones mentioned above.

5.2 Stratified Negation

The purpose of stratified negation is to eliminate the (problematic) case of recursion through negation. What makes this type of recursion problematic is that it may eliminate stable models and that the actual source may be spread over several rules. To give some concise examples, consider the programs $\{a \leftarrow \neg a\}$ and $\{a \leftarrow \neg b, b \leftarrow \neg c, c \leftarrow \neg a\}$ admitting no stable models. Following the dependencies in both examples, we count one and three dependencies, respectively, all of which pass through negated body literals. More generally, cyclic dependencies traversing an odd number of negated body literals (not necessarily consecutively) are known sources of incoherence. Conversely, an even number of such occurrences on a cycle is not harmful but spawns alternatives, usually manifested in multiple stable models. To see this, consider the program $\{a \leftarrow \neg b, b \leftarrow \neg a\}$ producing two stable models. Neither type of rule interaction is admitted in austere logic programs. Rather the idea is to confine the sources of multiple and eliminated stable models to dedicated components, namely, choices and integrity constraints. The same idea was put forward by Niemelä in [25] yet by admitting a more general setting than definite rules by advocating the concept of stratified negation.

To eliminate the discussed cyclic constellations, stratified negation imposes an additional constraint on the stratification of a logic program: Given the prerequisites of Definition 7, we define:

3. If a predicate symbol q occurs in a negative body literal of a rule in P_i, then $def(q) \subseteq P_j$ for some $j < i$.

In other words, while the definitions of predicates appearing positively in rule bodies may appear in a lower or equal partition, the ones of negatively occurring predicates are restricted to lower components. Although this condition tolerates positive recursion as in $\{a \leftarrow b, b \leftarrow a\}$, it rules out negative recursion as in the above programs. Since using programs with stratified negation rather than definite programs generalizes austere logic programs, their combination with choices and integrity constraints is also as expressive as full ASP [25].

An example of stratified negation can be found in Listing 1.3. The negative literal in Line 5 refers to a predicate defined—beforehand—in Line 8.

An attractive feature of normal logic programs with stratified negation is that they yield a unique stable model, just as with austere programs (cf. Observation 1). Hence, they provide an interesting generalization of definite rules maintaining the property of deterministically extending guessed solution candidates.

5.3   Complex Constraints

As mentioned, we aim at accommodating complex language constructs as aggregates in order to leverage the full expressiveness of ASP's modeling languages. For instance, we may replace lines 9 and 10 in Listing 1.1 by

```
9    :- { hc(U,V) } >= 2, node(U).
10   :- { hc(U,V) } >= 2, node(V).
```

without violating its stratification.

More generally, a rule with an aggregate '$\#op\{l_1, \ldots, l_m\} \prec k$' in the consequent can be represented with choice rules along with an integrity constraint, as shown in [27]. That is, we can replace any rule of form

$$\#op\{l_1, \ldots, l_m\} \prec k \leftarrow l_{m+1} \wedge \cdots \wedge l_n$$

by[8]

$$\{l_i\} \leftarrow l_{m+1} \wedge \cdots \wedge l_n \qquad\qquad \text{for } i = 1, \ldots, m \text{ and}$$
$$\bot \leftarrow \neg(\#op\{l_1, \ldots, l_m\} \prec k) \wedge l_{m+1} \wedge \cdots \wedge l_n .$$

This allows us to integrate aggregate literals into easy logic programs without sacrificing expressiveness.

In fact, many encodings build upon restricted choices that are easily eliminated by such a transformation. A very simple example is graph coloring. Assume a problem instance is given in terms of facts `node/1`, `edge/2`, and `color/1`. A corresponding encoding is given by the following two rules:

```
1    { assign(X,C) : color(C) } = 1 :- node(X).
2    :- edge(X,Y), assign(X,C), assign(Y,C).
```

Note that the aggregate in the consequent of Line 1 is a shortcut for a *#count* aggregate.

To eliminate the restricted choice from the consequent in Line 1, we may apply the above transformation to obtain the following easy encoding:

---

[8] In practice, a set of such choice rules can be represented by a single one of form $\{l_1, \ldots, l_m\} \leftarrow l_{m+1} \wedge \cdots \wedge l_n$.

```
1  { assign(X,C) } :- node(X), color(C).
2  :- not { assign(X,C) : color(C)} = 1, node(X).
3  :- edge(X,Y), assign(X,C), assign(Y,C).
```

Given some set of facts, F, this encoding amounts to the easy logic programs $(F, \{1\}, \{2\}, \{3\})$.

The decomposition into a choice and its restriction may appear unnecessary to the experienced ASP modeler. However, we feel that such a separation adds clarity and is preferable to language constructs combining several aspects, at least for ASP beginners. Also, it may be worth noting that this decomposition is done anyway by an ASP system and hence brings about no performance loss.

Two further examples of easy logic programs are given in Listing 1.2 and 1.3, solving the Queens and the Tower-of-Hanoi puzzles both with parameter n.[9] While the

```
1   { queen(1..n,1..n) }.
2
3   d1(I,J,I-J+n) :- I = 1..n, J = 1..n.
4   d2(I,J,I+J-1) :- I = 1..n, J = 1..n.
5
6   :- { queen(I,1..n) } != 1, I = 1..n.
7   :- { queen(1..n,J) } != 1, J = 1..n.
8
9   :- { queen(I,J) : d1(I,J,D) } > 1, D=1..n*2-1.
10  :- { queen(I,J) : d2(I,J,D) } > 1, D=1..n*2-1.
```

Listing 1.2. An easy logic program for the n-Queens puzzle

easy logic program for the n-Queens puzzle has the format

$$(\emptyset, \{1\}, \{3, 4\}, \{6, 7\}, \{9, 10\}),$$

the one for the Tower-of-Hanoi puzzle can be partitioned into

$$(\{1, 2, 3, 4\}, \{6\}, \{8\}, \{10, 11, 12\}, \{14, 15\}, \{17, 19, 20, 21, 23\}) .$$

5.4 Limitations

The methodology of ezASP has its limits. For instance, sometimes it is convenient to make choices depending on previous choices. Examples of this are the combination of routing and scheduling, as in train scheduling [1], or the formalization of frame axioms in (multi-valued) planning advocated in [18]. Another type of encodings escaping our methodology occurs in meta programming, in which usually a single predicate, like holds, is used and atoms are represented as its arguments. Thus, for applying the

---

[9] This parameter is either added from the command line via option --const or a default added via directive #const (see [13] for details).

```
1   peg(a;b;c).
2   disk(1..4).
3   init_on(1..4,a).
4   goal_on(1..4,c).
5
6   { move(D,P,T) : disk(D), peg(P) } :- T = 1..n.
7
8   move(D,T)              :- move(D,_,T).
9
10  on(D,P,0)              :- init_on(D,P).
11  on(D,P,T)              :- move(D,P,T).
12  on(D,P,T+1)            :- on(D,P,T), not move(D,T+1), T < n.
13
14  blocked(D-1,P,T+1) :- on(D,P,T), T < n.
15  blocked(D-1,P,T)   :- blocked(D,P,T), disk(D).
16
17  :- { move(D,P,T) : disk(D), peg(P) } != 1, T = 1..n.
18
19  :- move(D,P,T), blocked(D-1,P,T).
20  :- move(D,T), on(D,P,T-1), blocked(D,P,T).
21  :- not 1 { on(D,P,T) } 1, disk(D), T = 1..n.
22
23  :- goal_on(D,P), not on(D,P,n).
```

Listing 1.3. An easy logic program for a Towers-of-Hanoi puzzle (for plans of length n)

ezASP methodology, one had to refine the concept of stratification to access the term level in order to capture the underlying structure of the program. And finally, formalizations of planning and reasoning about actions involve the formalization of effect and inertia laws that are usually self-referential on the predicate level (sometimes resolved on the term level, through situation terms or time stamps). A typical example of circular inertia laws is the following:

```
holds(F,T)  :-  holds(F,T-1), not -holds(F,T).
-holds(F,T) :- -holds(F,T-1), not  holds(F,T).
```

Here, '-' denotes classical negation, and F and T stand for (reified) atoms and time points. On the other hand, the sophistication of the given examples illustrates that they are usually not addressed by beginners but rather experts in ASP for which the strict adherence to ezASP is less necessary.

6   Related Work

Apart from advocating the idea illustrated in the introduction, Ilkka Niemelä also showed in [25] that negative body literals can be replaced by a new atom for which a choice needs to be made whether to include it in the model or not; and such that a model cannot contain both the new atom and the atom of the replaced literal but one of them needs to be included. This technique amounts exactly to the transformation in Definition 2 and traces back to Abductive logic programming [7,9]. Indeed, it was already shown in [16] that for DATALOG queries the expressive power of stable model semantics can be achieved via stratified negation and choices.

We elaborated upon this idea in several ways. First, we have shown that the full expressiveness of normal logic programs can even be achieved with definite rules rather than normal ones with stratified negation. Second, we have provided a strong equivalence result that allows for applying the transformation in Definition 2 to selected rules only. Third, we have generalized the idea by means of the logic of Here-and-There, which made it applicable to other fragments of logic programs. And finally, this investigation has revealed that the roots of the idea lie in the logical principle of extension by definition.

Over the last decades many more related ideas were presented in the literature. For instance, in [10], normal logic programs are translated into positive disjunctive programs by introducing new atoms for negative literals. Also, strong negation is usually compiled away via the introduction of new atoms along with integrity constraints excluding that both the original atom and the atom representing its strong negation hold [15]. The principle of extension by definition was also used in [11] to prove properties about programs with nested expressions. EzASP is closely related to the paradigm of IDP [6], where the program parts F, C and I are expressed in first-order logic, while the D_i's form inductive definitions. Finally, in [8], the authors propose an informal semantics for logic programs based on the guess-define-check methodology, that are similar to the easy logic programs that we introduce in this paper.

7   Conclusion

We have revisited an old idea from the literature on logic programming under stable model semantics and elaborated upon it in several ways. We started by tracing it back to the principle of extension by definition. The resulting formalization in the setting of the logic of Here-and-there provides us with a logical framework that can be instantiated in various ways. Along these lines, we have shown that normal logic programs can be reduced to choices, definite rules, and integrity constraints, while keeping the same expressiveness as the original program. A major advantage of this austere format is that it confines non-determinism and incoherence to well-defined spots in the program. The resulting class of austere logic programs could play a similar role in ASP as formulas in conjunctive normal form in classical logic.

Drawing on the properties observed on austere logic program, we put forward the modeling methodology of ezASP. The idea is to compensate for the lacking guarantees provided by the restricted format of austere programs by following a sequential structure when expressing a problem in terms of a logic program. This makes use of the well-known concept of stratification to refine ASP's traditional guess-define-check methodology. Although the ordering of rules may seem to disagree with the holy grail of full declarativeness, we evidence its great value in introducing beginners to ASP. Also, many encodings by experienced ASP users follow the very same pattern.

Moreover, the ezASP paradigm aligns very well with that of *achievements* [21] that aims not only at easily understandable but moreover provably correct programs. To this end, formal properties are asserted in between a listing of rules to express what has been achieved up to that point. Extending ezASP with achievements and automatically guiding the program development with ASP verifiers, like *anthem* [22], appears to us as a highly interesting avenue of future research. In this context, it will also be interesting to consider the components of an easy logic program as modules with an attached input-output specification, so that the meaning of the overall program emerges from the composition of all components. This would allow for successive refinements of programs' components, while maintaining their specification.

References

1. Abels, D., Jordi, J., Ostrowski, M., Schaub, T., Toletti, A., Wanko, P.: Train scheduling with hybrid ASP. In: Balduccini et al. [4], pp. 3–17
2. Aguado, F., Cabalar, P., Fandinno, J., Pearce, D., Pérez, G., Vidal, C.: Forgetting auxiliary atoms in forks. Artif. Intell. **275**, 575–601 (2019)
3. Apt, K., Blair, H., Walker, A.: Towards a theory of declarative knowledge. In: Minker, J. (ed.) Foundations of Deductive Databases and Logic Programming, chap. 2, pp. 89–148. Morgan Kaufmann Publishers (1987)
4. Balduccini, M., Lierler, Y., Woltran, S. (eds.): Logic programming and nonmonotonic reasoning. In: Proceedings of the Fifteenth International Conference on Logic Programming and Nonmonotonic Reasoning (LPNMR 2019), LNAI, vol. 11481. Springer, Cham (2019). https://doi.org/10.1007/978-3-030-20528-7
5. Calimeri, F., et al.: ASP-Core-2 input language format. Theory Pract. Log. Program. **20**(2), 294–309 (2019)
6. De Cat, B., Bogaerts, B., Bruynooghe, M., Janssens, G., Denecker, M.: Predicate logic as a modeling language: the IDP system, pp. 121–177. ACM/Morgan, Claypool (2018)
7. Denecker, Marc, Kakas, Antonis: Abduction in logic programming. In: Kakas, Antonis C.., Sadri, Fariba (eds.) Computational Logic: Logic Programming and Beyond. LNCS (LNAI), vol. 2407, pp. 402–436. Springer, Heidelberg (2002). https://doi.org/10.1007/3-540-45628-7_16
8. Denecker, M., Lierler, Y., Truszczyński, M., Vennekens, J.: The informal semantics of answer set programming: A Tarskian perspective. CoRR abs/19C1.09125 (2019). http://arxiv.org/abs/1901.09125
9. Eshghi, K., Kowalski, R.: Abduction compared with negation by failure. In: Levi, G., Martelli, M. (eds.) Proceedings of the Sixth International Conference on Logic Programming (ICLP 1989), pp. 234–255. MIT Press (1989)
10. Fernández, J., Lobo, J., Minker, J., Subrahmanian, V.: Disjunctive LP + integrity constraints= stable model semantics. Ann. Math. Artif. Intell. **8**(3–4), 449–474 (1993)
11. Ferraris, P., Lifschitz, V.: Weight constraints as nested expressions. Theory Pract. Log. Program. **5**(1–2), 45–74 (2005)
12. Gebser, M., Harrison, A., Kaminski, R., Lifschitz, V., Schaub, T.: Abstract Gringo. Theory Pract. Log. Program. **15**(4–5), 449–463 (2015). https://doi.org/10.1017/S1471068415000150
13. Gebser, M., et al.: Potassco user guide. University of Potsdam, 2 edn. (2015). http://potassco.org
14. Gebser, M., Kaminski, R., Kaufmann, B., Schaub, T.: Multi-shot ASP solving with clingo. Theory Pract. Log. Program. **19**(1), 27–82 (2019). https://doi.org/10.1017/S1471068418000054

15. Gelfond, M., Lifschitz, V.: Logic programs with classical negation. In: Warren, D., Szeredi, P. (eds.) Proceedings of the Seventh International Conference on Logic Programming (ICLP 1990), pp. 579–597. MIT Press (1990)

16. Greco, S., Saccà, D., Zaniolo, C.: Extending stratified datalog to capture complexity classes ranging from P to QH. Acta Informatica **37**(10), 699–725 (2001)

17. Heyting, A.: Die formalen Regeln der intuitionistischen Logik. In: Sitzungsberichte der Preussischen Akademie der Wissenschaften, pp. 42–56. Deutsche Akademie der Wissenschaften zu Berlin (1930)

18. Lee, J., Lifschitz, V., Yang, F.: Action language BC: preliminary report. In: Rossi, F. (ed.) Proceedings of the Twenty-Third International Joint Conference on Artificial Intelligence (IJCAI 2013), pp. 983–989. IJCAI/AAAI Press (2013)

19. Leone, N., Pfeifer, G., Faber, W., Eiter, T., Gottlob, G., Perri, S., Scarcello, F.: The DLV system for knowledge representation and reasoning. ACM Trans. Comput. Log. **7**(3), 499–562 (2006)

20. Lifschitz, V.: Answer set programming and plan generation. Artif. Intell. **138**(1–2), 39–54 (2002)

21. Lifschitz, V.: Achievements in answer set programming. Theory Pract. Log. Program. **17**(5–6), 961–973 (2017)

22. Lifschitz, V., Lühne, P., Schaub, T.: Verifying strong equivalence of programs in the input language of GRINGO. In: Balduccini et al. [4], pp. 270–283

23. Lloyd, J.W.: Foundations of Logic Programming. Springer, Heidelberg (1987). https://doi.org/10.1007/978-3-642-83189-8

24. McCarthy, J.: Elaboration tolerance (1998). http://jmc.stanford.edu/articles/elaboration/elaboration.pdf

25. Niemelä, I.: Answer set programming without unstratified negation. In: Garcia de la Banda, M., Pontelli, E. (eds.) ICLP 2008. LNCS, vol. 5366, pp. 88–92. Springer, Heidelberg (2008). https://doi.org/10.1007/978-3-540-89982-2_15

26. Pearce, D.: Equilibrium logic. Ann. Math. Artif. Intell. **47**(1–2), 3–41 (2006). https://doi.org/10.1007/s10472-006-9028-z

27. Simons, P., Niemelä, I., Soininen, T.: Extending and implementing the stable model semantics. Artif. Intell. **138**(1–2), 181–234 (2002)

28. Van Gelder, A., Ross, K., Schlipf, J.: The well-founded semantics for general logic programs. J. ACM **38**(3), 620–650 (1991)

The Role of Abstraction in Model Checking

María-del-Mar Gallardo$^{(\boxtimes)}$ ⓘ, Pedro Merino ⓘ, and Laura Panizo ⓘ

Andalucía Tech, ITIS Software, Universidad de Málaga,
C/ Arquitecto Francisco Peñalosa, 18, 29010 Málaga, Spain
{mdgallardo,pmerino,laurapanizo}@uma.es

Abstract. The intimate relationship between model checking and abstract interpretation has been shown in a large number of relevant papers in literature. Maybe the use of abstract interpretation to reduce the well-known state space explosion problem in model checking was the first and most successful combination of these two techniques. However, this is not the only possible way both methods can collaborate to improve the software reliability. Along these last 20 years, our contributions in this area have been focussed on the practical application of abstract interpretation in the context of model checking tools. From our point of view, model checking tools such as SPIN can be hardly improved in terms of efficiency. Thus, we have concentrated on applying abstraction to completely reuse the underlying model checkers. We have applied our ideas to different modelling and programming languages, tools and real applications. In this paper, we summarize some of these contributions.

1   Introduction

As it is well known the process of applying model checking [6] consists of three main activities: (1) the modelling phase involves the construction of a formal model containing the behaviors of the original system (M); (2) in the specification phase, the desirable properties of the system are written using some variant of temporal logic (f), (3) the analysis phase makes use of an automatic tool (the model checker) to verify whether the model behavior conforms to the specifications, written as $M \models f$.

Modelling languages such as PROMELA (the input of SPIN [22]) are defined using the notion of transition system, i.e., $M = \langle \Sigma, \rightarrow, s_0 \rangle$, where Σ is the set of states, $\rightarrow \subseteq \Sigma \times \Sigma$ is the transition relation and s_0 is the initial state. Transition systems are both a simple and a powerful starting point for giving semantics to modelling languages, since they make it possible the description of sequential/concurrent systems, deterministic/non deterministic behaviors, finite/infinite state systems.

This work has been supported by the Spanish Ministry of Science, Innovation and Universities project RTI2018-099777-B-I00 and the European Union's Horizon 2020 research and innovation programme under grant agreement No 815178 (5GENESIS).

© Springer Nature Switzerland AG 2023
P. Lopez-Garcia et al. (Eds.): Hermenegildo Festschrift 2022, LNCS 13160, pp. 151–169, 2023.
https://doi.org/10.1007/978-3-031-31476-6_8

Although, in model checking, the set of states Σ from which the whole state space of systems is built must be finite, it may be huge, preventing tools from completely analyzing the whole model. For instance, in explicit model checking, where the reachability graph produced by the model is stored in memory, this usually occurs when the model contains complex data structures. This is why abstract interpretation is naturally used to reduce the computational charge of model checking algorithms, aiming to achieve feasible state spaces. The application of abstract interpretation to reduce the state space in model checking is called *abstract model checking*. In terms of transition systems, this abstraction process can be seen as the construction of an abstract transition system $M^\alpha = \langle \Sigma^\alpha, \rightarrow^\alpha, s_0^\alpha \rangle$ that *simulates* the original one M.

In Sect. 2, we discuss our particular approach to abstract model checking which is based on the idea that since model checker tools (such as SPIN) are very efficient, it is preferable to reuse them even though they have to deal with abstract models. The way of explicit model checking algorithms work will lead us to the need to also abstract the properties (f^α) to achieve the desired property preservation between the abstract and the original models ($M^\alpha \models f^\alpha \Rightarrow M \models f$). In that section, we describe the two dual methods for abstracting models and properties that can be utilized and how they affect the property preservation.

Usually, the input models for model checkers are written in the so-called modelling languages, such as PROMELA in the case of SPIN, which are simpler than standard programming languages as C or JAVA. Modelling languages make it possible the efficient handling of the state spaces produced by models since they used to limit the data types and syntax constructors. However, it possible to break the gap between the modelling and programming languages in model checking. For instance, in Sect. 3, we present the use of abstraction techniques to analyze concurrent software written in programming languages (such as C) making use of well defined APIs. In this line, Sect. 4 goes further and shows how abstraction may be also useful to carry out testing of programming languages as JAVA. We finalize in Sect. 5 pointing out other applications of the interaction between model checking and abstraction in which we have worked.

2   Abstracting PROMELA Models and LTL Formulae by Source-to-Source Transformation

In this section, we summed up several papers devoted to the application of abstract interpretation to PROMELA models aiming to carry out the so-called automatic source-to-source transformation [10,13,14] to reuse the model checker SPIN. The key point in these works is to find algorithms to transform a PROMELA model M into a *sound* abstract model M^α written also in PROMELA.

Assuming that $M = \langle \Sigma, \rightarrow, s_0 \rangle$ is a transition system, the small step operational semantics of transition system M (written as $\mathcal{O}(M)$) is built from the single computations of the form $s \rightarrow s'$ as the set of all maximal (in the sense they cannot be extended) execution paths $\pi = s_0 \rightarrow \cdots$ defined by M.

The abstraction of M is carried out via the construction of an abstract transition system $M^\alpha = \langle \Sigma^\alpha, \to^\alpha, s_0^\alpha \rangle$, where $\langle \Sigma^\alpha, \leq^\alpha \rangle$ is an ordered lattice related with the original set of states Σ by means of an abstraction function $\alpha : \wp(\Sigma) \to \Sigma^\alpha$ which, with the corresponding concretization function $\gamma : \Sigma^\alpha \to \wp(\Sigma)$, form the Galois connection $(\wp(\Sigma), \alpha, \gamma, \Sigma^\alpha)$.

Abstraction soundness is achieved if relation $\to^\alpha$ is a simulation of $\to$, that is, for all $s_1, s_2 \in \Sigma, s_1^\alpha \in \Sigma^\alpha$ such that $s_1 \to s_2$ and $\alpha(\{s_1\}) \leq^\alpha s_1^\alpha$, there exists s_2^α with $\alpha(\{s_2\}) \leq^\alpha s_2^\alpha$ and $s_1^\alpha \to^\alpha s_2^\alpha$. In practice, this means that M^α is an *over-approximation* of M, since it is easy to prove that for each execution trace $\pi = s_0 \to s_1 \cdots$ of $\mathcal{O}(M)$, there exists an abstract execution path $\pi^\alpha = s_0^\alpha \to s_1^\alpha \cdots$ of $\mathcal{O}(M^\alpha)$ such that for all $i \geq 0.\alpha(\{s_i\}) \leq^\alpha s_i^\alpha$. This simulation relation induces an abstraction relation $\preccurlyeq$ between the concrete and abstract small step semantics such as $\mathcal{O}(M) \preccurlyeq \mathcal{O}(M^\alpha)$ meaning that the abstract model is a sound approximation of the original one.

Relation $\preccurlyeq$ is key to transfer the analysis carried out on the abstract models to the original ones. Most abstract model checking approaches construct over-approximations of the behavior models, that is, abstract models are simplifications displaying more possible behaviors than the original models. However, as it will be explained later, it is also possible to follow a dual approach and use abstraction to construct *under-approximated models*. In this case, the relation between M and M^α is formalized as $\mathcal{O}(M^\alpha) \preccurlyeq \mathcal{O}(M)$. In fact, we will show that it is possible to construct an abstract model M^α such that $\mathcal{O}(M^\alpha) \subseteq \mathcal{O}(M)$ in Sect. 3.

2.1   Model Abstraction

PROMELA [21, 22] is a modelling language, with a syntax similar to that of C, suitable to specify non-trivial communication systems. Synchronization is embodied in the language using *Boolean expressions* that suspend the process in execution when they are evaluated to FALSE. It contains non-deterministic selection and iteration along with synchronous and asynchronous process communication via channels. Figure 1 shows an example of a PROMELA program with some language instructions. For instance, channel c is a synchronous channel that implements process communication via rendezvous. The code contains two processes that are initially alive thanks to the reserved word *active*. Process $p1$ contains a *do* iteration with two branches starting at symbols "::". The first instruction of each branch behaves as a guard, i.e., the branch is only selected to continue the execution if the guard is *executable*, which, in the case of Boolean expressions, means that the expression is TRUE. In the example, guards exclude themselves but it is possible to have non-deterministic selection if several guards are simultaneously TRUE. It is also worth noting the use of the *atomic* instruction that impedes the process interleaving. The code also shows the intensive use of the *goto* and label statements in PROMELA. This is because the language is thought to model transition systems where *goto*s naturally represent transitions. In the code, some other PROMELA instructions appear such as the *a unless b* constructor, whose semantics makes the system evolve by executing a whenever b is not

```
#define N 10
chan c=[0] of {int};
active proctype p1() {
      int i = 1;
L1:   do
      :: i < N -> atomic{c!i;  i = i+1}
      :: i >= N ->   i = 0;
      od;
}
active proctype p2() {
      int j = 1;
start:  {c?j; printf(j); goto start} unless {(j\%2) == 0};
even:   atomic{printf("Even"); j = 1; goto start}
}
```

Fig. 1. An example of PROMELA code

executable. When b becomes executable the execution of a finishes. Instructions $c!i$ and $c?j$ correspond to writing/reading to/from channel c using the CSP syntax. In this case, since c is a synchronous channel, both writing and reading instructions execute at the same time. In the case of bounded channels, $c!i$ and $c?j$ are asynchronously executed. The SPIN model checker may carry out random (interleaving processes arbitrarily, when it is possible) and guided system simulations. In addition, it can also make deadlock and assertion verification along with verification of LTL formulae.

The source-to-source transformation of PROMELA models guided by abstraction presented in [14] is based on two main ideas. The first one is that the PROMELA semantics may be organized in different levels of structured operational semantic (SOS) rules. From the lowest level, we have: the *process-level rules* that define the behavior of a process without taking into account the rest of system processes; the *interaction rules* that carry out the interleaving and other instructions that involve the evolution of several processes such as rendezvous; the *execution mode-based rules* that implement different execution constraints to be taken into account to avoid, for instance, the interleaving when a process is executing an *atomic* instruction. With these three levels, the so-called *simulation rules* can be defined, which formally establish the behavior of SPIN when simulating a PROMELA model.

The second idea is that all these levels of rules are supported by a given interpretation of the *data* that only affects the low-level PROMELA instructions that deal directly with them, that is, the Boolean and arithmetic expressions. In consequence, we can say that the semantics of a PROMELA model can be *generalized* with respect to the data interpretation, and so, changing the data interpretation does not change the rest of instructions. Thus, the source-to-source transformation is based on the substitution of Boolean and arithmetic expressions by their corresponding abstract versions that must observe *some natural correctness conditions* (see [14] for details). For instance, the code of Fig. 1 could be transformed into the one of Fig. 2 with the well-known *even-odd* abstraction for variables i and j.

```
#define N even
mtype = {even,odd}
chan c=[0] of {mtype};
active proctype p1() {
        int i = odd;
L1:     do
        :: true -> atomic{c!i; if
                            :: i == even -> i = odd
                            :: i== odd -> i=even
                            fi ;
                    }
        :: true -> i = even;
        od;
}
active proctype p2() {
        int j = odd;
start:  {c?j; printf(j); goto start} unless {j == even};
even:   atomic{printf("Even"); j = odd; goto start}
}
```

Fig. 2. An example of an abstract PROMELA code

Observe that the code of Figs. 1 and 2 are very similar, we have only changed the type for variables i and j which are now mtypes (the enumerated type in PROMELA) and the Boolean and arithmetic operations on these variables. Thus, for instance, increment $i = i + 1$ in the original code has been transformed into a selection depending on the actual value of i is *even* or *odd*. Similarly, guards $i \leq N$ and $i > N$ have been converted into TRUE, the top of the even-odd lattice since, as we have lost the information about the particular value of variable i, we cannot know if the guard is TRUE or FALSE. The substitution of guards by TRUE guarantees that the simulation condition described above is preserved by the transformation, that is, if it is possible to go through a given branch in the original model, then, it is also possible to go in this branch in the abstract model. Of course, the abstract model have many more behaviors than the original one. These are called *spurious* traces and are inevitable due to the loss of information intrinsic to the abstraction process. It is important to underline that the source-to-source transformation explicitly makes use of the non-determinism supported by the *do/od* and *if/fi* PROMELA sentences. If the language did not include them, the transformation would be more complicated.

2.2   LTL Abstraction

Assume we have abstracted the data of a PROMELA model M to construct an abstraction M^α following the methodology explained above. Now, if we want to prove whether M satisfy a LTL formula f by analyzing M^α, we also need to abstract the data in f to match their representation in M^α.

As in the case of models, the abstraction of formulae only affects the atomic propositions in the formulae and not the modal and logic operators. In [13], the authors show that unlike models, which are usually over-approximated in the context of abstract model checking, properties can be abstracted following two dual approaches, i.e., formulae may be over or under-approximated. The way formulae are abstracted determines the preservation of results. Thus, if a LTL formula f is under-approximated (which we will write as f_u^α from now on), meaning that it is more difficult for an abstract model to satisfy it, we obtain the preservation of *universal* properties: $M^\alpha \models \forall f_u^\alpha$ implies that $M \models \forall f$. We write quantifier $\forall$ to emphasize that f and f_u^α have to be satisfied by all behaviors displayed by M and M^α, respectively. Under-approximation of formulae is needed in the preservation of universal properties to someway compensate the loss of information in the model. Given a model M, an abstraction of M, M^α, and an atomic proposition a, the abstract formula a_u^α is an under-approximation of a iff given an abstract state s^α satisfying a_u^α, then *for all* concrete state s such that $\alpha(\{s\}) \leq^\alpha s^\alpha$, s satisfies a. For example, for the code of Fig. 1, we could prove that "i is even infinitely often" written as $\Box\Diamond(\texttt{i\%2} == 0)$ in LTL, by analyzing the abstract under-approximated formula $\Box\Diamond(\texttt{i} == \textbf{even})$ on the abstract model of Fig. 2. The key point here is that all concrete values $\texttt{i}$ abstracted by $\textbf{even}$ satisfy property $\texttt{i\%2} == 0$. However, property "$\texttt{i}$ takes value 0 infinitely often" written as $\Box\Diamond(\texttt{i} == 0)$ cannot be proved on the abstract model using $\Box\Diamond(\texttt{i} == \textbf{even})$ because this abstract formula is not an under-approximation of $\Box\Diamond(\texttt{i} == 0)$ as there exist many concrete values $\texttt{i}$ abstracted by $\textbf{even}$ that *do not* satisfy property $\texttt{i} == 0$.

Over-approximation of formulae is dually defined. Intuitively, it is easier for an abstract model to satisfy an over-approximated formula. In consequence, the preservation of results between a concrete model M and its abstract version M^α, when the formula f is over-approximated as f_o^α refers to the refutation of existential properties, that is, $M^\alpha \not\models \exists f_o^\alpha$ implies that $M \not\models f$. Here, we use the existential quantifier $\exists$ to denote that no behavior of M/M^α satisfies f/f_o^α. For instance, for the model of Fig. 1, we can prove that property "variable $\texttt{i}$ is always 0" written as $\Box(\texttt{i} == 0)$ is not satisfied since the abstract model of Fig. 2 does not satisfy the over-approximated formula $\Box(\texttt{i} == \textbf{even})$.

The preservation results $M^\alpha \models \forall f_u^\alpha \Rightarrow M \models \forall f$ and $M^\alpha \not\models \exists f_o^\alpha \Rightarrow M \not\models \exists f$ hold for each LTL formula f, independently of the modal operators nested in f, such as it is proved in [13]. It is worth noting that both results are dual, the two sides of the same coin. Intuitively, since f_u^α is harder to hold than f, if all executions of M^α satisfy f_u^α then all executions of M satisfy f. Inversely, since f_o^α is simpler to hold than f, if no execution of M^α satisfies f_o^α then no execution of M satisfies f. In addition, it is important to remark that the inverse results do not hold, i.e., $M \models \forall f \not\Rightarrow M^\alpha \models \forall f_u^\alpha$ and $M \not\models \exists f \not\Rightarrow M^\alpha \not\models \exists f_o^\alpha$.

For the case of SPIN, the distinction between under and over approximation of properties is of utmost importance, since SPIN works by refuting properties. That is, given a model M and a formula f, SPIN constructs the negation of the formula $\neg f$ and tries to prove that no behavior of M satisfies $\neg f$ or, written more formally, that $M \not\models \exists \neg f$. If it finds a trace satisfying $\neg f$, this is a counterexample for the original formula f. SPIN may make this transformation from f to $\neg f$ because, in the concrete scenario, expressions $M \models \forall f$ and $M \not\models \neg \forall f$ (or $M \not\models \exists \neg f$) are equivalent. But, as it has been discussed above, in the abstract setting, we cannot indistinctly use the same formula abstraction to prove and

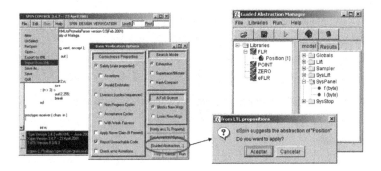

Fig. 3. One view of αSPIN

refute a property. In consequence, in order to reuse SPIN to analyze a formula over abstract models, we have to over-approximate it. Anyway, this involves no much work, because we can apply the same abstraction approach used to abstract models.

We implemented an automatic tool αSPIN [10], including all the functionalities described in this section. The user only has to introduce the abstract setting, and the tool automatically constructs the abstract model and is able to prove abstract over-approximated properties reusing the same original tool SPIN. Figure 3 shows a view of the new tool. αSPIN interface adds a new button with the label "guided abstraction" to SPIN that allows user to select the variables to be abstracted and introduce how this abstraction should work. Observe that the tool contains some predefined abstractions such as the *zero* or *point* abstractions.

3 Abstraction of Concurrent Software with Well Defined APIs

Model checking can be used beyond modelling languages using the "model-extraction" approach, where the programs are translated into modelling languages of an existing model checker (see Feaver [24], JPF [20] and Bandera [7]). In this approach, translation usually involves some *abstraction* to produce a model with only the relevant aspects for the properties to be analyzed. As far as the model should be self-contained, calls to external functions in the operating system through APIs should also be abstracted. The abstraction of the APIs also prevents the model checker to be suspended or stopped in case of execution errors. Ensuring the correctness of all the abstractions to preserve the results is the key aspect in model extraction. In [3,5,15], we developed translation and abstraction schemes and tools for concurrent C programs with APIs like *Berkeley sockets*, *dynamic memory* management and APEX interface for onboard avionics software, respectively. In [5] and [15], the correctness of the APIs models is granted thanks to the formalization of the operational semantics of the APIs to

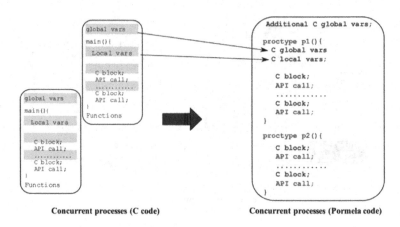

Concurrent processes (C code)   **Concurrent processes (Pormela code)**

Fig. 4. C to PROMELA mapping

drive the modelling process. In [3], we also followed a conformance testing approach, thanks to an existing battery of reference C based avionics applications
with well-known expected results. Furthermore, beyond these works to ensure
correctness in the translation, we developed *abstract matching*, a novel optimization technique that is compatible with abstracting APIs. Abstract matching
dramatically reduces the state space of the program model thanks to different
variants of the so-called *influence static analysis*.

In order to introduce abstract matching, we give an overview of the whole
translation approach. Figure 4 shows the general mapping scheme from concurrent C programs with well defined APIs to PROMELA. We use PROMELA extensions to work with embedded C code. To this end, the following primitives are
added to PROMELA: c_decl allows us to declare C data types and global variables; c_state is used to declare C variables and decide on the kind of visibility
for SPIN (e.g. local, global or hidden). The primitive c_expr is used to express
guard conditions to be evaluated in a side-effect free manner. Finally, the primitive c_code supports the use of embedded C code blocks inside the PROMELA
model.

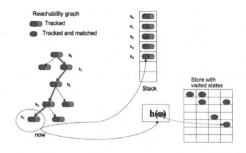

Fig. 5. Hiding part of the state with c_track

We should mention that SPIN makes use of two main structures to explore the state space produced by a model: the search **stack** that stores the states of the current trace which is being analyzing, and **state space** (the heap) that contains all states visited, and is used to backtrack when an already visited state is found during the current search. One of the most interesting extensions for our purpose is c_track. This construction allows the user to declare variables as UnMatched in order to be only stored into the SPIN stack (without registering into the heap). The effect of this mechanism is shown in Fig. 5, which represents the main data structures employed during verification (see [2] for details). Note that states in the stack contain all the information, whereas the store of visited states contains only part of the information. We exploit this mechanism to create abstract matching.

3.1   Abstract Matching and Influence Analysis

The technique to include abstract matching in SPIN and the problem of how to ensure the validity of abstract matching functions was originally presented by Holzmann and Joshi in [23]. The idea is to avoid starting a new search from a given state if an *essentially* equal state has been visited before. Thus, given a global state s, abstraction consists on replacing the usual operation "add s to States", that stores it as a visited state in the heap, by the new operation "add f(s) to States", where f() represents the abstraction function. It is worth noting that function f() is only used to cut the search tree, but the exploration is actually realized with the concrete state s, without losing information. Using this abstraction during the model checking process as explained above, we explore a subset of the original state space. Thus, in this case, abstraction produces an *under-approximation* of the original model, and similarly to the approach followed in Sect. 2, to assure that the explored tree via abstract matching is a correct under-approximation of the original one, function f() has to satisfy *some correctness conditions*. In [23], the authors do not address any particular method to generate f(), however, they present necessary conditions to define sound abstract functions that preserve CTL* properties. We contribute with implementable methods to produce abstraction functions, which are sound and oriented to the LTL property to be checked. In our scheme, abstraction functions are implemented in such a way that they can identify the variables to be hidden from the state-vector[1] in every global state, after the execution of every verification step. For instance, in the code of Fig. 6 variables x and y are visible in the state-vector. If we extract the model assuming, by default, that C variables do not influence the verification of the LTL property (i.e., their values are irrelevant for the evaluation of the property), then both variables x and y are declared as hidden (UnMatched) as represented in Fig. 7. However, if we also want to verify this code against a different property that needs the precise value of x after executing the code at L1, the model extracted must keep variable x

---

[1] The state-vector is the SPIN structure where each state is stored.

```
proctype p() {
    c_track "&x" "sizeof(int)" "Matched"
    c_track "&y" "sizeof(int)" "Matched"
    ....
    L0: initialize();
    L1: c_code{x = 1};
    L2: c_code{y = x};
    ...
}
```

Fig. 6. Initial PROMELA code generated from C

```
proctype p() {                                void f(int label) {
    c_track "&x" "sizeof(int)" "UnMatched"        switch(label) {
    c_track "&y" "sizeof(int)" "UnMatched"        ...
    c_track "&x_" "sizeof(int)" "Matched"         case L0: now.x_ = Hide()
    c_track "&y_" "sizeof(int)" "Matched"                  now.y_ = Hide()
    ...                                           case L1: now.x_ = Show(x)
    L0: atomic{initialize(); f(L0)};              case L2: now.x_ = Hide()
    L1: c_code{x = 1; f(L1)};                              now.y_ = Hide(y)
    L2: c_code{y = x; f(L2)};                     ...
    ...                                         }
}                                             }
```

Fig. 7. PROMELA code to read from the system and to build states for SPIN

visible after executing the instruction at L1. This is why, in Fig. 7, f() is called at any point where the global state should be stored.

Function f() uses its argument to check the current execution point in the model. The function updates the variables to be hidden or updated before matching them with the current set of visited states, depending on the current label. For instance, variable x can be hidden until it is updated in L1. In contrast, it is made visible at L2 because it will be used to update y, and it is again hidden after updating y. The extra variables x_ and y_ are used to store the values of the real (hidden) variables or a representation of their values. We propose to construct f() using the information provided by a static analysis of the model.

Let us denote with M_u^α the under-approximated abstraction of a concurrent C program M following the approach described above. M_u^α is an under-approximation of M in the sense that each execution trace produced by M_u^α is also an execution trace of M, i.e., $\mathcal{O}(M_u^\alpha) \subseteq \mathcal{O}(M)$. Given f is an LTL formula to be analyzed by SPIN, we need to assure the preservation of results written as $M_u^\alpha \models \forall f \Rightarrow M \models \forall f$.[2] This condition is guaranteed thanks to four variants of the so-called *influence analysis* (IA). IA is a data flow analysis [25] similar to the *live variable analysis* that calculates for each program point the set of variables that will be used in the future. IA is a more precise analysis oriented to annotate each program point with a set of *significant* variables to become visible for a given property to build the abstraction function f() (see [4]), that is, for IA a variable is *alive* if its current value will be used to evaluate f(). In short, we say that variable x *influences* variable y at a given program point, if there exists an

---

[2] Observe that f does not have to be abstracted due to execution traces of M_u^α *are* execution traces of M.

```
active proctype p1(int n) {              active proctype p2() {
  int x = n;                               int x1,x2,x3,x4;
  int y = 1;                             L1: if
L1: if                                       :: true -> L2: x2 = 0;
    :: x > 0 ->                              :: true -> L3: x2 = 1;
      L2: x = x - 1;                       fi;
      L3: y = 2 * y; goto L1            L4: x1 = x2;
    :: else -> L4: printf(y); goto End: L5: if
    fi;                                      :: x3 < 2 ->
End:                                         L6: x1 = x1 + 1; goto L5;
}                                            :: else -> L7: skip;
                                             L8: if
                                                 :: true -> L9:  x4 = 0;
                                                 :: true -> L10: x4 = -1;
                                             fi;
                                         L11: if
                                                 :: x4 >= 0 ->
                                                 L12: assert(x1 == 2);
                                                 :: else -> L3: skip
                                                 fi
                                          fi;
                                       End:}
```

Fig. 8. Two PROMELA processes

execution path in M from this point to an assignment $y = exp$ and the current value of x is used to calculate exp, that is, if the current value of x is *needed* to construct the value of y in the future. The way to build the four variants impacts on different preservation of results as follows.

IA_1 calculates the visible variables in each program point in order to preserve the *reachability tree* of the original PROMELA model. This analysis produces the *best* abstract matching function, i.e., the one inducing the best state space reduction. Since global variables must be dealt with very carefully, IA_1 assumes that the model under analysis has only local variables. The left diagram of Fig. 9 shows an example of the application of IA_1 to process p1 of Fig. 8.

IA_2 preserves state properties specified using the **assert** sentence. For instance, to analyze assertion x1 == 2 of process p2 in Fig. 8, we need to store not only the variables *influencing* the Boolean expressions in the code in order to completely simulate the reachability tree, but also those that influence the variables in the **assert** sentence (x1 in the example). The right diagram of Fig. 9 shows the result of IA_2 for process p2. Observe that variable x1 is attached to some labels of the process, since its value is needed at label $L12$. The third analysis IA_3 extends IA_2 to address models with global variables. And, finally, IA_4 focusses on the global variables present in the LTL formulae. More details of these analysis may be found in [4].

4   Abstracting Executions of Real Systems

The use of abstraction in previous sections relies on analyzing all the execution traces provided by a model written in a modelling language such as PROMELA. In [1,9,27], we showed how model checking tools like SPIN can also be used to carry out *testing* on traces produced by the execution of a real system such as, for

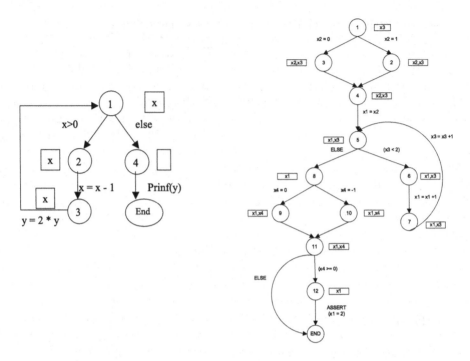

Fig. 9. Result of IA_1 for process p1 (left) and IA_2 for process p2 (right)

instance, a JAVA program. In this case, the real execution trace π to be analyzed is transformed using an abstraction/projection function ρ to generate a new trace $\rho(\pi)$ conveniently reduced. Thus, given $S = \langle \Sigma, \rightarrow, s_0 \rangle$ a transition system describing the behavior of a real system, we instrument the model checker with two goals: (1) to consider each trace π produced by S as an independent model to analyze; and (2) to abstract the *real states* of S using a projection function ρ. In consequence, the model checker takes a simplified representation $\rho(\pi)$ of the original trace π as the model to be analyzed and works as it normally does with the usual algorithms for checking duplicate states, deadlock or LTL formulae. The use of real execution traces as models opens new applications for SPIN. Our work for testing JAVA programs using SPIN as the testing engine in the tool TJT [1] is the most ambitious case because we consider infinite execution traces. The explanation in this section refers to the tool TJT for JAVA.

4.1 Building SPIN's Traces from Real Executions of JAVA Programs

Each possible execution of a JAVA program S may be represented as an infinite sequence of states $\pi = \sigma_0 \rightarrow \sigma_1 \rightarrow \sigma_2 \rightarrow \ldots$[3]. However, the internal representation of the states in SPIN is done with projections $\rho(\sigma_i)$ of such states as illustrated in the green box in Fig. 10 that shows the architecture of tool TJT.

---

[3] If the sequence is finite, we assume that the last state is infinitely repeated.

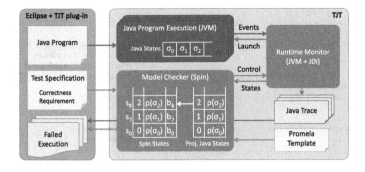

Fig. 10. TJT architecture and workflow

The tool is divided into three modules: the *model checking module*, the *runtime monitoring module* and the *Eclipse plug-in*. The programmer must supply two inputs in this workflow (left side of Fig. 10): the JAVA program being analyzed and an XML file with the *test* specification that includes the correctness requirement written in a formalism supported by SPIN, such as an LTL formula. This specification also contains additional information for carrying out the tests, like the program parameters, and their ranges, for generating test inputs.

In general, to produce the traces, the system S should be instrumented, for instance, using the JDI interface for JVM. SPIN is driven by a PROMELA code (shown in Fig. 11) that interacts with S to produce traces. The PROMELA code in Fig. 11 also provides the main logic that allows SPIN to backtrack and to exploit non-determinism to generate a new trace when the analysis of the current one has finished. The C code is used to communicate with the real system (connected via sockets to JDI) and to store part of the states in internal C structures. The code in Fig. 11 is the main entry point, where the `inline` function `explore()` launches the external system execution to produce traces. This function calls to `analyzeSystem()` displayed in Fig. 12. The most important function of this code is contained in the `analyzeExecution()` `inline`. We have omitted some details from this `inline`, including checking assertions, and left only the trace reconstruction core. This core is pretty simple: a loop that will retrieve the next state and update SPIN's global state accordingly, while there are more states available. The `nextState()` function hides the origin of this state: it may be a new state σ_i from the system execution trace π, or it may be an already visited state because SPIN backtracked during the analysis of the current trace (due to the non-determinism included in process `never_claim`)[4]. The `currentState` variable, which is stored in the state vector, has the index of the current state. When SPIN requests the state that follows the current one, it is first checked whether the stack contains it. If not, the stack is updated first with a new state from the execution trace, keeping the values of the variables that did not change.

---

[4] `never_claim` is the PROMELA process that implements the non-deterministic Büchi automata of the LTL formula.

```
inline explore() {
  generateConfig();
  cleanupPrevExecution();
  storeConfig();

  if
  :: c_expr { checkConfig() } ->
    executeSystem()
  :: else -> skip
  fi;

  cleanupExecution();
}
```

```
inline initialize() {
  c_code {
    os_init();
    os_launchServerSocket();
    initializeDatabase();
    initializeStateStack();
    initializeVariableTable();
  }
}

init {
  initialize();
  explore();
}
```

Fig. 11. Main PROMELA code to build the execution traces

```
c_code {
  void nextState(int fd) {
    now.currentState++;
    if (now.currentState > lastState)
    {
      copyPrevState();
      readState(fd);
    }
    else {
      // Backtracked
    }
    updateSpinStateFromStateStack();
  }
}
```

```
inline analyzeExecution() {
  do
  :: (running) -> c_code {
    nextState(os_getProxydata()->
      clientSocket);
  };
  :: (!running) -> break
  od
}

inline executeSystem() {
  setupNewExecution();
  startExecution();
  analyzeExecution();
}
```

Fig. 12. PROMELA code to read from the system and to build states for SPIN

Then, the variables in the SPIN's state vector are updated from the values of the corresponding state in the state stack.

4.2   The Abstraction *Projection*

The main drawback when applying model checking to programming languages is the state space explosion. Apart from taking advantage of some of the SPIN optimization methods, one practical approach consists of abstracting/projecting the JAVA states σ_i to be sent to the *model checking module*. We only send those states produced after relevant events in the JAVA execution (exceptions, deadlocks, update of designated variables, method entry and exit, interactions with monitors, breakpoints, and program termination). In addition, we only take some *visible* variables from the original state to be part of the *projection*, as shown in Fig. 13. In order to define a projection, if *Var* is the set of program variables and $\mathcal{A}$ and $\mathcal{D}$ are the set of possible memory references and the set of all possible values of JAVA primitive data types, a state of a JAVA program is a function $\sigma : Var \rightarrow \mathcal{A} \cup \mathcal{D}$ that associates each variable with its value. The *projection* of a state σ onto $V \subseteq Var$ can be defined as the function $\rho_V(\sigma) : V \rightarrow \mathcal{A} \cup \mathcal{D}$ such that $\forall v \in V.\rho_V(\sigma)(v) = \sigma(v)$. Given a JAVA trace $\pi = \sigma_0 \rightarrow \sigma_1 \rightarrow \sigma_2 \rightarrow \ldots$, the projection of π onto $V \subseteq Var$ is $\rho_V(t) = \rho_V(\sigma_0) \rightarrow \rho_V(\sigma_1) \rightarrow \rho_V(\sigma_2) \rightarrow \ldots$

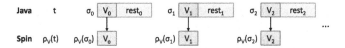

Fig. 13. Trace projection with selected variables and states

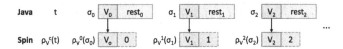

Fig. 14. Trace projection with state counting

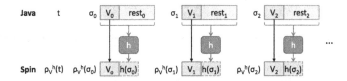

Fig. 15. Trace projection with state hashing

The effect of this projection is similar to that of the "cone of influence" technique [6]. The result is that when using a temporal formula f, if $Var(f)$ is the set of variables in f, and assuming that $Var(f) \subseteq V$, we can obtain the desired preservation relation $\pi \models f \iff \rho_V(\pi) \models f$.

However, such initial projection is not always suitable. Due to the elimination of most program variables in the projected states, it is very likely that a projected trace $\rho_V(\pi)$ contains many consecutive repeated states and makes the model checker to erroneously detect cycles[5]. To eliminate consecutive repeated states in traces, we propose the *counter projection* and the *hash projection* represented in Figs. 14 and 15, respectively.

Adding a new counter variable *count* to the set of visible variables V that is increased for every new state removes the possibility that SPIN erroneously find a non-existing cycle. The *counter projection of a state* $\sigma : V \to \mathcal{A} \cup \mathcal{D}$ is $\rho_V^i(\sigma) : V \cup \{count\} \to \mathcal{A} \cup \mathcal{D}$ defined as $\rho_V^i(\sigma)(v) = \rho_V(\sigma)(v)$, for all $v \in V$, and $\rho_V^i(\sigma)(count) = i$. Variable count is called state counter of $\rho_V^i(\sigma)$. Now, given a JAVA trace $\pi = \sigma_0 \to \sigma_1 \cdots$ we define the *counter projection of* π onto V, ρ_V^c, by projecting each state σ_i with the i-th counter projection, that is, $\rho_V^c(\pi) = \rho_V^0(\sigma_0) \to \rho_V^1(\sigma_1) \cdots$. We can keep the following result: given a temporal formula f in negation normal form using only the eventually "$\Diamond$" and until "U" temporal operators, if $V = var(f) \subseteq Var$ then $\rho_V^c(\pi) \models_s f \implies \pi \models f$, where $\models_s$ represents the evaluation algorithm implemented by SPIN.

---

[5] Note that this does not contradict the previous satisfaction result, since in this result we do not assume any particular algorithm to evaluate the property on the projected trace.

Counter projection ρ_V^c does not permit SPIN to detect cycles in the projected trace. Thus, properties that do not require the detection of cycles (i.e., those that use only operators *eventually* "$\Diamond$" and *until* "U")[6] can be properly checked over this projection. In contrast, since properties that use the *always* "$\Box$" temporal operator are checked by SPIN by searching for cycles, they cannot be analyzed over $\rho_V^c(\pi)$. So, we extend the notion of state projection onto V by adding the codification of the whole state σ (including the non-visible part) as $\rho_V^h(\sigma)$ using the hash function h as $\rho_V^h(\sigma) : V \cup \{hash\} \to \mathcal{A} \cup \mathcal{D}$ defined as $\rho_V^h(\sigma)(v) = \rho_V(\sigma)(v)$, for all $v \in V$, and $\rho_V^h(\sigma)(hash) = h(\sigma)$.

Now, given a JAVA trace $\pi = \sigma_0 \to \sigma_1 \cdots$, we define the *hash projection of* π onto V, ρ_V^h, by projecting each state σ_i with the hash projection, that is, $\rho_V^h(\pi) = \rho_V^h(\sigma_0) \to \rho_V^h(\sigma_1) \cdots$. And we keep the result $\rho_V^h(\pi) \models_s f \implies \pi \models f$ with the degree of probability allowed by h.

This section has summarized paper [1] by highlighting the contributions in (1) the implementation of tool TJT regarding the extraction of traces from a JAVA program and their handling by SPIN; and (2) the simplification of traces using different projection functions that preserve the correctness results.

5   Conclusions

In this paper, we highlight some contributions in the area of abstraction for model checking developed by the MORSE team at ITIS Software-University of Málaga. The first contribution is going deeper in the duality of over/under-approximation of models/properties wrt the usual over-approximation method in the classic papers on abstract model checking. The way we implement over-approximation of properties by source-to-source transformation allows us to reuse existing explicit model checkers like SPIN to support the analysis of LTL formulae. A second contribution is the method to inject real execution traces in the model checkers, opening many application areas, like model checking of concurrent programming languages. The third contribution is a new set of abstraction functions like projection, counter, hash projection, as well as the general abstract matching technique based on influence analysis.

The combination of these contributions allows us to apply model checking to complex systems. In the paper, we have provided some examples: infinite traces in JAVA programs and concurrent C programs using well-defined APIs. In particular, we have applied this last methodology to socket-based communication software in C [5], dynamic memory management in C programs [15,19], avionics software with APEX interface [3], apps for mobile networks [8] or models of communication network for simulation [27]. In addition, variants of the same ideas have been successfully applied in other areas, like building decision support systems for water management [11,12], model checking of hybrid systems [18,26] or extending the CADP framework to deal with well defined APIs based software [16].

We believe that mobile networks is one of the more relevant application areas in the near future due to the size of the market, the impact in society and the

---

[6] This is because SPIN transforms these properties into their corresponding negations.

increasing requirements in terms of reliability, latency and throughput. As an example, the work with execution traces in the project TRIANGLE [9] conducted us to detect potential underperformance scenarios in Spotify application [8]. Our current interest is to use abstraction and model checking for software based communication networks, like the 5G mobile networks as we proposed in [17]. This is part of the work to be done in the context of the 5GENESIS project funded under H2020 EC framework.

Acknowledgements. The three of us are very honoured to have had the opportunity to participate in this volume devoted to celebrating the Manuel Hermenegildo's achievements in research. In particular, the first author is very grateful for his advice early in her research career and for introducing her to the exciting field of abstract interpretation.

Finally, we want to recognize the contributions of former members of MORSE team, specially to Jesús Martínez, David Sanán, Alberto Salmerón, Pedro de la Cámara, Christophe Joubert, Ana Rosario Espada and Damián Adalid.

References

1. Adalid, D., Salmerón, A., Gallardo, M., Merino, P.: Using SPIN for automated debugging of infinite executions of java programs. J. Syst. Softw. **90**, 61–75 (2014). https://doi.org/10.1016/j.jss.2013.10.056

2. Bosnacki, D.: Enhancing state space reduction techniques for model checking. Ph.D. thesis, Department of Mathematics and Computer Science (2001). https://doi.org/10.6100/IR549628

3. de la Cámara, P., Castro, J.R., Gallardo, M., Merino, P.: Verification support for ARINC-653-based avionics software. Softw. Test. Verif. Reliab. **21**(4), 267–298 (2011). https://doi.org/10.1002/stvr.422

4. de la Cámara, P., del Mar Gallardo, M., Merino, P.: Abstract matching for software model checking. In: Valmari, A. (ed.) SPIN 2006. LNCS, vol. 3925, pp. 182–200. Springer, Heidelberg (2006). https://doi.org/10.1007/11691617_11

5. de la Cámara, P., Gallardo, M., Merino, P., Sanán, D.: Checking the reliability of socket based communication software. Int. J. Softw. Tools Technol. Transf. **11**(5), 359–374 (2009). https://doi.org/10.1007/s10009-009-0112-7

6. Clarke, E.M., Grumberg, O., Peled, D.A.: Model Checking. The MIT Press, Cambridge (2000)

7. Corbett, J.C., Dwyer, M.B., Hatcliff, J., Laubach, S., Pasareanu, C.S., Robby, Zheng, H.: Bandera: extracting finite-state models from java source code. In: Ghezzi, C., Jazayeri, M., Wolf, A.L. (eds.) Proceedings of the 22nd International Conference on on Software Engineering, ICSE 2000, Limerick Ireland, 4–11 June 2000, pp. 439–448. ACM (2000). https://doi.org/10.1145/337180.337234

8. Espada, A.R., Gallardo, M., Salmerón, A., Merino, P.: Performance analysis of spotify® for android with model-based testing. Mob. Inf. Syst. **2017**, 67–77 (2017). https://doi.org/10.1155/2017/2012696

9. Espada, A.R., Gallardo, M., Salmerón, A., Panizo, L., Merino, P.: A formal app-roach to automatically analyse extra-functional properties in mobile applications. Softw. Test. Verification Reliab. **29**(4–5), e1699 (2019). https://doi.org/10.1002/stvr.1699

10. Gallardo, M.M., Martínez, J., Merino, P., Pimentel, E.: aSPIN: a tool for abstract model checking. Softw. Tools Technol. Transf. **5**(2–3), 165–184 (2004)

11. Gallardo, M.M., Merino, P., Panizo, L., Linares, A.: Developing a decision support tool for dam management with SPIN. In: Alpuente, M., Cook, B., Joubert, C. (eds.) FMICS 2009. LNCS, vol. 5825, pp. 210–212. Springer, Heidelberg (2009). https://doi.org/10.1007/978-3-642-04570-7_20

12. Gallardo, M.M., Merino, P., Panizo, L., Linares, A.: A practical use of model checking for synthesis: generating a dam controller for flood management. Softw. Pract. Exp. **41**(11), 1329–1347 (2011)

13. Gallardo, M.M., Merino, P., Pimentel, E.: Refinement of LTL formulas for abstract model checking. In: Hermenegildo, M.V., Puebla, G. (eds.) SAS 2002. LNCS, vol. 2477, pp. 395–410. Springer, Heidelberg (2002). https://doi.org/10.1007/3-540-45789-5_28

14. Gallardo, M.M., Merino, P., Pimentel, E.: A generalized semantics of PROMELA for abstract model checking. Formal Aspects Comput. **16**(3), 166–193 (2004)

15. Gallardo, M.M., Merino, P., Sanán, D.: Model checking dynamic memory allocation in operating systems. J. Autom. Reasoning **42**(2–4), 229–264 (2009)

16. Gallardo, M., Joubert, C., Merino, P., Sanán, D.: A model-extraction approach to verifying concurrent C programs with CADP. Sci. Comput. Program. **77**(3), 375–392 (2012). https://doi.org/10.1016/j.scico.2011.10.003

17. Gallardo, M.-M., Luque-Schempp, F., Merino-Gómez, P., Panizo, L.: How formal methods can contribute to 5G networks. In: ter Beek, M.H., Fantechi, A., Semini, L. (eds.) From Software Engineering to Formal Methods and Tools, and Back. LNCS, vol. 11865, pp. 548–571. Springer, Cham (2019). https://doi.org/10.1007/978-3-030-30985-5_32

18. Gallardo, M., Panizo, L.: Extending model checkers for hybrid system verification: the case study of SPIN. Softw. Test. Verif. Reliab. **24**(6), 438–471 (2014). https://doi.org/10.1002/stvr.1505

19. Gallardo, M., Sanán, D.: Verification of complex dynamic data tree with mu-calculus. Autom. Softw. Eng. **20**(4), 569–612 (2013). https://doi.org/10.1007/s10515-012-0113-8

20. Havelund, K., Pressburger, T.: Model checking JAVA programs using JAVA pathfinder. Int. J. Softw. Tools Technol. Transf. **2**(4), 366–381 (2000). https://doi.org/10.1007/s100090050043

21. Holzmann, G.: The model checker SPIN. IEEE Trans. Softw. Eng. **23**(5), 279–295 (1997)

22. Holzmann, G.: The SPIN Model Checker?: Primer and Reference Manual. Addison-Wesley Professional, Boston (2003)

23. Holzmann, G. J., Joshi, R.: Model-driven software verification. In: Model Checking Software: 11th International SPIN Workshop, Barcelona, Spain, 1-3 April 2004. Proceedings 11, pp. 76-91. Springer, Berlin (2004). https://doi.org/10.1007/b96721

24. Holzmann, G.J., Smith, M.H.: Software model checking: extracting verification models from source code. Softw. Test. Verification Reliab. **11**(2), 65–79 (2001)

25. Nielson, F., Nielson, H.R., Hankin, C.: Principles of Program Analysis. Springer, Berlin (1998)
26. Panizo, L., Gallardo, M.: An extension of Java PathFinder for hybrid systems. ACM SIGSOFT Softw. Eng. Notes **37**(6), 1–5 (2012)
27. Salmerón, A., Merino, P.: Integrating model checking and simulation for protocol optimization. SIMULATION **91**(1), 3–25 (2015). https://doi.org/10.1177/0037549714557054

Justifications and a Reconstruction of Parity Game Solving Algorithms

Ruben Lapauw⬤, Maurice Bruynooghe⬤, and Marc Denecker(⊠)⬤

Department of Computer Science, KU Leuven, 3001 Leuven, Belgium
{ruben.lapauw,maurice.bruynooghe,marc.denecker}@cs.kuleuven.be

Abstract. Parity games are infinite two-player games played on directed graphs. Parity game solvers are used in the domain of formal verification. This paper defines parametrized parity games and introduces an operation, **Justify**, that determines a winning strategy for a single node. By carefully ordering **Justify** steps, we reconstruct three algorithms well known from the literature.

1 Introduction

Parity games are games played on a directed graph without leaves by two players, Even (0) and Odd (1). A node has an owner (a player) and an integer priority. A play is an infinite path in the graph where the owner of a node chooses which outgoing edge to follow. A play and its nodes is won by Even if the highest priority that occurs infinitely often is even and by Odd otherwise. A parity game is solved when the winner of every node is determined and proven.

Parity games are relevant for boolean equation systems [8,17], temporal logics such as LTL, CTL and CTL* [13] and μ-calculus [13,30]. Many problems in these domains can be reduced to solving a parity game. Quasi-polynomial time algorithm for solving them exist [7,12,24]. However, all current state-of-the-art algorithms (Zielonka's algorithm [31], strategy-improvement [27], priority promotion [1–3] and tangle learning [28]) are exponential.

We start the paper with a short description of the role of parity game solvers in the domain of formal verification (Sect. 2). In Sect. 3, we recall the essentials of parity games and introduce parametrized parity games as a generalization of parity games. In Sect. 4 we recall justifications, which we introduced in [20] to store winning strategies and to speed up algorithms. Here we introduce safe justifications and define a **Justify** operation and proof its properties. Next, in Sect. 5, we reconstruct three algorithms for solving parity games by defining different orderings over **Justify** operations. We conclude in Sect. 6.

© Springer Nature Switzerland AG 2023
P. Lopez-Garcia et al. (Eds.): Hermenegildo Festschrift 2022, LNCS 13160, pp. 170–187, 2023.
https://doi.org/10.1007/978-3-031-31476-6_9

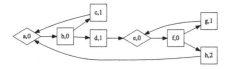

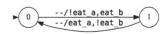

Fig. 1. A reduced parity game.

Fig. 2. The resulting Mealy machine with two states, alternating $\neg eat_A, eat_B$ and $eat_A, \neg eat_B$ regardless of the input of $hungry_A$ and $hungry_B$.

2   Verification and Parity Game Solving

Time logics such as LTL are used to express properties of interacting systems. Synthesis consists of extracting an implementation with the desired properties. Typically, formulas in such logics are handled by reduction to other formalisms. LTL can be reduced to Büchi-automata [18,29], determinized with Safra's construction [26], and transformed to parity games [25]. Other modal logics have similar reductions, CTL* can be reduced to automata [4], to μ-calculus [9], and recently to LTL-formulae [5]. All are reducible to parity games.

One of the tools that support the synthesis of implementations for such formulas is Strix [21,22], one of the winners of the SyntComp 2018 [15] and Synt-Comp 2019 competition. This program reduces LTL-formulae on the fly to parity games pitting a machine against the (uncontrollable) environment. A game has three possible outcomes: (i) the parity game needs further expansion, (ii) the machine wins the game, i.e., an implementation is feasible, (iii) the environment wins, i.e., no implementation exists. Strix also extracts an implementation with the specified behaviour, e.g., as a Mealy machine.

Consider a formula based on the well-known dining philosophers problem:

$$G(hungry_A \Rightarrow Feat_A) \wedge \quad \text{If A is hungry, he will eventually eat}$$
$$G(hungry_B \Rightarrow Feat_B) \wedge \quad \text{If B is hungry, he will eventually eat} \qquad (1)$$
$$G(\neg eat_A \vee \neg eat_B) \qquad \text{A and B cannot eat at the same time.}$$

Here $(G\phi)$ means ϕ holds in every future trace and $(F\phi)$ means ϕ holds in some future trace where a trace is a succession of states.

With a complex procedure, Strix transforms the LTL-formula 1 into the optimised parity game shown in Fig. 1. The machine (Even) plays in the square nodes and the environment (Odd) in the diamond nodes. By playing in state b to d, and in state f to h, Even wins every node as 2 is then the highest priority that occurs infinitely often in every play. From the solution, Strix extracts a 2-state Mealy machine (Fig. 2). Its behaviour satisfies Formula 1: both philosophers alternate eating regardless of their hunger.

3   Parametrized Parity Games

A parity game [11,23,30] is a two-player game of player 0 (Even) against 1 (Odd). We use $\alpha \in \{0,1\}$ to denote a player and $\bar{\alpha}$ to denote its opponent. Formally, we define a *parity game* as a tuple $\mathcal{PG} = (V, E, O, Pr)$ with V the set of nodes, E the set of possible moves represented as pairs (v, w) of nodes, $O : V \to \{0, 1\}$ the owner function, and Pr the priority function $V \to \mathbb{N}$ mapping nodes to their priority; (V, E) is also called the game graph. Each $v \in V$ has at least one possible move. We use O_α to denote nodes owned by α.

A *play* (in node v_1) of the parity game is an infinite sequence of nodes $\langle v_1, v_2, \ldots, v_n \ldots \rangle$ where $\forall i : v_i \in V \wedge (v_i, v_{i+1}) \in E$. We use π as a mathematical variable to denote a play. $\pi(i)$ is the i-th node v_i of π. In a play π, it is the owner of the node v_i that decides the move (v_i, v_{i+1}). There exists plays in every node. We call the player $\alpha = (n \mod 2)$ the *winner of priority n*. The winner of a play is the winner of the highest priority n through which the play passes infinitely often. Formally: $Winner(\pi) = \lim_{i \to +\infty} max\,\{Pr(\pi(j))|j \geq i\} \mod 2$.

The key questions for a parity game $\mathcal{PG}$ are, for each node v: Who is the winner? And how? As proven by [11], parity games are memoryless determined: every node has a unique winner and a corresponding memoryless winning strategy. A (memoryless) strategy for player α is a partial function σ_α from a subset of O_α to V. A play π is consistent with σ_α if for every v_i in π belonging to the domain of σ_α, v_{i+1} is $\sigma_\alpha(v_i)$. A strategy σ_α for player α is a *winning strategy* for a node v if every play in v consistent with this strategy is won by α, i.e. regardless of the moves selected by $\bar{\alpha}$. As such, a game $\mathcal{PG}$ defines a winning function $W_{\mathcal{PG}} : V \mapsto \{0, 1\}$. The set $W_{\mathcal{PG},\alpha}$ or, when $\mathcal{PG}$ is clear from the context, W_α denotes the set of nodes won by α. Moreover, for both players $\alpha \in \{0, 1\}$, there exists a memoryless winning strategy σ_α with domain $W_\alpha \cap O_\alpha$ that wins in all nodes won by α. A *solution* of $\mathcal{PG}$ consists of a function $W' : V \to \{0, 1\}$ and two winning strategies σ_0 and σ_1, with $dom(\sigma_\alpha) = W'_\alpha \cap O_\alpha$, such that every play in $v \in W'_\alpha$ consistent with σ_α is won by α. Solutions always exist; they may differ in strategy but all have $W' = W_{\mathcal{PG}}$, the winning function of the game. We can say that the pair (σ_0, σ_1) proves that $W' = W_{\mathcal{PG}}$.

In order to have a framework in which we can discuss different algorithms from the literature, we define a parametrized parity game. It consists of a parity game $\mathcal{PG}$ and a parameter function P, a partial function $P : V \rightharpoonup \{0, 1\}$ with domain $dom(P) \subseteq V$. Elements of $dom(P)$ are called parameters, and P assigns a winner to each parameter. Plays are the same as in a $\mathcal{PG}$ except that every play that reaches a parameter v ends and is won by $P(v)$.

Definition 1 (Parametrized parity game). *Let $\mathcal{PG} = (V, E, O, Pr)$ be a parity game and $P : V \rightharpoonup \{0, 1\}$ a partial function with domain $dom(P) \subseteq V$. Then $(\mathcal{PG}, P)$ is a* parametrized parity game *denoted $\mathcal{PG}_P$, with parameter set $dom(P)$. If $P(v) = \alpha$, we call α the assigned winner of parameter v. The sets P_0 and P_1 denote parameter nodes with assigned winner 0 respectively 1.*

A play of $(\mathcal{PG}, P)$ is a sequence of nodes $\langle v_0, v_1, \ldots \rangle$ such that for all i: if $v_i \in P_\alpha$ then the play halts and is won by α, otherwise v_{i+1} exists and $(v, v_{i+1}) \in E$. For infinite plays, the winner is as in the original parity game $\mathcal{PG}$.

Every parity game $\mathcal{PG}$ defines a class of parametrized parity games (PPG's), one for each partial function P. The original $\mathcal{PG}$ corresponds to one of these games, namely the one without parameters $(dom(P) = \emptyset)$; every total function $P : V \to \{0, 1\}$ defines a trivial PPG, with plays of length 0 and $P = W_{\mathcal{PG}_P}$.

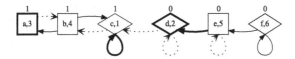

Fig. 3. A parametrized parity game with nodes $a, \ldots, f$, $P_0 = \{d\}$ and $P_1 = \{a\}$, and winning strategies for 0 and 1. The two parameter nodes are in bold. Square nodes are owned by Even, diamonds by Odd. The labels inside a node are the name and priority; the label on top of a node is the winner. A bold edge belongs to a winning strategy (of the owner of its start node). A slim edge is one starting in a node that is lost by its owner. All remaining edges are dotted.

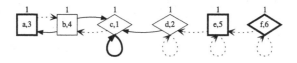

Fig. 4. A parametrized parity game and strategy, after withdrawing d from the parameter list.

A PPG $\mathcal{PG}_P$ can be reduced to an equivalent PG G: in each parameter $v \in dom(P)$ replace the outgoing edges with a self-loop and the priority of v with $P(v)$. We now have a standard parity game G. Every infinite play $\langle v_0, v_1, \ldots \rangle$ in $\mathcal{PG}_P$ is also an infinite play in G with the same winner. Every finite play $\langle v_0, v_1, \ldots, v_n \rangle$ with winner $P(v_n)$ in $\mathcal{PG}_P$ corresponds to an infinite play $\langle v_0, v_1, \ldots, v_n, v_n, \ldots \rangle$ with winner $P(v_n)$ in G. Thus, the two games are equivalent. It follows that any PPG $\mathcal{PG}_P$ is a zero-sum game defining a winning function W and having memory-less winning strategies σ_α with domain $(W_\alpha \setminus P_\alpha) \cap O_\alpha$ (for $\alpha = 0, 1$).

PPG's allow us to capture the behaviour of several state of the art algorithms as a sequence of solved PPG's. In each step, strategies and parameters are modified and a solution for one PPG is transformed into a solution for a next PPG and this until a solution for the input PG is reached.

Example 1. Figure 3 shows a parametrized parity game and its winning strategies. The parameter nodes a and d are won by the assigned winners, respectively 1 and 0. Player 1 owns node c and wins its priority. Hence, by playing from c to c, 1 wins in this node. Node b is owned by 0 but has only moves to nodes won by 1, hence it is also won by 1. Player 0 wins node e by playing to node d; 1 plays in node f but playing to f results in an infinite path won by 0, while playing to node e runs into a path won by 0, so f is won by 0.

Based on this PPG, we can construct a solved PPG where node d is removed from the parameters. The strategy is adjusted accordingly: Odd wins in d by playing to c. However, changing the winner of d breaks the strategies and winners of the nodes e and f. Figure 4 shows one way to obtain a solved PPG with further adjustments: nodes e and f are turned into parameters won by 1. Many other solutions exist, e.g., by turning e into a parameter won by 0.

4   Justifications

In Fig. 3 and Fig. 4, the solid edges form the subgraph of the game graph that was analysed to confirm the winners of all nodes. We formalize this subgraph as a *justification*, a concept introduced in [14] and described below. In the rest of the paper, we assume the existence of a parity game $\mathcal{PG} = (V, E, O, Pr)$ and a parametrized parity game $\mathcal{PG}_P = (\mathcal{PG}, P)$ with P a parameter function with set of parameters $dom(P)$. Also, we use $H : V \rightarrow \{0, 1\}$ as a function describing a "hypothesis" of who is winning in the nodes.

Definition 2 (Direct justification). *A direct justification dj for player α to win node v is a set containing one outgoing edge of v if $O(v) = \alpha$ and all outgoing edges of v if $O(v) = \bar{\alpha}$.*

A direct justification dj wins v for α under hypothesis H if for all $(v, w) \in dj$, $H(w) = \alpha$. We also say: α wins v by dj under H.

Definition 3 (Justification). *A justification J for $\mathcal{PG}$ is a tuple (V, D, H) such that (V, D) is a subgraph of (V, E). If a node has outgoing edges in D, it is justified in J, otherwise it is unjustified.*

Definition 4 (Weakly winning). *A justification (V, D, H) is weakly winning if for all justified nodes $v \in V$ the set of outgoing edges Out_v is a direct justification that wins v for $H(v)$ under H.*

We observe that any justification $J = (V, D, H)$ determines a PPG $\mathcal{PG}_{P_J}$ where the parameter function P_J is the restriction of H to unjustified nodes.

If J is weakly winning, the set of edges $\{(v, w) \in D \mid O(v) = H(v) = \alpha\}$ is a partial function on O_α, i.e., a strategy for α. We denote it as $\sigma_{J,\alpha}$.

Proposition 1. *Assume a weakly winning justification $J = (V, D, H)$. Then, (i) For every path π in D, all nodes v on π have the same hypothetical winner $H(v)$. (ii) All finite paths π starting in node v in D are won in $\mathcal{PG}_{P_J}$ by $H(v)$. (iii) Every path in D with nodes hypothetically won by α is consistent with $\sigma_{J,\alpha}$. (iv) Every play starting in v of $\mathcal{PG}_{P_J}$ consistent with $\sigma_{J,H(v)}$ is a path in D.*

Proof. (i) Since any edge $(v, w) \in D$ belongs to a direct justification that wins v for $H(v)$, it holds that $H(v) = H(w)$. It follows that every path π in D consists of nodes with the same hypothetical winner. (ii) If path π in v is finite and ends in parameter w, then $H(v) = H(w)$. The winner of π in $\mathcal{PG}_{P_J}$ is $P_J(w)$ which is equal to $H(v)$ as H expands P_J. (iii) Every path in D with hypothetical winner α, follows $\sigma_{J,\alpha}$ when it is in a node v with owner α. (iv) Let $H(v) = \alpha$ and π be a play in v of $\mathcal{PG}_P$ consistent with $\sigma_{J,\alpha}$. We can inductively construct a path from $v = v_1$ in D. It follows from (i) that the n'th node v_n has $H(v_n) = H(v_1) = \alpha$. For each non-parameter node v_n, if $O(v_n) = \alpha$, then $v_{i+1} = \sigma_{J,\alpha}(v_i)$ which is in D. If $O(v_n) = \bar{\alpha}$ then D contains all outgoing edges from v_n including the one to v_{n+1}. $\qquad\square$

Definition 5 (Winning). *A justification* $J = (V, D, H)$ *is* winning *if (i)* J *is weakly winning and (ii) all infinite paths* $\langle v_1, v_2, \ldots \rangle$ *in* D *are plays of* $\mathcal{PG}$ *won by* $H(v_1)$.

Observe that, if J is winning and $H(v) = \alpha$, all plays in $\mathcal{PG}_{P_J}$ starting in v and consistent with $\sigma_{(V,D,H),\alpha}$ are paths in (V, D) won by α. Hence:

Theorem 1. *If* $J = (V, D, H)$ *is a winning justification for* $\mathcal{PG}_{P_J}$ *then* H *is* $W_{\mathcal{PG}_{P_J}}$, *the winning function of* $\mathcal{PG}_{P_J}$, *with corresponding winning strategies* $\sigma_{J,0}$ *and* $\sigma_{J,1}$.

The central invariant of the algorithm presented below is that its data structure $J = (V, D, H)$ is a winning justification. Thus, in every stage, H is the winning function of $\mathcal{PG}_{P_J}$ and the graph (V, D) comprises winning strategies $\sigma_{J,\alpha}$ for both players. In a sense, (V, D) provides a proof that H is $W_{\mathcal{PG}_{P_J}}$.

4.1 Operations on Weakly Winning Justifications

We introduce an operation that modifies a justification $J = (V, D, H)$ and hence also the underlying game $\mathcal{PG}_{P_J}$. Let v be a node in V, α a player and dj either the empty set or a direct justification. We define $J[v : dj, \alpha]$ as the justification $J' = (V, D', H')$ where D' is obtained from D by replacing the outgoing edges of v by the edges in dj, and H' is the function obtained from H by setting $H'(v) := \alpha$. Modifications for a set of nodes are independent of application order. E.g., $J[v : \emptyset, H'(v) \mid v \in S]$ removes all out-going edges of v and sets $H'(v)$ for all $v \in S$. Multiple operations, like $J[v : dj, \alpha][v' : dj', \alpha']$, are applied left to right. Some useful instances, with their properties, are below.

In the proposition, a cycle in J is a finite sequence of nodes following edges in J that ends in its starting node.

Proposition 2. *For a weakly winning justification* J *and a node* v *with direct justification* dj *the following holds:*

(i) If $H(v) = \bar{\alpha}$, v *has no incoming edges and* dj *wins* v *for* α *under* H, *then* $J[v : dj, \alpha]$ *is weakly winning and there are no cycles in* J' *with edges of* dj.

(ii) Let S *be a set of nodes closed under incoming edges (if* $v \in S$ *and* $(w, v) \in D$, *then* $w \in S$), *let* H_f *be an arbitrary function mapping nodes of* S *to players. It holds that* $J[v : \emptyset, H_f(v) \mid v \in S]$ *is weakly winning. There are no cycles in* J' *with edges of* dj.

(iii) If $H(v) = \alpha$ *and* dj *wins* v *for* α *under* H, *then* $J[v : dj, \alpha]$ *is weakly winning. There are no new cycles when* $(v, v) \notin dj$ *and no* $w \in range(dj)$ *can reach* v *in* J. *Otherwise new cycles pass through* v *and have at least one edge in* dj.

Proof. We exploit the fact that J and J' are very similar.

(i) The direct justification dj cannot have an edge ending in v since $H(v) \neq H(w)$ for $(v, w) \in dj$ and no $w \in dj$ can reach v in J since v has no incoming edges, hence J' has no cycles through dj. As J is weakly winning and H is updated only in v, the direct justification of a justified node $w \neq v$ in J is still winning in J'. Since also dj wins v for α, J' is weakly winning.

(ii) Setting $H(v)$ arbitrary cannot endanger the weak support of J' as v has no direct justification and no incoming edges in J'. Hence J' is weakly winning. Also, removing direct justifications cannot introduce new cycles.

(iii) Let $H(v) = \alpha$ and dj wins v for α under H. Let $J' = J[v : dj, \alpha]$. We have $H' = H$ so the direct justifications of all nodes $w \neq v$ in J' win w for $H'(w)$. Since dj wins v for $H'(v)$, J' is weakly winning. Also, new cycles if any, pass through dj and v.

4.2   Constructing Winning Justifications

The eventual goal of a justification is to create a winning justification without unjustified nodes. Such a justification contains a solution for the parity game without parameters. To reach this goal we start with an empty winning justification and iteratively assign a direct justification to one of the nodes.

However, haphazardly (re)assigning direct justifications will violate the intended winning justification invariant. Three problems appear: First, changing the hypothesis of a node may violate weakly winning for incoming edges. The easiest fix is to remove the direct justification of nodes with edges to this node. Yet removing direct justifications decreases the justification progress. Thus a second problem is ensuring progress and termination despite these removals. Third, newly created cycles must be winning for the hypothesis. To solve these problems, we introduce safe justifications; we start with some auxiliary concepts.

Let J be a justification. The set of nodes *reaching* v in J, including v, is closed under incoming edges and is denoted with $J{\downarrow}_v$. The set of nodes *reachable* from v in J, including v, is denoted with $J{\uparrow}_v$. We define $Par_J(v)$ as the parameters reachable from the node v, formally $Par_J(v) = J{\uparrow}_v \cap dom(P)$. The *justification level* $jl_J(v)$ of a node v is the lowest priority of all its parameters and $+\infty$ if v has none. The *justification level* $jl_J(dj)$ of a direct justification $dj = \{(v, w_1), \ldots, (v, w_n)\}$ is $min\{jl_J(w_1), \ldots, jl_J(w_n)\}$, the minimum of the justification levels of the w_i. We drop the subscript J when it is clear from the context and write $Par(v)$, $jl(v)$ and $jl(dj)$ for the above concepts. The *default winner* of a node v is the winner of its priority, i.e., $Pr(v)$ mod 2; the *default hypothesis* H_d assigns default winners to all nodes, i.e., $H_d(v) = Pr(v)$ mod 2.

Definition 6 (Safe justification). *A justification is safe iff (i) it is a winning justification, (ii) all unjustified nodes v have $H(v) = H_d(v)$, that is, the winners of the current parameters of the PPG are their default winners, and (iii) $\forall v \in V : jl(v) \geq Pr(v)$, i.e., the justification level of a node is at least its priority.*

Fixing the invariants is easier for safe justifications. Indeed, for nodes w on a path to a parameter v, $Pr(v) \geq jl(w) \geq Pr(w)$, so when v is given a direct justification to w then $Pr(v)$ is the highest priority in the created cycle and $H(v)$ correctly denotes its winner. Furthermore, the empty safe justification $(V, \emptyset, H_d)$ will serve as initialisation of the solving process.

4.3   The Operation Justify

To progress towards a solution, we introduce a single operation, namely **Justify**. Given appropriate inputs, it can assign a direct justification to an unjustified node or replace the direct justification of a justified node. Furthermore, if needed, it manipulates the justification in order to restore its safety.

Definition 7 (Justify).   *The operation* **Justify**(J, v, dj) *is* executable *if*

- *Precondition 1: $J = (V, D, H)$ is a safe justification, v is a node in V, there exists a player α who wins v by dj under H.*
- *Precondition 2: if v is unjustified in J then $jl(dj) \geq jl(v)$ else $jl(dj) > jl(v)$.*

Let **Justify**(J, v, dj) *be executable. If $H(v) = \alpha$ then* **Justify**$(J, v, dj) = J[v : dj, H(v)]$, *i.e., dj becomes the direct justification of v.*

If $H(v) = \bar{\alpha}$, then **Justify**$(J, v, dj) = J[w : \emptyset, H_d(w) \mid w \in J{\downarrow}v][v : dj, \alpha]$, *i.e., α wins v by dj, while all other nodes w that can reach v become unjustified, and their hypothetical winner $H(w)$ is reset to their default winner.*

If **Justify**(J, v, dj) is executable, we say that v is *justifiable with dj* or *justifiable* for short; when performing the operation, we *justify v*.

Observe, when **Justify** modifies the hypothetical winner $H(v)$, then, to preserve weak winning, edges (w, v) need to be removed, which is achieved by removing the direct justification of w. Moreover, to preserve (iii) of safety, this process must be iterated until fixpoint and to preserve (ii) of safety, the hypothetical winner $H(w)$ of w needs to be reset to its default winner. This produces a situation satisfying all invariants. Furthermore, when **Justify** is applied on a justified v, it preserves $H(v)$ but it replaces v's direct justification by one with a strictly higher justification level. As the proof below shows, this ensures that no new cycles are created through v so we can guarantee that all remaining cycles still have the correct winner. So, cycles can only be created by justifying an unjustified node.

Lemma 1. *An executable operation* **Justify**(J, v, dj) *returns a safe justification.*

Proof. Assume **Justify**(J, v, dj) is executable, $J' =$ **Justify**(J, v, dj) and let α be the player that wins v by dj. First, we prove that J' is also a winning justification, i.e., that J' is weakly winning and that the winner of every infinite path in J' is the hypothetical winner $H(w)$ of the nodes w on the path.

The operations applied to obtain J' are the ones that have been analysed in Proposition 2 and for which it was proven that they preserve weakly winning. Note that, in case $H(v) = \bar{\alpha}$, the intermediate justification $J[v : \emptyset, H_d(v) \mid v \in J{\downarrow}v]$ removes all incoming edges of v. By case (ii) of Proposition 2, J' is weakly winning and all nodes v, w connected in J have $H'(v) = H'(w)$ (*). If no edge in dj belongs to a cycle, then every infinite path $\langle v_1, v_2, \ldots \rangle$ in J' has an infinite tail in J starting in $w \neq v$ which is, since J is winning, won by $H(w)$. By (*), this path is won by $H(v_1) = H(w)$ and J' is winning.

If J' has cycles through edges in dj, then, by (i) of Proposition 2, $H(v)$ must be α and we use case (iii) of Proposition 2. We analyse the nodes n on such a cycle. By safety of J, $Pr(n) \leq jl_J(n)$; as n reaches v in J, $jl_J(n) \leq jl_J(v)$. If v is unjustified in J then $jl_J(v) = Pr(v) \geq Pr(n)$, hence $Pr(v)$ is the highest priority on the cycle and $H(v)$ wins the cycle. If v is justified in J and $(v, w) \in dj$ is on the new cycle, then $jl_J(w) \geq jl_J(dj) > jl_J(v)$ (Precondition 2 of **Justify**). But w reaches v so $jl_J(w) \leq jl_J(v)$, which is a contradiction.

Next, we prove that J' is a safe justification (Definition 6). (i) Before, we proved that J' is a winning justification. (ii) For all unjustified nodes v of J', it holds that $H(v) = H_d(v)$, its default winner. Indeed, J has this property and whenever the direct justification of a node w is removed, $H'(w)$ is set to $H_d(w)$.

(iii) We need to prove that for all nodes w, it holds that $jl_{J'}(w) \geq Pr(w)$. We distinguish between the two cases of **Justify**(J, v, dj).

(a) Assume $H(v) = \alpha = H'(v)$ and $J' = J[v : dj, H(v)]$ and let w be an arbitrary node of V. If w cannot reach v in J', the parameters that w reaches in J and J' are the same and it follows that $jl_{J'}(w) = jl_J(w) \geq Pr(w)$. So, (iii) holds for w. Otherwise, if w reaches v in J', then w reaches v in J and any parameter x that w reaches in J' is a parameter that w reaches in J or one that an element of dj reaches in J. It follows that $jl_{J'}(w)$ is at least the minimum of $jl_J(w)$ and $jl_J(dj)$. As w reaches v in J, $jl_J(w) \leq jl_J(v)$. Also, by Precondition 2 of **Justify**, $jl_J(v) \leq jl_J(dj)$. It follows that $jl_{J'}(w) \geq jl_J(w) \geq Pr(w)$. Thus, (iii) holds for w.

(b) Assume $H'(v) \neq H(v) = \bar{\alpha}$ and $J' = J[w : \emptyset, H_d(w) \mid w \in J\downarrow_v][v : dj, \alpha]$ then for nodes w that cannot reach v in J, $Par_{J'}(w) = Par_J(w)$ hence $jl_{J'}(w) = jl_J(w) \geq Pr(w)$ and (iii) holds for w. All nodes $w \neq v$ that can reach v in J are reset, hence $jl_{J'}(w) = Pr(w)$ and (iii) holds. As for v, by construction $jl_{J'}(v) = jl_J(dj) \geq jl_J(v)$; also $jl_J(v) \geq Pr(v)$ hence (iii) also holds.   □

Lemma 2. *Let J be a safe justification for a parametrized parity game. Unless J defines the parametrized parity game $PG_\emptyset = \mathcal{PG}$, there exists a node v justifiable with a direct justification dj, i.e., such that* **Justify**(J, v, dj) *is executable.*

Proof. If J defines the parametrized parity game $PG_\emptyset$ then all nodes are justified and J is a solution for the original $\mathcal{PG}$. Otherwise let p be the minimal priority of all unjustified nodes, and v an arbitrary unjustified node of priority p and let its owner be α. Then either v has an outgoing edge (v, w) to a node w with $H(w) = \alpha$, thus a winning direct justification for α, or all outgoing edges are to nodes w for which $H(w) = \bar{\alpha}$, thus v has a winning direct justification for $\bar{\alpha}$. In both cases, this direct justification dj has a justification level larger or equal to p since no parameter with a smaller priority exist, so **Justify**(J, v, dj) is executable.   □

To show progress and termination, we need an order over justifications.

Definition 8 (Justification size and order over justifications). *Let $1, \ldots, n$ be the range of the priority function of a parity game PG $(+\infty > n)$ and J a winning justification for a parametrized parity game extending PG. The size*

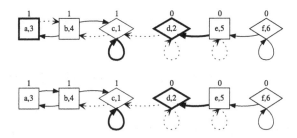

Fig. 5. Above, in solid line the edges of the justification graph of the winning but unsafe justification of Fig. 3 and below the result of justifying node a, a non-winning justification.

of J, $s(J)$ is the tuple $(s_{+\infty}(J), s_n(J), \ldots s_1(J))$ where for $i \in \{1, \ldots, n, +\infty\}$, $s_i(J)$ is the number of justified nodes with justification level i.

The order over justifications is the lexicographic order over their size: with i the highest index such that $s_i(J) \neq s_i(J')$, we have $J >_s J'$ iff $s_i(J) > s_i(J')$.

The order over justifications is a total order which is bounded as $\Sigma_i s_i(J) \leq |V|$.

Example 2. Let us revisit Example 1. The winning justification J of Fig. 3 is shown at the top of Fig. 5. For the justified nodes of J, we have $jl(b) = 3$, $jl(c) = +\infty$, $jl(e) = 2$ and $jl(f) = 2$. The justification is not safe as, e.g., $jl(b) = 3 < Pr(b) = 4$. Both unjustified nodes a and d have a winning direct justification, the direct justification $\{(a, b)\}$ wins a for player 1 and the direct justification $\{(d, c)\}$ wins d for 1. The figure at the bottom shows the justification resulting from inserting the direct justification winning a. There is now an infinite path $\langle a, b, a, b, \ldots \rangle$ won by Even but with nodes with hypothetical winner Odd. The justification **Justify**$(J, a, \{(a, b)\})$ is not winning. This shows that condition (iii) of safety of J is a necessary precondition for maintaining the desired invariants.

Lemma 3. *Let J be a safe justification with size s_J, v a node justifiable with dj and $J' = $ **Justify**(J, v, dj) a justification with size $s_{J'}$. Then $s_{J'} > s_J$.*

Proof. In case v is unjustified in J and is assigned a dj that wins v for $H(v)$, v is not counted for the size of J but is counted for the size of J'. Moreover, other nodes keep their justification level (if they cannot reach v in J) or may increase their justification level (if they can reach v in J). In any case, $s_{J'} > s_J$.

In case v is justified in J and is assigned a dj that wins v for $H(v)$, then $jl_J(dj) > jl_J(v)$, so $jl'_J(v) > jl_J(v)$. Other nodes keep their justification level or, if they reach v, may increase their justification level. Again, $s_{J'} > s_J$.

Finally, the case where dj wins v for the opponent of $H(v)$. Nodes can be reset; these nodes w have $jl_J(w) \leq Pr(v)$. As a node cannot have a winning direct justification for both players, v is unjustified in J. Hence, by precondition (2) of **Justify**, $jl_J(dj) \geq Pr(v)$. In fact, it holds that $jl_J(dj) > Pr(v)$. Indeed, if some $w \in dj$ would have a path to a parameter of v's priority, that path would be won by $H_d(v) = H(v)$ while $H(w)$ is its opponent. Thus, the highest index i where s_i changes is $jl_J(dj)$, and s_i increases. Hence, $s_{J'} > s_J$. □

Theorem 2. *Any iteration of* **Justify** *steps from a safe justification, in particular from* $(V, \emptyset, H_d)$, *with* H_d *the default hypothesis, eventually solves* $\mathcal{PG}$.

Proof. By induction: Let $\mathcal{PG} = (V, E, O, Pr)$ be a parity game. Clearly, the empty justification $J^0 = (V, \emptyset, H_d)$ is a safe justification. This is the base case.

Induction step: Let J^i be the safe justification after i successful **Justify** steps and assume that $J^i = (V, D^i, H^i)$ contains an unjustified node. By Lemma 2, there exists a pair v and dj such that v is justifiable with dj. For *any* pair v and dj such that **Justify**(J^i, v, dj) is executable, let $J^{i+1} = $ **Justify**(J^i, v, dj). By Lemma 1, J^{i+1} is a safe justification. By Lemma 3, there is a strict increase in size, i.e., $s(J^{i+1}) > s(J^i)$.

Since the number of different sizes is bounded, this eventually produces a safe $J^k = (V, D^k, H^k)$ without unjustified nodes. The parametrized parity game $\mathcal{PG}_{P_{J^k}}$ determined by J^k is $\mathcal{PG}$. Hence, H^k is the winning function of $\mathcal{PG}$, and J^k comprises winning strategies for both players.   □

Theorem 2 gives a basic algorithm to solve parity games. The algorithm has three features: it is (1) simple, (2) *nondeterministic*, and (3) in successive steps it may arbitrarily switch between different priority levels. Hence, by imposing different strategies, different instantiations of the algorithm are obtained.

Existing algorithms differ in the order in which they (implicitly) justify nodes. In the next section we simulate such algorithms by different strategies for selecting nodes to be justified. Another difference between algorithms is in computing the set R of nodes that is reset when dj wins v for the opponent of $H(v)$. Some algorithms reset more nodes; the largest reset set for which the proofs in this paper remain valid is $\{w \in V \mid jl(w) < jl(dj)\}$. To the best of our knowledge, the only algorithms that reset as few nodes as **Justify**(J, v, dj) are the ones we presented in [20]. As the experiments presented there show, the work saved across iterations by using justifications results in better performance.

5   A Reformulation of Three Existing Algorithms

In this section, by ordering justification steps, we obtain basic versions of different algorithms known from the literature. In our versions, we represent the parity game G as (V, E, O, Pr) and the justification J as (V, D, H). All algorithms start with the safe empty justification $(V, \emptyset, H_d)$. The recursive algorithms operate on a subgame SG determined by a set of nodes V_{SG}. This subgame determines the selection of **Justify**(J, v, dj) steps that are performed on G. For convenience of presentation, G is considered as a global constant.

Nested Fixpoint Iteration [6,10,20] is one of the earliest algorithms able to solve parity games. In Algorithm 1, we show a basic form that makes use of our **Justify**(J, v, dj) action. It starts from the initial justification $(V, \emptyset, H_d)$. Iteratively, it determines the lowest priority p over all unjustified nodes, it selects a node v of this priority and justifies it. Recall from the proof of Lemma 2, that all unjustified nodes of this priority are justifiable. Eventually, all nodes are

input: A parity game G

1 $J \leftarrow$ **Zielonka**$((V, \emptyset, H_d), V)$
2 **Fn Zielonka**(J, V_{SG}):

Fn Fixpoint(G):

1 **Fn Fixpoint**(G):
2 $J \leftarrow (V, \emptyset, H_d)$ the initial safe justification
3 **while** J *has unjustified nodes* **do**
4 $p \leftarrow min\{Pr(v) \mid v \text{ is unjustified}\}$
5 $v \leftarrow$ an unjustified node with $Pr(v) = p$
6 $dj \leftarrow$ a winning direct justification for v under H
7 $J \leftarrow$ **Justify**(J, v, dj)
8 **return** J

Algorithm 1: A fixpoint algorithm for justifying nodes

3 $p \leftarrow max\{Pr(v) \mid v \in V_{SG}\}$
4 $\alpha \leftarrow p \bmod 2$
5 **while** *true* **do**
6 $\quad$ **while** $\exists v \in V_{SG}, dj : v$ *is unjustified, v is justifiable with dj for α with* $jl(dj) \geq p$ **do**
7 $\quad \mid J \leftarrow$ **Justify**(J, v, dj)
8 $\quad V_{SSG} \leftarrow \{v \in V_{SG} \mid Pr(v) < p,$
9 $\quad \quad v \text{ is unjustified}\}$
10 $\quad$ **if** $V_{SSG} = \emptyset$ **then return** J;
11 $\quad J \leftarrow$ **Zielonka**(J, V_{SSG})
12 $\quad$ **while** $\exists v \in V_{SG}, dj : v$ *is unjustified, v is justifiable with dj for $\bar{\alpha}$ with* $jl(dj) \geq p + 1$ **do**
13 $\quad \mid J \leftarrow$ **Justify**(J, v, dj)

Algorithm 2: A **Justify** variant of Zielonka's algorithm.

---

justified and a solution is obtained. For more background on nested fixpoint algorithms and the effect of justifications on the performance, we refer to our work in [20].

A feature of nested fixpoint iteration is that it solves a parity game *bottom up*. It may take many iterations before it uncovers that the current hypothesis of some high priority unjustified node v is, in fact, wrong and so that playing to v is a bad strategy for α. The next algorithms are *top down*, they start out from nodes with the highest priority.

Zielonka's Algorithm [31], one of the oldest algorithms, is recursive and starts with a greedy computation of a set of nodes, called *attracted* nodes, in which the winner α of the top priority p has a strategy to force playing to nodes of top priority p. In our reconstruction, Algorithm 2, attracting nodes is simulated at Line 6 by repeatedly justifying nodes v with a direct justification that wins v for α and has a justification level $\geq p$. Observe that the while test ensures that the preconditions of **Justify**(J, v, dj) on the justification level of v are satisfied. Also, every node can be justified at most once.

The procedure is called with a set V_{SG} of nodes of maximal level p that cannot be attracted by levels $> p$. It follows that the subgraph determined by V_{SG} contains for each of its nodes an outgoing edge (otherwise the opponent of the owner of the node would have attracted the node at a level $> p$) , hence this subgraph determines a parity game. The main loop invariants are that (1) the justification J is safe; (2) the justification level of all justified nodes is $\geq p$ and (3) $\bar{\alpha}$ has no direct justifications of justification level $> p$ to win an unjustified node in V_{SG}. The initial justification is safe and it remains so as every **Justify** call satisfies the preconditions.

After the attraction loop at Line 6, no more unjustified nodes of V_{SG} can be attracted to level p for player α. Then, the set of V_{SSG} of unjustified nodes of priority $< p$ is determined. If this set is empty, then by Lemma 2 all unjustified nodes of priority p are justifiable with a direct justification dj with $jl(dj) \geq p$, hence they would be attracted to some level $\geq p$ which is impossible. Thus, there are no unjustified nodes of priority p. In this case, the returned justification J justifies all elements of V_{SG}. Else, V_{SSG} is passed in a recursive call to justify all its nodes. Upon return, if $\bar{\alpha}$ was winning some nodes in V_{SSG}, their justification level will be $\geq p + 1$. Now it is possible that some unjustified nodes of priority p can be won by $\bar{\alpha}$ and this may be the start of a cascade of resets and attractions for $\bar{\alpha}$. The purpose of Line 12 is to attract nodes of V_{SG} for $\bar{\alpha}$. Note that **Justify**(J, v, dj) resets all nodes that depend on nodes that switch to $\bar{\alpha}$. When the justification returned by the recursive call shows that α wins all nodes of V_{SSG}, the yet unjustified nodes of V_{SG} are of priority p, are justifiable by Lemma 2 and can be won only by α. So, at the next iteration, the call to $Attr_\alpha$ will justify all of them for α and V_{SSG} will be empty. Eventually the initial call of Line 1 finishes with a safe justification in which all nodes are justified thus solving the game G.

Whereas fixpoint iteration first justifies low priority nodes resulting in low justification levels, Zielonka's algorithm first justifies nodes attracted to the highest priority. Compared to fixpoint iteration, this results in large improvements in justification size which might explain its better performance. However, Zielonka's algorithm still disregards certain opportunities for increasing justification size as it proceeds by priority level, only returning to level p when all sub-problems at level $< p$ are completely solved. Indeed, some nodes computed at a low level $i \ll p$ may have a very high justification level, even $+\infty$ and might be useful to revise false hypotheses at high levels, saving much work, but this is not exploited. The next algorithm, priority promotion, overcomes this limitation.

Priority Promotion [1–3] follows the strategy of Zielonka's algorithm except that, when it detects that all nodes for priority p are justified, it does not make a recursive call but returns the set of nodes attracted to priority p nodes as a set R_p to a previous level q. There R_p is added to the attraction set at level q and the attraction process is restarted. In the terminology of [2], the set R_p is a *closed p-region* that is *promoted* to level q. A *closed p-region* of V_{SG}, with maximal priority p, is a subset $R_p \subseteq V_{SG}$ that includes all nodes of V_{SG} with priority p and for which $\alpha = p \bmod 2$ has a strategy winning all infinite plays in R_p and for which $\bar{\alpha}$ cannot escape from R_p unless to nodes of higher q-regions won by α. We call the latter nodes the *escape nodes* from R_p denote the set of them as $Escape(R_p)$. The level to which R_p is promoted is the lowest q-region that contains an escape node from R_p. It is easy to show that q is a lower bound of the justification level of R_p. In absence of escape nodes, R_p is promoted to $+\infty$.

input: A parity game G
1 $J \leftarrow (V, \emptyset, H_d)$
2 **while** $\exists v \in V_G : v$ *is unjustified*
   do
3     $R_{+\infty} \leftarrow \{v \mid jl(v) = +\infty\}$
4     $V_{SG} \leftarrow V \setminus R_{+\infty}$
5     $(J, \_, \_) \leftarrow$ **Promote**(V_{SG}, J)
6   **while** $\exists v \in V_{SG}, dj : v$ *is*
   justifiable with dj and
   $jl(dj) = +\infty$ **do**
7       $J \leftarrow$ **Justify**(J, v, dj)

Algorithm 3: A variant of priority promotion using **Justify**.

1 **Fn Promote**(V_{SG}, J):
2     $p \leftarrow max\{Pr(v) \mid v \in V_{SG}\}$
3     $\alpha \leftarrow p \bmod 2$
4   **while** *true* **do**
5   **while** $\exists v \in V_{SG}, dj : v$ *is unjustified*
      or $jl(v) < p$, v *is justifiable with dj*
      for α *with* $jl(dj) \geq p$ **do**
6         $J \leftarrow$ **Justify**(J, v, dj)
7       $R_p \leftarrow \{v \in V_{SG} \mid jl(v) \geq p\}$
8   **if** **Closed**(R_p, V_{SG}) **then**
9         $l \leftarrow min\{q \mid R_q$ contains an escape
      node of $R_p\}$
10   **return** (J, R_p, l)
11      $V_{SSG} \leftarrow V_{SG} \setminus R_p$
12      $(J, R_{p'}, l) \leftarrow$ **Promote**(V_{SSG}, J)
13   **if** $l > p$ **then**
14   **return** $(J, R_{p'}, l)$

Our variant of priority promotion (PPJ) is in Algorithm 3. Whereas **Zielonka** returned a complete solution J on V_{SG}, **Promote** returns only a partial J on V_{SG}; some nodes of V_{SG} may have an unfinished justification ($jl(v) < +\infty$). To deal with this, **Promote** is iterated in a while loop that continues as long as there are unjustified nodes. Upon return of **Promote**, all nodes attracted to the returned $+\infty$-region are justified. In the next iteration, all nodes with justification level $+\infty$ are removed from the game, permanently. Note that when promoting to some q-region, justified nodes of justification level $< q$ can remain. A substantial gain can be obtained compared to the original priority promotion algorithm which does not maintain justifications and loses all work stored in J.

By invariant, the function **Promote** is called with a set of nodes V_{SG} that cannot be justified with a direct justification of level larger than the maximal priority p. The function starts its main loop by attracting nodes for level p. The attraction process is identical to Zielonka's algorithm except that leftover justified nodes v with $jl(v) < p$ may be rejustified. As before, the safety of J is preserved. Then R_p consists of elements of V_{SG} with justification level $\geq p$. It is tested (**Closed**) whether R_p is a closed p-region. This is provably the case if all nodes of priority p are justified. If so, J, R_p and its minimal escape level are returned. If not, the game proceeds as in Zielonka's algorithm and the game is solved for the nodes not in R_p which have strictly lower justification level. Sooner or later, a closed region will be obtained. Indeed, at some point, a subgame is entered in which all nodes have the same priority p. All nodes are justifiable (Lemma 2) and the resulting region is closed. Upon return from the recursive call, it is checked whether the returned region ($R_{p'}$) promotes to the current level p. If not, the function exits as well (Line 14). Otherwise a new iteration starts with attracting nodes of justification level p for α. Note that contrary to Zielonka's algorithm, there is no attraction step for $\bar{\alpha}$: attracting for $\bar{\alpha}$ at p is the same as attracting for $\alpha' = \bar{\alpha}$ at $p' = p + 1$.

Discussion. Our versions of Zielonka's algorithm and priority promotion use the justification level to decide which nodes to attract. While maintaining justification levels can be costly, in these algorithms, it can be replaced by selecting nodes that are "forced to play" to a particular set of nodes (or to an already attracted node). In the first attraction loop of **Zielonka**, the set is initialised with all nodes of priority p, in the second attraction loop, with the nodes won by $\bar{\alpha}$; In **Promote**, the initial set consists also of the nodes of priority p.

Observe that the recursive algorithms implement a strategy to reach as soon as possible the justification level $+\infty$ for a group of nodes (the nodes won by the opponent in the outer call of **Zielonka**, the return of a closed region—for any of the players—to the outer level in **Promote**). When achieved, a large jump in justification size follows. This may explain why these algorithms outperform fixpoint iteration.

Comparing our priority promotion algorithm (PPJ) to other variants, we see a large overlap with region recovery (RR) [1] both algorithms avoid resetting nodes of lower regions. However, RR always resets the full region, while PPJ can reset only a part of a region, hence can save more previous work. Conversely, PPJ eagerly resets nodes while RR only validates the regions before use, so it can recover a region when the reset escape node is easily re-attracted. The equivalent justification of such a state is winning but unsafe, thus unreachable by applying **Justify**(J, v, dj). However, one likely can define a variant of **Justify**(J, v, dj) with modified safety invariants that can reconstruct RR. Delayed priority promotion [3] is another variant which prioritises the best promotion over the first promotion and, likely, can be directly reconstructed.

Tangle learning [28] is another state of the art algorithm that we have studied. Space restrictions disallow us to go in details. We refer to [20] for a version of tangle learning with justifications. For a more formal analysis, we refer to [19]). Interestingly, the updates of the justification in the nodes of a tangle cannot be modelled with a sequence of safe **Justify**(J, v, dj) steps. One needs an alternative with a precondition on the set of nodes in a tangle. Similarly as for **Justify**(J, v, dj), it is proven in [19] that the resulting justification is safe and larger than the initial one.

Justification are not only a way to explicitly model (evolving) winning strategies, they can also speed up algorithms. We have implemented justification variants of the nested fixpoint algorithm, Zielonka's algorithm, priority promotion, and tangle learning. For the experimental results we refer to [19,20].

Note that the data structure used to implement the justification graph matters. Following an idea of Benerecetti et al. [2], our implementations use a single field to represent the direct justification of a node; it holds either a single node, or *null* to represent the set of all outgoing nodes. To compute the reset set R of a node, we found two efficient methods to encode the graph J: (i) iterate over all incoming nodes in E and test if their justification contains v, (ii) store for every node a hash set of every dependent node. On average, the first approach is better, while the second is more efficient for sparse graphs but worse for dense graphs.

6   Conclusion

This paper explored the use of justifications in parity game solving. First, we generalized parity games by adding parameter nodes. When a play reaches a parameter it stops in favour of one player. Next, we introduced justifications and proved that a winning justification contains the solution of the parametrized parity game. Then, we introduced safe justifications and a **Justify** operation and proved that a parity game can be solved by a sequence of **Justify** steps. A **Justify** operation can be applied on a node satisfying its preconditions, it assigns a winning direct justification to the node, resets—if needed—other nodes as parameters, preserves safety of the justification, and ensures the progress of the solving process.

To illustrate the power of **Justify**, we reconstructed three algorithms: nested fixpoint iteration, Zielonka's algorithm and priority promotion by ordering applicable **Justify** operations differently. Nested fixpoint induction prefers operations on nodes with the lowest priorities; Zielonka's algorithm starts on nodes with the maximal priority and recursively descends; priority promotion improves upon Zielonka with an early exit on detection of a closed region (a solved subgame).

A distinguishing feature of a justification based algorithm is that it makes active use of the partial strategies of both players. While other algorithms, such as region recovery and tangle learning, use the constructed partial strategies while solving the parity game, we do not consider them justification based algorithms. For region recovery, the generated states are not always weakly winning, while tangle learning applies the partial strategies for different purposes. As shown in [20] where justifications improve tangle learning, combining different techniques can further improve parity game algorithms.

Interesting future research includes: (i) exploring the possible role of justifications in the quasi-polynomial algorithm of Parys [24], (ii) analysing the similarity between small progress measures algorithms [12,16] and justification level, (iii) analysing whether the increase in justification size is a useful guide for selecting the most promising justifiable nodes, (iv) proving the worst-case time complexity by analysing the length of the longest path in the lattice of justification states where states are connected by **Justify**(J, v, dj) steps.

References

1. Benerecetti, M., Dell'Erba, D., Mogavero, F.: Improving priority promotion for parity games. In: Bloem, R., Arbel, E. (eds.) HVC 2016. LNCS, vol. 10028, pp. 117–133. Springer, Cham (2016). https://doi.org/10.1007/978-3-319-49052-6_8
2. Benerecetti, M., Dell'Erba, D., Mogavero, F.: Solving parity games via priority promotion. In: Chaudhuri, S., Farzan, A. (eds.) CAV 2016. LNCS, vol. 9780, pp. 270–290. Springer, Cham (2016). https://doi.org/10.1007/978-3-319-41540-6_15
3. Benerecetti, M., Dell'Erba, D., Mogavero, F.: A delayed promotion policy for parity games. Inf. Comput. **262**, 221–240 (2018). https://doi.org/10.1016/j.ic.2018.09.005
4. Bernholtz, O., Vardi, M.Y., Wolper, P.: An automata-theoretic approach to branching-time model checking (Extended abstract). In: Dill, D.L. (ed.) CAV 1994.

LNCS, vol. 818, pp. 142–155. Springer, Heidelberg (1994). https://doi.org/10.1007/3-540-58179-0_50

5. Bloem, R., Schewe, S., Khalimov, A.: CTL* synthesis via LTL synthesis. In: Fisman, D., Jacobs, S. (eds.) Proceedings Sixth Workshop on Synthesis, SYNT@CAV 2017, Heidelberg, Germany, 22nd July 2017. EPTCS, vol. 260, pp. 4–22 (2017). https://doi.org/10.4204/EPTCS.260.4

6. Bruse, F., Falk, M., Lange, M.: The fixpoint-iteration algorithm for parity games. In: Peron, A., Piazza, C. (eds.) Proceedings Fifth International Symposium on Games, Automata, Logics and Formal Verification, GandALF 2014, Verona, Italy, 10–12 September 2014. EPTCS, vol. 161, pp. 116–130 (2014). https://doi.org/10.4204/EPTCS.161.12

7. Calude, C.S., Jain, S., Khoussainov, B., Li, W., Stephan, F.: Deciding parity games in quasipolynomial time. In: Hatami, H., McKenzie, P., King, V. (eds.) Proceedings of the 49th Annual ACM SIGACT Symposium on Theory of Computing, STOC 2017, Montreal, QC, Canada, 19–23 June 2017, pp. 252–263. ACM (2017). https://doi.org/10.1145/3055399.3055409

8. Cranen, S., et al.: An overview of the mCRL2 toolset and its recent advances. In: Piterman, N., Smolka, S.A. (eds.) TACAS 2013. LNCS, vol. 7795, pp. 199–213. Springer, Heidelberg (2013). https://doi.org/10.1007/978-3-642-36742-7_15

9. Cranen, S., Groote, J.F., Reniers, M.A.: A linear translation from CTL* to the first-order modal μ -calculus. Theor. Comput. Sci. **412**(28), 3129–3139 (2011). https://doi.org/10.1016/j.tcs.2011.02.034

10. van Dijk, T., Rubbens, B.: Simple fixpoint iteration to solve parity games. In: Leroux, J., Raskin, J. (eds.) Proceedings Tenth International Symposium on Games, Automata, Logics, and Formal Verification, GandALF 2019, Bordeaux, France, 2–3rd September 2019. EPTCS, vol. 305, pp. 123–139 (2019). https://doi.org/10.4204/EPTCS.305.9

11. Emerson, E.A., Jutla, C.S.: Tree automata, mu-calculus and determinacy (extended abstract). In: 32nd Annual Symposium on Foundations of Computer Science, San Juan, Puerto Rico, 1–4 October 1991, pp. 368–377. IEEE Computer Society (1991). https://doi.org/10.1109/SFCS.1991.185392

12. Fearnley, J., Jain, S., Schewe, S., Stephan, F., Wojtczak, D.: An ordered approach to solving parity games in quasi polynomial time and quasi linear space. In: Erdogmus, H., Havelund, K. (eds.) Proceedings of the 24th ACM SIGSOFT International SPIN Symposium on Model Checking of Software, Santa Barbara, CA, USA, 10–14 July 2017, pp. 112–121. ACM (2017). https://doi.org/10.1145/3092282.3092286

13. Grädel, E., Thomas, W., Wilke, T. (eds.): LNCS, vol. 2500. Springer, Heidelberg (2002). https://doi.org/10.1007/3-540-36387-4

14. Hou, P., Cat, B.D., Denecker, M.: FO(FD): extending classical logic with rule-based fixpoint definitions. TPLP **10**(4–6), 581–596 (2010). https://doi.org/10.1017/S1471068410000293

15. Jacobs, S., et al.: The 5th reactive synthesis competition (SYNTCOMP 2018): Benchmarks, participants & results. CoRR (2019). http://arxiv.org/abs/1904.07736

16. Jurdziński, M.: Small progress measures for solving parity games. In: Reichel, H., Tison, S. (eds.) STACS 2000. LNCS, vol. 1770, pp. 290–301. Springer, Heidelberg (2000). https://doi.org/10.1007/3-540-46541-3_24

17. Kant, G., van de Pol, J.: Efficient instantiation of parameterised Boolean equation systems to parity games. In: Wijs, A., Bosnacki, D., Edelkamp, S. (eds.) Proceedings First Workshop on GRAPH Inspection and Traversal Engineering,

GRAPHITE 2012, Tallinn, Estonia, 1st April 2012. EPTCS, vol. 99, pp. 50–65 (2012). https://doi.org/10.4204/EPTCS.99.7

18. Kesten, Y., Manna, Z., McGuire, H., Pnueli, A.: A decision algorithm for full propositional temporal logic. In: Courcoubetis, C. (ed.) CAV 1993. LNCS, vol. 697, pp. 97–109. Springer, Heidelberg (1993). https://doi.org/10.1007/3-540-56922-7_9

19. Lapauw, R.: Reconstructing and Improving Parity Game Solvers with Justifications. Ph.D. thesis, Department of Computer Science, KU Leuven, Leuven, Belgium (2021). [To appear]

20. Lapauw, R., Bruynooghe, M., Denecker, M.: Improving parity game solvers with justifications. In: Beyer, D., Zufferey, D. (eds.) VMCAI 2020. LNCS, vol. 11990, pp. 449–470. Springer, Cham (2020). https://doi.org/10.1007/978-3-030-39322-9_21

21. Luttenberger, M., Meyer, P.J., Sickert, S.: Practical synthesis of reactive systems from LTL specifications via parity games. Acta Inf. **57**(1), 3–36 (2020). https://doi.org/10.1007/s00236-019-00349-3

22. Meyer, P.J., Sickert, S., Luttenberger, M.: Strix: explicit reactive synthesis strikes back! In: Chockler, H., Weissenbacher, G. (eds.) CAV 2018. LNCS, vol. 10981, pp. 578–586. Springer, Cham (2018). https://doi.org/10.1007/978-3-319-96145-3_31

23. Mostowski, A.: Games with forbidden positions. University of Gdansk, Gdansk. Technical report, Poland (1991)

24. Parys, P.: Parity games: Zielonka's algorithm in quasi-polynomial time. In: Rossmanith, P., Heggernes, P., Katoen, J. (eds.) 44th International Symposium on Mathematical Foundations of Computer Science, MFCS 2019, August 26–30, 2019, Aachen, Germany. LIPIcs, vol. 138, pp. 10:1–10:13. Schloss Dagstuhl - Leibniz-Zentrum für Informatik (2019). https://doi.org/10.4230/LIPIcs.MFCS.2019.10

25. Piterman, N.: From nondeterministic Buchi and Streett automata to deterministic parity automata. In: 21th IEEE Symposium on Logic in Computer Science (LICS 2006), 12–15 August 2006, Seattle, WA, USA, Proceedings, pp. 255–264. IEEE Computer Society (2006). https://doi.org/10.1109/LICS.2006.28

26. Safra, S.: On the complexity of omega-automata. In: 29th Annual Symposium on Foundations of Computer Science, White Plains, New York, USA, 24–26 October 1988, pp. 319–327. IEEE Computer Society (1988). https://doi.org/10.1109/SFCS.1988.21948

27. Schewe, S.: An optimal strategy improvement algorithm for solving parity and payoff games. In: Kaminski, M., Martini, S. (eds.) CSL 2008. LNCS, vol. 5213, pp. 369–384. Springer, Heidelberg (2008). https://doi.org/10.1007/978-3-540-87531-4_27

28. Dijk, T.: Attracting tangles to solve parity games. In: Chockler, H., Weissenbacher, G. (eds.) CAV 2018. LNCS, vol. 10982, pp. 198–215. Springer, Cham (2018). https://doi.org/10.1007/978-3-319-96142-2_14

29. Vardi, M.Y., Wolper, P.: An automata-theoretic approach to automatic program verification (preliminary report). In: Proceedings of the Symposium on Logic in Computer Science (LICS 1986), Cambridge, Massachusetts, USA, 16–18 June 1986, pp. 332–344. IEEE Computer Society (1986)

30. Walukiewicz, I.: Monadic second order logic on tree-like structures. In: Puech, C., Reischuk, R. (eds.) STACS 1996. LNCS, vol. 1046, pp. 399–413. Springer, Heidelberg (1996). https://doi.org/10.1007/3-540-60922-9_33

31. Zielonka, W.: Infinite games on finitely coloured graphs with applications to automata on infinite trees. Theor. Comput. Sci. **200**(1–2), 135–183 (1998). https://doi.org/10.1016/S0304-3975(98)00009-7

SMT-Based Test-Case Generation and Validation for Programs with Complex Specifications

Ricardo Peña$^{(\boxtimes)}$, Jaime Sánchez-Hernández , Miguel Garrido,
and Javier Sagredo

Complutense University of Madrid, Madrid, Spain
{ricardo,jaime}@sip.ucm.es, migarr01@ucm.es

Abstract. We present a system which automatically generates an exhaustive set of black-box test-cases, up to a given size, for units under test requiring complex preconditions. The key of the approach is to translate a formal precondition into a set of constraints belonging to the decidable logics of SMT solvers. By checking the satisfiability of the constraints, then the models returned by the solver automatically synthesize the cases. We also show how to use SMT solvers to automatically check the validity of the test-case results, by using the postcondition as an oracle, and also how to complement the black-box cases with white-box ones automatically generated. Finally, we use the solver to perform what we call *automatic partial verification* of the program. In summary, we present a system in which exhaustive black-box and white-box testing, result validation, and partial verification, can all be done automatically. The only extra effort required from programmers is to write formal specifications.

Keywords: Black-box testing · SMT solvers · Test-case generation

1 Introduction

Testing is very important for increasing program reliability. Thorough testing ideally exercises all the different situations described by the specification, and all the instructions and conditions of the program under test, so that it achieves a high probability of finding bugs, if they are present in the code. Unfortunately, thorough testing is a time consuming activity and, as a consequence, less testing than the desirable one is performed in practice.

There is a general agreement that automatic tools can alleviate most of the tedious and error prone activities related to testing. One of them is test-case generation (TCG). Traditionally (see, for instance [1]), there are two TCG variants: black-box TCG and white-box TCG. In the first one, test-cases are based on the program specification, and in the second one, they are based on a particular

Work partially funded by the Spanish Ministry of Economy and Competitiveness, under the grant TIN2017-86217-R, and by the Madrid Regional Government, under the grant S2018/TCS-4339, co-funded by the European Union EIE funds.

P. Lopez-Garcia et al. (Eds.): Hermenegildo Festschrift 2022, LNCS 13160, pp. 188–205, 2023.
https://doi.org/10.1007/978-3-031-31476-6_10

reference implementation. Each one complements each other, so both are needed if we aim at performing thorough testing.

On white-box testing there is much literature, and sophisticated techniques such as symbolic and concolic TCG, have been proposed [5,6,10,17,20]. One of the problems arising when using the implementation as the basis to generate test-cases, is that less attention is paid to program specification, that usually is even not formalized. As a consequence, test cases can be generated that do not meet the input requirements expected by the program. Generating cases satisfying a given precondition may be not so easy when that precondition is complex. For instance, some programs require as input sorted arrays, sorted lists, or sophisticated data structures satisfying complex invariants such as red-black trees or binary heaps. When this happens, usually auxiliary boilerplate code is created to build these structures in order to generate valid input for the program under test. This approach increments the testing effort and may also introduce new errors in the boilerplate code.

Another problem related to testing automation is checking for validity the results returned by the program under test for each test-case. If this checking is done by humans, then again the testing effort and the possibility of errors increase. In order to automate this process, programmers must write formal postconditions, or formal assertions, and have executable versions of them, as it is done for instance in property-based testing [8,11]. Again, having executable assertions require programming effort and open more possibilities of introducing errors. Our group presented some years ago a tool [2] that transformed assertions written in a logic language supporting sets, multisets, sequences and arrays, into executable Haskell code, so that no extra code was needed in order to create executable versions of program postconditions. This system was used as an oracle for validating test results and could also be used to generate cases satisfying a complex precondition. The approach consisted of automatically generating a huge number of structures of the appropriate type, then executing the precondition on each of them, and then filtering out those satisfying it. For instance, if a precondition required a tree to be an AVL one, then all possible trees up to a given size were generated and only those satisfying the executable *isAVL* predicate were kept. The approach was fully automatic, but not very efficient, as sometimes less then 1% of the generated cases were kept.

In this work, we use an SMT solver [3] to directly generate test-cases satisfying a complex precondition, without needing a trial and error process, such as the above described one. The key idea is to transform the formal precondition into a set of constraints belonging to the logics supported by the SMT solver. This has been possible thanks to a recent facility introduced in such solvers: the theory of algebraic types and the support given to recursive function definitions on those types. If the constraints are satisfiable, then every model returned by the SMT solver can be easily converted into a test-case satisfying the precondition. In this way, we have been able to synthesise sorted arrays, sorted lists, AVL trees, red-black trees, and some other complex data structures. We apply the same approach to the postconditions: the result returned by the program under test is converted into an SMT term, and then the postcondition constraints are applied to it. If the resulting SMT problem is satisfiable, then the result is correct.

In many programs, the conditions occurring in **if** statements and **while** loops are simple enough to be converted into constraints supported by the SMT logics. If this is the case, then we can use SMT solvers to also generate white-box test-cases, as it is done in the symbolic testing approach. The execution paths along the program are converted into appropriate constraint sets, and then they are given to the solver. In this work, we add to these path constraints the precondition constraints, so we synthesise test-cases which are guaranteed to satisfy the precondition, and also to execute a given path.

A final contribution of this work is to use the SMT solver to do 'effortless' program verification. We call the approach *partial automatic verification* and consists of giving the solver formulas to be checked for validity instead of for satisfiability. Each formula expresses that all test-cases satisfying the precondition, satisfying the constraints of a given path, and returning some result in that path, must also satisfy the postcondition for the returned result. If the solver checks the validity of this formula, this is equivalent to proving that *all* valid inputs exercising that path are correct. If we apply this procedure to an exhaustive set of paths covering all the program under test up to a given depth, then we would be verifying the correctness of a high number of test-cases at once, without even executing the program.

Summarizing, we present a system in which exhaustive black-box and white-box testing, result validation, and partial verification, can all be done automatically. The only extra effort to be done by programmers is writing formal specifications for their programs. This may seem to be a big effort, since usually programmers are not very found of writing formal specifications. But our work has been performed in the context of our verification platform CAVI-ART[1] [14,15], where formal assertions are anyway mandatory because the platform has been specifically designed to assist in the formal verification of programs. Someone may wonder why testing is needed in a verification platform, since verification gives in general more guarantees than testing. The answer to this question is that, when forced to write formal specifications, programmers usually write incomplete ones in their first attempts. So, automatic testing may help them to debug, not only the code, but also their initially weak specifications, before embarking themselves into formal verification, which usually requires a bigger effort in the form of intermediate assertions and auxiliary lemmas. So, we propose automatic testing as a cheap alternative for removing the most obvious code and specification errors.

The plan of the paper is as follows: in Sect. 2, we explain how to program complex preconditions in the SMT language; Sect. 3 shows how to generate exhaustive black-box test-cases by only using the precondition; Sect. 4 explains the generation of exhaustive white-box test-cases, and Sect. 5 details the partial verification approach; Sect. 6 presents some experiments with the system, and draws some conclusions. Finally, Sect. 7 surveys some related and future work.

---

[1] Acronym of *Computer Assisted Validation by Analysis, Transformation and Proof.*

2 Specifying Pre- and Postconditions by Using the SMT Language

In the last fifteen years, SMT solvers have evolved very quickly. There has been a very much profitable feedback between SMT developers and SMT users. The latter have been asking for more and more complex verification conditions to be automatically proved by SMTs, and the former have improved the SMT heuristics and search strategies in order to meet these requirements. The result has been that SMT solvers support today a rich set of theories, and that more complex programs can be verified by using them.

Up to 2015, the available SMTs essentially supported the boolean theory, several numeric theories, and the theory of uninterpreted functions. With the addition of a few axioms, the latter one was easily extended in order to support arrays, set and multiset theories. This state of the art is reflected in the language described in the SMT-LIB Standard, Version 2.5.[2]

After that, in the last few years, SMT solvers have incorporated algebraic datatypes and the possibility of defining recursive functions on them. Reynolds et al. [19] proposed a strategy for translating terminating recursive functions into a set of universally quantified formulas. In turn, several techniques have been developed to find models for a large set of universally quantified formulas. From the user point of view, a satisfiability problem can be posed to a modern SMT solver in terms of a set of recursive function definitions. The SMT-LIB Standard, Version 2.6, of Dec. 2017, reflects this state of affairs.

It happens that many useful preconditions and postconditions of algebraic datatype manipulating programs can be expressed by means of recursively defined predicates and functions. For instance, the function that inserts an element into an AVL tree, needs as a precondition the input tree to be an AVL. An AVL is defined as either the empty tree, or as a non-empty tree whose two children are both AVL trees. Additionally, the tree must be a Binary Search Tree (i.e. a BST predicate holds), and the difference in height of the children should be at most one. Also, in each node there is an additional field containing the tree height. In turn, the BST property can be recursively defined, and so can it be the height function on trees. In Fig. 1, we show some of these definitions written in the SMT language. There, the predefined function `ite` has the same meaning as the `if-then-else` expression of functional languages. As it can be seen, the SMT language for writing recursive definitions is not very different from a functional language, except by the fact of using an uncomfortable prefix syntax. In a similar way, predicates for defining sorted lists, or invariants of data structures such as skew heaps, leftlist heaps, or red-black trees, can be defined.

The same idea applies to postconditions. For instance, after inserting an element in an AVL tree, we would like to express that the result is also an AVL tree, and that the set of elements of this result is the union of the set of elements of the input tree, and the element being inserted. The function giving the set of elements of a tree, or the multiset of elements of a heap, can also be recursively

---

[2] http://smtlib.cs.uiowa.edu/language.shtml.

```
(declare-datatypes (T) ((AVL leafA (nodeA (val T) (alt Int) (izq AVL) (der AVL)))))

(define-fun-rec
   heightA ((t (AVL Int))) Int
      (ite (= t leafA)
            0
            (+ 1 (max (heightA (izq t)) (heightA (der t)))))
      )
)

(define-fun-rec
   isAVL ((t (AVL Int))) Bool
      (ite (= t leafA)
            true
            (and (isBSTA t) (isAVL (izq t)) (isAVL (der t))
               (<= (absol (- (heightA (izq t)) (heightA (der t)))) 1)
               (= (alt t) (heightA  t))
            )
      )
)

(define-fun-rec
   isBSTA ((t (AVL Int))) Bool
      (
            ite(= t leafA)
               true
               (ite (and (= (izq t) leafA) (= (der t) leafA))
                     true
                     (ite (= (izq t) leafA)
                        (and (isBSTA (der t)) (< (val t) (minTA (der t))))
                        (ite (= (der t) leafA)
                           (and (isBSTA (izq t)) (< (maxTA (izq t)) (val t)))
                           (and (isBSTA (izq t)) (isBSTA (der t))
                                 (< (maxTA (izq t)) (val t)) (< (val t) (minTA (der t))))
                        )
                     )
               )
            )
      )
)
```

Fig. 1. Definition of the predicate isAVL and the function heightA in the SMT language

```
(define-sort Set (T) (Array T Bool))

(define-fun empty () (Set Int)
   ((as const (Array Int Bool)) false))

(define-fun unit ((i Int)) (Set Int)
   (store empty i true))

(define-fun set-union ((s1 (Set Int)) (s2 (Set Int))) (Set Int)
   ((_ map or) s1 s2 )  )

(define-fun-rec
   setA ((t (AVL Int))) (Set Int)
      (ite (= t leafA)
            empty
            (set-union (set-union (setA (izq t)) (setA (der t))) (unit (val t)))
      )
)
```

Fig. 2. Definition of the function setA giving the set of elements of an AVL tree

defined in the SMT-LIB language, as we show in Fig. 2. There, a set of elements is modeled as an infinite array of boolean values, i.e. as the characteristic function of the set. Having defined such predicates and functions, the specification of the insertion function for AVLs, can be written as follows:

$$\{ isAVL(t) \} \tag{1}$$

define $insertAVL \, (x :: int, t :: AVL \; int) :: (res :: AVL \; int)$

$$\{ isAVL \, (res) \wedge setA \, (res) = \textit{set-union} \, (setA \, (t), unit \, (x)) \} \tag{2}$$

3   Synthesizing Black-Box Test-Cases

The purpose of defining preconditions as a set of constraints written in the SMT-LIB language is to let solvers to check the satisfiability of these constraints and to generate models for their variables. Each model satisfying the constraints is then easily transformed into a test-case, since the generated values satisfy the precondition.

In our context, the Unit Under Test (UUT in what follows) is a set of related pure functions, of which only one is visible from outside the unit. The functions do not share any variable or object. The only allowed interaction between them is that the visible one may call any of the other functions, and the latter ones may call each other in a mutually recursive way. The visible top-level UUT function is specified by means of a formal precondition and postcondition.

Modern SMT solvers are very clever in finding models for constraints involving algebraic datatypes and recursive functions on them. In our experiments, we used the Z3 SMT solver [16], version 4.8.8, published in May 2020. When giving the following constraint to Z3:

```
(assert (= 3 (heightA t)))
```

it synthesizes a binary tree t having height 3. Previous versions of this solver were not able to process this constraint. They entered an endless loop when trying to solve it. This means that the search strategies of SMT solvers are continuously evolving, and that each time they can solve more complex problems.

Our preconditions are conjunctions of predicates usually involving recursive definitions, as those shown in Fig. 1. Our aim is to generate an exhaustive set of black-box test-cases so, in order to have a finite number of them, the user should fix a maximum size for each argument of the UUT. In the cases of trees and lists, their height and their length would be suitable sizes. In the case of integers, the user should specify a finite interval for them. If tree nodes and list elements consist of integer values, this latter constraint has the additional effect of limiting the values which will populate the nodes, so contributing to getting a finite number of models for the arguments.

In the example shown in Fig. 3, we have forced the tree t to satisfy the predicate $isAVL(t)$, to have 3 as its height, and to contain integer values comprised between -6 and $+6$. The solver generated the model shown in the drawing, which is just one of all the possible models. The annotation $h = xx$ in each node is the value of its height field.

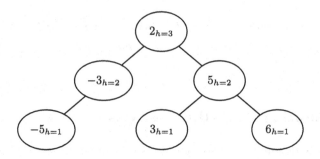

Fig. 3. AVL tree synthesized with the constraint (`assert` (`and` (`= 3` (`heightA t`)) (`isAVL t`))).

The next step is to be able to generate many different test cases. The most popular solvers, such as Z3 [16], only return one model for every satisfiable problem. There exist the so called All-SAT solvers, which give as a result *all* the models satisfying a set of constraints (see for instance [21]), but these only solve pure SAT problems, i.e. they lack the rich set of theories supported by SMT solvers. A common solution to force the SMT to give more models is adding constraints which negate the prior obtained models. This is what we did: we called the solver in a loop, by adding at each iteration a constraint forcing the result to be different from the previous one. For instance, for AVL trees having less than or equal to 7 nodes, and populated with values between 1 and 10, we obtained 3 353 trees. The solver entered an infinite loop trying to get the model number 3 354. In fact, our hand calculations gave us that there exist only 3 353 correct AVLs within the above restrictions. This means that the solver was trying to solve an unsatisfiable problem and got lost while searching new models. Getting timeouts in SMT problem solving is a frequent situation when the set of constraint reaches a high complexity, as it is the case here.

Then, summarizing our strategy for generating black-box test-cases, it consists of first fixing a maximum size for the data structure, then fixing an interval of values for populating the elements of the structure, and then letting the solver to find *all* the models satisfying the constraints. This amounts to perform exhaustive testing up to a given size. We consider the set of cases generated in this way to have a high probability of finding bugs, if they are present in the program. Successfully passing these tests will give us a high confidence in the UUT reliability, since it is infrequent for programmers to build programs that successfully pass exhaustive testing for small size test-cases, and still contain bugs, only showing up for bigger sizes.

The last step consists of checking that the result computed by the UUT for each test-case is really the correct one. Given the high number of test-cases we may generate, ideally this should be automatically done by the system. The result could be a value of a simple type, such as an integer or a boolean value, or it could be a term of an algebraic type, such as a list or a tree. Our system translates the returned term from the executable language to the solver language, and then uses the postcondition to check whether the term satisfies it. For instance, if *res* is the tree returned for the function inserting a value x into an AVL tree t, then the SMT solver performs a satisfiability check for the following constraint (see Eq. 2 above):

```
(assert (and (isAVL res) (= (setA res) (set-union (setA t) (unit x)))))
```

where t, x, and *res*, are instantiated variables. If the solvers returns sat, then the result is correct. Otherwise, it is not.

4   Synthesizing White-Box Test-Cases

The black-box test-cases are independent of the possible implementations of the UUT. Given a particular implementation, it may be the case that, after running an exhaustive set of black-box test-cases up to a given size, there still exist non exercised paths in the UUT. The usual testing strategies recommend to additionally generate implementation-based test-cases which complement the black-box ones. A common exhaustiveness criterium is to generate cases exercising all the paths in the UUT. When paths through loops are considered, then a bound on the number of iterations through the loop is set. For instance, a bound of 1 means that paths exercising at most one iteration of each loop are considered.

Our implementation language is a sort of core functional language which supports mutually recursive function definitions. It is the internal language (we call it IR, acronym of Intermediate Representation) of our verification platform CAVI-ART [14,15], to which real-life languages such as Java and Haskell are translated. In Fig. 4 we show its abstract syntax. Notice that all expressions are flattened in the sense that all the arguments in function and constructor applications, and also the **case** discriminants, are atoms. An additional feature is that IR programs are in **let** A-normal form [9], and also in SSA[3] form, i.e. all **let** bound variables in a nested sequence of **let** expressions are distinct, and also different to the function arguments, and to the **case** bound pattern variables.

As the abstract IR of Fig. 4 is the target and/or the origin of the many transformations available in our platform CAVI-ART, it also has a textual representation in order to store it in files. We call CLIR to this textual format, acronym of *Common Lisp IR*, because it has some resemblance with Lisp. In Fig. 5 we partially show the specification and the code of the *insertAVL* function written in this format.

---

[3]   Static Single Assignment.

$$
\begin{array}{llll}
a & ::= c & \{ \text{ constant } \} \\
& \mid x & \{ \text{ variable } \} \\
be & ::= a & \{ \text{ atomic expression } \} \\
& \mid f \ \overline{a_i} & \{ \text{ function/primitive operator application } \} \\
& \mid \langle \overline{a_i} \rangle & \{ \text{ tuple construction } \} \\
& \mid C \ \overline{a_i} & \{ \text{ constructor application } \} \\
e & ::= be & \{ \text{ binding expression } \} \\
& \mid \textbf{let } \langle \overline{x_i :: \tau_i} \rangle = be \textbf{ in } e & \{ \text{ sequential let. Left part of the binding can be a tuple } \} \\
& \mid \textbf{letfun } \overline{def_i} \textbf{ in } e & \{ \text{ let for mutually recursive function definitions } \} \\
& \mid \textbf{case } a \textbf{ of } \overline{alt_i}[; \ \_ \rightarrow e] & \{ \text{ case distinction with optional default branch } \} \\
tldef & ::= \textbf{define } \{\psi_1\} \ def \ \{\psi_2\} & \{ \text{ top level function def. with pre- and post-conditions } \} \\
def & ::= f \ (\overline{x_i :: \tau_i}) :: (\overline{y_j :: \tau_j}) = e & \{ \text{ function definition. Output results are named } \} \\
alt & ::= C \ \overline{x_i :: \tau_i} \rightarrow e & \{ \text{ case branch } \} \\
\tau & ::= \alpha & \{ \text{ type variable } \} \\
& \mid T \ \overline{\tau_i} & \{ \text{ type constructor application } \}
\end{array}
$$

Fig. 4. CAVI-ART IR abstract syntax

In Fig. 6 we show a more sweetened IR code for function *insertAVL*. In the **letfun** main expression, the code for functions *height*, *compose*, *leftBalance* and *rightBalance* is not shown. The first one computes the height of an AVL with a time cost in $O(1)$, by just getting the value stored in its root node. The second one just joins two trees and a value received as arguments to form an AVL tree. The other two are responsible for performing the LL, LR, RL and RR rotations that reestablish the height invariant of AVLs. In what follows, we will use the *insertAVL* function, together with all its auxiliary functions defined in the **letfun** expression, as a running example of UUT.

We define a *static path* through a set of mutually recursive functions defined together in an UUT, as a potential execution path starting at the top level function, and ending when this function produces a result. Not all static paths correspond to actual execution paths, since some static paths may be unfeasible. We define the *depth* of a static path, as the maximum number of unfoldings that a recursive function may undergone in the path. When all the recursive functions in the UUT are tail recursive, this definition of depth essentially corresponds to the number of iterations in imperative loops. Depth 1 corresponds to none iteration in all loops, depth 2 corresponds to at most one iteration, and so on. When there is at least one non-tail recursive function in the UUT, the depth of the path is the depth of the call tree deployed during the path execution, considering only the calls to the non-tail recursive function. Depth 1 means that each recursive function executes one of its base cases, depth 2 corresponds to that at least one recursive function has executed a recursive case, and then this recursive call has executed its base case, and so on. More details about how exhaustive static paths are generated can be found in [18].

In the *insertAVL* example there are two paths with depth 1. In the first one, the input tree is empty and the internal function *ins* immediately terminates by creating a new node with the value x and with height 1. In the second one,

```
(define insertAVL ((x Int) (t (AVL Int))) ((res (AVL Int)))
  (declare (assertion
    (precd
      (@ isAVL t))
    (postcd
      (and (@ isAVL res)
        (@ = (@ setA res)
          (let ((s1 (Set Int))) (@ setA t)
            (let ((s2 (Set Int))) (@ unit x)
              (@ union s1 s2)))))))))
  (letfun (
    (ins ((x Int) (t (AVL Int))) ((res (AVL Int)))
      (case t (
        ((@@ LeafA)
          (@@ NodeA x (the Int 1) t t))
        ((@@ NodeA y h l r)
          (let ((b1 Bool)) (@ < x y)
            (case b1 (
              ((@@ True)
                (let ((ia (AVL Int))) (@ ins x l)
                  (@ equil ia y r)))
              ((@@ False)
                (let ((b2 Bool)) (@ > x y)
                  (case b2 (
                    ((@@ True)
                      (let ((ib (AVL Int))) (@ ins x r)
                        (@ equil l y ib)))
                    ((@@ False)
                      t)))))))))))))))
```

Fig. 5. The function *insertAVL* written in the CLIR syntax.

the value x being inserted is already present at the root of the input tree, and the *ins* function terminates without inserting anything. With depth 2, there are at least 4 paths through the function *ins*: two of them recursively call to *ins* with the left subtree as an argument, and another two call to *ins* with the right one as an argument. The rest of the path inside these recursive calls is one of the depth 1 paths. After inserting the value, the static paths go on with a call to function *equil*, and there are two paths in this function. Combined with the other 4, this gives 8 paths. Then, we should consider paths through *leftBalance* or *rightBalance*, depending on the branch taken by *equil*, and so on. The combinatorics soon produces an exponential number of paths when the UUT is as complex as in our example. Notice however, that many of these paths are unfeasible. For instance, when inserting a new node in the left subtree, it may not happen that *equil* takes the branch calling to *rightBalance*: if any unbalance arises after inserting to the left, it should be in the left subtree.

Given an UUT written in the IR language, and the user having fixed a maximum depth, our system generates all the static paths having a depth smaller than or equal to this maximum depth. For each static path, it collects all the equalities occurring in the **let** bindings traversed by the path, and the conditions holding in each traversed **case** expression forcing the path to follow one of the branches. These equalities and conditions are converted into restrictions for the

```
define insertAVL (x::Int, t::AVL Int)::(res::AVL Int) =
  letfun
    ins (x::Int, t::AVL Int)::(res::AVL Int) =
      case t of
        LeafA                                          -> NodeA x 1 LeafA LeafA
        NodeA y::Int h::Int l::(AVL Int) r::(AVL Int) ->
                          let b1::Bool = x < y in
                          case b1 of
                            True  -> let ia::(AVL Int) = ins x l in
                                     equil ia y r
                            False -> let b2::Bool = x > y in
                                     case b2 of
                                       True  -> let ib::(AVL Int) = ins x r in
                                                equil l y ib
                                       False -> t
    equil (l::AVL Int, x::Int, r::AVL Int)::(res::AVL Int) =
      let hl::Int  = height l in
      let hr::Int  = height r in
      let hr2::Int = hr + 2 in
      let b::Bool  = hl == hr2 in
        case b of
          True  -> leftBalance l x r
          False -> let hl2::Int = hl + 2 in
                   let b2::Bool = hr == hl2 in
                   case b2 of
                     True  -> rightBalance l x r
                     False -> compose l x r
    ... definitions of height, compose, leftBalance and rightBalance
  in ins x t
```

Fig. 6. CAVI-ART IR for function *insertAVL*

SMT solver. For instance, for the *insertAVL* depth-1 path in which the inserted element is already in the tree, the following constraints are collected:

$$(t = nodeA \; y \; h \; l \; r) \wedge (b1 = x < y) \wedge (b1 = false) \wedge$$
$$(b2 = x > y) \wedge (b2 = false) \wedge (res = t)$$

Then, the solver is given the set of constraints corresponding to the UUT precondition, together with the set of constraints corresponding to a static path. If the solver finds a model, it means that it satisfies the precondition, and that the path is feasible. Then, the model assignment for the input arguments (in our example, for the tree t and for the value x) constitutes a test-case that, when run, it does not violate the precondition and exactly exercises that path.

In Fig. 7 we show the beginning of the set of constraints generated by our system for a path of depth 1 that inserts an element to the left of the input tree. As there are two calls to function *ins*, its variables must be renamed in each call. For instance, ins_2_t stands for argument t of the second call to *ins*. For this path, the solver finds the model $t = nodeA \; 3 \; 1 \; leafA \; leafA$, $x = 2$ and $res = nodeA \; 3 \; 2 \; (nodeA \; 2 \; 1 \; leafA \; leafA) \; leafA$, which corresponds to a path inserting the value $x = 2$ to the left of the tree t, being its left subtree an empty tree.

```
(declare-const res (AVL Int))
(declare-const ins_1_x Int)
(declare-const ins_1_t (AVL Int))
(assert (= x ins_1_x))
(assert (= t ins_1_t))
(declare-const ins_1_res (AVL Int))
(assert (= res ins_1_res))
(declare-const ins_1_y Int)
(declare-const ins_1_h Int)
(declare-const ins_1_l (AVL Int))
(declare-const ins_1_r (AVL Int))
(assert (= ins_1_t (nodeA ins_1_y ins_1_h ins_1_l ins_1_r)))
(declare-const ins_1_b1 Bool)
(assert (= ins_1_b1 (< ins_1_x ins_1_y)))
(assert (= ins_1_b1 true))
(declare-const ins_2_x Int)
(declare-const ins_2_t (AVL Int))
(assert (= ins_1_x ins_2_x))
(assert (= ins_1_l ins_2_t))
(declare-const ins_2_res (AVL Int))
(declare-const ins_1_ia (AVL Int))
(assert (= ins_1_ia ins_2_res))
(assert (= ins_2_t leafA))
(assert (= ins_2_res (nodeA ins_2_x 1 ins_2_t ins_2_t)))
(declare-const equil_1_l (AVL Int))
(declare-const equil_1_x Int)
(declare-const equil_1_r (AVL Int))
(assert (= ins_1_ia equil_1_l))
(assert (= ins_1_y equil_1_x))
(assert (= ins_1_r equil_1_r))
...
```

Fig. 7. Constraints for a path of depth 1 in *insertAVL*

5   Partial Automatic Verification

In prior sections, we have illustrated the use of SMTs for generating an exhaustive set of black-box test-cases up to a given size, and an exhaustive set of white-box ones covering all the UUT paths up to a given depth. Also, we have explained how to use SMTs to automatically check the validity of the results returned by the UUT.

By using the same strategy as that of black-box test-case generation, we could improve a bit the exhaustiveness of white-box cases by generating *all* models for every satisfiable path. This would probably result in generating a huge number of cases. We have not followed this idea, but instead have followed an equivalent solution involving much less computational effort. We call it *partial automatic verification*.

The idea consists of adding to each satisfiable path a constraint expressing that the result returned in that path must satisfy the postcondition. Let us call $Q(\overline{x})$ to the precondition applied to the input arguments $\overline{x}$, $path(\overline{x}, \overline{y})$ to the set of constraints collected by the path, which may depend on the input arguments and on some intermediate variables $\overline{y}$, and $R(\overline{z})$ to the postcondition applied to the result $\overline{z}$ returned by the path, where $\overline{z}$ is a subset of $\overline{x} \cup \overline{y}$. Then, we ask the solver to check whether the formula

$$(Q(\overline{x}) \wedge path(\overline{x}, \overline{y})) \Rightarrow R(\overline{z})$$

is valid, i.e. all possible models satisfy it. Equivalently, we ask the solver to check whether the formula

$$Q(\overline{x}) \wedge path(\overline{x}, \overline{y}) \wedge \neg R(\overline{z})$$

in unsatisfiable, because $\neg(A \rightarrow B) \equiv \neg(\neg A \vee B) \equiv A \wedge \neg B$. If it were so, then we would have proved that all the test-cases covering this path are correct. If we proved this kind of formulas for all the satisfiable paths up to a given depth, we would have proved the correctness of the UUT for all the possible executions exercising the UUT up to that depth. Since all this work is done without executing the UUT, in fact we are doing formal verification. And, as the automatic testing above described, by just pressing a button. In case we could automatically prove these formulas, we would forget about invariants, intermediate assertions, auxiliary lemmas, and all the effort usually implied by doing formal verification by hand.

If one of these formulas were satisfiable, then the models given by the SMT would constitute counter examples of correctness, i.e. test-cases for which the UUT will return an incorrect result. In this case, we would be doing debugging of our program at a very low cost.

We have applied this idea to the 10 satisfiable paths of *insertAVL* with *depth* ≤ 2. The result has been that the formulas corresponding to the two depth-1 paths are unsat, the ones of two of the eight depth-2 paths are also unsat, and for the remaining formulas, the solver gives unknown as a result. That is, at least for 4 of these paths, the solver can prove their correctness. For the other 6, we conclude that the formulas are too complex for the current SMT technology. To return unsat is clearly more costly for the solver, since it must explore all the proof space. We remind that the recursive functions and predicates are internally transformed to universally quantified first order formulas, and that first order logic is undecidable in general. We did also the experiment of introducing a bug in the program by returning nodeA x 0 leafA leafA in the base case of *insertAVL*, instead of nodeA x 1 leafA leafA. Then the solver returned sat for the path formula, and returned the model $t = leafA$, which is in fact a failing test-case.

6   Experiments

A picture of our integrated testing system, named CAVI-TEST, is shown in Fig. 8. The input to the tool is a CLIR file containing the UUT code written in the IR language, and its formal specification, written in the IR specification language. The CAVI-ART IR was thought as an intermediate representation for the platform, and it is not directly executable. In order to get an executable version, there is a translation from the IR code to Haskell, shown in the bottom part of the tool. The Test Driver is also Haskell code, and it is responsible for

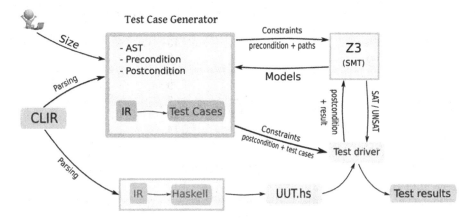

Fig. 8. A picture of CAVI-TEST, the CAVI-ART integrated testing system.

interacting with the UUT. It delivers the tests-cases to the UUT, and receives and checks the results the latter produces. The left part of the tool is the TCG. It receives from the user the desired size parameters and the desired depths for the static paths, converts the specifications and the paths into SMT constraints, and interacts with the SMT solver. Then, it translates the SMT results into Haskell test-cases. There is an inverse translation in the Test Driver from the Haskell results returned by the UUT to the SMT syntax, in order to check whether the postcondition is satisfied, again with the help of the SMT solver.

UUT	size	min Int	max Int	# cases
binSearch	3	1	3	60
DutchNationalFlag	3	0	2	40
linearSearchArray	3	1	3	120
insertArray	3	1	3	162
quicksortArray	3	1	3	40
insertList	3	1	4	60
deleteList	3	1	4	60
searchBST	3	1	5	560
insertBST	3	1	5	560
searchAVL	3	1	5	310
insertAVL	3	1	5	310
searchLLRB	3	1	5	250
unionLeftist	3	1	3	144
insertLeftist	3	1	4	504

Fig. 9. Black-box cases generated for a suit of UUTs.

UUT	depth	total paths	sat paths	unsat paths	unknown
binSearch	3	7	7	0	0
DutchNationalFlag	3	13	13	0	0
linearSearchArray	3	6	6	0	0
insertArray	3	6	4	2	0
quicksortArray	3	2549	9	2540	0
insertList	4	8	7	1	0
deleteList	4	12	10	2	0
searchBST	3	14	14	0	0
insertBST	3	14	14	0	0
searchAVL	3	14	14	0	0
insertAVL	2	10306	10	10257	39
searchLLRB	3	14	14	0	0
unionLeftist	3	20202	4	20197	1
insertLeftist	3	20202	6	20191	5

Fig. 10. White-box paths generated for a suit of UUTs.

We have prepared a UUT suit for our CAVI-TEST system, including functions dealing with a variety of data structures, such as sorted arrays, sorted lists, binary search trees, AVL trees, leftist heaps, and red-black trees. In Fig. 9 we show the results obtained for black-box test-cases. The column *size*, depending on the function, refers to the maximum size of the synthesized arrays, the maximum length of the lists, or the maximum height of the trees or heaps. Columns *min Int* and *max Int* show the limits used for integer values. Finally, column *#* *cases* shows the number of cases generated under the given constraints. These cases are *exhaustive* in the sense that they are all the cases satisfying the constraints. Notice that, even with these small sizes, we get a significant number of test-cases. Slightly increasing them leads very soon to thousands of cases. Of course, since running and checking the cases is also fully automatic, the user may always choose bigger sizes and let the system run thousands or millions of cases overnight.

In Fig. 10 we show the results obtained for white-box test-cases. The sizes used in the preconditions are the same shown in Fig. 9. The path depth was set to 3 for most of the examples, except for the simplest ones, such as *insertList* and *deleteList*, for which it was set to 4, and for *insertAVL*, which generated 10 306 paths for a path depth of 2, and a two million lines constraint file for depth 3. For complex UUTs such as this one, for the *quicksort* algorithm, and for the union of two leftist heaps, the number of unfeasible paths is very high. The insertion in a leftist heap is in fact a wrapper for the union function, and also gives a high number of unfeasible paths. Notice also that some unknown results are obtained for the most complex examples. We interpret this as an evidence of the complexity and size of the constraints associated to some paths and of the corresponding formulas given to the SMT solver. For each satisfiable path, our system produces a test-case that exercises that path. Notice that, within the depth constraints given here, together with the size constraints given in the precondition, the number of feasible paths obtained is rather small. If more (deeper) paths were desired, the sizes given in the precondition should be adjusted correspondingly. For instance, if we wish 5-depth paths in the *insertList* function, that means that at least 4 recursive calls should be performed, and then lists of at least size 4 should be allowed in the precondition.

For programs evaluating complex conditions in **let** bindings or in **case** expressions, it may happen that the solver cannot find a model, even if the set of constraints is satisfiable. In this situation, we would obtain neither sat nor unsat as the solver answer, but unknown. If the SMT answered sat for all the UUT feasible paths, then we would obtain a test suit covering all the UUT execution paths up to the given depth.

After running all the cases generated by the system, we found half a dozen of failing UUTs. For each failing case, the system reports the input arguments given to the UUT and the results obtained. As the cases were usually very small, it was easy to locate the error. In two of them, they were actual errors in the implementation and, in the remaining four, the code was correct, but the specification was not: some postconditions were wrong, or so were the definitions of some predicates.

As we anticipated in the Introduction section, the effort of writing formal specifications pays off. Thanks to them, our system was able to automatically generate, run, and validate a high number of test-cases, which helped us to refine both the specification and the implementation before embarking in a formal verification effort.

7   Related and Future Work

We have not found much literature for synthesizing test-cases from a precondition. The system Korat [4] was able to create relatively complex Java data structures such as binary search trees satisfying an executable JML assertion. The idea is similar to our previously cited work [2]: the system generates all possible trees and then filter out those satisfying the assertion. A more recent work [7] generates test-cases from Prolog predicates used as assertions in preconditions. Prolog predicates can be regarded both as executable assertions and as test-case generators. In the latter case, the logical variables used as arguments are not instantiated, so the predicate generates—if there are no cuts—all the ground terms satisfying it. The depth-first search is replaced by a random-search in order to generate a random set of test-cases.

A closer approach to the one presented here is the use of the Alloy system [12,13] for syntesizing complex data structures. The system uses an specification language based on the language Z, and translates these specifications into a SAT formula. The language gives neither support for recursion nor for quantified formulas, but it includes sets, relations, and regular expressions. Integers are encoded in the SAT formula as bit sequences. With some specification effort, they have been able to synthesize red-black trees. Given the lack of support of SAT solvers for complex theories, the generated formulas need a huge number of boolean variables, so only small cases could be synthesized in a reasonable time.

We have not found any literature on using SMT solvers and formal postconditions to validate the results returned by the program under test.

As future work, we plan to make the system more generic in the sense that it could process definitions of new datatypes and predicates, and could generate test-cases for them. For the moment, we can deal with a fix set of datatype definitions for arrays, lists, and a number of different trees. The recursive functions and predicates for these datatypes are currently directly defined in the SMT language.

References

1. Anand, S., et al.: An orchestrated survey of methodologies for automated software test case generation. J. Syst. Softw. **86**(8), 1978–2001 (2013). https://doi.org/10.1016/j.jss.2013.02.061
2. Aracil, M., García, P., Peña, R.: A tool for black-box testing in a multilanguage verification platform. In: Proceedings of the XVII Jornadas sobre Programación y Lenguajes, PROLE 2017, Tenerife, Spain, September 2017, pp. 1–15 (2017)
3. Barrett, C.W., Sebastiani, R., Seshia, S.A., Tinelli, C.: Satisfiability modulo theories. In: Biere, A., Heule, M., van Maaren, H., Walsh, T. (eds.) Handbook of Satisfiability, Frontiers in Artificial Intelligence and Applications, vol. 185, pp. 825–885. IOS Press (2009). https://doi.org/10.3233/978-1-58603-929-5-825
4. Boyapati, C., Khurshid, S., Marinov, D.: Korat: automated testing based on Java predicates. In: Frankl, P.G. (ed.) Proceedings of the International Symposium on Software Testing and Analysis, ISSTA 2002, Roma, Italy, 22–24 July 2002, pp. 123–133. ACM (2002). https://doi.org/10.1145/566172.566191, http://doi.acm.org/10.1145/566172.566191
5. Cadar, C., Dunbar, D., Engler, D.R.: KLEE: unassisted and automatic generation of high-coverage tests for complex systems programs. In: Draves, R., van Renesse, R. (eds.) 8th USENIX Symposium on Operating Systems Design and Implementation, OSDI 2008(December), pp. 8–10, 2008. San Diego, California, USA, Proceedings, pp. 209–224. USENIX Association (2008). http://www.usenix.org/events/osdi08/tech/full_papers/cadar/cadar.pdf
6. Cadar, C., Sen, K.: Symbolic execution for software testing: three decades later. Commun. ACM **56**(2), 82–90 (2013). https://doi.org/10.1145/2408776.2408795
7. Casso, I., Morales, J.F., López-García, P., Hermenegildo, M.V.: An integrated approach to assertion-based random testing in prolog. In: Gabbrielli, M. (ed.) LOPSTR 2019. LNCS, vol. 12042, pp. 159–176. Springer, Cham (2020). https://doi.org/10.1007/978-3-030-45260-5_10
8. Claessen, K., Hughes, J.: QuickCheck: a lightweight tool for random testing of Haskell programs. In: Odersky, M., Wadler, P. (eds.) Proceedings of the Fifth ACM SIGPLAN International Conference on Functional Programming (ICFP 2000), Montreal, Canada, 18–21 September 2000, pp. 268–279. ACM (2000). https://doi.org/10.1145/351240.351266, http://doi.acm.org/10.1145/351240.351266
9. Flanagan, C., Sabry, A., Duba, B.F., Felleisen, M.: The essence of compiling with continuations. In: Cartwright, R. (ed.) Proceedings of the Conference on Programming Language Design and Implementation (PLDI 1993), pp. 237–247. ACM (1993). https://doi.org/10.1145/155090.155113, http://doi.acm.org/10.1145/155090.155113

10. Godefroid, P., Klarlund, N., Sen, K.: DART: directed automated random testing. In: Sarkar, V., Hall, M.W. (eds.) Proceedings of the ACM SIGPLAN 2005 Conference on Programming Language Design and Implementation, Chicago, IL, USA, 12–15 June 2005, pp. 213–223. ACM (2005). https://doi.org/10.1145/1065010. 1065036

11. Hughes, J.: Software testing with QuickCheck. In: Horváth, Z., Plasmeijer, R., Zsók, V. (eds.) CEFP 2009. LNCS, vol. 6299, pp. 183–223. Springer, Heidelberg (2010). https://doi.org/10.1007/978-3-642-17685-2_6

12. Jackson, D., Schechter, I., Shlyakhter, I.: Alcoa: the Alloy constraint analyzer. In: Ghezzi, C., Jazayeri, M., Wolf, A.L. (eds.) Proceedings of the 22nd International Conference on on Software Engineering, ICSE 2000, Limerick Ireland, 4–11 June 2000, pp. 730–733. ACM (2000). https://doi.org/10.1145/337180.337616

13. Khurshid, S., Marinov, D.: TestEra: specification-based testing of Java programs using SAT. Autom. Softw. Eng. 11(4), 403–434 (2004). https://doi.org/10.1023/B:AUSE.0000038938.10589.b9

14. Montenegro, M., Nieva, S., Peña, R., Segura, C.: Liquid types for array invariant synthesis. In: D'Souza, D., Narayan Kumar, K. (eds.) ATVA 2017. LNCS, vol. 10482, pp. 289–306. Springer, Cham (2017). https://doi.org/10.1007/978-3-319-68167-2_20

15. Montenegro, M., Peña, R., Sánchez-Hernández, J.: A generic intermediate representation for verification condition generation. In: Falaschi, M. (ed.) LOPSTR 2015. LNCS, vol. 9527, pp. 227–243. Springer, Cham (2015). https://doi.org/10.1007/978-3-319-27436-2_14

16. de Moura, L., Bjørner, N.: Z3: an efficient SMT solver. In: Ramakrishnan, C.R., Rehof, J. (eds.) TACAS 2008. LNCS, vol. 4963, pp. 337–340. Springer, Heidelberg (2008). https://doi.org/10.1007/978-3-540-78800-3_24

17. Pasareanu, C.S., Visser, W.: A survey of new trends in symbolic execution for software testing and analysis. STTT 11(4), 339–353 (2009)

18. Peña, R., Sánchez-Hernández, J.: White-box path generation in recursive programs. In: Byrski, A., Hughes, J. (eds.) TFP 2020. LNCS, vol. 12222, pp. 121–135. Springer, Cham (2020). https://doi.org/10.1007/978-3-030-57761-2_6

19. Reynolds, A., Blanchette, J.C., Cruanes, S., Tinelli, C.: Model finding for recursive functions in SMT. In: Olivetti, N., Tiwari, A. (eds.) IJCAR 2016. LNCS (LNAI), vol. 9706, pp. 133–151. Springer, Cham (2016). https://doi.org/10.1007/978-3-319-40229-1_10

20. Sen, K., Marinov, D., Agha, G.: CUTE: a concolic unit testing engine for C. In: Wermelinger, M., Gall, H.C. (eds.) Proceedings of the 10th European Software Engineering Conference held jointly with 13th ACM SIGSOFT International Symposium on Foundations of Software Engineering, 2005, Lisbon, Portugal, 5–9 September 2005, pp. 263–272. ACM (2005). https://doi.org/10.1145/1081706. 1081750

21. Toda, T., Soh, T.: Implementing efficient all solutions SAT solvers. ACM J. Exp. Algorithmics 21(1), 1.12:1–1.12:44 (2016). https://doi.org/10.1145/2975585

Layerings of Logic Programs - Layer Decomposable Semantics and Incremental Model Computation

Alexandre Miguel Pinto[1] and Luís Moniz Pereira[2(✉)]

[1] Signal AI, London, UK
alexandre.pinto@signal-ai.com
[2] Department of Computer Science, Universidade Nova de Lisboa, Lisbon, Portugal
lmp@fct.unl.pt

Abstract. Model calculation of Logic Programs (LPs) is a computational task that depends both on the size of the LP and the semantics considered for it. With ever growing size and diversity of applications using logic programs as representations of knowledge bases, there is a corresponding growing need to optimize the efficiency of model computation. In this paper we define two graph-theoretical structures, which we dub the Rule Layering and the Atom Layering, induced by the LP's syntactic dependencies that allow us to develop an algorithm for incremental, and possibly distributed, model computation. This algorithm is parameterizable by the semantics considered for the LP, but because it relies on the Layerings notions it is suitable only for a certain family of semantics, which includes the Stable Models and the Well-Founded Semantics. We conclude the paper with some preliminary complexity results and a characterization of the family of semantics our approach captures.

Keywords: Logic Programs · Layerings · Model Computation · Stratification

1 Introduction

Logic Programs (LPs) are commonly used as one of the knowledge representation and reasoning formalisms for the development of knowledge bases, deductive databases and intelligent software agents in general. During the last decades the tools and results of this formalism have been continuously growing mature, and as a consequence LPs have been successfully used to model increasingly larger and more complex domains with accompanying growing complexity of reasoning tasks. Some of the most common reasoning tasks with LPs are *skeptical reasoning*, which corresponds to checking whether a conjunction of literals is *true* in all models of the LP, and *credulous reasoning*, which corresponds to checking whether a conjunction of literals is *true* in some model of the LP. Hence the computational complexity and performance of the reasoning tasks is highly dependent on the model computation task, and it is the role of the particular semantics chosen for the LP to dictate which interpretation(s) is (are) accepted as model(s). On the other hand, it is both the specific kinds of applications an LP is

© Springer Nature Switzerland AG 2023
P. Lopez-Garcia et al. (Eds.): Hermenegildo Festschrift 2022, LNCS 13160, pp. 206–221, 2023.
https://doi.org/10.1007/978-3-031-31476-6_11

being used for, and the overall properties required of the whole LP-based system, that determine which semantics one should choose for the LP. With ever growing size and diversity of applications using LP there is a corresponding growing need to optimize the efficiency of model computation.

In this paper we contribute to the optimization of model computation by devising a generic method and a distributable and incremental algorithm for model computation of LPs which is parameterizable by the particular semantics chosen by the user. We do so by first identifying and taking advantage of the graph-theoretical structure induced by the syntactic dependencies in an LP. As a consequence, we introduce two new graph-theoretical structural properties of LPs, the Rule Layering and the Atom Layering; and our generic method and algorithm for incremental model computation and show it can be used to compute the Stable Models [8], the Well-Founded Model [7], and also models of other semantics. Indeed, our approach allows us to define and characterize the family of semantics our method can capture, and we do so in the paper before presenting preliminary complexity results and conclusions and future work.

1.1 Background and Notation

We consider here the usual notions of alphabet, language, atom, literal, rule, and (logic) program. A literal is either an atom A or its default negation $not\ A$. We dub default literals those of the form $not\ A$. Without loss of generality we consider only ground normal logic programs, consisting of normal rules of the form $H \leftarrow B_1, \ldots, B_n, not\ C_1, \ldots, not\ C_m$, (with $m, n \geq 0$ and finite) where H, the B_i and the C_j are ground atoms. In conformity with the standard convention, we write rules of the form $H \leftarrow$ also simply as H (known as "facts"). An LP P is called definite if none of its rules contain default literals. If r is a rule we denote its head H by $head(r)$, and $body(r)$ denotes the set $\{B_1, \ldots, B_n, not\ C_1, \ldots, not\ C_m\}$ of all the literals in its body. We write $\mathcal{H}_P$ to denote the Herbrand Base of P.

We abuse the 'not' default negation notation applying it to sets of literals too: we write $not\ S$ to denote $\{not\ s : s \in S\}$, and confound $not\ not\ a \equiv a$. When S is an arbitrary, non-empty set of literals $S = \{B_1, \ldots, B_n, not\ C_1, \ldots, not\ C_m\}$ we use the following notation:

- S^+ denotes the set $\{B_1, \ldots, B_n\}$ of positive literals in S
- S^- denotes the set $\{not\ C_1, \ldots, not\ C_m\}$ of negative literals in S
- $|S|$ denotes the set $\{B_1, \ldots, B_n, C_1, \ldots, C_m\}$ of atoms of S

Besides containing normal rules as above, LPs may also include rules with a non-empty body and where the head is the special symbol $\perp$ which are known as a type of Integrity Constraints (ICs), specifically *denials*, and they are normally used to prune out unwanted models of the normal rules part. We write $heads(P)$ to denote the set of heads of non-IC rules of an LP P, and $facts(P)$ to denote the set of facts of P.

2 Layerings of Logic Programs

We aim at devising an incremental algorithm for model computation which should be parameterizable by a chosen semantics and it should allow some degree of parallelization. In order to develop such a generic and parameterizable method, we resort to a divide-and-conquer approach using the syntactic features of the LP: first we identify its syntactic components dividing the LP into, as much as possible, independent modules; then we use the chosen semantics to compute individual models for each component and module; and finally we combine the individual models to obtain a global one for the whole LP. As we will see, this approach is suitable only for a restricted family of semantics, which includes, among others, the Stable Models (SMs), and the Well-Founded Semantics (WFS), but not, e.g., the Minimal Models semantics.

2.1   The Structure of Logic Programs

The traditional approach to identify the knowledge structure in an LP considers the atom dependency graph of the LP.

Definition 1. *Atom graph.* *$DG(P)$ is the atom dependency (directed) graph of the LP P where the atoms of P are the vertices of $DG(P)$, and there is a directed edge from a vertex A to a vertex B iff there is a rule in P with head B such that A appears in its body.*

But as the author of [2] puts it, relating the Dependency Graph with the Answer Set semantics [8,11], "it is well-known, the traditional Dependency Graph (DG) is not able to represent programs under the Answer Set semantics: in fact, programs which are different in syntax and semantics, have the same Dependency Graph." Here we define a generic method and algorithm for model computation which, while encompassing SMs, is not limited to it and so the "traditional" atom DG is also not enough for our purposes. In the literature, we find also the rule graph, introduced in [4].

Definition 2. *Rule graph (Definition 3.8 of [4]).* *Let P be a reduced negative NLP (i.e., there are only negative literals in the bodies of rules). $RG(P)$ is the rule graph of P where the rules of P are the nodes of $RG(P)$, and there is an arc from a node r_1 to a node r_2 iff the head of rule r_1 appears in the body of the rule r_2.*

But, as the author of [2] says, "in our opinion it would be difficult to define any practical programming methodology on the basis of the rule graph, since it does not graphically distinguish among cases which are semantically very different." This sentence assumes not only that the underlying semantics is the SMs, but also that the arcs in the rule graph are supposed to contain all the semantic information of the program. Besides, the rule graph, as defined in [4], presupposes reduced negative programs. As we shall see below, our approach to rule graphs considers its structural information as a crucial necessary part in determining the semantics of the program, but not a sufficient one. Thus, we will be able to *define a practical programming methodology on the basis of the rule graph*, plus other semantic constructs, namely, hypotheses assumption, as per the sequel.

The next definition extends the rule graph one (Definition 2), in the sense that it is applicable to all LPs and not just to reduced negative logic programs.

Definition 3. *Complete Rule Graph.* *The complete rule graph of an LP P (denoted by $CRG(P)$) is the directed graph whose vertices are the rules of P, and there is a directed edge from vertex r_1 to vertex r_2 in $CRG(P)$ iff the head of rule r_1 appears, possibly default negated, in the body of r_2.*

In the rest of the paper we assume P is a Logic Program and $CRG(P)$ denotes its Complete Rule Graph. In order to identify and take advantage of the graph-like syntactic structure of an LP we need to introduce all the syntactic dependencies notions we will be using.

Definition 4. Dependencies in a program. *A rule r_2 directly depends on r_1 (written as $r_2 \leftarrow r_1$) iff there is a direct edge in $CRG(P)$ from r_1 to r_2; we say r_2 depends on r_1 ($r_2 \twoheadleftarrow r_1$) iff there is a directed path in $CRG(P)$ from r_1 to r_2.*

We also consider the other combinations of (direct) dependencies amongst atoms and rules, and use the same graphical notation $(\leftarrow, \twoheadleftarrow)$ to denote (direct, indirect) dependency. Rule r directly depends on atom a iff $a \in |body(r)|$; and r depends on a iff either r directly depends on atom a or r depends on some rule r' which directly depends on a. An atom a directly depends on rule r iff $head(r) = a$; and a depends on r iff either a directly depends on r or a directly depends on some rule r' such that r' depends on r. An atom b directly depends on atom a iff a appears (possibly default negated) in the body of a rule with head b, and b depends on a iff either b directly depends on a, or b directly depends on some rule r which depends on a.

Alongside with the graph perspective of logic programs is the classical notion of stratification, usually associated with the atom dependency graph.

Definition 5. Stratification [15]. *A program P is stratified if and only if it is possible to decompose the set S of all predicates of P into disjoint sets $S_1, \ldots, S_r$, called strata, so that for every clause $A \leftarrow B_1, \ldots, B_m, not\ C_1, \ldots, not\ C_n$, in P, where A's, B's and C are atoms, we have that: $\forall_i stratum(B_i) \leq stratum(A)$ and $\forall_j stratum(C_j) < stratum(A)$ where $stratum(A) = i$, if the predicate symbol of A belongs to S_i. Any particular decomposition $\{S_1, \ldots, S_r\}$ of S satisfying the above conditions is called a stratification of P.*

This notion fails to capture all the structural information of a program since it focuses only on the atoms', thereby confounding the specific dependencies for each particular rule. Moreover, there are cases of programs which have no stratification whatsoever, in particular ones with loops over negation. We now put forward the Layerings notions of LPs; these are applicable to all programs and capture all the structural information in each one.

Definition 6. Rule Layering. *Let P be an LP with no infinitely long descending chains of dependency. A rule layering function $Lf/1$ of P is a function mapping each vertex of $CRG(P)$ (a rule r of P) to a non-zero ordinal such that*

$$\forall_{r_1, r_2 \in P} \begin{cases} Lf(r_1) = Lf(r_2) \Leftarrow (r_1 \twoheadleftarrow r_2) \wedge (r_2 \twoheadleftarrow r_1) \\ Lf(r_1) > Lf(r_2) \Leftarrow (r_1 \twoheadleftarrow r_2) \wedge \neg (r_2 \twoheadleftarrow r_1) \end{cases}$$

A rule layering of P is thus a partition $\ldots, P^i, \ldots$ of P such that P^i contains all rules r having $Lf(r) = i$. We write $P^{<\alpha}$ as an abbreviation of $\bigcup_{\beta < \alpha} P^\beta$, and $P^{\leq \alpha}$ as an abbreviation of $P^{<\alpha} \cup P^\alpha$, and define $P^0 = P^{\leq 0} = \emptyset$. It follows immediately that $P = \bigcup_\alpha P^\alpha = \bigcup_\alpha P^{\leq \alpha}$, and also that the $\leq$ relation between layers is a total-order in the sense that $P^i \leq P^j$ iff $i \leq j$.

Amongst the several possible rule layerings of P we can always find the least one, i.e., the rule layering with least number of layers, where the ordinals of the layers are the smallest possible, and where the ordinals of $Lf(r)$, for each rule r, are also the smallest possible, whilst respecting the rule layering function assignments. This least rule layering is easily seen to be unique.

N.B.: In the following, when referring to the program's "layering", we mean just such least rule layering. Likewise, there is also a least stratification. We address the relationship between strata and layers in the sequel.[1]

The Rule Layering definition above states that two rules are placed in the same layer if they depend on each other. This is an *if*, not an *if and only if*. I.e., according to Rule Layering, two rules *can* be placed in the same layer when, e.g., they have no dependencies amongst them. In the following example, the rules $x \leftarrow not\ x$ and $e \leftarrow e$ are placed in the same layer despite there being no dependencies whatsoever between them.

Example 1. **Rule Layering example.** Consider the following program *P*, depicted along with the layer numbers for its least layering:

Program *P* with its rules distributed along the layers.

$b \leftarrow not\ b$	$d \leftarrow not\ c$	$c \leftarrow not\ d, not\ y, not\ a$	P^3 — Layer 3
$b \leftarrow not\ x$	$y \leftarrow not\ x$	$z \leftarrow f$	P^2 — Layer 2
$x \leftarrow not\ x$	$e \leftarrow e$	f	P^1 — Layer 1
$\emptyset$			P^0 — Layer 0

Atom f has a fact rule: its body is empty (it depends on no other rule), and therefore it is placed in the lowest possible layer: P^1. The unique rule for x is also placed in Layer 1 in the least layering of P because it depends only on itself. Likewise for rule $e \leftarrow e$. Rules $b \leftarrow not\ x$ and $y \leftarrow not\ x$ are necessarily placed strictly above Layer 1 because they both depend directly on the rule for x, which in turn does not depend on any of them. So, both these rules for y and for b are placed in Layer 2, P^2, in the least layering of P. For the same reason, rule $z \leftarrow f$ is placed in Layer 2, because it depends on the (fact) rule for f which is in Layer 1. Notice this important difference between Layering and Stratification: the Layering does not distinguish between positive and negative dependencies nor does it treat such cases differently, as the Stratification does (cf. Definition 5). For the Layering notion the only important factor is the existence

---

[1] The layers notion in [10] have some similarities with the ones presented in Definition 6 when applied to $CRG(P)$, but the former (Definition 6.2 of [10]) has the limited role of providing the scaffolding of a transfinite inductive definition of the *weakly perfect model* which is a subset of the Well-Founded Model (as per Corollary 6.9 of [10]). The layering notion presented here, although similar to [13], is not equivalent to it and has a standing of its own as an important syntactical ordering, besides its structuring influence inducing certain desirable characteristics of models of a semantics, as we shall see later.

of, or lack thereof, syntactic dependency, regardless of it being through a positive or negative literal. This is the reason why the Layering puts rule $z \leftarrow f$ in a layer strictly above that of the fact f (because $z \leftarrow f$ depends on fact f and not vice-versa), whereas Stratification would allow atom z to be in the same stratum as atom f (because $z \leftarrow f$ depends *positively* on fact f). I.e., Layering and the Stratification use different criteria to assign layer/stratum ordinal indices.

Rule $b \leftarrow not\ b$ is placed strictly above all other rules for b that do not depend on b, i.e., on Layer 3, P^3. The rule for c is placed strictly above the rule for y because it depends on *not y* and no rule for y depends on any rule for c. The rule for d is placed in the same Layer as the rule for c because they depend on each other. Hence, both rules for c and d are placed in Layer 3, P^3.

The Rule Layering tries to capture the *ordo cognoscendi* implicit in the knowledge expressed by the program. The algorithm we present in the sequel takes advantage of this ordering to incrementally construct models of the program. Building upon the (rule) layering we can now define the Atom Layering—a notion similar to that of stratification.

Definition 7. *Atom-Layering of a Logic Program* P. Let $Lf/1$ be a rule layering function of P. An atom layering function $ALf/1$ is defined over the atoms of P, assigning each $a \in \mathcal{H}_P$ an ordinal, s.t.

$$ALf(a) = \begin{cases} lub_{r \in P:head(r)=a}(Lf(r)) & if\ \exists_{r \in P}head(r) = a \\ 0 & otherwise \end{cases}$$

where lub stands for the least upper bound—in this case, the least upper bound of all the rule layer ordinals for layers containing a rule with the atom a as head.

An atom layering of program P is a partition $\ldots, A^i_P, \ldots$ of $\mathcal{H}_P$ s.t. A^i_P contains all atoms a having $ALf(a) = i$. We write $A^{<\alpha}_P$ as an abbreviation of $\bigcup_{\beta < \alpha} A^\beta_P$, and $A^{\leq\alpha}_P$ as an abbreviation of $A^{<\alpha}_P \cup A^\alpha_P$, and define $A^{\leq 0}_P = \emptyset$. It follows immediately that $\mathcal{H}_P = \bigcup_\alpha A^\alpha_P = \bigcup_\alpha A^{\leq\alpha}_P$, and also that the $\leq$ relation between layers of atoms is a total-order in the sense that $A^i_P \leq A^j_P$ iff $i \leq j$.

Amongst the several possible atom layerings of a program P we can always find the least one corresponding to the definition of "atom layering function" $ALf/1$ based upon the program's least rule layering function $Lf/1$. In the following, when referring to the program's "atom layering", we mean just such least atom layering, and we will explicitly mention "atom", as in "atom layering" to make the distinction from (rule) layering.

This notion of atom layering is a level-mapping [9, 10] because, as explained in [10], "Level mappings are mappings from Herbrand bases to ordinals, i.e. they induce orderings on the set of all ground atoms while disallowing infinite descending chains" and the atom layering does induce such an ordering while disallowing infinite descending chains. Moreover, the atom layering also exists for programs with loops, where in such cases there are no stratifications, and in that sense the atom layering is more general than the stratification notion. Also, due to the definition of dependency, in general, atom layerings do not coincide with stratifications [1], nor do rule layers coincide with the layers definition of [14]. When a program is not stratified there are nonetheless atom layerings.

However, when the program at hand is stratified (according to [1]) it can easily be seen that there is a relation between its atom layerings and its stratifications. A stratification, applicable to atoms, may put two atoms in the same stratum if one of them only depends through positive arcs on the other (without any reciprocal dependency), whereas, under the same conditions, an atom layering would put them in different layers—cf. Example 2 below concerning rule $z \leftarrow f$. So, for each stratification there is an atom layering, possibly with more layers than the strata there are in the stratification. On the other hand, assuming the program is stratified, for each atom layering there is a stratification. Moreover, there is a clear correspondence between a stratification and the least atom layering for acyclic programs—in this case the only difference relates to the atoms whose rules have only positive dependencies on some other atom. The motivation for this difference between layering and stratification, in what positive dependencies are concerned, is mainly a matter of uniformity and simplicity of the definition of layering, specifically regarding distinguishing reciprocal from non-reciprocal dependencies and layer/stratum ordinal assignment.

Example 2. **Atom Layering example.** Consider again the program from Example 1, now depicted along with both its least rule layering and least atom layering: Atom a has no rules, therefore it is placed in atom-layer 0: A_P^0. Atoms x, e, f have only one rule in Layer 1; they are placed in atom-layer 1: A_P^1. Atoms y, z have only one rule in Layer 2; they are placed in atom-layer 2: A_P^2. Atom b has two rules: one in Layer 2 and the other in Layer 3, therefore it is placed in atom-layer 3 which is the maximum of its rules' layers: A_P^3. Atoms c, d only have rules in Layer 3: they go in A_P^3.

NLP's rules and atoms distributed along the program's Rule and Atom least Layerings.

Rule Layer			Atom Layer	Layer Index
$P^3 = \{b \leftarrow not\ b$	$d \leftarrow not\ c$	$c \leftarrow not\ d, not\ y, not\ a\}$	$A_P^3 = \{b, c, d\}$	3
$P^2 = \{b \leftarrow not\ x$	$y \leftarrow not\ x$	$z \leftarrow f\}$	$A_P^2 = \{y, z\}$	2
$P^1 = \{x \leftarrow not\ x$	$e \leftarrow e$	$f\}$	$A_P^1 = \{x, e, f\}$	1
$P^0 = \emptyset$			$A_P^0 = \{a\}$	0

The following, results immediately from the previous definitions of (least) atom layering and (least) rule layering—the interested reader can find their formalizations and proofs in appendix.

Result: The least atom layering of an atom identifies the highest layer with rules for the atom; and a rule's layer is greater than or equal to each of the body's literals' atom-layering.

Result: Considering the Strongly Connected Components [12] (SCCs) of rules in the $CRG(P)$, rules in the same SCC are in the same layer.

Result: If SCC_1 and SCC_2 are two distinct SCCs of rules in $CRG(P)$, and some rule $r_2 \in SCC_2$ depends on some rule $r_1 \in SCC_1$ then all rules in SCC_2 are in layers strictly above that of the rules in SCC_1.

2.2 Layers and Strongly Connected Components of Rules

The mutual syntactic dependencies among rules are a central factor in the definitions of the Layerings notions. A parameterizable incremental ("layer-wise") algorithm to compute models according to a user-chosen semantics must be as general as possible, in what the particular chosen semantics is concerned. In that regard, the specific semantics might interpret the rules of the program in loop (in an SCC in $CRG(P)$) differently from the rules in non-circular dependencies. To that effect, our algorithm will need to be able to distinguish the parts of the bodies of rules which are in loop with the rule, i.e., which literals in the body of a rule have corresponding atoms appearing as heads of rules, depending on the considered rule.

Layers and Bodies of Rules. The (least) atom layering of a program allows to partition the body of any given rule into atom-layer indexed subsets.

Definition 8. *Atom-layer partition of a rule's body. The $body(r)$ of a rule r of an LP P can be partitioned into subsets $\dots, body(r)^{\alpha}, \dots$ such that each*

$$body(r)^{\alpha} = \{B_i \in body(r)^+ : ALf(B_i) = \alpha\} \cup \{not\ C_j \in body(r)^- : ALf(C_j) = \alpha\}$$

It follows immediately from previous results and this definition that:

Result: A rule's layer index is greater than or equal to each of the body's subsets indices, i.e.,
$\forall_{body(r)^{\alpha} \subseteq body(r)} Lf(r) \geq \alpha$, and also that:

Result: A rule's body literals in a loop have atom-layering equal to the rule's layer, i.e.,
$\forall_{\substack{a \in \mathcal{H}_p \\ r \in P}} (a \in |body(r)^{Lf(r)}| \Rightarrow ALf(a) = Lf(r))$.

$body(r)^{Lf(r)}$ is then the set of literals of $body(r)$ which are in loop with r, and $body(r) \setminus body(r)^{Lf(r)}$ the literals of $body(r)$ not in loop with r. In the sequel we write simply $\overline{body(r)}$ as an abbreviation of $body(r) \setminus body(r)^{Lf(r)}$, which represents the subset of literals in the body of r whose corresponding atoms have all their rules, if any, in layers strictly below that of r.

2.3 Transfinite Layering

Layering also copes with programs with a transfinite number of layers as long as there is no infinitely long *descending* chain of dependencies. In practice, all useful programs have a finite number of layers, but for theoretical completeness we show that this layering notion also deals with the transfinite case.

Example 3. **Program with transfinite number of layers.** Let $P =$

$$p(s(X)) \leftarrow p(X)$$
$$p(0)$$

The ground (layered) version of this program, assuming there is only one constant 0 (zero) is:

$$\vdots \leftarrow \vdots$$
$$p(s(s(0))) \leftarrow p(s(0))$$
$$p(s(0)) \leftarrow p(0)$$
$$p(0)$$

This program has a layering even though it has an infinite chain of dependencies. This is the case since that infinite chain is *ascending*—this program has a transfinite number of layers.

A typical case of a program with no layering (representing a whole class of programs with real theoretical interest) has an infinitely long *descending* chain of dependencies, and was presented by François Fages in [6]:

Example 4. **Program with no layering [6].**

$$p(X) \leftarrow p(s(X)) \qquad\qquad p(X) \leftarrow not\ p(s(X))$$

Its ground version, assuming only one constant 0 (zero), is:

$$p(0) \leftarrow p(s(0)) \qquad\qquad p(0) \leftarrow not\ p(s(0))$$
$$p(s(0)) \leftarrow p(s(s(0))) \qquad\qquad p(s(0)) \leftarrow not\ p(s(s(0)))$$
$$p(s(s(0))) \leftarrow p(s(s(s(0)))) \qquad p(s(s(0))) \leftarrow not\ p(s(s(s(0))))$$
$$\vdots \leftarrow \vdots \qquad\qquad\qquad \vdots \leftarrow \vdots$$

3   Layer-Decomposable Semantics and Incremental Model Computation

With the Layerings notions presented we have captured all the structural information behind the knowledge represented within an LP. We now argue that every semantics for LPs should comply with this structure in the sense that a model for the whole LP should be decomposable into mutually consistent individual models for each layer. Assuming this premise, we propose a bottom-up, and layer-wise incremental, algorithm that allows us to calculate the models of every semantics complying with this layer-decomposability principle. We show that, among others, the Stable Models and the Well-Founded Model can be computed in this way. Finally, we characterize the members of this Layer-Decomposable family of semantics.

Intuitively, we say a semantics for LPs is Layer-Decomposable iff all its models are decomposable into a partition of subsets, each of which is a model for an individual layer, containing all the atoms determined necessarily *true* in that layer, and the default negation of all atoms necessarily *false*, and, what is more, also compliant with all the models for the other layers, where compliance can be achieved by requiring consistency of the union of individual layers' models. The unique model for layer 0 is the set of default negated literals corresponding to the atoms of P with no rules.

As model computation is concerned, a pure guess-and-check algorithm, in the sense that we guess individual interpretations for each layer, and check if their union is a model (according to the chosen semantics) of the global program, would be too naïve. Instead, we propose an incremental layer-wise bottom-up algorithm where we progressively restrict the freedom of the guesses for each layer, by beforehand enforcing in that layer the truthfulness of the sub-model chosen for the layers below it. As pointed out before in Sect. 2.2, in order to build an algorithm that is correct also for computing models of semantics that distinguish circular dependencies from non-circular ones, we must have a syntactic method of restricting the freely available guesses in each layer, which is sensitive to circular dependencies. For comparison with classical approaches that do not make such a syntactic distinction, we also define a (classical) method of restricting the guesses regardless of circularity or otherwise of dependencies. We dub these, respectively, Layer Division and Classical Division.

Definition 9. Classical Division. *Let I be a 3-valued interpretation of the LP P. The classical division of P by I, denoted by $P :: I$, is the program we get after deleting from P all the rules r with $body(r)$ inconsistent with I, and deleting all literals in I from the bodies of the remaining rules. I.e., $P :: I = \{head(r) \leftarrow (body(r) \setminus I) : r \in P \wedge (not\ body(r)) \cap I = \emptyset\}$.*

Definition 10. Layer Division. *Let I be a 3-valued interpretation of the LP P. The layer division of P by I, denoted by $P : I$, is the program we get after deleting all the rules r from P with $\overline{body(r)}$ inconsistent with I and deleting all literals in I from the parts of bodies not in loop of the remaining rules. I.e., $P : I = \{head(r) \leftarrow (body^{Lf(r)} \cup (\overline{body(r)} \setminus I)) : r \in P \wedge (not\ body(r)) \cap I = \emptyset\}$.*

In both Definitions 9 and 10, the interpretation I is a set of assumed hypotheses.

We can now use the syntactic scaffolding of layers, along with the corresponding Layer Division, to define the Layer-Decomposable semantics family. Intuitively, a model M is Layer-Decomposable iff it can be decomposed into a set of sub-models $\{M_{\leq 0}, \ldots, M_{\leq \alpha}, \ldots, M_{\leq \omega}\}$, each of which referring to the set of layers $\leq \alpha$ of P, i.e., to $P^{\leq \alpha}$. Each sub-model $M_{\leq \alpha}$ takes as assumed hypotheses the truth values for all atoms in $M_{<\alpha}$, which include $A_P^{\leq \alpha}$. We then enforce $M_{<\alpha}$, in a Layer-support-consistent fashion, in the rules of P^α via Layer Division.

Definition 11. Layer Decomposable Model. *Let P be an LP, and M a model of P according to semantics Sem. M is Layer Decomposable in P iff there is a Layer Decomposition $\{M_{\leq 0}, \ldots, M_{\leq \alpha}, \ldots, M_{\leq \omega}\}$ of M in P, i.e., $M = \bigcup_{\alpha > 0} M_{\leq \alpha}$ such that every M_α is a model of $P^\alpha : M_{<\alpha}$ according to Sem, where $M_{<0} = M_{\leq 0}^+ = \emptyset$. If Sem is a 2-valued semantics, then $M_\alpha = M_\alpha^+$ and $M_{\leq \alpha}^+ = M_\alpha^+ \cup M_{<\alpha}^+$ and $M_{\leq \alpha}^- = not\ (A_P^{\leq \alpha} \setminus M_{\leq \alpha}^+)$. If Sem is 3-valued, then $M_{\leq \alpha}^+ = M_\alpha^+ \cup M_{<\alpha}^+$ and $M_{\leq \alpha}^- = M_\alpha^- \cup M_{<\alpha}^-$.*

Each $M_{\leq \alpha}$ is a 3-valued interpretation of P where $M_{\leq \alpha}^+$ states which atoms are believed to be *true* considering only the rules up to $P^{\leq \alpha}$, and for 2-valued semantics, $M_{\leq \alpha}^-$

states that all the atoms that were not determined *true* in $M^{\leq\alpha}$ and that have no more rules in layers above P^{α} are necessarily determined *false*. It follows immediately that $\forall_{\alpha\leq\beta} M_{\leq\alpha} \subseteq M_{\leq\beta}$; i.e. $(\{M_{\leq\alpha} : \alpha \geq 0\}, \subseteq)$ is a total order with $M_{\leq 0}$ and $M = \bigcup_{\alpha\geq 0} M_{\leq\alpha}$ as its lower and upper bound, respectively. *Sem* is said Layer Decomposable iff all of its models are Layer Decomposable.

The Layer Division is more conservative than Classical Division, in the sense that it deletes less rules and less literals from the bodies of the remaining rules. In this sense, we can also define a Classically-Decomposable (CD) family of semantics, in every way equal to the Layer-Decomposable one, except for that the CD family uses Classical Division to restrict the available guesses instead of Layer Division, i.e., where M_α is a model of $P^{\alpha} :: M_{<\alpha}$. In this regard, every CD model is also an LD model. Classical Division closely follows the Gelfond-Lifschitz program division [8], and so every model that complies with the GL division, like the SMs and the WFM, is also a CD model, and in turn an LD model. The LD family is not trivial, in the sense that not all semantics are LD; e.g., the Minimal Models are not LD. The program consisting of just the rule $a \leftarrow not\ b$ has two minimal models: $\{a\}$ and $\{b\}$, where the second one is not LD – since there are no rules for b it must be *false* in all LD models, which is not the case with the minimal model $\{b\}$. Also, Layer Division is necessary for any 2-valued semantics enjoying the Cumulativity property [5]—we illustrate this with example 5. This is also the reason why the SM semantics is not Cumulative: because it does Classical Division, and not Layer Division.

4   Constructive Method for Computing Layer Decomposable Models

From the above we now define a sound and complete constructive method, which is guaranteed to terminate, for obtaining all the LD models of a finite ground program.

Definition 12. *Constructive Method for Layer Decomposable models. Let P be an NLP with a finite number n of layers. Then, since by definition $P^{<\alpha+1} = P^{\leq\alpha}$, all the LD models of P can be constructed in the following manner*

For a 2-valued semantics *Sem*, the guessing step only guesses the positive part of the model for $P_{M_{<i}}^{i+1}$. The guessed positive part is then complemented with the negation of all atoms that have all the rules where they appear as head in layers up to $i+1$— if the atom was not determined, or chosen, to be *true*, and there are no more rules in the layers above that can render it *true*, then it must be assumed *false* right away and henceforth. If, on the other hand, *Sem* is 3-valued, then the guessing step guesses both a positive part M_{i+1}^+ and a negative M_{i+1}^-, where all the remaining atoms that still have no truth-value guessed/assigned remain *undefined* (Fig. 1).

This iterative algorithm performs an incremental computation of a model, according to the chosen *Sem* of the given program. By taking advantage of the layerings, the algorithm can split what would otherwise be a single guess of a model for the whole program, into a sequence of smaller guesses for the subsets of rules of the program in individual layers, and use previously computed sub-models to restrict the still available guesses in layers above. This method can also be modified to allow the parallelization

Algorithm Bottom-Up Construct an LDM

Input: An LP P, and a Layer-Decomposable semantics *Sem*

Output: An LD model of P according to *Sem*

$M_{\leq 0} := M_0 := not\ A_P^0;$

for each layer index $0 \leq i < n$

    $P_{M_{\leq i}}^{i+1} := P^{i+1} : M_{\leq i};$ // $M_{\leq i} = M_{<i+1}$

    Non-deterministically choose a model M_{i+1} of $P_{M_{\leq i}}^{i+1}$ according to *Sem*;

    $M_{\leq i+1}^+ := M_{i+1}^+ \cup M_{\leq i}^+;$

    if *Sem* is 2-valued

        $M_{\leq i+1}^- := not\ (A_P^{\leq i+1} \setminus M_{\leq i+1})^+;$

    else

        $M_{\leq i+1}^- := M_{i+1}^- \cup M_{\leq i}^-;$

    $M_{\leq i+1} := M_{\leq i+1}^+ \cup M_{\leq i+1}^-;$

return $M_{\leq n}$

Fig. 1. Algorithm BOTTOM-UP CONSTRUCT AN LDM PARAMETERIZED BY A SEMANTICS

of the computation of models for individual SCCs of rules within each layer, as they are necessarily syntactically independent. This parallelization will allow for further reduction of the combinatorics of each guess.

The complexity of identifying the Rule Layering is dominated by detecting the SCCs of rules in $CRG(P)$ which is known to be a polynomial task [12]. The Atom Layering can be computed in polynomial time from the Rule Layering. In our algorithm, apart from the non-deterministic step of guessing a model of $P_{M_{\leq i}}^{i+1}$, every step in computable in polynomial time. So the overall complexity of the algorithm is polynomial if guessing a model according to *Sem* is at most polynomial. Otherwise, the complexity of the algorithm is the complexity of the guessing step.

5   Conclusions and Future Work

We have analyzed the syntactic structure of Logic Programs and have presented the novel notions of Rule Layering and Atom Layering, which always exist for programs with no infinitely long descending chains, even if there is no Stratification. Our new notion of Layer Division allows us to define the Layer-Decomposable family of semantics, of which the Stable Models and the Well-Founded Semantics are members, and we present an incremental, and parallelizable, algorithm for bottom-up computation of LD models. We show the Layer Division is a crucial ingredient in defining 2-valued semantics that enjoy Cumulativity. Future work includes exploiting the semantic characterization possibilities opened up by layered decomposability, implementing its parameterizable LD model algorithm, and comparing its performance against current SM and WFS implementations.

Acknowledgements. L.M.P. is supported by NOVA LINCS (UIDB/04516/2020) with the financial support of FCT- Fundação para a Ciência e a Tecnologia, Portugal, through national funds.

A   Auxiliary Definitions, Results and Proofs

Proposition 1. *The least atom layering of an atom identifies the highest layer with rules for the atom. Let P be an LP, $Lf/1$ its least rule layering function, and $ALf/1$ its least atom layering function; then*

$$\forall_{a \in \mathcal{H}_P} ALf(a) = \alpha \Leftrightarrow \left(\forall_{r \in P: head(r)=a} r \in P^{\leq \alpha} \land (\alpha \neq 0 \Leftrightarrow \exists_{r' \in P^\alpha} head(r')=a) \right)$$

Proof. $\Rightarrow$:

Assume $a \in \mathcal{H}_P$ and $ALf(a) = \alpha$. If a has rules then, by definition of least atom layering function, we have $ALf(a) = max_{r \in P: head(r)=a}(Lf(r))$, i.e., $\alpha = max_{r \in P: head(r)=a}(Lf(r))$. This means that all rules $r \in P$ having $head(r) = a$ have $Lf(r) \leq \alpha$, and there is at least one rule r' such that $Lf(r') = \alpha$. I.e. $\forall_{r \in P: head(r)=a} r \in P^{\leq \alpha} \land \exists_{r' \in P^\alpha} head(r')=a$.

On the other hand, if a has no rules then, by definition of least atom layering function, we have $ALf(a) = 0$, i.e., $\alpha = 0$. Thus, $\forall_{r \in P: head(r)=a} r \in P^{\leq \alpha}$ becomes vacuously true because, by hypothesis, a has no rules.

$\Leftarrow$:

Assume $a \in \mathcal{H}_P$ and $\forall_{r \in P: head(r)=a} r \in P^{\leq \alpha}$. If a has rules then they are all in layers $\leq \alpha$. The layers ordinals' maximum is thus α. I.e. $max_{r \in P: head(r)=a}(Lf(r)) = \alpha = ALf(a)$.

If a has no rules then, $\forall_{r \in P: head(r)=a} r \in P^{\leq \alpha}$ vacuously holds for whichever ordinal. In particular, $\forall_{r \in P: head(r)=a} r \in P^{\leq 0}$ holds, i.e., $\alpha = 0$. Since a has no rules, by definition of atom least layering $ALf(a) = \alpha = 0$ also holds.

Proposition 2. *A rule's layer is greater than or equal to each of the body's literals' atom-layering.*
$$\forall_{\substack{r \in P \\ a \in |body(r)|}} Lf(r) \geq ALf(a).$$

Proof. Assume P an LP, r a rule of P and a an atom of $\mathcal{H}_P$ such that $a \in |body(r)|$. If a has no rules then, by definition of atom-layering function $ALf(a) = 0$, and since by definition of rule-layering function $\forall_{r \in P} Lf(r) \geq 0$ we conclude $\forall_{\substack{r \in P \\ a \in |body(r)|}} Lf(r) \geq ALf(a)$.

If a has rules then, because r depends on a we know that r depends on every rule r_a such that $head(r_a) = a$. By definition of rule-layering it must be either the case that r_a also depends on r—in which case $Lf(r) = Lf(r_a)$— or that r_a does not depend on r—in which case $Lf(r) > Lf(r_a)$. Either way, $Lf(r) \geq Lf(r_a)$ always holds for every rule r_a. In particular, $Lf(r) \geq max_{r_a \in P: head(r_a)=a}(Lf(r_a))$, i.e., $Lf(r) \geq= ALf(a)$.

Proposition 3. *Rules in the same SCC are in the same layer.* $\forall_{r,r' \in P}(r \twoheadleftarrow r' \land r' \twoheadleftarrow r) \Rightarrow Lf(r) = Lf(r')$.

Proof. By definition of SCC, two rules r and r' are in the same SCC iff $r \twoheadleftarrow r'$ and $r' \twoheadleftarrow r$ hold; and by Definition 6, in that case, $Lf(r) = Lf(r')$ holds. Two rules in the same SCC must also necessarily depend on each other, and, hence, be placed in the same layer.

Proposition 4. *Layering of SCCs.* If there is an edge from SCC_1 to SCC_2, with $SCC_1 \neq SCC_2$, in the $SCCG(P)$ then $\forall_{\substack{r_1 \in SCC_1 \\ r_2 \in SCC_2}} Lf(r_2) > Lf(r_1)$.

Proof. From Proposition 3 we know that all rules in SCC_1 are in the same layer. Likewise, all rules in SCC_2 are in the same layer. There is an arc from SCC_1 to SCC_2 in the Directed Acyclic Graph (DAG) of SCCs of $CRG(P)$ iff SCC_2 depends on SCC_1. Since all rules of SCC_2 depend on each other, they all also depend on SCC_1, i.e., all the rules of SCC_2 depend on all the rules of SCC_1. Since SCC_1 and SCC_2 are non-mutually-dependent (otherwise they would form a unique SCC) and SCC_2 depends on SCC_1, it must be the case, by Definition 6, that

$$\forall_{\substack{r_1 \in SCC_1 \\ r_2 \in SCC_2}} Lf(r_2) > Lf(r_1)$$

Proposition 5. *A rule's body literals in a loop have atom-layering equal to the rule's layer.*

$$\forall_{\substack{a \in \mathscr{H}_P \\ r \in P}} (a \in |body(r)^{Lf(r)}| \Rightarrow ALf(a) = Lf(r))$$

Proof. It follows trivially from Definition 8.

Our focus on Layer-Decomposable Semantics stems also from the importance of Layer Division (and, naturally, Layer Decomposability) versus Classical Division (and Classical Decomposability) which is tied to the Cumulativity property [5]. In [3] the authors stress the importance of the Cumulativity property and define an alternative more credulous version of this property (dubbing it Extended Cumulativity, ECM, for short). They also show that the SM semantics enjoys ECM although it does not enjoy cumulativity. A 2-valued semantics for NLP can only enjoy Cumulativity if all its models are compatible with Layer Division.

Example 5. **Layer Division is necessary for Cumulativity.** Let P be

$$b \leftarrow a$$
$$a \leftarrow not\ b, c$$
$$c \leftarrow not\ a$$

which has no stable models. All the rules depend on each other, so they are all in the same layer 1. This program has three classical models: $M_1 = \{a, b, not\ c\}$, $M_2 = \{not\ a, b, c\}$, and $M_3 = \{a, b, c\}$. b is *true* in all models. If a semantics enjoys Cumulativity then we can add b as a fact to P and the resulting semantics will remain unchanged. $P \cup \{b\}$ is

$$b \leftarrow a$$
$$a \leftarrow not\ b, c$$
$$c \leftarrow not\ a$$
$$b$$

where the fact b is in layer 1 of $P \cup \{b\}$ while the other three original rules are now in layer 2 of $P \cup \{b\}$. The unique model for layers up to 0 is $M_{\leq 0} = \emptyset$, and the unique model for layers up to 1 is $M_{\leq 1} = \{b\}$.

If we take a Classical Division then $P^2 :: M_{\leq 1}$ has the unique SM $\{b,c\}$. But now, after adding b as a fact to the program, c becomes also *true* in every (just one) model—the semantics has changed by the addition of an atom that was *true* in the semantics, i.e., the semantics is not Cumulative.

If instead we take the Layer Division, then $P^2 : M_{\leq 1} = P^2$ and its semantics remains unchanged, i.e., the semantics can enjoy Cumulativity. Let us see why: in this Layer Division case the rule $a \leftarrow not\ b, c$ is not deleted because, although b is a fact, there is also another rule $b \leftarrow a$ that depends on $a \leftarrow not\ b, c$, i.e., $\overline{body(a \leftarrow not\ b, c)} = \emptyset$.

The Layer Division is a crucial ingredient for Cumulativity exactly because it prevents facts (that are always placed in layer 1) from deleting rules involved in loops and depending on negation of the fact, and from deleting the facts from the bodies of rules when they are in loop through that atom. Layer Division thus guarantees that loops are not "broken" by facts, and so facts can safely be added to layer 1 without the risk of changing the semantics of loops of rules.

References

1. Apt, K.R., Blair, H.A.: Arithmetic classification of perfect models of stratified programs. Fundam. Inform. **14**(3), 339–343 (1991)
2. Costantini, S.: Comparing different graph representations of logic programs under the answer set semantics. In: Provetti, A., Son, T.C. (eds.) Answer Set Programming, Towards Efficient and Scalable Knowledge Representation and Reasoning, Proc. of the 1st Intl. ASP'01 Workshop (2001)
3. Costantini, S., Lanzarone, G.A., Magliocco, G.: Layer supported models of logic programs. In: Maher, M. (ed.) Procs. 1996 Joint International Conference and Symposium on Logic Programming (JICSLP 1996), pp. 438–452, MIT Press, Cambridge, USA (1996)
4. Dimopoulos, Y., Torres, A.: Graph theoretical structures in logic programs and default theories. Theor. Comput. Sci. **170**(1–2), 209–244 (1996)
5. Dix, J.: A classification theory of semantics of normal logic programs: I. strong properties. Fundam. Inform. **22**(3), 227–255 (1995)
6. Fages, F.: Consistency of Clark's completion and existence of stable models. J. Methods Log. Comput. Sci. **1**, 51–60 (1994)
7. Van Gelder, A., Ross, K.A., Schlipf, J.S.: The well-founded semantics for general logic programs. J. ACM **38**(3), 620–650 (1991)
8. Gelfond, M., Lifschitz, V.: The stable model semantics for logic programming. In: Procs. ICLP 1988, pp. 1070–1080 (1988)
9. Hitzler, P., Schwarz, S.: Level mapping characterizations of selector generated models for logic programs. In: Wolf, A., Frühwirth, T.W., Meister, M. (eds.) W(C)LP. volume 2005–01 of Ulmer Informatik-Berichte, pp. 65–75. Universität Ulm, Germany (2005)
10. Hitzler, P., Wendt, M.: A uniform approach to logic programming semantics. TPLP **5**(1–2), 93–121 (2005)
11. Lifschitz, V.: Answer set planning. In: Proceedings of the International Conference on Logic Programming, pp. 23–37 (1999)
12. Nuutila, E., Soisalon-Soininen, E.: On finding the strongly connected components in a directed graph. Inf. Process. Lett. **49**, 9–14 (1994)
13. Pereira, L.M., Pinto, A.M.: Layer supported models of logic programs. In: Erdem, E., Lin, F., Schaub, T. (eds.) LPNMR 2009. LNCS (LNAI), vol. 5753, pp. 450–456. Springer, Heidelberg (2009). https://doi.org/10.1007/978-3-642-04238-6_41

14. Przymusinski, T.C.: Every logic program has a natural stratification and an iterated least fixed point model. In: PODS, pp. 11–21. ACM Press (1989)
15. Przymusinski, T.C.: On the declarative and procedural semantics of logic programs. J. Autom. Reason. **5**(2), 167–205 (1989)

Modularization of Logic Programs

Alexandre Miguel Pinto[1] and Luís Moniz Pereira[2]([⊠])

[1] Signal AI, London, UK
alexandre.pinto@signal-ai.com
[2] Department of Computer Science, Universidade Nova de Lisboa, Lisbon, Portugal
lmp@fct.unl.pt

Abstract. Standard software and knowledge engineering best practices advise for modularity because, amongst other benefits, it facilitates development, debugging, maintenance, composition and interoperability. Knowledge bases written as Logic Programs are no exception, and their corresponding semantics should enable such modularity. In this paper we formally define several new syntactical notions and semantics properties that capture the notions of modularity and separation of concerns applied to the LPs domain. Furthermore, we set forth other notions necessary for top-down, call-graph oriented existential query answering with 2-valued semantics for LPs with Integrity Constraints.

Keywords: Modularization · Logic Programs · Credulous Reasoning · Properties · Semantics

1 Introduction

1.1 Context

Both in the academia and in the industry, development of intelligent software systems is becoming increasingly more frequent due to the need to offer systems and services that deliver more value to the end user. Larger and more distributed teams collaborate in the development of such systems, including the Knowledge Bases (KBs) they are built upon. In this paper we focus on the usage of Logic Programs (LPs) as the means to encode the KBs and the usual credulous and sceptical reasoning tasks as the mechanisms to solve the computational problem the system is intended to. LPs have been used successfully to represent and solve several kind of problems including combinatorial search, planning, abduction, diagnosis, constraint solving and many others.

The different kinds of problems and the respectively distinct intended usages of the LP-based systems require different reasoning mechanisms. Whenever the LP-based system is intended to allow the user to explore alternative scenarios a 2-valued semantics, e.g., Stable Models (SMs) [5], is the adequate choice for the LP as, in general, these allow for more than one model. Under this setting the individual models can represent the different scenarios. Credulous reasoning can then be used to find one, or more, of the individual models that satisfy a

© Springer Nature Switzerland AG 2023
P. Lopez-Garcia et al. (Eds.): Hermenegildo Festschrift 2022, LNCS 13160, pp. 222–232, 2023.
https://doi.org/10.1007/978-3-031-31476-6_12

user's query. On the other hand, if the intended usage of the LP-base system is to provide irrefutable answers, and warranted knowledge to the user, then a 3-valued semantics, like the Well-Founded Semantics (WFS) [4], may be more adequate as these usually provide exactly one model—sceptical reasoning allows the user to find out what consequences necessarily follow from the KB and is commonly implemented as checking if the user's query is entailed by the single 3-valued (sceptical) model, and where Integrity Constraints (ICs), in the form of denials, can then be satisfied when their bodies are false but also if undefined [7].

Basic notions: We consider here the usual notions of alphabet, language, atom, literal, rule, and (logic) program. A literal is either an atom A or its default negation *not A*. We dub default literals (or default negated literals—DNLs, for short) those of the form *not A*. Without loss of generality we consider only ground Normal Logic Programs (NLPs), which are sets of Normal Logic Rules (NLRs) of the form $H \leftarrow B_1, \ldots, B_n, not\ C_1, \ldots, not\ C_m$, (with $m, n \geq 0$ and finite) where H, the B_i and the C_j are ground atoms. In conformity with the standard convention, we write rules of the form $H \leftarrow$ also simply as H (known as "facts"). An NLP P is called definite if none of its rules contain default literals. If r is a rule we denote its head H by $head(r)$, and $body(r)$ denotes the set $\{B_1, \ldots, B_n, not\ C_1, \ldots, not\ C_m\}$ of all the literals in its body. We write $\mathcal{H}_P$ to denote the Herbrand Base of P.

Besides containing normal rules as above, LPs may also include rules with a non-empty body and where the head is the special symbol $\perp$ which are known as a type of Integrity Constraints (ICs), specifically *denials*, and they are normally used to prune out unwanted models of the normal rules part. An LP is thus the union of a set of normal rules with a (possibly empty) set of ICs.

1.2 Motivation

The development of LP-based intelligent systems are software engineering projects and as these, their teams, and the KBs developed grow larger, the adoption of the best practices and principles of the software engineering discipline become indispensable if one wishes to guarantee certain qualities of the overall intelligent system. In particular, the development and usage of the LP-based KB part must itself be subject to compliance with those guidelines. In this paper we focus on the assurance of the principles of Modularity and Separation of Concerns in LP-based KBs. We will see in the sequel that adopting these principles and ensuring those qualities in an LP-based KB has a number of implications regarding the properties the particular LP semantics must comply with, depending on whether it is a 3-valued or a 2-valued one. Our main goal within this paper is precisely to contribute with the definitions of those formal properties of semantics for LPs which ensure Modularity and Separation of Concerns, and to provide with mechanisms to define such semantics.

The approach we follow in the remainder of the paper goes as follows. First, we recap the most common properties of semantics in the literature [3] that are related to the principles of Modularity and Separation of Concerns. Since the concept of Modularity is intrinsically related to the notion of modules, or components, and their interdependencies, we translate these dependencies notions to the domain of LPs and in that regard we recap the definitions in the literature, define two new notions of syntactic structure of an LP and compare them to the standard ones. We translate the concept of Separation of Concerns into the LP domain by making explicitly distinct the role of Normal Logic Rules and Integrity Constraints and show how this explicit distinction implies certain properties of the semantics for the Normal Logic Rules part. Then we characterize the family of semantics complying with the properties we defined, compare them to SMs, and show an algorithm to compute models of these semantics. Final remarks and future work conclude the paper.

2   Background Review

2.1   Modularity and Separation of Concerns

Modularity and Separation of Concerns (henceforth abbreviated as Mod. and SoC, respectively) are two of the central qualities required of software systems developed according to the best practices of software engineering. Amongst other benefits, a modular, i.e., a component-based, system is easier to develop, test, debug, maintain, to compose, and to interoperate with others. According to [8]

> Component-based software engineering is a reuse-based approach to defining, implementing, and composing loosely coupled independent components into systems. A component is a software unit whose functionality and dependencies are completely defined by a set of public interfaces. Components can be composed with other components without knowledge of their implementation and can be deployed as an executable unit.

From this definitions we can infer a module, or component, in such a "component-based" system, should be easily replaceable by another with the same functionality, as long as its interface and externally observable behavior remain the same; modules can also be independently developed and later put together to form the entire system. When translating these notions to LP-based KBs we need to define what the modules are so that they exhibit these high (internal) cohesion and low (external) coupling [6] characteristics. In Sect. 3 we present new semantical properties and syntactic structure notions that will allows us to define such modules in LPs.

Also from [8] we learn that

> The separation of concerns is a key principle of software design and implementation. It means that you should organize your software so that each element in the program (...) does one thing and one thing only. You can then focus on that element without regard for the other elements in the program. You can understand each part of the program by knowing its concern, without the need to understand other elements. When changes are required, they are localized to a small number of elements.

From this definition it follows immediately that, in the LP domain (remember we are considering a LP to be the union of a NLP with a set of ICs), the normal rules in the NLP and the ICs are reifications of two very distinct Concerns: that of generating alternative scenarios, and that of filtering out the undesired candidates, respectively. Since it is the job of the ICs part to reject the bad candidates, by the SoC principle, the NLP part, or any subset of it, must not be allowed to prevent the existence of said candidates. Thus, compliance with the SoC principle implies the semantics for the NLP must guarantee model existence; to allow otherwise is to violate the SoC.

2.2   Semantics and Models

Taking the classical notions of (Herbrand) interpretation and model, [2] defines (def. 2.4) a semantics of LPs as follows:

A semantics SEM is a mapping from the class of all programs into the powerset of the set of all 3-valued Herbrand structures. SEM assigns to every program a set of 3-valued Herbrand models of P

and also a sceptical entailment relation (def. 2.5) as:

Let P be a program and U a set of atoms. Any semantics SEM induces a sceptical entailment relation SEM^{scept} as follows:

$$SEM^{scept}(U) := \bigcap_{\mathcal{M} \in SEM_P(U)} \{L : L \text{ is a pos. or neg. literal with } \mathcal{M} \models L\}$$

where $SEM_P(U) = SEM_{P \cup U}$, the set of models of $P \cup U$ according to SEM. In the following we write $SEM(P)$ to denote the set of all models of P according to SEM, whereas $SEM^{scept}(P)$ still denotes the intersection of all such models. For LPs including ICs, every model $M \in SEM(P)$ is such that $\bot \notin M$.

In [2], and its subsequent paper [3], the author defines several properties of semantics, including Relevance, Cumulativity, Modularity, and many others, but all of these regard SEM^{scept}, i.e., the intersection of all models of $P \cup U$ according to SEM. When SEM is a 3-valued semantics, e.g., the WFS, SEM already provides a single model, so in that case the intersection of all models coincides with the unique model. When SEM is a 2-valued semantics this means those properties pertain to the literals in the intersection of all 2-valued models of the semantics; not to each individual 2-valued model. However, when we are interested in using the individual 2-valued-models, e.g. for answering existential queries, we need properties analogous to that of Relevance and Cumulativity, but pertaining to individual models and not to their intersection. We have found no such properties in the literature and so we provide them below as part of our contribution. In [1] the authors stress the importance of the Cumulativity property and define an alternative more credulous version of this property (dubbing it Extended Cumulativity, ECM for short). They also show that the SM semantics enjoys ECM although it does not enjoy cumulativity.

2.3   Syntactic Dependencies

In [3] the author introduced a notion of Modularity (def. 5.7) as a formal property of semantics for LPs. We recap it here for self-containment, but first we need to include other auxiliary syntactic notions.

Definition 1. *Dependencies in a program.* *In a LP P, a rule r_2 directly depends on r_1 (written as $r_2 \leftarrow r_1$) iff the head of r_1 appears, possibly negated, in the body of r_2; we say r_2 depends on r_1 ($r_2 \twoheadleftarrow r_1$) iff either r_2 directly depends on r_1 or r_2 directly depends on some other rule r_3 which in turn depends on r_1.*

We also consider the other combinations of (direct) dependencies amongst atoms and rules, and use the same graphical notation ($\leftarrow, \twoheadleftarrow$) to denote (direct, indirect) dependency. Rule r directly depends on an atom a iff a appears, possibly negated, in the body of r; and r depends on a iff either r directly depends on a or r depends on some rule r' which directly depends on a. An atom a directly depends on rule r iff $head(r) = a$; and a depends on r iff either a directly depends on r or a directly depends on some rule r' such that r' depends on r. An atom b directly depends on atom a iff a appears (possibly default negated) in the body of a rule with head b, and b depends on a iff either b directly depends on a, or b directly depends on some rule r which depends on a.

In [3] Dix introduces the notion of *relevant rules*, which we restate here adapted to our notation.

Definition 2. *Sub-program Relevant for Atom.* *Let P be a NLP and a an atom of P. We write $Rel_P(a)$ to denote the set of rules of P which are relevant and enough for determining a's truth value. Formally, $Rel_P(a) = \{r \in P : a \text{ depends on } r\}$.*

Also in [3] we find the notion of Program Reduction (def. 3.8) which is similar, but not exactly equal, to the Gelfond-Lifschitz program division, and which will be necessary to the Modularity notion.

Definition 3. *P reduced by M (def. 3.8 of [3], adapted to our notation).* *Let P be a program and M be a set of literals. "P reduced by M" is the program $P^M := \{r^M : r \in P \text{ and } (body(r) \cup M) \text{ is a consistent set of literals}\}$, where $body(r^M) = body(r) \setminus M$.*

Now that we have the notions of Relevant Part and P reduced by M we can recap the notion of Modularity from [3].

Definition 4. *Modularity (def. 5.7 of [3] adapted to meet our notation).* *Let $P = P_1 \cup P_2$ be instantiated and for every $A \in \mathcal{H}_2 : Rel_P(A) \subseteq P_2$. The principle of Modularity is: $SEM^{scept}(P) = SEM^{scept}(P_1^{SEM^{scept}(P_2)} \cup P_2)$.*

These syntactical and semantical notions do not capture all the various aspects of the Modularity and Separation of Concerns of software engineering principles applied to LPs. For this reason we now introduce, as part of our contribution, the new ones we find necessary for that purpose.

3 New Notions and Properties

The concept of Modularity is intrinsically related to the notion of modules, or components, and their interdependencies, and in order to provide a rendering of that concept in the LP domain we need to translate these dependencies into syntactic features of LPs. The relevant rules (Definition 2) syntactic notion does part of this job but it still does not capture all the characteristics of a module. We introduce below the formal notion of a Module as well as some of its syntactic properties. Also, the semantical notion of modularity in Definition 4, besides being insufficient to fully grasp the Modularity concept applied to LPs, and like all other semantical properties in [2] and [3], regards only the intersection of models, and for that reason is suitable only for sceptical reasoning purposes. Since in our work we are especially interested in existential query answering with 2-valued semantics, we also provide new definitions of credulous reasoning oriented semantical properties that capture the various aspects of Modularity.

As stated before, regarding the concept of Separation of Concerns, it translates into the LP domain by making explicitly distinct the role of Normal Logic Rules from that of Integrity Constraints, and noticing this explicit distinction entails the property of guarantee of model existence for the semantics for the Normal Logic Rules part.

Finally, we introduce new notions supporting existential query answering with LPs, both syntactic and semantical, which allow us to formally compose a comprehensive framework for credulous reasoning with LPs (including ICs) with semantics that comply with both the Modularity and Separation of Concerns principles.

3.1 Modularity in Logic Programs

In a modular system, the components, or modules, have high internal cohesion (the elements inside the module are tightly related), and low external coupling (the elements from two distinct modules are lightly, if at all, related). The modularity semantic property in Definition 4 does not capture all these requirements associated with the Modularity principle.

In LPs we only have logic rules and the only dependency notion we can find is a syntactical one. By taking the transitive closure over this syntactic dependency, the *relevance* in Definition 2 captures a part of the *module* concept according to the description above, but not all of it. For this reason, we set forth a more encompassing notion of *module* and examine some of its properties.

Definition 5. *Modules of a Logic Program.* *Let P and P_1 be LPs such that $P_1 \subseteq P$. P_1 is said to be a* module *of P iff $\forall_{a \in \mathcal{H}_{P_1}} Rel_P(a) \subseteq P_1$. I.e., a module of P is any subset of rules of P that contains all, and only, the rules relevant to the atoms inside the module.*

Let P_1 and P_2 be modules of P. We say P_1 is nested *inside P_2 iff $P_1 \subseteq P_2$. In this case we also say P_1 is a* sub-module *of P_2.*

We say two modules P_1 and P_2 of P are independent *iff they do not share any atoms, i.e., $\mathcal{H}_{P_1} \cap \mathcal{H}_{P_2} = \emptyset$.*

It follows from this definition that if modules P_1 and P_2 are independent, then every sub-module of P_1 is independent from every sub-module of P_2. From a system-wide analysis perspective, it might be of interest to identify the unique set of maximal (w.r.t. set-inclusion) independent modules of a given program P—we denote this set by $MIM(P)$.

With the above definition, the "components" inside modules (the individual rules) are necessarily highly correlated, by virtue of syntactic dependency, thus embodying the high internal cohesion demanded of modules. On the other hand, the independent modules notion fully captures the low external coupling by virtue of their syntactical independence.

Example 1. **Modules in a program.** Let P be

$$c \leftarrow not\ a$$
$$a \leftarrow not\ b$$
$$b \leftarrow not\ a$$
$$x \leftarrow y$$

The pair of rules $a \leftarrow not\ b$ and $b \leftarrow not\ a$ form a module P_1 of P. $P_2 = P_1 \cup \{c \leftarrow not\ a\}$ is another module, $P_3 = \{x \leftarrow y\}$ is yet another module, and the whole program is also considered to be a module. P_1 is nested inside P_2, and every module of P is nested inside P. In this example, P_2 and P_3 are *independent*, and so are necessarily P_1 and P_3 as well.

As stated above, the Modularity property defined in [3] pertains to the sceptical entailment of a semantics SEM, i.e., when taking a 2-valued semantics, this property is defined only over the intersection of all its models for a given program. In our work, since we are intent on performing credulous reasoning with a 2-valued semantics, we need a corresponding credulous version of modularity, one that concerns each indvidual 2-valued-model, and not just the intersection of all models. Hence, we introduce now several new semantical properties that will be used to build our credulous modularity property.

Definition 6. *Credulous Module Replaceability.* Let P_1, P_2 and P_x be LPs such that P_1 is a module of $P_x \cup P_1$ and P_2 is a module of $P_x \cup P_2$, with $\mathcal{H}_{P_1} = \mathcal{H}_{P_2}$, and let SEM be a 2-valued semantics for LPs. When $SEM(P_1) = SEM(P_2)$—in which case we say P_1 and P_2 are $SEM-equivalent$—we say SEM enjoys Credulous Module Replaceability iff $SEM(P_x \cup P_1) = SEM(P_x \cup P_2)$.

Intuitively this means one can replace one module of a program with another as along as they have exactly the same models, all the while preserving the models of the global program. This notion intends to capture the idea of functional implementation independence of modules as far as interface and meaning are preserved, which is characteristic of modular systems.

The following two notions (Credulous Monotony and Cartesian Product) capture the black-box view on modules which allows the rapid composition of a prototypical system by knowing the possible behaviors of its composing modules.

Definition 7. *Credulous Monotony.* *Let P be an LP and P_1 a module of P. A 2-valued semantics SEM is said to enjoy* Credulous Monotony *iff*

$$\underset{M_1 \in SEM(P_1)}{\forall} \{M : M \in SEM(P) \wedge M \supseteq M_1\} = SEM((P \setminus P_1) \cup M_1)$$

Intuitively this means one can replace one module of the program by any one of its models, and rest assured that the models of the resulting program are exactly those models of the original program that set-included the model which was used to replace the module.

The Stable Models semantics fails this property as the following example shows.

Example 2. **Stable Models fail Credulous Monotony.**   Let P be

$$a \leftarrow not \ b$$
$$b \leftarrow not \ a$$
$$c \leftarrow not \ c, not \ a$$

P has $\{a\}$ as its unique SM. The rules for a and b form a module P_1 of P which has two SMs: $\{a\}$, and $\{b\}$. If we replace P_1 by its model $\{b\}$ we obtain the program $P' =$

$$b$$
$$c \leftarrow not \ c, not \ a$$

which has no SMs at all, thus showing the failure of SM semantics regarding Credulous Monotony.

Definition 8. *Cartesian Product.* *Let P_1 and P_2 be independent modules of $P_1 \cup P_2$, and SEM a 2-valued semantics for LPs. SEM is said to enjoy the* Cartesian Product *property iff*

$$SEM(P_1 \cup P_2) = \{M_1 \cup M_2 : M_1 \in SEM(P_1) \wedge M_2 \in SEM(P_2)\}$$

I.e., models of unions of independent modules are unions of models of the individual modules. If $\#SEM(P_1) = n$ and $\#SEM(P_2) = m$ then $\#SEM(P_1 \cup P_2) = nm$, hence the name *Cartesian Product*.

Definition 9. *Credulous Modularity.* *SEM is said to enjoy Credulous Modularity iff it enjoys all four properties of Credulous Module Replaceability, Credulous Monotony, Cartesian Product, and Model Existence (i.e., $\#SEM(P) \geq 1$ for any given NLP P).*

This definition considers the concept of Credulous Modularity as including the notion of Separation of Concerns (by demanding Model Existence for NLPs) as one of its characteristics.

3.2   A Framework for Credulous Reasoning with LPs

Credulous reasoning with LPs amounts to finding if there is some model M of the program P at hand that satisfies some user-specified criteria Q. This can either take the form of finding/computing one such model (if it exists), or finding/computing one sub-model of it (i.e. subset of a model) sufficient to answer the user's query. The former is a common way to, e.g., address combinatorial search problems, while the latter is more commonly used in top-down query-answering *a la* Prolog.

In our work we focus on the latter approach which is only realizable with semantics where the truth value of atoms in any given model depends only on their relevant rules. The Relevance notion in Definition 2 pertains only to the atoms in the intersection of all models. What we need here is a "per-model" version of the Relevance notion. We put if forward now.

Definition 10. *Credulous Relevance. Let P be an NLP. SEM is Credulously Relevant iff*

$$\mathop{\forall}_{a \in \mathcal{H}_P} \left(\mathop{\forall}_{M \in SEM(P)} a \in M \Rightarrow (\mathop{\exists}_{M_a \in SEM(Rel_P(a))} M_a \subseteq M \wedge a \in M_a) \right)$$

$$\wedge$$

$$\left(\mathop{\forall}_{M_a \in SEM(Rel_P(a))} \mathop{\exists}_{M \in SEM(P)} M_a \subseteq M \right)$$

I.e., in a Credulously Relevant semantics, an atom is *true* in *some* model of the whole program iff it is *true* in *some* sub-model of the part of the program *relevant* to the atom, where that sub-model is a subset of a model for the whole program where the atom is *true*.

This notion, however, is applicable only to NLPs, but not whole LPs (which may include ICs). When finding an existential answer to a query in a LP, it might be the case that a candidate answer found may turn out to be rejected by some IC. This means we need another notion of relevance that is applicable to LPs with ICs. We now present this notion, preceded by other auxiliary ones.

Definition 11. *Sub-program Influenced by Atom. Let P be a LP. We say atom $a \in \mathcal{H}_P$ influences rule $r \in P$ iff r depends on a. We write $Infl_P(a)$ to denote the set of such r, i.e., $Infl_P(a) = \{r \in P : r \leftarrow a\}$.*

Definition 12. *Constraint Directly Relevant Atoms. Let $P = NLP \cup ICs$ be a LP composed of the set of normal rules NLP and the set of ICs ICs, and $S \subseteq \mathcal{H}_P$ a subset of atoms of P. The set of atoms of P which are Constraint Directly Relevant for S contains exactly all the atoms relevant for the ICs in P which are influenced by the atoms in the Relevant part of P for any atom in S.*

Due to its complexity, we breakdown this definition in intermediate steps as follows. First we take each atom a of S and obtain the Relevant part of P for it. Taking the union over all such atoms of S we obtain all the atoms of P relevant for any atom in S, i.e.,

$$\bigcup_{a \in S} Rel_P(a)$$

Let us abuse notation are denote this set by $Rel_P(S)$. Next we take all the atoms in $Rel_P(S)$, i.e., $\mathcal{H}_{Rel_P(S)}$, and for each we find the rules of P which it influences, thus obtaining

$$\bigcup_{b \in \mathcal{H}_{Rel_P(S)}} Infl_P(b)$$

We abuse notation again and denote this set by $Infl_P(S)$, and now we find which ICs are included in this set of influenced rules, i.e., $Infl_P(S) \cap ICs$, denoted by $ICInfl_P(S)$. Finally, we take all atoms in the rules of P which are relevant to the atoms in $ICInfl_P(S)$, to obtain the set of Constraint Directly Relevant Atoms,

$$ICDirRel_P(S) = \mathcal{H}_{(\bigcup_{c \in \mathcal{H}_{ICInfl_P(S)}} Rel_P(c))}$$

Definition 13. Constraint Relevant Atoms. *Let $P = NLP \cup ICs$ be a LP composed of the set of normal rules NLP and the set of ICs ICs, and $S \subseteq \mathcal{H}_P$ a subset of atoms of P. The set of atoms of P which are Constraint Relevant for S, denoted by $ICRel_P(S)$ is S^ω, where*

$$S^0 = S$$
$$S^{i+1} = S^i \cup ICDirRel_P(S^i)$$
$$S^\alpha = \bigcup_{\beta < \alpha} S^\beta$$

Definition 14. Credulous Constraint Relevance. *Let P be a LP. SEM is Credulously Constraint Relevant iff*

$$\underset{\substack{a \in \mathcal{H}_P \\ M \in SEM(P)}}{\forall} a \in M \Rightarrow (\underset{M_a \in SEM(Rel_P(ICRel_P(\{a\})) \cup ICInfl_P(\{a\}))}{\exists} M_a \subseteq M \wedge a \in M_a))$$

I.e., in a Credulously Constraint Relevant semantics, if an atom is *true* in *some* model of the whole program then it is *true* in *some* sub-model of the part of the program *constraint relevant* to the atom, where that sub-model is a subset of a model for the whole program where the atom is *true*.

These definitions set forth a theoretical framework upon which formal existential query answering methods can be developed for LPs, including ICs, with a 2-valued semantics.

Definition 15. Credulous Constraint Relevant Knowledge Existential Answer to a Query. *Let $P = NLP \cup ICs$ be a LP composed of the set of normal rules NLP and the set of ICs ICs, and Q a set of literals formed with atoms from $\mathcal{H}_P$ dubbed the user's query.*

M_Q is a credulous constraint relevant knowledge existential answer to query Q according to SEM iff

$$M_Q \in SEM(Rel_P(ICRel_P(|Q|)) \cup ICInfl_P(|Q|)) \text{ and } M_Q \supseteq Q$$

where $|Q|$ denotes the set of atoms in the literals in Q, i.e.,

$$|Q| = \{q : q \in Q \vee not\ q \in Q\}$$

The existence of a Credulous Constraint Relevant Knowledge Existential Answer to a Query M_Q does not necessarily guarantee the existence of a model M of P such that $M \supseteq M_Q$, but only because independent ICs might prevent model existence at all. However, the credulous constraint relevance property still ensures yet another local degree of modularity which might be used to focus the scope of rules considered when answering an existential query.

4   Conclusions and Future Work

We have taken the concepts of Modularity and Separation of Concerns from the software engineering discipline and applied them to the Logic Programs domain. As a result we devised a set of semantical properties, and auxiliary syntactical notions, that a 2-valued semantics for LPs must comply with in order to ensure the LP respects those Modularity and SoC principles. We have provided new notions of relevance and modularity that extend the ones in the literature in two ways: by being applicable to individual models of a 2-valued semantics instead of just to their intersection, and by taking into account also the possible ICs in the LP. Future work includes the definition of a 2-valued semantics complying with all these properties, and respective implementations.

Acknowledgements. L.M.P. is supported by NOVA LINCS (UIDB/04516/2020) with the financial support of FCT- Fundação para a Ciência e a Tecnologia, Portugal, through national funds.

References

1. Costantini, S., Lanzarone, G.A., Magliocco, G.: Layer supported models of logic programs. In: Maher, M. (ed.) Proceedings of the 1996 Joint International Conference and Symposium on Logic Programming (JICSLP 1996), pp. 438–452. MIT Press. Cambridge, USA (1996)
2. Dix, J.: A classification theory of semantics of normal logic programs: I. strong properties. Fundam. Inform. **22**(3), 227–255 (1995)
3. Dix, J.: A classification theory of semantics of normal logic programs: II. weak properties. Fundam. Inform. **22**(3), 257–288 (1995)
4. Van Gelder, A., Ross, K.A., Schlipf, J.S.: The well-founded semantics for general logic programs. J. ACM **38**(3), 620–650 (1991)
5. Gelfond, M., Lifschitz, V.: The stable model semantics for logic programming. In: ICLP/SLP, pp. 1070–1080. MIT Press (1988)
6. Papazoglou, M., Yang, J.: Design methodology for web services and business processes. Technol. E-Serv. **2444**, 175–233 (2002)
7. Pereira, L.M., Aparicio, J.N., Alferes, J.J.: Hypothetical reasoning with well founded semantics. In: Mayoh, B. (ed.) Scandinavian Conference on Artificial Intelligence: Proceedings of the SCAI 1991, pp. 289–300. IOS Press, Amsterdam (1991)
8. Sommerville, I.: Software Engineering 9. Pearson Education, London (2011)

Proof-Theoretic Foundations of Normal Logic Programs

Elmer Salazar and Gopal Gupta[✉]

Department of Computer Science, University of Texas at Dallas, Richardson, USA
gupta@utdallas.edu

Abstract. There are several semantics in logic programming for negation as failure. These semantics can be realized with a combination of
induction and coinduction, and this realization can be used to develop
a goal-directed method of computing models. In essence, the difference
between these semantics is how they resolve the unstratified portions of
a program. In this paper, restricting ourselves to the propositional case,
we show how the semantics of normal logic programs is a mixture of
induction and coinduction, and how we can use coinduction to resolve
the cycles (or loops) formed by the rules in a program. We present denotational semantics based on a fixed point of a function and show its
equivalence to the use of induction and coinduction. We take a look at
the different ways a semantics may resolve cycles, and show how to implement two popular semantics, well-founded and stable models, as well as
co-stable model semantics. Finally, we present operational semantics as a
parametrized goal-directed execution algorithm that allows us to determine how cycles are resolved.

1 Introduction

Considerable amount of research has been done on adding negation to logic programming over the last 40 years [2,23]. Many semantics have been proposed:
well-founded semantics, Fittings 3-valued semantics, the stable model semantics, perfect model semantics, etc. Dix [8,9] has done a systematic study of these
semantics, proposing a number of properties that can be used to characterize a
semantics. In this paper we show that various semantics of negation can be more
elegantly characterized via a combination of induction and coinduction. Induction captures well-founded computations—well-founded in the sense of Russell
and Whitehead's characterization, i.e., terminating in a base case—while coinduction captures cyclical (non well-founded), consistent computations. Various
semantics are a combination of the two. They differ in what value they assign
to cyclically dependent computations. For example, given a cycle of calls where
p calls q and q calls p, then the well-founded semantics of Van Gelder, Ross and

---

Dedicated to Professor Manuel Hermenegildo on the occasion of his 60th birthday.
Authors are grateful for support from US NSF and US DoD.

P. Lopez-Garcia et al. (Eds.): Hermenegildo Festschrift 2022, LNCS 13160, pp. 233–252, 2023.
https://doi.org/10.1007/978-3-031-31476-6_13

Schlipf assigns p and q the value false, the Fitting 3-valued semantics assigns ⊥ (unknown), the stable model semantics false, and the co-stable model semantics will produce two models: one in which both p and q are assigned true and one in which both are assigned false. Note that in this paper we use the term cycle and loop interchangeably.

Induction and coinduction [1] both have an operational semantics, based on recursion and co-recursion, respectively [28]. Thus, our characterization of these semantics based on induction and coinduction also results in elegant, query-driven execution strategies discussed later. The ultimate benefit of this insight is that practical goal-directed execution strategies have been designed for predicate answer set programming [3,21].

In this paper we give the declarative and operational semantics for various semantics of normal logic programs in a unifying, systematic manner. We consider four semantics for normal logic programs: Fitting's 3-valued semantics, well-founded semantics, stable model semantics, and co-stable model semantics. Our systematic, unifying characterization not only increases our understanding of various semantics of normal logic programs, it also allows us to produce efficient, query-driven implementation of these semantics.

The intuition for our work, from a high level perspective, is the following. During execution of a query with respect to a logic program, the execution can be well-founded or it can contain cycles that can keep unfolding forever. If the execution is well-founded then all the goals will get resolved during a successful top-down execution of a query **g**, with the final goal in the final resolvent matching a fact. This case will result in successful execution of the goal **g**. Alternatively, the terminal call will be of the form **not p** with no matching rules for **p**. In such a case, **not p** will succeed and query will be resolved successfully. Essentially, if the execution is well-founded, i.e., there are no infinitely unfolding cycles, then there is a single, unique model for the program [2]. All semantics of negation will find this single, unique model. If the execution of **g** is not well-founded, then loops (possibly over negation) will arise. In such a case, different semantics of negation (well-founded semantics of Van Gelder, Ross and Schlipf [29], stable model semantics [11], Fitting's 3-valued semantics [10], and co-stable model semantics [12]) will make different choices in different situations. If we have goal **g**, and during execution, a recursive call to **g** is encountered again, resulting in a potentially infinitely unfolding computation, then there can be multiple possibilities (in all cases, we assume that the program is completed [7,18] and that only supported models [4] are considered):

1. There are no intervening negative calls between the query **g** and the recursive call **g**: Multiple possibilities exist in such a case and so multiple values for **g** are possible: ⊥ (Fitting's 3-valued semantics), False (well-founded semantics, stable model semantics, and co-stable model semantics), or True (co-stable model semantics).

2. There are even number of intervening negations between **g** and its recursive call: In such a case, multiple models are possible. Indeed, the well-founded semantics and Fitting's 3-valued semantics will assign ⊥, while the stable and

co-stable model semantics will assign true to **g** in one world and will assign false in another.

3. Query **g** leads to a recursive call to **g** with odd number of intervening negations: in such a case, the values possible for **g** are ⊥ (Fitting's 3-valued and well-founded semantics) or False (stable model and co-stable model semantics). In the latter case, the conjunction of goals leading from the query **g** to recursive call should be false. If this conjunction evaluates to true, then a model cannot exist.

p is a fact: Well-founded comp.	p is not defined: Well-founded comp.	positive loop: no intervening not.	even loop: intervening not.	odd loop
No choice: Same model for all semantics	No choice: Same model for all semantics	Many possibilities Assign False Assign ⊥ Assign True	Many possibilities Assign ⊥ Assign True Assign False	Assign ⊥ *or, only way a model exists if h is false and g is false*
p: true g: true	p: false g: true	F: WFS, SM, coSM ⊥ : Fitting True: coSM	⊥ : Fitting, WFS True: SM, coSM False: SM, coSM	⊥ : Fitting, WFS SM & coSM will falsify g & h

WFS = Well Founded Semantics; SM = Stable Model Semantics

Fig. 1. Commonalities Among Semantics

The above intuition is summarized in Fig. 1. Note that we only give a brief overview here of proof-theoretic semantics of normal logic programs. Detailed discussion can be found elsewhere [25,26]. The rest of the paper is organized as follows: In Sect. 2 we provide a review of negation-as-failure, CoSLD resolution, and various semantic definitions that are of interest for this paper. We will also formally define the language we will be working with. Section 3 presents the declarative semantics, and in Sect. 4 we give the operational semantics in the form of a query-driven algorithm. Finally, Sect. 5 briefly describes Dix's work [8,9], Seki's work [27] and founded semantics [17], and how they are related to our work.

Finally, we should add that goal-directed execution methods that have been designed and implemented thus far [3,21] are not as fast as state-of-the-art implementations (especially, those based on SAT solvers). Program analysis [15] can help in improving the execution speed. The declarative fixpoint semantics as well as the operational semantics we present in this paper will help in the design of static analyses tools needed to help speed up the implementation of various semantics of negation (Fittng's 3-valued, well-founded, stable model, and co-stable model). We hope that presentation of this research at the workshop to celebrate 60th birthday of Professor Manuel Hermenegildo, a pioneer in static analysis of logic programs, will also spur research in static analysis of *normal* logic programs.

2   Background

2.1   Negation-as-Failure and the Language

Negation-as-failure is an interpretation of negation stemming from the closed world assumption and adds a new global axiom: if a proposition is unable to be proved, assume it is false. The completion of a program is a way of identifying supported models and handling negation-as-failure [7,18]. Throughout this paper we will represent the negation of a proposition p as **not** p to indicate we are working with negation-as-failure.

Definition 1. *A* literal *is a proposition or its negation. For some literal L, $prop(L)$ is the proposition the literal is constructed from. If $prop(L) = L$ then we say L is positive. Otherwise, L is negative and $not\ L = prop(L)$.*

Definition 2. *A normal logic* program *is a set of rules R of the following form:*

$$H\text{:-}B_1, B_2, \cdots, B_n, \textbf{not } B_{n+1}, \textbf{not } B_{n+2}, \cdots, \textbf{not } B_{n+m}.$$

where $n, m \geq 0$, and $H, B_1, B_2, \cdots, B_{n+m}$ are propositions.
In addition, for convenience we define the following functions:

- $head(R) = H$,
- $pos(R) = \{B_1, B_2, \cdots, B_n\}$,
- $neg(R) = \{B_{n+1}, B_{n+2}, \cdots, B_{n+m}\}$,
- $props(R) = \{H\} \cup pos(R) \cup neg(R)$,
- $body(R) = pos(R) \cup \{\textbf{not } p \mid p \in neg(R)\}$
- *for some program P, $props(P) = \{p \mid R \in P, p \in props(R)\}$, and*
- *for some program P, $lit\,(P) = props(P) \cup \{\textbf{not } p \mid p \in props(P)\}$.*

A fact *is a rule (written as p.) for which no B_i exists, i.e., $pos(R) \cup neg(R) = \{\}$.*

We will be focusing on semantics that agree with the completion. In Horn clause logic, a rule is interpreted as an implication where the body implies the head. The completion of a program interprets a set of rules with the same head as a bi-implication with the head on one side and the disjunction of the bodies on the other. This agrees with the axiom: if a proposition cannot be proved assume it is false.

Definition 3. *Let P be a program. We can represent all facts as having a body of true and any proposition that is not the head of some rule we can imagine a rule with a body of false. Then, for all propositions $p \in props(P)$, let B be a disjunction of conjunctions such that each conjunction in B is the body of some rule in P with p as the head, and B contains all such conjunctions. Then, $p \iff B$ is the* completion rule *for p. The* completion *of P is the set of all such completion rules. In addition, we will assume $\bot \iff \bot$ is true.*

Definition 4. *Let S be some semantics. Then S is said to be a* completion semantics *if and only if for all programs P, every model with respect to S is also a model of the completion of P.*

The completion of a program can be simulated by adding new rules called dual rules to the program. For each proposition p in a program we can add a new symbol **not** p and rules for **not** p so that **not** p is true if and only we cannot prove p. The resulting program is called the extended program.

Definition 5. *For some program P, the* extended program, *$ext(P)$, is defined by extending P as follows: For each proposition $p \in props(P)$:*

- *If p is not the head of any rule in P, then add a fact for **not** p.*
- *If there is a fact for p in P, then ignore p.*
- *Otherwise, take the body of the Clark's Completion rule for p, negate it, and use De Morgan's Law and distribution until it is a disjunction of conjunctions. For each conjunction, add a rule with **not** p as the head and the conjunction as it's body.*

As an example consider the program below:

```
p :- s.
p :- not q.
q :- not p.
r :- p.
```

The extended (completed) program is generated by adding the dual rules below:

```
not p :- not s, q.
not q :- p.
not r :- not p.
not s.
```

As can be seen, the only difference between how a program and an extended program are defined is the fact that extended programs have negated literals in the head. We will extend our representation for programs to account for that.

Definition 6. *Let P be a program. For each rule $r \in ext(P)$ with a negative literal in the head, r is of the form:*

$$\textbf{not } H:-B_1, B_2, \cdots, B_n, \textbf{not } B_{n+1}, \textbf{not } B_{n+2}, \cdots, \textbf{not } B_{n+m}$$

where $n, m \geq 0$, and $H, B_1, B_2, \cdots, B_{n+m}$ are propositions. In addition,

- $head(r) = \textbf{not } H,$
- $pos(r) = \{B_1, B_2, \cdots, B_n\},$
- $neg(r) = \{B_{n+1}, B_{n+2}, \cdots, B_{n+m}\},$
- $props(r) = \{\textbf{not } H\} \cup pos(r) \cup neg(r),$ *and*
- $body(r) = pos(r) \cup \{\textbf{not } p \mid p \in neg(r)\}.$

All other rules are in P, and therefore follow our previous definition.

Note that we are only interested in supported models.

Definition 7. *A set $\mathcal{M}$ of atoms is supported by a normal logic program P, if for every $B \in \mathcal{M}$, there is a rule (Definition 2) such that $B = H, B_1, B_2, ..., B_n \in \mathcal{M}$ and $B_{n+1}, B_{n+2}, ... B_{n+m} \notin \mathcal{M}$*

We have defined the language, and can now define what a semantics is. A semantics can be viewed as a function that maps programs to sets of models, and we will use this definition throughout this paper.

Definition 8. *A semantics, S, is a function mapping programs to sets of models. If for some model M and some program P, $M \in S(P)$ then we say that M is a model of P with respect to S.*

2.2   Coinduction

Our approach is based on coinductive logic programming. Coinductive logic programming is based on the concept of coinduction (the dual of induction) from category theory [13]. Category theory is an abstraction of mathematical ideas such a sets, groups and rings [16]. A good introduction to the concepts of induction and coinduction that does not rely heavily on category theory can be found elsewhere [14].

2.3   SLD and CoSLD Resolution

SLD resolution can be viewed as an inductive proof method based on resolution theory. CoSLD resolution [22,28] is likewise a coinductive proof method and can be considered a form of circular coinduction [24]. It is our observation that the non-monotonic completion semantics require a combination of induction and coinduction. A modified CoSLD resolution algorithm is presented by Kyle Marple et al. [19] that incorporates induction to realize stable-model semantics. This modification uses the standard CoSLD resolution to detect cycles during execution, and decides to succeed or fail based on what is correct for the stable-model semantics. Due to space constraints this paper will not go into details, but they can be found in the original paper [19,25].

2.4   The Semantics

Given the call graph of a normal logic program, this paper divides cycles into three types: positive, even, and odd. Positive cycles contain no negations, odd and even cycles contain an odd and even number of negations, respectively. An odd (even) cycle is nothing but an *odd (even) loop over negation* [4]. A rule may be part of multiple types of cycles. For example, in the code below, rule (1) is part of an even cycle (1-2-1) as well as an odd cycle (1-3-4-1).

```
p :- not q.              ... ( 1 )
q :- not p.              ... ( 2 )
```

q :– **not** r.   ... (3)
r :– **not** p.   ... (4)

We will take a look at some semantics that have been devised for normal logic programs. We will present a brief review of how models are computed, and then discuss how the cycles are handled in each case. For this section we will be using the traditional definition of an interpretation. That is, we will assume interpretations are sets of propositions with the assumption that any missing propositions are false. Starting in Sect. 3 we will use a different definition.

Fitting's 3-Valued Semantics: Fitting's 3-value semantics [10] is a way to compute the value of predicates(or in our case propositions) that are locally stratified but in a program that is not stratified. Essentially, Fitting's 3-value semantics solves the problem by assigning $\perp$ (Unknown) to any proposition in a cycle. Due to the complexity of the computation method it is not formally reviewed in this paper, but can be found in Fitting's original paper [10].

Well-Founded Semantics. Well-founded semantics solve the same problem as Fitting's 3-value semantics, but to agree with traditional logic programs it handles positive cycles differently [29].

Definition 9. *For some program P with interpretation I , $A \subseteq lit(P)$ is an* unfounded set *with respect to I if for all $p \in A$ and all rules, R, of P with p as the head, at least on of the following holds:*

- *Some literal in the body of R is false in I,*
- *Some positive literal in the body of R is in A.*

Definition 10. $\mathbf{U}_P(I)$, *the union of all unfounded sets for P with respect to I, is called the* greatest unfounded set *of P with respect to I.*

Definition 11. *Let* $\mathbf{W}_P(I) = T_P(I) \cup \neg \cdot \mathbf{U}_P(I)$. *Then, the least fixed-point of* $\mathbf{W}_P$ *is the* well-founded partial model *of P. T_P is the standard least fixed-point operator used to compute the inductive meaning of a logic program [18].*

If a proposition is in a positive cycle, it will be in the greatest unfounded set, and thus assigned the value false. If the value of a proposition depends on a cycle containing a negation, it will not appear in the partial model (and thus assigned $\perp$). It can be seen that neither T_p nor U_p will add the proposition (as a positive or negative literal) to the model.

Stable Model Semantics: Stable models uses multiple worlds, rather than assigning $\perp$, to stratify a program [11].

Definition 12. *Let P be a program, and I be an interpretation. The* residual program *of P is the Horn clause logic program computed by the Gelfond-Lifshitz transformation as follows:*

- *for all propositions $p \in I$ and rules in P, R, remove R if **not** p is in the body.*
- *remove all negative literals from the resulting program.*

Definition 13. *Let P be a program, and $I \subseteq props(P)$. Then I is a* stable model *if and only if I equals the least-fixed point semantics of the residual program for P and I.*

If a positive cycle exists in the program, and the truth value of the propositions in the cycle depend only on that cycle then the least fixed-point of the residual program will not contain those propositions. Thus, positive cycles in stable-model semantics are resolved by assigning false to all propositions in the cycle. For even cycles, two worlds are created. One world for each possible assignment of truth values. For odd cycles if the value a proposition depends on its negation, no model will be found. This can be seen by looking at two different cases. In the first case we guess p is true. All rules containing **not** p will be removed in the residual program. Since p depended on its negation and the rule that it depend on was removed, p will be false in the least-fixed point semantics of the residual program. Thus, p cannot be true in any model.

For the second case we guess p is false. Since p depends on its negation there exists a rule with **not** p in the body with all other literals in the body being in the least-fixed point of the residual program, and p is in the least-fixed point of the residual program if and only if the body of that rule is true. If this were not the case then the value of p could not depend on its negation. But, if it is the case, **not** p will be removed from the rule, and since all other literals are in the least-fixed point then p must be in the least-fixed point. This does not match our guess, so no model can assign false to p.

Co-stable Model Semantics. Co-stable model semantics is a semantics based on a generalization of stable model semantics presented at the Co-LP 2016 workshop [12].

Definition 14. *The co-residual program of a program P for an interpretation I is computed by the following steps:*

- *for all propositions $p \in I$ and rules $R \in P$, remove R if **not** p is in the body.*
- *for all propositions $p \notin I$ and rules $R \in P$, remove R if p is in the body.*
- *Remove all literals from the body of the rules in the resulting program.*

Definition 15. *For some program P, a set of proposition $I \subseteq props(P)$ is a* co-stable model *of P if and only if I is the least fixed-point of the coresidual program of P and I.*

Co-stable model semantics is similar to stable model semantics – except how it handles positive cycles. It uses multiple worlds to allow a positive cycle to be true or false. If a set of propositions do not contain any of the propositions that are part of a positive cycle then all rules that form that cycle will be removed from the coresidual program and all such propositions will not be in the least model of the coresidual program. On the other hand if all of the propositions in a positive cycle is in the set then they will have facts in the coresidual program. Thus, given the program "p :- p.", the co-stable model semantics will generate two models {} (i.e., p false) and {p} (i.e., p true).

We can divide all the propositions in an even cycle into two sets A and B such that for all p $\in A$ and for all q $\in B$, p depends on **not** q. In addition we can interchange A and B and the property still holds. By choosing A or B to be a subset of the co-stable model candidate we can create multiple worlds one where one half is true and one where the other half is true.

Finally, there can be no odd cycles just like stable model semantics.

3   Fixed-Point Formalization Overview

In this section we present a generalized fixed-point semantics. In the interest of space, this will be a short summary. Since we are working with both 2-value and 3-value logics, and our goal is to create a proof theoretic, goal directed algorithm that computes partial models, we must change the way we define interpretations.

An interpretation is a set of literals (both positive and negative). For some proposition, p:

If p is in the interpretation, but not p is not, then p is true in that interpretation.

If not p is in the interpretation, but p is not, then p is false in that interpretation.

If both p and not p are not in the interpretation, then p is $\perp$ (unknown) in that interpretation.

If both p and not p are in the interpretation, then p is *unresolved* in that interpretation.

Furthermore, we say that an interpretation is *unresolved* if it contains a proposition that is unresolved in it. Now that we can specify interpretations we must be able to decide which interpretations are models. This will, of course, depend on the specific semantics we wish to view the interpretation in. Which, in turn, depends on how we handle the cycles.

We will identify these cycles using *cycle sets*. Cycle sets can be thought of as a minimal subset of the program such that each rule in that subset depends on some other rule in the subset. This allows us to filter out the non-cyclic portion of the program, but a cycle set in and of itself does not guarantee a cycle. Consider the program "p :− p,q.". This one rule forms a cycle set, but it is not a cycle. Since q does not have a rule it must be false. So, the body of the rule must be false, and therefore p must be false.

If a cycle actually exists, then we need to break the cycle. We will do this through *cycle resolutions*. A cycle resolution for a particular cycle set can be viewed as a consistent assignment of truth values to the head of each rule in that cycle set. Cycle resolutions can take care of the coinductive part of the program. After *resolving* all cycles, the rest of the program is inductive.

For a fixed-point semantics, we need to specify a function that inductively assign truth values, and when cycles block our progress, resolve them. A particular semantics is specified by specifying how to generate cycle resolutions. This is done with four functions. Two of these functions are *cycle resolution functions*.

A cycle resolution function maps an interpretation to a set of cycle resolutions. One of these cycle resolution functions is limited to resolving positive cycles, and the second is limited to resolving even cycles. The last two function are called *filter functions*. The first is the *local filter function* and maps an interpretation to another interpretation. The intention is to resolve unresolved propositions or add an unresolved proposition. Adding an unresolved proposition is equivalent to specifying the interpretation is not a model.

For this paper, a semantics will define two local filters The local filter function $\mathcal{L}^{WF}$ filters interpretations by assigning all unresolved literals $\perp$. This correspond to how well-founded semantics handles odd loops. As stated earlier, we assume all positive and even cycles will be resolved by the time the local filter function is used. So, all unresolved propositions must depend on an odd cycle. $\mathcal{L}^{SM}$ is an identity function for interpretation. Since the only unresolved literals in an interpretation given to $\mathcal{L}^{SM}$ should be part of an odd cycle, we can just keep them and it will be eliminated as a possible model (as will be described below). This is for semantics such as stable models that cannot have odd cycles.

The second type of filter function, is the *global filter function*. The global filter function maps a set of interpretation to a set of interpretations. In this paper we will only consider the identity function for a set of interpretations.

Overall, what we want is a function that maps a set of interpretations to a new set of interpretations with a fixed-point that is the set of models. Some decisions, however, cannot be made until we have made all the other decisions. In resolution form, these decisions are made with the filter functions. So, our final function will have three stages. First, starting with the set containing the interpretation where every proposition is unresolved we step-by-step apply the extended T_P operator to each interpretation and then resolve any positive or even cycles halting progress. The extended T_P operator is like the standard T_P operator of logic programming [18], but operates on the extended program [25, 26]. Recall that a cycle resolution function gives a set of cycle resolutions. So, each interpretation can be replaced with several "resolved" interpretations. This processes is continued until a fixed point is reached, and at this point there may be unresolved interpretations or interpretations that are not models and need to be filtered out. The second stage is applying the local filter function to each interpretation, remove any unresolved interpretation, and then apply the extended T_P operator until we reach a fix point. The last step is needed since it is possible that some propositions may be indirectly affected by the changes made. A good example of this is the well-founded semantics. Odd cycles at this step will not be resolved. So the filter function must resolve it by assigning $\perp$ to the involved propositions. This will, in turn, require propositions dependent on that cycle to also be assigned $\perp$. The final stage is to apply the global filter function. After applying the global filter function, any interpretations in the resulting set which contain unresolved propositions are removed. The final set of interpretations are the set of models for the program.

4   Proof-Theoretic Formalization

4.1   3-Value Modified CoSLD Resolution

Since we will be working with 3-value logics such as well founded semantics we must modify the algorithm from [19] further. To do this we must differentiate between the truth value of a proposition and the success/failure of its proof. We will say that a query succeeds if there exists a model such that the query is not false in that model.

Definition 16. *3-value Modified CoSLD resolution can be defined by modifying the original algorithm (from [19]) as follows.*

- *On success, the literals on the call stack are assigned a value in reverse order.*
- *On coinductive success, the last literal on the call stack is not assigned a value, and all others are assigned a value in reverse order.*
- *If a literal is to be assigned $\perp$, it is assigned the value temporarily and execution continues to the next branch (as if it had failed). If a success assigns true to the literal the previous $\perp$ value is overwritten and true is assigned to the literal. Otherwise it stays $\perp$.*

4.2   Restrictions

Besides the obvious restrictions that the semantics must use negation-as-failure and be a completion semantics, we impose some additional restrictions for the proof-theoretic method: (i) All semantics that require a filter function besides the three defined in Sect. 3 are unsupported. It is important to note that this is not a technical restriction, but one of convenience. All such semantics can be implemented by computing the consistency constraint imposed by the filter functions and appending it to the query as we do for $\mathcal{L}^{SM}$ [25]; and, (ii) We will assume that no semantics will allow a cycle to be resolved as both true/false and $\perp$. This restriction can be lifted by non-deterministically selecting a resolution rule and trying again if needed.

4.3   Preprocessing

The goal directed algorithm presented in this paper is a generalization of the algorithm for stable model semantics presented in [19] and demonstrated in [20]. More details on preprocessing a program can be found in those papers.

Internal IDs: The method we describe will require modifying the original program internally. This includes the generation of the consistency check as well as the creation of the extended program. This will sometimes require the use of new propositions. We want to hide these new propositions so that when the algorithm is viewed as a black box the modification is not apparent. So, we will need a means of marking these propositions. For the purpose of this paper we will surround a normal proposition name with "⟨" and "⟩" to represent an *internal name*. It is important to note that sample and ⟨*sample*⟩ are considered different propositions.

Dual Rule Generation: The method for generating the dual rules to be added to the extended program presented in Sect. 2.1 of this paper is not suitable for practical applications. For the proof-theoretic algorithm we will use the method presented in [19].

To generate the extended program we add rules as follows:

Definition 17. *Let P be some program. Then, for all propositions $p \in props(P)$:*

- *Collect all rules $r \in P$ for which head(r) = p.*
- *If no such rules exist add the rule "**not** p." otherwise:*
  - *for each rule r collected and each literal $L \in body(r)$, add a rule "⟨not_p_r⟩:− **not** L.", and*
  - *add a rule r′ with head(r′) = **not** p and the conjunction of all ⟨not_p_r⟩ generated in the above rule.*

Consistency Check: The filter functions defined in Sect. 3, can disqualify an interpretation from being a model or make an unresolved interpretation a model. The local filter functions make use of information about the entire interpretation and the global filter function makes use of information about the entire set of interpretations. There is no guarantee that the goal-directed execution provided in this paper will explore an entire interpretation, and it is very unlikely it will explore the set of all possible interpretations.

Since we are only considering the identity function as our global filter function, we do not need to worry about it. It makes no changes to the set of possible models. Likewise, we do not need to worry about the local filter function $\mathcal{L}^{WF}$. However, the local filter function $\mathcal{L}^{SM}$ may leave odd cycles unresolved. In such situations, to capture the decisions made in the filter functions we need to explicitly write a rule that ensures the generated partial model would not have been invalidated by the local filter function. The consistency check is the head of this rule. This head is appended to all queries to make sure that the partial model found conforms to any constraints imposed by the filter functions.

If we assume all positive and even cycles are resolved before reaching the filter function, then the only unresolved propositions that can be present in an interpretation are those that are dependent on an odd cycle. This is consistent with the fixed-point form discussed int Sect. 3 and [19], and the same consistency check proposed in [19] (also called an NMR check) can be used when a semantics uses $\mathcal{L}^{SM}$.

To generate the check we must first construct a call graph for the program, and decide what rules in the program form odd cycles. Each rule that is part of an odd cycle is called an OLON (Odd loop over negation) rule.

Definition 18. *Let P be some program.*

- *For each OLON rule $r :h:-L_1, L_2, \ldots, L_n$ create a new proposition ⟨chk_h_r⟩ and for each literal L_i, such that $L_i \neq$ **not** h, add a new rule "⟨chk_h_r⟩:− **not**L_i". Then, add rule "⟨chk_h_r⟩:− h".*

- *Create a new rule, r', with head$(r') = \langle chk \rangle$ and the conjunction of all $\langle chk\_h_r \rangle$'s from the previous step as the body.*

4.4   The Rules

A specific semantics is specified by three rules. Each rule decides how to resolve a cycle when detected.

Definition 19. *A cycle resolution rule can be one of three possible rules:*

- *SUCCESS(True) means a goal that results in a cycle will succeed with intended value true.*
- *SUCCESS($\perp$) means a goal that results in a cycle will succeed with the intended value $\perp$.*
- *FAIL means a goal that results in a cycle will fail.*

In addition to the above rules, odd cycle resolutions rules must also specify whether or not a consistency check is needed. This will be represented in this paper as CHK and NOCHK.

Definition 20. *A cycle resolution rule can be fixed or symmetric. A fixed cycle resolution rule applies to both the positive and negative goals. A symmetric cycle resolution rule will invert the truth value for negative goals.*

In this paper will specify a cycle resolution rule to be fixed by accompanying it with FIX. All rules are assumed to be symmetric unless accompanied by FIX. FAIL and SUCCESS(True) are symmetric of each other and SUCCESS($\perp$) is symmetric of itself.

We will assume that if a FAIL is FIXed there will be some sort of consistency check to ensure that the model does not have any cycles of that type. For our work we will only allow FAIL to be FIXed for odd cycles for which we already have a consistency check. With the current restrictions there is no way to determine if an even cycle should fail or if its negation should fail. So, we will also require even cycle rules to be FIXed.

Semantics	Positive Cycles	Even Cycles	Odd Cycles
Fittings 3-Val	SUCCESS($\perp$)	SUCCESS($\perp$) FIX	SUCCESS($\perp$) NOCHK
Well-Founded	FAIL	SUCCESS($\perp$) FIX	SUCCESS($\perp$) NOCHK
Stable-Models	FAIL	SUCCESS(True) FIX	FAIL FIX,CHK
co-stable Models	SUCCESS(True) FIX	SUCCESS(True) FIX	FAIL,FIX,CHK

4.5   The Algorithm

The following algorithm assumes that the program had already been transformed with dual rules and the consistency check, and that cycle resolutions rules for positive, even, and odd cycles have been defined. We present the algorithm in a top-down manner, with the mutually recursive functions `prove_goals` and `prove_goal` as the core. Given some list of goals Q, query(Q) computes the partial model, for which each member of Q is not false , if it exists and fails otherwise. Note that CoSLD resolution maintains a coinductive hypothesis set (CHS) where it keeps the list of all literals that are either true or hypothesized to be true. The algorithm produces a partial model, which is determined by the CHS at the time the query succeeds. Multiple partial models can be generated by extending the algorithm to backtrack after a success. Each partial model is part of a complete model for the program [25,26], and multiple partial models could be associated with the same model.

```
prove_goals(Goals,CallStack,CHS) begin
    Let [L₁, L₂, ..., Lₙ] for some n ≥ 0 be a permutation of Goals;
    if n = 0 then
    |   return (True , CHS)
    else
        for x ∈ CHS do
            if x = (L₁, T) then return (T, CHS) ;
            if x = (not L₁, ⊥) then return (⊥, CHS) ;
            if x = (not L₁, True) then return (False, CHS) ;
        end
        Let T = prove_cycle(L₁, CallStack);
        if T ≠ NOCYCLE then
        |   return (T, CHS)
        else
            Let (T, CHS2) = prove_goal(L₁, CallStack, CHS);
            if T = False then
            |   return (T, {}, {})
            else
                Let (T2, CHS2) ← prove_goals([L₂, ..., Lₙ], CallStack, CHS2);
                if T2 = True then
                |   return (T, CHS2)
                else
                |   return (T2, CHS2)
                end
            end
        end
    end
end
```

The function `prove_goals` tries to find a proof for a conjunction of goals while constructing the partial candidate model. The `prove_cycle` function is the coinductive portion of the algorithm. It searches the call stack to see if the current goal (or its negation) is already in it, signaling a cycle. If the current proof depends on a cycle, `prove_cycle` also detects what kind of cycle it is and applies the proper rule to resolve it.

The `apply_*_cycle_rule` function calls in `prove_cycle` function represent assigning a truth value based on the rule for the cycle. False is used to represent FAIL. If the argument to the function is negative and the rule is not FIXed then the symmetric value is used. Next, `prove_goal` tries to find a proof for a single goal by expanding rules.

```
prove_cycle(L,CallStack) begin
    Let CS ← CallStack;
    Let NegCycle ← False;
    while CS ≠ [] do
        Let CS = [L' | CS2];
        if L' is positive and L is negative then
            | Let NegCycle ← True;
        else if L' is negative and L is positive then
            | Let NegCycle ← True;
        end
        if L' = L then
            if NegCycle then
                | Let X ← apply_even_cycle_rule(L);
            else
                | Let X ← apply_positive_cycle_rule(L);
            end
            return X
        else if L' = not L then
            Let X ← apply_odd_cycle_rule(L);
            return X
        end
        Let CS ← CS2;
    end
    return NOCYCLE
end
```

When computing a model, the proof-theoretic algorithm is essentially computing the results of applying the extended T_P operator as we do in the fixed-point semantics. Coinductive success is essentially applying the cycle resolution rules. Any literals not in the resulting partial model can be computed independently and added to the partial model to form a model for the program. It is important to note that with our current restrictions, the only way to invalidate a potential model is if there exists an odd cycle. This is checked with the consistency constraint, so the result must be a model of the program.

```
prove_goal(L,CallStack,CHS) begin
    Let RS be a list of the bodies of all rules with L as the head;
    Let Unknown ← False;
    while RS ≠ [] do
        Let RS = [R | RS2];
        Let (T,CHS2) ← prove_goals(R,[L|CallStack],CHS);
        if T = True then
            if L is an internal id then return (True, CHS2) ;
            else return (True, CHS2 ∪ {(L, True)}) ;
        else if T = ⊥ then
            Let Unknown ← True;
            Let CHS ← CHS2;
        end
    end
    if Unknown then
        if L is an internal id then return (⊥, CHS) ;
        else return (⊥, CHS ∪ {(L, ⊥)}) ;
    else
        return (False, CHS)
    end
end
```

Our algorithm generates partial models, which have a different format from interpretations as presented in this paper. So we will present some tools for working with them.

Definition 21. *Let M_1 and M_2 be partial models. M_1 conflicts with M_2 if there exists a pair $(L_1, T_1) \in M_1$ and pair $(L_2, T_2) \in M_2$ such that*

- $L_1 = \textbf{not } L_2$ and either $T_1 \neq \perp$ or $T_2 \neq \perp$, or
- $L_1 = L_2$ and $T_1 \neq T_2$.

L_1 and L_2 are called conflicting *literals, and we say L_1 conflicts with M_2 and L_2 conflicts with M_1.*

To prove the correctness of our algorithm we must show that the query can be extended until a full model is generated. We must also show that model is a superset of the original partial model and that it is a model with respect to the semantics.

Lemma 1. *Let S be a semantics represented by cycle resolution rules. Let P be a program with at least one model with respect to S, M a partial model of P, and L a coinductive literal of P that succeeds. If for all partial models, D, that is generated when L succeeds(ignoring any consistency check) there exists some proposition p that is assigned different values by D and M then $\textbf{not } L$ can succeed and there exists a partial model D' generated when $\textbf{not } L$ succeeds(ignoring any consistency check) such that D' does not conflict M.*

Theorem 1. *Let Q be a list of literals to be proved, and P be a program. Let S be the semantics represented by cycle resolution rules. Then,*

1. **query**(Q) *succeeds with partial model M implies the literals in Q are in M and there exists a model M' of P with respect to S such that $M \subseteq M'$, and*
2. *if there exists a model M' of P with respect to S with the literals of Q are in M' there exists $M \subseteq M'$ with the literals of Q in M such that* **query**(Q) *succeeds with partial model M.*

5   Related Work

Jürgen Dix has studied properties of semantics for normal logic programs quite extensively [8,9]. The multiple semantics examined in his papers include the semantics considered in this paper plus many others. Dix's work does not try to generalize semantics as we do. Instead it looks at how different semantics are similar and dissimilar and how the various properties enable or restrict the use of a semantics.

Seki has considered application of non-stratified co-LP to Answer Set Programming (ASP) and the well-founded semantics [27]. He has given iterated fixed-point characterizations of stable models as well as the well-founded semantics via dual programs in a spirit similar to ours. Some of Seki's work was in collaboration with the authors of this paper and therefore there are common grounds between his work and ours. However, the main thrust of Seki's work is to show that Horn μ-calculus can be used as an extension of co-logic programming for handling "non- stratified" co-LPs.

More recently, Liu and Stoller have done work in unifying the semantics discussed in this paper, but have taken a different approach. They designed two new semantics (founded semantics and constraint semantics) that subsume the other semantics. Instead of a parametrized algorithm for computing models, their semantics make use of metalogical properties that are assigned to predicates to determine how they are handled. This allows them to simulate the behavior of the other semantics, and can even simulate other semantics not covered by our work [17]. It is our belief, however, that with some modifications to our algorithm and assumptions, such as allowing metalogical properties and modifying $\mathbf{T}'_{\mathbf{p}}$ to use dual rules only for *complete* (a metalogical property) predicates instead of all predicates, we can compute models for the semantics in [17]. Given that we define the semantics of normal logic programs as a mixture of induction and coinduction, then, as demonstrated, we can derive efficient query-driven implementations with ease.

6   Conclusion

In this paper we demonstrated that normal logic program semantics, for which the models of a program is a subset of its completion, can be expressed as a combination of induction and coinduction. We explored the role of both induction and coinduction, and showed that the major difference between such semantics is in how they assign values to cyclic dependent computations. We then presented the declarative and operational semantics of four semantics of normal logic programs in a unifying, systematic manner (Fitting's 3-valued semantics, well-founded semantics, stable model semantics, and co-stable model semantics).

We presented a fixed-point declarative semantics. This fixed-point formalization constructs the set of all models for a program by starting from the set of all its positive and negative literals (representing having no information about the model) and removing literals (ignoring literals that form an odd cycle) in each iteration when we know that cannot be true. Multiple worlds such as those generated by even cycles in stable model semantics are represented by creating two models in the next step. One will have the proposition removed and the other will have its negation removed. Finally when a fixed point is reached, odd cycles are resolved before any remaining models that do not conform to the current semantics based on all cycles or even other models are removed.

Finally, we gave a parametric goal-directed algorithm for computing partial models of these semantics. The psuedocode for the algorithm, example executions, and proof of correctness was also presented.

The main significance of our work is that goal-directed, i.e., query-driven, implementations of normal logic programs with predicates and terms can be realized, e.g., the s(ASP) and s(CASP) systems [3,21]. Such implementations allow us to develop applications that are not possible otherwise, for example, to natural language question answering [5] and medical expert systems that outperform doctors [6].

References

1. Aczel, P.: Non-well-founded sets, CSLI lecture notes series, vol. 14. CSLI (1988)
2. Apt, K.R., Bol, R.N.: Logic programming and negation: a survey. J. Log. Program. **19**(20), 9–71 (1994). https://doi.org/10.1016/0743-1066(94)90024-8
3. Arias, J., Carro, M., Salazar, E., Marple, K., Gupta, G.: Constraint answer set programming without grounding. TPLP **18**(3–4), 337–354 (2018)
4. Baral, C.: Knowledge Representation, Reasoning and Declarative Problem Solving. Cambridge University Press, Cambridge (2003)
5. Basu, K., Shakerin, F., Gupta, G.: AQuA: ASP-based visual question answering. In: Komendantskaya, E., Liu, Y.A. (eds.) PADL 2020. LNCS, vol. 12007, pp. 57–72. Springer, Cham (2020). https://doi.org/10.1007/978-3-030-39197-3_4
6. Chen, Z., Marple, K., Salazar, E., Gupta, G., Tamil, L.: A physician advisory system for chronic heart failure management based on knowledge patterns. Theory Pract. Log. Program. **16**(5–6), 604–618 (2016)
7. Clark, K.: Negation as failure. In: Gallaire, H., Minker, J. (eds.) Logic and Data Bases, pp. 293–322. Springer, Boston, MA (1978). https://doi.org/10.1007/978-1-4684-3384-5_11
8. Dix, J.: A classification theory of semantics of normal logic programs: I. strong properties. Fundam. Inform. **22**(3), 227–255 (1995)
9. Dix, J.: A classification theory of semantics of normal logic programs: II. weak properties. Fundam. Inform. **22**(3), 257–288 (1995)

10. Fitting, M., Ben-Jacob, M.: Stratified and three-valued logic programming semantics. In: Logic Programming, Proceedings of the Fifth International Conference and Symposium, Seattle, Washington, 15–19 August 1988 (2 Volumes), pp. 1054–1069 (1988)

11. Gelfond, M., Lifschitz, V.: The stable model semantics for logic programming. In: Logic Programming, Proceedings of the Fifth International Conference and Symposium, Seattle, Washington, 15–19 August 1988 (2 Volumes), pp. 1070–1080 (1988)

12. Gupta, G., Marple, K., Others: Coinductive answer set programming or consistency-based computing (2012). Co-LP 2012 - A workshop on Coinductive Logic Programming, https://utdallas.edu/~gupta/coasp.pdf

13. Gupta, G., Saeedloei, N., DeVries, B., Min, R., Marple, K., Kluźniak, F.: Infinite computation, co-induction and computational logic. In: Proceedings of the Coalgebra and Algebra in Computer Science (CALCO), pp. 40–54 (2011)

14. Jacobs, B., Rutten, J.: A tutorial on (co)algebras and (co)induction. EATCS Bull. **62**, 62–222 (1997)

15. Klemen, M., Stulova, N., López-García, P., Morales, J.F., Hermenegildo, M.V.: Static performance guarantees for programs with runtime checks. In: Sabel, D., Thiemann, P. (eds.) Proceedings of the PPDP, pp. 13:1–13:13. ACM (2018)

16. Leinster, T.: Basic Category Theory. Cambridge University Press, Cambridge (2016)

17. Liu, Y.A., Stoller, S.D.: Founded semantics and constraint semantics of logic rules. J. Log. Comput. **30**(8), 1609–1668 (2020)

18. Lloyd, J.W.: Foundations of Logic Programming. Springer, Berlin, Heidelberg (1987). https://doi.org/10.1007/978-3-642-83189-8

19. Marple, K., Bansal, A., Min, R., Gupta, G.: Goal-directed execution of answer set programs. In: Principles and Practice of Declarative Programming, PPDP 2012, Leuven, Belgium - 19–21 September 2012, pp. 35–44 (2012)

20. Marple, K., Gupta, G.: Galliwasp: a goal-directed answer set solver. In: Logic-Based Program Synthesis and Transformation, 22nd International Symposium, LOPSTR 2012, Leuven, Belgium, 18–20 September 2012, Revised Selected Papers, pp. 122–136 (2012)

21. Marple, K., Salazar, E., Gupta, G.: Computing stable models of normal logic programs without grounding (2017). arXiv preprint arXiv:1709.00501

22. Min, R.K.: Predicate Answer Set Programming with Coinduction. Ph.D. thesis, University of Texas at Dallas, Richardson, TX, USA (2009)

23. Minker, J. (ed.): Foundations of Deductive Databases and Logic Programming. Morgan Kaufmann Publishers Inc., Burlington (1988)

24. Roşu, G., Lucanu, D.: Circular coinduction: a proof theoretical foundation. In: Kurz, A., Lenisa, M., Tarlecki, A. (eds.) CALCO 2009. LNCS, vol. 5728, pp. 127–144. Springer, Heidelberg (2009). https://doi.org/10.1007/978-3-642-03741-2_10

25. Salazar, E.E.: NAF-Based Logic Semantics: Proof-Theoretic Generalization and Non-Ground Extension. Ph.D. thesis, Dept of Computer Science, UT Dallas (2019)

26. Salazar, E.E., Gupta, G.: Proof-theoretic foundations of normal logic programs, Technical report, dept of comp. sci., UT Dallas (2017). https://utdallas.edu/~gupta/prooftheoretic.pdf

27. Seki, H.: On dual programs in co-logic programming. In: Falaschi, M. (ed.) LOPSTR 2015. LNCS, vol. 9527, pp. 21–35. Springer, Cham (2015). https://doi.org/10.1007/978-3-319-27436-2_2

28. Simon, L., Bansal, A., Mallya, A., Gupta, G.: Co-logic programming: extending logic programming with coinduction. In: Arge, L., Cachin, C., Jurdziński, T., Tarlecki, A. (eds.) ICALP 2007. LNCS, vol. 4596, pp. 472–483. Springer, Heidelberg (2007). https://doi.org/10.1007/978-3-540-73420-8_42
29. Van Gelder, A., Ross, K.A., Schlipf, J.S.: The well-founded semantics for general logic programs. J. Assoc. Comput. Mach. **38**(03), 620–650 (1991)

A Discourse on Guessing and Reasoning

Enric Trillas$^{(\boxtimes)}$

European Centre for Soft Computing, Mieres, Spain
etrillas@gmail.com

Abstract. Computer Science studies the possibility of mechanizing reasoning, an activity of the human brain often confused with thinking, but more or less distinguished from guessing. This paper is devoted to considering, at not too much length, the links between thinking, guessing and reasoning.

Keywords: Reasoning · Thinking · Commonsense Reasoning

1 Introduction

1.1 Thinking, Guessing and Reasoning

Computer Science studies the possibility of mechanizing reasoning, an activity of the human brain often confused with thinking, but more or less distinguished from guessing [5,6], and this paper is devoted to considering, at not too much length, the links between thinking, guessing and reasoning. The first is seldom linguistic, the second is often linguistically expressed, but the third is almost always so; actually, reasoning and language are interwoven. If thinking can be spontaneous, both guessing and reasoning require the thinker's will [4].

Thinking is an activity of the brain in which guessing and reasoning are grounded, and it is produced as soon as the thinker's attention directs to some goal departing from some previous and linguistically expressed information or knowledge; that is, expressing everything by means of statements she/he tries to get a conclusion. Both guessing and reasoning are "directed thinking". The reasoning's goal is, in turn, usually guessed before a correct reasoning can establish it, and is also linguistically expressed; reasoning's correctness is essential for finally accepting whether what was previously guessed can be effectively obtained and consequently believed [6–8].

Thinking is, in itself, a natural phenomenon whose scientific study, including how a person recognizes and expresses it, corresponds to neuroscience. In principle, thinking is independent of correction and will; it only ceases with death, when the electroencephalogram stops. As far as guessing and reasoning, which require the will of the thinker, are concerned, they can be, at least partially,

---

To professor Manuel Hermenegildo. Dear Manuel, Pax et Bonum!.

© Springer Nature Switzerland AG 2023
P. Lopez-Garcia et al. (Eds.): Hermenegildo Festschrift 2022, LNCS 13160, pp. 253–265, 2023.
https://doi.org/10.1007/978-3-031-31476-6_14

studied from a formal point of view; that is, by means of a mathematical model. It should be noticed that if p is the starting statement or premise, reasoning is essentially understood as either establishing a consequence q of p, or an explanation or hypothesis h for p. Statements p, q, h, etc., are not always elemental (that is, of the type subject-predicate, "x is P"); they often are complex, composed from other statements. Consider, for instance, the statement serving to define Natural Numbers, namely the conjunction of the three axioms of Peano, as well as the conclusions reached from them, namely the theorems expressing the properties of Natural Numbers that, "hidden" in the axioms, are revealed by inference from them. If thinking can be seen as a free neural activity, reasoning is, up to some level, rule-governed and it is just what permits the analysis of its correctness as well as its study through formal models.

Reasoning is done thanks to the binary relation $<$, the *inference* or *illation* relation. It is produced through conditional statements "If p, then q", shortened by $p < q$, and only required to universally comply with the *reflexive* law $p < p$, for all statements p. Consequences of p are those statements q such that $p < q$, and hypotheses for p those statements h such that $h < p$. When trying to reach consequences, reasoning is known as *deduction*, and when trying to reach hypotheses as *abduction*; the first is forwards inference, and the second backwards inference. It should be noticed that conditional statements $p < q$, are not always understood in the same way [6–8]; this point will be considered later on.

1.2   The Universal Laws Relation

The question on the universal laws relation $<$ can be required to comply with, is certainly relevant. It is so since ordinary or natural reasoning and language, cannot be supposed to constantly enjoy the same properties. For instance, conjunction "and", symbolized by a dot ($\cdot$), representing "p and q" by $p \cdot q$, is not always commutative, $p \cdot q = q \cdot p$, as it is shown by "Cries and runs", not necessarily the same as "Runs and cries". Analogously, disjunction "or", symbolized by a cross ($+$), representing "p or q" by $p + q$, is not always associative $[p + (q + r) = (p + q) + r]$ since "moving commas" easily can change what is understood by a linguistic statement, as it is shown by the fact that "(Stand up or fall) or cry" and "Stand up or (fall or cry)", are not necessarily the same. Often, sequencing is important in language, and, in it, these properties are not purely syntactic but semantic; meaning plays an essential role in language, and hence in reasoning [11].

Both in ordinary language and reasoning, almost every statement is situational, that is, depends on the context and usually also on its purpose; all is *context-dependent* and *purpose-driven*. It is at least for this reason that, when trying to represent a complex statement by a formula, every part of it should be carefully designed, and, for instance, it can't be supposed that all appearances of "and", "or", and "not", can be represented in the same way. Great care should be taken regarding the way in which connectives, linguistic hedges, quantifiers, etc., are used [6,11].

For instance, the statement "(x is big, and y is small), and z is big", corresponds to the fuzzy proto-form $T_1(T_2(m_{big}(x), m_{small}(y)), m_{big}(z))$, where T_1 and T_2 are suitable functions for "and", and m_{big}, m_{small} the corresponding membership functions for the attributes "big" and "small" [6,11]. If the universe of discourse is the interval $[0, 10]$, $m_{big}(x) = x/10$ and $m_{small}(y) = 1 - y/10$, then the proto-form will be $T_1(T_2(x/10, 1 - y/10), z/10)$; only the functions T_1 and T_2 remain to be specified in it. If the contextual information consists of $T_1 = prod$ and $T_2 = min$, the final equation will be $min((x/10)(1 - y/10), z/10)$, representing a surface in R^4 and thus given $x = 10$, $y = 5$, $z = 2$, corresponds the value $min(1/2, 1/5) = 1/5$ as the degree up to which the statement holds at point $(10, 5, 2)$. Such specifications can come, for instance, from knowing that both functions are commutative, that T_1 represents an interactive conjunction ($p \cdot p$ is not p), but T_2 represents an idempotent one ($p \cdot p$ is just p). Obviously, if the contextual information consisted of different functions T_1 and T_2, the final result will be different [11].

It should also be remarked that "and" is not always idempotent, for instance, sometimes "stupid and stupid" is understood as "very stupid" and not as simply "stupid"; capturing such linguistic but relevant nuances requires attending both the context and the use of the statements in it. Ordinary language and reasoning are *situational* [6–8].

1.3   Thinking

As regards thinking, it is often relational, and a difference with reasoning is that this is based on the single relation $<$, but on the other hand, thinking manages many relations several of which may be imprecise, in a simultaneous form and without necessarily trying to reach a conclusion. For this reason, building up a mathematical model of thinking is difficult; the difficulty is usually increased by a lack of previous information, and because many times thinking is not directed by the thinker, and is helped by analogy with what lies in her/his memory. Often, thinking appears in blurred images, incomplete and distorted situations, old and unconsciously forgotten sensations, etc. Thinking is pervasive, it always works and not always in the same direction, moves from one to another direction; even during reasoning, thinking continues either in parallel, or together with reasoning [8].

In what follows we will limit ourselves to consider a general but naïve model for reasoning, departing from the primitive relation $<$ that, being in language, is considered a primitive relation analogously to how "point", "line" and "plane" are seen in Euclid's "Elements" [7,8].

2   A Naïve Formal Model of Reasoning

§2.1. As previously mentioned, given two statements p (taken as the premise) and q, it can be $p < q$, or $q < p$, or neither the first, nor the second. In the first case, q is a *consequence* of p, in the second q is a *hypothesis* for p. In the third, q

is said to be inferentially *orthogonal* to p, and it is written $p \lozenge q$ [$\Leftrightarrow p \not< q$ & $q \not< p$]. Whenever both the first and the second hold, it is said that p and q are inferentially *equivalent*, and it is written $p \sim q$ [$\Leftrightarrow p < q$ & $q < p$]. Notice that if h were both a hypothesis for p and a consequence of p, from $p < h$ and $h < p$, it follows that $h \sim p$. Usually, hypotheses are presumed not to be equivalent to the premise, that is $h < p$ and $p \not< h$; hypotheses equivalent to the premise are avoided. Thus, reasoning leads to conclusions being either a consequence of p, or a hypothesis for p, or orthogonal to p.

Relation $\sim$ is, obviously, symmetrical and reflexive, and $\lozenge$ is symmetrical but not reflexive.

§2.2. Each q is supposed to have a unique linguistic *negation* q', satisfying the law: $p < q \Rightarrow q' < p'$; negation just *inverts* relation $<$. There are some q occurring in language with *opposite* statements, also called *antonyms*, written q^a and assumed to satisfy the law of coherence $q^a < q'$. As it is shown by examples such as, "if the bottle is not full, it is not empty", it is not always the case that $q' < q^a$; usually it is not $q^a \sim q'$. Negation bounds opposites by above; inferentially, is their superior limit [6]. When a statement q does not have an opposite, it is called "irregular", and it is assumed that $q^a \sim q'$, that is, its negation is "defined" as its unique antonym.

As regards negation, it can be of the following four types for each statement q: 1) $q < (q')'$; 2) $(q')' < q$; 3) $q \sim (q')'$; 4) $q \lozenge (q')'$. In the first, negation is *weak* at q, in the second *intuitionistic* at q, in the third *strong* at q, and in the fourth *wild* at q; negation's character is "local". By definition, opposites are always supposed strong, $(q^a)^a \sim q$, except if q is irregular in which case its character depends on its negation's character.

It is important to notice the singularity of statement q'; if q is in the dictionary, all its opposites q^a are also in it, but its negation q' is not as, for instance, "young" is in the dictionary, "old" is also in the dictionary, but neither "not young" nor "not old" is in it. That is, if statement q can be considered a linguistic term, also q^a is a linguistic term, but q' is not so. Hence and in principle, if it makes sense to consider $(q^a)'$, it is doubtful to consider $(q')^a$; nevertheless, if the latter exists, it will verify $(q')^a < (q')'$, provided negation is intuitionistic or strong at q, $(q')' < q$, and $<$ transitive, implies $(q')^a < q$. Notice that if p were an elemental statement subject-predicate, "x is P", p' is the statement "x is P' (= not P)", simply meaning that x does not exhibit the property named by the word P; instead, "x is P^a" means that x exhibits a concrete property, that specified by the antonym of the word P^a. In a non irregular case, the meanings of words P' and P^a are not coincidental.

§2.3. The transitive property of $<$ is not always valid in language, as it is shown by examples like "The light is red $<$ I stop my car", "I stop my car $<$ A car crosses the orthogonal street", does not necessarily imply "The light is red $<$ A car crosses the orthogonal street" when lacking knowledge of the car's driver. We will see soon the relevance of being $<$ transitive, a property that, like negation, only can be locally considered, and that examples like the former can motivate its substitution by forms like: $[p < q$, and $q < r \Rightarrow p{\cdot}q < r]$, a form of transitivity weaker than the usual: $[p < q$, and $q < r \Rightarrow p < r]$, as will be seen shortly. In the former example, the conclusion will be "The light is red and I stop my car $<$ A car crosses the orthogonal street", which seems more reasonable since a driver ("I") observes the fact.

Concerning linguistic concepts conjunction (and, $\cdot$), and disjunction (or, $+$), they are just assumed to satisfy the universal laws:

1. $p \cdot q < p$, $p \cdot q < q$; both p and q are consequences of "p and q";
2. $p < p + q$, $q < p + q$; both p and q are hypotheses for "p or q",

for all statements p, q. It is just from law 1 that the above-mentioned weaker character of the former type of transitivity follows: If $p < q$ and $q < r$, since it is $p \cdot q < q$ then, under the usual type of transitivity, it follows that $p \cdot q < r$.

§2.4. It is said that q *contradicts* p, or *refutes* p whenever $p < q'$. In particular, p is said to be *self-contradictory* if it is $p < p'$, if contradicts, refutes itself. Self-contradiction is considered a "Mortal Sin" in reasoning, and neither self-contradictory premises are accepted as conveying departing sensory information, nor are self-contradictory conclusions taken into account but avoided.

Theorem 1. *Provided $<$ is transitive in the involved corresponding statements, no two consequences of a non self-contradictory premise p ($p \not< p'$) can be contradictory.*

Proof. If $p < q$ and $p < r$ and it were $q < r'$, since $p < r \Rightarrow r' < p'$, it will follow from $p < q$, $q < r'$, and $r' < p'$, the absurd $p < p'$. Notice that the transitive character of $<$ in the triplet (p, q, r') suffices.   □

No analogous "theorem" can be proven for hypotheses; it is a matter of experience that contradictory hypotheses do exist, and were such a result proven, the confidence in the above definitions would suggest serious doubts [7,8].

§2.5. Let's now enter in what is an actually distinctive part of commonsense, ordinary or everyday reasoning, that on which people usually ground their decisions for daily actions. For instance, why do people buy lottery tickets? Of course, they don't buy a lottery ticket because of "If I buy this ticket, it will be rewarded", but because of "If I buy this ticket, I cannot state that it will not be rewarded", that is, the reasoning for the decision of buying a lottery's ticket is not $p < q$, with $p =$ "I buy a ticket" and $q =$ "This ticket will be rewarded", but $p \not< q'$. Since q is not contradictory with the premise p, the conclusion does not refute the premise; that is, q can be conjectured from p.

Definition 1. *Given a premise p, $p \not< p'$, it is said that q is a* conjecture *from p if $p \not< q'$, if q does not refute p.*

Hence, regarding reasoning from a not self-contradictory premise, it only can consist in either refuting or conjecturing. Notice that premises are statements supposed to be both consequences and conjectures of itself, $p < p$ and $p \not< p'$. But, what about consequences and hypotheses?

Theorem 2. *If* $<$ *is transitive in the involved statements, then* $p < q \Rightarrow p \not< q'$, *consequences are conjectures; deducing is a particular case of conjecturing.*

Proof. If $p < q'$, since $p < q \Rightarrow q' < p'$, the transitivity of $<$ leads to the absurd $p < p'$. Notice that transitivity in the triplet (p, q', p') suffices. □

Theorem 3. *If* $<$ *is transitive in the involved statements, then* $h < p \Rightarrow p \not< h'$, *provided* $h \not< h'$; *abducing is a particular case of conjecturing.*

Proof. If $p < h'$, from $h < p$ it will follow that $h < h'$, which is absurd. Notice that the transitivity of $<$ in the triplet (h, p, h') suffices. □

Thus, in presence of local transitivity, both consequences and not self-refuting hypotheses are conjectures; but in total absence of transitivity there can exist consequences and hypotheses that are not conjectures. Transitivity simplifies the classification of conjectures; under that assumption, reasoning just consists in refuting, deducing, abducing, and in finding orthogonal conjectures.

A forwards chain of elemental steps like $p < q$, $q < r$, $r < t$ allows us to conclude $p < t$, provided $<$ is transitive in the involved statements; if it is not, the only thing that can be immediately stated is 1) q is a consequence of p; 2) r is a consequence of q, and 3) t is a consequence of r, but the possibility of $p < t$ should be directly checked. Analogously, with a backwards chain $p > q > r > t$ ($p > q \Leftrightarrow q < r$), transitivity allows us to conclude $p > t$; without transitivity such conclusion is undecided and it should be directly checked.

Notwithstanding this, in general, conjectures are not only consequences or hypotheses; there can exist conjectures that are orthogonal to the premise, that is, those statements s such that $p \not< s'$ and $p \Diamond s$. They are called *speculations* from p, and these belong to the two disjoint families of those, namely: 1) $p \Diamond s$ and $s' < p$, called *weak speculations*, and 2) $p \Diamond s$ and $p \Diamond s'$, called *strong speculations*. Hence, under transitivity, reasoning just consists in refuting, deducing, abducing and speculating [5–8, 10].

§2.6. Weak speculations can be obtained deductively provided the negation is not wild in them. In fact, from $s' < p$, s' can be backwards attained from p, and once s' is known, its negation $(s')'$, the double negation of s, allows forwards reaching s when it is $(s')' < s$, and backwards when $s < (s')'$; such a result is undecided if the negation is wild. Of course, if negation is strong, $(s')' \sim s$, a single step from s' to reach s suffices. As well as this, strong speculations cannot be attained directly from p because of being $p \Diamond s$, and $p \Diamond s'$.

Reaching strong speculations, or weak ones with a wild negation, is just *guessing, inducing*; thus, guessing is a particular but extreme type of reasoning. Nevertheless, it does not obviously mean the non-existence of chains of elemental steps $p < q$, some forwards and some backwards, allowing us to reach speculation s from p; what is actually impossible is to arrive from p to s through either only forwards, or only backwards chains. What is sure is that at the end of such mixed chains there neither will be consequences, nor hypotheses, but some element orthogonal to p. Let us show an example in a finite Boolean Algebra with five atoms a, b, c, d, e, $32 = 2^5$ elements, and with $p = a + b$.

In this case, since $s = a + c + d$ $(s' = b + e)$ verifies $p \Diamond s$ and $p \Diamond s'$, s is a strong speculation, and the mixed chain $p > a < s$ leads from p to s. Analogously, $s = b + e + d$ $(s' = a + c)$, verifies $p \Diamond s$ and $s' \Diamond p$ is a strong speculation attainable through the mixed chain $p > b < s$. On the other hand, $s = c + d + e$ $(s' = a + b)$, verifies $p \Diamond s$ and $p = s'$, is a weak speculation attainable by $p > a < s'$ and passing from s' to $(s')' = c + d + e = s$.

All this corresponds to a general result in finite Boolean Algebras [10]. Hence, in such an extremely rigid structure, speculations can be attained by a computer program even at the risk of a combinatorial explosion (consider a large number of atoms). Given p, it suffices to find all the elements orthogonal to p, and then selecting among them those that are speculations of both types. Perhaps what can be surprising is just the possibility of attaining strong speculations by means of a computer program; it is but just a first step towards mechanizing induction, guessing. It can be said that strong speculations are in the border between directed thinking and reasoning; in general, the thinker obtains them by reflecting on what she/he guesses will follow from p and, perhaps, by analogy with a former and similar case. Sometimes, such reflection is done by a retrocession, a kind of backwards chaining, from the final guess up to the premise.

§2.7. Let us finally show how speculations can help to obtain consequences and hypotheses, how guessing helps deducing and abducing. Obviously, $p \cdot q < q$ and $q < p + q$, show that for all statements q, its conjunction with the premise p is a hypothesis, and its disjunction a consequence. Both conclusions are independent of transitivity.

When directing the thinking to some question concerning the information conveyed by p, that is, when reflecting on such a question or problem, and if it leads to a speculation s from p, a consequence $p + s$, and a hypothesis $p \cdot s$, are obtained. Of course, their suitability for the current problem is not at all guaranteed, and it is the thinker who should decide to stop or to continue the search; if the decision were to continue, what was reached counts as new knowledge that can help such a continuation. That is, by respectively departing from $p \cdot s$, or from $p + s$.

Any researcher can recognize these results from his or her own experiences when searching for something new. Guessing, inducing, or speculating, is a variety of reasoning that is at the heart of creativity. If it were finally confirmed that all speculations can always be attained through a computer program, the mystery around creativity will disappear or, at least, reduced [7]. It should be noticed that tracking p^a instead of s, the obtained hypothesis $p \cdot p^a$ plays an important role in Dialectic Synthesis [12], provided it is not self-contradictory.

3   Additional Remarks

§3.1. Relation $\sim$ is not always transitive, and, as is obvious, the transitivity of $<$ suffices for being $\sim$ transitive also. In this case, $\sim$ is not only reflexive and symmetric, but also transitive, and thus it is an equivalence relation, whose classes are the sets of statements $\{q; q \sim p\} = [p]$, usually known as "propositions" and mainly considered by logicians. Nevertheless, language and ordinary reasoning manage statements but not always propositions that can reveal something out of language; it is, for instance, that inferential equivalence $p \sim q$ translates into identity $[p] = [q]$, which can cause some confusion when, as is usual, statements p and q are not actually identical but expressed in different words and, consequently, possibly showing some nuances that don't permit their full identification. Language is not as simple as logic seems to be, and, as has already been said, ordinary reasoning is interwoven with it.

§3.2. It was supposed that premises are single statements p, but usually the initial information is conveyed by a set of statements $\{p_1, \ldots, p_n\}$ with $n > 1$. Such statements can be aggregated into a *résumé* p, usually consisting in their conjunction even if it can be done through some "packages" of the p_i [3]. A comment is needed in regard to this, since in ordinary language conjunction neither can be always considered commutative, nor associative; notice, for instance, that with $n = 3$, the statements $p_1 \cdot (p_2 \cdot p_3)$ and $(p_2 \cdot p_3) \cdot p_1$, can be actually different. Hence, when lacking the commutative and the associative laws, the thinker should decide, in advance, a suitable ordering for the p_i; a decision based on some criteria coming from his/her contextual knowledge on the "n premises", or by considering, for instance, their complexity. Once the premises are ordered, $p_1, \ldots, p_n$, its résumé can be defined by $p = p_1 \cdot (p_2 \cdot (p_3 \cdot (\ldots) \cdot p_n))))$, which can then be written without parentheses, $p = p_1 \cdot p_2 \cdot p_3 \ldots p_n$, provided conjunction is associative. When, in addition, conjunction is commutative the order in which the p_i appear in the former expression does not matter [6,7].

Notice that without these laws, we have $p \cdot (q \cdot r) < p$, and $p \cdot (q \cdot r) < q \cdot r$, from which, since $q \cdot r < q$ and $q \cdot r < r$, can only be continued to give $p \cdot (q \cdot r) < q$, and $p \cdot (q \cdot r) < r$ if $<$ is transitive.

§3.3. The naïve model presented above allows, with local transitivity, the proof of the Aristotle's old "principles" of Non Contradiction and Excluded Middle as "theorems". The first proof below contradicts Aristotle's statement, "this principle cannot be submitted to proof" [4].

1. <u>Theorem of Non Contradiction</u>: $p \cdot p' < p$ implies $p' < (p \cdot p')'$. Hence, since it is also $p \cdot p' < p'$, by transitivity in the triplet $(p \cdot p', p', (p \cdot p')')$, it follows that $p \cdot p' < (p \cdot p')'$. That is, the statement "p and not p" is self-contradictory for all p.
2. <u>Theorem of Excluded Middle</u>: $p < p + p'$ implies $(p + p')' < p'$. Since it is also $p' < p + p'$, by transitivity in the triplet $((p + p')', p', p + p')$, it follows $(p + p')' < p + p'$, and $(p + p')' < ((p + p')')'$. That is, the statement "not $(p$ or not $p)$" is self-contradictory for all p.

Thus, it suffices to accept the equivalence [impossible $\sim$ self-contradictory], to have the principles in the old form presented by Aristotle: "p and not p is impossible", and "p or not p is sure" (just accepting that "sure" is equivalent to "not impossible"). It should be remarked that both theorems hold for any kind of negation, their proofs are independent of the negation's character.

Notice that, in Ortho-lattices, these "principles" reduce, respectively, to $p \cdot p' = 0$, and $p + p' = 1$, since in them $p < p' \Leftrightarrow p = 0$, the only self-contradictory element is its lattice's minimum (0): In Ortho-lattices, the "principles" appear among its axioms, as it is in the particular cases of Ortho-modular lattices and Boolean algebras. The situation is different in De Morgan algebras, where $p \cdot p' = 0$ and $p + p' = 1$ are not axioms, there can be more self-contradictory elements than just 0, and such two properties only hold for its "Boolean elements"; nevertheless, since the former proofs also hold in these algebras, the principles are valid in them as just stated by the former two theorems.

Notice also that in all those lattices [1], and since in them the laws of duality hold, $(p + q)' = p' \cdot q'$ and $(p \cdot q)' = p' + q'$, one equivalent to the other, both "principles" are equivalent. For instance, $p \cdot p' < (p \cdot p')' = p' + (p')' = p' + p = p + p' \Rightarrow (p + p')' < (p \cdot p')' = p' + p = ((p + p')')'$ since, in addition, negation is strong ($\Leftrightarrow (r')' = r$, for all r). Just as the commutative and associative laws of conjunction are not always admissible, the laws of duality are not always admissible; in ordinary language and reasoning, their validity is, like that of transitivity, a local property; furthermore, they are not equivalent and it may be that none holds, or that one holds but not the other [6]. It was in the setting of Ortho-lattices that conjectures were defined by the first time [9], and introduced the idea of speculation.

Anyway, given a conjunction ($\cdot$) its "dual disjunction" expressed by $p \vee q = (p' \cdot q')'$ exists; similarly, given a disjunction ($+$) there exists its "dual conjunction" $p \wedge q = (p' + q')'$. In fact, and provided the negation is weak or strong, and transitivity holds, the first verifies $p < p \vee q$ and $q < p \vee q$, since $p' \cdot q' < p' \Rightarrow (p')' < (p' \cdot q')' = p \vee q$, and $p < (p')'$ implies $p < p \vee q$; analogously it follows $q < p \vee q$, as well as it is proven that $p \wedge q < p$ and $p \wedge q < q$.

Concerning the algebras of fuzzy sets [11], which are lattices only when conjunction is represented by the function min, and disjunction by max, in which case are De Morgan-Kleene algebras [6,11], the two former theorems hold in all cases. It is a fact leaving out the usual affirmation that fuzzy sets don't verify the two "principles", an affirmation that is also not true for some representations of "not", "and", "or", and as it is, for instance, with $W(x, y) = max(0, x + y - 1)$ for "and", $W^*(x, y) = min(1, x + y)$ for "or", and $N(x) = 1 - x$ for "not", functions verifying $W(x, 1 - x) = max(0, x + 1 - x - 1) = 0$, and $W^*(1, 1 - x) = min(1, x + 1 - x) = 1$.

Actually, the former two theorems are very general, since they hold in very different situations. Both theorems only can fail in absence of local transitivity. Thus, if the principle of *Non Contradiction* is considered essential for having one's feet on solid ground (as it was, and still is, believed by most thinkers), it seems that the given definitions of conjunction and disjunction, as well as the law of inversion of negation, should be preserved jointly with the existence of some type of transitivity that differentiates, at the end, formal from ordinary reasoning.

§3.4. As it was said at the start of this paper, people don't uniformly understand the illation conditional statements $p < q$. It depends on the context and the use and purpose of $<$. There is not a single way of understanding $p < q$ in language. Perhaps the most usual form of understanding $p < q$ is identifying it with the unconditional statement "not p or q", $p' + q$. In this form, "If it rains, then I take an umbrella" means "It does not rain, or I take an umbrella", a statement that seems to hide the possibility of going with an umbrella with rain. For this reason, the equivalence with "It does not rain or (it rains and I take an umbrella)" seems more suitable, that is, identifying $p < q$ with the unconditional statement $p' + (p \cdot q)$, coincidental in Ortho-lattices with $p' \cdot (q + q') + (p \cdot q)$, and making clear that the umbrella is taken when raining but leaving it open in the case of not raining. Notice that, provided $<$ is transitive, and the negation weak or strong, $p \cdot q$ and p' are contradictory since $p \cdot q < p$, and $p < (p')'$ imply $p \cdot q < (p')'$, something that is not with p' and q in the first form $p' + q$. Hence, the form $p' + p \cdot q$ consists of the disjunction of two contradictory statements; a kind of "partition" of $p < q$.

Notice that in the Ortho-lattices, $p' \cdot (p \cdot q) = (p' \cdot p) \cdot q = 0 \cdot q = 0$, and in the particular case of Boolean algebras, $p' + p \cdot q = (p' + p) \cdot (p' + q) = 1 \cdot (p' + q) = p' + q$, thanks to the distributive law; that is, in these algebras both expressions $p' + q$ and $p' + p \cdot q$ are identical. The first is typically used in the so called Logic of Quantum Physics and the second in the classical Propositional Calculus [1]. If in the second, statements are represented by subsets of a universe of discourse, in the first are represented by vector subspaces of an infinite dimensional Hilbert space, whose respective models are Boolean algebras and Ortho-modular lattices. In the case of Quantum Physics the expression $q + (p' \cdot q')$ is also considered to mean $p < q$; this form also reduces in Boolean algebras to $p' + q : q + (p' \cdot q') = (q + p') \cdot (q + q') = (q + p') \cdot 1 = q + p' = p' + q$.

The large amount of laws in Boolean algebras make indistinguishable many "forms" that, without them, are different [2]; for instance, there is the "contradiction" $(p < q')$ indistinguishable from "incompatibility" $(p \cdot q = 0)$, since: 1) If p and q are contradictory $\Leftrightarrow p < q'$, then by the monotony of $(\cdot)$ respect to $<$, it is $p \cdot q < q' \cdot q = 0$; thus $p \cdot q = 0$; 2). If p and q are incompatible $\Leftrightarrow p \cdot q = 0$, and since it always holds the law of "perfect repartition", $p = p \cdot q + p \cdot q'$, it follows that $p = 0 + p \cdot q' = p \cdot q' \Leftrightarrow p < q'$. It should be noticed that in Boolean algebras the law of perfect repartition is a direct consequence of the distributive law: $p = p \cdot 1 = p \cdot (q + q') = p \cdot q + p \cdot q'$.

Let us mention yet another form appearing in ordinary language. It is the understanding of $p < q$ as "p and q", $p \cdot q$, a form requiring that the conjunction is not commutative, since $p < q$ is different from $q < p$. Remember that $p' + q$ ($p < q$) is different from $q' + p$ ($q < p$), as well as that $p' + p \cdot q$ does not coincide with $q' + q \cdot p$. This conjunctive interpretation is the preferred one in Fuzzy Logic's applications in Control Theory [11], but there are more forms of understanding the statement $p < q$; for instance, in Fuzzy Logic more than forty of them are used. At least and as far as the author knows, the use of the forms $p' + q$, $p' + p \cdot q$, and $p \cdot q$, are present, registered in ordinary language.

§3.5. It is important to realize that relation $<$ should be "effective", that is, once statements p and $p < q$ are known, q should be also known. This is what is translated by the formal expression $[(p \cdot (p < q)) < q]$, called the Modus Ponens Rule (MP) by shortening the old Latin expression "Modus Ponendo Ponens", the mode of posing q after posing p. MP is the fundamental rule of inference, and from it follows the Modus Tollens Rule (MT), by shortening the old Latin "Modus Tollendo Tollens", the mode of removing p after removing q: $[(q' \cdot (p < q)) < p']$. MT follows from MP because of the inversion $p < q \Rightarrow q' < p'$, since from $(q' \cdot (p < q)$ follows $(q' \cdot (q' < p')$ that, by MP, allows to arrive at p'.

When the "calculus" accepts more laws than the few presumed in the model presented in Sect. 2, the adopted representations by unconditional statements can be checked to satisfy MP. For instance, in Boolean algebras $p \cdot (p' + q) = (p \cdot p') + (p \cdot q) = p \cdot q < q$ holds. In the same vein, in Ortho-modular lattices it is proven that $p \cdot (p' + p \cdot q) < q$, and $p \cdot (q + p' \cdot q') < q$. With the model's few laws, and provided that conjunction is associative, $p \cdot (p \cdot q) = (p \cdot p) \cdot q < q$; that is, MP holds. It happens analogously with MT; for instance, in Boolean algebras, $q' \cdot (p' + q) = q' \cdot p' < p'$, and $q' \cdot (p \cdot q) = p \cdot (q' \cdot q) = p \cdot 0 = 0 < p'$ hold.

Nevertheless, Rules MP and MT can show limitations due to the necessity that their reasoning's premises, $p \cdot (p < q)$ in MP, and $q' \cdot (p < q)$ in MT, should be not self-contradictory. In Boolean algebras, as it was proven, that means that both expressions should be different from 0. Hence, in Boolean algebras, MT with the conjunctive interpretation of $p < q$ by $p \cdot q$ is not effective and hence it can't be used. In these algebras, the expression $p \cdot (p < q) < q$, allows the proof that the interpretation of $p < q$ as $p' + q$ is the "maximum" possible in the lattice order of the Boolean algebra; it implies that $p' + p \cdot (p < q) < p' + q \Leftrightarrow (p < q) < p' + (p < q) < p' + q$. In the Ortho-modular lattices it can be proven that a greatest expression for $p < q$ does not exist, but that both $p' + p \cdot q$ and $q + p' \cdot q'$ are maximal.

As regards Fuzzy Logic, if "x is $P < y$ is Q" is represented by means of a function $J : [0,1] \times [0,1] \to [0,1]$, such that $m_{P<Q}(x,y) = J(m_P(x), m_Q(y))$, for all x and y, then there exists a function $T : [0,1] \times [0,1] \to [0,1]$, representing conjunction, such that $T(m_P(x), J(m_P(x), m_Q(y))) \leq m_Q(y)$, for all x and y. For instance, if $<$ were represented by a function J, then and provided that the former T is a left-continuous t-norm [11], such an inequality is proven to be equivalent to $J(m_P(x), m_Q(y)) \leq J_T(m_P(x), m_Q(y)) = max\{z \in [0,1]; T(z, m_P(x)) \leq m_Q(y)\}$. In addition, J_T reduces to the form $p' + q$ when membership functions m_P and m_Q only take the values 0 or 1, that is, reduces to the classical or crisp case. A similar result to that in Boolean algebras is obtained, that is, with classical or crisp sets [6,11].

4 Conclusion

A model able to represent ordinary language and reasoning cannot be endowed with too many "universal laws"; the rigidity of the model increases with the number of presumed laws or axioms, and rising to a maximum in Boolean algebras. Instead, language and reasoning (which everyone relies on for everything) needs to cover all situations; both usually lack too much rigidity and, in part, by the pervasive appearance of imprecision and uncertainty; language will always resist any attempt to enclose it in any "axiomatic setting" [8].

In any case, the model presented in Sect. 2 and called the "Skeleton" of Commonsense Reasoning [4], permits, with very few universal laws, the proof of some results that are considered relevant in reasoning as it is, for instance as it was reclaimed by William Whewell in the 19th Century, when consequences are conjectures [8]. In addition it manifests the importance of local transitivity, and allows the study of Hegel's Dialectic Synthesis [12]. Of course, for each case of reasoning more suitable laws can be added to the few presumed in the model. It is a model just following the Ockham-Menger's Razor: neither more hypotheses should be presumed than those strictly necessary, nor less than those sufficient for reaching significant results [8]. In addition, the model not only reveals when reasoning is reduced to conjecturing and refuting, but shows the existence of speculations, the not purely deductive but inductive conclusions, whose relevance for ordinary reasoning is now not doubted, even if speculations are not generally recognized in the literature on logic. All this tries to further the old maxim of Leibniz: *Instead of discussing, let's compute!*, inspired in the Middle Age's work of Ramon Llull on the way towards seeing reasoning as a "calculus" [7,8].

Acknowledgements. The author thanks the referees whose corrections did improve this paper.

References

1. Birkhoff, G.: Lattice Theory. American Mathematical Society, Colloquium Publications (1967)
2. Bodiou, G.: Théorie dialectique des probabilités, englobant leurs calculs classique et quantique. Gauthier-Villars (1964)
3. Trillas, E., Castiñeira, E., Cubillo, S.: Averaging premises. Mathware Soft Comput. **8**(2), 83–91 (2001)
4. Trillas, E., Termini, S., Tabacchi, M.E.: Reasoning and Language at Work. A Critical Essay. Springer, Cham (2022)
5. Trillas, E.: Glimpsing at guessing. Fuzzy Sets Syst. **281**, 32–43 (2015)
6. Trillas, E.: On the Logos: A Naïve View on Ordinary Reasoning and Fuzzy Logic. SFSC, vol. 354. Springer, Cham (2017). https://doi.org/10.1007/978-3-319-56053-3
7. Trillas, E.: El desafío de la creatividad. Universidade de Santiago de Compostela, Servizo de Publicacións e Intercambio Científico (2018)
8. Trillas, E.: Narrar, conjeturar y computar. Editorial Universidad de Granada, El pensamiento (2020)

9. Trillas, E., Cubillo, S., Castiñeira, E.: On conjectures in orthocomplemented lattices. Artif. Intell. **117**(2), 255–275 (2000)
10. Trillas, E., de Soto, A.R.: On the search of speculations. New Math. Nat. Comput. **18**(1), 9–18 (2022) ·
11. Trillas, E., Eciolaza, L.: Fuzzy Logic. SFSC, vol. 320. Springer, Cham (2015). https://doi.org/10.1007/978-3-319-14203-6
12. Trillas, E., García-Honrado, I.: A reflection on the dialectic synthesis. New Math. Nat. Comput. **15**(1), 31–46 (2019)

Reversible Debugging in Logic Programming

Germán Vidal[(✉)] [iD]

MiST, VRAIN, Universitat Politècnica de València, Valencia, Spain
gvidal@dsic.upv.es

Abstract. Reversible debugging is becoming increasingly popular for locating the source of errors. This technique proposes a more natural approach to debugging, where one can explore a computation from the observable misbehaviour *backwards* to the source of the error. In this work, we propose a reversible debugging scheme for logic programs. For this purpose, we define an appropriate instrumented semantics (a so-called Landauer embedding) that makes SLD resolution reversible. An implementation of a reversible debugger for Prolog, rever, has been developed and is publicly available.

This paper is dedicated to Manuel Hermenegildo on his 60th birthday, for his many contributions to logic programming as well as his energetic leadership within the community. I wish him many springs more to come.

1 Introduction

Reversible debugging allows one to explore a program execution back and forth. In particular, if one observes a misbehaviour in some execution (e.g., a variable that takes a wrong value or an unexpected exception), reversible debugging allows us to analyse the execution backwards from this point. This feature is particularly useful for long executions, where a step-by-step forward inspection from the beginning of the execution would take too much time, or be even impractical.

One can already find a number of tools for reversible debugging in different programming languages, like Undo [12], rr [9] or CauDEr [6], to name a few. In this work, we consider reversible debugging in *logic programming* [7]. In this context, one has to deal with two specific features that are not common in other programming languages: nondetermism and a bidirectional parameter passing mechanism (unification).

Typically, the *reversibilization* of a (reduction) semantics can be obtained by instrumenting the states with an appropriate *Landauer embedding* [5], i.e., by

This work has been partially supported by grant PID2019-104735RB-C41 funded by MCIN/AEI/ 10.13039/501100011033, by the *Generalitat Valenciana* under grant Prometeo/2019/098 (DeepTrust), and by the COST Action IC1405 on Reversible Computation - extending horizons of computing.

P. Lopez-Garcia et al. (Eds.): Hermenegildo Festschrift 2022, LNCS 13160, pp. 266–280, 2023.
https://doi.org/10.1007/978-3-031-31476-6_15

introducing a *history* where the information required to undo the computation steps is stored. Defining a Landauer embedding for logic programming is a challenging task because of nondetermism and unification. On the one hand, in order to undo backtracking steps, a deterministic semantics that models the complete traversal of an SLD tree is required (like the linear operational semantics introduced in [10]). On the other hand, unification is an irreversible operation: given two terms, s and t, with most general unifier σ, we cannot obtain s from t and σ (nor t from s and σ).

Let us note that, in this work, we aim at reversibility in the sense of being able to *deterministically* undo the steps of a computation. In general, (pure) logic programs are *invertible* (e.g., the same relation can be used for both addition and subtraction), but they are not reversible in the above sense.

This paper extends the preliminary results reported in the short paper [13]. In particular, our main contributions are the following:

- First, we define a reversible operational semantics for logic programs that deals explicitly with backtracking steps. In particular, we define both a *forward* and a *backward* transition relation that model forward and backward computations, respectively.
- Moreover, we state and prove some formal properties for our reversible semantics, including the fact that it is indeed a conservative extension of the standard semantics, that it is deterministic, and that any forward computation can be undone.
- Finally, we present the design of a reversible debugger for Prolog that is based on our reversible semantics, and discuss some aspects of the implemented tool, the reversible debugger rever.

We consider that our work can be useful in the context of existing techniques for program validation in logic programming, like run-time verification (e.g., [11]) or concolic testing (e.g., [8]), in order to help locating the bugs of a program.

The paper is organised as follows. After introducing some preliminaries in the next section, we introduce our reversible operational semantics in Sect. 3. Then, Sect. 4 presents the design of a reversible debugger based on the previous semantics. Finally, Sect. 5 compares our approach with some related work and Sect. 6 concludes and points out some directions for further research.

2   Preliminaries

In this section, we briefly recall some basic notions from logic programming (see, e.g., [1, 7] for more details).

In this work, we consider a first-order language with a fixed vocabulary of predicate symbols, function symbols, and variables denoted by Π, Σ and $\mathcal{V}$, respectively, with $\Sigma \cap \Pi = \emptyset$ and $(\Sigma \cup \Pi) \cap \mathcal{V} = \emptyset$. Every element of $\Sigma \cup \Pi$ has an *arity* which is the number of its arguments. We write $f/n \in \Sigma$ (resp. $p/n \in \Pi$) to denote that f (resp. p) is an element of Σ (resp. Π) whose arity is

$n \geq 0$. A *constant symbol* is an element of Σ whose arity is 0. We let $\mathcal{T}(\Sigma, \mathcal{V})$ denote the set of *terms* constructed using symbols from Σ and variables from $\mathcal{V}$.

An *atom* has the form $p(t_1, \ldots, t_n)$ with $p/n \in \Pi$ and $t_i \in \mathcal{T}(\Sigma, \mathcal{V})$ for $i = 1, \ldots, n$. A *query* is a finite conjunction of atoms which is denoted by a sequence of the form $A_1, \ldots, A_n$, where the *empty query* is denoted by **true**. A *clause* has the form $H \leftarrow B_1, \ldots, B_n$, where H (the *head*) and $B_1, \ldots, B_n$ (the *body*) are atoms, $n \geq 0$ (thus we only consider *definite* logic programs, i.e., logic programs without negated atoms in the body of the clauses). Clauses with an empty body, $H \leftarrow$ **true**, are called *facts*, and are typically denoted by H. In the following, atoms are ranged over by $A, B, C, H, \ldots$ while queries (possibly empty sequences of atoms) are ranged over by $\mathcal{A}, \mathcal{B}, \ldots$

$Var(s)$ denotes the set of variables in the syntactic object s (i.e., s can be a term, an atom, a query, or a clause). A syntactic object s is *ground* if $Var(s) = \emptyset$. In this work, we only consider *finite* ground terms.

Substitutions and their operations are defined as usual; they are typically denoted by (finite) sets of bindings like, e.g., $\{x_1/s_1, \ldots, x_n/s_n\}$. We let *id* denote the identity substitution. Substitutions are ranged over by $\sigma, \theta, \ldots$ In particular, the set $\mathcal{D}om(\sigma) = \{x \in \mathcal{V} \mid \sigma(x) \neq x\}$ is called the *domain* of a substitution σ. Composition of substitutions is denoted by juxtaposition, i.e., $\sigma\theta$ denotes a substitution γ such that $\gamma(x) = \theta(\sigma(x))$ for all $x \in \mathcal{V}$. We follow a postfix notation for substitution application: given a syntactic object s and a substitution σ the application $\sigma(s)$ is denoted by $s\sigma$. The *restriction* $\theta\restriction_V$ of a substitution θ to a set of variables V is defined as follows: $x\theta\restriction_V = x\theta$ if $x \in V$ and $x\theta\restriction_V = x$ otherwise. We say that $\theta = \sigma\ [V]$ if $\theta\restriction_V = \sigma\restriction_V$.

A syntactic object s_1 is *more general* than a syntactic object s_2, denoted $s_1 \leqslant s_2$, if there exists a substitution θ such that $s_2 = s_1\theta$. A *variable renaming* is a substitution that is a bijection on $\mathcal{V}$. Two syntactic objects t_1 and t_2 are *variants* (or equal up to variable renaming), denoted $t_1 \approx t_2$, if $t_1 = t_2\rho$ for some variable renaming ρ. A substitution θ is a unifier of two syntactic objects t_1 and t_2 iff $t_1\theta = t_2\theta$; furthermore, θ is the *most general unifier* of t_1 and t_2, denoted by $\mathsf{mgu}(t_1, t_2)$ if, for every other unifier σ of t_1 and t_2, we have that $\theta \leqslant \sigma$.

A logic *program* is a finite sequence of clauses. Given a program P, we say that $A, \mathcal{B}' \rightsquigarrow_{P,\sigma} (\mathcal{B}, \mathcal{B}')\sigma$ is an *SLD resolution step*[1] if $H \leftarrow \mathcal{B}$ is a renamed apart clause (i.e., with fresh variables) of program P, in symbols, $H \leftarrow \mathcal{B} \ll P$, and $\sigma = \mathsf{mgu}(A, H)$. The subscript P will often be omitted when the program is clear from the context. An *SLD derivation* is a (finite or infinite) sequence of SLD resolution steps. As is common, $\rightsquigarrow^*$ denotes the reflexive and transitive closure of $\rightsquigarrow$. In particular, we denote by $\mathcal{A}_0 \rightsquigarrow^*_\theta \mathcal{A}_n$ a derivation

$$\mathcal{A}_0 \rightsquigarrow_{\theta_1} \mathcal{A}_1 \rightsquigarrow_{\theta_2} \ldots \rightsquigarrow_{\theta_n} \mathcal{A}_n$$

where $\theta = \theta_1 \ldots \theta_n$ if $n > 0$ (and $\theta = id$ otherwise).

An SLD derivation is called *successful* if it ends with the query **true**, and it is called *failed* if it ends in a query where the leftmost atom does not unify

---

[1] In this paper, we only consider Prolog's *computation rule*, so that the selected atom in a query is always the leftmost one.

with the head of any clause. Given a successful SLD derivation $\mathcal{A} \leadsto_\theta^* \text{true}$, the associated *computed answer*, $\theta\restriction_{\mathcal{V}ar(\mathcal{A})}$, is the restriction of θ to the variables of the initial query $\mathcal{A}$. SLD derivations are represented by a (possibly infinite) finitely branching tree, which is called *SLD tree*. Here, *choice points* (queries with more than one child) correspond to queries where the leftmost atom unifies with the head of more than one program clause.

Example 1. Consider the following (labelled) logic program:[2]

$$\ell_1 : \mathsf{p}(\mathsf{X},\mathsf{Y}) \;{:}\text{-}\; \mathsf{q}(\mathsf{X}), \mathsf{r}(\mathsf{X},\mathsf{Y}).$$
$$\ell_2 : \mathsf{q}(\mathsf{a}). \qquad\qquad\qquad \ell_5 : \mathsf{r}(\mathsf{b},\mathsf{b}).$$
$$\ell_3 : \mathsf{q}(\mathsf{b}). \qquad\qquad\qquad \ell_6 : \mathsf{r}(\mathsf{b},\mathsf{c}).$$
$$\ell_4 : \mathsf{q}(\mathsf{c}). \qquad\qquad\qquad \ell_7 : \mathsf{r}(\mathsf{c},\mathsf{c}).$$

Given the query $\mathsf{p}(\mathsf{X},\mathsf{Y})$, we have, e.g., the following (successful) SLD derivation:

$$\mathsf{p}(\mathsf{A},\mathsf{B}) \leadsto_{\{\mathsf{X}/\mathsf{A},\mathsf{Y}/\mathsf{B}\}} \mathsf{q}(\mathsf{A}), \mathsf{r}(\mathsf{A},\mathsf{B})$$
$$\leadsto_{\{\mathsf{A}/\mathsf{b}\}} \quad \mathsf{r}(\mathsf{b},\mathsf{B})$$
$$\leadsto_{\{\mathsf{B}/\mathsf{c}\}} \quad \text{true}$$

with computer answer $\{\mathsf{A}/\mathsf{b}, \mathsf{B}/\mathsf{c}\}$.

3   A Reversible Semantics for Logic Programs

In this section, we present a reversible semantics for logic programs that constitutes a good basis to implement a reversible debugger for Prolog (cf. Sect. 4). In principle, one of the main challenges for defining a reversible version of SLD resolution is dealing with unification, since it is an irreversible operation. E.g., given the SLD resolution step

$$\mathsf{p}(\mathsf{X},\mathsf{a}), \mathsf{q}(\mathsf{a}) \leadsto_{\{\mathsf{X}/\mathsf{a},\mathsf{Y}/\mathsf{a}\}} \mathsf{q}(\mathsf{a}), \mathsf{q}(\mathsf{a})$$

using clause $\mathsf{p}(\mathsf{a},\mathsf{Y}) \;{:}\text{-}\; \mathsf{q}(\mathsf{Y})$, there is no deterministic way to get back the query $\mathsf{p}(\mathsf{X},\mathsf{a}), \mathsf{q}(\mathsf{a})$ from the query $\mathsf{q}(\mathsf{a}), \mathsf{q}(\mathsf{a})$, the computed mgu $\{\mathsf{X}/\mathsf{a}, \mathsf{Y}/\mathsf{a}\}$, and the applied clause. For instance, one could obtain the query $\mathsf{p}(\mathsf{X},\mathsf{X}), \mathsf{q}(\mathsf{X})$ since the following SLD resolution step

$$\mathsf{p}(\mathsf{X},\mathsf{X}), \mathsf{q}(\mathsf{X}) \leadsto_{\{\mathsf{X}/\mathsf{a},\mathsf{Y}/\mathsf{a}\}} \mathsf{q}(\mathsf{a}), \mathsf{q}(\mathsf{a})$$

is also possible using the same clause and computing the same mgu.

In order to overcome this problem, [13] proposed a reversible semantics where

- computed mgu's are not applied to the atoms of the query, and
- the selected call at each SLD resolution step is also stored.

---

[2] We consider Prolog notation in examples (so variables start with an uppercase letter). Clauses are labelled with a unique identifier of the form ℓ_i.

Queries are represented as pairs $\langle \mathcal{A}; [(A_n, H_n, m_n), \ldots, (A_1, H_1, m_1)] \rangle$, where the first component is a sequence of atoms (a query), and the second component stores, for each SLD resolution step performed so far, the selected atom (A_i), the head of the selected clause (H_i), and the number of atoms in the body of this clause (m_i). Here, mgu's are not stored explicitly but can be inferred from the pairs (A_i, H_i). The number m_i is used to determine the number of atoms in the current query that must be removed when performing a backward step. A reversible SLD resolution step has then the form[3]

$$\langle A, \mathcal{B}; \mathcal{H} \rangle \rightharpoonup \langle B_1, \ldots, B_m, \mathcal{B}; (A, H, m) : \mathcal{H} \rangle$$

if there exists a clause $H \leftarrow B_1, \ldots, B_m \ll P$ and $\mathsf{mgu}(A\sigma, H) \neq \mathsf{fail}$, where σ is the substitution obtained from $\mathcal{H}$ by computing the mgu's associated to each triple (A_i, H_i, m) in $\mathcal{H}$ and, then, composing them. A simple proof-of-concept implementation that follows this scheme can be found at https://github.com/mistupv/rever/tree/rc2020.

The proposal in [13], however, suffers from several drawbacks:

- First, it is very inefficient, since one should compute the mgu's of each SLD resolution step once and again. This representation was chosen in [13] for clarity and, especially, because it allowed us to easily implement it without using a ground representation for queries and programs, so that there was no need to reimplement all basic operations (mgu, substitution application and composition, etc.).
- The second drawback is that the above definition of reversible SLD resolution cannot be used to undo a *backtracking* step, since the structure of the SLD tree is not explicit in the considered semantics.

In the following, we introduce a reversible operational semantics for logic programs that overcomes the above shortcomings.

3.1 A Deterministic Operational Semantics

First, we present a deterministic semantics (inspired by the linear operational semantics of [10]) that deals explicitly with backtracking.

Our semantics is defined as a transition relation on states. In the following, queries are represented as pairs $\langle \mathcal{A}; \theta \rangle$ instead of $\mathcal{A}\theta$, where θ is the composition of the mgu's computed so far in the derivation. This is needed in order to avoid undoing the application of mgu's, which is an irreversible operation.

Definition 1 (state). *A state is denoted by a sequence* $Q_1 | Q_2 | \ldots | Q_n$, *where each* Q_i *is a (possibly labelled) query of the form* $\langle \mathcal{B}; \theta \rangle$. *In some cases, a query* Q *is labelled with a clause label, e.g.,* Q^ℓ, *which will be used to denote that the query* Q *can be unfolded with the clause labelled with* ℓ *(see below).*

A state will often be denoted by $\langle \mathcal{B}; \theta \rangle | S$ so that $\langle \mathcal{B}; \theta \rangle$ is the first query of the sequence and S denotes a (possibly empty) sequence of queries. In the following, an empty sequence is denoted by ϵ.

---

[3] Here, $(A, H, m) : \mathcal{H}$ denotes a list with head element (A, H, m) and tail $\mathcal{H}$.

$$\text{(backtrack)} \ \frac{S \neq \epsilon}{\langle \text{fail}, \mathcal{B}; \theta \rangle \,|\, S \rightarrow S} \qquad \text{(next)} \ \frac{S \neq \epsilon}{\langle \text{true}; \theta \rangle \,|\, S \rightarrow S}$$

$$\text{(choice)} \ \frac{A \neq \text{fail} \wedge A \neq \text{true} \wedge \text{clauses}(A\theta, P) = \{\ell_1, \ldots, \ell_m\} \wedge m > 0}{\langle A, \mathcal{B}; \theta \rangle \,|\, S \rightarrow \langle A, \mathcal{B}; \theta \rangle^{\ell_1} \,|\, \ldots \,|\, \langle A, \mathcal{B}; \theta \rangle^{\ell_m} \,|\, S}$$

$$\text{(choice\_fail)} \ \frac{A \neq \text{fail} \wedge A \neq \text{true} \wedge \text{clauses}(A\theta, P) = \emptyset}{\langle A, \mathcal{B}; \theta \rangle \,|\, S \rightarrow \langle \text{fail}, \mathcal{B}; \theta \rangle \,|\, S}$$

$$\text{(unfold)} \ \frac{\text{cl}(\ell, P) = H \leftarrow B_1, \ldots, B_n \wedge \text{mgu}(A\theta, H) = \sigma}{\langle A, \mathcal{B}; \theta \rangle^{\ell} \,|\, S \rightarrow \langle B_1, \ldots, B_n, \mathcal{B}; \theta\sigma \rangle \,|\, S}$$

Fig. 1. A deterministic operational semantics

In this paper, we consider that program clauses are labelled, so that each label uniquely identifies a program clause. Here, we use the auxiliary function clauses(A, P) to obtain the labels of those clauses in program P whose heads unify with atom A, i.e.,

$$\text{clauses}(A, P) = \{\ell \mid \ell : H \leftarrow \mathcal{B} \ll P \wedge \text{mgu}(A, H) \neq \text{fail}\}$$

and $\text{cl}(\ell, P)$ to get a renamed apart variant of the clause labelled with ℓ, i.e., $\text{cl}(\ell, P) = (H \leftarrow \mathcal{B})\vartheta$ if $\ell : H \leftarrow \mathcal{B} \in P$ and ϑ is a variable renaming with fresh variables.

The rules of the semantics can be found in Fig. 1. An *initial state* has the form $\langle A, \mathcal{B}; id \rangle$, where A is an atom, $\mathcal{B}$ is a (possibly empty) sequence of atoms, and id is the identity substitution. Initially, one can either apply rule choice or choice_fail. Let us assume that A unifies with the head of some clauses, say $\ell_1, \ldots, \ell_m$. Then, rule choice derives a new state by replacing $\langle A, \mathcal{B}; id \rangle$ with m copies labelled with $\ell_1, \ldots, \ell_m$:

$$\langle A, \mathcal{B}; id \rangle \rightarrow \langle A, \mathcal{B}; id \rangle^{\ell_1} \,|\, \ldots \,|\, \langle A, \mathcal{B}; id \rangle^{\ell_m}$$

Now, let assume that $\text{cl}(\ell_1, P)$ returns $H \leftarrow B_1, \ldots, B_n$. Then, rule unfold applies so that the following state is derived:

$$\langle B_1, \ldots, B_n, \mathcal{B}; \sigma \rangle \,|\, \langle A, \mathcal{B}; id \rangle^{\ell_2} \,|\, \ldots \,|\, \langle A, \mathcal{B}; id \rangle^{\ell_m}$$

Let us consider now that $B_1\sigma$ does not match any program clause, i.e., we have clauses$(B_1\sigma, P) = \emptyset$. Then, rule choice_fail applies and the following state is derived:

$$\langle \text{fail}, B_2, \ldots, B_n, \mathcal{B}; \sigma \rangle \,|\, \langle A, \mathcal{B}; id \rangle^{\ell_2} \,|\, \ldots \,|\, \langle A, \mathcal{B}; id \rangle^{\ell_m}$$

Then, rule backtrack applies so that we jump to a choice point with some pending alternative (if any). In this case, we derive the state

$$\langle A, \mathcal{B}; id \rangle^{\ell_2} \,|\, \ldots \,|\, \langle A, \mathcal{B}; id \rangle^{\ell_m}$$

so that unfolding with clause ℓ_2 is tried now, and so forth.

Here, we say that a derivation is *successful* if the last state has the form $\langle \text{true}; \theta \rangle \mid S$. We have also included a rule called next to be able to reach all solutions of an SLD tree (which has a similar effect as rule backtrack). Therefore, θ is not necessarily the first computed answer, but an arbitrary one (as long as it is reachable from the initial state after a finite number of steps).

A computation is *failed* if it ends with a state of the form $\langle \text{fail}, \mathcal{B}; \theta \rangle$, so no rule is applicable (note that rule backtrack is not applicable when there is a single query in the state).

Example 2. Consider the program of Example 1 and the same initial query: $\langle \text{p}(\text{X}, \text{Y}); id \rangle$. In order to reach the same computed answer, $\{\text{A}/\text{b}, \text{B}/\text{c}\}$, we now perform the following (deterministic) derivation:[4]

$$
\begin{aligned}
\langle \text{p}(\text{A}, \text{B}); id \rangle \;&\rightarrow_{\text{choice}} && \langle \text{p}(\text{A}, \text{B}); id \rangle^{\ell_1} \\
&\rightarrow_{\text{unfold}} && \langle \text{q}(\text{A}), \text{r}(\text{A}, \text{B}); id \rangle \\
&\rightarrow_{\text{choice}} && \langle \text{q}(\text{A}), \text{r}(\text{A}, \text{B}); id \rangle^{\ell_2} \mid \langle \text{q}(\text{A}), \text{r}(\text{A}, \text{B}); id \rangle^{\ell_3} \mid \langle \text{q}(\text{A}), \text{r}(\text{A}, \text{B}); id \rangle^{\ell_4} \\
&\rightarrow_{\text{unfold}} && \langle \text{r}(\text{A}, \text{B}); \{\text{A}/\text{a}\} \rangle \mid \langle \text{q}(\text{A}), \text{r}(\text{A}, \text{B}); id \rangle^{\ell_3} \mid \langle \text{q}(\text{A}), \text{r}(\text{A}, \text{B}); id \rangle^{\ell_4} \\
&\rightarrow_{\text{choice\_fail}} && \langle \text{fail}; \{\text{A}/\text{a}\} \rangle \mid \langle \text{q}(\text{A}), \text{r}(\text{A}, \text{B}); id \rangle^{\ell_3} \mid \langle \text{q}(\text{A}), \text{r}(\text{A}, \text{B}); id \rangle^{\ell_4} \\
&\rightarrow_{\text{backtrack}} && \langle \text{q}(\text{A}), \text{r}(\text{A}, \text{B}); id \rangle^{\ell_3} \mid \langle \text{q}(\text{A}), \text{r}(\text{A}, \text{B}); id \rangle^{\ell_4} \\
&\rightarrow_{\text{unfold}} && \langle \text{r}(\text{A}, \text{B}); \{\text{A}/\text{b}\} \rangle \mid \langle \text{q}(\text{A}), \text{r}(\text{A}, \text{B}); id \rangle^{\ell_4} \\
&\rightarrow_{\text{choice}} && \langle \text{r}(\text{A}, \text{B}); \{\text{A}/\text{b}\} \rangle^{\ell_5} \mid \langle \text{r}(\text{A}, \text{B}); \{\text{A}/\text{b}\} \rangle^{\ell_6} \mid \langle \text{q}(\text{A}), \text{r}(\text{A}, \text{B}); id \rangle^{\ell_4} \\
&\rightarrow_{\text{unfold}} && \langle \text{true}; \{\text{A}/\text{b}, \text{B}/\text{b}\} \rangle \mid \langle \text{r}(\text{A}, \text{B}); \{\text{A}/\text{b}\} \rangle^{\ell_6} \mid \langle \text{q}(\text{A}), \text{r}(\text{A}, \text{B}); id \rangle^{\ell_4} \\
&\rightarrow_{\text{next}} && \langle \text{r}(\text{A}, \text{B}); \{\text{A}/\text{b}\} \rangle^{\ell_6} \mid \langle \text{q}(\text{A}), \text{r}(\text{A}, \text{B}); id \rangle^{\ell_4} \\
&\rightarrow_{\text{unfold}} && \langle \text{true}; \{\text{A}/\text{b}, \text{B}/\text{c}\} \rangle \mid \langle \text{q}(\text{A}), \text{r}(\text{A}, \text{B}); id \rangle^{\ell_4}
\end{aligned}
$$

with computer answer $\{\text{A}/\text{b}, \text{B}/\text{c}\}$.

Clearly, the semantics in Fig. 1 is deterministic. In the following, we assume that a fixed program P is considered for stating formal properties.

Theorem 1. *Let S be a state. Then, at most one rule from the semantics in Fig. 1 is applicable.*

Proof. The proof is straightforward since the conditions of the rules do not overlap:

- If the leftmost query is not headed by true nor fail and the query is not labelled, only rule choice and choice_fail are applicable, and the conditions trivially do not overlap.
- If the leftmost query is labelled, only rule unfold is applicable.
- Finally, if the leftmost query is headed by fail (resp. true) then only rule backtrack (resp. next) is applicable.

Now, we prove that the deterministic operational semantics is sound in the sense that it explores the SLD tree of a query following Prolog's depth-first search strategy:

---

[4] For clarity, we only show the bindings for the variables in the initial query. Moreover, the steps are labelled with the applied rule.

Theorem 2. *Let $\langle \mathcal{A}; id \rangle$ be an initial state. If $\langle \mathcal{A}; id \rangle \rightarrow^* \langle \text{true}; \theta \rangle \mid S$, then $\mathcal{A} \leadsto_\theta^* \text{true}$, up to variable renaming.*

Proof. Here, we prove a more general claim. Let us consider an arbitrary query, $\langle \mathcal{A}; \sigma \rangle$ with $\langle \mathcal{A}; \sigma \rangle \rightarrow^* Q_1 \mid \ldots \mid Q_m$, where Q_i is either $\langle \mathcal{B}_i; \sigma\theta_i \rangle$ or $\langle \mathcal{B}_i; \sigma\theta_i \rangle^{\ell_i}$, $i = 1, \ldots, m$. Then, we have $\mathcal{A}\sigma \leadsto_{\theta_i}^* \mathcal{B}_i\sigma\theta_i$ for all $i = 1, \ldots, m$ such that $\mathcal{B}_i \neq (\text{fail}, \mathcal{B}')$ for some $\mathcal{B}'$, up to variable renaming. We exclude the queries with fail since failures are not made explicit in the definition of SLD resolution (this is just a device of our deterministic semantics to point out that either a backtracking step should be performed next or the derivation is failed).

We prove the claim by induction on the number n of steps in the former derivation: $\langle \mathcal{A}; \sigma \rangle \rightarrow^* Q_1 \mid \ldots \mid Q_m$. Since the base case ($n = 0$) is trivial, let us consider the inductive case ($n > 0$). Here, we assume a derivation of $n + 1$ steps from $\langle \mathcal{A}; \sigma \rangle$. By the induction hypothesis, we have $\mathcal{A}\sigma \leadsto_{\theta_i}^* \mathcal{B}_i\sigma\theta_i$ for all $i = 1, \ldots, m$ such that $\mathcal{B}_i \neq (\text{fail}, \mathcal{B}')$ for some $\mathcal{B}'$. We now distinguish several possibilities depending on the applied rule to the state $Q_1 \mid \ldots \mid Q_m$:

- If the applied rule is backtrack or next, we have

$$Q_1 \mid Q_2 \mid \ldots \mid Q_m \rightarrow Q_2 \mid \ldots \mid Q_m$$

  and the claim trivially holds by the induction hypothesis.
- If the applied rule is choice, we have

$$Q_1 \mid \ldots \mid Q_m \rightarrow Q_1^{\ell_1} \mid \ldots \mid Q_1^{\ell_k} \mid Q_2 \mid \ldots \mid Q_m$$

  for some $k > 0$, and the claim also follows trivially from the induction hypothesis.
- If the applied rule is choice_fail, the claim follows immediately by the induction hypothesis since a query of the form $(\text{fail}, \mathcal{B}')$ is not considered.
- Finally, let us consider that the applied rule is unfold. Let $Q_1 = \langle A, \mathcal{B}; \sigma\theta_1 \rangle^{\ell_1}$. Then, we have

$$\langle A, \mathcal{B}; \sigma\theta_1 \rangle^{\ell_1} \mid Q_2 \mid \ldots \mid Q_m \rightarrow \langle \mathcal{B}', \mathcal{B}; \sigma\theta_1\theta' \rangle \mid Q_2 \mid \ldots \mid Q_m$$

  if $\text{cl}(\ell_1, P) = H \leftarrow \mathcal{B}'$ and $\text{mgu}(A\sigma\theta_1, H) = \theta'$. Then, we also have an SLD resolution step of the form $(A, \mathcal{B})\sigma\theta_1 \leadsto_{\theta'} (\mathcal{B}', \mathcal{B})\sigma\theta_1\theta'$ using the same clause[5] and computing the same mgu and, thus, the claim follows from the induction hypothesis.

Note that the deterministic semantics is sound but *incomplete* in general since it implements a depth-first search strategy.

---

[5] For simplicity, we assume that the same renamed clauses are considered in both derivations.

(backtrack) $$\frac{}{\langle \mathsf{fail}, \mathcal{B}; \theta \rangle \,|\, \langle A, \mathcal{B}'; \theta' \rangle \,|\, S \bullet \Pi \;\rightharpoonup\; \langle A, \mathcal{B}'; \theta' \rangle \,|\, S \bullet \mathsf{bck}(\mathcal{B}, \theta) : \Pi_{\mathsf{redo}(A\theta')}}$$

(next) $$\frac{S \neq \epsilon}{\langle \mathsf{true}; \theta \rangle \,|\, S \bullet \Pi_{\mathsf{answer}(\theta)} \;\rightharpoonup\; S \bullet \mathsf{next}(\theta) : \Pi}$$

(choice) $$\frac{A \neq \mathsf{true} \wedge A \neq \mathsf{fail} \wedge A \neq \mathsf{ret}(A') \wedge \mathsf{clauses}(A\theta, P) = \{\ell_1, \dots, \ell_m\} \wedge m > 0}{\langle A, \mathcal{B}; \theta \rangle \,|\, S \bullet \Pi_{\mathsf{call}(A\theta)} \;\rightharpoonup\; \langle A, \mathcal{B}; \theta \rangle^{\ell_1} \,|\, \dots \,|\, \langle A, \mathcal{B}; \theta \rangle^{\ell_m} \,|\, S \bullet \mathsf{ch}(m) : \Pi}$$

(choice_fail) $$\frac{A \neq \mathsf{true} \wedge A \neq \mathsf{fail} \wedge A \neq \mathsf{ret}(A') \wedge \mathsf{clauses}(A\theta, P) = \emptyset}{\langle A, \mathcal{B}; \theta \rangle \,|\, S \bullet \Pi_{\mathsf{call}(A\theta)} \;\rightharpoonup\; \langle \mathsf{fail}, \mathcal{B}; \theta \rangle \,|\, S \bullet \mathsf{fail}(A) : \Pi_{\mathsf{fail}(A\theta)}}$$

(unfold) $$\frac{A \neq \mathsf{ret}(A') \wedge \mathsf{cl}(\ell, P) = H \leftarrow B_1, \dots, B_n \wedge \mathsf{mgu}(A\theta, H) = \sigma}{\langle A, \mathcal{B}; \theta \rangle^{\ell} \,|\, S \bullet \Pi \;\rightharpoonup\; \langle B_1, \dots, B_n, \mathsf{ret}(A), \mathcal{B}; \theta\sigma \rangle \,|\, S \bullet \mathsf{unf}(A, \theta, \ell) : \Pi}$$

(exit) $$\frac{}{\langle \mathsf{ret}(A), \mathcal{B}; \theta \rangle \,|\, S \bullet \Pi_{\mathsf{exit}(A\theta)} \;\rightharpoonup\; \langle \mathcal{B}; \theta \rangle \,|\, S \bullet \mathsf{exit}(A) : \Pi}$$

Fig. 2. Forward reversible semantics

3.2 A Reversible Semantics

Now, we extend the deterministic operational semantics of Fig. 1 in order to make it reversible. Our reversible semantics is defined on *configurations*:

Definition 2 (configuration). *A configuration is defined as a pair* $S \bullet \Pi$ *where* S *is a state (as defined in Definition 1) and* Π *is a list representing the history of the configuration. Here, we consider the following history events:*

- $\mathsf{ch}(n)$: *denotes a choice step with* n *branches;*
- $\mathsf{unf}(A, \theta, \ell)$: *represents an unfolding step where the selected atom is* A, *the answer computed so far is* θ, *and the selected clause is labelled with* ℓ;
- $\mathsf{fail}(A)$: *is associated to rule* choice_fail *and denotes that the selected atom* A *matches no rule;*
- $\mathsf{exit}(A)$: *denotes that the execution of atom* A *has been completed (see below);*
- $\mathsf{bck}(\mathcal{B}, \theta)$: *represents a backtracking step, where* $\langle \mathsf{fail}, \mathcal{B}; \theta \rangle$ *is the query that failed;*
- $\mathsf{next}(\theta)$: *denotes an application of rule* next *after an answer* θ *is obtained.*

We use Haskell's notation for lists and denote by $s : \Pi$ *a history with first element* s *and tail* Π; *an empty history is denoted by* $[\,]$.

The reversible (forward) semantics is shown in Fig. 2.[6] The rules of the reversible semantics are basically self-explanatory. They are essentially the same as in the standard deterministic semantics of Fig. 1 except for the following differences:

- First, configurations now keep a *history* with enough information for undoing the steps of a computation.

---

[6] The subscripts of some configurations: call, exit, fail, redo, and answer, can be ignored for now. They will become useful in the next section.

– And, secondly, unfolding an atom A now adds a new call of the form $\mathsf{ret}(A)$ after the atoms of the body (if any) of the considered program clause. This is then used in rule exit in order to determine when the call has been completed successfully ($\mathsf{ret}(A)$ marks the exit of a program clause). This extension is not introduced for reversibility, but it is part of the design of our reversible debugger (see Sect. 4, where the reversible debugger rever is presented). Here, and in the following, we assume that programs contain no predicate named $\mathsf{ret}/1$.

We note that extending our developments to SLD resolution with an arbitrary computation rule (i.e., different from Prolog's rule, which always selects the leftmost atom) is not difficult. Basically, one would only need to extend the unf elements as follows: $\mathsf{unf}(A, \theta, i, \ell)$, where i is the position of the selected atom in the current query.

Example 3. Consider again the program of Example 1 and the initial query: $\langle \mathsf{p}(\mathsf{X}, \mathsf{Y}); id \rangle \bullet [\,]$. In order to reach the first computed answer, $\{\mathsf{A}/\mathsf{b}, \mathsf{B}/\mathsf{b}\}$, we perform the derivation shown in Fig. 3.

It is worthwhile to observe that the drawbacks of [13] mentioned before are now overcome by using substitutions with the answer computed so far, together with a deterministic semantics where backtracking is dealt with explicitly.

Trivially, the instrumented semantics of Fig. 2 is a conservative extension of the deterministic semantics of Fig. 1 since the rules impose no additional condition. The only difference is the addition of atoms $\mathsf{ret}(A)$ that mark the exit of a program clause. In the following, given two states, S, S', we let $S \sim S'$ if they are equal after removing all atoms of the form $\mathsf{ret}(A)$.

Theorem 3. *Let Q be an initial state. Then, $Q \rightarrow^* S$ iff $Q \bullet [\,] \rightharpoonup^* S' \bullet \Pi$ such that $S \sim S'$ for some history Π, up to variable renaming.*

Let us now consider backward steps. Here, our goal is to be able to explore a given derivation backwards. For this purpose, we introduce a backward operational semantics that is essentially obtained by switching the configurations in each rule of the forward semantics, and removing all unnecessary premises. The resulting backward semantics is shown in Fig. 4. Let us just add that, in rule $\underline{\mathsf{unfold}}$, we use the auxiliary function $\mathsf{body}(\ell, P)$ to denote the body of clause labelled with ℓ in program P, and, thus, $|\mathsf{body}(\ell, P)|$ represents the number of atoms in the body of this clause.[7] This information was stored explicitly in our previous approach [13].

Example 4. If we consider the configurations of Fig. 3 from bottom to top, they constitute a backward derivation using the rules of Fig. 4.

The following result states the reversibility of our semantics:

---

[7] As is common, $|S|$ denotes the cardinality of the set or sequence S.

$\langle p(A, B); id \rangle \bullet [\,]$

$\rightharpoonup_{choice} \langle p(A, B); id \rangle^{\ell_1} \bullet [ch(1)]$

$\rightharpoonup_{unfold} \langle q(A), r(A, B), ret(p(A, B)); id \rangle \bullet [unf(p(A, B), id, \ell_1), ch(1)]$

$\rightharpoonup_{choice} \langle q(A), r(A, B), ret(p(A, B)); id \rangle^{\ell_2} \,|\, \langle q(A), r(A, B), ret(p(A, B)); id \rangle^{\ell_3}$
$\qquad |\, \langle q(A), r(A, B), ret(p(A, B)); id \rangle^{\ell_4} \bullet [ch(3), unf(p(A, B), id, \ell_1), ch(1)]$

$\rightharpoonup_{unfold} \langle ret(q(A)), r(A, B), ret(p(A, B)); \{A/a\} \rangle \,|\, \langle q(A), r(A, B), ret(p(A, B)); id \rangle^{\ell_3}$
$\qquad |\, \langle q(A), r(A, B), ret(p(A, B)); id \rangle^{\ell_4}$
$\qquad \bullet [unf(q(A), id, \ell_2), ch(3), unf(p(A, B), id, \ell_1), ch(1)]$

$\rightharpoonup_{exit} \langle r(A, B), ret(p(A, B)); \{A/a\} \rangle \,|\, \langle q(A), r(A, B), ret(p(A, B)); id \rangle^{\ell_3}$
$\qquad |\, \langle q(A), r(A, B), ret(p(A, B)); id \rangle^{\ell_4}$
$\qquad \bullet [exit(q(A)), unf(q(A), id, \ell_2), ch(3), unf(p(A, B), id, \ell_1), ch(1)]$

$\rightharpoonup_{choice\_fail} \langle fail, ret(p(A, B)); \{A/a\} \rangle \,|\, \langle q(A), r(A, B), ret(p(A, B)); id \rangle^{\ell_3}$
$\qquad |\, \langle q(A), r(A, B), ret(p(A, B)); id \rangle^{\ell_4}$
$\qquad \bullet [fail(r(A, B)), exit(q(A)), unf(q(A), id, \ell_2), ch(3), unf(p(A, B), id, \ell_1), ch(1)]$

$\rightharpoonup_{backtrack} \langle q(A), r(A, B), ret(p(A, B)); id \rangle^{\ell_3} \,|\, \langle q(A), r(A, B), ret(p(A, B)); id \rangle^{\ell_4}$
$\qquad \bullet [bck(ret(p(A, B)), \{A/a\}), fail(r(A, B)), exit(q(A)), unf(q(A), id, \ell_2), ch(3),$
$\qquad unf(p(A, B), id, \ell_1), ch(1)]$

$\rightharpoonup_{unfold} \langle ret(q(A)), r(A, B), ret(p(A, B)); \{A/b\} \rangle \,|\, \langle q(A), r(A, B), ret(p(A, B)); id \rangle^{\ell_4}$
$\qquad \bullet [unf(q(A), id, \ell_3), bck(ret(p(A, B)), \{A/a\}), fail(r(A, B)), exit(q(A)),$
$\qquad unf(q(A), id, \ell_2), ch(3), unf(p(A, B), id, \ell_1), ch(1)]$

$\rightharpoonup_{exit} \langle r(A, B), ret(p(A, B)); \{A/b\} \rangle \,|\, \langle q(A), r(A, B), ret(p(A, B)); id \rangle^{\ell_4}$
$\qquad \bullet [exit(q(A)), unf(q(A), id, \ell_3), bck(ret(p(A, B)), \{A/a\}), fail(r(A, B)), exit(q(A)),$
$\qquad unf(q(A), id, \ell_2), ch(3), unf(p(A, B), id, \ell_1), ch(1)]$

$\rightharpoonup_{choice} \langle r(A, B), ret(p(A, B)); \{A/b\} \rangle^{\ell_5} \,|\, \langle r(A, B), ret(p(A, B)); \{A/b\} \rangle^{\ell_6}$
$\qquad |\, \langle q(A), r(A, B), ret(p(A, B)); id \rangle^{\ell_4}$
$\qquad \bullet [ch(2), exit(q(A)), unf(q(A), id, \ell_3), bck(ret(p(A, B)), \{A/a\}), fail(r(A, B)),$
$\qquad exit(q(A)), unf(q(A), id, \ell_2), ch(3), unf(p(A, B), id, \ell_1), ch(1)]$

$\rightharpoonup_{unfold} \langle ret(r(A, B)), ret(p(A, B)); \{A/b, B/b\} \rangle \,|\, \langle r(A, B), ret(p(A, B)); \{A/b\} \rangle^{\ell_6}$
$\qquad |\, \langle q(A), r(A, B), ret(p(A, B)); id \rangle^{\ell_4}$
$\qquad \bullet [unf(r(A, B), \{A/b\}, \ell_5), ch(2), exit(q(A)), unf(q(A), id, \ell_3),$
$\qquad bck(ret(p(A, B)), \{A/a\}), fail(r(A, B)), exit(q(A)), unf(q(A), id, \ell_2), ch(3),$
$\qquad unf(p(A, B), id, \ell_1), ch(1)]$

$\rightharpoonup_{exit} \langle ret(p(A, B)); \{A/b, B/b\} \rangle \,|\, \langle r(A, B), ret(p(A, B)); \{A/b\} \rangle^{\ell_6}$
$\qquad |\, \langle q(A), r(A, B), ret(p(A, B)); id \rangle^{\ell_4}$
$\qquad \bullet [exit(r(A, B)), unf(r(A, B), \{A/b\}, \ell_5), ch(2), exit(q(A)), unf(q(A), id, \ell_3),$
$\qquad bck(ret(p(A, B)), \{A/a\}), fail(r(A, B)), exit(q(A)), unf(q(A), id, \ell_2), ch(3),$
$\qquad unf(p(A, B), id, \ell_1), ch(1)]$

$\rightharpoonup_{exit} \langle true; \{A/b, B/b\} \rangle \,|\, \langle r(A, B), ret(p(A, B)); \{A/b\} \rangle^{\ell_6} \,|\, \langle q(A), r(A, B), ret(p(A, B)); id \rangle^{\ell_4}$
$\qquad \bullet [exit(p(A, B)), exit(r(A, B)), unf(r(A, B), \{A/b\}, \ell_5), ch(2), exit(q(A)),$
$\qquad unf(q(A), id, \ell_3), bck(ret(p(A, B)), \{A/a\}), fail(r(A, B)), exit(q(A)),$
$\qquad unf(q(A), id, \ell_2), ch(3), unf(p(A, B), id, \ell_1), ch(1)]$

Fig. 3. Example derivation with the reversible (forward) semantics.

(backtrack) $S \bullet \mathsf{bck}(\mathcal{B}, \theta) : \Pi \;\leftharpoonup\; \langle \mathsf{fail}, \mathcal{B}; \theta \rangle \,|\, S \bullet \Pi$

(next) $S \bullet \mathsf{next}(\theta) : \Pi \;\leftharpoonup\; \langle \mathsf{true}; \theta \rangle \,|\, S \bullet \Pi$

(choice) $\langle A, \mathcal{B}; \theta \rangle^{\ell_1} \,|\, \ldots \,|\, \langle A, \mathcal{B}; \theta \rangle^{\ell_m} \,|\, S \bullet \mathsf{ch}(m) : \Pi \;\leftharpoonup\; \langle A, \mathcal{B}; \theta \rangle \,|\, S \bullet \Pi$

(choice_fail) $\langle \mathsf{fail}, \mathcal{B}; \theta \rangle \,|\, S \bullet \mathsf{fail}(A) : \Pi \;\leftharpoonup\; \langle A, \mathcal{B}; \theta \rangle \,|\, S \bullet \Pi$

(unfold) $\langle B_1, \ldots, B_n, \mathsf{ret}(A), \mathcal{B}; \theta\sigma \rangle \,|\, S \bullet \mathsf{unf}(A, \theta, \ell) : \Pi \;\leftharpoonup\; \langle A, \mathcal{B}; \theta \rangle^{\ell} \,|\, S \bullet \Pi$
where $|\mathsf{body}(\ell, P)| = n$

(exit) $\langle \mathcal{B}; \theta \rangle \,|\, S \bullet \mathsf{exit}(A) : \Pi \;\leftharpoonup\; \langle \mathsf{ret}(A), \mathcal{B}; \theta \rangle \,|\, S \bullet \Pi$

Fig. 4. Backward reversible semantics

Lemma 1. *Let $\mathcal{C}, \mathcal{C}'$ be configurations. If $\mathcal{C} \rightharpoonup \mathcal{C}'$, then $\mathcal{C}' \leftharpoonup \mathcal{C}$, up to variable renaming.*

Proof. The claim follows by a simple case distinction on the applied rule and the fact that the backward semantics of Fig. 4 is trivially deterministic since each rule requires a different element on the top of the history.

In principle, one could also prove the opposite direction, i.e., that $\mathcal{C}' \leftharpoonup \mathcal{C}$ implies $\mathcal{C} \rightharpoonup \mathcal{C}'$, by requiring that $\mathcal{C}'$ is not an arbitrary configuration but a "legal" one, i.e., a configuration that is reachable by a forward derivation starting from some initial configuration.

The above result could be straightforwardly extended to derivations as follows:

Theorem 4. *Let $\mathcal{C}, \mathcal{C}'$ be configurations. If $\mathcal{C} \rightharpoonup^* \mathcal{C}'$, then $\mathcal{C}' \leftharpoonup^* \mathcal{C}$, up to variable renaming.*

4 A Reversible Debugger for Prolog

In this section, we present the design of a reversible debugger for Prolog. It is based on the standard 4-port tracer introduced by Byrd [2,3]. The ports are call (an atom is called), exit (a call is successfully completed), redo (backtracking requires trying again some call), and fail (an atom matches no clause). In contrast to standard debuggers that can only explore a computation forward, our reversible debugger allows us to move back and forth.

The implemented debugger, rever, is publicly available from https://github. com/mistupv/rever. It can be used in two modes:

- *Debug mode.* In this case, execution proceeds silently (no information is shown) until the execution of a special predicate rtrace/0 is reached (if any). The user can include a call to this predicate in the source program in order to start tracing the computation (i.e., it behaves as trace/0 in most Prolog

```
Call: p(A,B)                ^Exit: p(b,b)
Call: q(A)                  ^Exit: r(b,b)
Exit: q(a)                  ^Call: r(b,B)
Call: r(a,B)                ^Exit: q(b)
Fail: r(a,B)                ^Redo: q(A)
Redo: q(A)                  ^Fail: r(a,B)
Exit: q(b)                  ^Call: r(a,B)
Call: r(b,B)                ^Exit: q(a)
Exit: r(b,b)                ^Call: q(A)
Exit: p(b,b)                ^Call: p(A,B)
**Answer:  A = b, B = b
```

           (a)   (b)

Fig. 5. Trace Example with rever

systems). Tracing also starts if an *exception* is produced during the evaluation of a query. This mode is invoked with a call of the form rdebug(query), where query is the initial query whose execution we want to explore.

– *Trace mode.* In this mode, port information is shown from the beginning. One can invoke the trace mode with rtrace(query). Note that it is equivalent to calling rdebug((rtrace, query)).

Our reversible debugger essentially implements the transition rules in Figs. 2 and 4. As the reader may have noticed, some configurations in Fig. 2 are labeled with a subscript: it denotes the output of a given port. Moreover, there is an additional label in rule next which denotes that, at this point, an answer must be shown to the user.

In tracing mode, every time that a configuration with a subscript is reached, the execution stops, shows the corresponding port information, and waits for the user to press some key. We basically consider the following keys: ↓ (or Enter) proceeds with the next (forward) step; ↑ performs a backward step; s (for skip) shows the port information without waiting for any user interaction; t enters the tracing mode; q quits the debugging session.

For instance, given the initial call rtrace(p(A, B)), and according to the forward derivation shown in Fig. 3, our debugger displays the sequence shown in Fig. 5 (a). Now, if one presses "↑" repeatedly, the sequence displayed in Fig. 5 (b) is shown. Note that ports are prefixed by the symbol "^" in backward derivations. Of course, the user can move freely back and forth.

Reversible debugging might be especially useful when we have an execution that produces some exception at the end. With our tool, one can easily inspect the execution backwards from the final state that produced the error.

Let us mention that, in order to avoid the use of a ground representation and having to implement all basic operations (mgu, substitution application and composition, etc.), substitutions are represented in its equational form. E.g., substitution {A/a, B/b} is represented by A = a, B = b. This equational representation of a mgu can be easily obtained by using the predefined predicate unify/3. This representation is much more efficient than storing pairs of atoms (as in [13]), that must be unified once and again at each execution step.

Finally, let us mention that, despite the simplicity of the implemented system (some 500 lines of code in SWI Prolog), our debugger is able to deal with medium-sized programs (e.g., it has been used to debug the debugger itself).

5   Related Work

The closest approach is clearly the preliminary version of this work in [13]. There are, however, several significant differences: [13] presents a reversible version of the usual, nondeterministic SLD resolution. Therefore, backtracking steps cannot be undone. This is improved in this paper by considering a deterministic semantics that models the traversal of the complete SLD tree. Moreover, [13] considers a simple but very inefficient representation for the history, which is greatly improved in this paper. Finally, we provide proofs of some formal properties for our reversible semantics, as well as a publicly available implementation of the debugger, the system rever.

Another close approach we are aware of is that of Opium [4], which introduces a trace query language for inspecting and analyzing trace histories. In this tool, the trace history of the considered execution is stored in a database, which is then used for trace querying. Several analysis can then be defined in Prolog itself by using a set of given primitives to explore the trace elements. In contrast to our approach, Opium is basically a so-called "post-mortem" debugger that allows one to analyze the trace of an execution. Therefore, the goal is different from that of this paper.

6   Concluding Remarks and Future Work

We have proposed a novel reversible debugging scheme for logic programs by defining an appropriate Landauer embedding for a deterministic operational semantics. Essentially, the states of the semantics are extended with a *history* that keeps track of all the information which is needed to be able to undo the steps of a computation. We have proved a number of formal properties for our reversible semantics. Moreover, the ideas have been put into practice in the reversible debugger rever, which is publicly available from https://github. com/mistupv/rever. Our preliminary experiments with the debugger have shown promising results.

As for future work, we are currently working on extending the debugger in order to cope with negation and the cut. Also, we plan to define a more compact representation for the history, so that it can scale up better to larger programs and derivations.

Acknowledgements. The author gratefully acknowledges the editors, John Gallagher, Roberto Giacobazzi and Pedro López-García, for the opportunity to contribute to this volume, dedicated to Manuel Hermenegildo on the occasion of his 60th birthday.

References

1. Apt, K.R.: From Logic Programming to Prolog. Prentice Hall, London (1997)
2. Byrd, L.: Understanding the control flow of prolog programs. In: Tarnlund, S.A. (ed.) Proceedings of the 1980 Logic Programming Workshop, pp. 127–138 (1980)
3. Clocksin, W.F., Mellish, C.S.: Programming in PROLOG, 4th edn. Springer, Cham (1994)
4. Ducassé, M.: Opium: an extendable trace analyzer for prolog. J. Log. Program. **39**(1–3), 177–223 (1999). https://doi.org/10.1016/S0743-1066(98)10036-5
5. Landauer, R.: Irreversibility and heat generation in the computing process. IBM J. Res. Develop. **5**, 183–191 (1961)
6. Lanese, I., Palacios, A., Vidal, G.: Causal-consistent replay debugging for message passing programs. In: Pérez, J.A., Yoshida, N. (eds.) FORTE 2019. LNCS, vol. 11535, pp. 167–184. Springer, Cham (2019). https://doi.org/10.1007/978-3-030-21759-4_10
7. Lloyd, J.W.: Foundations of Logic Programming, 2nd Edition. Springer, Cham (1987). https://doi.org/10.1007/978-3-642-83189-8
8. Mesnard, F., Payet, É., Vidal, G.: Concolic testing in logic programming. Theory Pract. Log. Program. **15**(4–5), 711–725 (2015). https://doi.org/10.1017/S1471068415000332
9. O'Callahan, R., Jones, C., Froyd, N., Huey, K., Noll, A., Partush, N.: Engineering record and replay for deployability: Extended technical report. CoRR abs/1705.05937 (2017). http://arxiv.org/abs/1705.05937
10. Ströder, T., Emmes, F., Schneider-Kamp, P., Giesl, J., Fuhs, C.: A linear operational semantics for termination and complexity analysis of ISO Prolog. In: Vidal, G. (ed.) LOPSTR 2011. LNCS, vol. 7225, pp. 237–252. Springer, Heidelberg (2012). https://doi.org/10.1007/978-3-642-32211-2_16
11. Stulova, N., Morales, J.F., Hermenegildo, M.V.: Assertion-based debugging of higher-order (C)LP programs. In: Chitil, O., King, A., Danvy, O. (eds.) Proceedings of the 16th International Symposium on Principles and Practice of Declarative Programming (PPDP 2014), pp. 225–235. ACM (2014). https://doi.org/10.1145/2643135.2643148
12. Undo Software: Increasing software development productivity with reversible debugging (2014). https://undo.io/media/uploads/files/Undo_ReversibleDebugging_Whitepaper.pdf
13. Vidal, G.: Reversible computations in logic programming. In: Lanese, I., Rawski, M. (eds.) RC 2020. LNCS, vol. 12227, pp. 246–254. Springer, Cham (2020). https://doi.org/10.1007/978-3-030-52482-1_15

Towards Systematically Engineering Autonomous Systems Using Reinforcement Learning and Planning

Martin Wirsing[1(✉)] and Lenz Belzner[2]

[1] Ludwig-Maximilians-Universität München, Munich, Germany
wirsing@lmu.de
[2] Technische Hochschule Ingolstadt, Ingolstadt, Germany
lenz.belzner@thi.de

Abstract. Autonomous systems need to be able dynamically adapt to changing requirements and environmental conditions without redeployment and without interruption of the systems functionality. The EU project ASCENS has developed a comprehensive suite of foundational theories and methods for building autonomic systems. In this paper we specialise the EDLC process model of ASCENS to deal with planning and reinforcement learning techniques. We present the "AIDL" life cycle and illustrate it with two case studies: simulation-based online planning and the PSyCo reinforcement learning approach for synthesizing agent policies from hard and soft requirements. Related work and potential avenues for future research are discussed.

1 Introduction

An autonomous system is able to adapt at runtime to uncertain and dynamically changing environments and to new requirements. Autonomous systems can be single autonomous entities or collective ones that consist of several collaborating entities. Classical examples are intelligent agents [67], and autonomic systems [26], more recent are ensembles [28,64], and collective adaptive systems [33].

Reinforcement learning [53] and online planning are methods for automatically computing sequential controllers - so-called policies - of autonomous systems. Given an uncertain probabilistic environment, reinforcement learning is about learning from interactions with the environment. It is an interactive process with the goal to learn a policy that maximises the sum of future rewards. Planning requires a (simulation) model and is a "computational process that takes a model as input and produces or improves a policy for interacting with the modelled environment".

Systematic engineering approaches for intelligent agents and multi-agent systems such as Gaia [68], Tropos [14] support a sequential development process

---

Dedicated to Manuel Hermenegildo.

© Springer Nature Switzerland AG 2023
P. Lopez-Garcia et al. (Eds.): Hermenegildo Festschrift 2022, LNCS 13160, pp. 281–306, 2023.
https://doi.org/10.1007/978-3-031-31476-6_16

or focus on software architecture such as IBM's MAPE-K architecture [30] for autonomic systems.

The modern industrial agile development approaches MLOps [3] and AIOps [2] aim at machine learning methods for big data applications and IT operations. [22] proposes an engineering process exhibiting the central activities necessary for the successful application of machine learning.

The EU project ASCENS [1, 65] has developed a comprehensive suite of foundational theories and methods for building autonomic systems. The ASCENS methods cover system specification and development as well as monitoring and dynamic system adaptation. Also machine-learning approaches have been studied in ASCENS but they were not systematically related to the software development life cycle. In particular, the ASCENS project has proposed the Ensemble Development Life Cycle EDLC [27] for engineering adaptive and autonomous systems. The EDLC is an agile process covering the whole software life cycle including development and runtime phases and provides mechanisms for enabling system changes at runtime.

In this paper we review the EDLC life cycle and specialise it to the construction of autonomous policies using planning and reinforcement learning techniques. We call this life cycle "AIDL" and illustrate it with two existing case studies: simulation-based online planning for autonomously adapting the behaviour of a robot [10] and the PSyCo reinforcement learning approach for synthesizing agent policies from hard and soft requirements [12]. Related work and future directions for research are discussed.

Personal Note. Martin has known Manuel for almost 20 years when they met and contributed to initiatives of the Future Emerging Technologies section of the European Commission, e.g. in 2005 at the "Beyond-the-Horizon" Workshop on Anticipating Future and Emerging Information Society.

In 2007 Manuel invited Martin to become a member of the Scientific Board of IMDEA Software and later in 2011, to be a guest researcher at IMDEA Software for three months. In this way, Martin had the chance in participating in the extraordinary raise of IMDEA Software to one of Europe's leading research institutes. Cooperating and discussing with Manuel is a very pleasant experience. He is not only an outstanding scientist and an excellent coordinator of scientific work; he is also a warm-hearted and kind friend and colleague. We are looking forward to many further inspiring exchanges with him.

Outline. In Sect. 2 we shortly review reinforcement learning, planning, and the EDLC life cycle. In Sect. 3 we present the AIDL Life Cycle. Section 4 illustrates AIDL by two case studies. Finally, Section 5 presents related work and Section 6 concludes the paper.

2 Preliminaries: Reinforcement Learning, Planning, and the Life Cycle EDLC

2.1 Reinforcement Learning and Planning

Reinforcement learning and (online-) planning are well-suited methods for computing optimising goals in a probabilistic domain. The standard case is that the domain is given by a Markov decision process (MDP) (for a formal definition see Appendix A) and the goal is to compute a policy which maximises an expected reward.

Model-Free and Model-Based Reinforcement Learning. Reinforcement learning is an interactive process between an agent and the environment. The goal is to learn a policy for maximising the discounted cumulative return the agent receives over time (for definitions see Appendix A). In each step the agent makes an action and receives an immediate reward. Typically, positive values express good actions, negative values express bad actions.

There is a rich family of reinforcement learning algorithms. For small or middle size state and action spaces classical algorithms such as value iteration, policy iteration, and temporal difference learning are widely used. If the state space is large one can only hope to find approximate solutions and thus uses so-called function approximation methods such as gradient-descent over artificial neural networks (see e.g. [53,54]).

The latter algorithms are model-free in that they do not have any knowledge of the domain and thus start from an arbitrary distribution. Model-based algorithms have access to or learn a (probabilistic) digital twin[1] of the environment which predicts state transitions and rewards. This allows the algorithm to plan its next steps based on a range of possible choices. In many cases this considerably improves the learning efficiency; however, if the model does not faithfully match the reality the algorithm may behave badly in the real environment.

Some modern algorithms combine model-free with model-based learning. E.g. AlphaGo combines a model-free reinforcement learning algorithm with (model-based) Monte Carlo tree search; it was the first program to win the game Go against a human champion [51]. Reinforcement learning algorithms are also combined with evolutionary methods in order to improve stability and quality of the results [20].

[54] gives an overview on classical reinforcement learning algorithms (until 2010). For a taxonomy of reinforcement learning algorithms see [4], an excellent survey on model-based reinforcement learning is given in [40].

Safe Learning. In the algorithms above, learning is used for optimizing the system behavior but not for guaranteeing the safety of the system. But in many applications, the system requirements comprise different kinds of goals including achieve goals that optimize behaviours, and maintain goals that restrict the space of feasible solutions.

---

[1] also called internal model or simulation model in the literature.

There are three broad classes for dealing with such situations: shielding [6], safe exploration [24], and reward-shaping methods [12,47]. Shielding ensures at runtime that the chosen action is safe whereas in safe exploration, the learning process is restricted to learn only safe actions. Reward-shaping methods are based on Constrained Markov Decision Processes (CMDP) [7] (see also Appendix A) and try to balance optimization of return and costs incurred by constraint violation. E.g. [12] uses a Lagrangian for transforming the costs of the safety constraints and the rewards into a single optimizing problem. The safety of the solution is ensured by runtime Bayesian model checking.

Non-stationary Environments. In non-stationary environments the probability transition function and/or the reward change over time. Main approaches are transfer learning, and meta-learning (see e.g. [40]).

Transfer learning [55,59] explores the idea that experience gained in learning to perform one task can help improve learning performance in a related, but different, task. Meta-learning [56] is concerned with accumulating experience on the performance of multiple applications of a learning system. Typically, an adaptation space is given by a distribution of environments and a shared common structure that can be exploited for fast learning. For fast online adaptation in dynamic environments, [18] uses an distribution of MDPs whereas [42] meta-trains a global model.

Planning. Planning is a large and longtime established field. In "classical" offline-planning algorithms the policy is constructed for the entire state space before the system is interacting with the environment. This is only feasible for small and mid-size problems. Instead, an online algorithm is computing a near-optimal action for the current state. When interacting with the environment an online-algorithm encounters only a small subset of the entire state space and has to tune its decisions only for a single time step.

The key idea of online planning is to perform planning and execution of an action iteratively at runtime. At each planning step, the agent performs forward search on a digital twin, e.g. by Monte Carlo Tree Search [15,34] (in discrete domain) or by Cross Entropy Open Loop Planning [62] (in continuous state and action spaces). Online planning is suitable for MDPs as well as for partially observable MDPs (POMDPs) (see formal def. in Appendix A). A survey of classical online POMDP methods is given in [49]. For the trade-off between online planning and model-based reinforcement learning see [41].

2.2   The Ensemble Development Life Cycle EDLC

The "Ensemble Development Life Cycle" EDLC [27] is an agile software process model that explicitly deals with autonomous systems, in particular with ensembles and collective adaptive systems. EDLC has been used in the development of several autonomic systems such as swarm robots [44,66], peer-to-peer cloud [38], and e-mobility applications [17,25]. The construction of autonomous systems using EDLC is supported by eight engineering principles [11]. System construction according to EDLC emphasises mathematically well-founded approaches to validate and verify the properties of the collective autonomic system and enable the prediction of the behaviour of such complex software.

The EDLC life cycle is arranged in three cycles (see Fig. 1). In the development cycle Dev (called "design time cycle" in [27]) the classical development phases - requirements engineering, modelling and programming, verification and validation - are iterated; in the operations cycle Ops (called "runtime cycle" in [27]), the entities of the ensemble iterate a "runtime feedback control loop" comprising the monitoring, awareness, and (self-) adaptation mechanisms. They consist of observing the running system and the environment, reasoning on such observations and using the results of the analysis for adapting the system and providing feedback data that can be used in the development activities for improving the system. The connection between the two cycles is established by a third evolutionary cycle consisting of system deployment or hot update to the operations and providing feedback data from runtime to the development cycle.

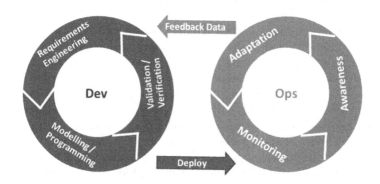

Fig. 1. Ensemble Development Life Cycle EDLC.

Development Cycle Dev. The phases of the Dev cycle rely on mathematically well-founded approaches that support the correct construction and the analysis of autonomic systems.

Requirements. EDLC supports two goal-oriented methods - SOTA [5] and ARE [58] - for elicitating and specifying the requirements. In both cases the final requirements specification consists of a model of the domain together with hard goals that the system has to satisfy and soft goals that describe behaviours that should be optimised.

The notion of adaptation domain [29,66] describes the "borders of validity" of an autonomous system. The adaptation domain determines the variety of different environments, goals, and adverse system states the system should be able to tolerate and in which it should be able to continue working "correctly." In some cases the adaptation space is complemented by so-called "resilience goals" which determine those environments and system states outside the adaptation space the system should be able to recover from and return back into the adaptation space.

Modelling and Programming. For this task, the EDLC relies on well-known methods for modelling and implementing adaptation and autonomy. This ranges from a method for stepwise refinement and the development of high-level modelling languages (such as SCEL [19]) to classical adaptation techniques (such as programming using modes and dynamic reconfiguration) as well as AI adaptation techniques (such as swarm algorithms as well as planning, learning, and reasoning).

A main ingredient are pattern catalogues [21,45,63] to help developers to make appropriate design choices for models and implementations. For example, architectural patterns such as "knowledge-equipped component" describe the architecture of a system or a component, and adaptation patterns such as "centralised autonomic manager" are concerned with adaptation mechanisms [27,45].

Validation and Verification. Analysis techniques for adaptive and autonomous systems have to cover the "normal" system behaviour as well as essential aspects such as adaptive behaviour and changing environments. This comprises qualitative methods ensuring that the system behaves without any flaw, and quantitative analyses that target non-functional properties and evaluate expected performances according to predefined metrics.

Qualitative methods range from reviews and testing to the automated verification of invariants and security properties. Quantitative methods are well-suited for performance analysis and studying the behaviour of a system in different environments and under changing requirements (for a comprehensive collection of papers see [13]). Main techniques are statistical modelchecking (see e.g. [36]), simulation tools (see e.g. [37]) and the analysis of Markov chains using differential equations (see e.g. [57,66]).

Operations Cycle Ops. In the operations cycle, the entities of the autonomic system iterate a "runtime feedback control loop" consisting of monitoring, awareness, and self-adaptation activities.

Montoring. The task of monitoring is to collect data at runtime for providing information about the environment (e.g. by the collecting sensor data) and the functional and non-functional properties of the system (e.g. by instrumenting the code and collecting runtime data). The monitoring information is passed to the awareness mechanism and may also give feedback to developers about the state of the system and the environment.

Awareness. Conventional systems can react directly to the data obtained by the monitor but autonomous systems often need a deeper analysis. The awareness mechanism uses reasoning, planning and learning methods to determine the current situation of the system and to prepare the subsequent system behaviour.

Self-adaptation. The adaptation mechanism implements the results of the awareness deliberations. In case of weak adaptation some control parameters of the system are modified or new functions are added or existing functions are modified. Strong adaptation means to modify the architecture of the system.

Deployment and Feedback Data. The evolutionary loop connects the development cycle and the operations cycle. During deployment the system is prepared it for its execution. This involves installing, configuring and launching the application. The deployment may also involve executable code generation and compilation/linking.

The feedback data are collected by monitoring and in the awareness process. They may trigger a new Dev cycle and are used to provide information for system redesign, validation, verification, and redeployment.

3   The AIDL Life Cycle for Autonomous Systems

The AIDL life cycle specialises EDLC to techniques for systematically constructing autonomous policies that are based on reinforcement learning and planning techniques. We focus here on the specific issues of learning and planning. For simplicity, we restrict ourselves in this paper to systems with a single agent in an uncertain and possibly changing environment which may be noisy but is fully observable.

In AIDL, the modelling and programming phase of EDLC is extended by activities for constructing a digital twin. The use of a digital twin, i.e. a generative model of the environment dynamics, enables modeling of highly complex transition dynamics that would be unfeasible to capture by closed-form specification. Note that components of the twin (e.g. environment dynamics) can be learned from or adjusted to data collected from the environment.

At development time, the twin is used for training the system using learning algorithms. Validation is leveraging simulation for performing quantitative, sample-based statistical evaluation of a trained system. At runtime, the awareness mechanism is enriched with the twin for online planning.

Figure 2 shows the adjusted life cycle. The three new, small runtime cycles representing the digital twin are very similar to the operations cycle. In each of these cycles, the entities of the system iterate a "runtime feedback control loop" consisting of monitoring, awareness, and self-adaptation activities. The difference is that typically the additional cycles operate on the digital twin and not directly on the system.

The digital twin is not present in the requirements engineering phase. This is a natural choice, since the twin itself is specified here: It should comprise all relevant information about the application domain and cannot possibly inform itself.

Note that leveraging a digital twin could also be possible for further learning/training online at runtime, and simulation-based runtime verification in the monitoring phase. We do not treat these two applications of simulation at run-time in the following, and think that integrating them into AIDLE is an interesting avenue for future research.

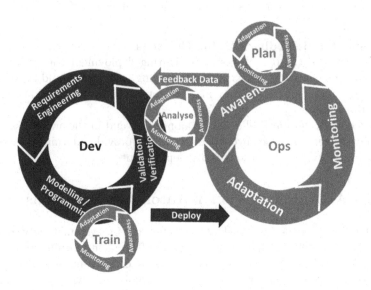

Fig. 2. AIDL life cycle.

3.1   Requirements

For engineering the system requirements we follow the ASCENS ideas and propose a goal-oriented approach where e.g. requirements elicitation can be performed using the ARE ontology. The requirement specification is the end product of the requirements elicitation process; it is defined by descriptions of the environment and of the domain of the envisaged system, adaptation requirements, and by a set of goals.

Domain Description. For systems which have to take autonomous decisions about the actions of the system, the environment and the required reliability of the system play an important role.

Often there is uncertainty on the behaviour of the environment which may also change dynamically. If the system contains embedded or IoT components, then it may not be fully reliable and certain system actions or components may fail. Such uncertain environments and systems are expressed by probability distributions. Formally, they form a kind of an MDP.

In many applications, in the beginning neither the initial distribution nor the transition distribution are known to the agent but they have to be learned based on the observations of the agent. In the case of a changing environment, or a changing system reliability, or changing goals, these distributions may change as well. Then the adaptation domain consists of a set of goals and MDPs, or of a probability distribution over goals and MDPs.

Goals. A goal represents a desirable system state or property that a software systems should achieve. For an autonomic system this is not always possible but one rather "strives to achieve" such a property, in spite of uncertainties and obstacles.

We distinguish optimisation goals and safety goals. Optimisation goals are soft goals that strive to achieve a property. Typically they are expressed with the help of an objective function and their goal is to find values that maximize or minimize this function.

Safety goals are hard goals which require that certain properties have to be preserved; in KAOS these are called maintain goals (if a property must always to hold) or avoid goals (if a property should never hold). For "classical" software systems such goals can be expressed by temporal logic formulae of the form "$\phi \implies \Box\psi$" (where ϕ and ψ are linear temporal logic formulae). But in presence of uncertainties, these safety properties cannot be universally true. They must consider probabilities for expressing the aleatoric uncertainty. It is also recommendable to estimate the epistemic uncertainty, i.e. the confidence in the validity of the result. Formally, we choose a probabilistic temporal logic such as PCTL [23] and express "soft" safety properties by formulas of the form "$P_{\geq p}(\psi)$ and $\mathbb{C}_{\geq c}$" which state that the goal ψ holds with at least probability p and at least confidence c ($p, c \in (0, 1)$).

3.2 Modelling and Programming

In this phase the system design and the implementation are developed. We focus here on the specific issues of learning and planning, i.e. the choice of the appropriate domain model and of the learning and planning algorithms, their implementation and the training of the agent.

Choice of Domain Model. The choice of the domain model depends on the kind of uncertainty of the environment and on the translation of goals into rewards and costs.

Aleatoric Uncertainty of the Environment. In the standard case of an (aleatoric) uncertainty, the environment can be described by a probability distribution, possibly depending on the current state and the action of the agent. Then the system can be modelled by (a variant of) a Markov decision process. For a specification comprising optimising and safety goals constrained Markov decision processes [7] are a good choice whereas for a specification with only one optimising goal a classical MDP is sufficient. If the application has noisy or unreliable sensors and the autonomic entity may not be able to determine the current state with complete reliability one may resort to Partially Observable Markov decision processes (POMDP) [32] as system model.

Changing Environment. A more difficult situation arises if the changes of environment are not stationary. Then one can try to model this by a probability distribution over the set of possible environments or - if also the goals and the system may change - one may model the adaptation domain as a probability distribution over MDPs [18].

Specification of Rewards and Costs. Another issue is the definition of of the immediate rewards and costs. Often their values can be directly derived from the corresponding optimization and safety goals but the correspondence is not always obvious. In this case one can explore different reward and cost functions or try to adjust the rewards and costs in a next round of the development cycle.

Choice of Algorithm. There is a wealth of learning and planning algorithms; none of them is known to outperform the others. The choice depends on several factors including the kind of domain model and goals, the size of the state and action space, the real-time performance requirements, and the availability of a digital twin. For a more detailed set of criteria see [39].

Kind of Domain Model and Goals. For MDPs with only one optimising goal, there is wide selection of model-free reinforcement learning algorithms, model-based reinforcement learning algorithms, and online planning algorithms. For applications with safety constraints a scalarisation approach can be followed if during training and learning a policy, actions are not required to be always safe. Otherwise shielding and safe exploration algorithms can be used. Partially Observable Markov Decision Processes (POMDPs) can be solved by online planning algorithms or by combinations of reinforcement learning with planning [40]).

The case of complex adaptation domains with changing environments can be tackled by meta-learning and online planning. Meta-learning algorithms are well-suited for dealing with non-stationary environments that can be described as a probability distribution over a set of environments. Online planning methods are able to react to non-stationary changes of the environment as well as to changes of goals and to noisy actions.

Size of State and Action Space. For small state and action spaces classical tabular model-free algorithms can be used, e.g. Q-learning and Temporal Difference learning for discrete sets of actions or Gaussian processes in the continuous case. Also planning algorithms use tabular representation methods. When the state space becomes too large, one has to resort to approximate representations of the value function. These function approximations can be linear (such as Fourier transform) or nonlinear (such as deep or forward neural networks). Also combining function approximation and local tabular methods as in [52] is promising.

Because of the computational intractability of belief states, algorithms for POMDPs are mostly only applicable to small and mid size problems. These issues can be partially resolved by factorisation of the state space or by exploiting full observability whenever possible [43].

Performance and Availability of a Digital Twin. By using function approximation, model-free methods scale to complex tasks (such as robotics and motion
animation) but they need large amounts of samples and training. Instead, model-
based algorithms and pure online planning require less training but need to rely
on a faithful model of the environment. Errors in the model undermine the quality of the solutions but recent methods such as uncertainty estimation of the
learned models can mitigate the model-bias [18].

The real-time performance of model-based algorithms such as PETS may
be another issue, e.g. in case that action selection of the algorithm needs more
time than a default time-step of the environment. In [61] T. Wang et al. provide
benchmarks for several state-of-the-art reinforcement learning algorithms and
show that model-based and model-free algorithms can achieve similar performances. Benchmarks for algorithms with safety constraints are given in [47].

Implementation and Training. The task of implementing an autonomous
agent by reinforcement learning is twofold: (1) implementing the model, the
algorithm and the training pipeline and (2) synthesis of the policy via training
(i.e. execution of the training cycle).

Implementation. For implementing the model and algorithm one needs to define
a software architecture for the appropriate variant of Markov Decision Processes,
the learning algorithm, and the application. E.g. this can be an object-oriented
architecture, differential equations, or a neural network architecture. For standard applications a reinforcement learning framework can be used such as the
Reinforcement Learning Toolbox of MathWorks[2] or Gym of OpenAI[3]. Neural
networks for function approximation can be implemented with the help of deep
learning frameworks such as PyTorch[4] and TensorFlow[5].

Training. The objective of training is to synthesize a policy which achieves the
required optimizing goals and safety goals constraints.

Training is executed in a training cycle in which the learning agent interacts
with the environment through a repeated trial-and-error process. A certain number of finite episodes are performed and the parameters of the policy are tuned
for maximizing the cumulative reward, minimizing the loss, and for ensuring
the required probability and confidence of the safety goals. Typically, after each
episode the parameters of the policy are updated and - if possible - the environment is reset. Training options comprise the length of an episode, the maximum
number of episodes, the individual or the average rewards and costs.

Training can be performed in the real environment or by simulations on a
digital model. The latter has the advantage that typically many more training
cycles are possible and that it is reversible, i.e. that the environment can be

---

[2] https://de.mathworks.com/products/reinforcement-learning.html.
[3] https://gym.openai.com/.
[4] https://pytorch.org/.
[5] https://www.tensorflow.org/.

reset. For many applications, training consists of two parts, a simulation on a digital twin of the application and training of the autonomous agent in the real environment.

A good training practice is to start with a simplified setting consisting of a simple simulated environment and a simple reinforcement learning algorithm. The algorithm and environment are then refined until the desired setting is achieved. Note that this approach means to iteratively run through deployment, operations cycle, feedback, validation, and re-adjustment of requirements and design until the model is accepted and then can be deployed for operation. For comparing the learning algorithms and choosing the most suitable one, a good practice is to deploy and train different algorithms in parallel.

3.3 Validation and Verification

Because of the large size of and the uncertainties about the environment, the construction of policies for autonomic systems requires extensive validation and verification. This is includes the validation and verification methods of ASCENS as well as all classical verification and testing methods such as unit, integration, system, and user testing, static analysis, and runtime verification.

A key issue is the statistical analysis of the training results such as the analysis of cumulative and average episode return. Statistical model checking [36] and Bayesian model checking [69] are the main tools for verifying safety constraints. Both methods use a runtime cycle for performing simulations and statistical analysis. In statistical model checking, finitely many randomised simulations of the system are executed and statistical methods are used for deciding whether the samples provide a statistical evidence for the satisfaction or violation of the specification. Bayesian model checking is a variant of statistical model checking which - instead of randomised sampling - incorporates prior information about the model being verified. The advantage is that it this often requires a significantly smaller number of sampled episodes.

The operation of autonomous systems has also to be validated in the real environment. This leads to several additional problems such as recognizing an environment which is different from the training environment, guaranteeing safe exploration of the real environment, and avoiding actions which disturb the real environment. For a discussion and possible solutions see [8].

3.4 Deployment and Feedback Data

Deployment. Deployment is used in three phases of the AIDL life cycle: for connecting the development cycle with the operations cycle, for executing the training cycle, and during validation and verification. During deployment the system is prepared for execution in a simulated ("in vitro") or in a real environment ("in vivo"). This involves the choice of the runtime infrastructure and the choice of the real environment and in case of simulation, the choice of the parameters of the digital twin.

Other tasks are compilation, linking, and generation of executable code. Microcontrollers and GPUs are typical infrastructures for autonomous systems operating in real environments. Simulations are deployed into GPUs, clouds and clusters of cpus, the latter two for executing in parallel to improve training performance.

Feedback. Feedback is based on the data collected by monitoring and in the awareness process. The feedback data are used for validation and verification and for evaluating and improving the design, the implementation, and the requirements.

3.5   The Operations Cycle

The Ops cycle of AIDL is almost the same as the one of EDLC. It can run in the real environment or in a digital model. The only change is that it emphasizes an additional Ops cycle for simulations which are executed in the awareness phase.

Monitoring. As in EDLC, monitoring employs mechanisms such as sensor information and code instrumentation for collecting data about the state of the environment, of some components of the autonomous system or of the whole system. In the context of MDPs, monitoring comprises also runtime validation of design assumptions about MDP by observing statistical properties and simulation results and their relations with other factors. This includes uncertainty quantification and detecting non-functional changes such as drift and anomalies.

An important task is MDP identification, i.e. in case the agent is able to work in several environment the current environment is monitored and if a change of the environment is detected, the adaptation mechanism of the agent is triggered; using feedback, also a new development cycle may be activated.

For systems with several digital twins, monitoring can check the status of these twins and inform the awareness mechanism. Another use of monitoring is to survey the learning results in case the system continues learning during operation.

Awareness. In this phase reasoning and planning is carried out. The monitored data are evaluated and analysed w.r.t. required (functional) properties. Often simulations on the digital twin are performed for predicting the behaviour of system and environment. The results can then be used e.g. for online planning and deciding on the next steps of the agent.

Adaptation. Based on the awareness results, different forms of adaptation are possible. Weak adaptation amounts simply to execute the action selected by the policy or to change some control parameters of the algorithm such as the change of the direct reward. Strong adaptation means e.g. to change the dynamic model (MDP) by updating the direct reward or the transition distribution. Also the system may be reconfigured, e.g. by exchanging system components or sensor functions.

4   Case Studies

In this section we illustrate AIDL by two existing case studies: a simple search-and-rescue case study [10] and a so-called particle dance case study [12]. The search-and-rescue scenario is solved by online planning whereas the particle dance illustrates the systematic development of a reinforcement learning solution. In Subsects. 4.1 and 4.2 the two case studies are presented along the phases of the AIDL life cycle. Subsection 4.3 gives a short comparison of both approaches.

4.1   Case Study: Engineering Adaptation by Simulation-Based Online Planning

The first example [10] is a simple search-and-rescue scenario which is solved by online planning. The experimental results shows that the generated planning policy of the agent is able to act autonomously and is robust w.r.t. unexpected events and changes of system goals at runtime.

Search-and-Rescue Scenario. A robot is deployed in a damaged area and must rescue victims by bringing them to an ambulance. If the robot encounters a fire, it has first extinguish the fire, and only then it can continue its way.

Requirements. The domain model consists of victims, fires, and ambulances in an environment with an unknown topology which is represented by a finite graph. The rescue robot can move (to a neighbor position), load or drop a victim (at its position), do nothing, and extinguish a fire (at a neighbor position). The robot has two goals. Its achieve goal is to find the victims and bring them to an ambulance. The safety constraint requires the agent to ignite all fires that are adjacent to its current position.

$$\textbf{Goal} \text{ Achieve } \textit{SaveVictims2Amb} : \diamond(\bigwedge_{i=1,\dots,n} victim_i \text{ at ambulance}) \qquad (1)$$

$$\textbf{Goal} \text{ Constraint } \textit{IgniteFire} : \Box(\forall Fire f : adjacent(f) \Rightarrow ignite(f)) \qquad (2)$$

There are also several adaptation requirements. First, the environment and the system may change: fires probabilistically ignite and cease; the actions of the robot are not reliable and may fail with a certain probability. The robot may also inadvertently drop the victim it is bringing to the ambulance. Moreover, the goals of the robot may change: the goal of saving victims from fire may change to the SaveVictims2Amb goal of "saving victims and bringing them to an ambulance."

Modelling and Programming. For modelling and implementing the search-and-rescue scenario, an object-oriented domain model of the scenario and a generic framework, called OnPlan, were developed. Then the domain model was plugged into OnPlan. Figure 3 shows the class diagram of the domain model.

OnPlan is a framework for modelling autonomous systems based on online planning [10]. it has a generic object-oriented architecture which realises an arbitrary MDP. It comprises components for states, actions, rewards, and also for the transition probabilities that define the policy (called strategy in [10]) of the robot. In addition, the architecture has a monitoring component for observing the environment and an abstract planning component which has a concrete simulation-based online planning component as realisation.

The latter makes use of a digital twin of the application domain for gathering information about potential system episodes. During the planning steps, future episodes are simulated at runtime. Simulation provides information about probability and value of the different state space regions, thus guiding system behaviour execution. After simulating possible choices of actions and behavioural alternatives, the transition probabilities of the MDP are updated and the agent executes an action (in reality) that performed well in simulation.

The dynamic model of OnPlan realises the behaviour of an Operations cycle (see below) and performs monitoring of the environment and planning and execution of actions iteratively at runtime.

Training is not necessary for OnPlan but the digital twin has to be a true model of the real environment.

OnPlan comes with two instantiations for online planning, Monte Carlo Tree Search [34] for discrete domains and the Gaussian approach of Cross Entropy Open Loop Planning [62] for continuous state and action spaces. For the search-and-rescue scenario, the former was used and plugged into the OnPlan architecture.

Validation. Validation is performed by statistical model checking using the MultiVesta tool [50]. Measurements include the estimation of the mean expected future reward.

A main aspect is the validation of the quality of the autonomous behaviour and of the robustness to changes. Concerning the autonomous behaviour, we test the system in an environment exhibiting aleatoric uncertainty: fires probabilistically ignite and cease and the actions of the robot are not reliable and may fail with a certain probability. Figure 4 shows that the planning component is able to generate a policy for transporting victims to safe positions autonomously.

Figures 5 and 6 address the adaptability and robustness of the system. Figure 5 shows the robot is able to recover from the unexpected events efficiently. The transportation of victims to safety is only marginally impaired by the sudden unexpected changes of the situation. The framework is also able to react adequately to a re-specification of system goals. In Fig. 6 before step 40, the robot was given a reward for keeping the number of fires low resulting in a reduction of the number of burning victims. On-wards from step 40, reward was instead provided for victims that have been transported to safety.

In all three Figs. 4, 5, and 6 the blue line indicates the percentage of saved victims, the red line the percentage of victims in fire, and the green line the percentage of positions in fire. Dotted lines indicate 0.95 confidence intervals.

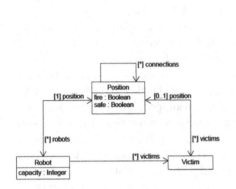

Fig. 3. Class diagram of search-and-rescue domain.

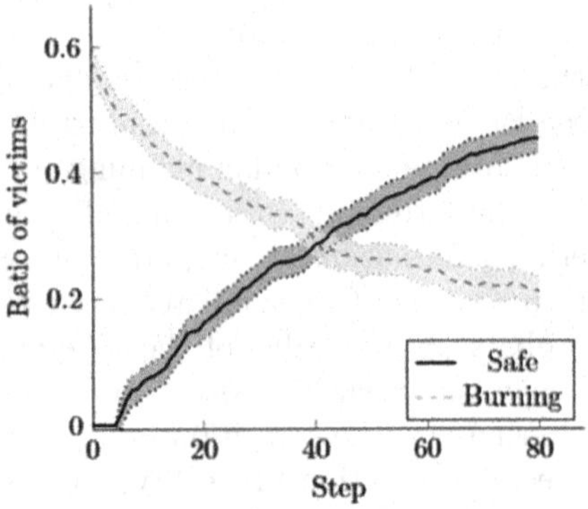

Fig. 4. Autonomous agent performance. Reward is given for victims at safe positions.

Operations Cycle. Monitoring of the environment is performed by OnPlan through an operation "observe" which senses the whole graph including the current position of the robot, the victims and fires. In addition, it counts the fires and victims, and monitors the success of the rescue actions.

By simulating iteratively future episodes at runtime, the robot becomes aware of the current situation.

Short term weak self-adaptation is achieved by online planning. The policy is iteratively updated according to the results of the Monte Carlo Search and to the observations of the robot action.

Deployment, Feedback, and New Development Cycle. Deploying the OnPlan scenario is standard and consists of packaging the software and deploying it on the infrastructure. Feedback comes from the monitoring data which inform the developers about the current status of fires and victims as well the (victim saving and fire fighting) performance of the agent. Strong adaptation arises in case of goal revision. If e.g. the current agent goal was to extinguish fires but new victims are detected, then a new development cycle is initiated for changing the goal and giving rewards for saving the victims.

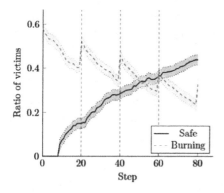

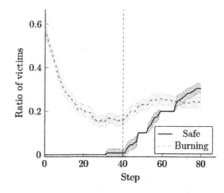

Fig. 5. Autonomous agent performance despite unexpected events at runtime. Every 20th step, all victims carried by the agent fall to the ground, and the number of fires raises to 10.

Fig. 6. Autonomous agent performance with a re-specification of system goal at runtime. Before step 40, the agent is given a reward for keeping the number of fires low, resulting in a reduction of the number of burning victims. Onwards from step 40, reward is provided for victims that have been transported to safety.

4.2 Case Study Safe Learning: Policy SYnthesis with Safety Constraints (PSyCo)

In line with the AIDL life cycle, the PSyCo approach is a systematic method for specifying and implementing agents that shape rewards dynamically over the learning process based on their confidence in requirement satisfaction [12]. It is centered around a safe reinforcement learning algorithm which combines evolutionary learning with Bayesian model checking. The basic idea is to emphasize return optimization when the learner is confident, and to focus on satisfying given constraints otherwise. This enables to explicitly distinguish requirements wrt. aleatoric uncertainty that is inherent to the domain, and epistemic uncertainty arising from an agent's learning process based on limited observations.

Particle Dance Scenario. In the Particle Dance scenario, an agent has to learn to follow a randomly moving particle as closely as possible.

Requirements. The domain is modelled as an MDP with an unknown transition distribution. State and action space are bounded continuous subsets of R. The reward computes the negative distance between particle and agent.

Minimising the distance means maximizing the reward. Thus the optimising goal is to maximise the expectation of the cumulative return $\mathcal{R}$:

$$\textbf{Goal } \textit{Optimize Return} : \max \mathbb{E}(\mathcal{R}) \tag{3}$$

The safety constraint requires the agent to keep a minimum distance of the particle except in a fixed small number of cases. We require that the particle satisfies this requirement with a high probability and a high confidence.

$$\textbf{Goal} \text{ Constraint } \textit{BoundedCollisions} : \mathbb{P}_{\geq p_{\text{req}}}(\Box\phi) \text{ and } \mathbb{C}_{\geq c_{\text{req}}} \qquad (4)$$

Here the formula ϕ expresses that the distance between particle and agent is greater than the minimum distance. Typically, we set the required probability for satisfying the constraint $p_{\text{req}} = 0.85$ and the required confidence $c_{\text{req}} = 0.98$.

Modelling, Programming, and Training. For dealing with the safety constraint, the MDP domain model of the Particle Dance is extended to form a Constrained MDP over continuous state and action spaces. The safety requirement $\Box\phi$ is transformed into a notion of cost $\mathcal{C}_\phi$ which (for each episode of Particle Dance) counts the number of violations of the safety property ϕ. The transformed goal is the following constrained optimization problem.

$$\max \mathbb{E}(\mathcal{R}) \text{ s.t. } \mathbb{P}_{\geq p_{\text{req}}}(\mathcal{C}_\phi = 0) \text{ and } \mathbb{C}_{\geq c_{\text{req}}} \qquad (5)$$

To solve this goal, we developed the so-called Safe Neural Evolutionary Strategies (SNES) reinforcement learning algorithm. As usual in deep learning, SNES models a policy as neural network. SNES synthesises such policies by combining a safe evolutionary learning algorithm with an algorithm for Bayesian model checking. The basis of the safe learning algorithm is the Lagrangian approach for solving constrained MDPs [7] where the constrained problem

$$\max \mathcal{R} \text{ s.t. } \mathcal{C}_\phi = 0 \qquad (6)$$

is transformed to a Lagrange formulation:

$$\max \mathcal{R} - (1 - \lambda)\mathcal{C}_\phi \qquad (7)$$

where $\lambda \in \mathbb{R}^+$ is a Lagrangian multiplier [9].

The resulting optimisation algorithm adaptively weights return and cost such that the resulting policy is likely to be positively verified. The algorithm does not ensure safety while learning, but only when converging to a solution of the Lagrangian. Bayesian model checking serves for modelling the epistemic uncertainty about the satisfaction probability of the results. We use it in two ways: To guide the learning process towards feasible solutions and to verify synthesized policies. The learning procedure of SNES is based on an evolutionary algorithm, called Evolutionary strategies (ES). This is a gradient free, search-based optimization algorithm that has shown competitive performance in reinforcement learning tasks.

Function approximation for SNES is realised by a feedforward neural network with one hidden layer. Training is performed over 60000 episodes (of length 50). Every 1000 episodes, Bayesian model checking is performed for a maximum of 1000 episodes (outside the learning loop of SNES) to evaluate the policy synthesized by SNES up to that point.

Validation. Validation is performed by Bayesian model checking and an analysis of e.g. the proportion of constraint satisfaction and the confidence in the results. For example, we can observe that the SNES agent learns to follow the particle closely. Figure 7 illustrates this by sample trajectories of the particle and the agent (color gradients denote time).

Figure 8 shows the proportion of episodes that satisfy the given requirement. We can see that the proportion closely reaches the defined bound of $p_{req} = 0.85$, shown by the dashed vertical line. Note that the satisfying proportion is closely above the required bound.

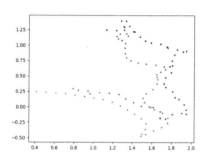

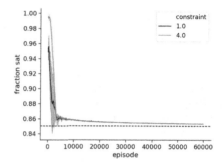

Fig. 7. Sample trajectories of the particle (light to dark blue, color gradient denotes time) and the agent (light to dark red). (Color figure online)

Fig. 8. Proportion of episodes satisfying cost requirement.

Figure 9 shows the confidence of the learning agent in its ability to satisfy the given requirement based on the observations made in the learning process. Note that the confidence is mostly kept above the confidence requirement $c_{req} = 0.98$ given in the specification. This shows SNES is effectively incorporating observations, probability requirements, and confidence into its learning process.

Operations Cycle. Monitoring consists in sensing the distance of the agent to the particle and in recording the number of distance violations and the cumulative reward. Since the policy is synthesised the operations cycle consists of monitoring and executing the policy. Thus there is no explicit adaptation and awareness phase in this loop.

Deployment, Feedback and New Development Cycle. As for OnPlan, deployment is standard and consists of packaging the software and deploying it on the infrastructure.

Feedback is given e.g. in case the monitor detects that the particle behaviour is changing or the agent behaviour is degrading so that the agent is not following closely the particle. Then a new development cycle is initiated for revising the requirements and the algorithm, new training and validation rounds, and finally the deployment of a revised policy.

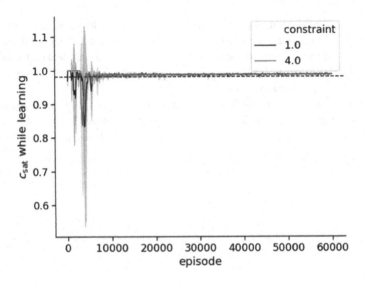

Fig. 9. Confidence c_{sat} in satisfying specification based on observations in the course of learning.

4.3   Comparison

The above results show that although the requirements are similar the two solutions are complementary in many ways.

Both case studies have goals requiring a high level of confidence. The search-and-rescue scenario is modelled as an MDP whereas as the particle dance is modelled as a CMDP. The sets of states and actions are discrete and finite for the search-and-rescue case but infinite and continuous for the particle dance.

Reinforcement learning is model-free; but it needs many training cycles and thus is "slow" at "programming" time. Online planning is model-based; but it does not need any training and thus is fast at "programming" time. During the Ops cycle, the synthesised reinforcement policy is directly executed and thus is fast, whereas online planning uses runtime simulation which may be too slow for real-time applications.

Adaptation of the synthesised policy requires a new Dev cycle, whereas the online planning policy is able to act autonomously and is robust w.r.t. unexpected events at runtime. For a change of system goals, also online planning requires an adjustment of the rewards and thus a new development cycle.

5   Related Work

Systematic engineering approaches for intelligent agents and multi-agent systems such as Gaia [68], Tropos [14] support a sequential development process starting with the collection of goal-oriented requirements and the model of the environment and then proceeding with architectural design, detailed design, and implementation. Gaia follows an organisational metaphore where agents play roles whereas Tropos is founded on the BDI (*Belief, Desire,* and *Intention*) agent architecture [46]. The AgentComponent approach [35] proposes a component-based software development process fully based on UML models. IBM's approach to autonomic systems is based on the MAPE-K architecture [30] built around an "autonomic manager" that iterates a feedback control loop consisting of four activities: *Monitoring, Analysing, Planning,* and *Executing.* The "generic life cycle for context-aware adaptive systems" based on MAPE-K addresses foreseen and unforeseen evolution of the environment [31].

More recent development approaches for autonomous systems focus on specialised goal-oriented requirements (such as SOTA [5], GEM [29], and ARE [58]) and on feedback control loops (such as [16,60]). The SOTA [5] approach is an extension of existing goal-oriented requirements engineering that integrates elements of dynamic systems modelling. Semantically, SOTA is built on the General Ensemble Model GEM [29]. The Autonomous Requirements Engineering approach ARE [58] focusses on systematically eliciting so-called autonomy requirements.

Similar to AIDL and EDLC, DevOps [48] is an agile software development method which connects software development with runtime management based on a software life cycle. DevOps does not specialize on autonomous systems and its life cycle consists of only one life cycle instead of three. MLOps [3] instantiates DevOps to the development of machine learning applications but different from AIDL, it focusses on big data applications. AIOps [2] aims at automating and enhancing IT operations through analytics and machine learning, but it does not consider software development.

The engineering process [22] for machine learning is closely related to AIDL. It follows a different life cycle and addresses adaptive instead of autonomous systems, but as AIDL it proposes central activities necessary for developing machine learning applications.

The FRAP framework [39] does not aim for a full engineering life cycle; instead it identifies fine grain design decisions for reinforcement learning and planning algorithms. In addition to computational effort and function representation, criteria such as trial selection, return estimation, update procedure, and back-up are considered.

6   Concluding Remarks

In this paper we proposed a systematic development process, called AIDL, for constructing/synthesizing policies of autonomous systems using planning and reinforcement learning techniques. AIDL can be seen as an instance of the EDLC development process for collective autonomic systems. It emphasizes the particular issues of machine learning techniques such as training, digital environment and agent models, and additional runtime cycles in almost all phases of development. We illustrated AIDL with two existing complementary case studies for reinforcement learning and online planning.

AIDL is not yet complete. Our two case studies address autonomic systems with single agents; a next step will be to refine and extend AIDL to AIDL-E for engineering collective autonomic systems. Also further learning/training online at runtime, simulation-based runtime verification in the monitoring phase, and additional non-functional requirements such as reliability, robustness, and security of policies should be discussed and integrated into our development approach. An ambitious mid term objective is to build an integrated development environment for AIDL.

An interesting methodical research question is how to use abstraction and refinement for stepwise learning of digital twin and how abstraction can help to learn policies. Also the relationship between aleatoric and epistemic uncertainty is not always straightforward and deserves further investigation.

Acknowledgement. We thank the anonymous reviewer for constructive criticisms and helpful suggestions.

A   Markov Decision Processes

A Markov Decision Process (MDP) M defines a domain as a set S of states consisting of all states of the environment and the agent, a set of A of agent actions, and a probability distribution $T : p(S|S, A)$ describing the transition probabilities of reaching some successor state when executing an action in a given state. For expressing optimisation goals the labelled transition system is extended by a reward function $R : S \times A \times S \to \mathbb{R}$ which gives the expected immediate reward gained by the agent for taking each action in each state. Moreover, an initial state distribution $\rho : p(S)$ is given.

An episode $e \in E$ is a finite or infinite sequence of transitions (s_i, a_i, s_{i+1}, r_i), $s_i, s_{i+1} \in S$, $a_i \in A$, $r_i = R(s_i, a, s_{i+1})$ in the MDP. For a given discount parameter $\gamma \in [0, 1]$ and any finite or infinite episode e, the cumulative return $\mathcal{R}$ is the discounted sum of rewards $\mathcal{R} = \sum_{i=1}^{|e|} \gamma^i r_i$. Depending on the application, the agent behaves in an environment according to a memoryless stationary policy $\pi : S \to p(A)$ or according to a deterministic memoryless policy $\pi : S \to A$ with the goal to maximise the expectation of the cumulative return $\mathbb{E}(\mathcal{R})$.

A partially observable Markov Decision Process (POMDP) [32] is a Markov decision process together with a set Ω of observations and an observation probability distribution $O : p(\Omega|S, A)$.

A Constrained Markov Decision Process (CMDP) has an additional cost function $C : S \times A \times S \to \mathbb{R}$ which can be used for expressing constraints and safety goals.

References

1. ASCENS: Autonomic Component Ensembles. Integrated Project, 01 Oct 2010–31 Mar 2015, Grant agreement no: 257414, EU 7th Framework Programme. http://www.ascens-ist.eu/. Accessed 21 April 2020

2. Gartner Inc.: Market Guide for AIOps Platforms (2019). https://www.bmc.com/forms/tools-and-strategies-for-effective-aiops.html. Accessed 07 Oct 2020

3. Google Cloud Solutions: MLOps: Continuous delivery and automation pipelines in machine learning. https://cloud.google.com/solutions/machine-learning/mlops-continuous-delivery-and-automation-pipelines-in-machine-learning. Accessed 07 Oct 2020

4. OpenAI. Spinning Up in Deep RL! Part 2: Kinds of RL Algorithms (2018). https://spinningup.openai.com. Accessed 07 July 2020

5. Abeywickrama, D., Bicocchi, N., Mamei, M., Zambonelli, F.: The SOTA approach to engineering collective adaptive systems. Int. J. Softw. Tools Technol. Transf. **22**(4), 399–415 (2020)

6. Alshiekh, M., Bloem, R., Ehlers, R., Könighofer, B., Niekum, S., Topcu, U.: Safe reinforcement learning via shielding. In: AAAI, pp. 2669–2678. AAAI Press (2018)

7. Altman, E.: Constrained Markov Decision Processes, vol. 7. CRC Press, Boca Raton (1999)

8. Amodei, D., Olah, C., Steinhardt, J., Christiano, P., Schulman, J., Mané, D.: Concrete problems in AI safety. CoRR, abs/1606.06565 (2016)

9. Beavis, B., Dobbs, I.: Optimisation and Stability Theory for Economic Analysis. Cambridge University Press, Cambridge (1990)

10. Belzner, L., Hennicker, R., Wirsing, M.: OnPlan: a framework for simulation-based online planning. In: Braga, C., Ölveczky, P.C. (eds.) FACS 2015. LNCS, vol. 9539, pp. 1–30. Springer, Cham (2016). https://doi.org/10.1007/978-3-319-28934-2_1

11. Belzner, L., Hölzl, M.M., Koch, N., Wirsing, M.: Collective autonomic systems: towards engineering principles and their foundations. Trans. Found. Mastering Chang. **1**, 180–200 (2016)

12. Belzner, L., Wirsing, M.: Synthesizing safe policies under probabilistic constraints with reinforcement learning and Bayesian model checking. Sci. Comput. Program. **206**, 102620 (2021)

13. Bernardo, M., De Nicola, R., Hillston, J.: Formal Methods for the Quantitative Evaluation of Collective Adaptive Systems, SFM 2016, vol. 9700, Lecture Notes in Computer Science. Springer, Cham (2016). https://doi.org/10.1007/978-3-319-34096-8

14. Bresciani, P., Perini, A., Giorgini, P., Giunchiglia, F., Mylopoulos, J.: Tropos: an agent-oriented software development methodology. JAAMAS **8**(3), 203–236 (2004)

15. Browne, C., et al.: A survey of Monte Carlo tree search methods. IEEE Trans. Comput. Intell. AI Games **4**(1), 1–43 (2012)

16. Brun, Y., et al.: Engineering self-adaptive systems through feedback loops. In: Cheng, B.H.C., de Lemos, R., Giese, H., Inverardi, P., Magee, J. (eds.) Software Engineering for Self-Adaptive Systems. LNCS, vol. 5525, pp. 48–70. Springer, Heidelberg (2009). https://doi.org/10.1007/978-3-642-02161-9_3

17. Bureš, T., et al.: A life cycle for the development of autonomic systems: the e-mobility showcase. In: SASO Workshops, pp. 71–76 (2013)

18. Clavera, I., Rothfuss, J., Schulman, J., Fujita, Y., Asfour, T., Abbeel, P.: Model-based reinforcement learning via meta-policy optimization. In: CoRL 2018, Proceedings of Machine Learning Research, vol, 87, pp. 617–629. PMLR (2018)

19. Nicola, R. D., Loreti, M., Pugliese, R., Tiezzi, F.: A formal approach to autonomic systems programming: the SCEL language. ACM Trans. Auton. Adapt. **9**(2), 7:1–7:29 (2014)

20. Drugan, M.M.: Reinforcement learning versus evolutionary computation: a survey on hybrid algorithms. Swarm Evol. Comput. **44**, 228–246 (2019)

21. Fernandez-Marquez, J.L., Serugendo, G.D.M., Montagna, S., Viroli, M., Arcos, J.L.: Description and composition of bio-inspired design patterns: a complete overview. Nat. Comput. **12**(1), 43–67 (2013)

22. Gabor, T., et al.: The scenario coevolution paradigm: adaptive quality assurance for adaptive systems. Int. J. Softw. Tools Technol. Transf. **22**, 457–476 (2020)

23. Hansson, H., Jonsson, B.: A logic for reasoning about time and reliability. Formal Asp. Comput. **6**(5), 512–535 (1994)

24. Hasanbeig, M., Abate, A., Kroening, D.: Cautious reinforcement learning with logical constraints. In: AAMAS, pp. 483–491. International Foundation for Autonomous Agents and Multiagent Systems (2020)

25. Hoch, N., Bensler, H.-P., Abeywickrama, D., Bureš, T., Montanari, U.: The E-mobility case study. In: Wirsing, M., Hölzl, M., Koch, N., Mayer, P. (eds.) Software Engineering for Collective Autonomic Systems. LNCS, vol. 8998, pp. 513–533. Springer, Cham (2015). https://doi.org/10.1007/978-3-319-16310-9_17

26. Horn, P.: Autonomic computing: IBM perspective on the state of information technology. IBM T.J. Watson Labs, NY (2001)

27. Hölzl, M., Koch, N., Puviani, M., Wirsing, M., Zambonelli, F.: The ensemble development life cycle and best practices for collective autonomic systems. In: Wirsing, M., Hölzl, M., Koch, N., Mayer, P. (eds.) Software Engineering for Collective Autonomic Systems. LNCS, vol. 8998, pp. 325–354. Springer, Cham (2015). https://doi.org/10.1007/978-3-319-16310-9_9

28. Hölzl, M., Rauschmayer, A., Wirsing, M.: Engineering of software-intensive systems: state of the art and research challenges. In: Wirsing, M., Banâtre, J.-P., Hölzl, M., Rauschmayer, A. (eds.) Software-Intensive Systems and New Computing Paradigms. LNCS, vol. 5380, pp. 1–44. Springer, Heidelberg (2008). https://doi.org/10.1007/978-3-540-89437-7_1

29. Hölzl, M., Wirsing, M.: Towards a system model for ensembles. In: Agha, G., Danvy, O., Meseguer, J. (eds.) Formal Modeling: Actors, Open Systems, Biological Systems. LNCS, vol. 7000, pp. 241–261. Springer, Heidelberg (2011). https://doi.org/10.1007/978-3-642-24933-4_12

30. IBM: An architectural blueprint for autonomic computing. Technical report, IBM Corporation (2005)

31. Inverardi, P., Mori, M.: A software lifecycle process to support consistent evolutions. In: de Lemos, R., Giese, H., Müller, H.A., Shaw, M. (eds.) Software Engineering for Self-Adaptive Systems II. LNCS, vol. 7475, pp. 239–264. Springer, Heidelberg (2013). https://doi.org/10.1007/978-3-642-35813-5_10

32. Kaelbling, L.P., Littman, M.L., Cassandra, A.R.: Planning and acting in partially observable stochastic domains. Artif. Intell. **101**(1–2), 99–134 (1998)

33. Kernbach, S., Schmickl, T., Timmis, J.: Collective adaptive systems: challenges beyond evolvability. CoRR abs/1108.5643 (2011)

34. Kocsis, L., Szepesvári, C.: Bandit based Monte-Carlo planning. In: Fürnkranz, J., Scheffer, T., Spiliopoulou, M. (eds.) ECML 2006. LNCS (LNAI), vol. 4212, pp. 282–293. Springer, Heidelberg (2006). https://doi.org/10.1007/11871842_29

35. Krutisch, R., Meier, P., Wirsing, M.: The AgentComponent approach, combining agents, and components. In: Schillo, M., Klusch, M., Müller, J., Tianfield, H. (eds.) MATES 2003. LNCS (LNAI), vol. 2831, pp. 1–12. Springer, Heidelberg (2003). https://doi.org/10.1007/978-3-540-39869-1_1

36. Legay, A., Delahaye, B., Bensalem, S.: Statistical model checking: an overview. In: Barringer, H., et al. (eds.) RV 2010. LNCS, vol. 6418, pp. 122–135. Springer, Heidelberg (2010). https://doi.org/10.1007/978-3-642-16612-9_11

37. Loreti, M., Hillston, J.: Modelling and analysis of collective adaptive systems with CARMA and its tools. In: Bernardo, M., De Nicola, R., Hillston, J. (eds.) SFM 2016. LNCS, vol. 9700, pp. 83–119. Springer, Cham (2016). https://doi.org/10. 1007/978-3-319-34096-8_4

38. Mayer, P., et al.: The autonomic cloud. In: Wirsing, M., Hölzl, M., Koch, N., Mayer, P. (eds.) Software Engineering for Collective Autonomic Systems. LNCS, vol. 8998, pp. 495–512. Springer, Cham (2015). https://doi.org/10.1007/978-3-319-16310-9_16

39. Moerland, T.M., Broekens, J., Jonker, C.M.: A framework for reinforcement learning and planning. CoRR, abs/2006.15009 (2020)

40. Moerland, T.M., Broekens, J., Jonker, C.M.: Model-based reinforcement learning: a survey. CoRR, abs/2006.16712 (2020)

41. Moerland, T.M., Deichler, A., Baldi, S., Broekens, J., Jonker, C.M.: Think too fast nor too slow: The computational trade-off between planning and reinforcement learning. CoRR, abs/2005.07404 (2020)

42. Nagabandi, A., et al.: Learning to adapt in dynamic, real-world environments through meta-reinforcement learning. In: ICLR 2019. OpenReview.net (2019)

43. Ong, S.C.W., Png, S.W., Hsu, D., Lee, W.S.: Planning under uncertainty for robotic tasks with mixed observability. Int. J. Robot. Res. **29**(8), 1053–1068 (2010)

44. Pinciroli, C., Bonani, M., Mondada, F., Dorigo, M.: Adaptation and awareness in robot ensembles: scenarios and algorithms. In: Wirsing, M., Hölzl, M., Koch, N., Mayer, P. (eds.) Software Engineering for Collective Autonomic Systems. LNCS, vol. 8998, pp. 471–494. Springer, Cham (2015). https://doi.org/10.1007/978-3-319-16310-9_15

45. Puviani, M., Cabri, G., Zambonelli, F.: Patterns for self-adaptive systems: agent-based simulations. EAI Endorsed Trans. Self-Adapt. Syst. **1**(1), e4 (2015)

46. Rao, A.S., Georgeff, M.P.: Modeling rational agents within a BDI-architecture. In: Proceedings of the Knowledge Representation and Reasoning, pp. 473–484 (1991)

47. Ray, A., Achiam, J., Amodei, D.: Benchmarking safe exploration in deep reinforcement learning. Technical report, Open AI (2019)

48. Roche, J.: Adopting DevOps practices in quality assurance. Commun. ACM **56**(11), 38–43 (2013)

49. Ross, S., Pineau, J., Paquet, S., Chaib-draa, B.: Online planning algorithms for POMDPs. J. Artif. Intell. Res. **32**, 663–704 (2008)

50. Sebastio, S., Vandin, A.: MultiVeStA: statistical model checking for discrete event simulators. In: ValueTools 2013, pp. 310–315. ICST/ACM (2013)

51. Silver, D., et al.: Mastering the game of go with deep neural networks and tree search. Nature **529**(7587), 484–489 (2016)

52. Silver, D.: Mastering the game of go without human knowledge. Nature **550**(7676), 354–359 (2017)

53. Sutton, R.S., Barto, A.G.: Reinforcement Learning - an Introduction. Adaptive Computation and Machine Learning, 2nd edn. MIT Press, Cambridge (2018)

54. Szepesvári, C.: Algorithms for Reinforcement Learning. Synthesis Lectures on Artificial Intelligence and Machine Learning, vol. 4, pp. 1–103. Morgan & Claypool Publishers, California (2010)

55. Taylor, M.E., Stone, P.: Transfer learning for reinforcement learning domains: a survey. J. Mach. Learn. Res. **10**, 1633–1685 (2009)

56. Thrun, S., Pratt, L.Y.: Learning to learn: introduction and overview. In: Thrun, S., Pratt, L.Y. (eds.) Learning to Learn, pp. 3–17. Springer, Boston (1998). https://doi.org/10.1007/978-1-4615-5529-2_1

57. Tschaikowski, M., Tribastone, M.: A unified framework for differential aggregations in Markovian process algebra. J. Log. Alg. Meth. Prog. **84**(2), 238–258 (2015)
58. Vassev, E., Hinchey, M.: Engineering requirements for autonomy features. In: Wirsing, M., Hölzl, M., Koch, N., Mayer, P. (eds.) Software Engineering for Collective Autonomic Systems. LNCS, vol. 8998, pp. 379–403. Springer, Cham (2015). https://doi.org/10.1007/978-3-319-16310-9_11
59. Vilalta, R., Giraud-Carrier, C., Brazdil, P., Soares, C.: Inductive transfer. In: Sammut, C., Webb, G.I. (eds.) Encyclopedia of Machine Learning and Data Mining, pp. 666–671. Springer, Boston (2017). https://doi.org/10.1007/978-1-4899-7687-1_138
60. Šerbedžija, N., Fairclough, S.: Biocybernetic loop: from awareness to evolution. In: IEEE Evolutionary Computation 2009, pp. 2063–2069. IEEE (2009)
61. Wang, T., et al.: Benchmarking model-based reinforcement learning. CoRR, abs/1907.02057 (2019)
62. Weinstein, A., Littman, M.: Open-loop planning in large-scale stochastic domains. In: AAI 2013. AAAI Press (2013)
63. Weyns, D., et al.: On patterns for decentralized control in self-adaptive systems. In: de Lemos, R., Giese, H., Müller, H.A., Shaw, M. (eds.) Software Engineering for Self-Adaptive Systems II. LNCS, vol. 7475, pp. 76–107. Springer, Heidelberg (2013). https://doi.org/10.1007/978-3-642-35813-5_4
64. Wirsing, M., Banâtre, J.-P., Hölzl, M., Rauschmayer, A.: Software-Intensive Systems and New Computing Paradigms - Challenges and Visions, vol. 5380. Lecture Notes in Computer Science. Springer, Heidelberg (2008). https://doi.org/10.1007/978-3-540-89437-7
65. M. Wirsing, M. M. Hölzl, N. Koch, and P. Mayer, editors. Software Engineering for Collective Autonomic Systems - The ASCENS Approach, volume 8998 of Lecture Notes in Computer Science. Springer, Cham (2015). https://doi.org/10.1007/978-3-319-16310-9
66. Wirsing, M., Hölzl, M., Tribastone, M., Zambonelli, F.: ASCENS: engineering autonomic service-component ensembles. In: Beckert, B., Damiani, F., de Boer, F.S., Bonsangue, M.M. (eds.) FMCO 2011. LNCS, vol. 7542, pp. 1–24. Springer, Heidelberg (2013). https://doi.org/10.1007/978-3-642-35887-6_1
67. Wooldridge, M.J., Jennings, N.R.: Intelligent agents: theory and practice. Knowl. Eng. Rev. **10**(2), 115–152 (1995)
68. Zambonelli, F., Jennings, N.R., Wooldridge, M.J.: Developing multiagent systems: the Gaia method. ACM Trans. Softw. Eng. Meth. **12**(3), 317–370 (2003)
69. Zuliani, P., Platzer, A., Clarke, E.M.: Bayesian statistical model checking with application to Simulink verification. Formal Meth. Syst. Des. **43**(2), 338–367 (2013)

Strand Spaces with Choice via a Process Algebra Semantics

Fan Yang[1], Santiago Escobar[2][(✉)], Catherine Meadows[3], Jose Meseguer[1], and Sonia Santiago[4]

[1] University of Illinois at Urbana-Champaign, Champaign, USA
{fanyang6,meseguer}@illinois.edu
[2] VRAIN, Universitat Politècnica de València, Valencia, Spain
sescobar@upv.es
[3] Naval Research Laboratory, Washington, D.C., USA
meadows@itd.nrl.navy.mil
[4] ITI, Universitat Politècnica de València, Valencia, Spain
ssantiago@iti.es

Abstract. Roles in cryptographic protocols do not always have a linear execution, but may include choice points causing the protocol to continue along different paths. In this paper we address the problem of representing choice in the strand space model of cryptographic protocols, particularly as it is used in the Maude-NPA cryptographic protocol analysis tool.

To achieve this goal, we develop and give formal semantics to a process algebra for cryptographic protocols that supports a rich taxonomy of choice primitives for composing strand spaces. In our taxonomy, deterministic and non-deterministic choices are broken down further. Non-deterministic choice can be either *explicit*, i.e., one of two paths is chosen, or *implicit*, i.e., the value of a variable is chosen non-deterministically. Likewise, deterministic choice can be either an *explicit if-then-else* choice, i.e., one path is chosen if a predicate is satisfied, while the other is chosen if it is not, or *implicit deterministic choice*, i.e., execution continues only if a certain pattern is matched. We have identified a class of choices which includes finite branching and some cases of infinite branching, which we address in this paper.

We provide a bisimulation result between the expected forwards execution semantics of the new process algebra and the original symbolic backwards semantics of Maude-NPA that preserves attack reachability. We have fully integrated the process algebra syntax and its transformation into strands in Maude-NPA. We illustrate its expressive power and

This work has been partially supported by the grants RTI2018-094403-B-C32 and PID2021-122830OB-C42 funded by MCIN/AEI/10.13039/501100011033 and ERDF "A way of making Europe", by the grant PROMETEO/2019/098 funded by Generalitat Valenciana, and by the grant PCI2020-120708-2 funded by MICIN/AEI/10.13039/501100011033 and the European Union NextGenerationEU/PRTR.

P. Lopez-Garcia et al. (Eds.): Hermenegildo Festschrift 2022, LNCS 13160, pp. 307–350, 2023.
https://doi.org/10.1007/978-3-031-31476-6_17

naturalness with various examples, and show how it can be effectively used in formal analysis. This allows users to write protocols from now on using the process syntax, which is more convenient for expressing choice than the strand space syntax, in which choice can only be specified implicitly, via two or more strands that are identical until the choice point.

1   Introduction

Formal analysis of cryptographic protocols has become one of the most successful applications of formal methods to security, with a number of tools available and many successful applications to the analysis of protocol standards. In the course of developing these tools it has become clear that there are certain universal features that can best be handled by accounting for them directly in the syntax and the semantics of the formal specification language, e.g., unguessable nonces, communication across a network controlled by an attacker, and support for the equational properties of cryptographic primitives. Thus a number of different languages have been developed that include these features.

At the same time, it is necessary to provide support for more commonly used constructs, such as *choice points* that cause the protocol to continue in different ways, and to do so in such a way that they are well integrated with the more specifically cryptographic features of the language. However, in their original form most of these languages do not support choice, or support it only in a limited way.

In particular, the strand space model [12], one of the most popular models designed for use in cryptographic protocol analysis, does not support choice in its original form; strands describe linear sequences of input and output messages, without any branching. One response to dealing with this limitation, and to formalizing strand spaces in general, has been to embed the strand space model in some other formal system that supports choice, e.g., event-based models for concurrency [5], Petri nets [13], or multi-set rewriting [3]. However, we believe that there are advantages in introducing choice in the strand space model itself, while proving soundness and completeness with another formal system in order to validate the augmented model. This allows us to concentrate on handling the types of choices that commonly arise in cryptographic protocols. A detailed discussion of related work can be found at Sect. 9.

We wish to honor Manuel Hermenegildo with this paper in his Festschrift volume. Besides Manuel's landmark contributions to Declarative Programming and Formal Methods, we wish to emphasize the close links that the work we present —which might at first sight appear to be somewhat distant from Manuel's interests— has with his seminal contributions to Constraint Logic Programming. Solving of equality and disequality constraints modulo user-definable equational theories, and narrowing-based symbolic search using semantic unification modulo such theories are some of the key symbolic techniques that we use to formally analyze the security of protocols modulo the equational properties of their cryptographic functions. Therefore, this is a way for us to continue a dialogue with

Manuel that for one of us started in California in the 1980s, and to wish him health and many more successes in the years to come.

1.1 Contributions

This paper is an extended version of the conference paper [21]. We address the problem of representing choice in the strand space model, particularly as it is used in the Maude-NPA cryptographic protocol analysis tool. We have identified several kinds of choices, including both finite branching and some cases of infinite branching. At the theoretical level, we provide a bisimulation result between the expected forwards execution semantics of the new process algebra and the original symbolic backwards semantics of Maude-NPA. This requires extra intermediate forwards and backwards semantics that are included in this paper, together with all the proofs, but were not included in the conference paper [21]. What these results make possible is a sound and complete symbolic reachability analysis method for cryptographic protocols with choice *modulo* equational properties of the cryptographic functions satisfying the finite variant property (FVP) (see [8] for a detailed explanation of how FVP theories are supported in Maude-NPA). At the tool level, we have fully integrated the process algebra syntax, and its transformation into strands, and have developed new methods to specify attack states using the process notation in the recent release of Maude-NPA 3.1.4 (see Sect. 8.1, and [8]). None of this was available at the time of the conference paper [21]. Furthermore, we illustrate the expressive power and naturalness of adding choice to strand spaces with various examples, and show how it can be effectively used in formal analysis.

1.2 Choice in Maude-NPA

Previous to this work, Maude-NPA offered some ways of handling choice, but its scope was limited, and a uniform semantics of choice was lacking. Several kinds of branching could be handled by a protocol composition method in which a single parent strand is composed with one or more child strands. Although protocol composition is intended for modular construction of protocols, with suitable restrictions it can also be used to express both non-deterministic branching and deterministic branching predicates on pattern matching of output parameters of the parent with the input parameters of the child. However, repurposing composition to branching has its limitations. First of all, it is possible to inadvertently introduce non-deterministic choice into what was intended to be deterministic choice by unwise choice of input and output parameters. Secondly, the limitation to pattern matching rules out certain types of deterministic choice conditioned on predicates that cannot be expressed this way, e.g., disequality[1] predicates. Finally, implementation of choice via composition can be inefficient,

---

[1] As discussed in [4], a disequality is a negated equality $t_1 \neq t_2$, whereas an inequality is a predicate $t_1 \leq t_2$, which is only meaningful if an interpretation of the $\leq$ symbol has been given.

since Maude-NPA must evaluate all possible child strands that match a parent strand.

Maude-NPA, in common with many other cryptographic protocol analysis tools, also offers a type of implicit choice that does not involve branching: non-deterministic choice of the values of certain variables. For example, a strand that describes an initiator communicating with a responder generally uses variables for both the initiator and responder names; this represents a non-deterministic choice of initiator and responder identities. However, the semantic implications of this kind of choice were not that well understood, which made it difficult to determine where it could safely be used. Clearly, a more unified treatment of choice was necessary, together with a formal semantics of choice.

In support of this work we have developed a taxonomy of choice in which the categories of deterministic and non-deterministic choice are further subdivided. First of all, non-deterministic choice is subdivided into *explicit* and *implicit* non-deterministic choice. In explicit non-deterministic choice a role[2] chooses either one branch or another at a choice point non- deterministically. In implicit non-deterministic choice a logical *choice variable* is introduced which may be non-deterministically instantiated by the role. Deterministic choice is subdivided into (explicit) *if-then-else* choice and *implicit deterministic choice*. In if-then-else choice a predicate is evaluated. If the predicate evaluates to true one branch is chosen, and if it evaluates to false another branch is chosen. Deterministic choice with more than two choices can be modeled by nesting of if-then-else choices. In implicit deterministic choice, a term pattern is used as an implicit guard, so that only messages matching such pattern can be chosen i.e., accepted, by the role. Although implicit deterministic choice can be considered a special case of if-then-else choice in which the second branch is empty, it is often simpler to treat it separately. Classifying choice in this way allows us to represent all possible behaviors of a protocol by a finite number of strands modeling possible executions, while still allowing the variables used in implicit non-deterministic and deterministic choice to be instantiated in an infinite number of ways.

1.3   A Motivating Example

In this section we introduce a protocol that we will use as a running example. It is a simplified version of the handshake protocol in TLS 1.3 [20], a proposed update to the TLS standard for client-server authentication. This protocol is chosen because, like most other protocol standards, offers a number of different alternatives and it exemplifies all the different kinds of choice considered in this paper, although, as explained in Sect. 8.4, it produces a very deep and wide analysis tree; see [15] for a more detailed presentation of the protocol. In order to make the presentation and discussion manageable, we present only a subset

---

[2] As further explained later, the behaviors of protocol participants, called *principals*, e.g., sender, receiver, server, etc., are described by their respective *roles*. Since a protocol may have multiple sessions, various participants may play a different role in each session.

here: the client chooses a Diffie-Hellman group, and proposes it to the server. The server can either accept it or request that the client proposes a different group. In addition, the server has the option of requesting that the client authenticates itself. We present the protocol at a high level similar to the style used in [20].

Example 1. We let a dashed arrow --→ denote an optional message, and an asterisk * denote an optional field.

1. $C \rightarrow S$: ClientHello, Key_Share
   The client sends a Hello message containing a nonce and the Diffie-Hellman group it wants to use. It also sends a Diffie-Hellman key share.
   - 1.1 S --→ C : HelloRetryRequest
     The server may optionally reject the Diffie-Hellman group proposed by the client and request a new one.
   - 1.2 C --→ S : DHGroup, Key_Share
     The client proposes a new group and sends a new key share.
2. $S \rightarrow C$: ServerHello, Key_Share, {AuthReq*},{CertificateVerify}, {Finished}
   The server sends its own Hello message and a Diffie-Hellman key share. It may optionally send an AuthReq to the client to authenticate itself with a public key signature from its public key certificate. It then signs the entire handshake using its own public key in the CertificateVerify field. Finally, in the Finished field it computes a MAC over the entire handshake using the shared Diffie-Hellman key. The {} notation denotes a field encrypted using the shared Diffie-Hellman key.
3. $C \rightarrow S$: {CertificateVerify*}, {Finished}
   If the client received an AuthReq from the server it returns its own CertificateVerify and Finished fields.

1.4   Plan of the Paper

The rest of the paper is organized as follows. After some preliminaries in Sect. 2 and a high level introduction of the Maude-NPA tool in Sect. 3, we first define the process algebra syntax and operational semantics in Sect. 4. In Sect. 5 we extend Maude-NPA's strand space syntax to include choice operators. The main bisimulation results between the expected forwards semantics of the process algebra in Sect. 4 and the original symbolic backwards strand semantics of Maude-NPA of Sect. 3 are stated in Theorems 2 and 3. They are proved by introducing an intermediate semantics, a forward strand space semantics originally introduced in [9]. First, in Sect. 5 we extend the strand space model with constraints, since strands are the basis of both the forwards semantics and the backwards semantics of Maude-NPA. In Sect. 6 we augment the forwards strand space semantics of [9] with choice operators and operational semantic rules to produce a *constrained forwards semantics*. In Sect. 6.2 we prove bisimilarity of the process algebra semantics of Sect. 4 and the constrained forwards semantics. In [9] the forwards strand space semantics was proved sound and complete w.r.t. the original symbolic backwards semantics of Maude-NPA and, therefore, such proofs had to be extended to handling constraints. In Sect. 7 we augment the original symbolic backwards semantics of Maude-NPA with choice operators and operational semantic rules to produce a *constrained backwards semantics*. In Sect. 7.2 we then prove that the constrained backwards semantics is sound and complete with respect to the constrained forwards semantics. By combining the bisimulation between the process algebra and the constrained forwards semantics on the one hand (Theorem 1) and the bisimulation between the constrained forwards semantics and the constrained backwards semantics on the other hand (Theorems 5 and 4) we obtain the main bisimulation results (Theorems 2 and 3). Finally, in Sect. 8 we describe how the process algebra has been fully integrated into Maude-NPA and show some experiments that we have run using Maude-NPA on various protocols exhibiting both deterministic and non-deterministic choice. In Sect. 9 we discuss related and future work, in particular the potential of using the process algebra syntax as a specification language. Finally, we conclude in Sect. 10. Proofs can be found in the Appendix.

2   Preliminaries

We follow the classical notation and terminology for term rewriting and for rewriting logic and order-sorted notions, see [17]. We assume an order-sorted signature $\Sigma = (S, \leqslant, \Sigma)$ with poset of sorts $(S, \leqslant)$. We also assume an S-sorted family $\mathcal{X} = \{\mathcal{X}_s\}_{s \in S}$ of disjoint variable sets with each $\mathcal{X}_s$ countably infinite. $\mathcal{T}_\Sigma(\mathcal{X})_s$ is the set of terms of sort s, and $\mathcal{T}_{\Sigma,s}$ is the set of ground terms of sort s. We write $\mathcal{T}_\Sigma(\mathcal{X})$ and $\mathcal{T}_\Sigma$ for the corresponding order-sorted term algebras. For a term t, $Var(t)$ denotes the set of variables in t.

Positions are represented by sequences of natural numbers. The top or root position is denoted by the empty sequence Λ. The set of positions of a term t is written $Pos(t)$, and the set of non-variable positions $Pos_\Sigma(t)$. The subterm of t at position p is $t|_p$ and $t[u]_p$ denotes the term t with subterm $t|_p$ replaced by u.

A *substitution* $\sigma \in Subst(\Sigma, \mathcal{X})$ is a sorted mapping from a finite subset of $\mathcal{X}$ to $\mathcal{T}_\Sigma(\mathcal{X})$. Substitutions are written as $\sigma = \{X_1 \mapsto t_1, \ldots, X_n \mapsto t_n\}$ where the domain of σ is $Dom(\sigma) = \{X_1, \ldots, X_n\}$ and the set of variables introduced by terms $t_1, \ldots, t_n$ is written $Ran(\sigma)$. The identity substitution is denoted *id*. Substitutions are homomorphically extended to $\mathcal{T}_\Sigma(\mathcal{X})$. The application of a substitution σ to a term t is denoted by $t\sigma$. For simplicity, we assume that every substitution is idempotent, i.e., σ satisfies $Dom(\sigma) \cap Ran(\sigma) = \varnothing$. This ensures $t\sigma = (t\sigma)\sigma$. The restriction of σ to a set of variables V is $\sigma|_V$. Composition of two substitutions σ and σ' is denoted by $\sigma\sigma'$. A substitution σ is a ground substitution if $Ran(\sigma) = \varnothing$.

A Σ-*equation* is an unoriented pair $t = t'$, where $t, t' \in \mathcal{T}_\Sigma(\mathcal{X})_s$ for some sort $s \in S$. Given Σ and a set E of Σ-equations, order-sorted equational logic induces a congruence relation $=_E$ on terms $t, t' \in \mathcal{T}_\Sigma(\mathcal{X})$. The E-equivalence class of a term t is denoted by $[t]_E$ and $\mathcal{T}_{\Sigma/E}(\mathcal{X})$ and $\mathcal{T}_{\Sigma/E}$ denote the corresponding order-sorted term algebras modulo E. Throughout this paper we assume that $\mathcal{T}_{\Sigma,s} \neq \varnothing$ for every sort s, because this affords a simpler deduction system. An *equational theory* (Σ, E) is a pair with Σ an order-sorted signature and E a set of Σ-equations. The *E-subsumption* preorder $\sqsupseteq_E$ (or just $\sqsupseteq$ if E is understood) holds between $t, t' \in T_\Sigma(\mathcal{X})$, denoted $t \sqsupseteq_E t'$ (meaning that t is *more general than* t' modulo E), if there is a substitution σ such that $t\sigma =_E t'$; such a substitution σ is said to be an *E-match* from t' to t.

An *E-unifier* for a Σ-equation $t = t'$ is a substitution σ such that $t\sigma =_E t'\sigma$. For $Var(t) \cup Var(t') \subseteq W$, a set of substitutions $CSU_E^W(t = t')$ is said to be a *complete* set of unifiers for the equality $t = t'$ modulo E away from W iff: (i) each $\sigma \in CSU_E^W(t = t')$ is an E-unifier of $t = t'$; (ii) for any E-unifier ρ of $t = t'$ there is a $\sigma \in CSU_E^W(t = t')$ such that $\sigma|_W \sqsupseteq_E \rho|_W$; (iii) for all $\sigma \in CSU_E^W(t = t')$, $Dom(\sigma) \subseteq (Var(t) \cup Var(t'))$ and $Ran(\sigma) \cap W = \varnothing$. If the set of variables W is irrelevant or is understood from the context, we write $CSU_E(t = t')$ instead of $CSU_E^W(t = t')$. An E-unification algorithm is *complete* if for any equation $t = t'$ it generates a complete set of E-unifiers. A unification algorithm is said to be *finitary* and complete if it always terminates after generating a finite and complete set of solutions.

A *rewrite rule* is an oriented pair $l \to r$, where[3] $l \notin \mathcal{X}$ and $l, r \in T_\Sigma(\mathcal{X})_s$ for some sort $\mathsf{s} \in \mathsf{S}$. An *(unconditional) order-sorted rewrite theory* is a triple (Σ, E, R) with Σ an order-sorted signature, E a set of Σ-equations, and R a set of rewrite rules.

The rewriting relation on $T_\Sigma(\mathcal{X})$, written $t \to_R t'$ or $t \to_{p,R} t'$ holds between t and t' iff there exist $p \in Pos_\Sigma(t)$, $l \to r \in R$ and a substitution σ, such that $t|_p = l\sigma$, and $t' = t[r\sigma]_p$. The subterm $t|_p$ is called a *redex*. The relation $\to_{R/E}$ on $T_\Sigma(\mathcal{X})$ is $=_E; \to_R; =_E$, i.e., $t \to_{R/E} t'$ iff there exists u, u' s.t. $t =_E u \to_R u' =_E t'$. Note that $\to_{R/E}$ on $T_\Sigma(\mathcal{X})$ induces a relation $\to_{R/E}$ on the free (Σ, E)-algebra $T_{\Sigma/E}(\mathcal{X})$ by $[t]_E \to_{R/E} [t']_E$ iff $t \to_{R/E} t'$. The transitive (resp. transitive and reflexive) closure of $\to_{R/E}$ is denoted $\to_{R/E}^+$ (resp. $\to_{R/E}^*$).

The $\to_{R/E}$ relation can be difficult to compute. However, under the appropriate conditions it is equivalent to the R, E relation in which it is enough to compute the relationship on any representatives of two E-equivalence classes. A relation $\to_{R,E}$ on $T_\Sigma(\mathcal{X})$ is defined as: $t \to_{p,R,E} t'$ (or just $t \to_{R,E} t'$) iff there exist $p \in Pos_\Sigma(t)$, a rule $l \to r$ in R, and a substitution σ such that $t|_p =_E l\sigma$ and $t' = t[r\sigma]_p$.

Let t be a term and W be a set of variables such that $Var(t) \subseteq W$, the R, E-*narrowing* relation on $T_\Sigma(\mathcal{X})$ is defined as $t \leadsto_{p,\sigma,R,E} t'$ ($\leadsto_{\sigma,R,E}$ if p is understood, $\leadsto_\sigma$ if R, E are also understood, and $\leadsto$ if σ is also understood) if there is a non-variable position $p \in Pos_\Sigma(t)$, a rule $l \to r \in R$ properly

---

[3] We do not impose the requirement $Var(r) \subseteq Var(l)$, since extra variables (e.g., choice variables) may be introduced in the righthand side of a rule. Rewriting with extra variables in righthand sides is handled by allowing the matching substitution to instantiate these extra variables in any possible way. Although this may produce an infinite number of one-step concrete rewrites from a term due to the infinite number of possible instantiations, the symbolic, narrowing-based analysis used by Maude-NPA and explained below can cover all those infinite possibilities in a finitary way.

renamed s.t. $(Var(l) \cup Var(r)) \cap W = \emptyset$, and a unifier $\sigma \in CSU_E^{W'}(t|_p = l)$ for $W' = W \cup Var(l)$, such that $t' = (t[r]_p)\sigma$. For convenience, in each narrowing step $t \leadsto_\sigma t'$ we only specify the part of σ that binds variables of t. The transitive (resp. transitive and reflexive) closure of $\leadsto$ is denoted by $\leadsto^+$ (resp. $\leadsto^*$). We may write $t \leadsto_\sigma^k t'$ if there are $u_1, \ldots, u_{k-1}$ and substitutions $\rho_1, \ldots, \rho_k$ such that $t \leadsto_{\rho_1} u_1 \cdots u_{k-1} \leadsto_{\rho_k} t'$, $k \geqslant 0$, and $\sigma = \rho_1 \cdots \rho_k$.

Maude-NPA uses *backwards narrowing* (i.e., uses protocol rules $l \to r$ "in reverse" as rules $r \to l$) *modulo* the algebraic properties of cryptographic functions as a *sound and complete* reachability analysis method. Section 7.2 gives a detailed proof of the soundness and completeness of this method for strands with choice.

3   Overview of Maude-NPA

Here we give a high-level summary of Maude-NPA. For further details please see [8].

Given a protocol $\mathcal{P}$, we define its specification in the strand space model as a rewrite theory of the form $(\Sigma_{SS_\mathcal{P}}, E_{SS_\mathcal{P}}, R_{B_\mathcal{P}^{-1}})$, where (i) the signature $\Sigma_{SS_\mathcal{P}}$ is split into predefined symbols Σ_{SS} for strand syntax and user-definable symbols $\Sigma_\mathcal{P}$ based on a parametric sort Msg of messages, (ii) the algebraic properties $E_{SS_\mathcal{P}}$ are also split into the algebraic properties of the strand notation E_{SS} and the user-definable algebraic properties $E_\mathcal{P}$ for the cryptographic functions, and (iii) the transition rules $R_{B_\mathcal{P}^{-1}}$ are defined on states, i.e., terms of a predefined sort State. They are *reversed* for backwards execution.

Example 2. The first action in Example 1, the hello message, contains a nonce, the Diffie-Hellman group it wants to use, and the Diffie-Hellman key share. This could be represented by the term "$hs \; ; \; n(C, r_1) \; ; \; G \; ; \; gen(G) \; ; \; keyG(G, C, r_2)$" where ; is the concatenation symbol, hs is a fixed constant, C is a variable denoting the Client identifier, $n(C, r_1)$ denotes a nonce created by the client using a randomly generated constant r_1, G is a variable denoting the chosen Diffie-Hellman group, $gen(G)$ is the generator associated to G, and $keyG(G, C, r_2)$ is the key created by the client using the chosen G and another randomly generated constant r_2.

In Maude-NPA states are modeled as elements of an initial algebra $\mathcal{T}_{\Sigma_{SS_\mathcal{P}}/E_{SS_\mathcal{P}}}$, i.e., an $E_{SS_\mathcal{P}}$-equivalence class $[t]_{E_{SS_\mathcal{P}}} \in \mathcal{T}_{\Sigma_{SS_\mathcal{P}}/E_{SS_\mathcal{P}}}$ with t a ground $\Sigma_{SS_\mathcal{P}}$-term. A state has the form $\{S_1 \& \cdots \& S_n \& \{IK\}\}$ where $\&$ is an associative-commutative union operator with identity symbol $\emptyset$. Each element in the set is either a *strand* S_i or the *intruder knowledge* $\{IK\}$ at that state.

The *intruder knowledge* $\{IK\}$ belongs to the state and is represented as a set of facts using the comma as an associative-commutative union operator with identity element *empty*. There are two kinds of intruder facts: *positive* knowledge facts (the intruder knows message m, i.e., $m \in \mathcal{I}$), and *negative* knowledge facts (the intruder *does not yet know* m but *will know it in a future state*, i.e., $m \notin \mathcal{I}$), where m is a message expression.

A *strand* [12] specifies the sequence of messages sent and received by a principal executing a given role in the protocol and is represented as a sequence of messages $[msg_1^{\pm}, msg_2^{\pm}, msg_3^{\pm}, \ldots, msg_{k-1}^{\pm}, msg_k^{\pm}]$ with $msg_i^{\pm}$ either msg_i^{-} (also written $-msg_i$) representing an input message, or msg_i^{+} (also written $+msg_i$) representing an output message. Note that each msg_i is a term of a special sort Msg.

Strands are used to represent both the actions of honest principals (with a strand specified for each protocol role) and the actions of an intruder (with a strand for each action an intruder is able to perform on messages). In Maude-NPA strands evolve over time; the symbol | is used to divide past and future. That is, given a strand $[\ msg_1^{\pm},\ \ldots,\ msg_i^{\pm}\ |\ msg_{i+1}^{\pm},\ \ldots,\ msg_k^{\pm}\ ]$, messages $msg_1^{\pm}, \ldots, msg_i^{\pm}$ are the *past messages*, and messages $msg_{i+1}^{\pm}, \ldots, msg_k^{\pm}$ are the *future messages* ($msg_{i+1}^{\pm}$ is the immediate future message). A strand $[msg_1^{\pm}, \ldots, msg_k^{\pm}]$ is shorthand for $[nil \mid msg_1^{\pm}, \ldots, msg_k^{\pm}, nil]$. An *initial state* is a state where the bar is at the beginning for all strands in the state, and the intruder knowledge has no fact of the form $m \in \mathcal{I}$. A *final state* is a state where the bar is at the end for all strands in the state and there is no intruder fact of the form $m \notin \mathcal{I}$.

Since Fresh variables must be treated differently from other variables by Maude-NPA, we make them explicit by writing $:: r_1, \ldots, r_k :: [m_1^{\pm}, \ldots, m_n^{\pm}]$, where each r_i first appears in an output message $m_{j_i}^{+}$ and can later appear in any input and output message of $m_{j_i+1}^{\pm}, \ldots, m_n^{\pm}$. If there are no Fresh variables, we write $:: nil :: [m_1^{\pm}, \ldots, m_n^{\pm}]$.

Example 3. For example, the Needham-Schroeder Public Key protocol is described as follows:

1. $A \rightarrow B : pk(B, A; N_A)$
2. $B \rightarrow A : pk(A, N_A; N_B)$
3. $A \rightarrow B : pk(B, N_B)$

where ; is the concatenation symbol, $pk(A, M)$ denotes encryption of message M using the public key of principal A, and N_A denotes a nonce generated by principal A. Its representation using strands would be as follows:

$$:: r_A :: [+(pk(B, A; n(A, r_A))), -(pk(A, n(A, r_A); N_B)), +(pk(B, N_B))]$$

$$:: r_B :: [-(pk(B, A; N_A)), +(pk(A, N_A; n(B, r_B))), -(pk(B, n(B, r_B)))]$$

Since the number of states in $T_{\Sigma_{SS_P}/E_{SS_P}}$ is in general infinite, rather than exploring concrete protocol states $[t]_{E_{SS_P}} \in T_{\Sigma_{SS_P}/E_{SS_P}}$ Maude-NPA explores *symbolic strand state patterns* $[t(x_1, \ldots, x_n)]_{E_{SS_P}} \in T_{\Sigma_{SS_P}/E_{SS_P}}(\mathcal{X})$ on the free $(\Sigma_{SS_P}, E_{SS_P})$-algebra over a set of variables $\mathcal{X}$. In this way, a state pattern $[t(x_1, \ldots, x_n)]_{E_{SS_P}}$ represents not a single concrete state but a possibly infinite set of such states, namely all the *instances* of the pattern $[t(x_1, \ldots, x_n)]_{E_{SS_P}}$ where the variables $x_1, \ldots, x_n$ have been instantiated by concrete ground terms.

The semantics of Maude-NPA is expressed in terms of the following *forward rewrite rules* that describe how a protocol moves from one state to another via the intruder's interaction with it.

$$\{SS \ \& \ [L \mid M^-, L'] \ \& \ \{M \in \mathcal{I}, IK\}\} \rightarrow \{SS \ \& \ [L, M^- \mid L'] \ \& \ \{M \in \mathcal{I}, IK\}\} \qquad (\text{-})$$

$$\{SS \ \& \ [L \mid M^+, L'] \ \& \ \{IK\}\} \rightarrow \{SS \ \& \ [L, M^+ \mid L'] \ \& \ \{IK\}\} \qquad (+)$$

$$\{SS \ \& \ [L \mid M^+, L'] \ \& \ \{M \notin \mathcal{I}, IK\}\} \rightarrow \{SS \ \& \ [L, M^+ \mid L'] \ \& \ \{M \in \mathcal{I}, IK\}\} \quad (++)$$

$$\forall \ [l_1, u^+, l_2] \in \mathcal{P} : \{SS \ \& \ [l_1 \mid u^+, l_2] \ \& \ \{u \notin \mathcal{I}, IK\}\} \rightarrow \{SS \ \& \ \{u \in \mathcal{I}, IK\}\} \qquad (\&)$$

where L and L' are variables denoting a list of strand messages, IK is a variable for a set of intruder facts ($m \in \mathcal{I}$ or $m \notin \mathcal{I}$), SS is a variable denoting a set of strands, and l_1, l_2 denote a list of strand messages. The set $R_{B_{\mathcal{P}}^{-1}}$ of *backwards state transition rules* is defined by reversing the direction of the above set of rules $\{(\text{-}), (+), (++)\} \cup (\&)$. In the backwards executions of $(\&)$, $(++)$, $u \notin \mathcal{I}$ marks when the intruder learnt u.

One uses Maude-NPA to find an attack by specifying an insecure state pattern called an *attack pattern*. Secrecy, authentication, and indistinguishability properties, among others, can be specified as attack patterns in Maude-NPA (see [8]). Maude-NPA attempts to find a path from an initial state to the attack pattern via backwards narrowing (narrowing using the rewrite rules with the orientation reversed). That is, a narrowing sequence from an initial state to an attack state is searched *in reverse* as a *backwards path* from the attack state to the initial state.

Example 4. A secrecy attack pattern for the protocol of Example 3 would be as follows:

$$:: r_B :: [-(pk(B, A; N_A)), +(pk(A, N_A; n(B, r_B))), -(pk(B, n(B, r_B))) \mid nil] \& \{n(B, r_B) \in \mathcal{I}\}$$

where Bob's strand is completed and the intruder has learnt his nonce $n(B, r_B)$. Maude-NPA adds extra strands, e.g. for Alice and for the intruder capabilities, along the path from the attack pattern to an initial state.

Maude-NPA attempts to find paths until it can no longer form any backwards narrowing steps, at which point it terminates. If at that point it has not found an initial state, the attack pattern is shown to be *unreachable* modulo $E_{SS_{\mathcal{P}}}$. Section 7.2 gives a detailed proof of the soundness and completeness of this symbolic method for the Maude-NPA extension supporting strands with choice. Note that Maude-NPA places *no bound on the number of sessions*, so reachability is undecidable in general. Note also that Maude-NPA does not perform any data abstraction such as a bounded number of nonces. However, the tool makes use of a number of sound and complete state space reduction techniques that help to identify unreachable and redundant states [10], and thus make termination more likely.

4   A Process Algebra for Protocols with Choice

In this section we define a process algebra that extends the strand space model to naturally specify protocols exhibiting choice points. Throughout the paper we refer to this process algebra as the *protocol process algebra*.

The rest of this section is organized as follows. First, in Sect. 4.1 we define the syntax of the protocol process algebra and state the requirements that a *well-formed process* must satisfy. Then in Sect. 4.2, we explain how *protocol specifications* can be defined in this process algebra. In Sect. 4.3 we then define the *operational semantics* of the protocol process algebra. Note that the operational semantics of Maude-NPA given in Sect. 3 corresponds to a symbolic backwards semantics, while in Sect. 4.3 we give a rewriting-based forwards semantics for process algebra. Sections 6.2 and 7.2 will relate these two semantics using *bisimulations*.

4.1   Syntax of the Protocol Process Algebra

In the *protocol process algebra* the behaviors of both honest principals and the intruder are represented by *labeled processes*. Therefore, a protocol is specified as a set of labeled processes. Each process performs a sequence of actions, namely, sending or receiving a message, and may perform deterministic or non-deterministic choices. The protocol process algebra's syntax is parameterized[4] by a sort Msg of messages and has the following syntax:

$$
\begin{aligned}
ProcConf &::= LProc \mid ProcConf \; \& \; ProcConf \mid \varnothing \\
LProc &::= (Role, I, J) \; Proc \\
Proc &::= nilP \mid \; + Msg \mid \; - Msg \mid Proc \cdot Proc \mid \\
&\qquad Proc \; ? \; Proc \mid if \; Cond \; then \; Proc \; else \; Proc \\
Cond &::= Msg \; \neq \; Msg \mid Msg \; = \; Msg
\end{aligned}
$$

- *ProcConf* stands for a *process configuration*, that is, a set of labeled processes. The symbol & is used to denote set union for sets of labeled processes.
- *LProc* stands for a *labeled process*, that is, a process *Proc* with a label $(Role, I, J)$. *Role* refers to the role of the process in the protocol (e.g., initiator or responder). I is a natural number denoting the identity of the process, which distinguishes different instances (sessions) of a process specification. J indicates that the action at stage J of the process specification will be the next one to be executed, that is, the first $J-1$ actions of the process for role *Role* have already been executed. Note that we omit I and J in the protocol specification when both I and J are 0.
- *Proc* defines the actions that can be executed within a process. $+Msg$, and $-Msg$ respectively denote sending out or receiving a message *Msg*. We assume a single channel, through which all messages are sent or received

---

[4] More precisely, as explained in Sect. 4.2, they are parameterized by a user-definable equational theory $(\Sigma_\mathcal{P}, E_\mathcal{P})$ having a sort Msg of messages.

by the intruder. "*Proc · Proc*" denotes *sequential composition* of processes, where symbol $\_\cdot\_$ is associative and has the empty process *nilP* as identity. "*Proc ? Proc*" denotes an explicit *nondeterministic choice*, whereas "*if Cond then Proc else Proc*" denotes an explicit *deterministic choice*, whose continuation depends on the satisfaction of the constraint *Cond*.

– *Cond* denotes a constraint that will be evaluated in explicit deterministic choices. In this work we only consider constraints that are either equalities (=) or disequalities ($\neq$) between message expressions.

Let PS, QS, and RS be process configurations, and P, Q, and R be protocol processes. Our protocol syntax satisfies the following *structural axioms*:

$$PS \,\&\, QS = QS \,\&\, PS \quad (1) \qquad (P \cdot Q) \cdot R = P \cdot (Q \cdot R) \quad (3) \qquad P \cdot nilP = P \quad (5)$$

$$(PS \,\&\, QS) \,\&\, RS = PS \,\&\, (QS \,\&\, RS) \quad (2) \qquad PS \,\&\, \varnothing = PS \quad (4) \qquad nilP \cdot P = P \quad (6)$$

Example 5. The strands of Example 3 are described using processes as follows:

$$(Alice) + (pk(B_?, A_?; n(A_?, r_A))) \cdot -(pk(A_?, n(A_?, r_A); N_B)) \cdot +(pk(B_?, N_B))$$

$$(Bob) - (pk(B, A; N_A)) \cdot +(pk(A, N_A; n(B, r_B))) \cdot -(pk(B, n(B, r_B)))$$

An alternative definition, forcing conditional expressions for pattern matching is:

$$(Alice) + (pk(B_?, A_?; n(A_?, r_A))) \cdot -(X) \cdot$$
$$if\ X = pk(A_?, n(A_?, r_A); N_B)\ then\ +(pk(B_?, N_B))\ else\ nilP$$

$$(Bob) - (X) \cdot if\ X = pk(B, A; N_A)$$
$$then\ +(pk(A, N_A; n(B, r_B))) \cdot -(Y) \cdot$$
$$if\ Y = pk(B, n(B, r_B))\ then\ nilP\ else\ nilP$$
$$else\ nilP$$

The specification of the processes defining a protocol's behavior may contain some variables denoting information that the principal executing the process does not yet have, or that will be different in different executions. In all protocol specifications we assume three disjoint kinds of variables:

– **fresh variables:** these are not really variables in the standard sense, but *names* for *constant values* in a data type V_{fresh} of unguessable values such as nonces. For instance, the randomly generated r_1 and r_2 of Example 2 or r_A and r_B of Examples 3 and 5 are fresh variables. A *fresh variable* r is always associated with a role $ro \in Role$ in the protocol. For each protocol session i, we associate to r a unique name $r.ro.i$ for a constant in the data type V_{fresh}. What is assumed is that if $r.ro.i \neq r'.ro'.j$ (including the case

$r.ro.i \neq r.ro.j$), the values interpreting $r.ro.i$ and $r'.ro'.j$ in $\mathsf{V_{fresh}}$ are both *different* and *unguessable*. In particular, for role $ro \in Role$, the interpretation mapping $I : \{r.ro.i \mid i \in \mathbb{N}\} \to \mathsf{V_{fresh}}$ is *injective* and *random*. In our semantics, a constant $r.ro.i$ denotes its (unguessable) interpretation $I(r.ro.i) \in \mathsf{V_{fresh}}$. Throughout this paper we will denote this kind of variables as $r, r_1, r_2, \ldots$.

- **choice variables:** variables first appearing in a *sent message* $+M$, which can be substituted by any value arbitrarily chosen from a possibly infinite domain. For instance, the chosen Diffie-Hellman group G of Example 2 is a choice variable. A choice variable indicates an *implicit non-deterministic choice*. Given a protocol with choice variables, each possible substitution of these variables denotes a possible continuation of the protocol. We always denote choice variables by uppercase letters postfixed with the symbol "?" as a subscript, e.g., $A_?, B_?, \ldots$.

- **pattern variables:** variables first appearing in a *received message* $-M$. These variables will be instantiated when matching sent and received messages. For instance, the generator for the chosen group G of Example 2 is received by the server using a pattern variable. Likewise, the variables used in Example 5 for the case with conditional expressions are also pattern variables. *Implicit deterministic choices* are indicated by terms containing pattern variables, since failing to match a pattern term may lead to the rejection of a message. A pattern term plays the implicit role of a guard, so that, depending on the different ways of matching it, the protocol can have different continuations. This kind of variables will be written with uppercase letters, e.g., $A, B, N_A, \ldots$.

Note that fresh variables are distinguished from other variables by having a specific sort Fresh. Choice variables or pattern variables can never have sort Fresh.

To guarantee the requirements on different kinds of variables that can appear in a given process, we consider only *well-formed* processes in Fig. 1. We make this notion precise by defining a function $wf : Proc \to Bool$ checking whether a given process is well-formed. A labeled process is *well-formed* if the process it labels is well-formed. A process configuration is *well-formed* if all the labeled process in it are well-formed. The definition of wf uses an auxiliary function $shVar : Proc \to VarSet$ in Fig. 2, retrieving the "shared variables" of a process, i.e., the set of variables that show up in all branches. Below we define both functions, where P, Q, and R are processes, M is a message, and T is a constraint.

$$wf(P \cdot +M) = wf(P) \qquad\qquad if\ (Var(M) \cap Var(P)) \subseteq shVar(P)$$
$$wf(P \cdot -M) = wf(P) \qquad\qquad if\ (Var(M) \cap Var(P)) \subseteq shVar(P)$$
$$wf(P \cdot (if\ T\ then\ Q\ else\ R)) = wf(P \cdot Q) \wedge wf(P \cdot R) \quad if\ P \neq nilP\ and\ Q \neq nilP\ and$$
$$Var(T) \subseteq shVar(P)$$
$$wf(P \cdot (Q\ ?\ R)) = wf(P \cdot Q) \wedge wf(P \cdot R) \qquad if\ Q \neq nilP\ or\ R \neq nilP$$
$$wf(P \cdot\ nilP) = wf(P)$$
$$wf(nilP) = True.$$

Fig. 1. Well-formed processes

$$shVar(+M \cdot P) = Var(M) \cup shVar(P)$$
$$shVar(-M \cdot P) = Var(M) \cup shVar(P)$$
$$shVar((if\ T\ then\ P\ else\ Q) \cdot R) = Var(T) \cup (shVar(P) \cap shVar(Q)) \cup shVar(R)$$
$$shVar((P\ ?\ Q) \cdot R) = (shVar(P) \cap shVar(Q)) \cup shVar(R)$$
$$shVar(nilP) = \varnothing$$

Fig. 2. Shared variables of a process

Remark 1. Note that the well-formedness property implies that if a process begins with a deterministic choice action *if T then Q else R*, then all variables in T must be instantiated, and thus only one branch may be taken. For this reason, it is undesirable to specify processes that begin with such an action. Furthermore, note that the well-formedness property avoids explicit choices where both possibilities are the *nilP* process. That is, processes containing either *(if T then nilP else nilP)*, or *(nilP ? nilP)*, respectively.

We illustrate the notion of well-formed process below.

Example 6. The behavior of a Client initiating an instance of the handshake protocol from Example 1 with the Server, where the Server may or may not request the Client to authenticate itself, may be specified by the well-formed process shown below:

$$
\begin{aligned}
(Client)\ & + (hs; n(C_?, r_1); G_?; gen(G_?); keyG(G_?, C_?, r_2)) \cdot \\
& - (hs; N; G_?; gen(G_?); E; Z(AReq, G_?, E, C_?, r_1, S, HM)) \cdot \\
& if\ (AReq = authreq)\ then \\
& + (e(keyE(G_?, E, C_?, r_1), \\
& \qquad sig(C, W(HM, AReq, S_?, G_?, E, C_?, r_1)); \\
& \qquad mac(keyE(G_?, E, , C_?, r_1), W(HM, AReq, S, G_?, E, C_?, r_1)))) \cdot \\
& else \\
& + (e(keyE(G_?, E, C_?, r_2), mac(keyE(G_?, E, C_?, r_2), W(HM, AReq, S, G_?, E, C_?, r_1))))
\end{aligned}
$$

where $keyG$, Z and W are macros used to construct messages sent in the protocol. The variables $C_?$ and $G_?$ are choice variables denoting the client and Diffie-Hellman group respectively, and the variables r_1 and r_2 are fresh variables. All other variables are pattern variables. In particular, the variable $AReq$ is a pattern variable that can be instantiated to either *authreq* or *noauthreq*. The Client makes a deterministic choice whether or not to sign its next message with its digital signature, depending on which value of $AReq$ it receives.

Example 7. The behavior of a Server who may or may not request a retry from a Client in an instance of the handshake protocol from Example 1 may be specified as follows:

$(Server):\ -(hs; N; G; gen(G); E)\cdot$
$\qquad (((+(hs; retry)\cdot$
$\qquad\qquad -(hs; N'; G'; gen(G'); E')\cdot$
$\qquad\qquad +(hs; n(S_?, r1); G'; gen(G'); keyG(G', S_?, r_2); Z(AReq_?, G', E', S, r_2, S_?, HM)))$
$\qquad ?$
$\qquad (+(hs; n(S_?, r1); G; gen(G); keyG(G, S, r_2); Z(AReq_?, G, E, S, r_2, S_?, HM)))))$

In this case the server nondeterministically chooses to request or not to request a retry. In the case of a retry it waits for the retry message from the client, and then proceeds with the handshake message using the new key information from the client. In the case when it does not request a retry, it sends the handshake message immediately after receiving the client's Hello message. The variable r_2 is a fresh variable, while $S_?$ and $AReq_?$ are choice variables. $S_?$ denotes the name of the server, and $AReq_?$ is nondeterministically instantiated to *authreq* or *noauthreq*.

Example 8. The following process does not satisfy the well-formedness property.

$(Resp)-(pk(B, A; NA))\cdot\ (+(pk(A, 1; n(B, r)))\ ?\ +(pk(A, 2)))\ \cdot\ +(pk(C_?, n(B, r)))$

The problem with this process is the fresh variable r appearing in $+(pk(C_?, n(B, r)))$, since $r \notin shVar(-(pk(B, A; NA))\cdot(+(pk(A, 1; n(B, r)))\ ?\ +(pk(A, 2))))$. More specifically, because it does not appear in message $+(pk(A, 2))$, but $r \in Var(-(pk(B, A; NA))\cdot(+(pk(A, 1; n(B, r)))\ ?\ +(pk(A, 2))))$.

4.2 Protocol Specification in Process Algebra

Given a protocol $\mathcal{P}$, we define its specification in the protocol process algebra, written $\mathcal{P}_{PA}$, as a pair of the form $\mathcal{P}_{PA} = ((\Sigma_{PA_\mathcal{P}}, E_{PA_\mathcal{P}}), P_{PA})$, where $(\Sigma_{PA_\mathcal{P}}, E_{PA_\mathcal{P}})$ is an equational theory explained below, and P_{PA} is a term denoting a *well-formed* process configuration representing the behavior of the honest principals as well as the capabilities of the attacker. That is, $P_{PA} = (ro_1)P_1\ \&\ \ldots\ \&\ (ro_i)P_i$, where each ro_k, $1 \leqslant k \leqslant i$, is either the role of an honest principal or identifies one of the capabilities of the attacker. P_{PA} cannot contain two processes with the same label, i.e., the behavior of each honest principal, and each attacker capability are represented by a *unique* process. $E_{PA_\mathcal{P}} = E_\mathcal{P} \cup E_{PA}$ is a set of equations with $E_\mathcal{P}$ denoting the protocol's cryptographic properties and E_{PA} denoting the properties of process constructors. The set of equations $E_\mathcal{P}$ is user-definable and can vary for different protocols. Instead, the set of equations E_{PA} is always the same for all protocols. $\Sigma_{PA_\mathcal{P}} = \Sigma_\mathcal{P} \cup \Sigma_{PA}$ is the signature defining the sorts and function symbols as follows:

- $\Sigma_{\mathcal{P}}$ is an order-sorted signature defining the sorts and function symbols for the messages that can be exchanged in protocol $\mathcal{P}$. However, independently of protocol $\mathcal{P}$, $\Sigma_{\mathcal{P}}$ must always have a sort Msg as the top sort in one of its connected components. We call a sort S a *data sort* iff it is either a subsort of Msg, or there is a message constructor $c : S_1...S...S_n \rightarrow S'$, with S' a subsort of Msg. The specific sort Fresh for fresh variables is an example of *data sort*. Choice and pattern variables have sort Msg or any of its subsorts.
- Σ_{PA} is an order-sorted signature defining the sorts and function symbols of the *process algebra infrastructure*. Σ_{PA} corresponds exactly to the BNF definition of the protocol process algebra's syntax in Sect. 4.1. Although it has a sort Msg for messages, it leaves this sort totally unspecified, so that different protocols $\mathcal{P}$ may use completely different message constructors and may satisfy different equational properties $E_{\mathcal{P}}$. Therefore, Σ_{PA} will be the same signature for any protocol specified in the process algebra. More specifically, Σ_{PA} contains the sorts for process configurations (ProcConf), labeled processes (LProc), processes (Proc), constraints (Cond), and messages(Msg), as well as the subsort relations LProc < ProcConf. Furthermore, the function symbols in Σ_{PA} are also defined according to the BNF definition.

Therefore, the syntax $\Sigma_{PA_{\mathcal{P}}}$ of processes for $\mathcal{P}$ will be in the union signature $\Sigma_{PA} \cup \Sigma_{\mathcal{P}}$, consisting of the protocol-specific syntax $\Sigma_{\mathcal{P}}$, and the generic process syntax Σ_{PA} through the shared sort Msg.

4.3   Operational Semantics of the Protocol Process Algebra

Given a protocol $\mathcal{P}$, a *state* of $\mathcal{P}$ consists of a set of (possibly partially executed) *labeled processes*, and a set of terms in the intruder's knowledge $\{IK\}$. That is, a state is a term of the form $\{LP_1 \& \cdots \& LP_n \mid \{IK\}\}$. Given a state St of this form, we abuse notation and write $LP_k \in St$ if LP_k is a labeled process in the set $LP_1 \& \cdots \& LP_n$.

The intruder knowledge IK models the *single* channel through which all messages are sent and received. We consider an active attacker who has complete control of the channel, i.e, can read, alter, redirect, and delete traffic as well as create its own messages by means of *intruder processes*. That is, the purpose of some $LP_k \in St$ is to perform message-manipulation actions for the intruder.

State changes are defined by a set $R_{PA_{\mathcal{P}}}$ of *rewrite rules*, such that the rewrite theory $(\Sigma_{PA_{\mathcal{P}}+State}, E_{PA_{\mathcal{P}}}, R_{PA_{\mathcal{P}}})$ characterizes the behavior of protocol $\mathcal{P}$, where $\Sigma_{PA_{\mathcal{P}}+State}$ extends $\Sigma_{PA_{\mathcal{P}}}$ by adding state constructor symbols. We assume that a protocol's execution begins with an empty state, i.e., a state with an empty set of labeled processes, and an empty intruder knowledge. That is, the initial state is always of the form $\{\varnothing \mid \{empty\}\}$. Each transition rule in $R_{PA_{\mathcal{P}}}$ is labeled with a tuple of the form (ro, i, j, a, n), where:

- ro is the role of the labeled process being executed in the transition.
- i denotes the identifier of the labeled process being executed in the transition. Since there can be more than one process instance of the same role in a

process state, i is used to distinguish different instances, i.e., ro and i together uniquely identify a process in a state.

- j denotes the process' step number since its beginning.
- a is a ground term identifying the action that is being performed in the transition. It has different possible values: "$+m$" or "$-m$" if the message m was sent (and added to the intruder's knowledge) or received, respectively; "m" if the message m was sent but did not increase the intruder's knowledge, "?" if the transition performs an explicit non-deterministic choice, or "T" if the transition performs a explicit deterministic choice.
- n is a number that, if the action that is being executed is an explicit choice, indicates which branch has been chosen as the process continuation. In this case n takes the value of either 1 or 2. If the transition does not perform any explicit choice, then $n = 0$.

Below we describe the set of transition rules that define a protocol's execution in the protocol process algebra, that is, the set of rules $R_{PA_{\mathcal{P}}}$. Note that in the transition rules shown below, PS denotes the rest of labeled processes of the state (which can be the empty set $\varnothing$).

- The action of *sending a message* is represented by the two transition rules below. Since we assume that the intruder has complete control of the network, it can learn any message sent by other principals. Rule (PA++) denotes the case in which the sent message is added to the intruder's knowledge. Note that this rule can only be applied if the intruder has not already learnt that message. Rule (PA+) denotes the case in which the intruder chooses not to learn the message, i.e., the intruder's knowledge is not modified, and, thus, no condition needs to be checked. Since choice variables denote messages that are nondeterministically chosen, all (possibly infinitely many) admissible ground substitutions for the choice variables are possible behaviors.

$$\{(ro, i, j)\ (+M \cdot P)\ \&\ PS \mid \{IK\}\}$$
$$\longrightarrow_{(ro,i,j,+M\sigma,0)} \{(ro, i, j+1)\ P\sigma\ \&\ PS \mid \{M\sigma \in \mathcal{I}, IK\}\} \quad \text{if } (M\sigma \in \mathcal{I}) \notin IK$$
$$\text{where } \sigma \text{ is a ground substitution binding choice variables in } M \qquad \text{(PA++)}$$

$$\{(ro, i, j)\ (+M \cdot P)\ \&\ PS \mid \{IK\}\}$$
$$\longrightarrow_{(ro,i,j,M\sigma,0)} \{(ro, i, j+1)\ P\sigma\ \&\ PS \mid \{IK\}\}$$
$$\text{where } \sigma \text{ is a ground substitution binding choice variables in } M \qquad \text{(PA+)}$$

- As shown in the rule below, a process can *receive a message* matching a pattern M if there is a message M' in the intruder's knowledge, i.e., a message previously sent either by some honest principal or by some intruder process, that matches the pattern message M. After receiving this message the process will continue with its variables instantiated by the matching substitution, which takes place modulo the equations $E_{\mathcal{P}}$. Note that the intruder can "delete" a message via choosing not to learn it (executing Rule PA+ instead of Rule PA++) or not to deliver it (failing to execute Rule PA-).

$$\{(ro, i, j) \ (-M \cdot P) \ \& \ PS \mid \{M' \in \mathcal{I}, IK\}\}$$
$$\longrightarrow_{(ro,i,j,-M\sigma,0)} \{(ro, i, j+1) \ P\sigma \ \& \ PS \mid \{M' \in \mathcal{I}, IK\}\} \qquad \textit{if } M' =_{E_\mathcal{P}} M\sigma$$
$$\text{(PA-)}$$

– The two transition rules shown below define the operational semantics of *explicit deterministic choices*. That is, the operational semantics of an *if T then P else Q* expression. More specifically, rule (PAif1) describes the *then* case, i.e., if the constraint T is satisfied, the process will continue as P. Rule (PAif2) describes the *else* case, that is, if the constraint T is *not* satisfied, the process will continue as Q. Note that, since we only consider well-formed processes, these transition rules will only be applied if $j \geqslant 1$. Note also that since T has been fully substituted by the time the if-then-else is executed, and the constraints that we considered in this paper are of the form $m \neq_{E_\mathcal{P}} m'$ or $m =_{E_\mathcal{P}} m'$, the satisfiability of T can be checked by checking whether the corresponding ground equality or disequality holds.

$$\{(ro, i, j) \ ((\textit{if } T \textit{ then } P \textit{ else } Q) \ \cdot R) \ \& \ PS \mid \{IK\}\}$$
$$\longrightarrow_{(ro,i,j,T,1)} \{(ro, i, j+1) \ (P \cdot R) \ \& \ PS \mid \{IK\}\} \ \textit{if } T \qquad \text{(PAif1)}$$
$$\{(ro, i, j) \ ((\textit{if } T \textit{ then } P \textit{ else } Q) \ \cdot R) \ \& \ PS \mid \{IK\}\}$$
$$\longrightarrow_{(ro,i,j,T,2)} \{(ro, i, j+1) \ (Q \cdot R) \ \& \ PS \mid \{IK\}\} \ \textit{if } \neg T \qquad \text{(PAif2)}$$

– The two transition rules below define the semantics of *explicit non-deterministic choice* $P \ ? \ Q$. In this case, the process can continue either as P, denoted by rule (PA?1), or as Q, denoted by rule (PA?2). Note that this decision is made non-deterministically.

$$\{(ro, i, j) \ ((P \ ? \ Q) \cdot R) \ \& \ PS \mid \{IK\}\}$$
$$\longrightarrow_{(ro,i,j,?,1)} \{(ro, i, j+1) \ (P \cdot R) \ \& \ PS \mid \{IK\}\} \qquad \text{(PA?1)}$$
$$\{(ro, i, j) \ ((P \ ? \ Q) \cdot R) \ \& \ PS \mid \{IK\}\}$$
$$\longrightarrow_{(ro,i,j,?,2)} \{(ro, i, j+1)(Q \cdot R) \ \& \ PS \mid \{IK\}\} \qquad \text{(PA?2)}$$

– The transition rules shown below describe the *introduction of a new process* from the specification into the state, which allows us to support an unbounded session model. Recall that fresh variables are associated with a role and an identifier. Therefore, whenever a new process is introduced: (a) the largest process identifier (i) will be increased by 1, and (b) new names will be assigned to the fresh variables in the new process. The function $MaxProcId(PS, ro)$ in the transition rule below is used to get the largest process identifier (i) of role ro in the process configuration PS. The substitution $\rho_{ro,i+1}$ in the transition rule below takes a labeled process and assigns new names to the fresh variables according to the label. More specifically, $(ro, i+1, 1) \ P_k(r_1, \ldots, r_n)\rho_{ro,i+1} =$

$(ro, i+1, 1) \; P_k(r_1, \ldots, r_n)\{r_1 \mapsto r_1.ro.i+1, \ldots, r_n \mapsto r_n.ro.i+1\}$. In a process state, a role name together with an identifier uniquely identifies a process. Therefore, there is a unique subset of fresh names for each process in the state. In the rest of this paper we will refer to this kind of substitutions as *fresh substitutions*.

$$\left\{ \begin{array}{l} \forall \; (ro) \; P_k \in P_{PA} \\ \{PS \mid \{IK\}\} \\ \longrightarrow_{(ro, i+1, 1, A, Num)} \{(ro, i+1, 2) \; P_k' \; \& \; PS \mid \{IK'\}\} \\ \mathsf{IF} \; \{(ro, i+1, 1) \; P_k \rho_{ro, i+1} \mid \{IK\}\} \longrightarrow_{(ro, i+1, 1, A, Num)} \{(ro, i+1, 2) \; P_k' \mid \{IK'\}\} \\ where \; \rho_{ro, i+1} \; is \; a \; fresh \; substitution, \; i = MaxProcId(PS, ro) \end{array} \right\}$$

$$(\text{PA\&})$$

Note that A denotes the action of the state transition, and can be of any of the forms explained above. The function *MaxProcId* is defined as follows:

$$MaxProcId(\varnothing, ro) = 0$$
$$MaxProcId((ro, i, j)P\&PS, ro) = max(MaxProcId(PS, ro), i)$$
$$MaxProcId((ro', i, j)P\&PS, ro) = MaxProcId(PS, ro) \qquad if \; ro \neq ro'$$

where PS denotes a process configuration, P denotes a process, and ro, ro' denote role names.

Therefore, the behavior of a protocol in the process algebra is defined by the set of transition rules $R_{PA_P} = \{(\text{PA++}), \; (\text{PA+}), (\text{PA-}), (\text{PAif1}), (\text{PAif2}), (\text{PA?1}), (\text{PA?2})\} \cup (\text{PA\&})$.

Example 9. Continuing Example 5, a possible run of the protocol using the case with conditional expressions is displayed in Fig. 3. We use letters a and b to denote concrete values chosen for variables $A_?$ and $B_?$, respectively.

Our main result is the existence of a bisimulation between the state space generated by the transition rules $R_{B_P^{-1}}$, associated to the symbolic backwards semantics of Sect. 3, and the transition rules R_{PA_P} above, associated to the forwards semantics for process algebra. This is nontrivial, since there are three major ways in which the two semantics differ. The first is that processes "forget" their past, while strands "remember" theirs. The second is that Maude-NPA uses backwards search, while the process algebra proceeds forwards. The third is that Maude-NPA performs symbolic reachability analysis using terms with variables, while the process algebra considers only ground terms.

We systematically relate these different semantics by introducing an intermediate semantics, a forward strand space semantics extending that in [9]. First, in Sect. 5 we extend the strand space model with constraints, since strands are the

$$\{\varnothing|\{\varnothing\}\} \quad \rightarrow_{Alice,1,1New} \{Alice:+(m_1)\cdots \mid \{\varnothing\}\} \; m_1 = pk(b,a;n(a,r_a))$$

$$\rightarrow_{Alice,1,2,+m_1,0,PA++} \{Alice:-(XA)\cdots \mid \{m_1 \in \mathcal{I}\}\}$$

$$\rightarrow_{Bob,1,1New} \begin{cases} Alice:-(XA)\cdots \\ Bob:-(XB)\cdots \end{cases} \bigg| \{m_1 \in \mathcal{I}\}\}$$

$$\rightarrow_{Bob,1,2,-m_1,0,PA-} \begin{cases} Alice:-(XA)\cdots \\ Bob: if\, m_1 = pk(B,A;N_A)\, then\, \cdots\, else\, nilP \end{cases} \bigg| \{m_1 \in \mathcal{I}\}\}$$

$$\rightarrow_{Bob,1,3,=,1,PAif1} \begin{cases} Alice:-(XA)\cdots \\ Bob:+(m_2)\cdots \end{cases} \bigg| \{m_1 \in \mathcal{I}\}\} \; m_2 = pk(a,n(a,r_a);n(b,r_b))$$

$$\rightarrow_{Bob,1,4,+m_2,0,PA++} \begin{cases} Alice:-(XA)\cdots \\ Bob:-(YB)\cdots \end{cases} \bigg| \{m_1 \in \mathcal{I}, m_2 \in \mathcal{I}\}\}$$

$$\rightarrow_{Alice,1,3,-m_2,0,PA-} \begin{cases} Alice: if\, m_2 = pk(a,n(a,r_a);n(b,r_b))\, then\, \cdots\, else\, nilP \\ Bob:-(YB)\cdots \end{cases} \bigg| \{m_1 \in \mathcal{I}, m_2 \in \mathcal{I}\}\}$$

$$\rightarrow_{Alice,1,4,=,1,PAif1} \begin{cases} Alice:+(m_3) \\ Bob:-(YB)\cdots \end{cases} \bigg| \{m_1 \in \mathcal{I}, m_2 \in \mathcal{I}\}\} \; m_3 = pk(b,n(b,r_b))$$

$$\rightarrow_{Alice,1,5,+m_3,0,PA++} \begin{cases} Alice: nilP \\ Bob:-(YB)\cdots \end{cases} \bigg| \{m_1 \in \mathcal{I}, m_2 \in \mathcal{I}, m_3 \in \mathcal{I}\}\}$$

$$\rightarrow_{Bob,1,5,-m_3,0,PA-} \begin{cases} Alice: nilP \\ Bob: if\, m_3 = pk(b,n(b,r_b))\, then\, nilP\, else\, nilP \end{cases} \bigg| \{m_1 \in \mathcal{I}, m_2 \in \mathcal{I}, m_3 \in \mathcal{I}\}\}$$

$$\rightarrow_{Bob,1,6,=,1,PAif1} \begin{cases} Alice: nilP \\ Bob: nilP \end{cases} \bigg| \{m_1 \in \mathcal{I}, m_2 \in \mathcal{I}, m_3 \in \mathcal{I}\}\}$$

Fig. 3. Process Execution for Example 5

basis of both the forwards semantics and the backwards semantics of Maude-NPA. In Sect. 6 we augment the forwards strand space semantics of [9] with choice operators and operational semantic rules to produce a *constrained forwards semantics*. In Sect. 6.2 we prove bisimilarity of the process algebra semantics of Sect. 4 and the constrained forwards semantics of Sect. 6.1. In [9] the forwards strand space semantics was proved sound and complete w.r.t. the original symbolic backwards semantics of Maude-NPA. But now such proofs have to be extended to handle constraints. In Sect. 7 we also augment the original symbolic backwards semantics of Maude-NPA with choice operators and operational semantic rules to produce a *constrained backwards semantics*. In Sect. 7.2, we then prove that the constrained backwards semantics of Sect. 7.1 is sound and complete with respect to the constrained forwards semantics of Sect. 6.1. By combining the bisimulation between the process algebra and the constrained forwards semantics on the one hand, and the bisimulation between the constrained forwards semantics and the constrained backwards semantics on the other hand, we obtain the main bisimulation result.

Besides providing a detailed semantic account of how the strand model can be extended with choice features, the key practical importance of these bisimulation results is that, with the relatively modest extensions to Maude-NPA described in Sect. 8.1 and supported by its recent 3.1 release, sound and complete analysis of protocols with choice features specified in process algebra is made possible.

5   Constrained Protocol Strands with Choice

To specify and analyze protocols with choices in Maude-NPA, in this section we extend Maude-NPA's strand notation by adding new symbols to support explicit choices. We refer to the strands in this extended syntax as *constrained protocol strands*.

In Sect. 5.1 we describe the syntax for constrained protocol strands. Then, in Sect. 5.2 we define a mapping from a protocol specification in the protocol process algebra, as described in Sect. 4.2, to a specification based on constrained protocol strands.

5.1   Constrained Protocol Strands Syntax

In this section we extend Maude-NPA's syntax by adding *constrained messages*, which are terms of the form $\{Cstr, Num\}$, where $Cstr$ is a constraint, and Num is a natural number that identifies the continuation of the protocol's execution, among the two possibilities after an explicit choice point. More specifically, we extend the Σ_{SS} part of the signature Σ_{SS_P} of the Maude-NPA's syntax we defined in Sect. 3 as follows:

- A new sort Cstr represents the constraints allowed in constrained messages, containing three symbols: (i) ? : → Cstr, (ii) _=_ : Msg Msg → Cstr, and (iii) _≠_ : Msg Msg → Cstr.
- A new sort CstrMsg for constrained messages, such that CstrMsg < SMsg, where SMsg is an existing Maude-NPA sort denoting signed messages (i.e., messages with + or -). Therefore, now a strand is a sequence of output, input and constrained messages.
- A new operator $\{\_,\_\}$: Cstr Nat → CstrMsg constructs constrained messages.

We refer to this extended signature as Σ_{CstrSS_P}. Note that the protocol signature Σ_P is contained in Σ_{SS_P}, and therefore in Σ_{CstrSS_P}. Furthermore, in the constrained semantics we allow each honest principal or intruder capability strand to be *labeled* by the "role" of that strand in the protocol (e.g., (Client) or (Server)). Therefore, strands are now terms of the form $(ro, i)[u_1, \ldots, u_n]$, where ro denotes the role of the strand in the protocol, i is a unique identifier distinguishing different instances of strands of the same role, and each u_i can be a sent or received message, i.e., a term of the form $M^{\pm}$, or a constraint message of the form $\{Cstr, Num\}$. We often omit i, or both ro and i for clarity when they are not relevant.

5.2   Protocol Specification Using Constrained Protocol Strands

The behavior of a protocol involving choices can be specified using the syntax presented in Sect. 5.1 as described below.

Definition 1 (Constrained protocol strand specification). *Given a protocol* $\mathcal{P}$, *we define its specification by means of constrained protocol strands, written* $\mathcal{P}_{CstrSS}$, *as a tuple of the form* $\mathcal{P}_{CstrSS} = ((\Sigma_{CstrSS_\mathcal{P}}, E_{SS_\mathcal{P}}), P_{CstrSS})$, *where* $\Sigma_{CstrSS_\mathcal{P}}$ *is the protocol's signature (see Sect. 5.1), and* $E_{SS_\mathcal{P}} = E_\mathcal{P} \cup E_{SS}$ *is a set of equations as we defined in Sect. 3, where* $E_\mathcal{P}$ *denotes the protocol's cryptographic properties and* E_{SS} *denotes the protocol-independent equational properties of constructors of strands. That is, the set of equations* $E_\mathcal{P}$ *may vary depending on different protocols, but the set of equations* E_{SS} *is always the same for all protocols.* P_{CstrSS} *is a set of constrained protocol strands as defined in Sect. 5.1, representing the behavior of the honest principals as well as the capabilities of the attacker. That is,* P_{CstrSS} *is a set of labeled strands of the form:* $P_{CstrSS} = \{(ro_1)[u_{1,1}, \ldots, u_{1,n_1}] \ \& \ \ldots \ \& \ (ro_m)[u_{m,1}, \ldots, u_{m,n_m}]\}$, *where, for each* ro_k *such that* $1 \leqslant k \leqslant i$, ro_k *is either the role of an honest principal, or identifies one of the capabilities of the attacker. We note that* P_{CstrSS} *may contain several strands with the same label, each defining one of the possible paths of such a principal.*

The protocol specification described above can be obtained by *transforming* a specification in the process algebra of Sect. 4.2 as follows. Given a protocol $\mathcal{P}$, its specification in the process algebra P_{PA}, consists of a set of *well-formed* labeled processes. We transform a term denoting a set of labeled processes into a term denoting a set of constrained protocol strands by the mapping *toCstrSS*. The intuitive idea is that, since our process contains no recursion, each process can be "deconstructed" as a set of constrained protocol strands, where each such strand represent a possible execution path of the process.

The mapping *toCstrSS* is specified in Definition 2 below.

Definition 2 (Mapping labeled processes *toCstrSS*). *Given a labeled process LP and a process configuration LPS, we define the mapping* $toCstrSS$: $\mathcal{T}_{\Sigma_{PA_\mathcal{P}}}(\mathcal{X}) \to \mathcal{T}_{\Sigma_{CstrSS_\mathcal{P}}}(\mathcal{X})$ *recursively as follows:*

$$toCstrSS(LP \ \& \ LPS) = toCstrSS^*(LP, nilP) \ \& \ toCstrSS(LPS)$$
$$toCstrSS(\varnothing) = \varnothing$$

where $\varnothing$ *is the empty set of strands.* $toCstrSS^*$ *is an auxiliary mapping that maps a term denoting a labeled process to a term that denotes a set of constrained protocol strands. It takes two arguments: a labeled process, and a temporary store that keeps a sequence of messages. More specifically,* $toCstrSS^* : \mathcal{T}_{\Sigma_{PA_\mathcal{P}}}(\mathcal{X}) \times \mathcal{T}_{\Sigma_{CstrSS_\mathcal{P}}}(\mathcal{X}) \to \mathcal{T}_{\Sigma_{CstrSS_\mathcal{P}}}(\mathcal{X})$ *is defined as follows:*

$toCstrSS^*((ro, i, j) \ nilP, L) = (ro, i) \ [\ L \ ]$
$toCstrSS^*((ro, i, j) \ (+M \ . \ P), L) = toCstrSS^*((ro, i, j) \ P, (L, +M))$
$toCstrSS^*((ro, i, j) \ (-M \ . \ P), \ L) = toCstrSS^*((ro, i, j) \ P, (L, -M))$
$toCstrSS^*((ro, i, j) \ (if \ T \ then \ P \ else \ Q) \ . \ R, L)$
     $= \ toCstrSS^*((ro, i, j) \ (P \ . \ R), (L, \{T, 1\})) \ \& \ toCstrSS^*((ro, i, j) \ (Q \ . \ R), (L, \{\neg T, 2\}))$
$toCstrSS^*((ro, i, j) \ (P \ ? \ Q) \ . \ R, L)$
     $= \ toCstrSS^*((ro, i, j) \ (P \ . \ R), (L, \{?, 1\})) \ \& \ toCstrSS^*((ro, i, j) \ (Q \ . \ R), (L, \{?, 2\}))$

where P, Q, and R denote processes, M is a message, T is a constraint, and L denotes a list of messages, i.e., input, output or constraint messages.

Note that *toCstrSS* does not modify output and input messages, since messages are actually terms in $\mathcal{T}_{\Sigma_\mathcal{P}/E_\mathcal{P}}(\mathcal{X})$ in both the protocol process algebra, and the constrained forwards semantics. *toCstrSS* can be used both as a map between specifications, and as a map from process configurations and strand sets appearing in states.

We illustrate the *toCstrSS* transformation with the example below.

Example 10. If we apply the mapping *toCstrSS* to the process in Example 7 we obtain the following term which denotes a set of strands:

$(Server)$ [$\{?, 1\}$,
  $- (hs; N; G; gen(G); E)$,
  $+ (hs; retry)$,
  $- (hs; N'; G'; gen(G'); E'))$,
  $+ (hs; n(S_?, r1); G'; gen(G'); keyG(G', S_?, r_2); Z(AReq_?, G', E', S, r_2, S_?, HM))$] &
$(Server)$ [$\{?, 2\}$,
  $- (hs; N; G; gen(G); E)$,
  $+ (hs; n(S_?, r1); G; gen(G); keyG(G, S, r_2); Z(AReq_?, G, E, S, r_2, S_?, HM))$]

A protocol specification in the protocol process algebra is transformed into a specification of that protocol in the constrained protocol strands described below using *toCstrSS*.

Definition 3 (Specification transformation). *Given a protocol $\mathcal{P}$ and its protocol process algebra specification $\mathcal{P}_{PA} = ((\Sigma_{PA_\mathcal{P}}, E_\mathcal{P} \cup E_{PA}), P_{PA})$, with $P_{PA} = (ro_1)P_1 \& \ldots \& (ro_n)P_n$, its specification by means of constrained protocol strands is $\mathcal{P}_{CstrSS} = ((\Sigma_{CstrSS_\mathcal{P}}, E_\mathcal{P} \cup E_{SS}), P_{CstrSS})$ with $P_{CstrSS} = toCstrSS(P_{PA})$.*

6 Constrained Forwards Strand Semantics

In this section we extend Maude-NPA's rewriting-based forwards semantics in [9] by adding new transition rules for constrained messages. We refer to this extended forwards semantics as *constrained forwards strand semantics*. We show that the process algebra semantics and the constrained forwards strand semantics are label bisimilar. Therefore, protocols exhibiting choices can be specified and executed in an equivalent way in both semantics.

6.1 Transition Rules of the Constrained Forwards Strand Semantics

In the constrained forwards strand semantics, state changes are defined by a set $R_{CstrF_\mathcal{P}}$ of *rewrite rules*, so that the rewrite theory $(\Sigma_{CstrSS_\mathcal{P}}, E_{SS_\mathcal{P}}, R_{CstrF_\mathcal{P}})$ characterizes the behaviors of protocol $\mathcal{P}$.

The set of transition rules $R_{CstrF_\mathcal{P}}$ is an extension of the transition rules $R_{F_\mathcal{P}}$ in [9]. The transition rules are generated from the protocol specification. A *state* consists of a multiset of partially executed strands and a set of terms denoting the intruder's knowledge. The main differences between the sets $R_{CstrF_\mathcal{P}}$ and $R_{F_\mathcal{P}}$ are: (i) new transition rules are added in $R_{CstrF_\mathcal{P}}$ to appropriately deal with constraint messages, (ii) strands are labeled with the role name, together with the identifier for distinguishing different instances, as explained in Sect. 5.1, (iii) transitions are also labeled, similarly as in the protocol process algebra, (iv) the global counter for generating fresh variables is deleted from the state. Instead, special unique names are assigned to fresh variable, which simplifies our notation.

In the constrained forwards strand semantics we label each transition rule similarly as in Sect. 4.3, that is, using labels of the form (ro, i, j, a, n), where ro, i, a, and n are as explained in Sect. 4.3, and j in this case is the position of the message that is being exchanged in the state transition. Also, similar to Sect. 4.3, for transitions that send out messages containing choice variables, all (possibly infinitely many) admissible ground substitutions for the choice variables are possible behaviors. A similar mechanism for distinguishing different fresh variables is used as that explained in Sect. 4.3. Since messages are introduced into strands in the state incrementally, we instantiate the fresh variables incrementally as well. Recall that fresh variables always first show up in a sent message. Therefore, each time a sent message is introduced into a strand in the state, we assign new names to the fresh variables in the message being introduced. The function *MaxStrId* for getting the max identifier for a constrained strand of a certain role is similar to *MaxProcId* in Sect. 4.3.

Since now messages in a strand can be sent or received messages, i.e., terms of the form m^+ or m^-, as well as constraint messages $\{Cstr, Num\}$, we represent them in the rules below simply as terms of the form u_i when their exact form is not relevant. We will use the precise form of the message when disambiguation is needed.

Before explaining the new transition rules for constraint messages, we show how the transition rules in [9] are labeled.

The constrained forwards strand semantics extends Maude-NPA's forwards semantics in [9] by adding transition rules to handle constraint messages, i.e., messages of the form $\{Cstr, Num\}$, where Num can be either 1 or 2. First, we add the two transition rules below for the cases when such a constrained message comes from explicit choices. Note that, as a consequence of well-formedness, the constraints introduce no new variables, and since the constraints that we consider are of the form $m \neq_{E_\mathcal{P}} m'$ or $m =_{E_\mathcal{P}} m'$, the satisfiability of $Cstr$ can be checked by checking whether the corresponding ground equality or disequality holds.

$$
\left\{
\begin{aligned}
&\forall\ (ro)\ [u_1, \ldots, u_{j-1}, u_j^+, u_{j+1}, \ldots, u_n] \in P_{CstrSS} \wedge j{>}1: \\
&\{SS \,\&\, \{IK\} \,\&\, (ro, i)\ [u_1, \ldots, u_{j-1}]\} \\
&\ \rightarrow_{(ro, i, j, (u_j \rho_{ro,i} \sigma)^+, 0)} \\
&\{SS \,\&\, \{(u_j \rho_{ro,i} \sigma) \in \mathcal{I}, IK\} \,\&\, (ro, i)[u_1, \ldots, u_{j-1}, (u_j \rho_{ro,i} \sigma)^+]\} \mathsf{IF}((u_j \rho_{ro,i} \sigma) \in \mathcal{I}) \notin IK \\
&where\ \sigma\ is\ a\ ground\ substitution\ binding\ choice\ variables\ in\ u_j, \\
&\rho_{ro,i} = \{r_1 \mapsto r_1.ro.i, \ldots, r_n \mapsto r_n.ro.i\}\ is\ a\ fresh\ substitution.
\end{aligned}
\right\}
$$

$$(\mathrm{F}{+}{+})$$

$$
\left\{
\begin{aligned}
&\forall\ (ro)\ [u_1, \ldots, u_{j-1}, u_j^+, u_{j+1}, \ldots, u_n] \in P_{CstrSS} \wedge j{>}1: \\
&\{SS \,\&\, \{IK\} \,\&\, (ro, i)\ [u_1, \ldots, u_{j-1}]\} \\
&\ \rightarrow_{(ro, i, j, u_j \rho_{ro,i} \sigma, 0)} \\
&\{SS \,\&\, \{IK\} \,\&\, (ro, i)\ [u_1, \ldots, u_{j-1}, (u_j \rho_{ro,i} \sigma)^+]\} \\
&where\ \sigma\ is\ a\ ground\ substitution\ binding\ choice\ variables\ in\ u_j, \\
&\rho_{ro,i} = \{r_1 \mapsto r_1.ro.i, \ldots, r_n \mapsto r_n.ro.i\}\ is\ a\ fresh\ substitution.
\end{aligned}
\right\}
$$

$$(\mathrm{F}{+})$$

$$
\left\{
\begin{aligned}
&\forall\ (ro)\ [u_1^+, \ldots, u_n] \in P_{CstrSS}: \\
&\{SS \,\&\, \{IK\}\} \\
&\ \rightarrow_{(ro, i+1, j, (u_1 \rho_{ro,i+1} \sigma)^+, 0)} \\
&\{SS \,\&\, (ro, i+1)\ [(u_1 \rho_{ro,i+1} \sigma)^+] \,\&\, \{u_1 \rho_{ro,i+1} \sigma \in \mathcal{I}, IK\}\} \mathsf{IF}\ (u_1 \rho_{ro,i+1} \sigma \in \mathcal{I}) \notin IK \\
&where\ \sigma\ is\ a\ ground\ substitution\ binding\ choice\ variables\ in\ u_1, \\
&i = MaxStrId(SS, ro), \\
&\rho_{ro,i+1} = \{r_1 \mapsto r_1.ro.i+1, \ldots, r_n \mapsto r_n.ro.i+1\}\ is\ a\ fresh\ substitution.
\end{aligned}
\right\}
$$

$$(\mathrm{F}{+}{+}\&)$$

$$
\left\{
\begin{aligned}
&\forall\ (ro)\ [u_1^+, \ldots, u_n] \in P_{CstrSS}: \\
&\{SS \,\&\, \{IK\}\} \\
&\ \rightarrow_{(ro, i+1, j, u_1 \rho_{ro,i+1} \sigma, 0)} \\
&\quad \{SS \,\&\, (ro, i+1)\ [(u_1 \rho_{ro,i+1} \sigma)^+] \,\&\, \{IK\}\} \\
&where\ \sigma\ is\ a\ ground\ substitution\ binding\ choice\ variables\ in\ u_1, \\
&i = MaxStrId(SS, ro), \\
&\rho_{ro,i+1} = \{r_1 \mapsto r_1.ro.i+1, \ldots, r_n \mapsto r_n.ro.i+1\}\ is\ a\ fresh\ substitution.
\end{aligned}
\right\}
$$

$$(\mathrm{F}{+}\&)$$

$$
\left\{
\begin{aligned}
&\forall\ (ro)\ [u_1, \ldots, u_{j-1}, u_j^-, u_{j+1}, \ldots, u_n] \in P_{CstrSS} \wedge j > 1: \\
&\{SS \,\&\, \{u_j \in \mathcal{I}, IK\} \,\&\, (ro, i)\ [u_1, \ldots, u_{j-1}]\} \\
&\ \rightarrow_{(ro, i, j, u_j^-, 0)} \{SS \,\&\, \{u_j \in \mathcal{I}, IK\} \,\&\, (ro, i)\ [u_1, \ldots, u_{j-1}, u_j^-]\}
\end{aligned}
\right\}
$$

$$(\mathrm{F}{-})$$

$$\left\{\begin{array}{l} \forall (ro)\ [u_1^-, u_2, \ldots, u_n] \in P_{CstrSS} : \\ \{SS \& \{u_1 \in \mathcal{I}, IK\}\} \rightarrow_{(ro, i+1, 1, u_1^-, 0)} \{SS \& (ro, i+1)\ [u_1^-] \& \{u_1 \in \mathcal{I}, IK\}\} \\ where\ i = MaxStrId(SS, ro) \end{array}\right\}$$

$$(\text{F-\&})$$

$$\left\{\begin{array}{l} \forall (ro)\ [u_1, \ldots, u_{j-1}, \{Cstr, Num\}, u_{j+1}, \ldots, u_n] \in P_{CstrSS} \wedge j > 1 : \\ \{SS \& \{IK\} \& (ro, i)\ [u_1, \ldots, u_{j-1}]\} \\ \rightarrow_{(ro, i, j, T, Num)} \{SS \& \{IK\} \& (ro, i)\ [u_1, \ldots, u_{j-1}, \{Cstr, Num\}]\}\ \text{IF}\ Cstr \end{array}\right\} \quad (\text{Fif})$$

$$\left\{\begin{array}{l} \forall (ro)\ [u_1, \ldots, u_{j-1}, \{?, Num\}, u_{j+1}, \ldots, u_n] \in P_{CstrSS} \wedge j > 1 : \\ \{SS \& \{IK\} \& (ro, i)\ [u_1, \ldots, u_{j-1}]\} \\ \rightarrow_{(ro, i, j, ?, Num)} \{SS \& \{IK\} \& (ro, i)\ [u_1, \ldots, u_{j-1}, \{?, Num\}]\} \end{array}\right\} \quad (\text{F?})$$

The following set of transition rules adds to the state a new strand whose first message is a constraint message of the form $\{?, Num\}$:

$$\left\{\begin{array}{l} \forall (ro)\ [\{?, Num\}, u_2, \ldots, u_n] \in P_{CstrSS} : \\ \{SS \& \{IK\}\} \\ \rightarrow_{(ro, i+1, 1, ?, Num)} \{SS \& (ro, i+1)\ [\{?, Num\}] \& \{IK\}\} \\ where\ i = MaxStrId(SS, ro) \end{array}\right\} \quad (\text{F?\&})$$

Definition 4. *Let $\mathcal{P}$ be a protocol with signature $\Sigma_{CstrSS_{\mathcal{P}}}$ and equational theory $E_{SS_{\mathcal{P}}}$. We define the constrained forwards rewrite theory characterizing $\mathcal{P}$ as $(\Sigma_{CstrSS_{\mathcal{P}}}, E_{SS_{\mathcal{P}}}, R_{CstrF_{\mathcal{P}}})$ where $R_{CstrF_{\mathcal{P}}} = (\text{F++}) \cup (\text{F+}) \cup (\text{F++\&}) \cup (\text{F+\&}) \cup (\text{F-}) \cup (\text{F-\&}) \cup (\text{Fif}) \cup (\text{F?}) \cup (\text{F?\&})$.*

6.2 Bisimulation Between Constrained Forwards Strand Semantics and Process Algebra Semantics

In this section we show that the process algebra semantics and the constrained forwards strand semantics are label bisimilar. We first define PA-State and FW-State, the respective notions of state in each semantics.

Definition 5 (PA-State). *Given a protocol $\mathcal{P}$, a PA-State of $\mathcal{P}$ is a state in the protocol process algebra semantics that is reachable from the initial state. The initial PA-State is $P_{init} = \{\varnothing \mid \{empty\}\}$.*

Definition 6 (FW-State). *Given a protocol $\mathcal{P}$, a FW-State of $\mathcal{P}$ is a state in the constrained forwards strand semantics that is reachable from the initial state. The initial FW-State is $F_{init} = \{\varnothing \& \{empty\}\}$.*

The bisimulation relation is defined based on reachability, i.e., if a PA-State and a FW-State are in the relation $\mathcal{H}$, then they both can be reached from their corresponding initial states by the same label sequence. Note that we only consider states that are reachable from the initial states.

Let us first define the notation of label sequence that we will use throughout.

Definition 7 (Label Sequence). *An ordered sequence α of transition labels is defined by using $\_.\_$ as an associative concatenation operator with nil as an identity. The length of a label sequence α is denoted by $|\alpha|$. Given a label sequence α, we denote by $\alpha|_{(ro,i)}$ the sub-sequence of labels in α that have ro as role name, and i as identifier, i.e., labels of the form $(ro, i, \_, \_, \_)$ ($\_$ is a shorthand for denoting any term).*

Definition 8 (Relation $\mathcal{H}$). *Given a protocol $\mathcal{P}$, the relation $\mathcal{H}$ is defined as: $\mathcal{H} = \{(Pst, Fst) \in PA\text{-}State \times FW\text{-}State \mid \exists \text{ label sequence } \alpha \text{ s.t. } P_{init} \rightarrow_{\alpha} Pst, \ F_{init} \rightarrow_{\alpha} Fst\}.$*

Recall that a process can be "deconstructed" by the mapping $toCstrSS$ into a set of constrained protocol strands, each representing a possible execution path. If a PA-State Pst and a FW-State Fst are related by $\mathcal{H}$, then an important observation is that there is a *duality* between individual processes in Pst and strands in Fst: if there is a process in the Pst describing a role's *continuation* in the future, there will be a corresponding strand in Fst describing the part of the process that has *already been executed*, and vice versa. Another observation is that, since the intruder's knowledge is extracted from the communication history, following the definition of $\mathcal{H}$, the states Pst and Fst have the same communication history, therefore they have the same intruder's knowledge. We formalize these observations in Lemmas 1 and 2, which are moved to the Appendix. These lemmas then lead us to the main result that $\mathcal{H}$ is a bisimulation relation.

Theorem 1 (Bisimulation). *$\mathcal{H}$ is a bisimulation.*

7   Constrained Backwards Strand Semantics

In this section we extend Maude-NPA's symbolic backwards semantics with rules for constrained messages of the form described in Sect. 5.1, so that it can analyze protocols exhibiting explicit choices. We refer to this extended backwards semantics as *constrained backwards strand semantics*. We then show that the *constrained backwards strand semantics* is sound and complete with respect to the constrained forwards strand semantics presented in Sect. 6, and the process algebra semantics presented in Sect. 4. This result allows us to use Maude-NPA for analyzing protocols exhibiting choice, including both implicit and explicit choices, and in particular any protocol specified using the *protocol process algebra*.

7.1 Transition Rules of the Constrained Backwards Strand Semantics

The strand space model used in the constrained backwards strand semantics is the same as the one already used in Maude-NPA [7], except for the following differences:

- Maude-NPA explores *constrained states* as defined in [11], that is, states that have an associated constraint store. More specifically, a *constrained state* is a pair $\langle St, \Psi \rangle$ consisting of a state expression St and a *constraint*, i.e., a set Ψ understood as a conjunction $\Psi = \bigwedge_{i=1}^{n} u_i \neq v_i$ of disequality constraints.
- Strands are now of the form $[u_1, \ldots, u_i \mid u_{i+1}, \ldots u_n]$, where each u_k can be of one of these forms: (i) m^+ if it is a sent message, (ii) m^- if it is a received message, or (iii) $\{Cstr, Num\}$ if it is a constrained message.

State changes are described by a set $R_{CstrB_{\mathcal{P}}^{-1}}$ of *rewrite rules*, so that the rewrite theory $(\Sigma_{CstrSS_{\mathcal{P}}}, E_{SS_{\mathcal{P}}}, R_{CstrB_{\mathcal{P}}^{-1}})$ characterizes the behavior of protocol $\mathcal{P}$ modulo the equations $E_{SS_{\mathcal{P}}}$ for *backwards* execution. The set of rules $R_{CstrB_{\mathcal{P}}^{-1}}$ is obtained as follows. First, we adapt the set of rules $R_{B_{\mathcal{P}}^{-1}}$ in Sect. 3 to constrained states, which is an embedding of rules in $R_{B_{\mathcal{P}}^{-1}}$. Their forwards version is shown below; these rules are identical to those of Sect. 3, except that the constraint Ψ is added:

$$\langle \{SS \& (ro)[L \mid M^-, L'] \ \& \ \{M \in \mathcal{I}, IK\}\}, \Psi \rangle \rightarrow \langle \{SS \& (ro)[L, M^- \mid L'] \ \& \ \{M \in \mathcal{I}, IK\}\}, \Psi \rangle$$
$$\text{(B-)}$$

$$\langle \{SS \& (ro)[L \mid M^+, L'] \ \& \ \{IK\}\}, \Psi \rangle \rightarrow \langle \{SS \& (ro)[L, M^+ \mid L'] \ \& \ \{IK\}\}, \Psi \rangle \qquad \text{(B+)}$$

$$\langle \{SS \& (ro)[L \mid M^+, L'] \& \{M \notin \mathcal{I}, IK\}\}, \Psi \rangle \rightarrow \langle \{SS \& (ro)[L, M^+ \mid L'] \& \{M \in \mathcal{I}, IK\}\}, \Psi \rangle$$
$$\text{(B++)}$$

$$\forall \, [l_1, u^+, l_2] \in \mathcal{P} : \langle \{\{SS \& [l_1 \mid u^+, l_2] \& \{u \notin \mathcal{I}, IK\}\}, \Psi \rangle \rightarrow \langle \{SS \& \{u \in \mathcal{I}, IK\}\}, \Psi \rangle \quad \text{(B\&)}$$

where L and L' are variables denoting a list of strand messages, IK is a variable for a set of intruder facts ($m \in \mathcal{I}$ or $m \notin \mathcal{I}$), SS is a variable denoting a set of strands, and l_1, l_2 denote a list of strand messages.

Then, we define new transition rules for constrained messages. That is, we add the reversed version of the following rules; note that (Bif$\neq$) is the only rule adding a constraint to Ψ:

$$\langle \{SS \& \{IK'\} \& (ro)[L \mid \{?, Num\}, L']\}, \Psi \rangle \rightarrow \langle \{SS \& \{IK'\} \& (ro)[L, \{?, Num\} \mid L']\}, \Psi \rangle$$
$$\text{(B?)}$$

$$\langle \{SS \& \{IK\} \& (ro)[L \mid \{M =_{E_{\mathcal{P}}} M, Num\}, L']\}, \Psi \rangle$$
$$\rightarrow \langle \{SS \& \{IK\} \& (ro)[L, \{M =_{E_{\mathcal{P}}} M, Num\} \mid L']\}, \Psi \rangle \qquad \text{(Bif=)}$$

$$\langle \{SS \,\&\, \{IK\} \,\&\, (ro)[L \mid \{M \neq M', Num\}, L']\}, (\Psi \wedge M \neq M') \rangle$$
$$\rightarrow \langle \{SS \,\&\, \{IK\} \,\&\, (ro)[L, \{M \neq M', Num\} \mid L']\}, \Psi \rangle$$
$$\text{if } (\Psi \wedge M \neq_{E_{\mathcal{P}}} M') \text{ is satisfiable in } \mathcal{T}_{\Sigma_{CstrSS_{\mathcal{P}}}/E_{\mathcal{P}}}(\mathcal{X}) \hspace{2cm} \text{(Bif≠)}$$

Rule (B?) processes a constraint message denoting an explicit non-deterministic choice with constant "?". The constraint store is not changed and no satisfiability check is required.

Rules (Bif=) and (Bif≠) deal with constrained messages associated to explicit deterministic choices. Since the only constraints we allow in explicit deterministic choices are equalities and disequalities, rule (Bif=) is for the case when the constraint is an equality, rule (Bif≠) is for the case when the constraint is a disequality. The equality constraint is solved by $E_{\mathcal{P}}$-unification. The constraint in a *constrained state* is therefore a *disequality constraint*, i.e., $\Psi = \bigwedge_{i=1}^{n} u_i \neq_{E_{\mathcal{P}}} v_i$. The *semantics* of such a constrained state, written $[\![\langle St, \Psi \rangle]\!]$ is the set of all ground substitution instances of the form:

$$[\![\langle St, \Psi \rangle]\!] = \{St\theta \mid \theta \in [\mathcal{X} \rightarrow \mathcal{T}_{\Sigma_{\mathcal{P}}}] \wedge u_i\theta \neq_{E_{\mathcal{P}}} v_i\theta, 1 \leqslant i \leqslant n\}$$

The disequality constraints are then solved the same way as in [11].

Definition 9. *Let $\mathcal{P}$ be a protocol with signature $\Sigma_{CstrSS_{\mathcal{P}}}$ and equational theory $E_{\mathcal{P}}$. We define the* constrained *backwards rewrite theory characterizing $\mathcal{P}$ to be $(\Sigma_{CstrSS_{\mathcal{P}}}, E_{SS_{\mathcal{P}}}, R_{CstrB_{\mathcal{P}}^{-1}})$ where $E_{SS_{\mathcal{P}}}$ is same as explained in Sect. 3. $R_{CstrB_{\mathcal{P}}^{-1}}$ is the result of reversing the rewrite rules $\{(B-), (B+), (B++), (B?), (Bif=), (Bif\neq)\} \cup (B\&)$.*

7.2 Soundness and Completeness of Constrained Backwards Strand Semantics

The soundness and completeness proofs generalize the proofs in [9]. Recall that the state in the constrained states of constrained backwards strand semantics is a symbolic strand state, i.e., a state with variables. A state in the forwards strand semantics is a ground strand state, i.e., a state without variables. The lifting relation defines the instantiation relation between symbolic and ground states.

We define a symbolic state and a ground state as follows.

Definition 10 (Symbolic Strand State). *Given a protocol $\mathcal{P}$, a symbolic strand state S of $\mathcal{P}$ is a term of the form:*

$$S = \{ :: r_{1_1}, \ldots, r_{m_1} :: [u_{1_1}, \ldots u_{i_1 - 1} \mid u_{i_1}, \ldots, u_{n_1}] \,\&$$
$$\vdots$$
$$:: r_{1_k}, \ldots, r_{m_k} :: [u_{1_k}, \ldots, u_{i_k - 1} \mid u_{i_k}, \ldots, u_{n_k}] \,\&\, SS$$
$$\{w_1 \in \mathcal{I}, \ldots, w_m \in \mathcal{I}, \ w_1' \notin \mathcal{I}, \ldots, w_{m'}' \notin \mathcal{I}, IK\}\}$$

where for each $1 \leqslant j \leqslant k$, there exists a strand $[m_{1_j}, \ldots m_{i_j-1}, m_{i_j}, \ldots, m_{n_j}] \in P_{CstrSS}$ and a substitution $\rho_j : \mathcal{X} \rightarrow \mathcal{T}_{\Sigma_P}(\mathcal{X})$ such that $m_{1_j}\rho_j =_{E_P} u_{1_j}, \ldots, m_{n_j}\rho_j =_{E_P} u_{n_j}$, SS is a variable denoting a (possibly empty) set of strands, and IK is a variable denoting a (possibly empty) set of intruder's knowledge facts.

Definition 11 (Ground Strand State). *Given a protocol $\mathcal{P}$, a ground strand state s of $\mathcal{P}$ is a term without variables of the form:*

$$s = \{[u_{1_1}, \ldots u_{i_1-1}] \& \cdots \& [u_{1_k}, \ldots, u_{i_k-1}] \& \{w_1 \in \mathcal{I}, \ldots, w_m \in \mathcal{I}\} \}$$

where for each $1 \leqslant j \leqslant k$, there exists a strand $[m_{1_j}, \ldots m_{i_j-1}, m_{i_j}, \ldots, m_{n_j}] \in P_{CstrSS}$ and a substitution $\rho_j : \mathcal{X} \rightarrow \mathcal{T}_{\Sigma_P}$ such that $m_{1_j}\rho_j =_{E_P} u_{1_j}, \ldots, m_{i_j}\rho_j =_{E_P} u_{i_j}$.

The lifting relation in [9] is extended with constraints and constrained messages. Note that the u_i in the definition below can be sent messages, received messages, or constrained messages.

Definition 12 (Lifting Relation). *Given a protocol $\mathcal{P}$, a constrained symbolic strand state $CstrS = \langle S, \Psi \rangle$ and a ground strand state s, we say that s lifts to CstrS, or that CstrS instantiates to s with a ground substitution $\theta : (Var(S) - \{SS, IK\}) \rightarrow \mathcal{T}_{\Sigma_P}$, written $CstrS >^{\theta} s$ iff*

- *for each strand $:: r_1, \ldots, r_m :: [u_1, \ldots u_{i-1} \mid u_i, \ldots, u_n]$ in S, there exists a strand $[v_1, \ldots v_{i-1}]$ in s such that $\forall 1 \leqslant j \leqslant i-1, v_j =_{E_P} u_j\theta$.*
- *for each positive intruder fact $w \in \mathcal{I}$ in S, there exists a positive intruder fact $w' \in \mathcal{I}$ in s such that $w' =_{E_P} w\theta$, and*
- *for each negative intruder fact $w \notin \mathcal{I}$ in S, there is no positive intruder fact $w' \in \mathcal{I}$ in s such that $w' =_{E_P} w\theta$.*
- *$E_P \models \Psi\theta$.*

In the following we show the soundness and completeness of transitions in constrained backwards strand semantics w.r.t. the constrained forwards strand semantics by proving two lemmas (Lemmas 3 and 4 in Appendix A.2) stating the completeness and soundness of one-step transition in the constrained backwards strand semantics w.r.t. the constrained forwards strand semantics. The soundness and completeness results follow from these two lemmas. In the proofs we consider only transition rules added in both semantics to deal with explicit choices, that is, rules (Fif) ∪ (F?) ∪ (F?&) in the constrained forwards strand semantics and rules {(B?), (Bif=), (Bif≠)} in the constrained backwards strand semantics. The proof of the soundness and completeness of one-step transitions performed in the constrained backwards strand semantics using rules {(B-), (B+), (B++) ∪ (B&) w.r.t to one-step transitions performed in the constrained forwards strand semantics using rules (F++) ∪ (F+) ∪ (F++&) ∪ (F+&) ∪ (F-) ∪ (F-&) is the same as in [9], since in these transitions no constraint is involved. Note that although in [9], *Choice Variables* were not defined explicitly, the proof extends to strands with choice variables naturally, since the lifting relation between a ground state and a symbolic state does not need to be changed to cover choice variables. Since the strand labels are irrelevant for the result of this section, we will omit the strand labels to simplify the notation from now on. Also, we include the fresh substitution in the substitutions and do not separate the fresh substitutions explicitly.

Theorem 2 (Soundness). *Given a protocol $\mathcal{P}$, two constrained symbolic strand states $CstrS_0, CstrS$, the initial FW-State F_{init}, a substitution θ, and the initial PA-State P_{init} s.t. (i) $CstrS_0$ is a symbolic initial strand state, and (ii) $CstrS_0 \overset{*}{\leftsquigarrow}_\mu CstrS$, and (iii) $CstrS_0 >^\theta F_{init}$. Then there exists a FW-State Fst such that $CstrS >^{\theta'} Fst$, and therefore, there is a PA-State Pst such that $Pst \; \mathcal{H} \; Fst$.*

Theorem 3 (Completeness). *Given a protocol $\mathcal{P}$, a PA-State Pst, a FW-State Fst, a constrained symbolic strand state CstrS s.t. (i) $Pst \; \mathcal{H} \; Fst$, (ii) $CstrS >^{\theta'} Fst$. Then there is a backwards symbolic execution $CstrS_0 \overset{*}{\leftsquigarrow}_\mu CstrS$ s.t. $CstrS_0$ is a symbolic initial strand state as defined in Sect. 3, and $CstrS_0 >^\theta F_{init}$.*

8 Protocol Experiments

In this section we describe some experiments[5] that we have performed on protocols with choice. We have fully integrated the process algebra syntax, and its transformation into strands, and have developed new methods to specify attack states using the process notation in the recent release of Maude-NPA 3.1 (see [8]).

8.1 Integration of the Protocol Process Algebra in Maude-NPA

We have fully implemented the process algebra notation in Maude-NPA. Strands represent each role behavior as a linear sequence of message outputs and inputs but processes represent each role behavior as a possibly non-linear sequence of message outputs and inputs. The honest principal specification is specified in the process algebra syntax. In order for Maude-NPA to accept process specifications, we have replaced the section **STRANDS-PROTOCOL** from the protocol template by a new section **PROCESSES-PROTOCOL**; see [8] for details. The intruder capabilities as well as the states generated by the tool still use the strand syntax.

Attack patterns may be specified using the process algebra syntax, under the label **ATTACK-PROCESS**, or strand syntax, under the label **ATTACK-STATE**. We describe how they are specified in the process algebra syntax below. An attack pattern describes a state consisting of zero or more processes that must have executed, and zero or more terms in the intruder knowledge. It may also contain *never patterns*, that is, descriptions of processes that must *not* be executed at the time the state is reached. Never patterns can be used to reason about

---

[5] Available at http://personales.upv.es/sanesro/Maude-NPA-choice/choice.html.

authentication properties, e.g., can Alice execute an instance of the protocol, apparently with Bob, without Bob executing an instance of the protocol with Alice.

Note that processes in an attack pattern cannot contain explicit nondeterminism (?) or explicit deterministic choice (if), since one and only one behavior is provided in an attack pattern. This is achieve by requiring that any constraint c appearing in an attack pattern must be *strongly irreducible*, that is, it must not only be irreducible, but for any irreducible substitution σ to the variables of c, σc must be irreducible as well.

That is, imagine a process i the form

$$-(m1) \, . \, + (m2) \, . \, if \; exp1 \; = \; exp2 \; then \; + (m3) \; else \; + (m4)$$

where each of the expressions $exp1$ and $exp2$ can evaluate to yes or no depending on the substitutions made to them.

Then in the attack pattern one must specify one and only one of the following possibilities

$$-(m1) \, . \, + (m2) \, . \, yes = yes \, . \, + (m3)$$
$$-(m1) \, . \, + (m2) \, . \, yes \neq no \, . \, + (m4)$$
$$-(m1) \, . \, + (m2) \, . \, no = no \, . \, + (m3)$$
$$-(m1) \, . \, + (m2) \, . \, no \neq yes \, . \, + (m4)$$

Finally, never patterns must satisfy a stronger condition: the entire never pattern must be strongly irreducible. This condition is inherited from the original Maude-NPA.

8.2   Choice of Encryption Type

This protocol allows either public key encryption or shared key encryption to be used by Alice to communicate with Bob. Alice initiates the conversation by sending out a message containing the chosen encryption mode, then Bob replies by sending an encrypted message containing his session key. The encryption mode is chosen nondeterministically by Alice. Therefore, it exhibits an *explicit nondeterministic choice*. Below we show the protocol description: the first one reflects the case in which public key encryption (denoted by $PubKey$) is chosen.

1. $A \to B : A \; ; \; B \; ; \; PubKey$
2. $B \to A : pk(A, B \; ; \; SK)$
3. $A \to B : pk(B, A \; ; \; SK \; ; \; N_A\}$
4. $B \to A : pk(A, B \; ; \; N_A)$

The second one reflects the case in which a shared key encryption (denoted by $SharedKey$) is chosen.

1. $A \to B : A \; ; \; B \; ; \; SharedKey$

2. $B \rightarrow A$: $shk(key(A, B), B$; $SK)$
3. $A \rightarrow B$: $shk(key(A, B), A$; SK ; $N_A)$
4. $B \rightarrow A$: $shk(key(A, B), B$; $N_A)$

Note that A and B are names of principals, SK denotes the session key generated by B, and N_A denotes a nonce generated by A.

There are different ways of encoding this protocol as two process expressions. We have chosen to treat the encryption mode as a choice variable which can be either public key encryption or shared key encryption, and then the receiver will perform an explicit deterministic choice depending on the value of this choice variable. The process specification is as follows:

$(Init)$ $((+(A_? ; B_? ; PubKey) \cdot -(pk(A_?, B_? ; SK)) \cdot$
$\quad + (pk(B_?, A_? ; SK ; n(A_?, r))) \cdot -(pk(A_?, B_? ; n(A_?, r))))$
$\quad ?$
$\quad\quad (+(A_? ; B_? ; SharedKey) \cdot -(e(key(A_?, B_?), B_? ; SK)) \cdot$
$\quad\quad + (e(key(A_?, B_?), A_? ; SK; n(A_?, r))) \cdot -(e(key(A_?, B_?), B_? ; n(A_?, r)))))$

$(Resp)$ $- (A ; B ; TEnc) \cdot$
$\quad if\ TEnc = PubKey\ then\ (+(pk(A, B ; skey(A, B, r')))\cdot$
$\quad\quad\quad\quad\quad\quad\quad\quad\quad - (pk(B, A ; skey(A, B, r') ; n(A, r))) \cdot$
$\quad\quad\quad\quad\quad\quad\quad\quad\quad + (pk(A, B ; n(A, r))))$
$\quad\quad\quad\quad\quad else\ (+(e(key(A, B), B ; skey(A, B, r'))))\cdot$
$\quad\quad\quad\quad\quad\quad\quad\quad\quad - (e(key(A, B), A ; skey(A, B, r') ; n(A, r))) \cdot$
$\quad\quad\quad\quad\quad\quad\quad\quad\quad + (e(key(A, B), B ; n(A, r))))$

We analyzed whether the intruder can learn the session key generated by Bob, when either the public key encryption or shared key encryption is chosen, assuming both principals are honest. For this property, Maude-NPA terminated without any attack being found for any of the two attack states.

8.3 Rock-Paper-Scissors

To evaluate our approach on protocols with explicit deterministic choices, we have used a simple protocol which simulates the famous Rock-Paper-Scissors game, in which Alice and Bob are the two players of the game. In this game, Alice and Bob commit to each other their hand shapes, which are later on revealed to each other after both players committed their hand shapes. The result of the game is then agreed upon between the two players according to the rule: rock beats scissors, scissors beats paper and paper beats rock. They finish by verifying with each other that they both reached the same conclusion. Thus, at the end of the protocol each party should know the outcome of the game and whether or not the other party agrees to the outcome. This protocol exhibits *explicit deterministic choice*, because the result of the game depends on the evaluation of the committed hand shapes according to the game's rule. Note that this protocol also exhibits *implicit nondeterministic choice*, since the hand shape of the players are chosen by the players during the game.

The protocol proceeds as follows. First, both initiator and responder choose their hand shapes and send them to each other using a secure commitment scheme. Next, they both send each other the nonces that are necessary to open the commitments. Each of them then compares the two hand shapes and decides if the initiator wins, the responder wins, or there is a tie. The initiator then sends the responder the outcome. When the responder receives the initiator's verdict, it compares it against its own. It responds with "finished" if it agrees with the initiator and "cheater" if it doesn't. All messages are signed and encrypted, and the initiator's and responder's nonces are included in the messages concerning the outcome of the game. The actual messages sent and choices made are described in more detail below.

1. $A \rightarrow B : pk(B, sign(A, commit(N_A, X_A)))$
2. $B \rightarrow A : pk(A, sign(B, commit(N_B, X_B)))$
3. $A \rightarrow B : pk(B, sign(A, N_A))$
4. $B \rightarrow A : pk(A, sign(B, N_B))$
5. $if\ (X_A\ beats\ X_B)\ then\ R = Win$
   $else\ if\ (X_B\ beats\ X_A)\ then\ R = Lose$
   $\qquad else\ if\ (X_B = X_A)\ then\ R = Tie\ else\ nilP$
6. $A \rightarrow B : pk(B, sign(A, N_A; N_B; R))$
7. $if\ (R = Win\ \&\ X_A\ beats\ X_B)\ or\ (R = Lose\ \&\ X_B\ beats\ X_A)\ or\ (R = Tie\ \&\ X_A = X_B)\ then\ B \rightarrow A : pk(A, sign(B, N_A; N_B; finished))\ else\ B \rightarrow A : pk(A, sign(B, N_A; N_B;\ cheater))$

One interesting feature of the Rock-Scissors-Paper protocol, is that, in order to verify that the commitment has been opened successfully, i.e., that the nonce received is the nonce used to create the commitment, one must verify that the result of opening it is well-typed, i.e., that it is equal to "rock", "scissors", or "paper". This can be done via the evaluation of predicates. First, we create a sort Item and declare the constants "rock", "scissors", and "paper" to be of sort Item. Then we create a variable $X{:}Item$ of sort Item. We then define a predicate *item?* such that *item?* $X{:}Item$ evaluates to true. Since only terms of sort Item can be unified with $X{:}Item$, this predicate can be used to check whether or not a term is of sort Item. We first tried to see whether the protocol can simulate the game successfully, so we asked for different scenarios in which the player Alice or Bob can win in a round of the game. Maude-NPA was able to generate the expected scenarios, and it did not generate any others. We then gave Maude-NPA a secrecy attack state, in which the intruder, playing the role of initiator against an honest responder, attempts to guess its nonce before the responder receives its commitment. Finally we specified an authentication attack state in which we asked if a responder could complete a session with an honest initiator with the conclusion that the initiator had carried out its rule faithfully, without that actually having happened. For both of these attack states Maude-NPA finished its search without finding any attacks.

8.4   TLS

In Sect. 1.3 we introduced a simplified version of the handshake protocol in TLS 1.3 [20]. Even this simplified version produced a very large search space, because of the long list of messages and the concurrent interactions of a big amount of choices. We are however able to check the correctness of our specification by producing legal executions in Maude-NPA. Unlike TLS 1.3, we intentionally introduced a "downgrade attack" in our version in which the attacker can trick the principals into using a weaker crypto system. However, we have not yet been able to produce this attack because of the very deep and wide analysis tree (i.e., long reachability sequences with many branches) that is produced. See [15] for a more detailed specification of TLS in Maude-NPA that is able to terminate, find attacks, and prove security against some classes of attacks.

9   Related Work

As we mentioned in the introduction, there is a considerable amount of work on adding choice to the strand space model that involves embedding it into other formal systems, including event-based models for concurrency [5], Petri nets [13], or multi-set rewriting [3]. Crazzolara and Winskel model nondeterministic choice as a form of composition, where a conflict relation is defined between possible child strands so that the parent can compose with only one potential child. In [13] Fröschle uses a Petri net model to add branching to strand space *bundles*, which represent the concurrent execution of strand space roles. Note that we have taken the opposite approach of representing bundles as traces of non-branching strands, where a different trace is generated for each choice taken. Although this results in more bundles during forward execution, it makes little difference in backwards execution, and is more straightforward to implement in an already existing analysis tool.

We also note that deterministic choice has been included in the applied pi calculus for cryptographic protocols [2], another widely used formal model, based on Milner's pi calculus [18]. The applied pi calculus includes the rule *if $M = N$ then P else Q*, where P and Q are terms. This is similar to our syntax for deterministic choice. However our long-term plan is to add other types or predicates as well (e.g., *M subsumes N*). Indeed our approach extends to any type of predicate that can be evaluated on a ground state. Although the applied pi calculus in its original form does not include nondeterministic choice, both nondeterministic and probabilistic choice have been added in subsequent work [14].

In addition, Olarte and Valencia show in [19] how a cryptographic protocol modeling language can be expressed in their universal timed concurrent con-

342 F. Yang et al.

straint programming (utcc) model, a framework that extends the timed concurrent constraint programming model to express mobility. The language does not support choice, but utcc does. It seems that it would not be difficult to extend the language to incorporate the utcc choice mechanisms.

The Tamarin protocol analysis tool [16] includes deterministic branching, which was used extensively in the analysis of TLS 1.3 [6]. In particular, it includes an optimization for roles of the form $P.(if\ T\ then\ Q\ else\ R).S$; when backwards search is used, it is sometimes possible to capture such an execution in terms of just one strand until the conditional is encountered, thus reducing the state space. Our approach produces two strands, but since the process algebra semantics makes it easy to tell whether or not R behaves "essentially" the same no matter if P or Q is chosen, we believe that we have a pathway for including such a feature if desired.

10   Conclusions

We have provided an extension to the strand space model that allows for both deterministic and nondeterministic choice, together with an operational semantics for choice in strand spaces that not only provides a formal foundation for choice, but allows us to implement it directly in the Maude-NPA cryptographic protocol analysis tool. In particular, we have applied Maude-NPA to several protocols that rely on choice in order to validate our approach.

This work not only provides a choice extension to strand spaces, but extends them in other ways as well. First of all, it provides a process algebra for strand spaces. This potentially allows us to relate the strand space model to other formal systems (e.g., the applied pi calculus [1]) giving a better understanding of how it compares with other formal models. In addition, the process algebra semantics provides a new specification language for Maude-NPA that we believe is more natural for users than the current strand-space language.

Another contribution of this work is that it provides a means for evaluating both equality and disequality predicates in the strand space model and in Maude-NPA. This allows us to implement features such as type checking in Maude-NPA, via predicates such as $foocheck(X)$, where $foocheck(0 : Foo) = tt$, that is, $foocheck(X)$ succeeds only if X is of sort Foo. This proved to be very helpful, for example, in our specification of the Rock-Scissors-Paper protocol as we described earlier. We believe the expressiveness of Maude-NPA can be further increased at little cost by extending the types of predicates that can be evaluated, e.g., by including predicates for subsumption and their negations. This is another subject for further investigation.

A   Proofs

A.1   Proofs of Section 6.2

The relation $\mathcal{H}$ relies on the relations $\mathcal{H}_{LP\_Str}$ and $\mathcal{H}_{PS\_FS}$. We define the relation $\mathcal{H}_{LP\_Str}$, which relates a possibly partially executed labeled process and a constrained strand. This relation defines the *duality* relation between a labeled process and a constrained strands. If a labeled process LP is related to a constrained strand Str by the relation $\mathcal{H}_{LP\_Str}$, then: (i) LP and Str denote the behavior of the same role with the same identity in the same protocol, and (ii) for any strand Str_{LP}, Str_{LP} denotes a possible execution path of LP iff Str followed by Str_{LP} forms a valid possible execution path of the protocol.

Definition 13 (Relation $\mathcal{H}_{LP\_Str}$). *Given a protocol $\mathcal{P}$, and a possibly partially executed labeled process LP of $\mathcal{P}$, a possibly partially executed constrained strand Str of $\mathcal{P}$, then $(LP, Str) \in \mathcal{H}_{LP\_Str}$ iff*

$$toCstrSS(LP) = \&\{(ro, i)[u_{j+1}, \ldots, u_n]\rho_{ro,i}\theta \mid \exists \text{ ground substitution } \theta$$
$$\exists (ro)[u_1, \ldots u_j, u_{j+1}, \ldots, u_n] \in \mathcal{P}_{Cstr} \text{ s.t. } Str = (ro, i)[u_1, \ldots u_j]\rho_{ro,i}\theta\}$$

where $\&\{S_1, S_2, \ldots, S_n\}$ is a shorthand for a term $S_1 \& S_2 \& \ldots \& S_n$ denoting a set of strands. $\rho_{ro,i} = \{r_1 \mapsto r_1.ro.i, \ldots, r_m \mapsto r_m.ro.i\}$ for fresh variables $r_1, \ldots, r_m$ in $[u_1, \ldots u_j, u_{j+1}, \ldots, u_n]$.

Example 11. Following Examples 7 and 10, we show a process LP and a strand Str that are related by the relation $\mathcal{H}_{LP\_Str}$. LP (resp. Str) is the labeled process (resp. constrained strand) of the Server role after making the first explicit nondeterministic choice.

$$LP = (Server, 1, 2) \; \sigma(+(hs; retry) \cdot -(hs; N'; G'; gen(G'); E') \cdot$$
$$+ (hs; n(S_?, r1); G'; gen(G'); keyG(G', S_?, r_2); Z(AReq_?, G', E', S, r_2, S_?, HM)))$$
$$Str = (Server, 1) \; \sigma[\; \{?, 1\}, -(hs; N; G; gen(G); E)]$$

where σ is a ground substitution to the pattern variables N, G, and E.

We then lift the duality relation between individual processes and strands to a duality relation between PA-State and FW-State.

Definition 14 (Relation $\mathcal{H}_{PS\_FS}$). *Let $Pst = \{LP_1 \& \ldots \& LP_n \mid \{IK\}\}$ be a PA-State and $Fst = \{Str_1 \& \ldots \& Str_m \& \{IK'\}\}$ be a FW-State, if $(Pst, Fst) \in \mathcal{H}_{PS\_FS}$, then:*

(i) *For each labeled process $LP_k \in Pst$, $1 \leqslant k \leqslant n$, there exists a strand $Str_{k'} \in Fst$, $1 \leqslant k' \leqslant m$, such that $(LP_k, Str_{k'}) \in \mathcal{H}_{LP\_Str}$.*
(ii) *For each strand $Str_{k'} \in Fst$, $1 \leqslant k' \leqslant m$, there exists a labeled process $LP_k \in Pst$, $1 \leqslant k \leqslant n$, such that $(LP_k, Str_{k'}) \in \mathcal{H}_{LP\_Str}$.*

The lemma below states that the relation $\mathcal{H}$ induces the *duality* relation $\mathcal{H}_{PS\_FS}$.

Lemma 1. *Let $Pst = \{LP_1 \& \ldots \& LP_n \mid \{IK\}\}$ be a PA-State and $Fst = \{Str_1 \& \ldots \& Str_m \& \{IK'\}\}$ be a FW-State, if $(Pst, Fst) \in \mathcal{H}$, i.e., exists a label sequence α such that $P_{init} \rightarrow_\alpha Pst$, and $F_{init} \rightarrow_\alpha Fst$, then $(Pst, Fst) \in \mathcal{H}_{PS\_FS}$.*

Proof. We first prove property (i). If $|\alpha| = 0$, since both the strand set and the process configuration are empty, the statement is vacuously true.

Now suppose that $|\alpha| > 0$. Then, without loss of generality, assume there exists a labeled process $LP_k = ((ro, i, j)\ P_k)$ in Pst, with $i, j \geq 1$. Then there is at least one label in α of the form $(ro, i, \_, \_, \_)$ (_ is a short hand for any content), therefore, there is a strand $St_{k'}$ in Fst of the form $(ro, i)[v_1, \ldots, v_{j'}]$.

We then show that the above-mentioned LP_k and $Str_{k'}$ are related by $\mathcal{H}_{LP\_Str}$, i.e., $(LP_k, Str_{k'}) \in \mathcal{H}_{LP\_Str}$. Since the state Fst is reachable from the initial state by the label sequence α, and $Str_{k'} \in Fst$, $[v_1, \ldots, v_{j'}]$ denotes exactly the sequence of messages in the unique sequence of labels $\alpha|_{(ro,i)}$. Moreover, $j' = j - 1$.

Since the process state Pst is reachable from the initial state P_{init} by label sequence α, there exists a unique process $(ro)P_{spec}$ in the specification P_{PA}, and LP_k represents all possible behaviors of $(ro)P_{spec}$ after the sequence of transitions $\alpha|_{(ro,i)}$. Therefore, $toCstrSS(LP_k) =$

$$\&\{(ro, i)[u_j, \ldots, u_n]\rho_{ro,i}\theta \mid$$
$$\exists \text{ ground substitution } \theta$$
$$\exists (ro)[u_1, \ldots, u_{j-1}, u_j, \ldots, u_n] \in toCstrSS((ro)P_{spec})$$
$$s.t.\ (ro, i)[u_1, \ldots, u_{j-1}]\rho_{ro,i}\theta = (ro, i)[v_1, \ldots, v_{j-1}]\}$$

By the correspondence between protocol specifications defined in Definition 3 , $\mathcal{P}_{CstrF} = toCstrSS(P_{PA})$. Also note that $(ro)P_{spec}$ is the only process in P_{PA} that has ro as its role name, therefore, $toCstrSS((ro)P_{spec}) = \{(ro)[u_1, \ldots, u_n] \mid (ro)[u_1, \ldots, u_n] \in \mathcal{P}_{CstrF}\}$. Therefore, $toCstrSS(LP_k) =$

$$\&\{(ro, i)[u_j, \ldots u_n]\rho_{ro,i}\theta \mid$$
$$\exists \text{ ground substitution } \theta,$$
$$\exists (ro)[u_1, \ldots, u_{j-1}, u_j, \ldots, u_n] \in \mathcal{P}_{CstrF}$$
$$s.t.\ (ro, i)[u_1, \ldots, u_{j-1}]\rho_{ro,i}\theta = (ro, i)[v_1, \ldots, v_{j-1}]\}.$$

Therefore, $(LP_k, Str_{k'}) \in \mathcal{H}_{LP\_Str}$. The proof for property (ii) is similar to the one for property (i). □

Lemma 2 below formalizes the observation that the equivalence of label sequence implies the same intruder knowledge.

Lemma 2. *Given a PA-State Pst and a FW-State Fst such that $(Pst, Fst) \in \mathcal{H}$, i.e., there exists a label sequence α such that $P_{init} \rightarrow_\alpha Pst$ and $F_{init} \rightarrow_\alpha Fst$, then the contents of intruder knowledge in Pst and in Fst are syntactically equal.*

Proof. In both semantics the only transition rules that add new elements to the intruder's knowledge are the ones whose label is of the form $(ro, i, j, +m, n)$. Therefore, given the two states Pst and Fst as described above, their intruder's knowledge can be computed from the sequence of labeled transitions α as $IK(Pst) = \{m \in \mathcal{I} \mid (\_, \_, \_, +m, \_) \in \alpha\} = IK(Fst)$. □

Based on the lemmas above, we can now show that the relation $\mathcal{H}$ is a bisimulation.

Theorem 1 (Bisimulation). $\mathcal{H}$ is a bisimulation.

Proof. Since $P_{init} \rightarrow_{nil} P_{init}$ and $F_{init} \rightarrow_{nil} F_{init}$, therefore, $(P_{init}, F_{init}) \in \mathcal{H}$. We then prove that: for all PA-State Pst_n, and FW-State Fst_n, if $(Pst_n, Fst_n) \in \mathcal{H}$, and there exists a PA-State Pst_{n+1} such that $Pst_n \rightarrow_a Pst_{n+1}$, then there exists a FW-State Fst_{n+1} such that $Fst_n \rightarrow_a Fst_{n+1}$ and $(Pst_{n+1}, Fst_{n+1}) \in \mathcal{H}$.. If $(Pst_n, Fst_n) \in \mathcal{H}$, by definition of the relation $\mathcal{H}$, there exists a label sequence α s.t. $P_{init} \rightarrow_\alpha Pst_n$ and $F_{init} \rightarrow_\alpha Fst_n$. Suppose there exists state Pst_{n+1} such that $Pst_n \rightarrow_a Pst_{n+1}$. We prove by case analysis on label a that there exists Fst_{n+1} such that $Fst_n \rightarrow_a Fst_{n+1}$. The fact that $(Pst_{n+1}, Fst_{n+1}) \in \mathcal{H}$ then follows this by the definition of relation $\mathcal{H}$.

In the rest of this proof, $\overrightarrow{L}, \overrightarrow{L_1}$ and $\overrightarrow{L_2}$ denote lists of messages, M, M' and m denote messages, P, Q and R denote processes, PS denotes a process configuration, SS denotes a set of constrained protocol strands, IK and IK' denote the set of messages in the intruder's knowledge.

1) $a = (ro, i, j, +m, 0)$: if $j > 1$, according to the semantics, $Pst_n \rightarrow_a Pst_{n+1}$ by applying rule (PA++), the state Pst_n is of the form $\{(ro, i, j) \ (+M \cdot P) \ \& \ PS \mid \{IK\}\}$ s.t. there exists a ground substitution σ binding the choice variables in M and $m = M\sigma$, the state $Pst_{n+1} = \{(ro, i, j+1) \ P\sigma \ \& \ PS \mid \{m \in \mathcal{I}, IK\}\}$ and $m \in \mathcal{I} \notin IK$. Since $Pst_n \ \mathcal{H} \ Fst_n$, by Lemmas 1 and 2, Fst_n is of the form $\{(ro, i) \ [\overrightarrow{L}] \ \& \ SS \ \& \ \{IK\}\}$ s.t. $(ro, i, j) \ (+M \cdot P) \ \mathcal{H}_{LP\_Str} \ (ro, i) \ [\overrightarrow{L}]$. Let $(ro) \ [\overrightarrow{L_1}, \overrightarrow{L_2}]$ be a constrained strand in P_{CstrSS} s.t. there exists a ground substitution θ s.t. $\overrightarrow{L_1}\rho_{ro,i}\theta = \overrightarrow{L}$. By the definition of relation $\mathcal{H}_{LP\_Str}$ and mapping $toCstrSS$, the first message of $\overrightarrow{L_2}$ is $+M'$, s.t. $M'\rho_{ro,i}\theta = M$. Then since $M\sigma = m$ and $m \in \mathcal{I} \notin IK$, the rule (F++) can be applied for the rewrite $Fst_n \rightarrow_a Fst_{n+1}$, where $Fst_{n+1} = \{(ro, i) \ [\overrightarrow{L}, +m] \ \& \ SS \ \& \ \{m \in \mathcal{I}, IK\}\}$.

If $j = 1$, $Pst_n \rightarrow_a Pst_{n+1}$ by applying rule (PA&), there exists a process $(ro) \ (+M \cdot P)$ in P_{PA} and a ground substitution σ s.t. $M\rho_{ro,i}\sigma = m$. Since $toCstrSS(P_{PA}) = P_{CstrSS}$, by the definition of $toCstrSS$, for all strands of role ro in P_{CstrSS}, the first message is $+M$. Without loss of generality, let Pst_n be $\{PS \mid \{IK\}\}$, and Fst_n be $\{SS \ \& \ \{IK'\}\}$. Since the rule (PA&) can be applied, $m \in \mathcal{I} \notin IK$. By Lemma 2, $IK = IK'$. Moreover, by Lemma 1, $MaxStrId(SS, ro) = MaxProcId(PS, ro)$, and since $MaxProcId(PS, ro) + 1 = i$, by applying the rule (F++&) we get $Fst_n \rightarrow_a Fst_{n+1}$.

2) $a = (ro, i, j, M\sigma, 0)$: similar to case 1.

3) $a = (ro, i, j, -m, 0)$: if $j > 1$, according to the semantics, $Pst_n \rightarrow_a Pst_{n+1}$ by applying rule (PA-), Pst_n is of the form $\{(ro, i, j) \ (-M \cdot P) \ \& \ PS \mid \{m \in \mathcal{I}, IK\}\}$ s.t. $m =_{E_P} M\sigma$ for some ground substitution σ and $Pst_{n+1} = \{(ro, i, j + 1) \ P\sigma \ \& \ PS \mid \{m \in \mathcal{I}, IK\}\}$. Since $Pst_n \ \mathcal{H} \ Fst_n$, by Lemmas 1 and 2, $Fst_n = \{(ro, i) \ [\overrightarrow{L}] \ \& \ SS \ \& \ \{m \in \mathcal{I}, IK\}\}$ s.t. $(ro, i, j) \ (-M \cdot P) \ \mathcal{H}_{LP\_Str} \ (ro) \ [\overrightarrow{L}]$. Let $(ro) \ [\overrightarrow{L_1}, \overrightarrow{L_2}] \in P_{CstrSS}$ s.t. there exists a ground substitution θ s.t. $\overrightarrow{L_1}\rho_{ro,i}\theta = \overrightarrow{L}$, then by definition of $\mathcal{H}_{LP\_Str}$

and $toCstrSS$, the first message of $\vec{L_2}$ is $-M'$ s.t. $M'\rho_{ro,i}\theta = M$. Since $m =_{E_P} M\sigma$, rule (F-) can be applied to get the transition $Fst_n \rightarrow_a Fst_{n+1}$, where $Fst_{n+1} = \{(ro,i)\,[\vec{L},-m]\ \&\ SS\ \&\ \{m\in\mathcal{I},IK\}\}$.

If $j = 1$, $Pst_n \rightarrow_a Pst_{n+1}$ by applying rule (PA&), there exists a process $(ro)\ (-M \cdot P)$ in P_{PA} and a ground substitution σ s.t. $M\rho_{ro,i}\sigma = m$. Without loss of generality, let Pst_n be $\{PS \mid \{IK\}\}$. Then $m\in\mathcal{I} \in IK$. Since $toCstrSS(P_{PA}) = P_{CstrSS}$, by the definition of $toCstrSS$, for all strands of role ro in P_{CstrSS}, the first message is $-M$. By Lemma 2, $m\in\mathcal{I}$ is in the intruder knowledge of Fst_n. Moreover, by Lemma 1, $MaxStrId(SS,ro) = MaxProcId(PS,ro)$, and since $MaxProcId(PS,ro) + 1 = i$, by applying the rule (F-&) we get $Fst_n \rightarrow_a Fst_{n+1}$.

4) $a = (ro,i,j,T,1)$: according to the transition rules, $Pst_n \rightarrow_a Pst_{n+1}$ by applying rule (PAif1). Therefore Pst_n is of the form $\{(ro,i,j)\ ((if\ c\ then\ P\ else\ Q)\ \cdot R)\ \&\ PS \mid \{IK\}\}$, $Pst_{n+1} = \{(ro,i,j + 1)\ (P\cdot R)\ \&\ PS \mid \{IK\}\}$ and $c =_{E_P} true$. Since $Fst_n\ \mathcal{H}\ Pst_n$, by Lemma 1, $Fst_n = \{(ro)\,[\vec{L}]\ \&\ SS\ \&\ \{IK'\}\}$ s.t. $(ro,i,j)\ ((if\ c\ then\ P\ else\ Q)\ \cdot R)\ \mathcal{H}_{LP\_Str}\ (ro,i)\,[\vec{L}]$. By the definition of the relation $\mathcal{H}_{LP\_Str}$ and the mapping $toCstrSS$, there exists $(ro)\,[\vec{L_1},\{C,1\},\vec{L_2}] \in P_{CstrSS}$ and a ground substitution θ s.t. $\vec{L} = \vec{L_1}\rho_{ro,i}\theta$, and $C\rho_{ro,i}\theta = c$. Since $c =_{E_P} true$, the rule (Fif) can be applied for the rewrite $Fst_n \rightarrow_a Fst_{n+1}$, where $Fst_{n+1} = \{\{(ro)\,[\vec{L},\{t,1\}]\ \&\ SS\ \&\ \{IK'\}\}$

5) $a = (ro,i,j,T,2)$: similar to case 4.

6) $a = (ro,i,j,?,1)$: if $j > 1$, $Pst_n \rightarrow_a Pst_{n+1}$ by applying rule (PA?1). Therefore Pst_n is of the form $\{(ro,i,j)\ ((P\ ?\ Q)\cdot R)\ \&\ PS \mid \{IK\}\}$ and $Pst_{n+1} = \{(ro,i,j + 1)\ (P\cdot R)\ \&\ PS \mid \{IK\}\}$. Since $Fst_n\ \mathcal{H}\ Pst_n$, by Lemma 1, $Fst_n = \{(ro,i)\,[\vec{L}]\ \&\ SS\ \&\ \{IK'\}\}$ s.t. $(ro,i,j)\ ((P\ ?\ Q)\ \cdot R)\ \mathcal{H}_{LP\_Str}(ro,i)\,[\vec{L}]$. By the definition of $\mathcal{H}_{LP\_Str}$ and $toCstrSS$, there is a strand $(ro,i)\,[\vec{L_1},\{?,1\},\vec{L_2}] \in P_{CstrSS}$ s.t. $\vec{L} = \vec{L_1}\theta$. Therefore, rule (F?) can be applied for the rewrite $Fst_n \rightarrow_a Fst_{n+1}$, and $Fst_{n+1} = \{(ro,i)\,[\vec{L},\{?,1\}]\ \&\ SS\ \&\ \{IK'\}\}$.

If $j = 1$, $Pst_n \rightarrow_a Pst_{n+1}$ by applying rule (PA&). Therefore, there exists a process $(ro)\ ((P\ ?\ Q)\cdot R)$ in P_{PA}. Since $toCstrSS(P_{PA}) = P_{CstrSS}$, by the definition of $toCstrSS$, there is a strand of role ro whose first message is $(?,1)$ in P_{CstrSS}. Moreover, by Lemma 1, $MaxStrId(SS,ro) = MaxProcId(PS,ro)$, and since $MaxProcId(PS,ro) + 1 = i$, by applying the rule (F?&) we get $Fst_n \rightarrow_a Fst_{n+1}$.

7) $a = (ro,i,j,?,2)$ similar to case 6.

Similarly, we can prove that for all PA-State Pst_n, and FW-State Fst_n, if $(Pst_n, Fst_n) \in \mathcal{H}$, and there exists a FW-State Fst_{n+1} such that $Fst_n \rightarrow_a Fst_{n+1}$, then there exists a PA-State Pst_{n+1} such that $Pst_n \rightarrow_a Pst_{n+1}$ and $(Pst_{n+1}, Fst_{n+1}) \in \mathcal{H}$ □

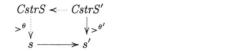

Fig. 4. Lemma 3   **Fig. 5.** Lemma 4

A.2   Proofs of Section 7.2

Extending the proofs in [9], we first prove how the lifting of a ground state to a symbolic state induces a lifting of a forwards rewriting step in the forwards semantics to a backwards narrowing step in the backwards semantics, i.e., the completeness of one-step transition. The lemma below extends the lifting lemma in [9] to strands with constrained messages.

Lemma 3 (Lifting Lemma). *Given a protocol $\mathcal{P}$, two ground strand states s and s', a constrained symbolic strand state $CstrS' = \langle S', \Psi' \rangle$ and a substitution θ' s.t. $s \to s'$ and $CstrS' >^{\theta'} s'$, then there exists a constrained symbolic strand state $CstrS = \langle S, \Psi \rangle$ and a substitution θ s.t. $CstrS >^{\theta} s$ and either $CstrS \overset{\mu}{\leadsto} CstrS'$ or $CstrS = CstrS'$.*

The Lifting Lemma is illustrated by Fig. 4.

Proof. As has been explained before, we only need to consider the new rules: (Fif), (F?), (F?&). The proof in [9] is structured by cases, some of which having specific requirements on intruder knowledge, or involve changes made to the intruder knowledge. Since all the new rules we are considering do not have specific requirements on the intruder knowledge, and do not change the intruder knowledge either, the cases that we need to consider are the following (cases e and f in the proof in [9]), which involve the appearance or non-appearance of certain strand(s):

e: There is a strand $[u_1, \ldots, u_{j-1}, u_j, \ldots, u_n]$ in P_{CstrSS}, $n \geqslant 1$, $1 \leqslant j \leqslant n$, and a substitution ρ such that $[u_1, \ldots, u_{j-1}, u_j]\rho$ is a strand in s' and $[u_1, \ldots, u_{j-1}, u_j \mid u_{j+1}, \ldots, u_n]\rho$ is a strand in $S'\theta'$.

f: There is a strand $[u_1, \ldots, u_{j-1}, u_j, \ldots, u_n]$ in P_{CstrSS}, $n \geqslant 1$, $1 \leqslant j \leqslant n$, and a substitution ρ such that $[u_1, \ldots, u_{j-1}, u_j]\rho$ is a strand in s' but $[u_1, \ldots, u_{j-1}, u_j \mid u_{j+1}, \ldots, u_n]\rho$ is not a strand in $S'\theta'$.

Now we consider for the forward rewrite rule application in the step $s \to s'$.

– Given ground states s and s' s.t. $s \to s'$ using a rule in set (Fif), then there exists a ground substitution τ, variables SS' and IK', and strand $[u_1, \ldots, u_{j-1}, \{T, Num\}, u_{j+1}, \ldots, u_n]$ in P_{CstrSS}, such that $s = \{SS'\tau \& \{IK'\tau\} \& (ro) [u_1\tau, \ldots, u_{j-1}\tau]\}$, and $s' = \{SS'\tau \& \{IK'\tau\} \& [u_1\tau, \ldots, u_{j-1}\tau, \{T\tau, Num\}]\}$ and $T\tau =_{E_{\mathcal{P}}} true$. Since there exists a substitution θ' s. t. $CstrS' >^{\theta'} s'$, we consider the following two cases:

- Case e) The strand appears in $S'\theta'$. More specifically, $[u_1\sigma, \ldots, u_{j-1}\sigma, \{T\sigma, Num\} \mid u_{j+1}\sigma, \ldots, u_n\sigma]$ is a strand in S' s.t. $\sigma\theta' =_{E_\mathcal{P}} \tau$. If the constraint T is an equality constraint, since $T\tau =_{E_\mathcal{P}} T\sigma\theta' =_{E_\mathcal{P}} true$, and by the lifting relation, $E_\mathcal{P} \models \Psi'\theta'$, rule (Bif=) can be applied for the backwards narrowing $CstrS' \xleftarrow{\mu} CstrS$, and $CstrS >^\theta s$ such that $\mu\theta =_{E_\mathcal{P}} \theta'$. If the constraint T is a disequality constraint, since $T\tau =_{E_\mathcal{P}} T\sigma\theta' =_{E_\mathcal{P}} true$, and by the lifting relation, $E_\mathcal{P} \models \Psi'\theta'$, we have $E_\mathcal{P} \models T\sigma\theta' \wedge \Psi'\theta'$. Therefore, rule (Bif≠) can be applied for the backwards narrowing, and $CstrS >^\theta s$.
- Case f) The strand does not appear in $S'\theta'$. Then θ' makes S' as a valid symbolic strand state of s, i.e., $S = S'$ and $CstrS >^{\theta'} s$.

- Given ground strand states s and s' s.t. $s \to s'$ using a rule in set (F?), then we consider the following two applicable cases:
  - Case e) The strand appears in $S'\theta'$ and thus we can perform a backwards narrowing step from $CstrS'$ with rule (B?), i.e., $CstrS' \rightsquigarrow CstrS$, and $CstrS >^{\theta'} s$.
  - Case f) The strand does not appear in $S'\theta'$. Then θ' makes $CstrS'$ as a valid constraint symbolic state of s, i.e., $CstrS = CstrS'$ and $CstrS >^{\theta'} s$.
- Given states s and s' s.t. $s \to s'$ using a rule in set (F?&), the proof is similar with using a rule in the set (F?).

$\square$

The Completeness Theorem below shows that the backwards symbolic reachability analysis is *complete* with respect to the forwards rewriting-based strand semantics.

Theorem 4 (Completeness). *Given a protocol $\mathcal{P}$, two ground strand states s, s_0, a constrained symbolic strand state $CstrS$ and a substitution θ s.t. (i) s_0 is an initial state, (ii) $s_0 \to^n s$, and (iii) $CstrS >^\theta s$. There exists a constrained symbolic initial strand state $CstrS_0$, two substitutions μ and θ', and $k \leq n$, s.t. $CstrS_0 \xleftarrow{k}_\mu CstrS$, and $CstrS_0 >^{\theta'} s_0$.*

The Soundness Theorem from [9] can also be extended to constrained backwards and forwards strand semantics. We first show that Lemma 2 in [9], which states the soundness of one-step transition, still holds after extending to constrained states. The Soundness Theorem then follows straightforwardly.

Lemma 4. *Given a protocol $\mathcal{P}$, two constrained symbolic states $CstrS = \langle S, \Psi \rangle$ and $CstrS' = \langle S', \Psi' \rangle$, a ground strand state s and a ground substitution θ, if $CstrS \xleftarrow{\mu} CstrS'$ and $CstrS >^\theta s$, then there exists a ground strand state s' and a ground substitution θ' such that $s \to s'$, and $CstrS' >^{\theta'} s'$.*

Lemma 4 is illustrated by Fig. 5.

Proof. We only need to consider the new rules: rule (Bif=), (Bif≠) and (B?).

1) If $CstrS \overset{\mu}{\leftsquigarrow} CstrS'$ using rule (B?), then there are associated rules in the sets (F?) and (F?&).

2) If $CstrS \overset{\mu}{\leftsquigarrow} CstrS'$ using rule (Bif=), there is a strand $[u_1\sigma, \ldots, u_{j-1}\sigma \mid \{(u = v)\sigma, Num\}, u_{j+1}\sigma, \ldots, u_n\sigma]$ in S, $[u_1\sigma', \ldots, u_{j-1}\sigma', \{(u = v)\sigma', Num\} \mid u_{j+1}\sigma', \ldots, u_n\sigma']$ in S' s.t. $\sigma =_{E_P} \sigma'\mu$, $\Psi =_{E_P} \Psi'\mu$ and $u\sigma =_{E_P} v\sigma$, where $[u_1, \ldots, u_{j-1}, \{u = v, Num\}, u_{j+1}, \ldots, u_n]$ is a strand in P_{CstrSS}. Since $CstrS >^\theta s$, there is a ground strand $[u_1\sigma\theta, \ldots, u_{j-1}\sigma\theta]$ in s, and $E_P \models \Psi\theta$. Therefore, $E_P \models \Psi'\mu\theta$ and $u\sigma\theta =_{E_P} v\sigma\theta$. By rule (Fif), $s \to s'$, and $CstrS' >^{\mu\theta} s'$.

If $CstrS \overset{\mu}{\leftsquigarrow} CstrS'$ using rule (Bif≠), there is a strand $[u_1\sigma, \ldots, u_{j-1}\sigma \mid \{(u \neq v)\sigma, Num\}, u_{j+1}\sigma, \ldots, u_n\sigma]$ in S, $[u_1\sigma', \ldots, u_{j-1}\sigma', \{(u \neq v)\sigma', Num\} \mid u_{j+1}\sigma', \ldots, u_n\sigma']$ in S' s.t. $\sigma =_{E_P} \sigma'\mu$ and $\Psi =_{E_P} \Psi'\mu \wedge (u \neq v)\sigma'\mu$, where $[u_1, \ldots, u_{j-1}, \{u \neq v, Num\}, u_{j+1}, \ldots, u_n]$ is a strand in P_{CstrSS}. Since $CstrS >^\theta s$, there is a ground strand $[u_1\sigma\theta, \ldots, u_{j-1}\sigma\theta]$ in s, and $E_P \models \Psi\theta$. Therefore, $E_P \models \Psi'\mu\theta \wedge (u \neq v)\sigma'\mu\theta$. By rule (Fif), $s \to s'$, and $CstrS' >^{\mu\theta} s'$. □

The Soundness Theorem below shows that the backwards symbolic reachability analysis is *sound* with respect to the forwards rewriting-based strand semantics.

Theorem 5 (Soundness). *Given a protocol $\mathcal{P}$, two constrained symbolic strand states $CstrS_0$, $CstrS'$, an initial ground strand state s_0 and a substitution θ s.t. (i) $CstrS_0$ is a symbolic initial state, and (ii) $CstrS_0 \overset{*}{\leftsquigarrow} CstrS'$, and (iii) $CstrS_0 >^\theta s_0$. Then there exists a ground strand state s' and a substitution θ', s.t. (i) $s_0 \to^* s'$, and (ii) $CstrS' >^{\theta'} s'$.*

The soundness and completeness results in Theorems 5 and 4 together with the bisimulation proved in Theorem 1 show that the backwards symbolic reachability analysis is *sound*, Theorem 2, and *complete*, Theorem 3, with respect to the process algebra semantics.

References

1. Abadi, M.: Leslie Lamport's properties and actions. In: Proceedings of the Twentieth Annual ACM Symposium on Principles of Distributed Computing, PODC 2001, p. 15 (2001)
2. Abadi, M., Fournet, C.: Mobile values, new names, and secure communication. In: Conference Record of POPL 2001: The 28th ACM SIGPLAN-SIGACT Symposium on Principles of Programming Languages, pp. 104–115 (2001)
3. Cervesato, I., Durgin, N.A., Mitchell, J.C., Lincoln, P., Scedrov, A.: Relating strands and multiset rewriting for security protocol analysis. In: Proceedings of the 13th IEEE Computer Security Foundations Workshop, CSFW 2000, pp. 35–51 (2000)
4. Comon, H.: Disunification: a survey. In: Lassez, J.-L., Plotkin, G.D. (eds.) Computational Logic - Essays in Honor of Alan Robinson, pp. 322–359. The MIT Press (1991)

5. Crazzolara, F., Winskel, G.: Composing strand spaces. In: Agrawal, M., Seth, A. (eds.) FSTTCS 2002. LNCS, vol. 2556, pp. 97–108. Springer, Heidelberg (2002). https://doi.org/10.1007/3-540-36206-1_10

6. Cremers, C., Horvat, M., Scott, S., van der Merwe, T.: Automated analysis and verification of TLS 1.3: 0-RTT, resumption and delayed authentication. In: IEEE Symposium on Security and Privacy, SP 2016, San Jose, CA, USA, 22–26 May 2016, pp. 470–485. IEEE Computer Society (2016)

7. Escobar, S., Meadows, C., Meseguer, J.: Maude-NPA: cryptographic protocol analysis modulo equational properties. In: Aldini, A., Barthe, G., Gorrieri, R. (eds.) FOSAD 2007-2009. LNCS, vol. 5705, pp. 1–50. Springer, Heidelberg (2009). https://doi.org/10.1007/978-3-642-03829-7_1

8. Escobar, S., Meadows, C., Meseguer, J.: Maude-NPA manual version 3.1 (2017). http://maude.cs.illinois.edu/w/index.php?title=Maude_Tools:_Maude-NPA

9. Escobar, S., Meadows, C., Meseguer, J., Santiago, S.: A rewriting-based forwards semantics for Maude-NPA. In: Proceedings of the 2014 Symposium and Bootcamp on the Science of Security, HotSoS 2014. ACM (2014)

10. Escobar, S., Meadows, C., Meseguer, J., Santiago, S.: State space reduction in the Maude-NRL protocol analyzer. Inf. Comput. **238**, 157–186 (2014)

11. Escobar, S., Meadows, C., Meseguer, J., Santiago, S.: Symbolic protocol analysis with disequality constraints modulo equational theories. In: Bodei, C., Ferrari, G.-L., Priami, C. (eds.) Programming Languages with Applications to Biology and Security. LNCS, vol. 9465, pp. 238–261. Springer, Cham (2015). https://doi.org/10.1007/978-3-319-25527-9_16

12. Thayer Fabrega, F.J., Herzog, J., Guttman, J.: Strand spaces: what makes a security protocol correct? J. Comput. Secur. **7**, 191–230 (1999)

13. Fröschle, S.B.: Adding branching to the strand space model. Electr. Notes Theor. Comput. Sci. **242**(1), 139–159 (2009)

14. Goubault-Larrecq, J., Palamidessi, C., Troina, A.: A probabilistic applied pi-calculus. In: Shao, Z. (ed.) APLAS 2007. LNCS, vol. 4807, pp. 175–190. Springer, Heidelberg (2007). https://doi.org/10.1007/978-3-540-76637-7_12

15. Lluch-Palop, J.: Verificación automática del protocolo TLS 1.3 usando Maude-NPA. Master's thesis, Universitat Politècnica de València (2019). http://hdl.handle.net/10251/130041

16. Meier, S., Schmidt, B., Cremers, C., Basin, D.: The TAMARIN prover for the symbolic analysis of security protocols. In: Sharygina, N., Veith, H. (eds.) CAV 2013. LNCS, vol. 8044, pp. 696–701. Springer, Heidelberg (2013). https://doi.org/10.1007/978-3-642-39799-8_48

17. Meseguer, J.: Conditional rewriting logic as a unified model of concurrency. Theor. Comput. Sci. **96**(1), 73–155 (1992)

18. Milner, R.: Communicating and Mobile Systems - The Pi-Calculus. Cambridge University Press, Cambridge (1999)

19. Olarte, C., Valencia, F.D.: The expressivity of universal timed CCP: undecidability of monadic FLTL and closure operators for security. In: 2008 Proceedings Principles and Practice of Declarative Programming, pp. 8–19 (2008)

20. Rescorla, E.: The transport layer security (TLS) protocol version 1.3. Technical report draft-ietf-tls-tls13-12, IETF (2016)

21. Yang, F., Escobar, S., Meadows, C.A., Meseguer, J., Santiago, S.: Strand spaces with choice via a process algebra semantics. In: Cheney, J., Vidal, G. (eds.) Proceedings of the 18th International Symposium on Principles and Practice of Declarative Programming, Edinburgh, UK, 5–7 September 2016, pp. 76–89. ACM (2016)

Author Index

Printed in the United States
by Baker & Taylor Publisher Services